PREACHER

WAR IN THE SUN

Garth Ennis
writer

Steve Dillon
Peter Snejbjerg
artists

Grant Goleash
Pamela Rambo
colorists

Clem Robins
letterer

Glenn Fabry
original covers

PREACHER created by
Garth Ennis and Steve Dillon

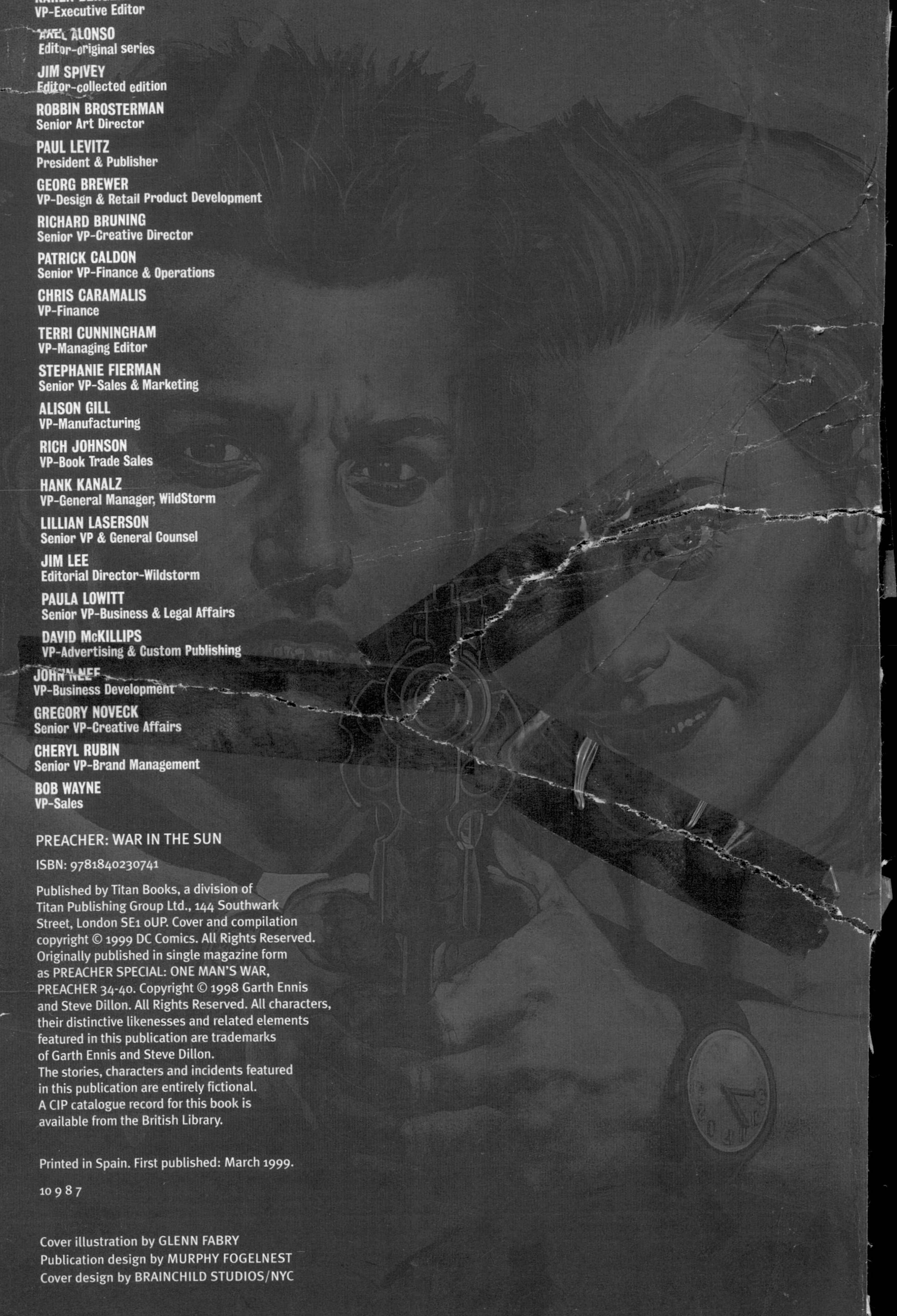

PREACHER: WAR IN THE SUN

ISBN: 9781840230741

Published by Titan Books, a division of
Titan Publishing Group Ltd., 144 Southwark
Street, London SE1 0UP. Cover and compilation
copyright © 1999 DC Comics. All Rights Reserved.
Originally published in single magazine form
as PREACHER SPECIAL: ONE MAN'S WAR,
PREACHER 34-40. Copyright © 1998 Garth Ennis
and Steve Dillon. All Rights Reserved. All characters,
their distinctive likenesses and related elements
featured in this publication are trademarks
of Garth Ennis and Steve Dillon.
The stories, characters and incidents featured
in this publication are entirely fictional.
A CIP catalogue record for this book is
available from the British Library.

Printed in Spain. First published: March 1999.

10 9 8 7

Cover illustration by GLENN FABRY
Publication design by MURPHY FOGELNEST
Cover design by BRAINCHILD STUDIOS/NYC

What's happened so far?
Well, thereby hangs a tale...

Reverend Jesse Custer was your run-o'-the-mill Texas minister preachin' to the simple folk of Annville, Texas on Sundays and crawling inside a bottle the rest of the week until GENESIS—a spirit conceived in a union between angel and demon—broke free of its bonds and charged outta Heaven like a fiery comet...straight toward Jesse and his flock. Two hundred people died in Annville...all except Jesse, possessed by Genesis and wielding the Word of God. When Jesse spoke, he could make anyone do as he said.

Fate or a divine hand reunited Jesse with his long-lost lover Tulip O'Hare and linked 'em both to Cassidy, an Irish vampire with a taste for whiskey. Jesse decided it was high time God was made accountable for his sins, having abandoned his post in Heaven to walk the earth. And Jesse aimed to find the Almighty to do just that.

For his troubles, Jesse met the Saint of Killers, an awakened angel of death sent by Genesis' keepers in Heaven. The Saint's aim was always true, and he left a bloody trail in his wake. And then there was Herr Starr, an agent of the Grail— a secret society dating back to the Crucifixion—which had designs on just what mankind's path *should* be in the face of the coming Armageddon. Starr plotted to replace his order's flawed messiah with...well, someone like Jesse Custer, a charismatic figure who spoke with the voice of God. To do so, Starr captured Cassidy and led Jesse on a bloody chase from San Francisco to the Grail's mountain fortress of Masada in France. The Saint of Killers, of course, was about two steps behind.

In the end, the Saint pretty much took out the entire Grail army. Starr dropped Allfather D'Aronique, leader of the Grail, out of a helicopter and right on top of the Grail's retarded messiah. Jesse and Cassidy got away...as did Starr. Meanwhile, the Saint of Killers was buried under a mountain, but he's had worse to deal with in his life and death.

Just recently, Jesse took part in some good ol' New Orleans voodoo to mine the memories of Genesis. And he got some of what he needed, learning the tragic origins of the Saint of Killers and just who was behind the Saint's damnation. But Jesse knows that for the whole truth, he's gotta access GENESIS directly. And he knows that the answers lie somewhere West.

Starr, now Allfather of the Grail, vows that Jesse will be the Grail's messiah if it kills him.

In Monument Valley, Jesse and Starr converge for an apocalyptic showdown...

REVEREND JESSE CUSTER

Possessed by the entity GENESIS—a child born of a union between Heaven and Hell that should never have existed—

Jesse Custer's on a quest to find God and the reason He's abandoned his post. Because of GENESIS, Jesse's voice is the literal Word of God, commanding those who hear him to do whatever he says. Jesse drinks too much, smokes too much and has a peculiar habit of taking advice from the spirit of John Wayne.

TULIP O'HARE

Five years ago, Tulip and Jesse were pretty much joined at the hip—that is, until Jesse was hauled back to his childhood home of Angelville by good ol' boys Jody and T.C., disappearing on Tulip. Since that time, Tulip made a bungling attempt to be a paid assassin to pay the bills and forget about Jesse Custer. Guns came easy, forgetting Jesse didn't. Jesse's promised to love her until the end of the world. Tulip aims to make him keep his word this time.

CASSIDY

A hard-drinkin' Irish vampire nearly a century old, Proinsias Cassidy has been with Jesse and Tulip since Tulip tried to steal his truck after a botched hit in Texas. He's promised to stay with them until Jesse's found God— mostly out of friendship...and mostly because he's in love with Tulip, a fact he's kept hidden from Jesse. Call him Cassidy, Cass, or even a total wanker. Just don't ever call him Proinsias.

THE SAINT OF KILLERS

Once, the Saint's hatred snuffed the flames of Hell and left it an icy wasteland. For that, the Devil flayed the skin from his bones. But even that didn't stop the Saint from hating, and so he replaced the Angel of Death and was sent forth to be the patron martyr for all who take up the gun, leading the dead to the afterlife—above or below. The Saint shot the Devil before he left Hell. Now, he stalks Jesse Custer for the secret he has.

ARSEFACE

Sheriff Hugo Root's only son decided life wasn't worth livin' when Nirvana frontman Kurt Cobain up and killed himself. His father's 12-gauge missed all the vital stuff, and six operations rebuilt the rest. Arseface blamed

Jesse Custer for Sheriff Root's suicide, but Jesse and Cass convinced him otherwise. They even got him laid, and helped him land a recording contract. Now he's a pop icon...with a face like an arse. Go figure.

STARR

Recruited by the centuries-old Grail, Starr rose through the ranks to become the order's most respected agent, answering only to Allfather D'Aronique. Starr killed D'Aronique, realizing that the Grail's efforts were wasted on a tainted messiah. In Jesse Custer, Starr sees the future of the Grail...a future the newly risen Allfather Starr would gladly kill to see a reality.

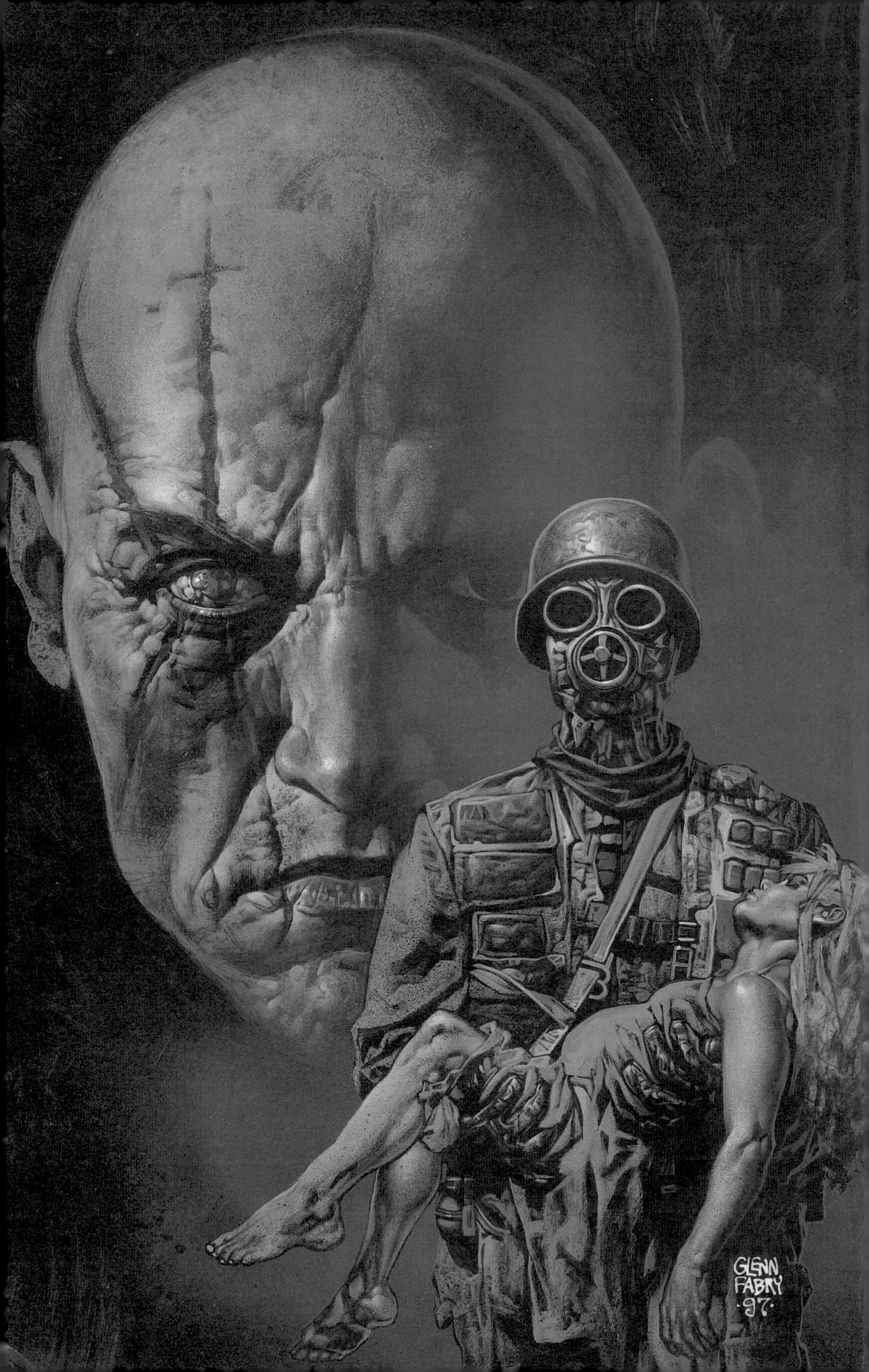
GLENN
FABRY
·97·

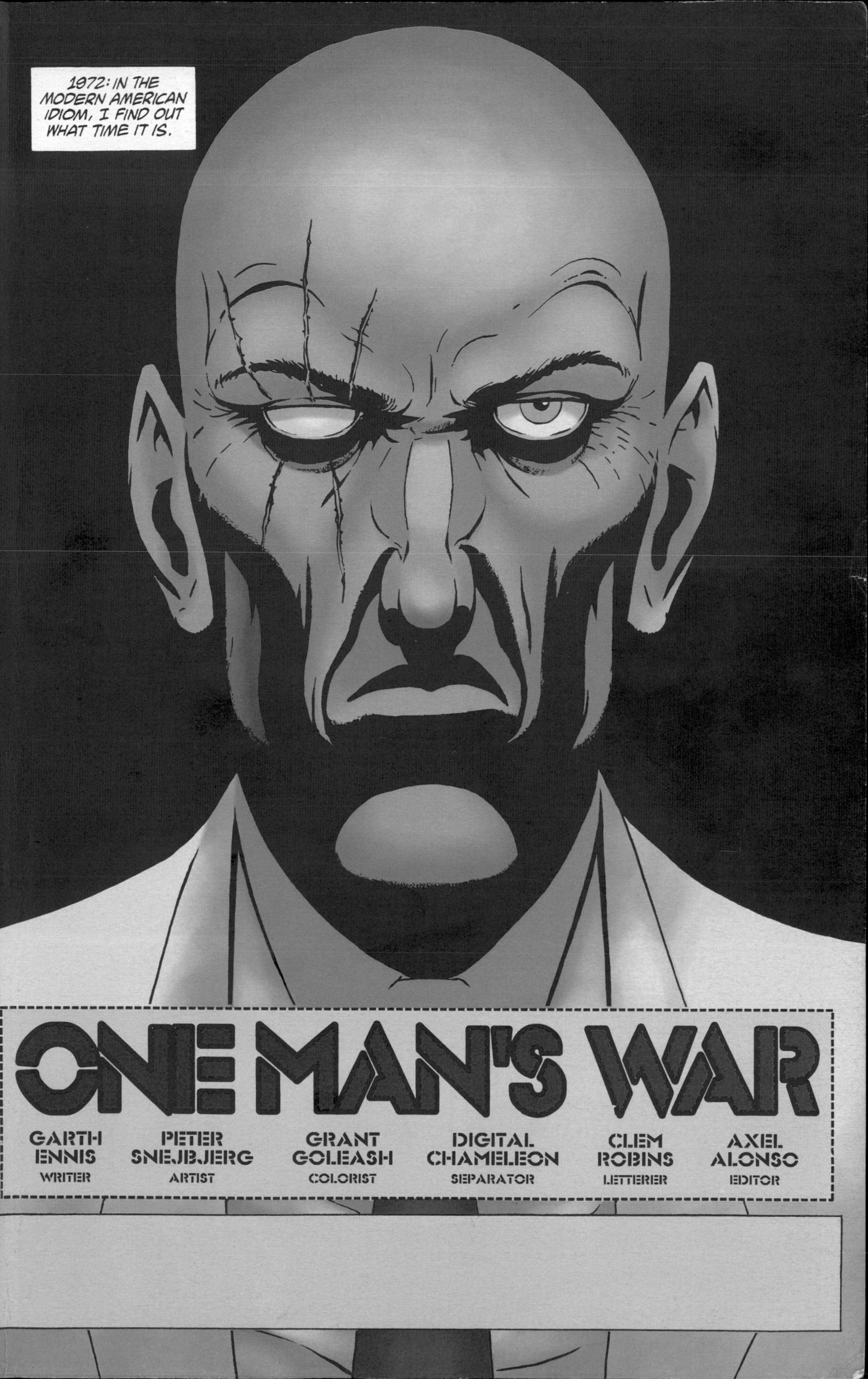
1972: IN THE MODERN AMERICAN IDIOM, I FIND OUT WHAT TIME IT IS.
ONE MAN'S WAR
GARTH ENNIS WRITER
PETER SNEJBJERG ARTIST
GRANT GOLEASH COLORIST
DIGITAL CHAMELEON SEPARATOR
CLEM ROBINS LETTERER
AXEL ALONSO EDITOR

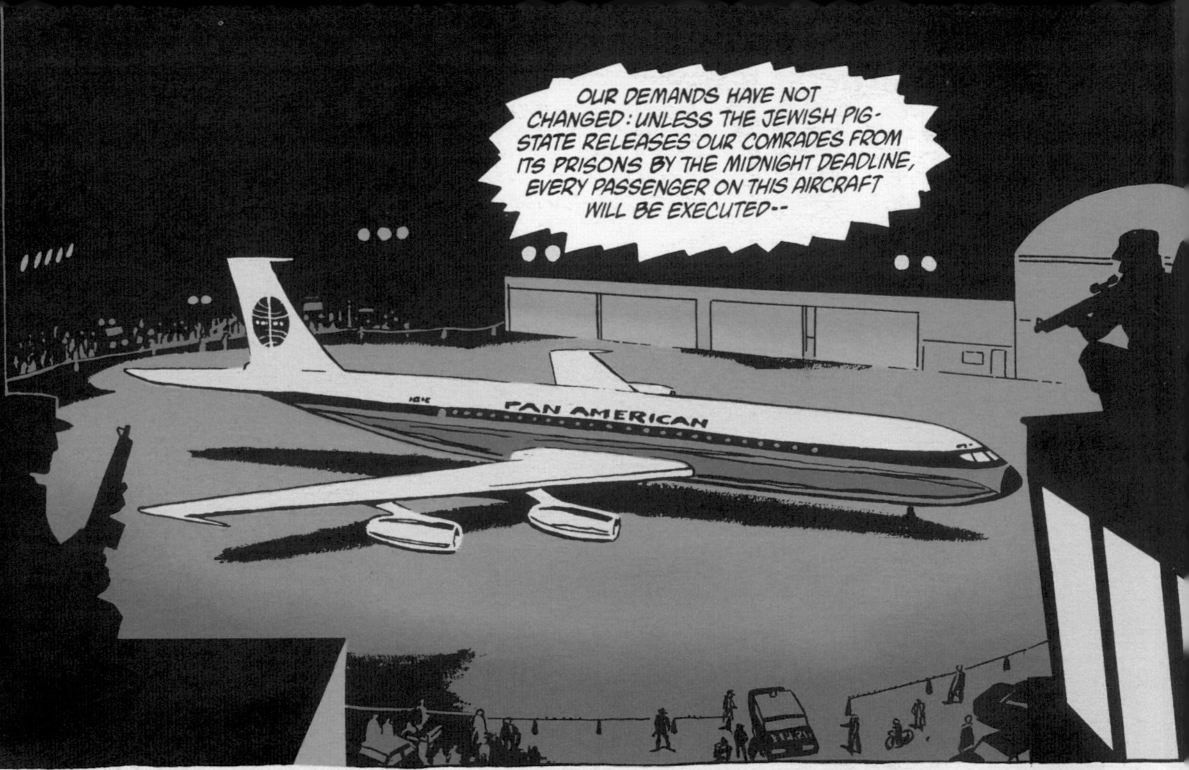
OUR DEMANDS HAVE NOT CHANGED: UNLESS THE JEWISH PIG-STATE RELEASES OUR COMRADES FROM ITS PRISONS BY THE MIDNIGHT DEADLINE, EVERY PASSENGER ON THIS AIRCRAFT WILL BE EXECUTED--
PAN AMERICAN

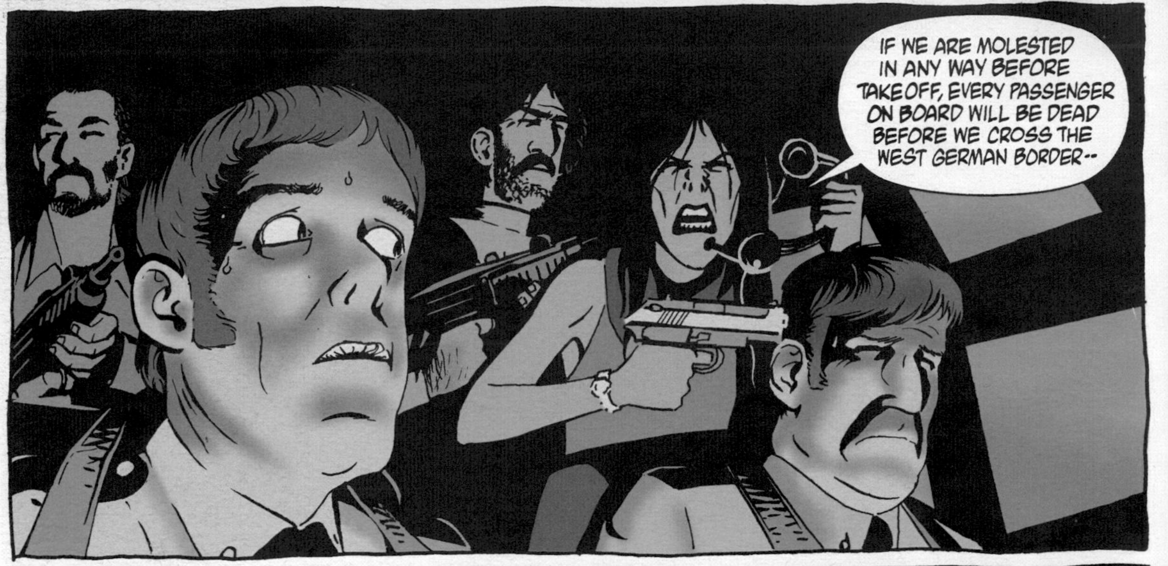
IF WE ARE MOLESTED IN ANY WAY BEFORE TAKEOFF, EVERY PASSENGER ON BOARD WILL BE DEAD BEFORE WE CROSS THE WEST GERMAN BORDER--

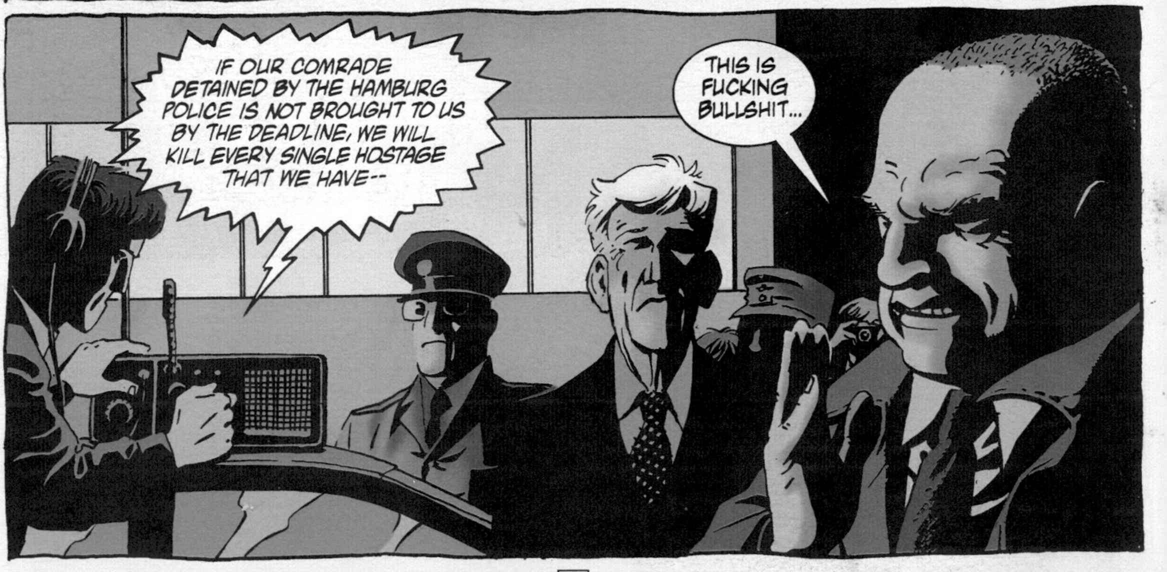
IF OUR COMRADE DETAINED BY THE HAMBURG POLICE IS NOT BROUGHT TO US BY THE DEADLINE, WE WILL KILL EVERY SINGLE HOSTAGE THAT WE HAVE--
THIS IS FUCKING BULLSHIT...

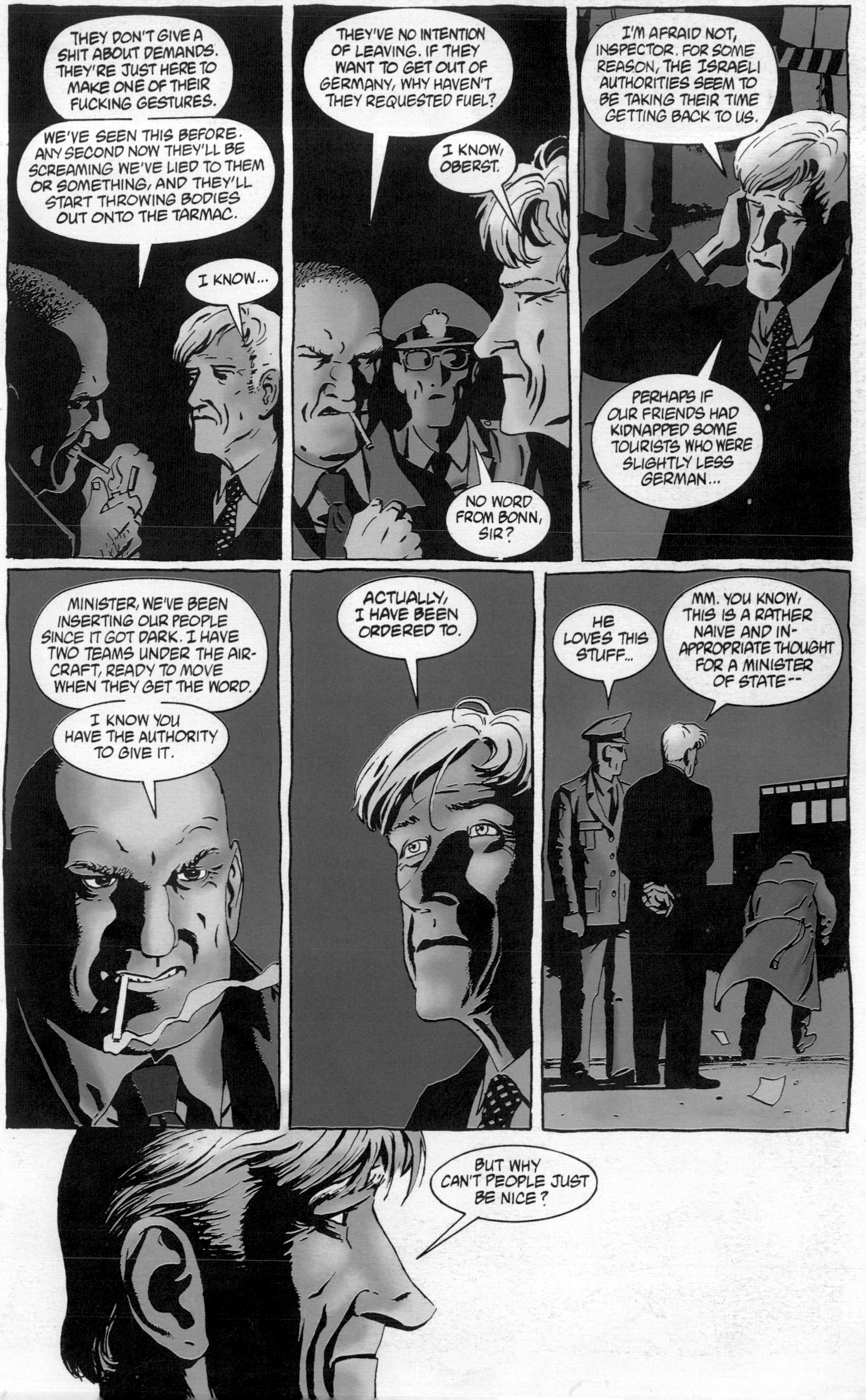
THEY DON'T GIVE A SHIT ABOUT DEMANDS. THEY'RE JUST HERE TO MAKE ONE OF THEIR FUCKING GESTURES.
WE'VE SEEN THIS BEFORE. ANY SECOND NOW THEY'LL BE SCREAMING WE'VE LIED TO THEM OR SOMETHING, AND THEY'LL START THROWING BODIES OUT ONTO THE TARMAC.
I KNOW...
THEY'VE NO INTENTION OF LEAVING. IF THEY WANT TO GET OUT OF GERMANY, WHY HAVEN'T THEY REQUESTED FUEL?
I KNOW, OBERST.
NO WORD FROM BONN, SIR?
I'M AFRAID NOT, INSPECTOR. FOR SOME REASON, THE ISRAELI AUTHORITIES SEEM TO BE TAKING THEIR TIME GETTING BACK TO US.
PERHAPS IF OUR FRIENDS HAD KIDNAPPED SOME TOURISTS WHO WERE SLIGHTLY LESS GERMAN...
MINISTER, WE'VE BEEN INSERTING OUR PEOPLE SINCE IT GOT DARK. I HAVE TWO TEAMS UNDER THE AIRCRAFT, READY TO MOVE WHEN THEY GET THE WORD.
I KNOW YOU HAVE THE AUTHORITY TO GIVE IT.
ACTUALLY, I HAVE BEEN ORDERED TO.
HE LOVES THIS STUFF...
MM. YOU KNOW, THIS IS A RATHER NAIVE AND INAPPROPRIATE THOUGHT FOR A MINISTER OF STATE--
BUT WHY CAN'T PEOPLE JUST BE NICE?

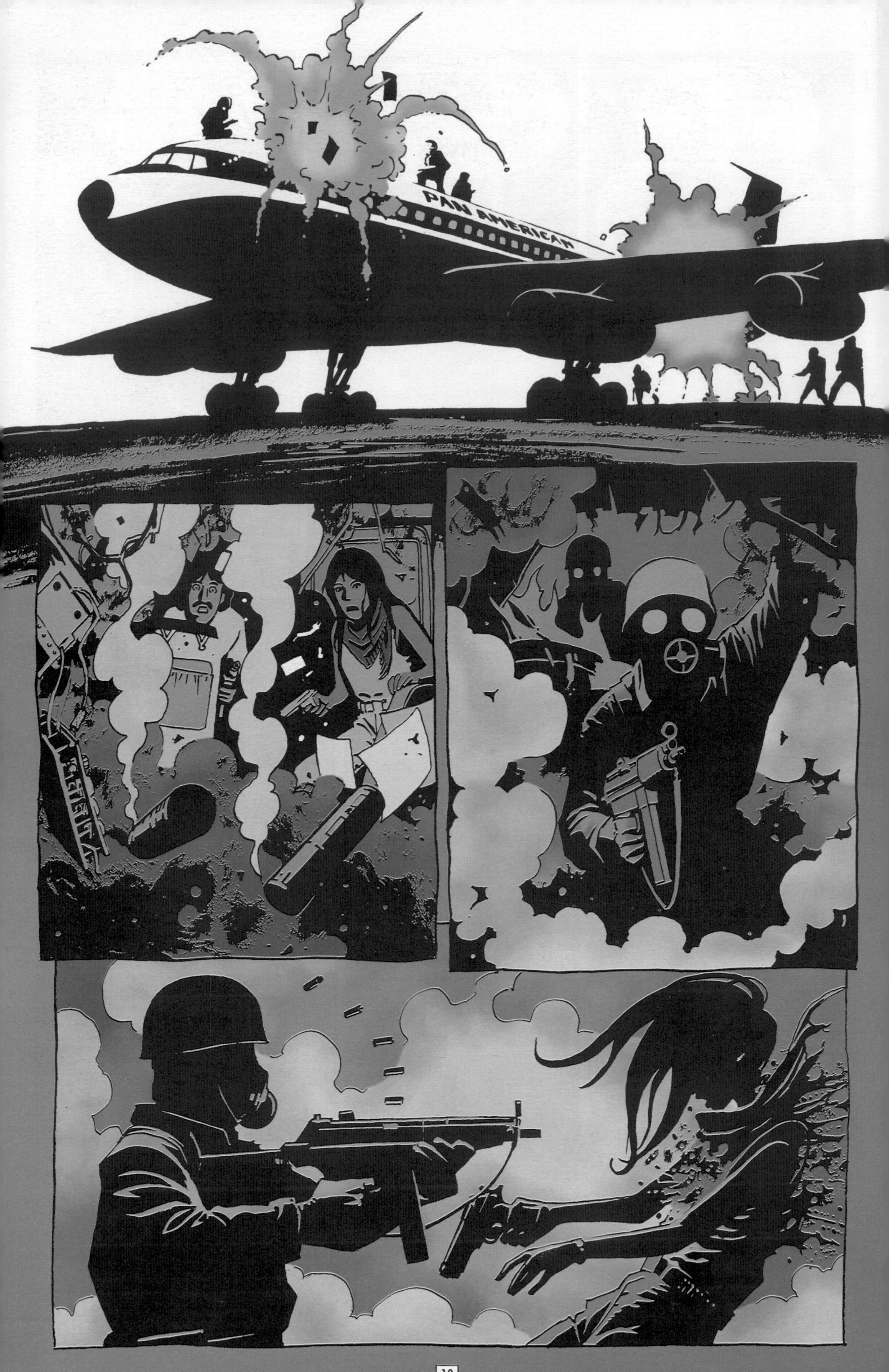
PAN AMERICAN

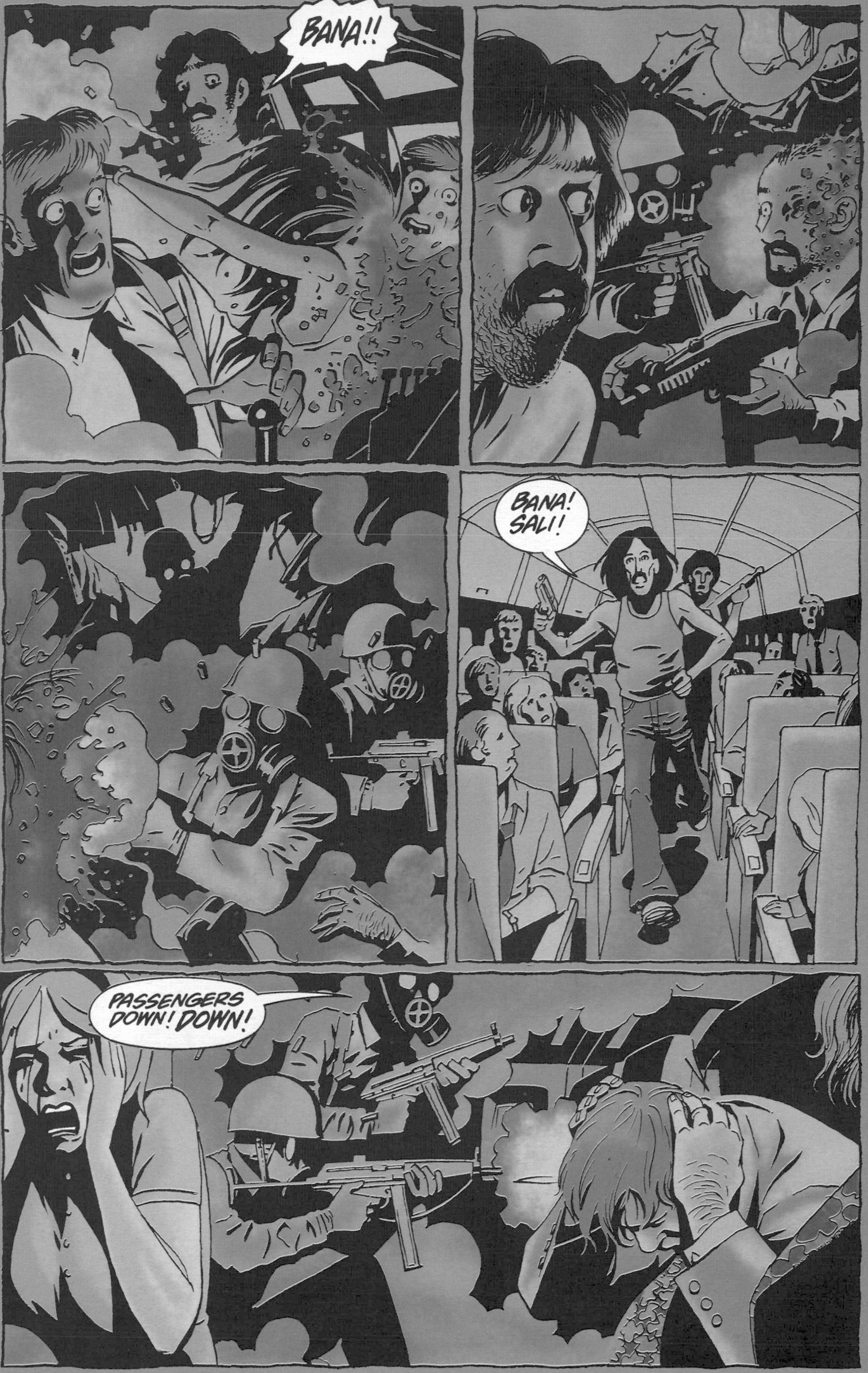
BANA!!
BANA!
SALI!
PASSENGERS
DOWN! DOWN!

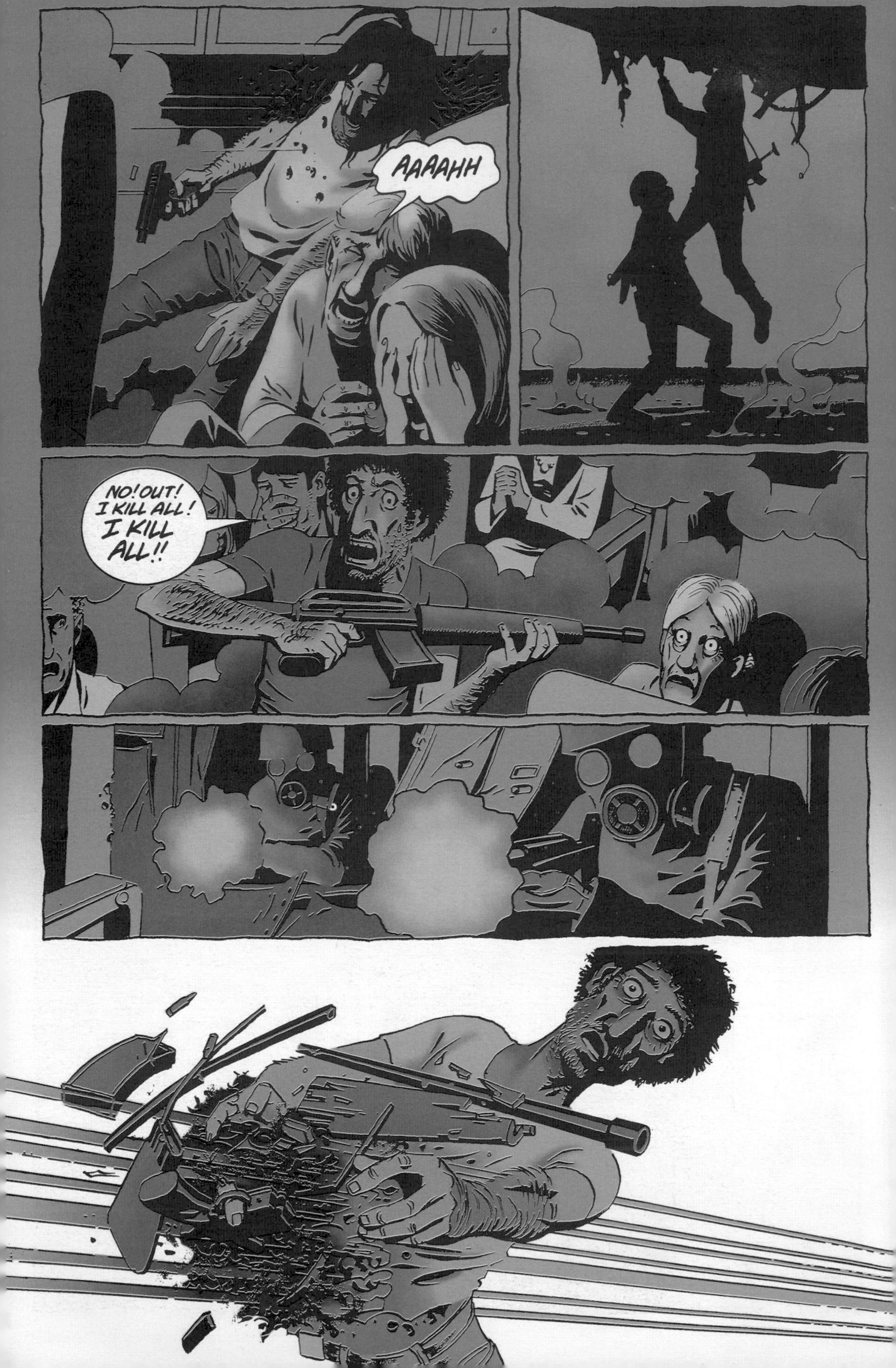
AAAAHH
NO! OUT! I KILL ALL! I KILL ALL!!

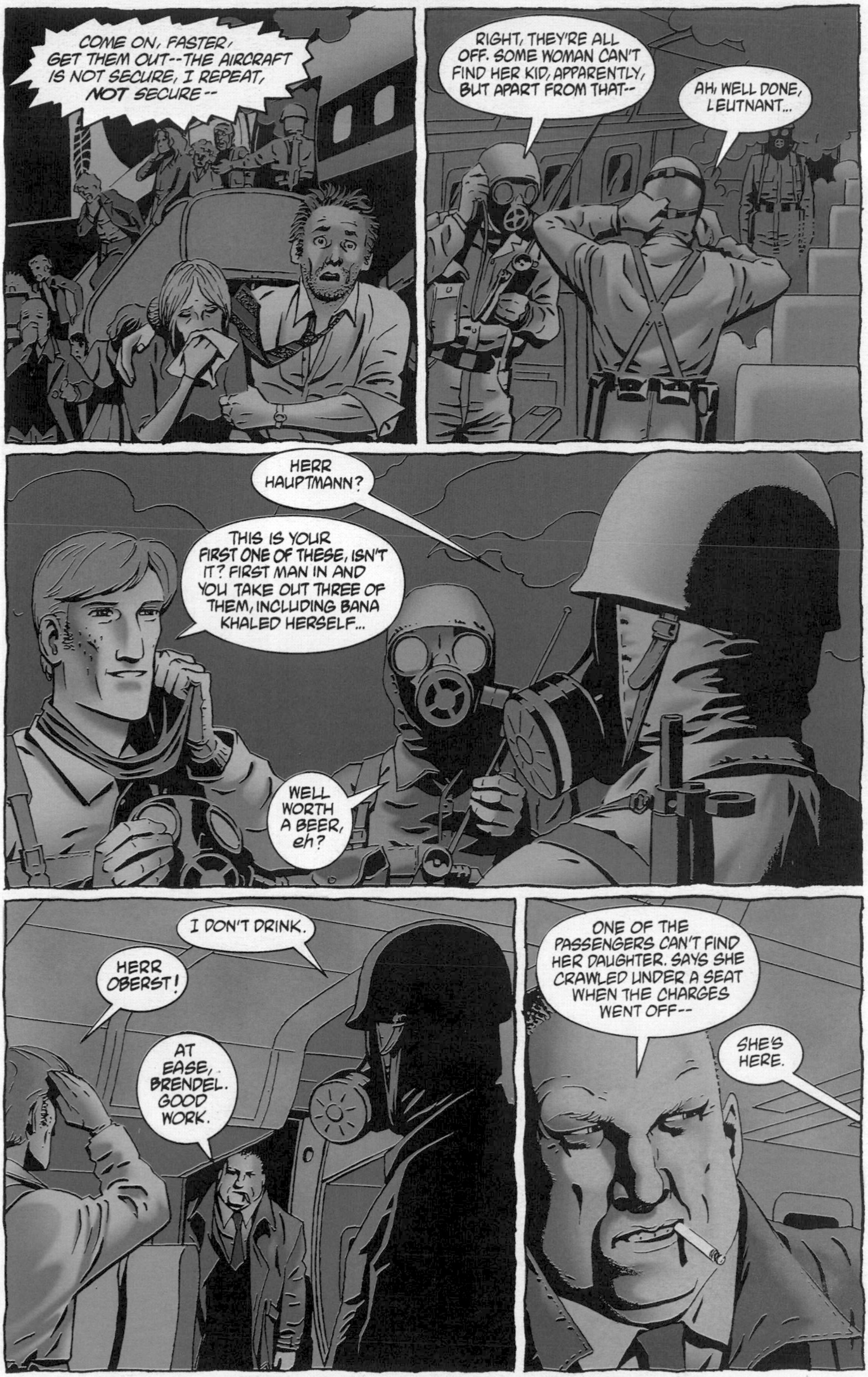
COME ON, FASTER, GET THEM OUT--THE AIRCRAFT IS NOT SECURE, I REPEAT, NOT SECURE--
RIGHT, THEY'RE ALL OFF. SOME WOMAN CAN'T FIND HER KID, APPARENTLY, BUT APART FROM THAT--
AH, WELL DONE, LEUTNANT...
HERR HAUPTMANN?
THIS IS YOUR FIRST ONE OF THESE, ISN'T IT? FIRST MAN IN AND YOU TAKE OUT THREE OF THEM, INCLUDING BANA KHALED HERSELF...
WELL WORTH A BEER, eh?
I DON'T DRINK.
HERR OBERST!
AT EASE, BRENDEL. GOOD WORK.
ONE OF THE PASSENGERS CAN'T FIND HER DAUGHTER. SAYS SHE CRAWLED UNDER A SEAT WHEN THE CHARGES WENT OFF--
SHE'S HERE.

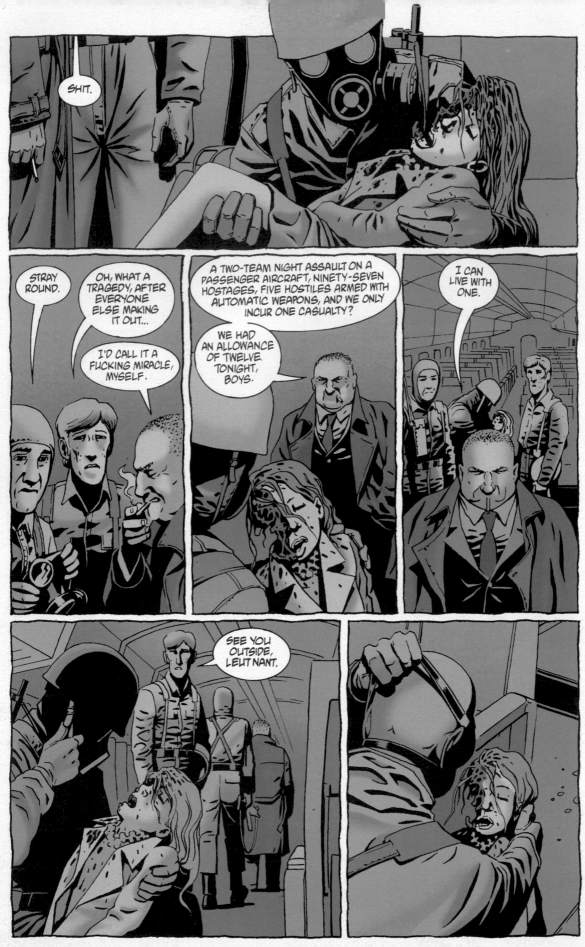

SHIT.

STRAY ROUND.

OH, WHAT A TRAGEDY, AFTER EVERYONE ELSE MAKING IT OUT...

I'D CALL IT A FUCKING MIRACLE, MYSELF.

A TWO-TEAM NIGHT ASSAULT ON A PASSENGER AIRCRAFT, NINETY-SEVEN HOSTAGES, FIVE HOSTILES ARMED WITH AUTOMATIC WEAPONS, AND WE ONLY INCUR ONE CASUALTY?

WE HAD AN ALLOWANCE OF TWELVE. TONIGHT, BOYS.

I CAN LIVE WITH ONE.

SEE YOU OUTSIDE, LEUTNANT.

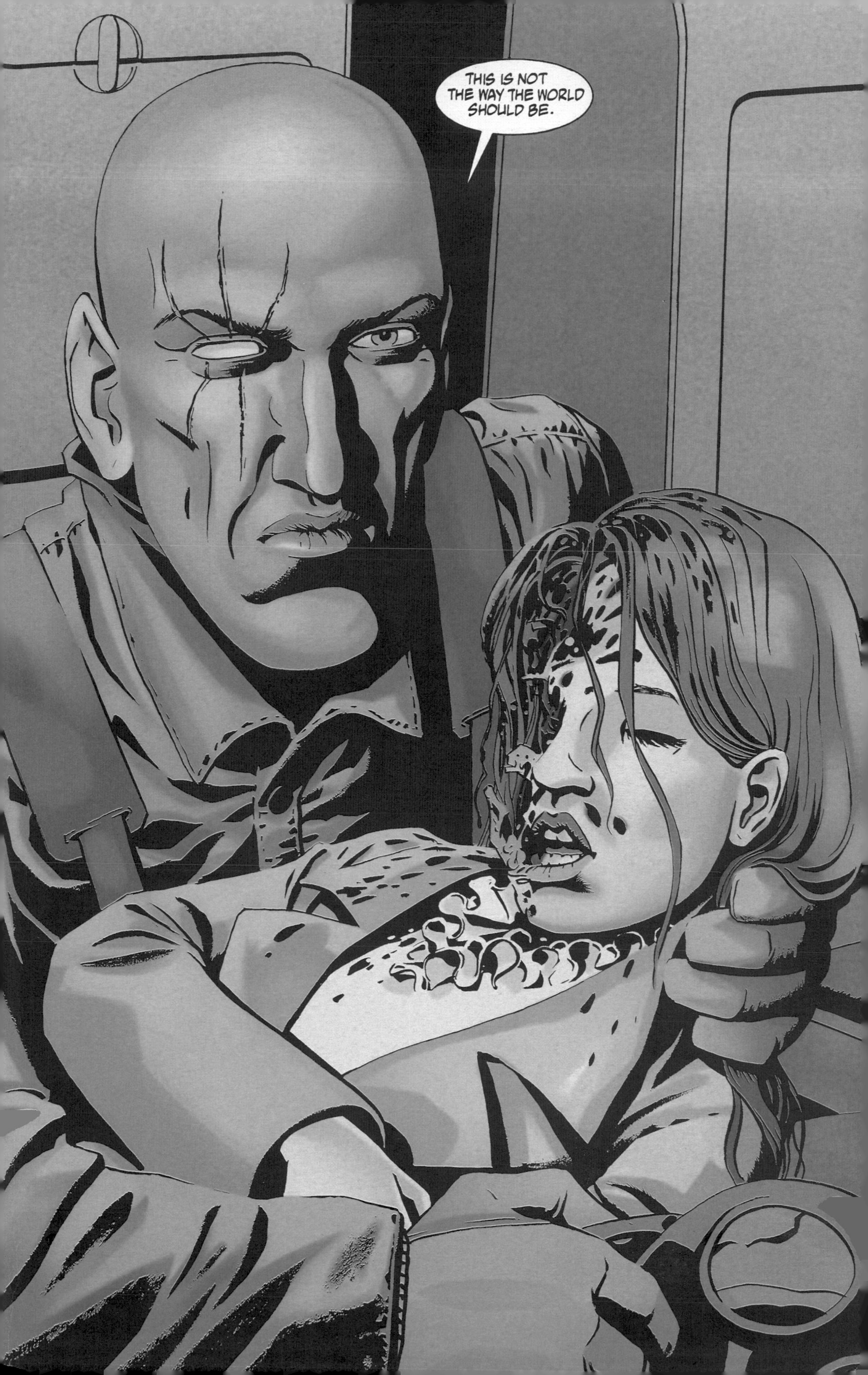
THIS IS NOT THE WAY THE WORLD SHOULD BE.

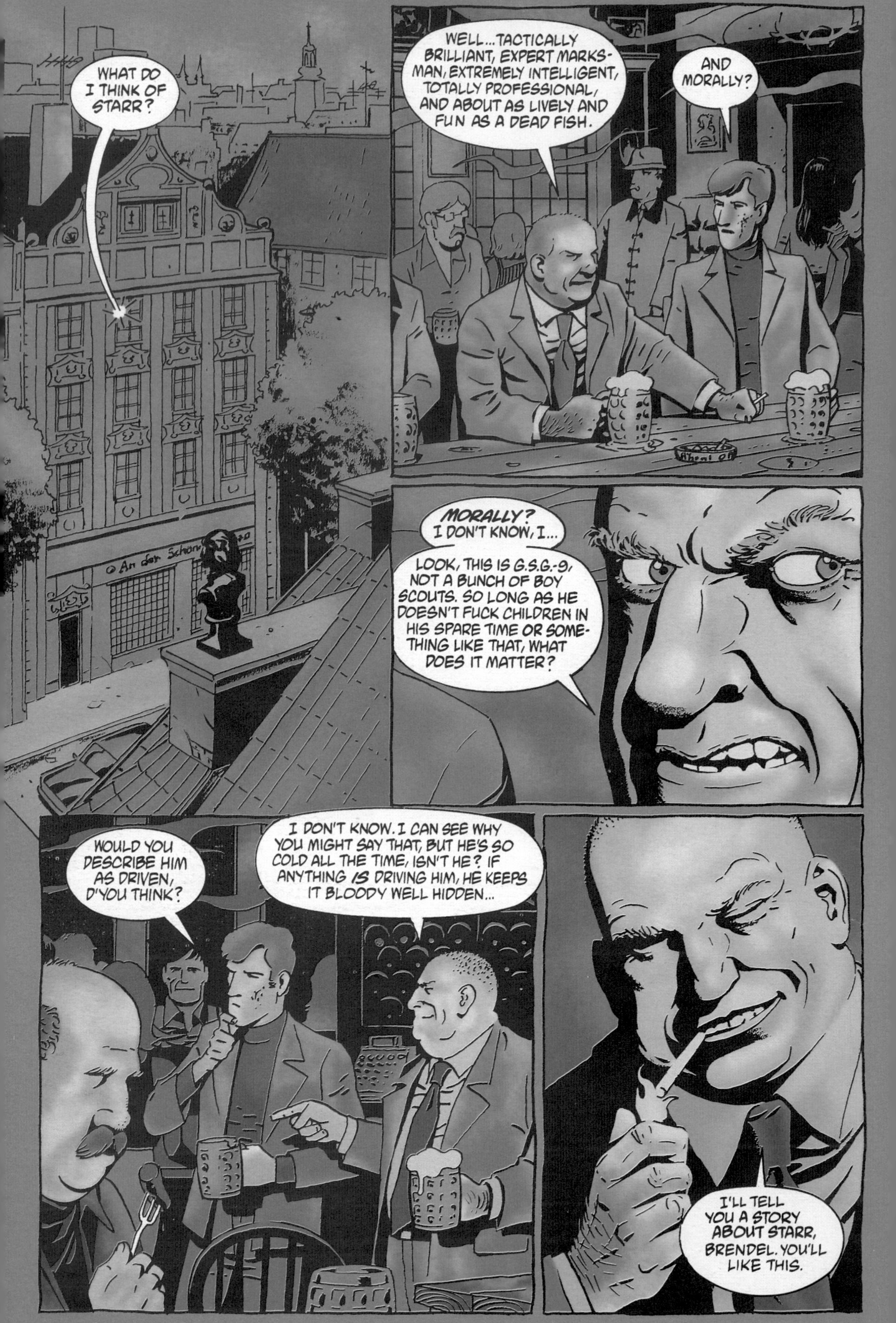

WHAT DO I THINK OF STARR?
WELL... TACTICALLY BRILLIANT, EXPERT MARKSMAN, EXTREMELY INTELLIGENT, TOTALLY PROFESSIONAL, AND ABOUT AS LIVELY AND FUN AS A DEAD FISH.
AND MORALLY?
MORALLY? I DON'T KNOW, I...
LOOK, THIS IS G.S.G.-9, NOT A BUNCH OF BOY SCOUTS. SO LONG AS HE DOESN'T FUCK CHILDREN IN HIS SPARE TIME OR SOMETHING LIKE THAT, WHAT DOES IT MATTER?
WOULD YOU DESCRIBE HIM AS DRIVEN, D'YOU THINK?
I DON'T KNOW. I CAN SEE WHY YOU MIGHT SAY THAT, BUT HE'S SO COLD ALL THE TIME, ISN'T HE? IF ANYTHING IS DRIVING HIM, HE KEEPS IT BLOODY WELL HIDDEN...
I'LL TELL YOU A STORY ABOUT STARR, BRENDEL. YOU'LL LIKE THIS.

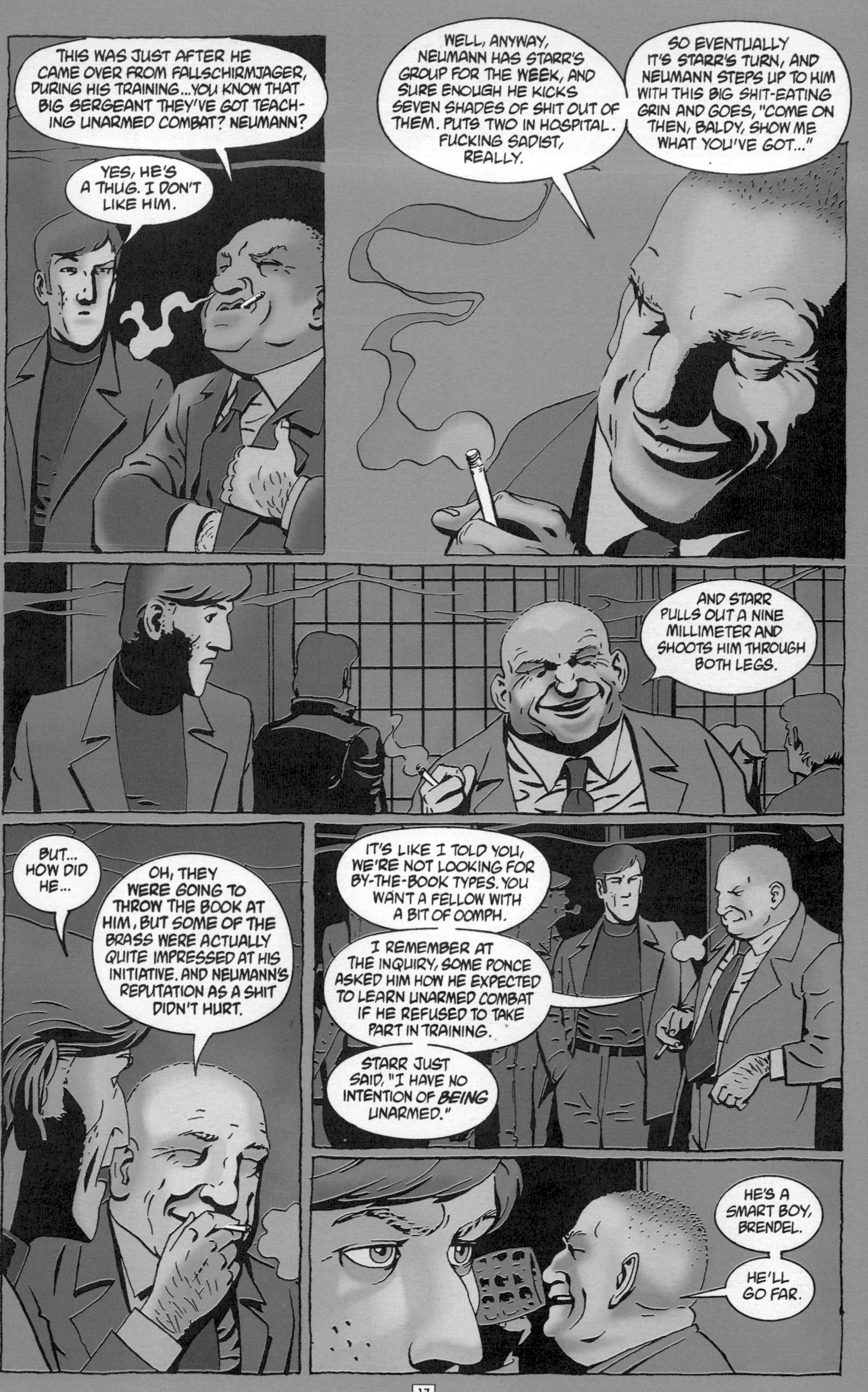
THIS WAS JUST AFTER HE CAME OVER FROM FALLSCHIRMJAGER, DURING HIS TRAINING...YOU KNOW THAT BIG SERGEANT THEY'VE GOT TEACHING UNARMED COMBAT? NEUMANN?
YES, HE'S A THUG. I DON'T LIKE HIM.
WELL, ANYWAY, NEUMANN HAS STARR'S GROUP FOR THE WEEK, AND SURE ENOUGH HE KICKS SEVEN SHADES OF SHIT OUT OF THEM. PUTS TWO IN HOSPITAL. FUCKING SADIST, REALLY.
SO EVENTUALLY IT'S STARR'S TURN, AND NEUMANN STEPS UP TO HIM WITH THIS BIG SHIT-EATING GRIN AND GOES, "COME ON THEN, BALDY, SHOW ME WHAT YOU'VE GOT..."
AND STARR PULLS OUT A NINE MILLIMETER AND SHOOTS HIM THROUGH BOTH LEGS.
BUT... HOW DID HE...
OH, THEY WERE GOING TO THROW THE BOOK AT HIM, BUT SOME OF THE BRASS WERE ACTUALLY QUITE IMPRESSED AT HIS INITIATIVE. AND NEUMANN'S REPUTATION AS A SHIT DIDN'T HURT.
IT'S LIKE I TOLD YOU, WE'RE NOT LOOKING FOR BY-THE-BOOK TYPES. YOU WANT A FELLOW WITH A BIT OF OOMPH.
I REMEMBER AT THE INQUIRY, SOME PONCE ASKED HIM HOW HE EXPECTED TO LEARN UNARMED COMBAT IF HE REFUSED TO TAKE PART IN TRAINING.
STARR JUST SAID, "I HAVE NO INTENTION OF *BEING* UNARMED."
HE'S A SMART BOY, BRENDEL.
HE'LL GO FAR.

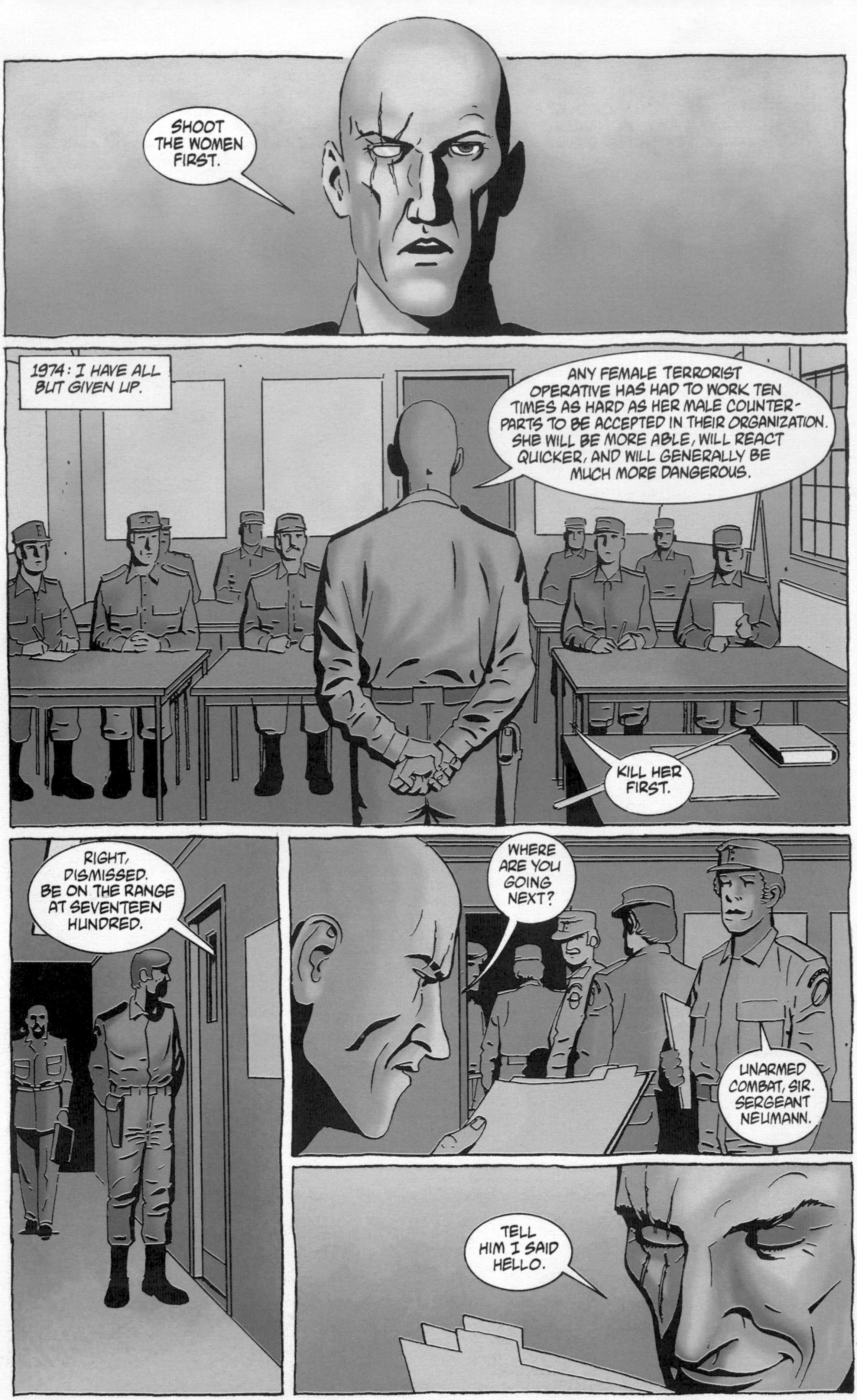
SHOOT THE WOMEN FIRST.
1974: I HAVE ALL BUT GIVEN UP.
ANY FEMALE TERRORIST OPERATIVE HAS HAD TO WORK TEN TIMES AS HARD AS HER MALE COUNTER-PARTS TO BE ACCEPTED IN THEIR ORGANIZATION. SHE WILL BE MORE ABLE, WILL REACT QUICKER, AND WILL GENERALLY BE MUCH MORE DANGEROUS.
KILL HER FIRST.
RIGHT, DISMISSED. BE ON THE RANGE AT SEVENTEEN HUNDRED.
WHERE ARE YOU GOING NEXT?
UNARMED COMBAT, SIR. SERGEANT NEUMANN.
TELL HIM I SAID HELLO.

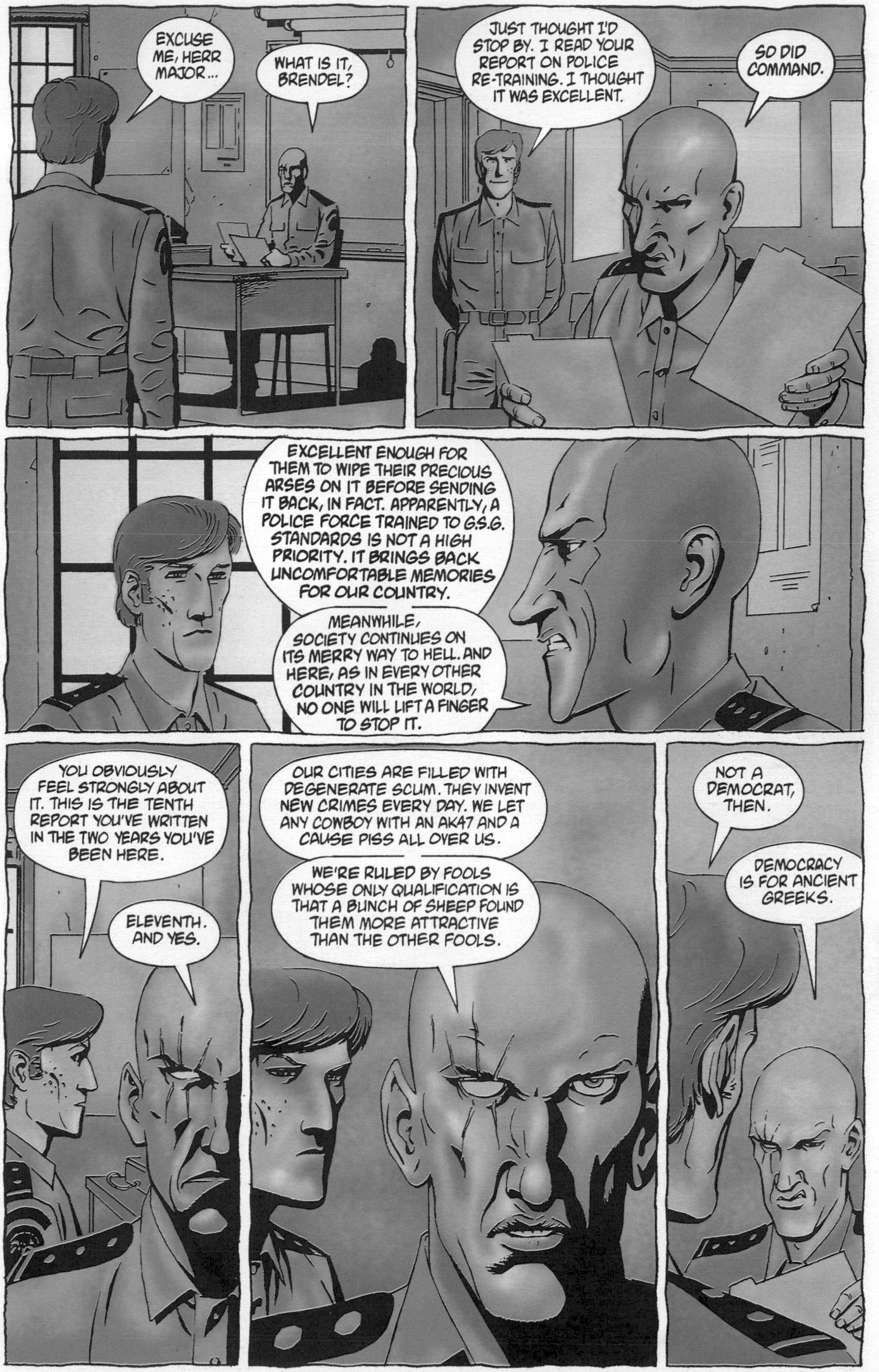
EXCUSE ME, HERR MAJOR...
WHAT IS IT, BRENDEL?
JUST THOUGHT I'D STOP BY. I READ YOUR REPORT ON POLICE RE-TRAINING. I THOUGHT IT WAS EXCELLENT.
SO DID COMMAND.
EXCELLENT ENOUGH FOR THEM TO WIPE THEIR PRECIOUS ARSES ON IT BEFORE SENDING IT BACK, IN FACT. APPARENTLY, A POLICE FORCE TRAINED TO G.S.G. STANDARDS IS NOT A HIGH PRIORITY. IT BRINGS BACK UNCOMFORTABLE MEMORIES FOR OUR COUNTRY.
MEANWHILE, SOCIETY CONTINUES ON ITS MERRY WAY TO HELL. AND HERE, AS IN EVERY OTHER COUNTRY IN THE WORLD, NO ONE WILL LIFT A FINGER TO STOP IT.
YOU OBVIOUSLY FEEL STRONGLY ABOUT IT. THIS IS THE TENTH REPORT YOU'VE WRITTEN IN THE TWO YEARS YOU'VE BEEN HERE.
ELEVENTH. AND YES.
OUR CITIES ARE FILLED WITH DEGENERATE SCUM. THEY INVENT NEW CRIMES EVERY DAY. WE LET ANY COWBOY WITH AN AK47 AND A CAUSE PISS ALL OVER US.
WE'RE RULED BY FOOLS WHOSE ONLY QUALIFICATION IS THAT A BUNCH OF SHEEP FOUND THEM MORE ATTRACTIVE THAN THE OTHER FOOLS.
NOT A DEMOCRAT, THEN.
DEMOCRACY IS FOR ANCIENT GREEKS.

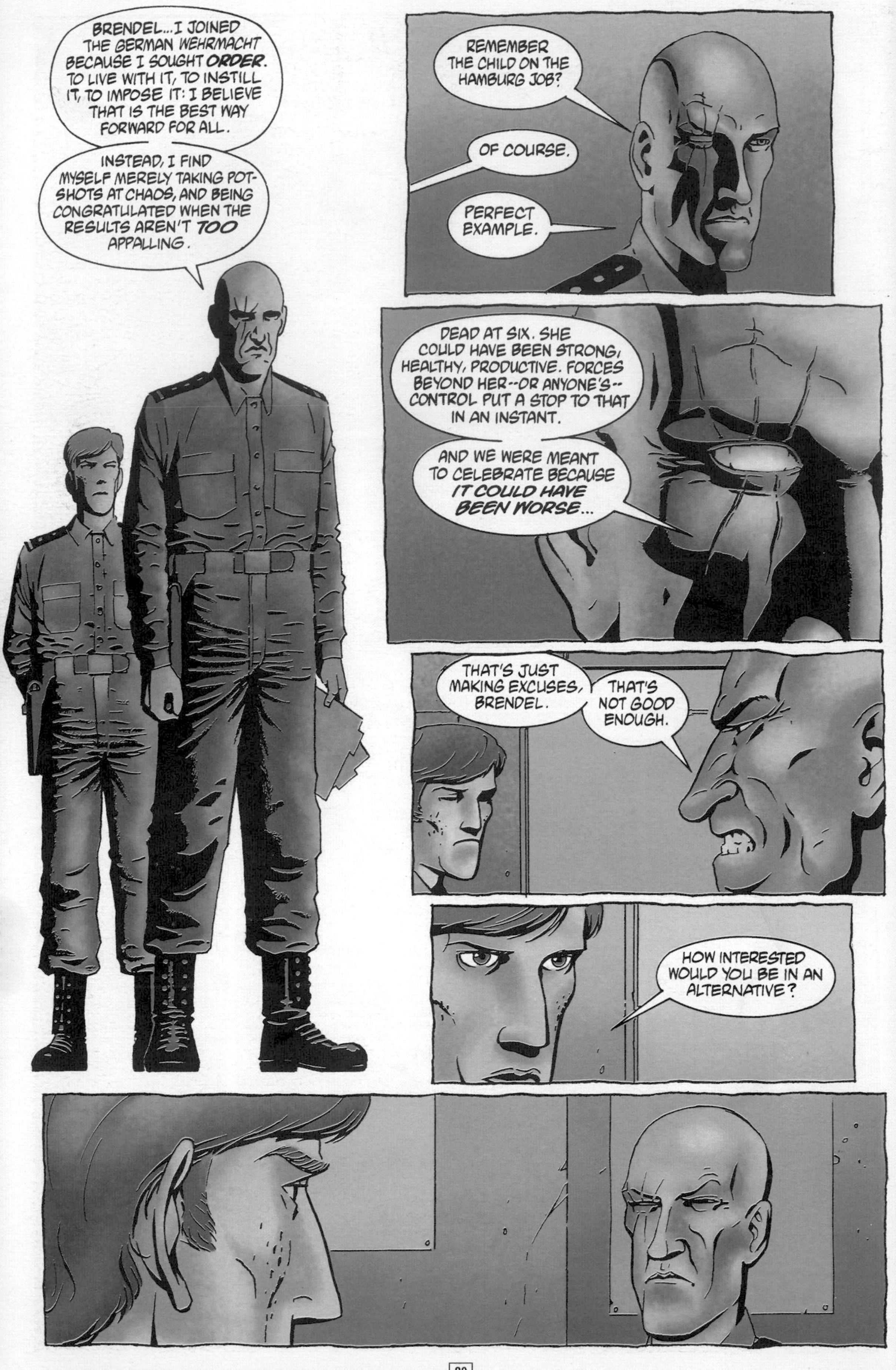
BRENDEL... I JOINED THE GERMAN WEHRMACHT BECAUSE I SOUGHT **ORDER**. TO LIVE WITH IT, TO INSTILL IT, TO IMPOSE IT: I BELIEVE THAT IS THE BEST WAY FORWARD FOR ALL.
INSTEAD, I FIND MYSELF MERELY TAKING POT-SHOTS AT CHAOS, AND BEING CONGRATULATED WHEN THE RESULTS AREN'T ***TOO*** APPALLING.
REMEMBER THE CHILD ON THE HAMBURG JOB?
OF COURSE.
PERFECT EXAMPLE.
DEAD AT SIX. SHE COULD HAVE BEEN STRONG, HEALTHY, PRODUCTIVE. FORCES BEYOND HER--OR ANYONE'S--CONTROL PUT A STOP TO THAT IN AN INSTANT.
AND WE WERE MEANT TO CELEBRATE BECAUSE ***IT COULD HAVE BEEN WORSE***...
THAT'S JUST MAKING EXCUSES, BRENDEL.
THAT'S NOT GOOD ENOUGH.
HOW INTERESTED WOULD YOU BE IN AN ALTERNATIVE?

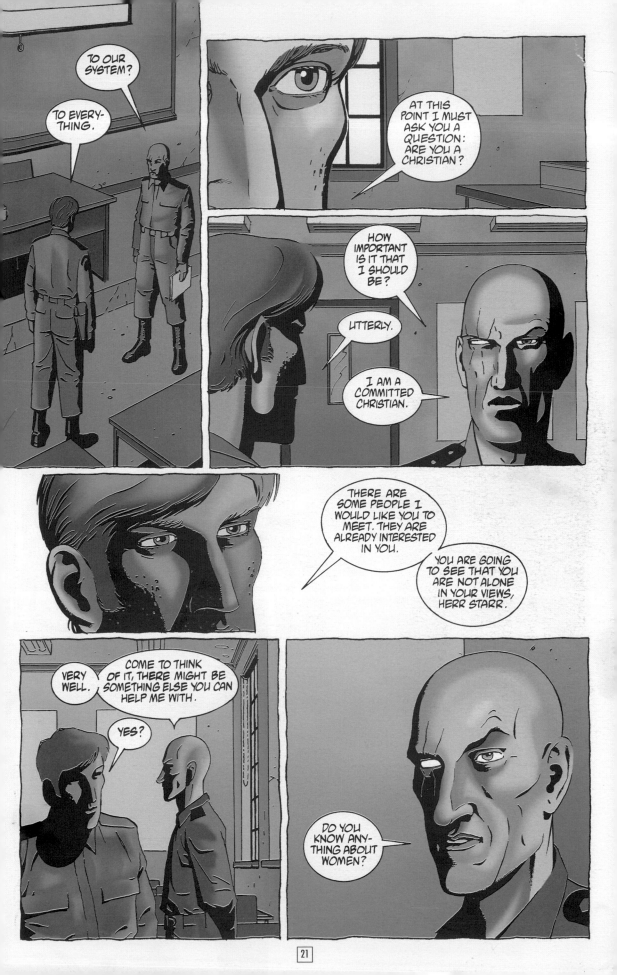

TO OUR SYSTEM?

TO EVERYTHING.

AT THIS POINT I MUST ASK YOU A QUESTION: ARE YOU A CHRISTIAN?

HOW IMPORTANT IS IT THAT I SHOULD BE?

UTTERLY.

I AM A COMMITTED CHRISTIAN.

THERE ARE SOME PEOPLE I WOULD LIKE YOU TO MEET. THEY ARE ALREADY INTERESTED IN YOU.

YOU ARE GOING TO SEE THAT YOU ARE NOT ALONE IN YOUR VIEWS, HERR STARR.

VERY WELL.

COME TO THINK OF IT, THERE MIGHT BE SOMETHING ELSE YOU CAN HELP ME WITH.

YES?

DO YOU KNOW ANYTHING ABOUT WOMEN?

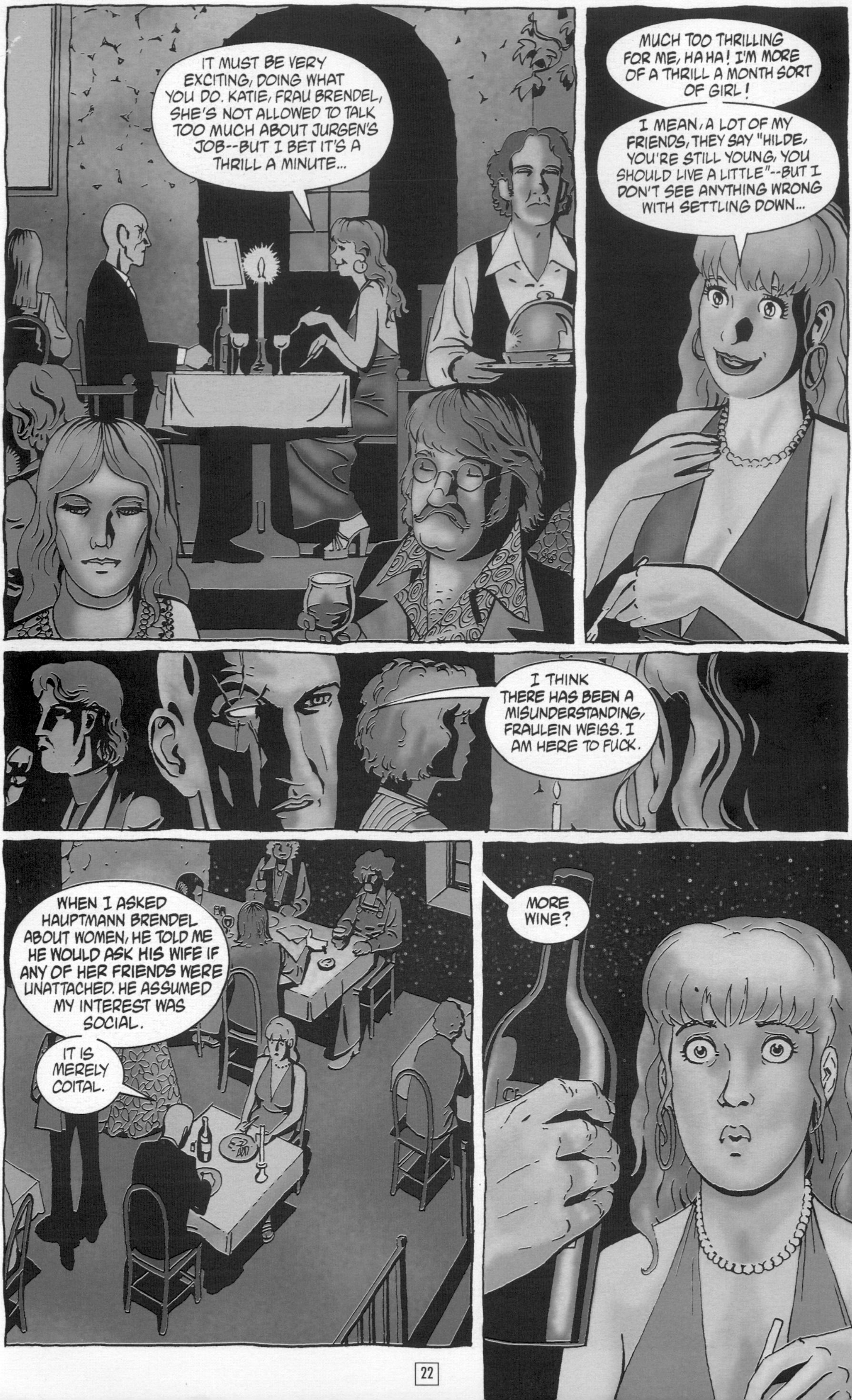
IT MUST BE VERY EXCITING, DOING WHAT YOU DO. KATIE, FRAU BRENDEL, SHE'S NOT ALLOWED TO TALK TOO MUCH ABOUT JURGEN'S JOB--BUT I BET IT'S A THRILL A MINUTE...
MUCH TOO THRILLING FOR ME, HA HA! I'M MORE OF A THRILL A MONTH SORT OF GIRL!
I MEAN, A LOT OF MY FRIENDS, THEY SAY "HILDE, YOU'RE STILL YOUNG, YOU SHOULD LIVE A LITTLE"--BUT I DON'T SEE ANYTHING WRONG WITH SETTLING DOWN...
I THINK THERE HAS BEEN A MISUNDERSTANDING, FRAULEIN WEISS. I AM HERE TO FUCK.
WHEN I ASKED HAUPTMANN BRENDEL ABOUT WOMEN, HE TOLD ME HE WOULD ASK HIS WIFE IF ANY OF HER FRIENDS WERE UNATTACHED. HE ASSUMED MY INTEREST WAS SOCIAL.
IT IS MERELY COITAL.
MORE WINE?

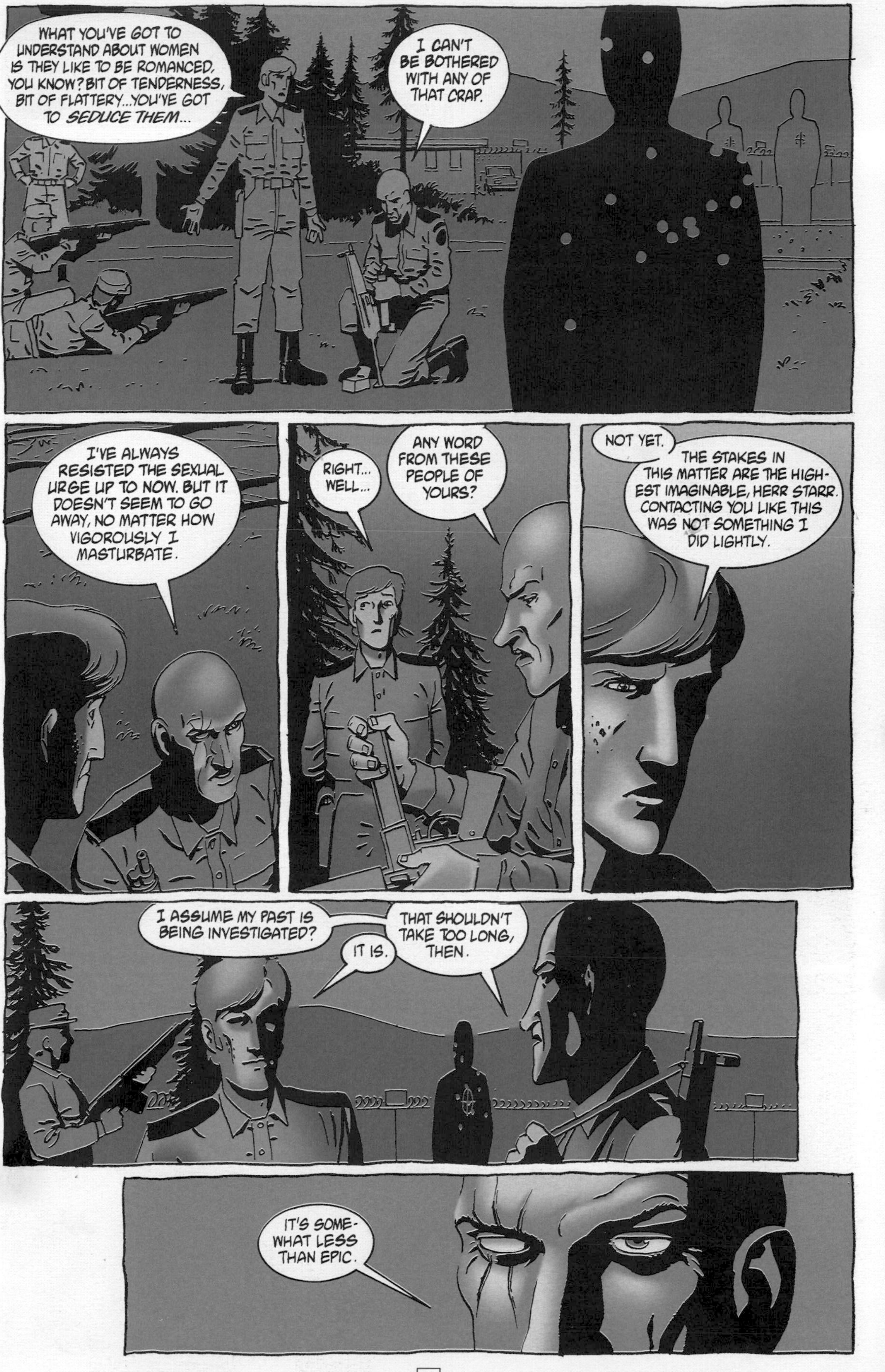

WHAT YOU'VE GOT TO UNDERSTAND ABOUT WOMEN IS THEY LIKE TO BE ROMANCED, YOU KNOW? BIT OF TENDERNESS, BIT OF FLATTERY...YOU'VE GOT TO *SEDUCE THEM*...
I CAN'T BE BOTHERED WITH ANY OF THAT CRAP.
I'VE ALWAYS RESISTED THE SEXUAL URGE UP TO NOW. BUT IT DOESN'T SEEM TO GO AWAY, NO MATTER HOW VIGOROUSLY I MASTURBATE.
RIGHT... WELL...
ANY WORD FROM THESE PEOPLE OF YOURS?
NOT YET.
THE STAKES IN THIS MATTER ARE THE HIGHEST IMAGINABLE, HERR STARR. CONTACTING YOU LIKE THIS WAS NOT SOMETHING I DID LIGHTLY.
I ASSUME MY PAST IS BEING INVESTIGATED?
IT IS.
THAT SHOULDN'T TAKE TOO LONG, THEN.
IT'S SOMEWHAT LESS THAN EPIC.

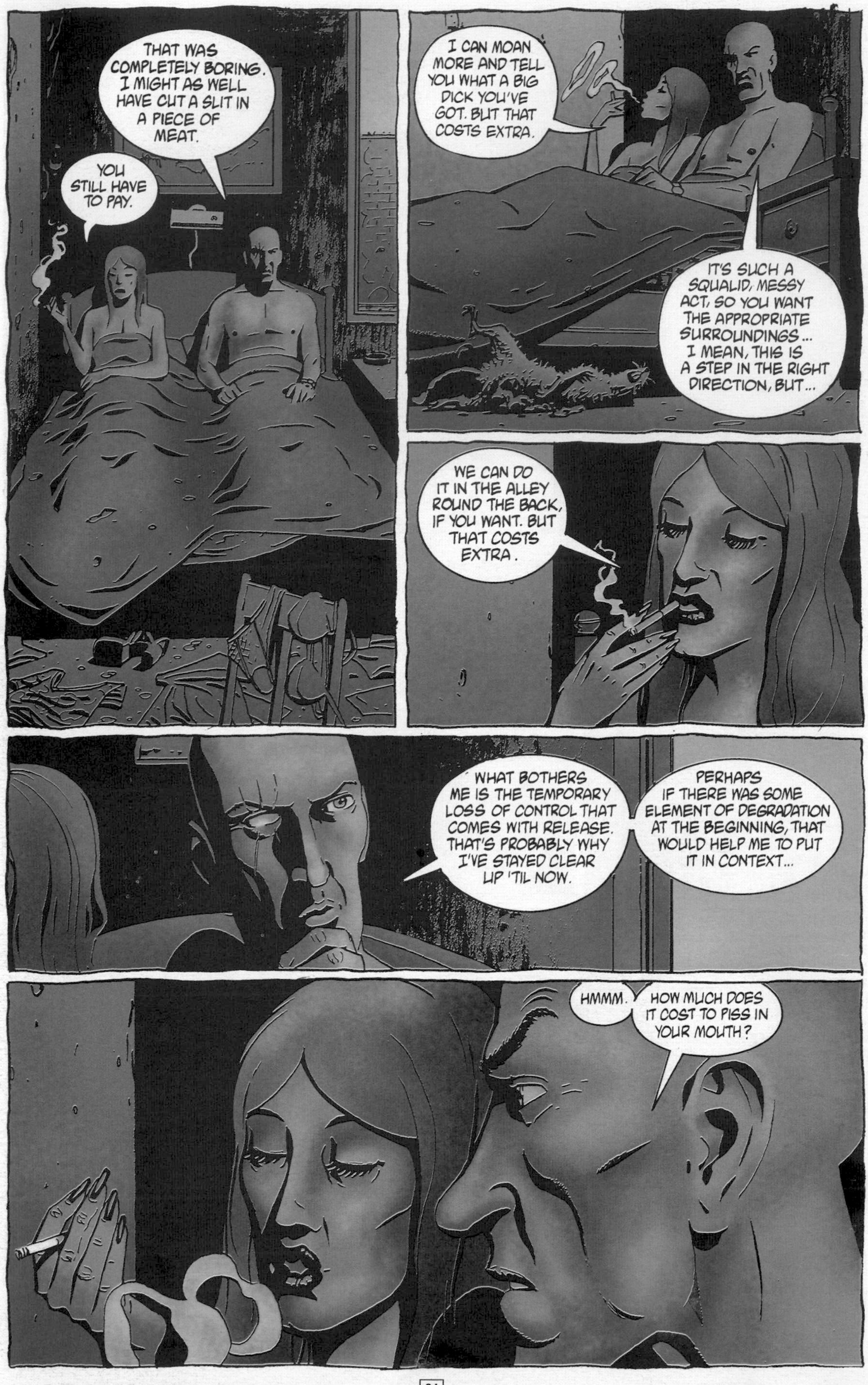
THAT WAS COMPLETELY BORING. I MIGHT AS WELL HAVE CUT A SLIT IN A PIECE OF MEAT.
YOU STILL HAVE TO PAY.
I CAN MOAN MORE AND TELL YOU WHAT A BIG DICK YOU'VE GOT. BUT THAT COSTS EXTRA.
IT'S SUCH A SQUALID, MESSY ACT, SO YOU WANT THE APPROPRIATE SURROUNDINGS... I MEAN, THIS IS A STEP IN THE RIGHT DIRECTION, BUT...
WE CAN DO IT IN THE ALLEY ROUND THE BACK, IF YOU WANT. BUT THAT COSTS EXTRA.
WHAT BOTHERS ME IS THE TEMPORARY LOSS OF CONTROL THAT COMES WITH RELEASE. THAT'S PROBABLY WHY I'VE STAYED CLEAR UP 'TIL NOW.
PERHAPS IF THERE WAS SOME ELEMENT OF DEGRADATION AT THE BEGINNING, THAT WOULD HELP ME TO PUT IT IN CONTEXT...
HMMM.
HOW MUCH DOES IT COST TO PISS IN YOUR MOUTH?

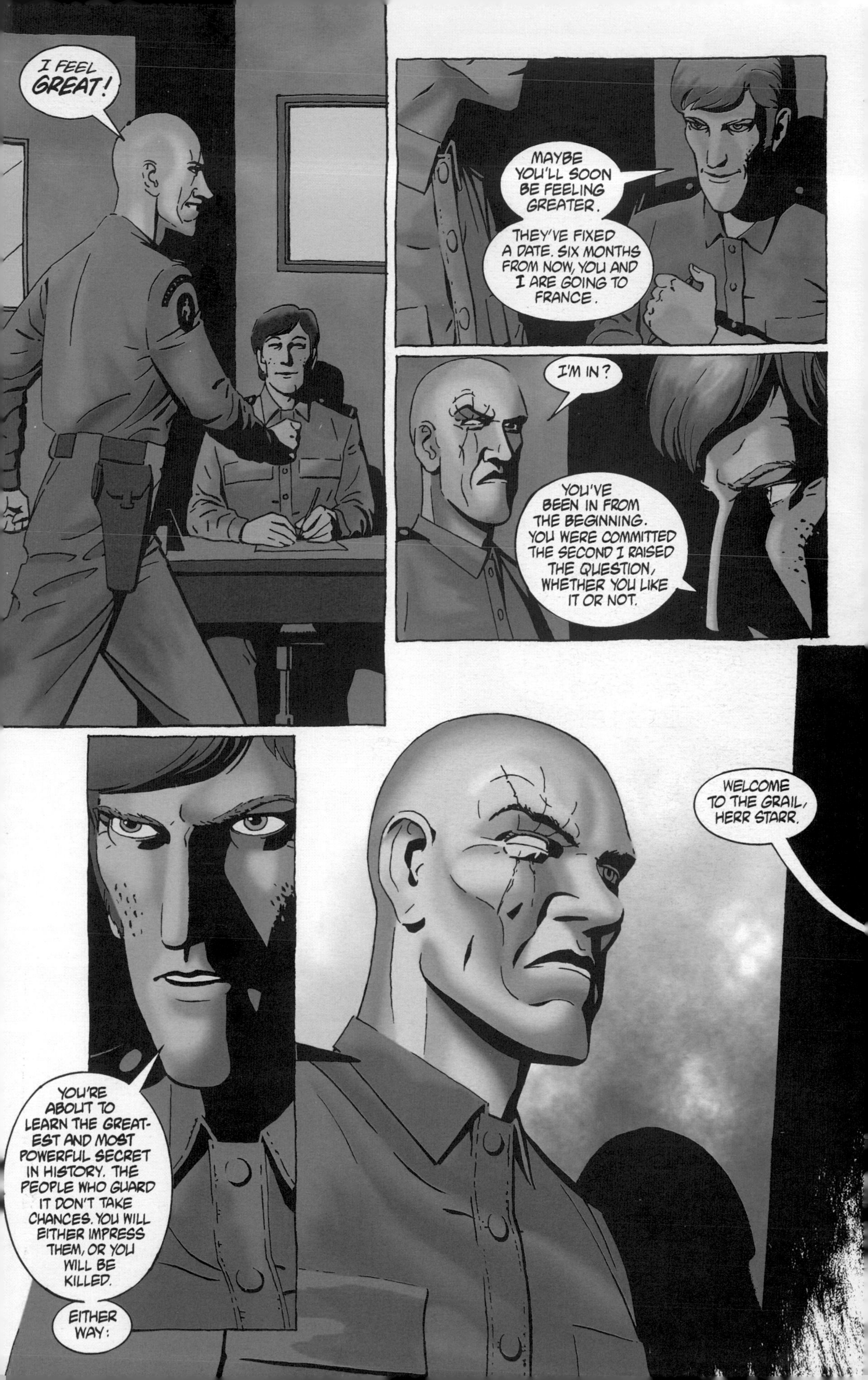
I FEEL GREAT!
MAYBE YOU'LL SOON BE FEELING GREATER.
THEY'VE FIXED A DATE. SIX MONTHS FROM NOW, YOU AND I ARE GOING TO FRANCE.
I'M IN?
YOU'VE BEEN IN FROM THE BEGINNING. YOU WERE COMMITTED THE SECOND I RAISED THE QUESTION, WHETHER YOU LIKE IT OR NOT.
WELCOME TO THE GRAIL, HERR STARR.
YOU'RE ABOUT TO LEARN THE GREATEST AND MOST POWERFUL SECRET IN HISTORY. THE PEOPLE WHO GUARD IT DON'T TAKE CHANCES. YOU WILL EITHER IMPRESS THEM, OR YOU WILL BE KILLED.
EITHER WAY:

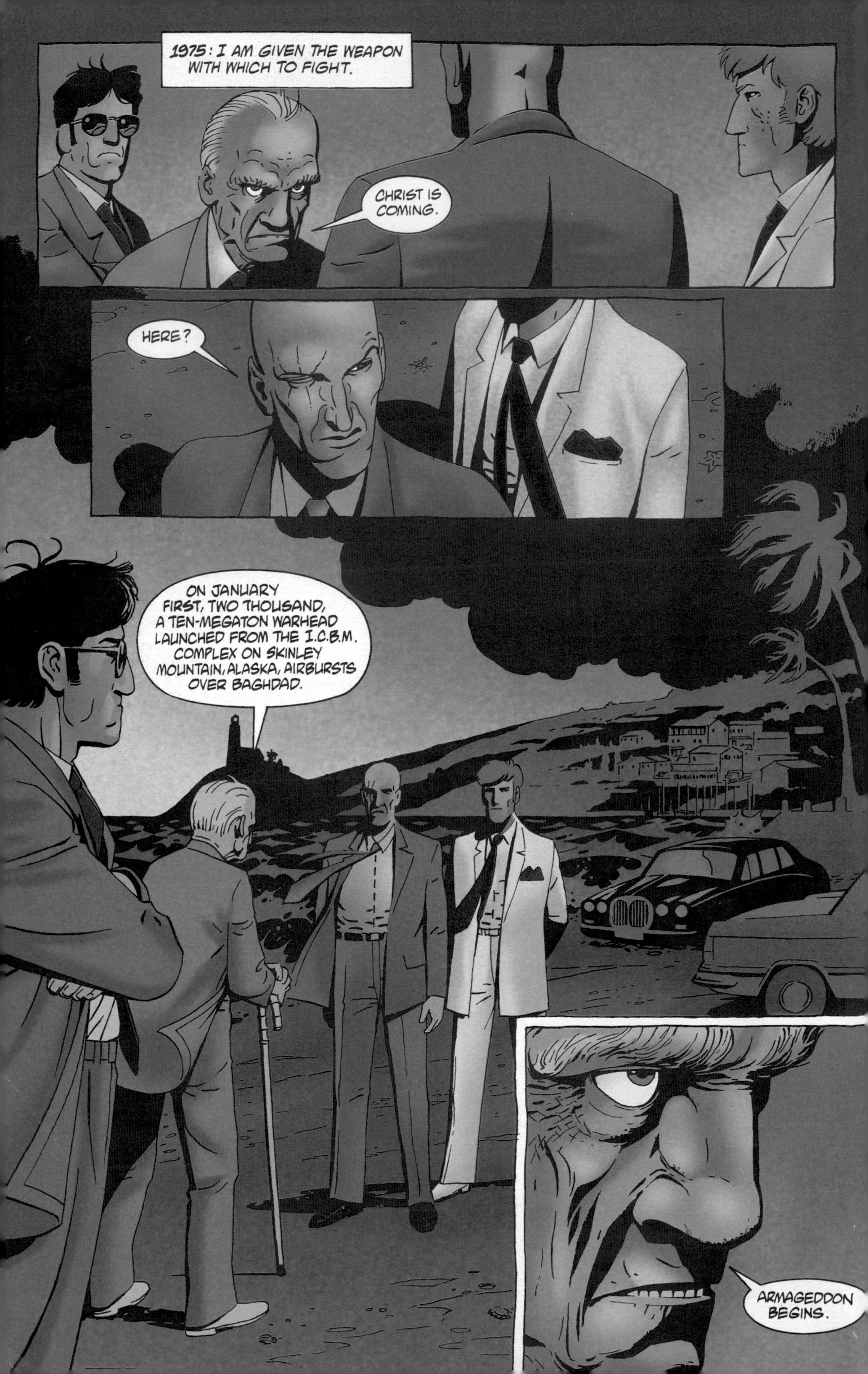
1975: I AM GIVEN THE WEAPON WITH WHICH TO FIGHT.
CHRIST IS COMING.
HERE?
ON JANUARY FIRST, TWO THOUSAND, A TEN-MEGATON WARHEAD LAUNCHED FROM THE I.C.B.M. COMPLEX ON SKINLEY MOUNTAIN, ALASKA, AIRBURSTS OVER BAGHDAD.
ARMAGEDDON BEGINS.

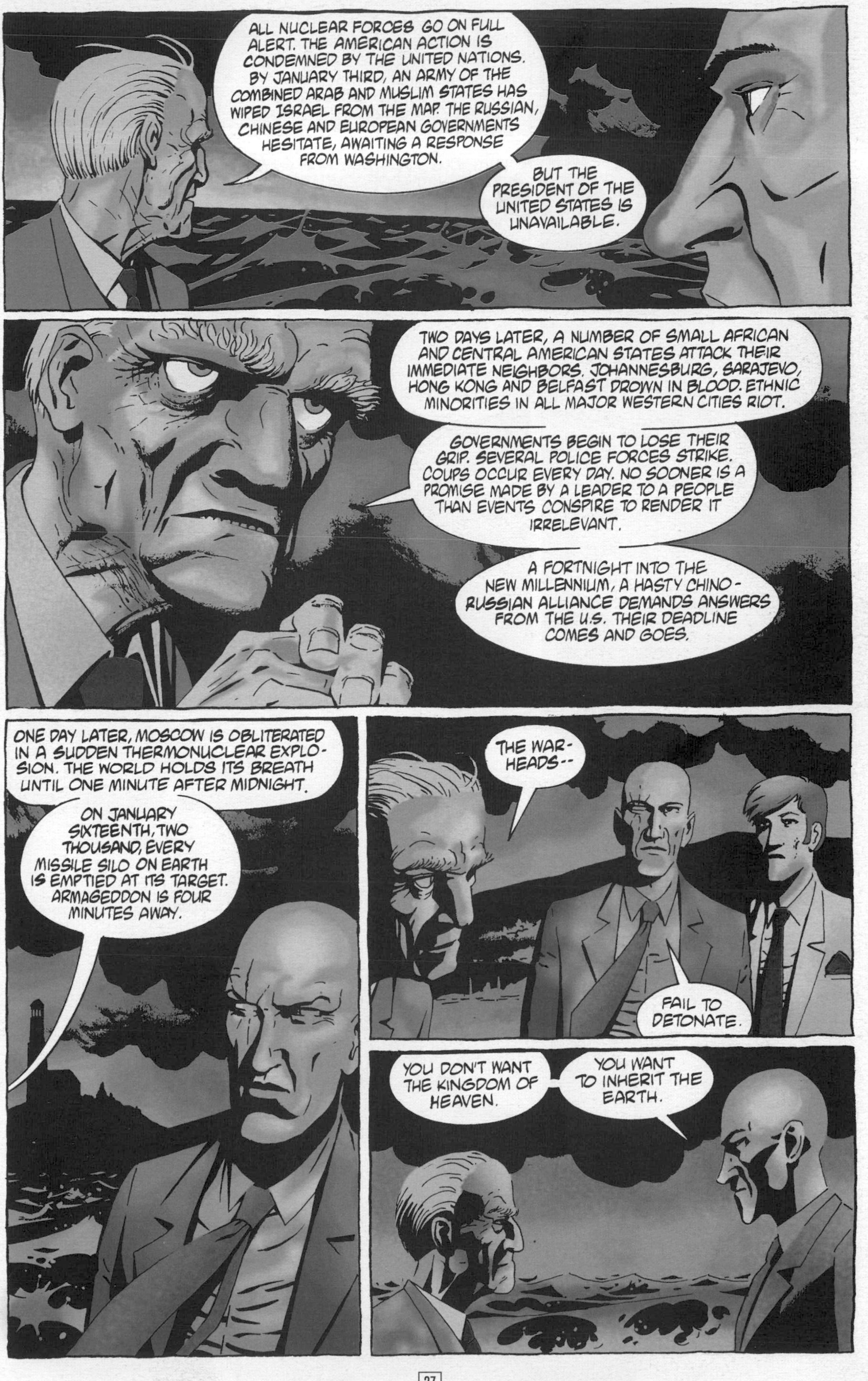
ALL NUCLEAR FORCES GO ON FULL ALERT. THE AMERICAN ACTION IS CONDEMNED BY THE UNITED NATIONS. BY JANUARY THIRD, AN ARMY OF THE COMBINED ARAB AND MUSLIM STATES HAS WIPED ISRAEL FROM THE MAP. THE RUSSIAN, CHINESE AND EUROPEAN GOVERNMENTS HESITATE, AWAITING A RESPONSE FROM WASHINGTON.
BUT THE PRESIDENT OF THE UNITED STATES IS UNAVAILABLE.
TWO DAYS LATER, A NUMBER OF SMALL AFRICAN AND CENTRAL AMERICAN STATES ATTACK THEIR IMMEDIATE NEIGHBORS. JOHANNESBURG, SARAJEVO, HONG KONG AND BELFAST DROWN IN BLOOD. ETHNIC MINORITIES IN ALL MAJOR WESTERN CITIES RIOT.
GOVERNMENTS BEGIN TO LOSE THEIR GRIP. SEVERAL POLICE FORCES STRIKE. COUPS OCCUR EVERY DAY. NO SOONER IS A PROMISE MADE BY A LEADER TO A PEOPLE THAN EVENTS CONSPIRE TO RENDER IT IRRELEVANT.
A FORTNIGHT INTO THE NEW MILLENNIUM, A HASTY CHINO-RUSSIAN ALLIANCE DEMANDS ANSWERS FROM THE U.S. THEIR DEADLINE COMES AND GOES.
ONE DAY LATER, MOSCOW IS OBLITERATED IN A SUDDEN THERMONUCLEAR EXPLOSION. THE WORLD HOLDS ITS BREATH UNTIL ONE MINUTE AFTER MIDNIGHT.
ON JANUARY SIXTEENTH, TWO THOUSAND, EVERY MISSILE SILO ON EARTH IS EMPTIED AT ITS TARGET. ARMAGEDDON IS FOUR MINUTES AWAY.
THE WAR-HEADS--
FAIL TO DETONATE.
YOU DON'T WANT THE KINGDOM OF HEAVEN.
YOU WANT TO INHERIT THE EARTH.

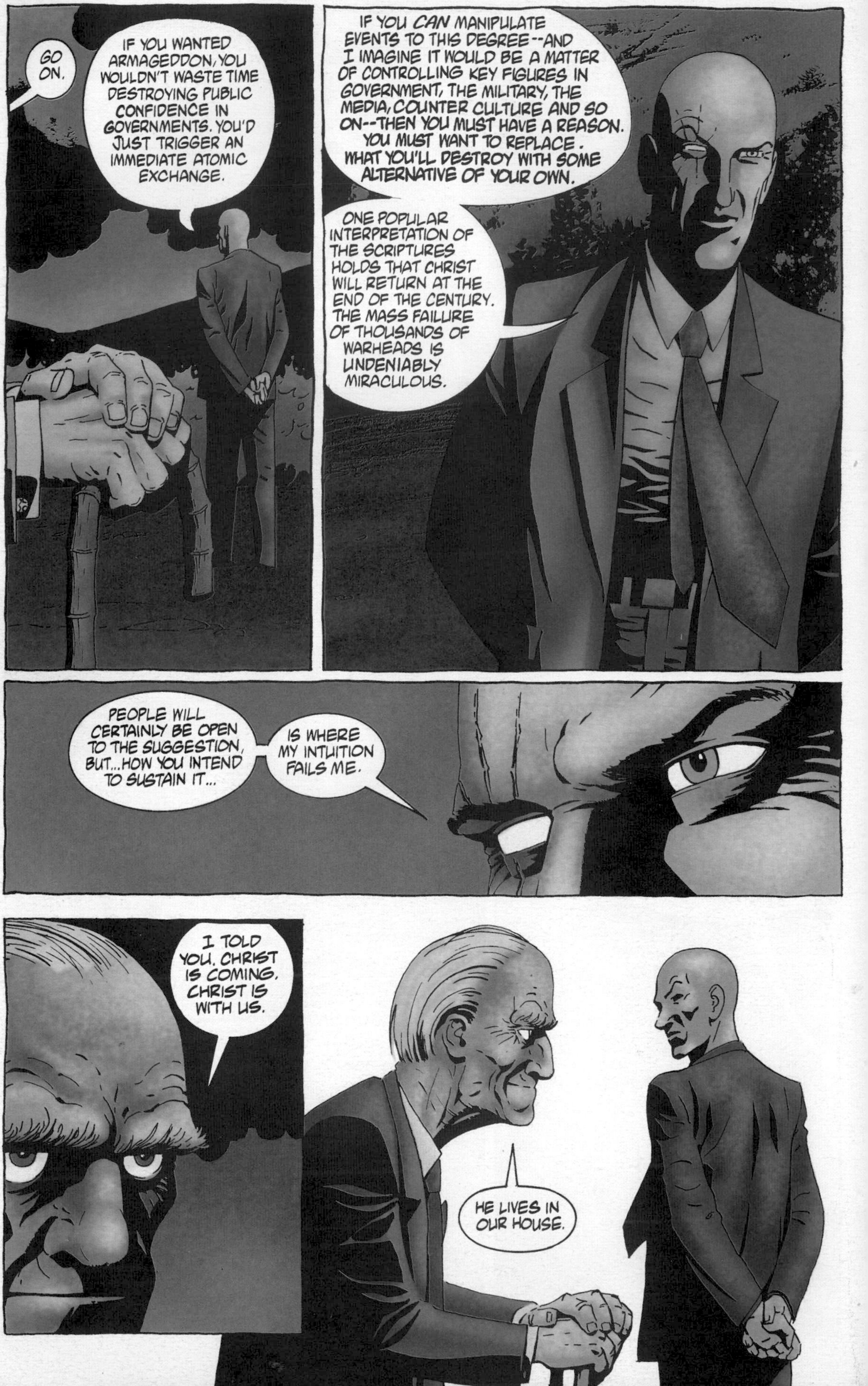
GO ON.
IF YOU WANTED ARMAGEDDON, YOU WOULDN'T WASTE TIME DESTROYING PUBLIC CONFIDENCE IN GOVERNMENTS. YOU'D JUST TRIGGER AN IMMEDIATE ATOMIC EXCHANGE.
IF YOU CAN MANIPULATE EVENTS TO THIS DEGREE--AND I IMAGINE IT WOULD BE A MATTER OF CONTROLLING KEY FIGURES IN GOVERNMENT, THE MILITARY, THE MEDIA, COUNTER CULTURE AND SO ON--THEN YOU MUST HAVE A REASON. YOU MUST WANT TO REPLACE. WHAT YOU'LL DESTROY WITH SOME ALTERNATIVE OF YOUR OWN.
ONE POPULAR INTERPRETATION OF THE SCRIPTURES HOLDS THAT CHRIST WILL RETURN AT THE END OF THE CENTURY. THE MASS FAILURE OF THOUSANDS OF WARHEADS IS UNDENIABLY MIRACULOUS.
PEOPLE WILL CERTAINLY BE OPEN TO THE SUGGESTION, BUT...HOW YOU INTEND TO SUSTAIN IT...
IS WHERE MY INTUITION FAILS ME.
I TOLD YOU. CHRIST IS COMING. CHRIST IS WITH US.
HE LIVES IN OUR HOUSE.

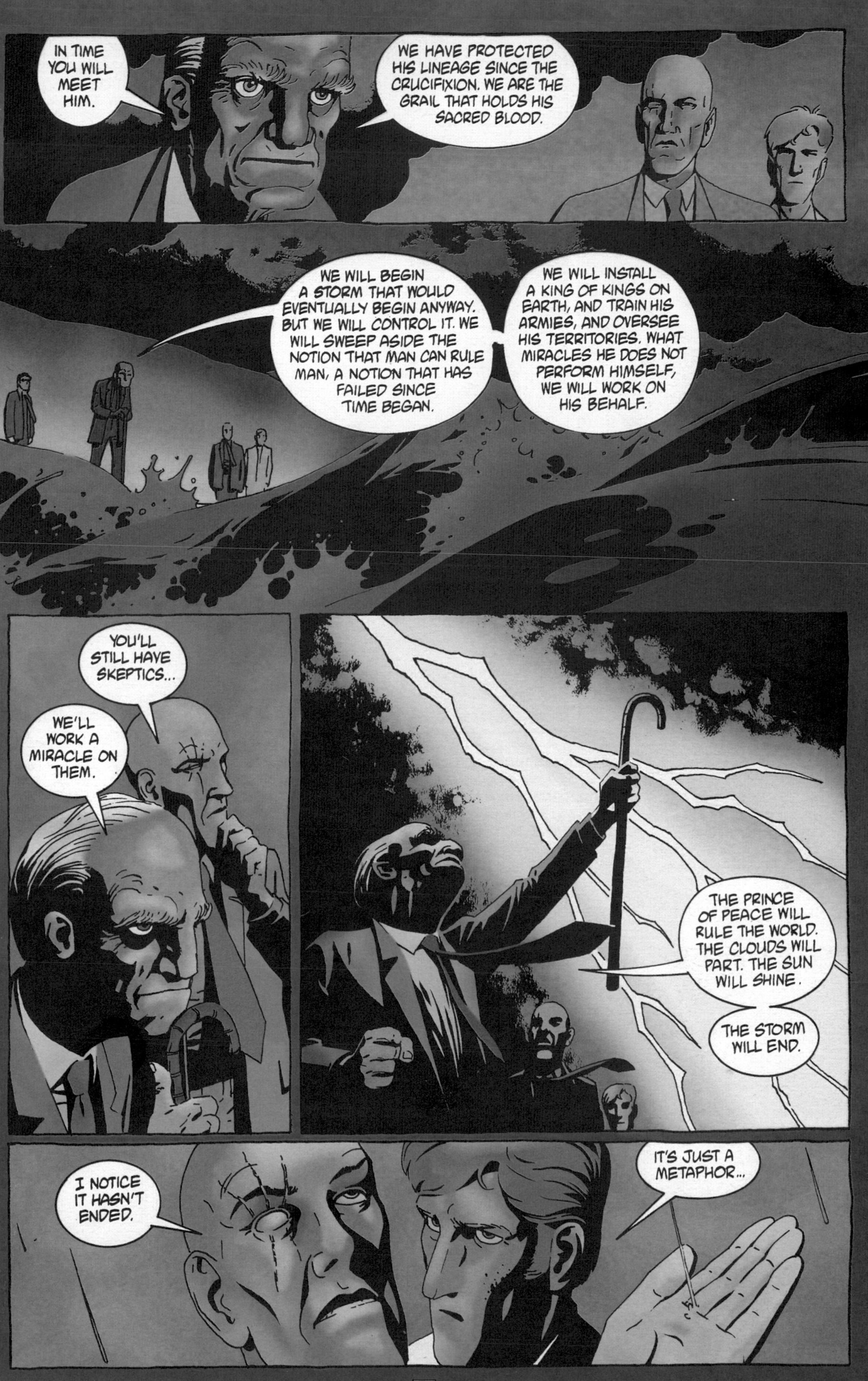
IN TIME YOU WILL MEET HIM.
WE HAVE PROTECTED HIS LINEAGE SINCE THE CRUCIFIXION. WE ARE THE GRAIL THAT HOLDS HIS SACRED BLOOD.
WE WILL BEGIN A STORM THAT WOULD EVENTUALLY BEGIN ANYWAY. BUT WE WILL CONTROL IT. WE WILL SWEEP ASIDE THE NOTION THAT MAN CAN RULE MAN, A NOTION THAT HAS FAILED SINCE TIME BEGAN.
WE WILL INSTALL A KING OF KINGS ON EARTH, AND TRAIN HIS ARMIES, AND OVERSEE HIS TERRITORIES. WHAT MIRACLES HE DOES NOT PERFORM HIMSELF, WE WILL WORK ON HIS BEHALF.
YOU'LL STILL HAVE SKEPTICS...
WE'LL WORK A MIRACLE ON THEM.
THE PRINCE OF PEACE WILL RULE THE WORLD. THE CLOUDS WILL PART. THE SUN WILL SHINE.
THE STORM WILL END.
I NOTICE IT HASN'T ENDED.
IT'S JUST A METAPHOR...

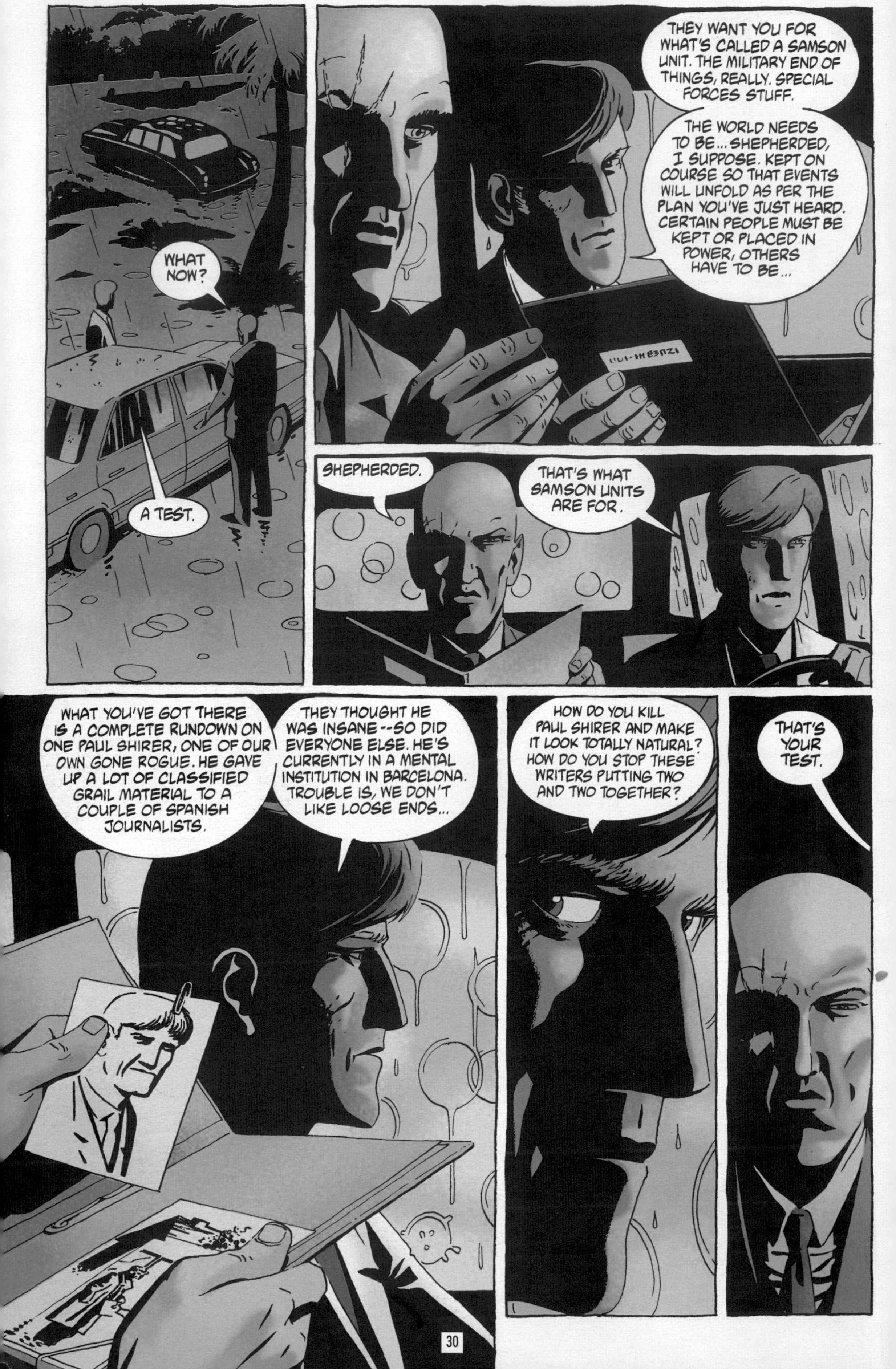
WHAT NOW?
A TEST.
THEY WANT YOU FOR WHAT'S CALLED A SAMSON UNIT. THE MILITARY END OF THINGS, REALLY. SPECIAL FORCES STUFF.
THE WORLD NEEDS TO BE... SHEPHERDED, I SUPPOSE. KEPT ON COURSE SO THAT EVENTS WILL UNFOLD AS PER THE PLAN YOU'VE JUST HEARD. CERTAIN PEOPLE MUST BE KEPT OR PLACED IN POWER, OTHERS HAVE TO BE...
SHEPHERDED.
THAT'S WHAT SAMSON UNITS ARE FOR.
WHAT YOU'VE GOT THERE IS A COMPLETE RUNDOWN ON ONE PAUL SHIRER, ONE OF OUR OWN GONE ROGUE. HE GAVE UP A LOT OF CLASSIFIED GRAIL MATERIAL TO A COUPLE OF SPANISH JOURNALISTS.
THEY THOUGHT HE WAS INSANE --SO DID EVERYONE ELSE. HE'S CURRENTLY IN A MENTAL INSTITUTION IN BARCELONA. TROUBLE IS, WE DON'T LIKE LOOSE ENDS...
HOW DO YOU KILL PAUL SHIRER AND MAKE IT LOOK TOTALLY NATURAL? HOW DO YOU STOP THESE WRITERS PUTTING TWO AND TWO TOGETHER?
THAT'S YOUR TEST.

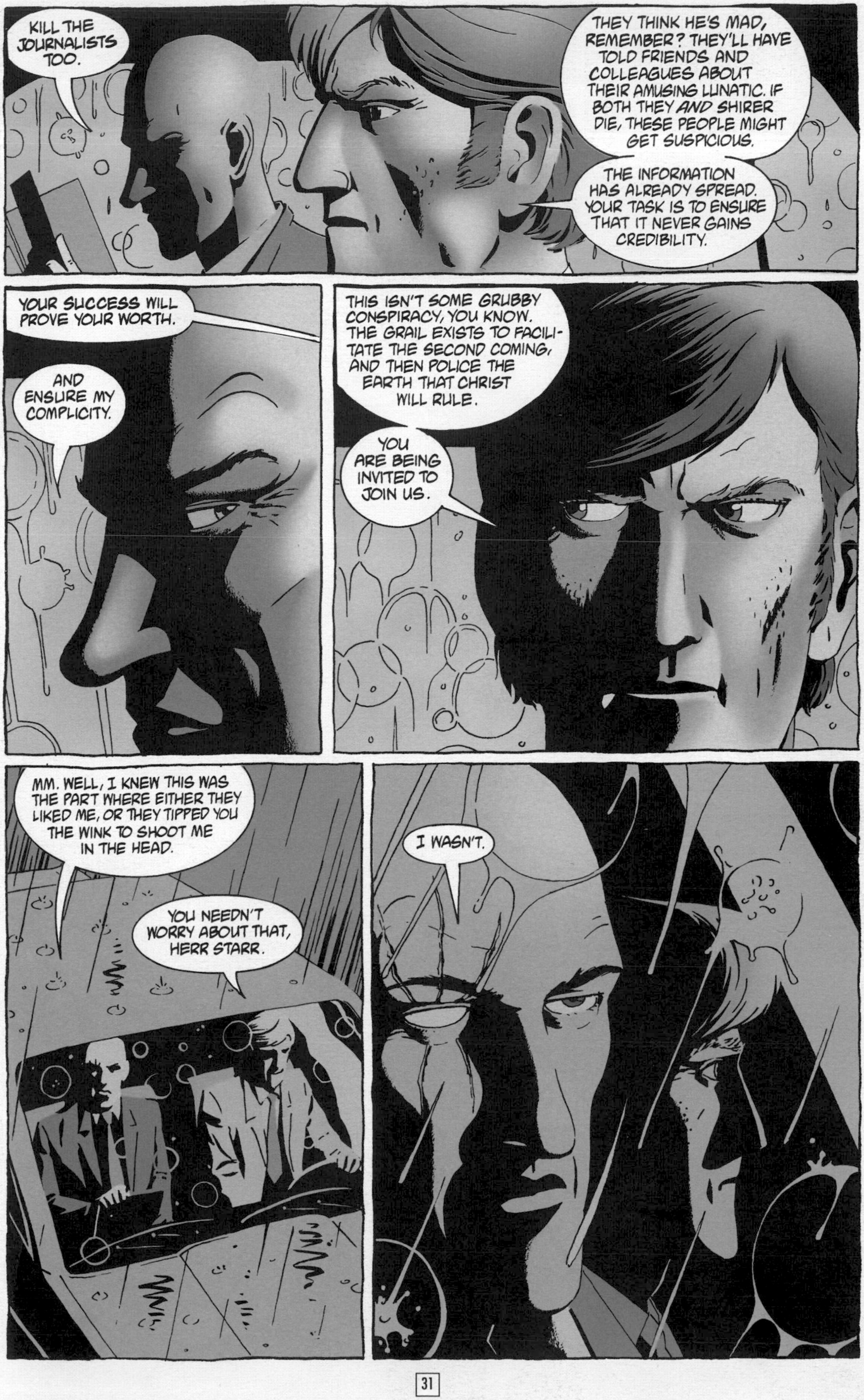
KILL THE JOURNALISTS TOO.
THEY THINK HE'S MAD, REMEMBER? THEY'LL HAVE TOLD FRIENDS AND COLLEAGUES ABOUT THEIR AMUSING LUNATIC. IF BOTH THEY AND SHIRER DIE, THESE PEOPLE MIGHT GET SUSPICIOUS.
THE INFORMATION HAS ALREADY SPREAD. YOUR TASK IS TO ENSURE THAT IT NEVER GAINS CREDIBILITY.
YOUR SUCCESS WILL PROVE YOUR WORTH.
AND ENSURE MY COMPLICITY.
THIS ISN'T SOME GRUBBY CONSPIRACY, YOU KNOW. THE GRAIL EXISTS TO FACILITATE THE SECOND COMING, AND THEN POLICE THE EARTH THAT CHRIST WILL RULE.
YOU ARE BEING INVITED TO JOIN US.
MM. WELL, I KNEW THIS WAS THE PART WHERE EITHER THEY LIKED ME, OR THEY TIPPED YOU THE WINK TO SHOOT ME IN THE HEAD.
YOU NEEDN'T WORRY ABOUT THAT, HERR STARR.
I WASN'T.

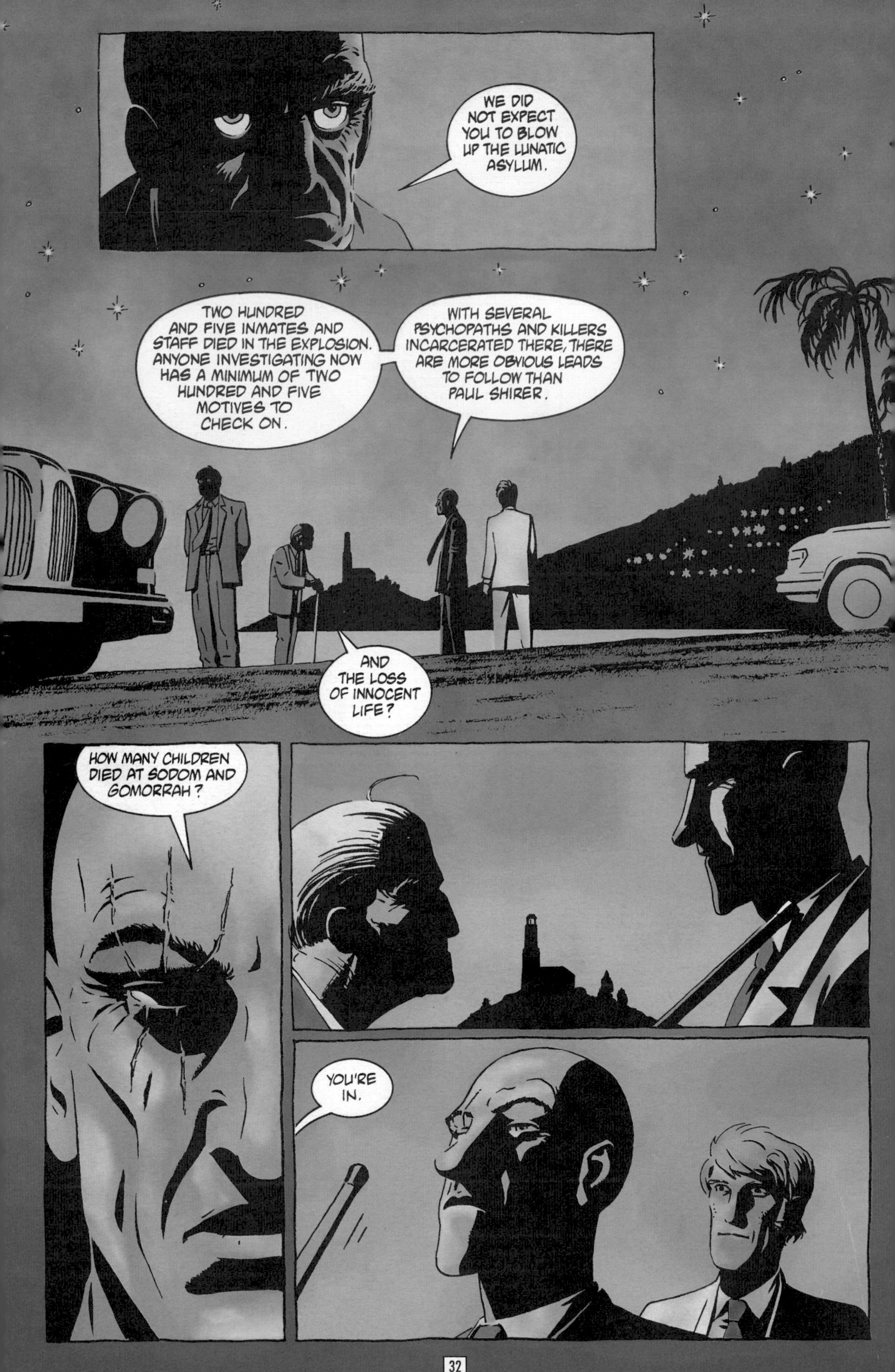
WE DID NOT EXPECT YOU TO BLOW UP THE LUNATIC ASYLUM.
TWO HUNDRED AND FIVE INMATES AND STAFF DIED IN THE EXPLOSION. ANYONE INVESTIGATING NOW HAS A MINIMUM OF TWO HUNDRED AND FIVE MOTIVES TO CHECK ON.
WITH SEVERAL PSYCHOPATHS AND KILLERS INCARCERATED THERE, THERE ARE MORE OBVIOUS LEADS TO FOLLOW THAN PAUL SHIRER.
AND THE LOSS OF INNOCENT LIFE?
HOW MANY CHILDREN DIED AT SODOM AND GOMORRAH?
YOU'RE IN.

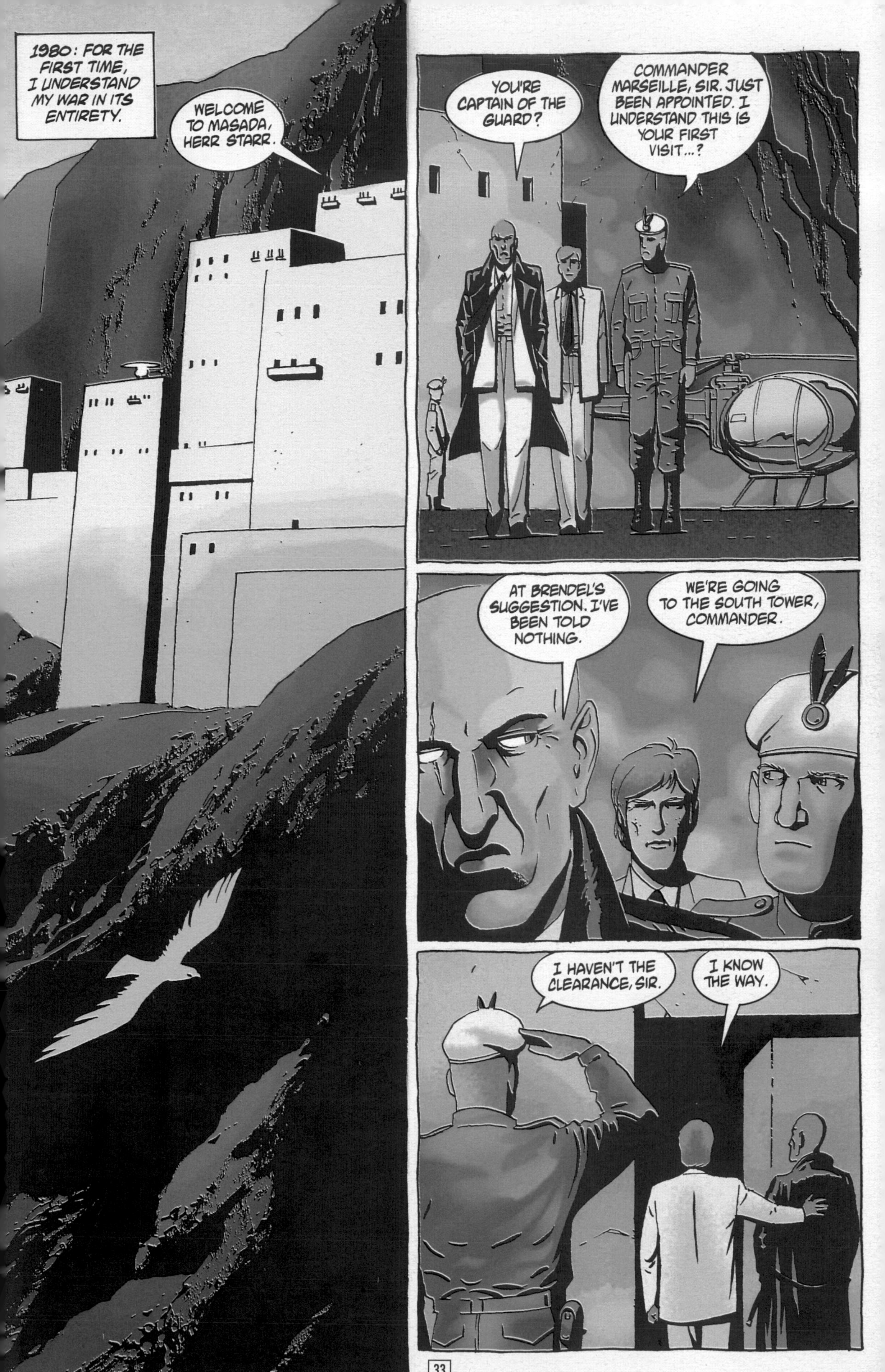

1980: FOR THE FIRST TIME, I UNDERSTAND MY WAR IN ITS ENTIRETY.
WELCOME TO MASADA, HERR STARR.
YOU'RE CAPTAIN OF THE GUARD?
COMMANDER MARSEILLE, SIR. JUST BEEN APPOINTED. I UNDERSTAND THIS IS YOUR FIRST VISIT...?
AT BRENDEL'S SUGGESTION. I'VE BEEN TOLD NOTHING.
WE'RE GOING TO THE SOUTH TOWER, COMMANDER.
I HAVEN'T THE CLEARANCE, SIR.
I KNOW THE WAY.

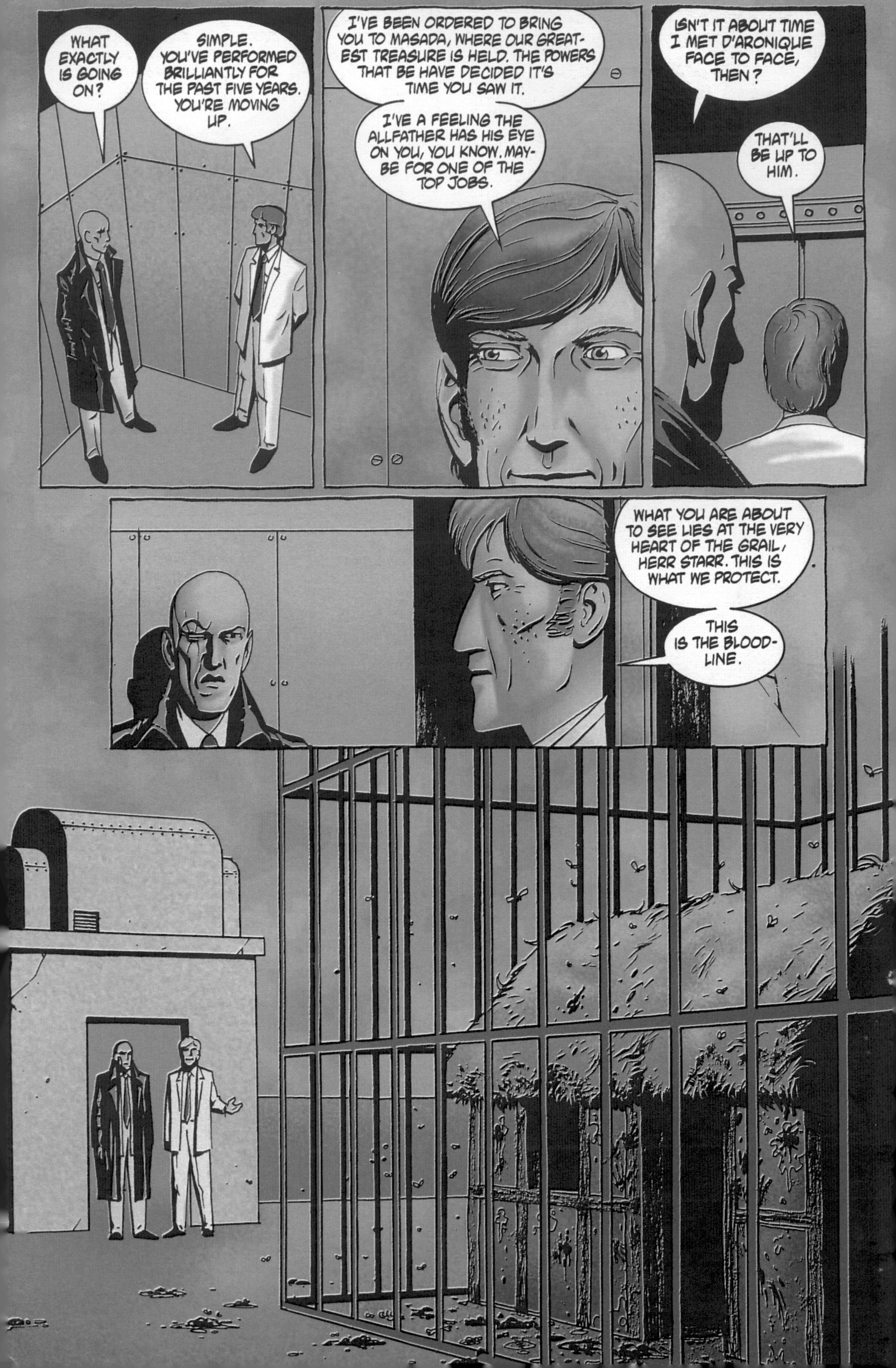
WHAT EXACTLY IS GOING ON?
SIMPLE. YOU'VE PERFORMED BRILLIANTLY FOR THE PAST FIVE YEARS. YOU'RE MOVING UP.
I'VE BEEN ORDERED TO BRING YOU TO MASADA, WHERE OUR GREAT-EST TREASURE IS HELD. THE POWERS THAT BE HAVE DECIDED IT'S TIME YOU SAW IT.
I'VE A FEELING THE ALLFATHER HAS HIS EYE ON YOU, YOU KNOW. MAY-BE FOR ONE OF THE TOP JOBS.
ISN'T IT ABOUT TIME I MET D'ARONIQUE FACE TO FACE, THEN?
THAT'LL BE UP TO HIM.
WHAT YOU ARE ABOUT TO SEE LIES AT THE VERY HEART OF THE GRAIL, HERR STARR. THIS IS WHAT WE PROTECT.
THIS IS THE BLOOD-LINE.

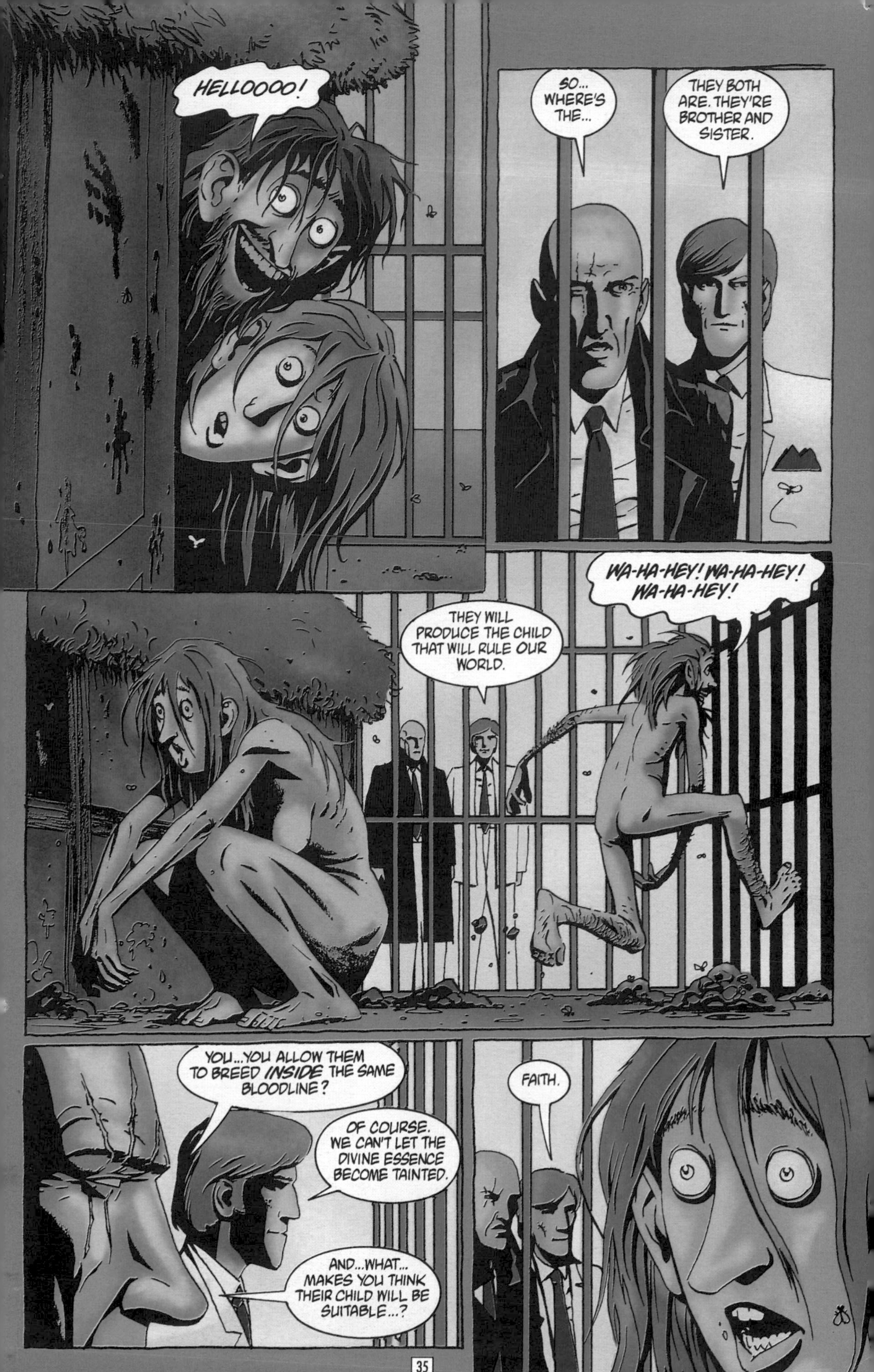
HELLOOOO!
SO... WHERE'S THE...
THEY BOTH ARE. THEY'RE BROTHER AND SISTER.
WA-HA-HEY! WA-HA-HEY! WA-HA-HEY!
THEY WILL PRODUCE THE CHILD THAT WILL RULE OUR WORLD.
YOU...YOU ALLOW THEM TO BREED *INSIDE* THE SAME BLOODLINE?
OF COURSE. WE CAN'T LET THE DIVINE ESSENCE BECOME TAINTED.
AND...WHAT... MAKES YOU THINK THEIR CHILD WILL BE SUITABLE...?
FAITH.

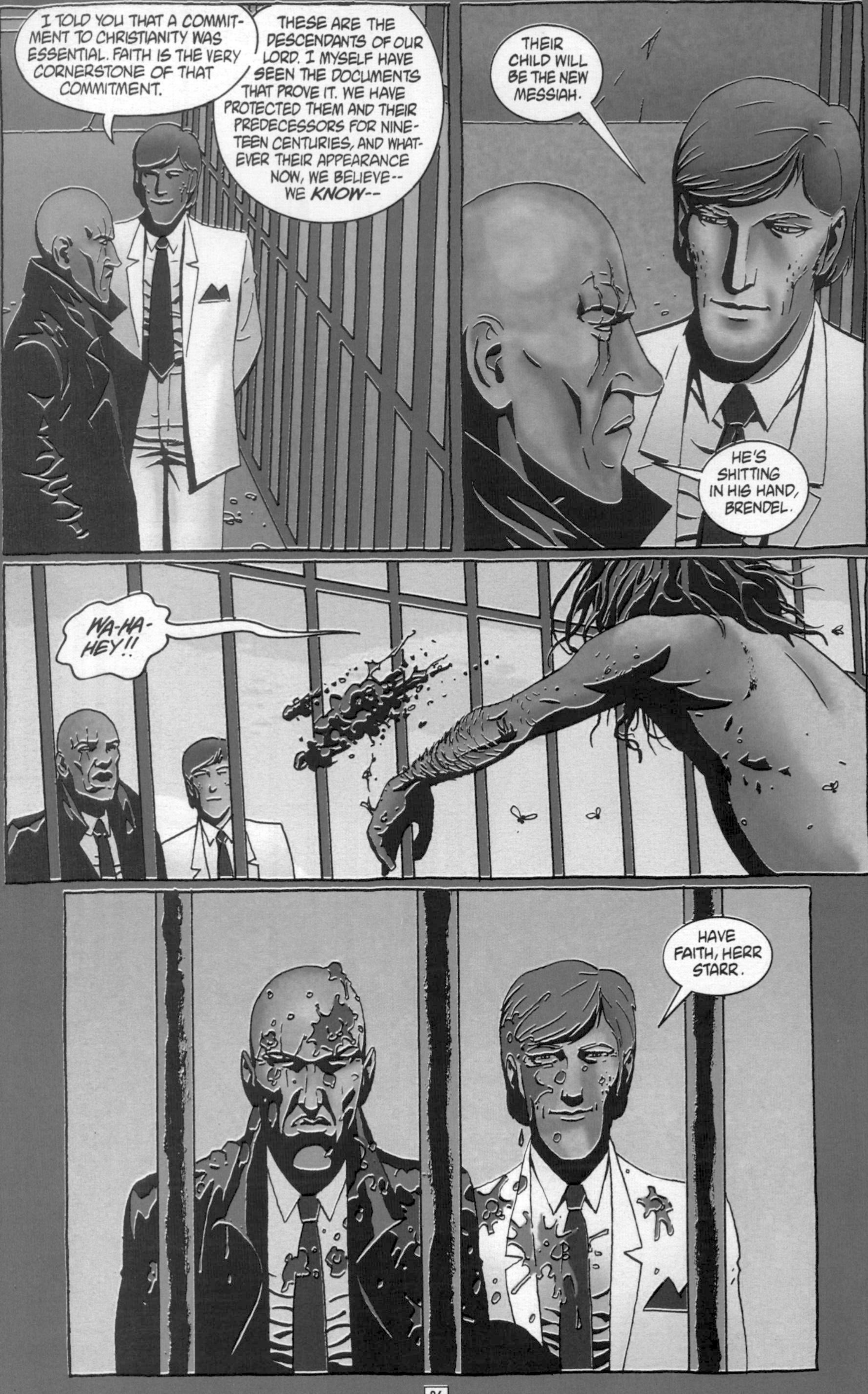

I TOLD YOU THAT A COMMITMENT TO CHRISTIANITY WAS ESSENTIAL. FAITH IS THE VERY CORNERSTONE OF THAT COMMITMENT.
THESE ARE THE DESCENDANTS OF OUR LORD. I MYSELF HAVE SEEN THE DOCUMENTS THAT PROVE IT. WE HAVE PROTECTED THEM AND THEIR PREDECESSORS FOR NINETEEN CENTURIES, AND WHATEVER THEIR APPEARANCE NOW, WE BELIEVE-- WE *KNOW*--
THEIR CHILD WILL BE THE NEW MESSIAH.
HE'S SHITTING IN HIS HAND, BRENDEL.
WA-HA-HEY!!
HAVE FAITH, HERR STARR.

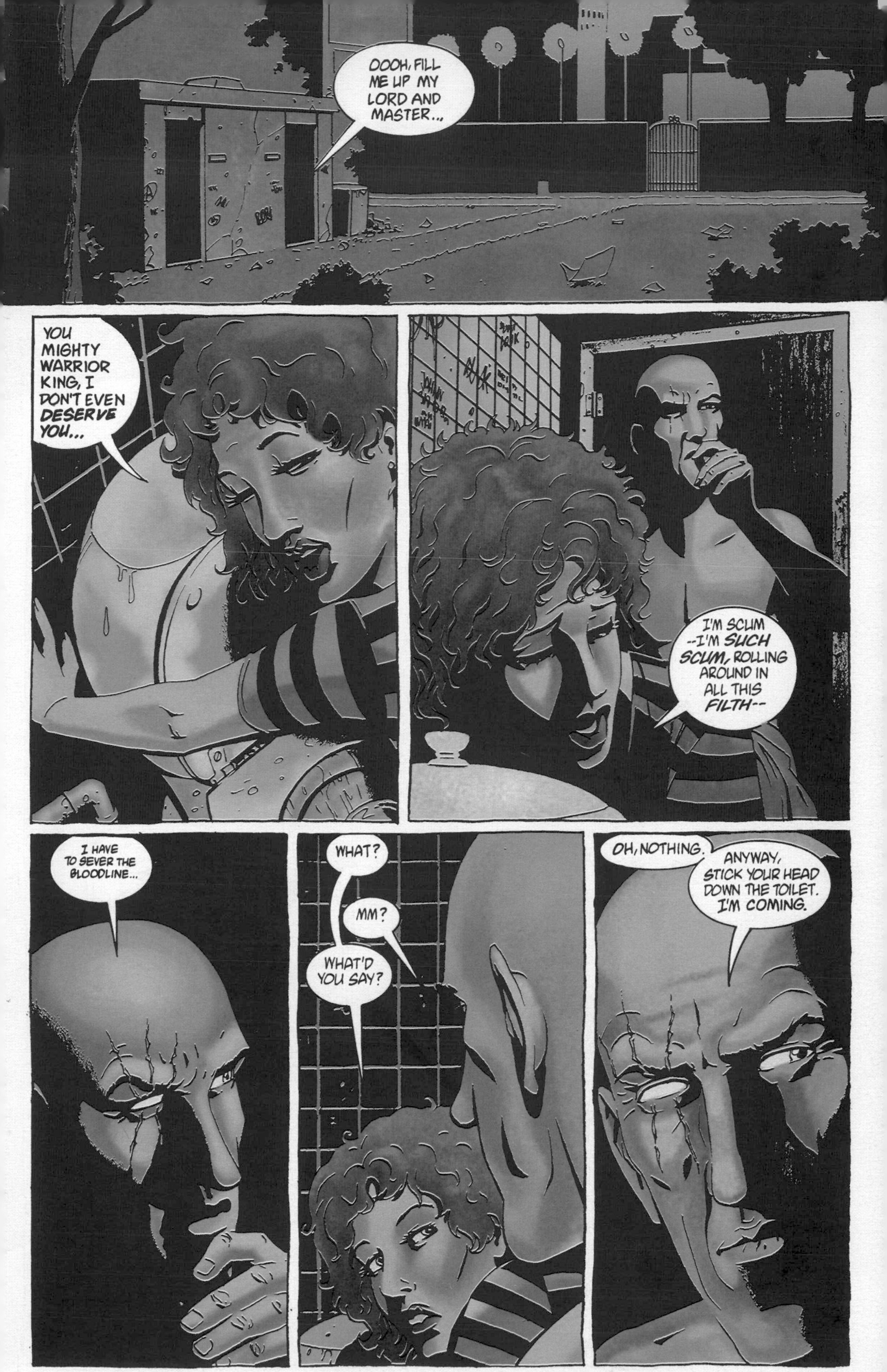
OOOH, FILL ME UP MY LORD AND MASTER...
YOU MIGHTY WARRIOR KING, I DON'T EVEN DESERVE YOU...
I'M SCUM --I'M SUCH SCUM, ROLLING AROUND IN ALL THIS FILTH--
I HAVE TO SEVER THE BLOODLINE...
WHAT?
MM?
WHAT'D YOU SAY?
OH, NOTHING.
ANYWAY, STICK YOUR HEAD DOWN THE TOILET. I'M COMING.

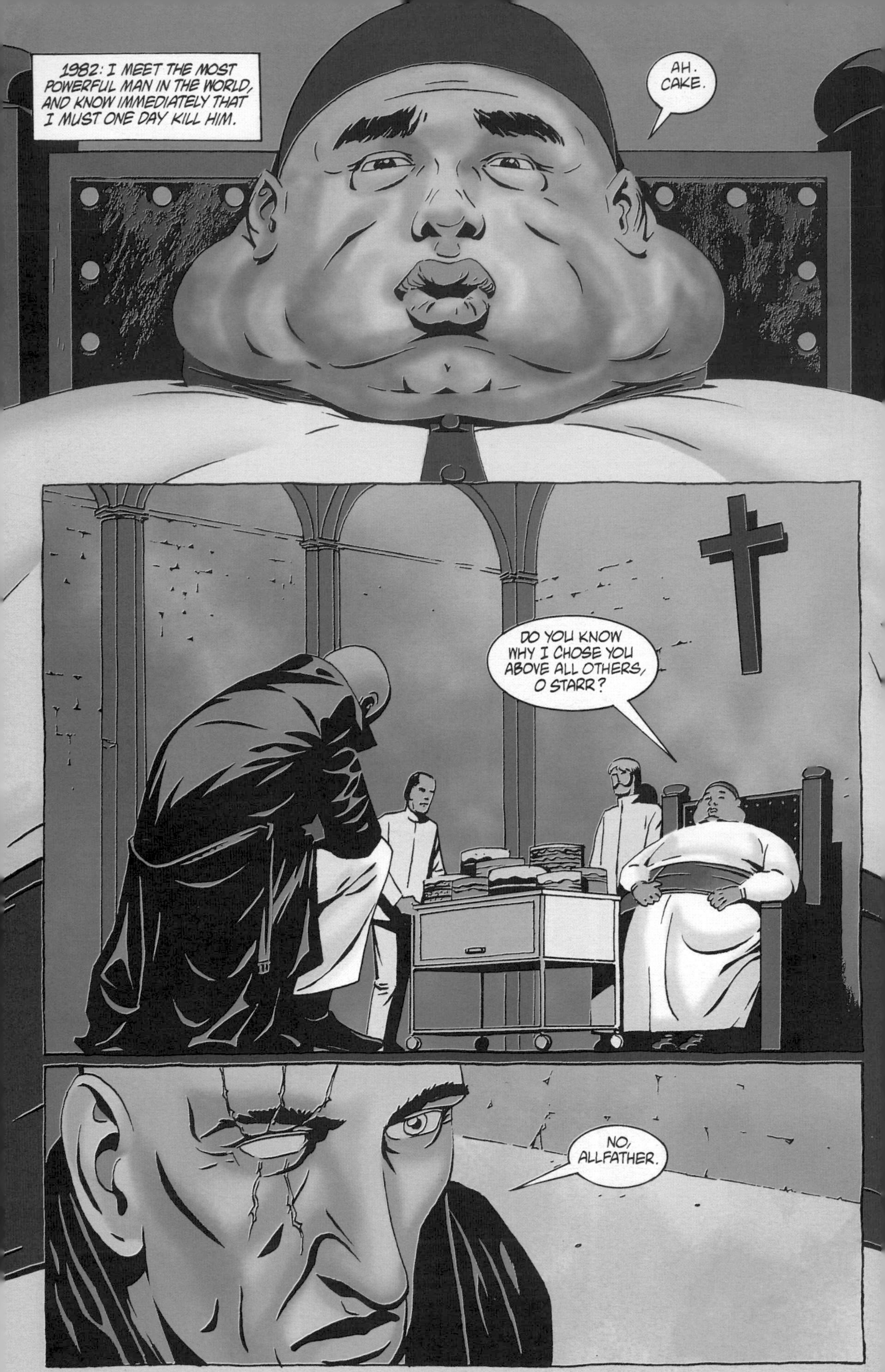
1982: I MEET THE MOST POWERFUL MAN IN THE WORLD, AND KNOW IMMEDIATELY THAT I MUST ONE DAY KILL HIM.
AH. CAKE.
DO YOU KNOW WHY I CHOSE YOU ABOVE ALL OTHERS, O STARR?
NO, ALLFATHER.

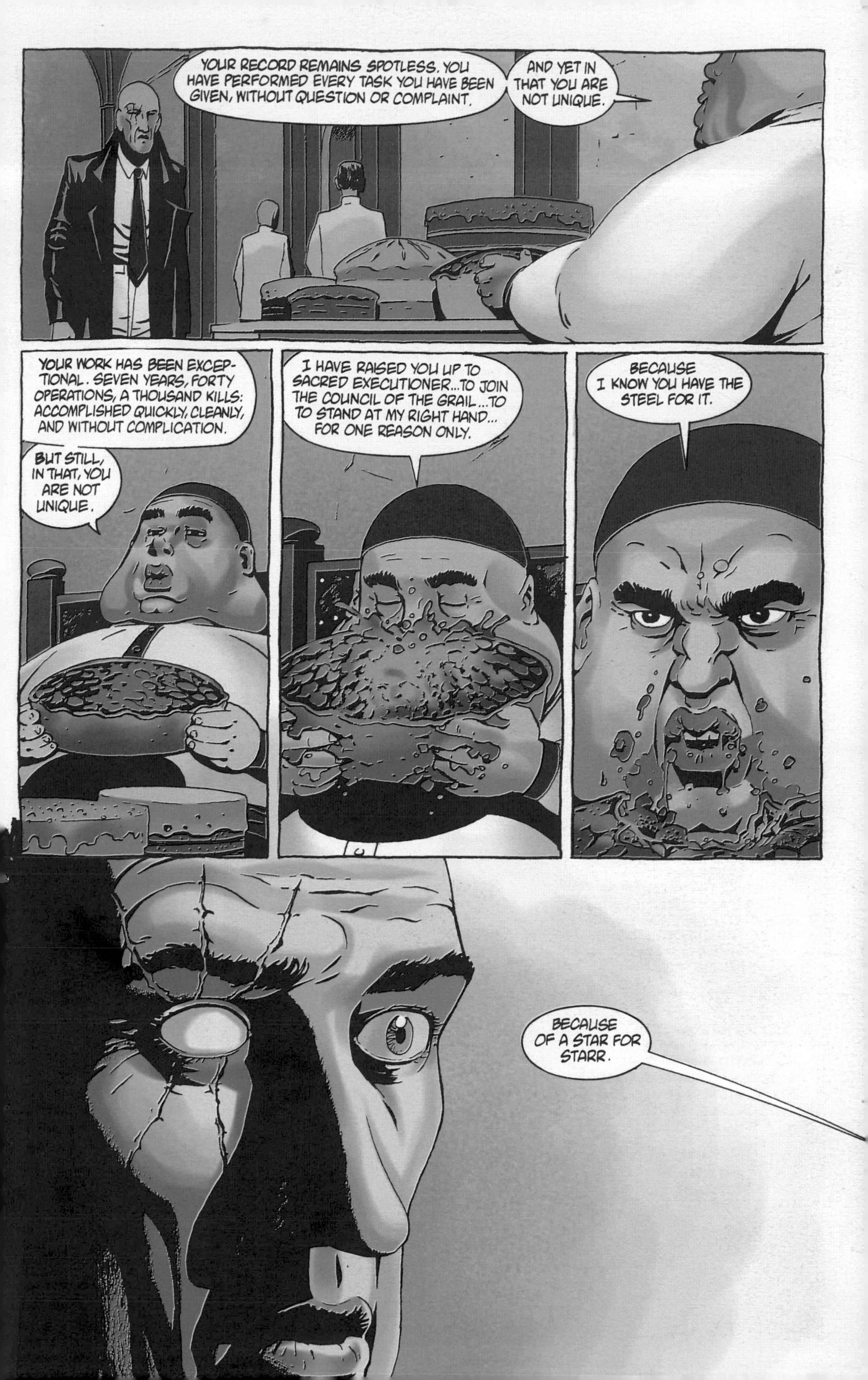
YOUR RECORD REMAINS SPOTLESS. YOU HAVE PERFORMED EVERY TASK YOU HAVE BEEN GIVEN, WITHOUT QUESTION OR COMPLAINT.
AND YET IN THAT YOU ARE NOT UNIQUE.
YOUR WORK HAS BEEN EXCEPTIONAL. SEVEN YEARS, FORTY OPERATIONS, A THOUSAND KILLS: ACCOMPLISHED QUICKLY, CLEANLY, AND WITHOUT COMPLICATION.
BUT STILL, IN THAT, YOU ARE NOT UNIQUE.
I HAVE RAISED YOU UP TO SACRED EXECUTIONER...TO JOIN THE COUNCIL OF THE GRAIL...TO TO STAND AT MY RIGHT HAND... FOR ONE REASON ONLY.
BECAUSE I KNOW YOU HAVE THE STEEL FOR IT.
BECAUSE OF A STAR FOR STARR.

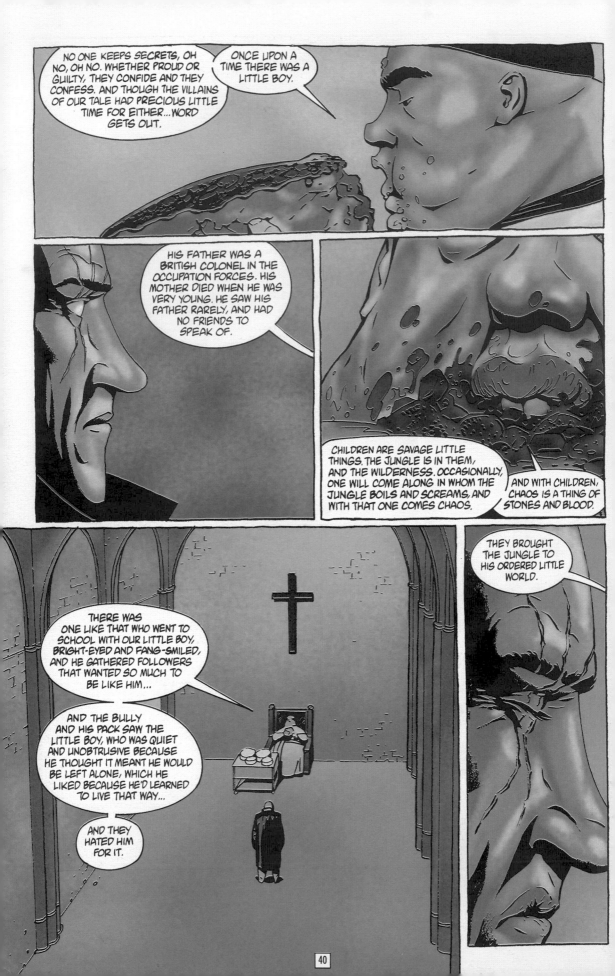

NO ONE KEEPS SECRETS, OH NO, OH NO. WHETHER PROUD OR GUILTY, THEY CONFIDE AND THEY CONFESS. AND THOUGH THE VILLAINS OF OUR TALE HAD PRECIOUS LITTLE TIME FOR EITHER...WORD GETS OUT.

ONCE UPON A TIME THERE WAS A LITTLE BOY.

HIS FATHER WAS A BRITISH COLONEL IN THE OCCUPATION FORCES. HIS MOTHER DIED WHEN HE WAS VERY YOUNG. HE SAW HIS FATHER RARELY, AND HAD NO FRIENDS TO SPEAK OF.

CHILDREN ARE SAVAGE LITTLE THINGS. THE JUNGLE IS IN THEM, AND THE WILDERNESS. OCCASIONALLY, ONE WILL COME ALONG IN WHOM THE JUNGLE BOILS AND SCREAMS, AND WITH THAT ONE COMES CHAOS.

AND WITH CHILDREN, CHAOS IS A THING OF STONES AND BLOOD.

THEY BROUGHT THE JUNGLE TO HIS ORDERED LITTLE WORLD.

THERE WAS ONE LIKE THAT WHO WENT TO SCHOOL WITH OUR LITTLE BOY, BRIGHT-EYED AND FANG-SMILED, AND HE GATHERED FOLLOWERS THAT WANTED SO MUCH TO BE LIKE HIM...

AND THE BULLY AND HIS PACK SAW THE LITTLE BOY, WHO WAS QUIET AND UNOBTRUSIVE BECAUSE HE THOUGHT IT MEANT HE WOULD BE LEFT ALONE, WHICH HE LIKED BECAUSE HE'D LEARNED TO LIVE THAT WAY...

AND THEY HATED HIM FOR IT.

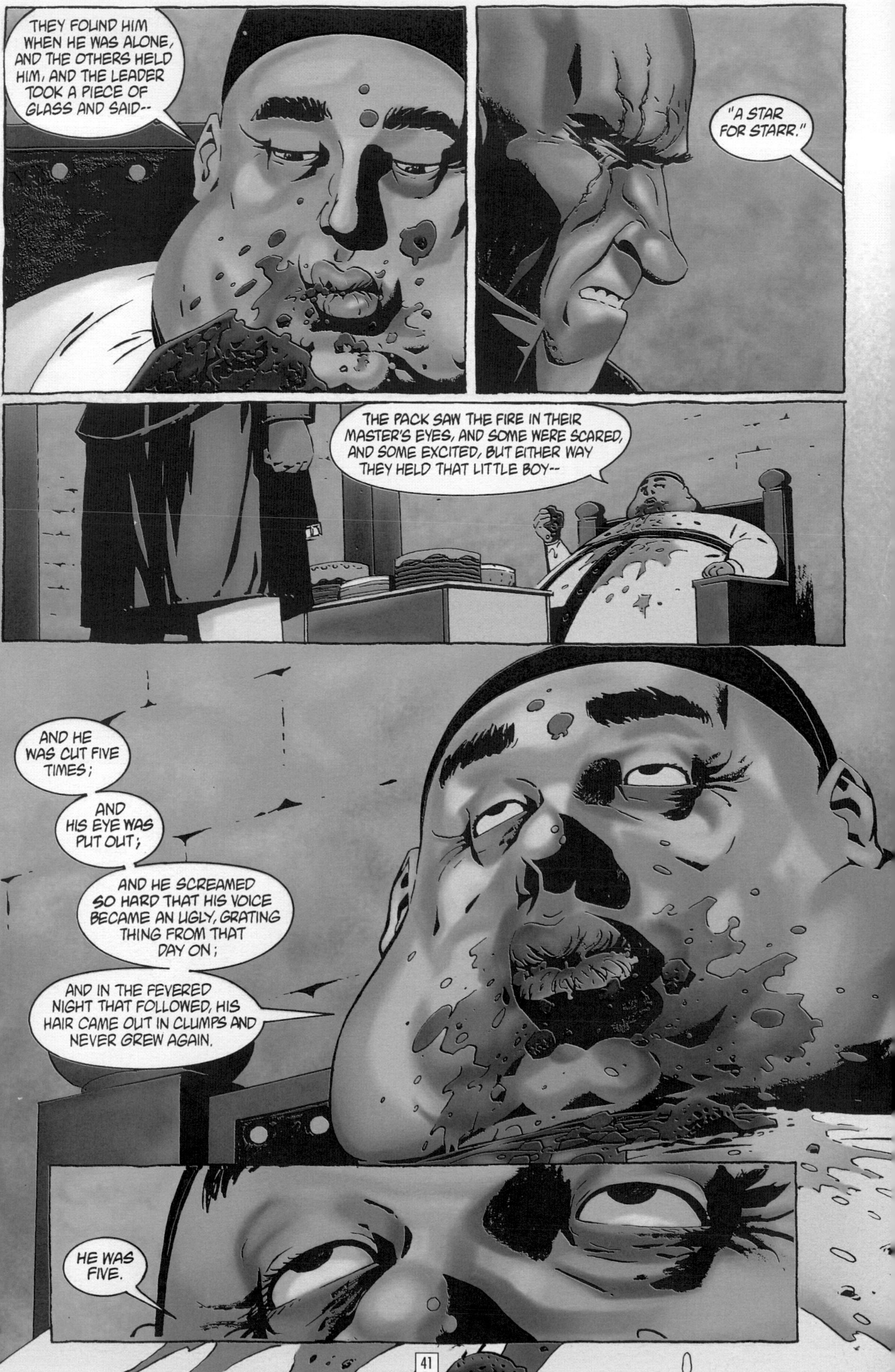
THEY FOUND HIM WHEN HE WAS ALONE, AND THE OTHERS HELD HIM, AND THE LEADER TOOK A PIECE OF GLASS AND SAID--
"A STAR FOR STARR."
THE PACK SAW THE FIRE IN THEIR MASTER'S EYES, AND SOME WERE SCARED, AND SOME EXCITED, BUT EITHER WAY THEY HELD THAT LITTLE BOY--
AND HE WAS CUT FIVE TIMES;
AND HIS EYE WAS PUT OUT;
AND HE SCREAMED SO HARD THAT HIS VOICE BECAME AN UGLY, GRATING THING FROM THAT DAY ON;
AND IN THE FEVERED NIGHT THAT FOLLOWED, HIS HAIR CAME OUT IN CLUMPS AND NEVER GREW AGAIN.
HE WAS FIVE.

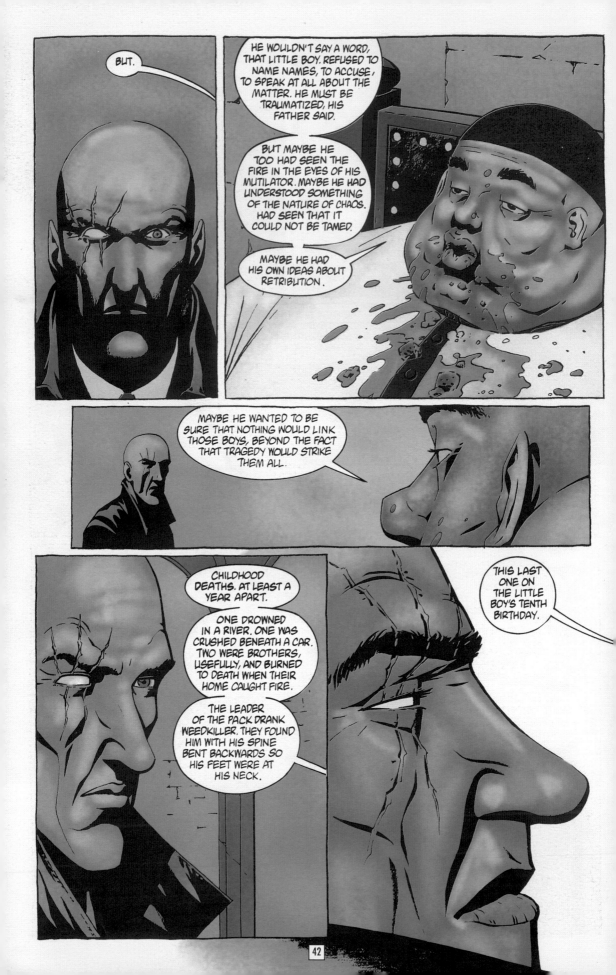

BUT.

HE WOULDN'T SAY A WORD, THAT LITTLE BOY. REFUSED TO NAME NAMES, TO ACCUSE, TO SPEAK AT ALL ABOUT THE MATTER. HE MUST BE TRAUMATIZED, HIS FATHER SAID.

BUT MAYBE HE TOO HAD SEEN THE FIRE IN THE EYES OF HIS MUTILATOR. MAYBE HE HAD UNDERSTOOD SOMETHING OF THE NATURE OF CHAOS. HAD SEEN THAT IT COULD NOT BE TAMED.

MAYBE HE HAD HIS OWN IDEAS ABOUT RETRIBUTION.

MAYBE HE WANTED TO BE SURE THAT NOTHING WOULD LINK THOSE BOYS, BEYOND THE FACT THAT TRAGEDY WOULD STRIKE THEM ALL.

CHILDHOOD DEATHS. AT LEAST A YEAR APART.

ONE DROWNED IN A RIVER. ONE WAS CRUSHED BENEATH A CAR. TWO WERE BROTHERS, USEFULLY, AND BURNED TO DEATH WHEN THEIR HOME CAUGHT FIRE.

THE LEADER OF THE PACK DRANK WEEDKILLER. THEY FOUND HIM WITH HIS SPINE BENT BACKWARDS SO HIS FEET WERE AT HIS NECK.

THIS LAST ONE ON THE LITTLE BOY'S TENTH BIRTHDAY.

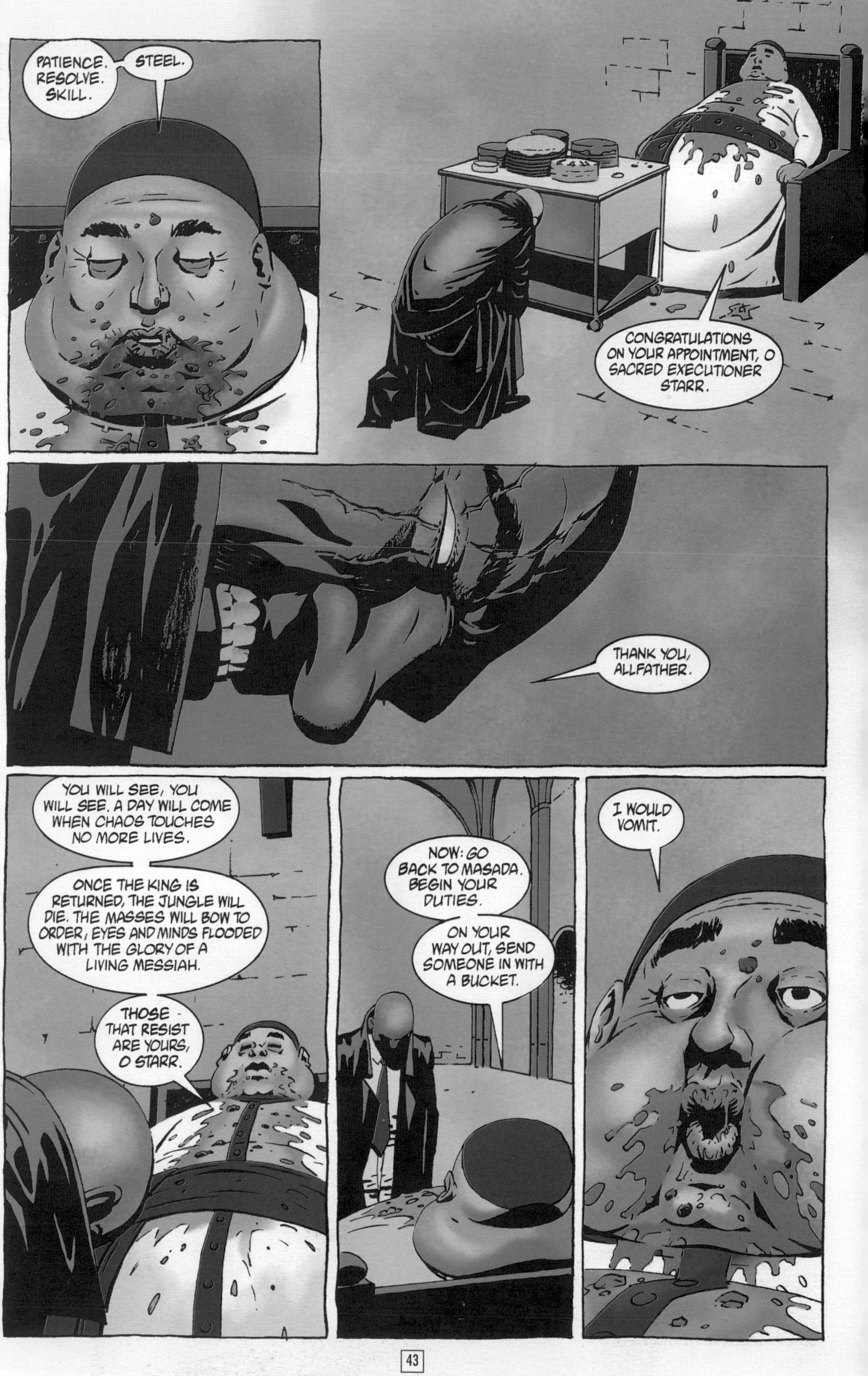
PATIENCE. RESOLVE. SKILL.
STEEL.
CONGRATULATIONS ON YOUR APPOINTMENT, O SACRED EXECUTIONER STARR.
THANK YOU, ALLFATHER.
YOU WILL SEE, YOU WILL SEE. A DAY WILL COME WHEN CHAOS TOUCHES NO MORE LIVES.
ONCE THE KING IS RETURNED, THE JUNGLE WILL DIE. THE MASSES WILL BOW TO ORDER, EYES AND MINDS FLOODED WITH THE GLORY OF A LIVING MESSIAH.
THOSE THAT RESIST ARE YOURS, O STARR.
NOW: GO BACK TO MASADA. BEGIN YOUR DUTIES.
ON YOUR WAY OUT, SEND SOMEONE IN WITH A BUCKET.
I WOULD VOMIT.

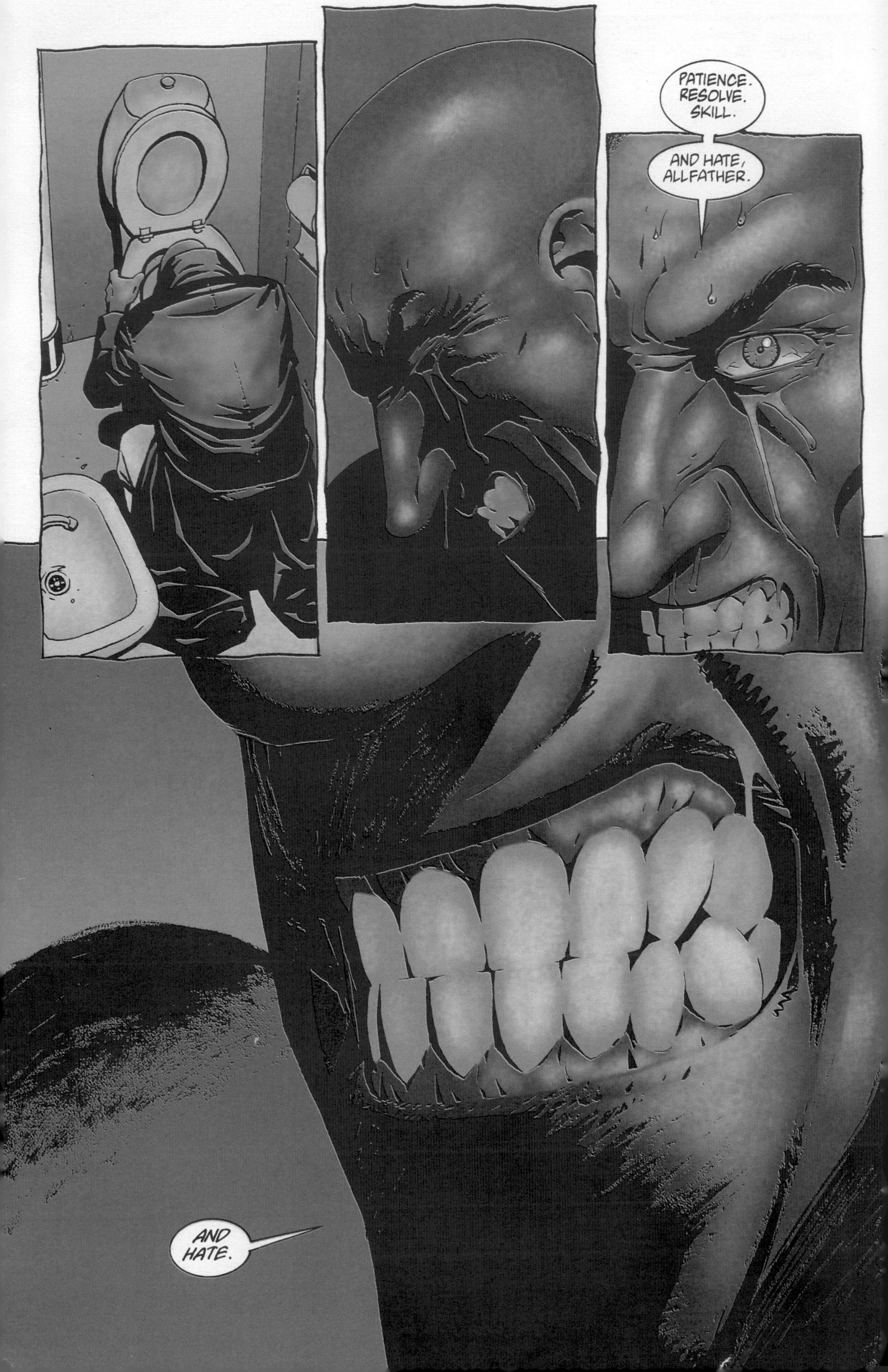
PATIENCE. RESOLVE. SKILL.
AND HATE, ALLFATHER.
AND HATE.

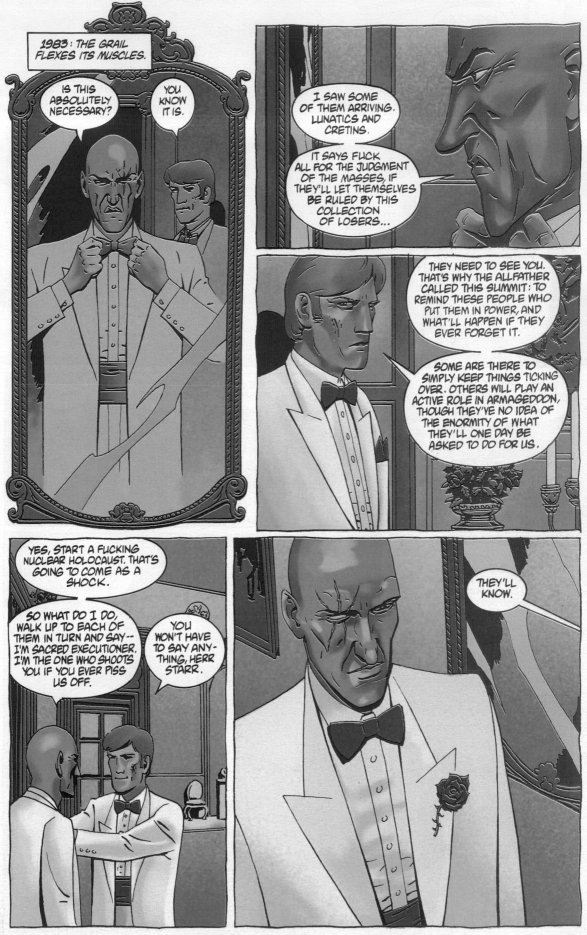

1983: THE GRAIL FLEXES ITS MUSCLES.

IS THIS ABSOLUTELY NECESSARY?

YOU KNOW IT IS.

I SAW SOME OF THEM ARRIVING. LUNATICS AND CRETINS.

IT SAYS FUCK ALL FOR THE JUDGMENT OF THE MASSES, IF THEY'LL LET THEMSELVES BE RULED BY THIS COLLECTION OF LOSERS...

THEY NEED TO SEE YOU. THAT'S WHY THE ALLFATHER CALLED THIS SUMMIT: TO REMIND THESE PEOPLE WHO PUT THEM IN POWER, AND WHAT'LL HAPPEN IF THEY EVER FORGET IT.

SOME ARE THERE TO SIMPLY KEEP THINGS TICKING OVER. OTHERS WILL PLAY AN ACTIVE ROLE IN ARMAGEDDON, THOUGH THEY'VE NO IDEA OF THE ENORMITY OF WHAT THEY'LL ONE DAY BE ASKED TO DO FOR US.

YES, START A FUCKING NUCLEAR HOLOCAUST. THAT'S GOING TO COME AS A SHOCK.

SO WHAT DO I DO, WALK UP TO EACH OF THEM IN TURN AND SAY-- I'M SACRED EXECUTIONER. I'M THE ONE WHO SHOOTS YOU IF YOU EVER PISS US OFF.

YOU WON'T HAVE TO SAY ANY-THING, HERR STARR.

THEY'LL KNOW.

45

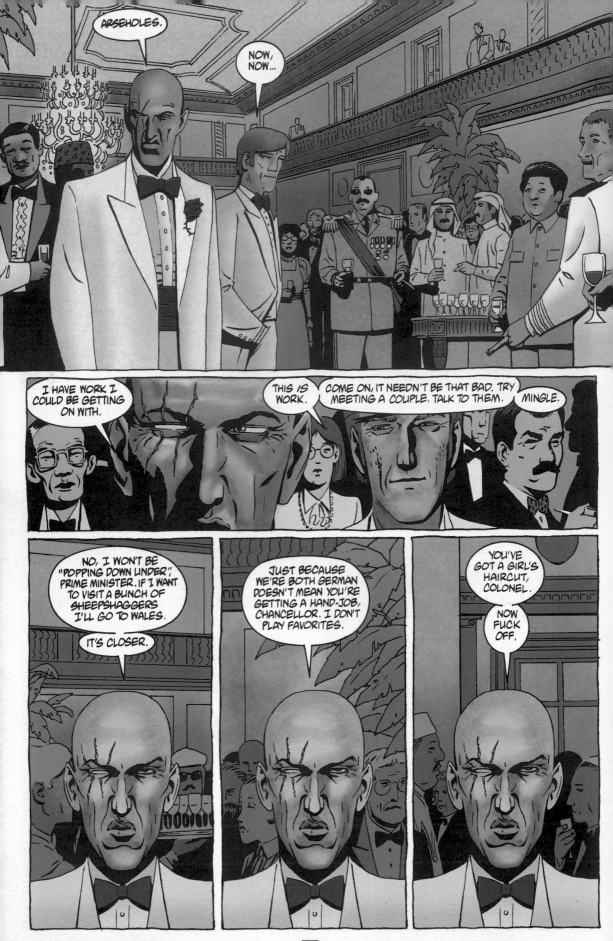

ARSEHOLES.

NOW, NOW...

I HAVE WORK I COULD BE GETTING ON WITH.

THIS IS WORK.

COME ON, IT NEEDN'T BE THAT BAD. TRY MEETING A COUPLE. TALK TO THEM.

MINGLE.

NO, I WON'T BE "POPPING DOWN UNDER", PRIME MINISTER. IF I WANT TO VISIT A BUNCH OF SHEEPSHAGGERS I'LL GO TO WALES.

IT'S CLOSER.

JUST BECAUSE WE'RE BOTH GERMAN DOESN'T MEAN YOU'RE GETTING A HAND-JOB, CHANCELLOR. I DON'T PLAY FAVORITES.

YOU'VE GOT A GIRL'S HAIRCUT, COLONEL.

NOW FUCK OFF.

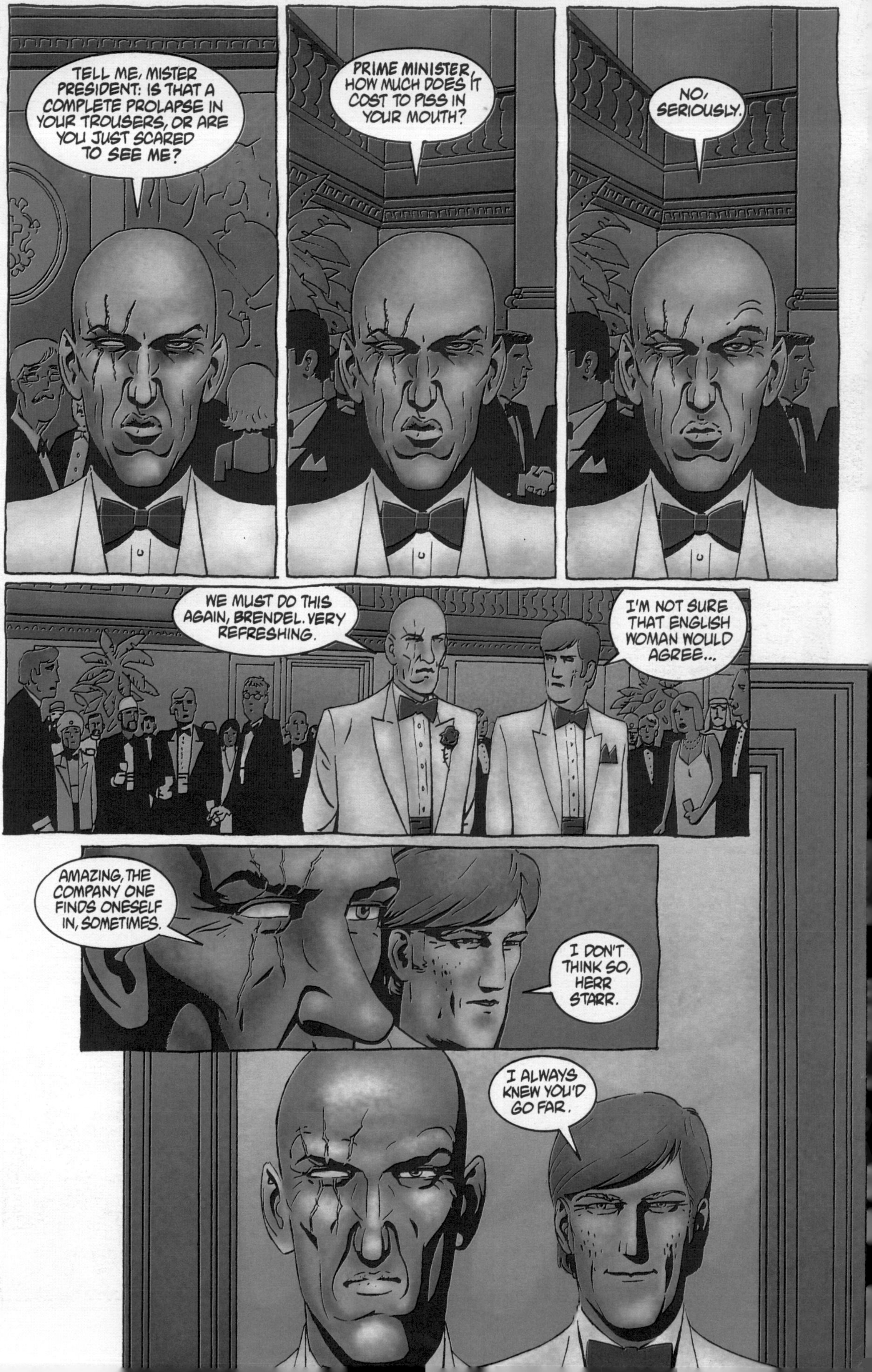
TELL ME, MISTER PRESIDENT: IS THAT A COMPLETE PROLAPSE IN YOUR TROUSERS, OR ARE YOU JUST SCARED TO SEE ME?
PRIME MINISTER, HOW MUCH DOES IT COST TO PISS IN YOUR MOUTH?
NO, SERIOUSLY.
WE MUST DO THIS AGAIN, BRENDEL. VERY REFRESHING.
I'M NOT SURE THAT ENGLISH WOMAN WOULD AGREE...
AMAZING, THE COMPANY ONE FINDS ONESELF IN, SOMETIMES.
I DON'T THINK SO, HERR STARR.
I ALWAYS KNEW YOU'D GO FAR.

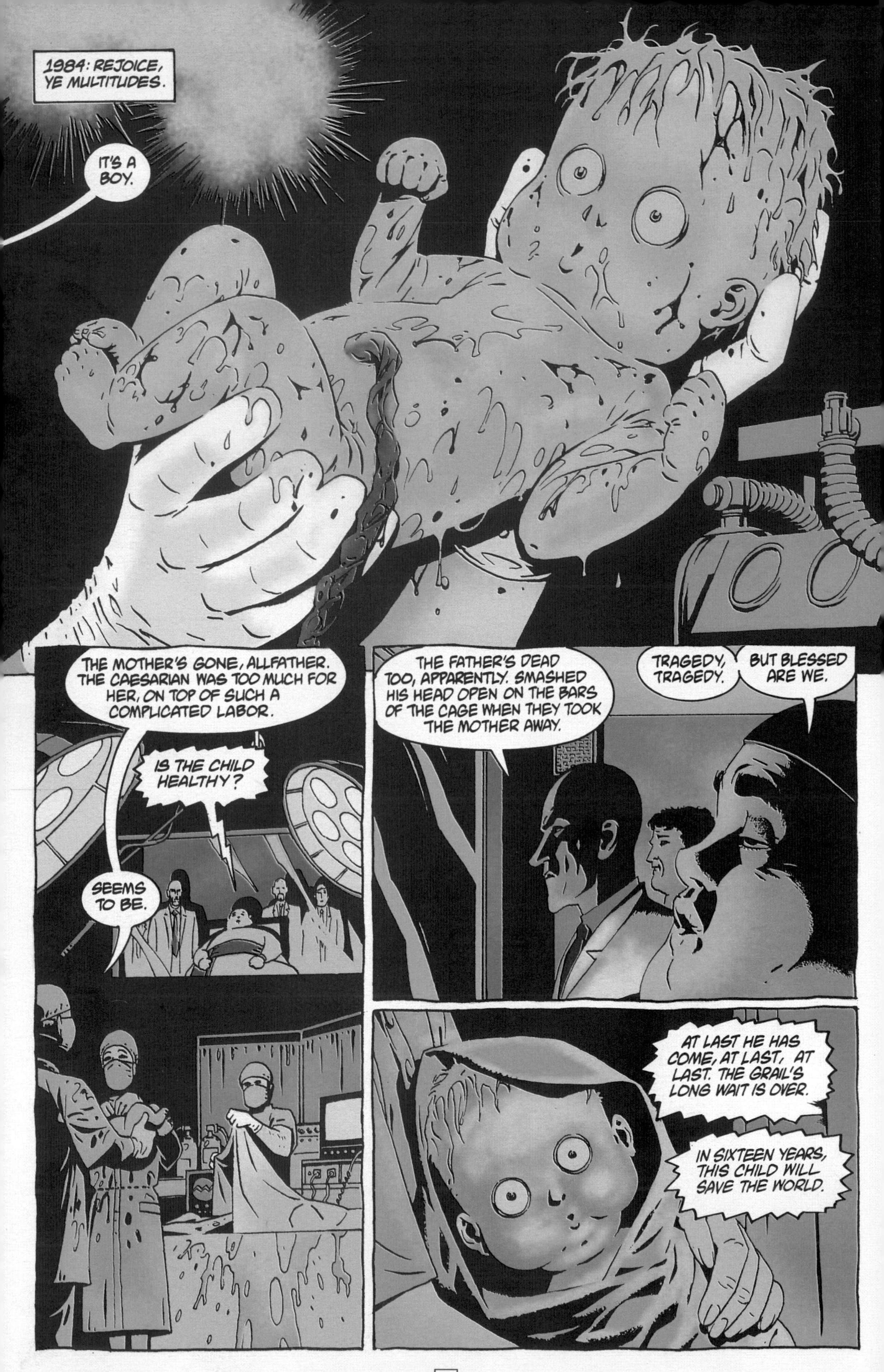
1984: REJOICE, YE MULTITUDES.
IT'S A BOY.
THE MOTHER'S GONE, ALLFATHER. THE CAESARIAN WAS TOO MUCH FOR HER, ON TOP OF SUCH A COMPLICATED LABOR.
IS THE CHILD HEALTHY?
SEEMS TO BE.
THE FATHER'S DEAD TOO, APPARENTLY. SMASHED HIS HEAD OPEN ON THE BARS OF THE CAGE WHEN THEY TOOK THE MOTHER AWAY.
TRAGEDY, TRAGEDY.
BUT BLESSED ARE WE.
AT LAST HE HAS COME, AT LAST, AT LAST. THE GRAIL'S LONG WAIT IS OVER.
IN SIXTEEN YEARS, THIS CHILD WILL SAVE THE WORLD.

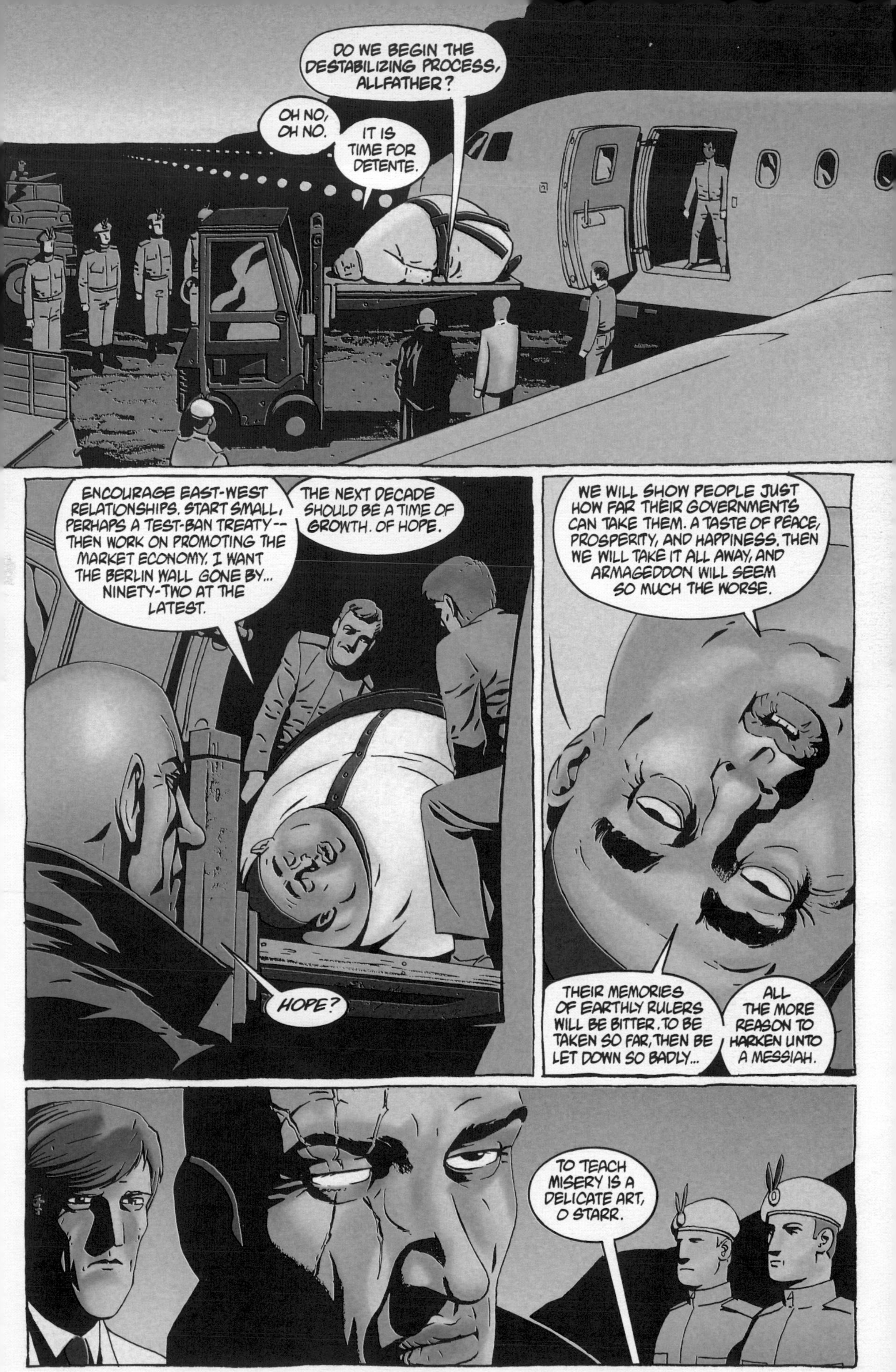
DO WE BEGIN THE DESTABILIZING PROCESS, ALLFATHER?
OH NO, OH NO.
IT IS TIME FOR DETENTE.
ENCOURAGE EAST-WEST RELATIONSHIPS. START SMALL, PERHAPS A TEST-BAN TREATY -- THEN WORK ON PROMOTING THE MARKET ECONOMY. I WANT THE BERLIN WALL GONE BY... NINETY-TWO AT THE LATEST.
THE NEXT DECADE SHOULD BE A TIME OF GROWTH. OF HOPE.
HOPE?
WE WILL SHOW PEOPLE JUST HOW FAR THEIR GOVERNMENTS CAN TAKE THEM. A TASTE OF PEACE, PROSPERITY, AND HAPPINESS. THEN WE WILL TAKE IT ALL AWAY, AND ARMAGEDDON WILL SEEM SO MUCH THE WORSE.
THEIR MEMORIES OF EARTHLY RULERS WILL BE BITTER. TO BE TAKEN SO FAR, THEN BE LET DOWN SO BADLY...
ALL THE MORE REASON TO HARKEN UNTO A MESSIAH.
TO TEACH MISERY IS A DELICATE ART, O STARR.

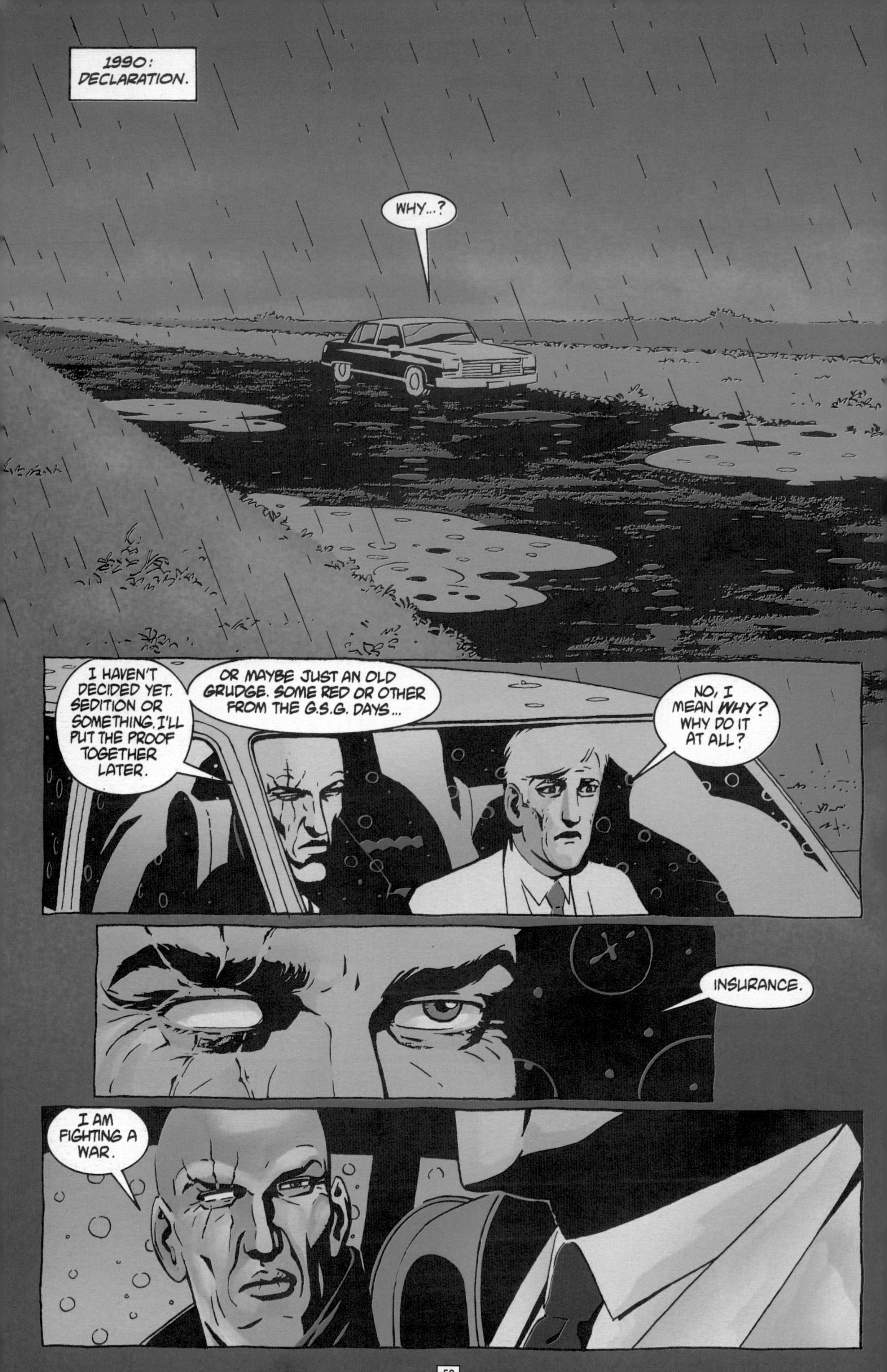
1990: DECLARATION.
WHY...?
I HAVEN'T DECIDED YET. SEDITION OR SOMETHING. I'LL PUT THE PROOF TOGETHER LATER.
OR MAYBE JUST AN OLD GRUDGE. SOME RED OR OTHER FROM THE G.S.G. DAYS...
NO, I MEAN WHY? WHY DO IT AT ALL?
INSURANCE.
I AM FIGHTING A WAR.

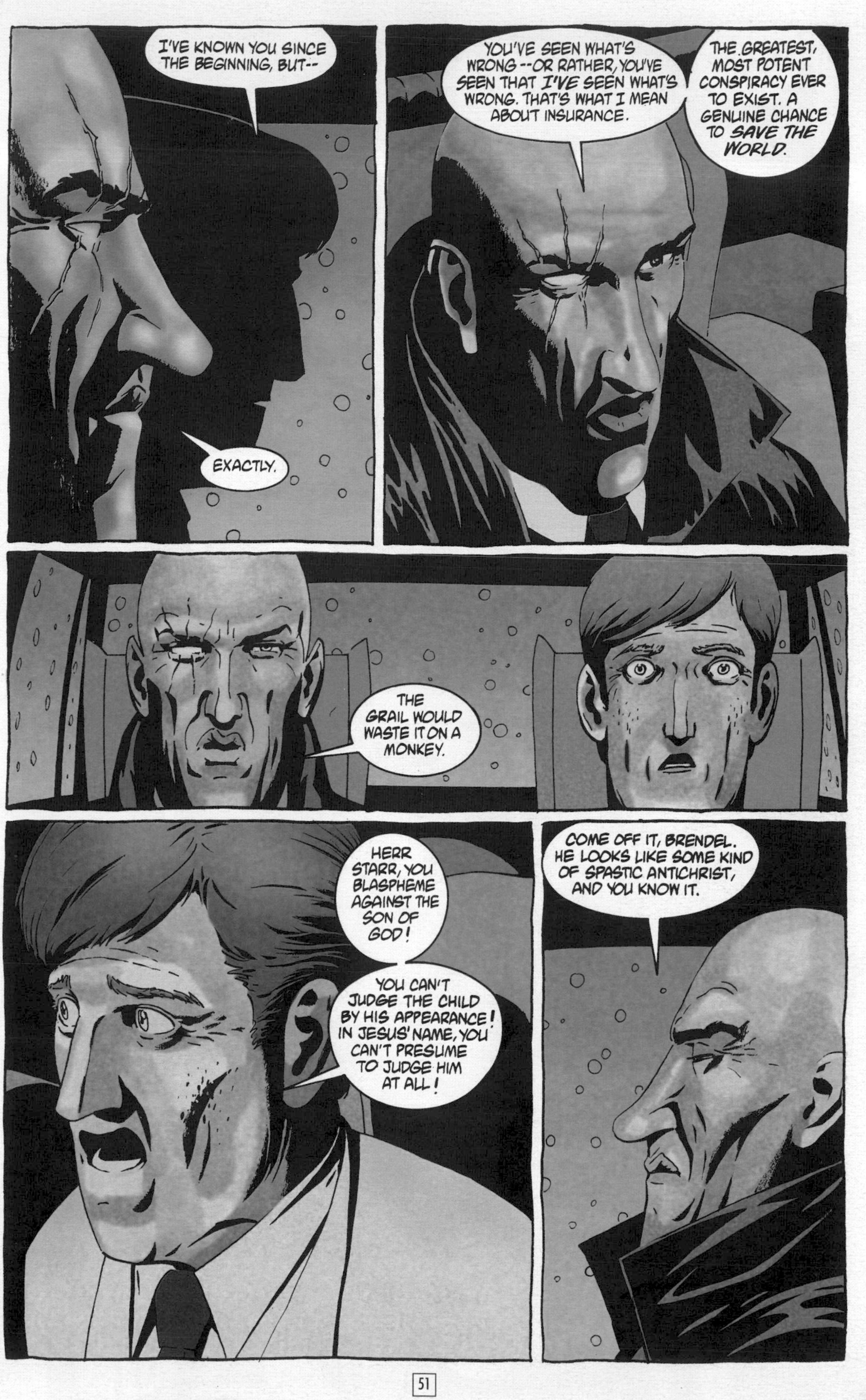
I'VE KNOWN YOU SINCE THE BEGINNING, BUT--
EXACTLY.
YOU'VE SEEN WHAT'S WRONG--OR RATHER, YOU'VE SEEN THAT I'VE SEEN WHAT'S WRONG. THAT'S WHAT I MEAN ABOUT INSURANCE.
THE GREATEST, MOST POTENT CONSPIRACY EVER TO EXIST. A GENUINE CHANCE TO SAVE THE WORLD.
THE GRAIL WOULD WASTE IT ON A MONKEY.
HERR STARR, YOU BLASPHEME AGAINST THE SON OF GOD!
YOU CAN'T JUDGE THE CHILD BY HIS APPEARANCE! IN JESUS' NAME, YOU CAN'T PRESUME TO JUDGE HIM AT ALL!
COME OFF IT, BRENDEL. HE LOOKS LIKE SOME KIND OF SPASTIC ANTICHRIST, AND YOU KNOW IT.

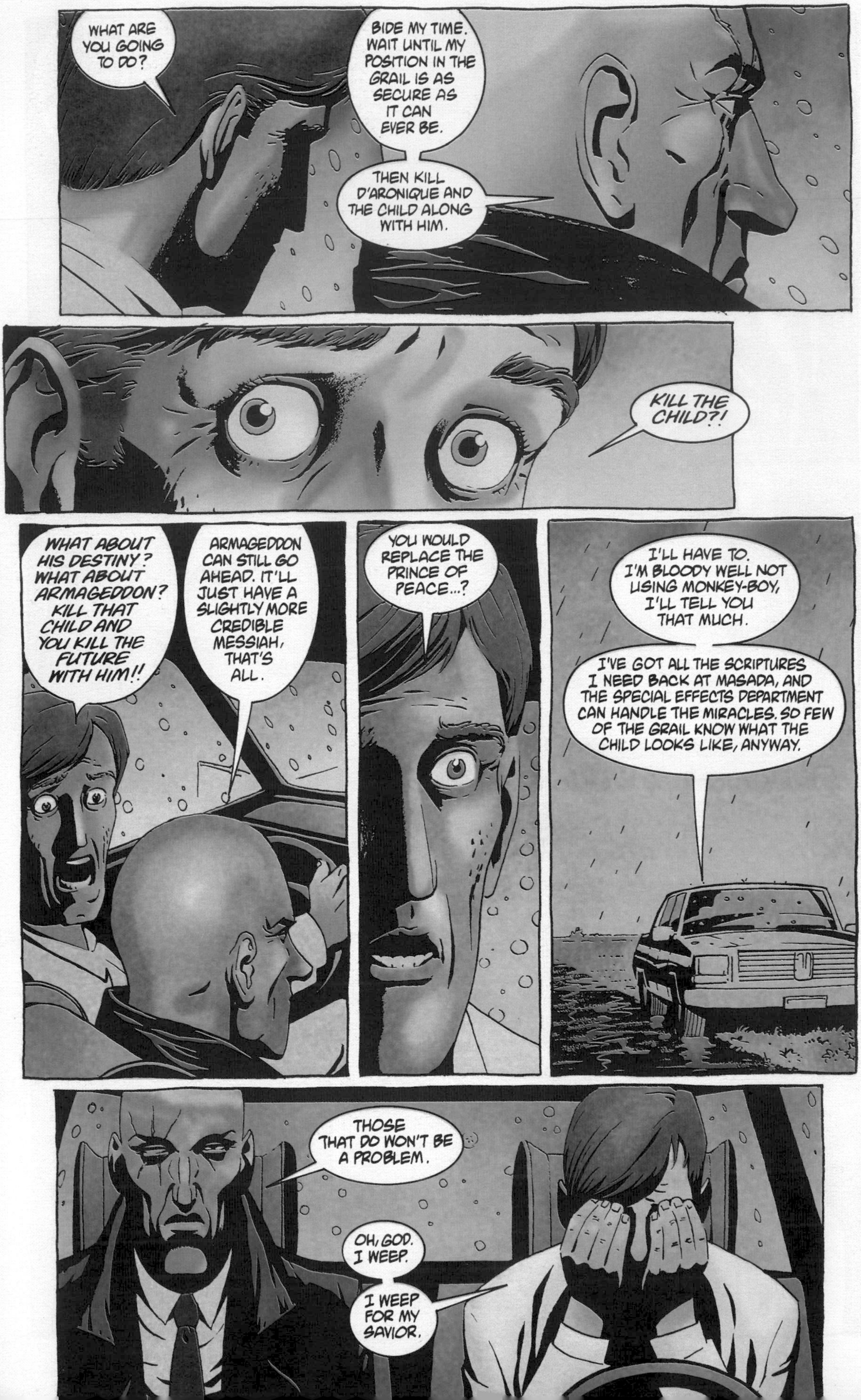
WHAT ARE YOU GOING TO DO?
BIDE MY TIME. WAIT UNTIL MY POSITION IN THE GRAIL IS AS SECURE AS IT CAN EVER BE.
THEN KILL D'ARONIQUE AND THE CHILD ALONG WITH HIM.
KILL THE CHILD?!
WHAT ABOUT HIS DESTINY? WHAT ABOUT ARMAGEDDON? KILL THAT CHILD AND YOU KILL THE FUTURE WITH HIM!!
ARMAGEDDON CAN STILL GO AHEAD. IT'LL JUST HAVE A SLIGHTLY MORE CREDIBLE MESSIAH, THAT'S ALL.
YOU WOULD REPLACE THE PRINCE OF PEACE...?
I'LL HAVE TO. I'M BLOODY WELL NOT USING MONKEY-BOY, I'LL TELL YOU THAT MUCH.
I'VE GOT ALL THE SCRIPTURES I NEED BACK AT MASADA, AND THE SPECIAL EFFECTS DEPARTMENT CAN HANDLE THE MIRACLES. SO FEW OF THE GRAIL KNOW WHAT THE CHILD LOOKS LIKE, ANYWAY.
THOSE THAT DO WON'T BE A PROBLEM.
OH, GOD. I WEEP.
I WEEP FOR MY SAVIOR.

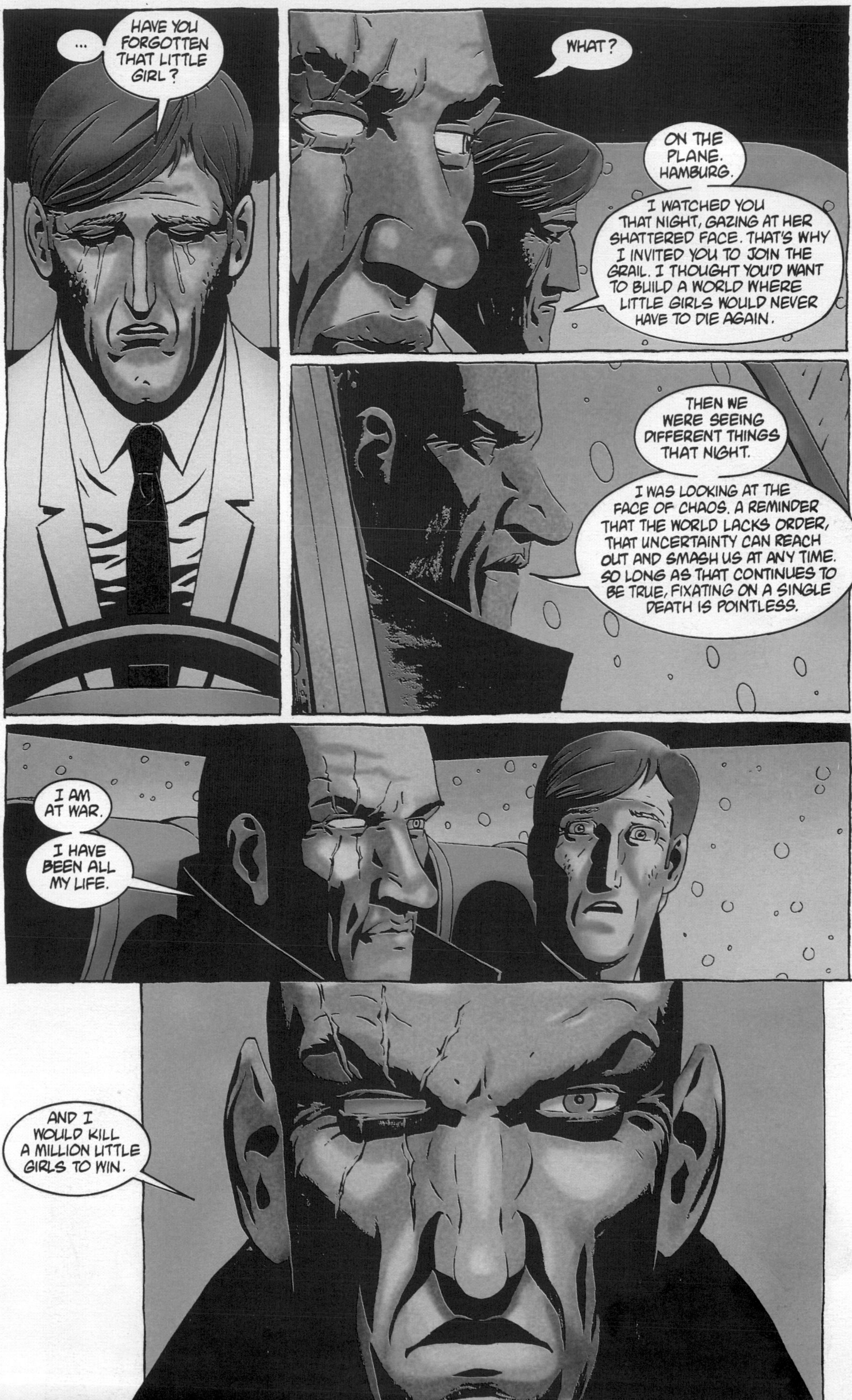
...
HAVE YOU FORGOTTEN THAT LITTLE GIRL?
WHAT?
ON THE PLANE. HAMBURG.
I WATCHED YOU THAT NIGHT, GAZING AT HER SHATTERED FACE. THAT'S WHY I INVITED YOU TO JOIN THE GRAIL. I THOUGHT YOU'D WANT TO BUILD A WORLD WHERE LITTLE GIRLS WOULD NEVER HAVE TO DIE AGAIN.
THEN WE WERE SEEING DIFFERENT THINGS THAT NIGHT.
I WAS LOOKING AT THE FACE OF CHAOS. A REMINDER THAT THE WORLD LACKS ORDER, THAT UNCERTAINTY CAN REACH OUT AND SMASH US AT ANY TIME. SO LONG AS THAT CONTINUES TO BE TRUE, FIXATING ON A SINGLE DEATH IS POINTLESS.
I AM AT WAR.
I HAVE BEEN ALL MY LIFE.
AND I WOULD KILL A MILLION LITTLE GIRLS TO WIN.

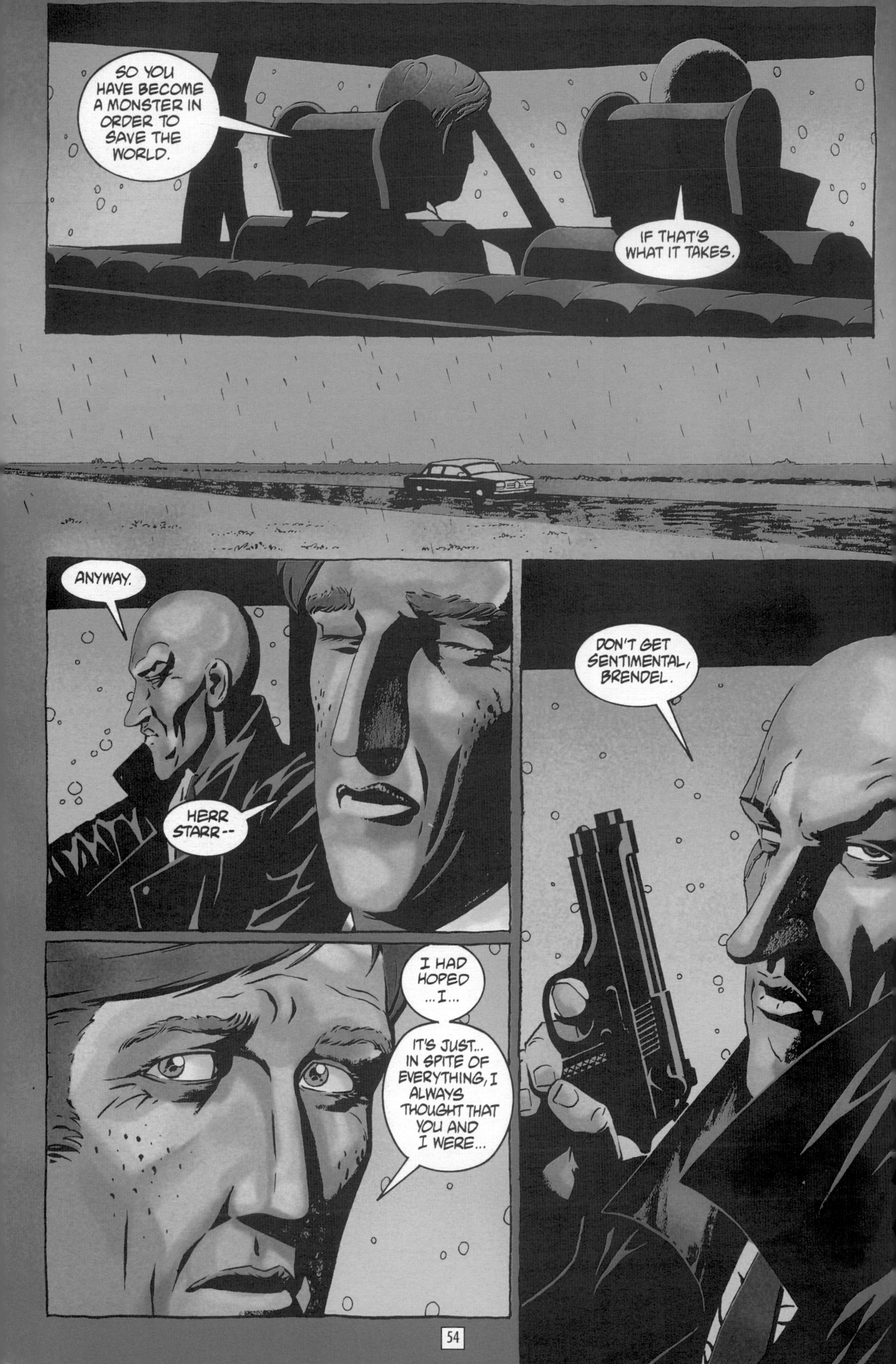
SO YOU HAVE BECOME A MONSTER IN ORDER TO SAVE THE WORLD.
IF THAT'S WHAT IT TAKES.
ANYWAY.
HERR STARR--
DON'T GET SENTIMENTAL, BRENDEL.
I HAD HOPED ...I...
IT'S JUST... IN SPITE OF EVERYTHING, I ALWAYS THOUGHT THAT YOU AND I WERE...

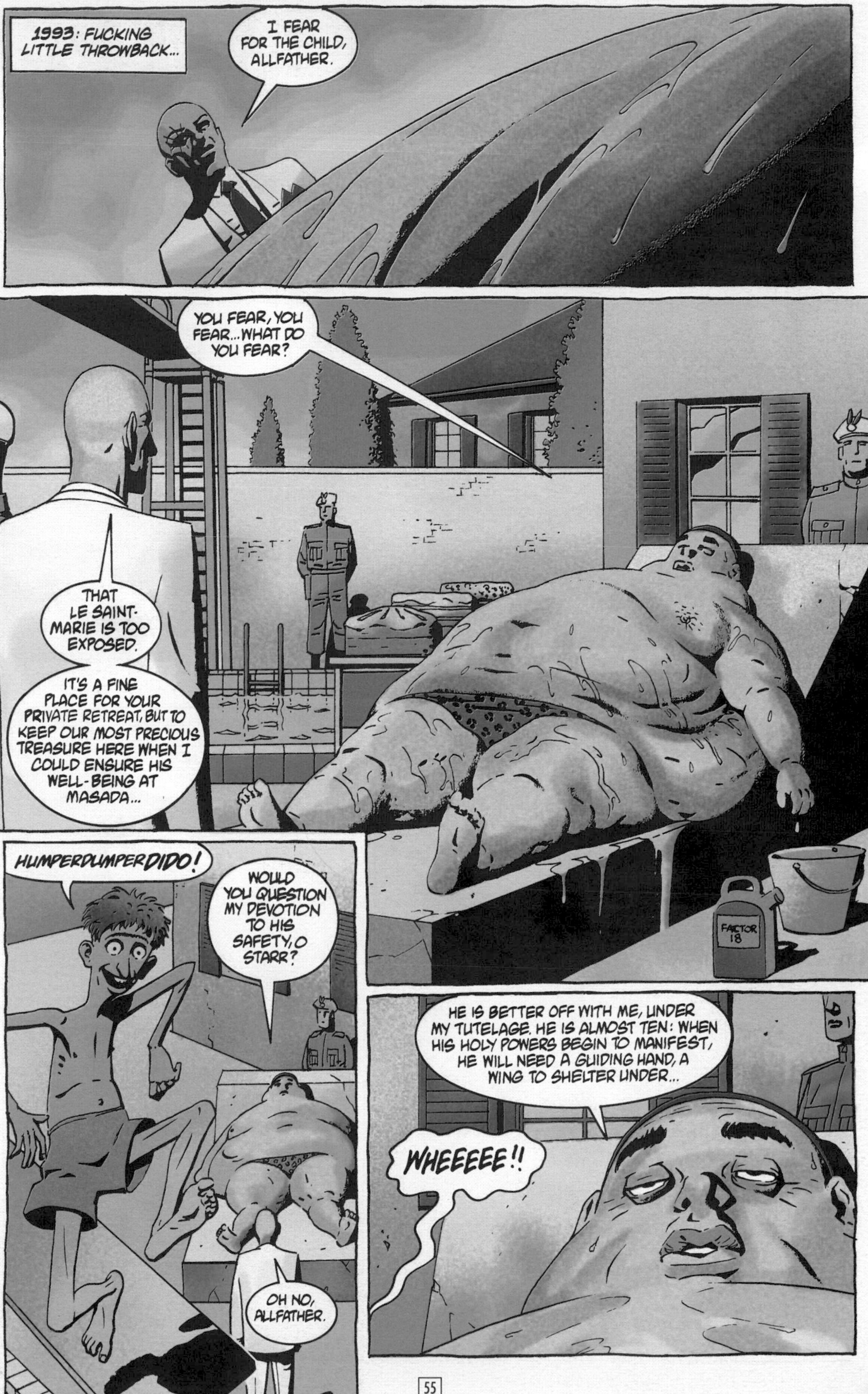
1993: FUCKING LITTLE THROWBACK...
I FEAR FOR THE CHILD, ALLFATHER.
YOU FEAR, YOU FEAR...WHAT DO YOU FEAR?
THAT LE SAINT-MARIE IS TOO EXPOSED.
IT'S A FINE PLACE FOR YOUR PRIVATE RETREAT, BUT TO KEEP OUR MOST PRECIOUS TREASURE HERE WHEN I COULD ENSURE HIS WELL-BEING AT MASADA...
FACTOR 18
HUMPERDUMPERDIDO!
WOULD YOU QUESTION MY DEVOTION TO HIS SAFETY, O STARR?
OH NO, ALLFATHER.
HE IS BETTER OFF WITH ME, UNDER MY TUTELAGE. HE IS ALMOST TEN: WHEN HIS HOLY POWERS BEGIN TO MANIFEST, HE WILL NEED A GUIDING HAND, A WING TO SHELTER UNDER...
WHEEEEE!!

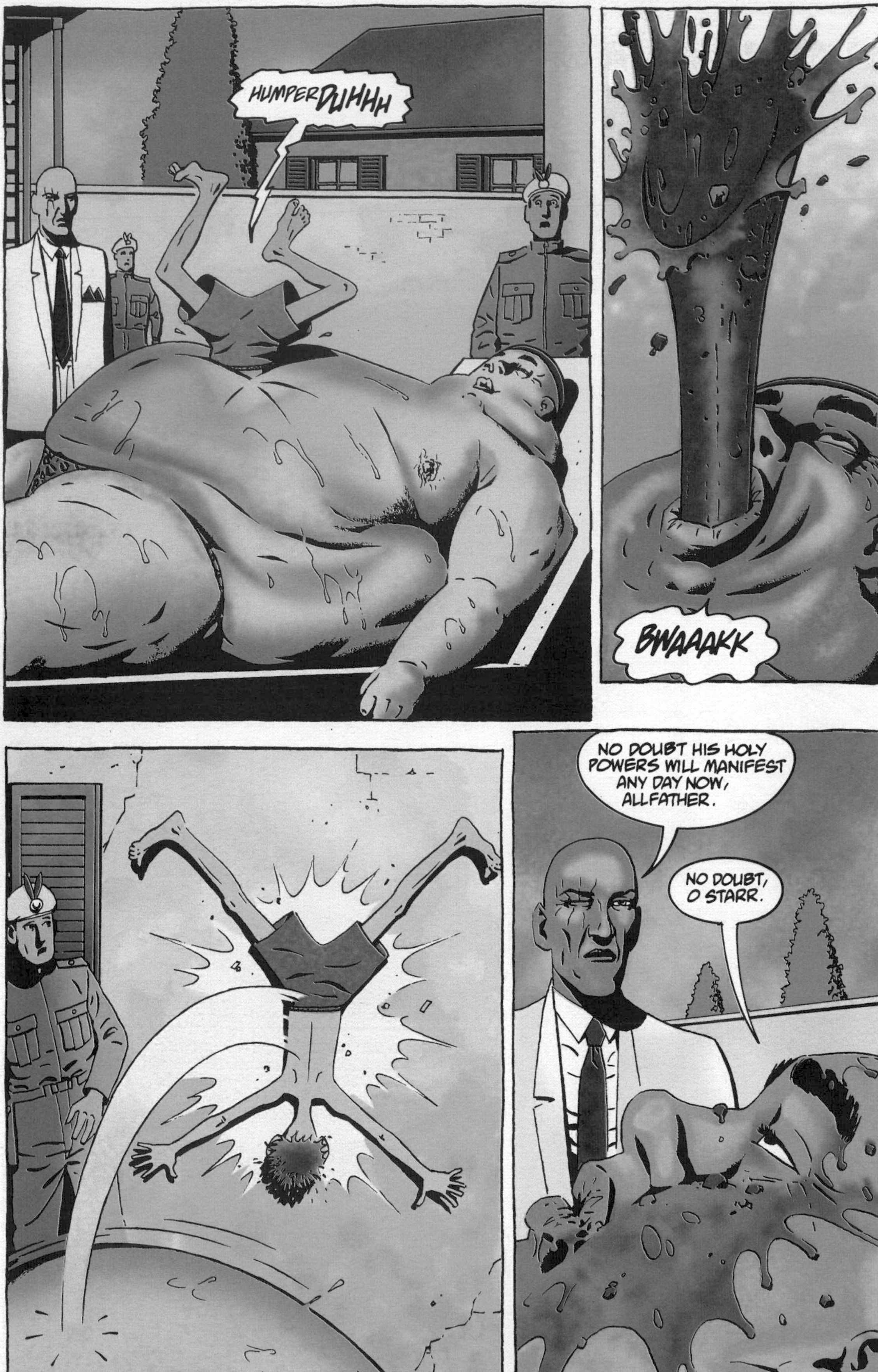
HUMPERDUHHH
BWAAAKK
NO DOUBT HIS HOLY POWERS WILL MANIFEST ANY DAY NOW, ALLFATHER.
NO DOUBT, O STARR.

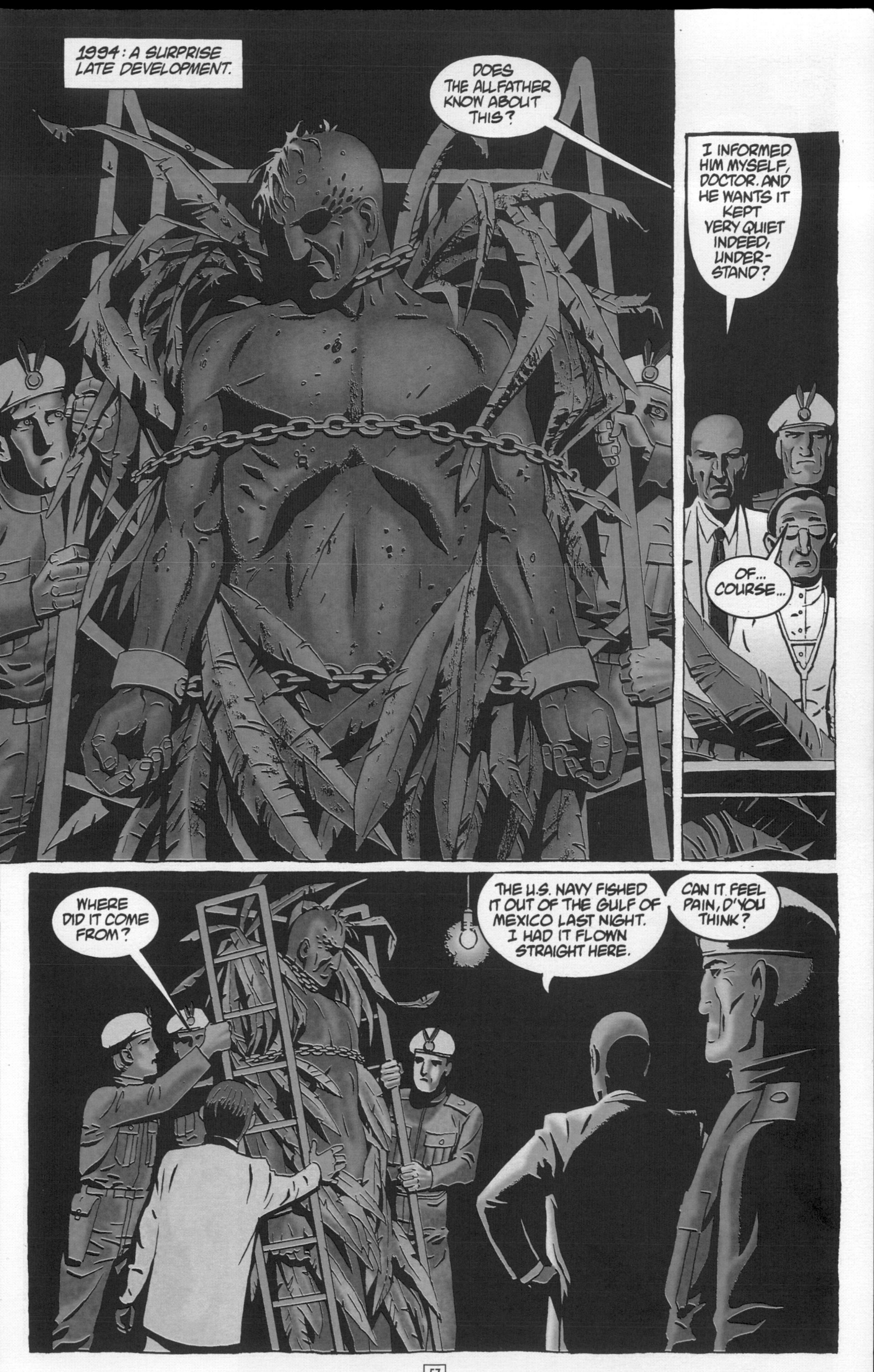
1994: A SURPRISE LATE DEVELOPMENT.
DOES THE ALLFATHER KNOW ABOUT THIS?
I INFORMED HIM MYSELF, DOCTOR. AND HE WANTS IT KEPT VERY QUIET INDEED, UNDER-STAND?
OF... COURSE...
WHERE DID IT COME FROM?
THE U.S. NAVY FISHED IT OUT OF THE GULF OF MEXICO LAST NIGHT. I HAD IT FLOWN STRAIGHT HERE.
CAN IT FEEL PAIN, D'YOU THINK?

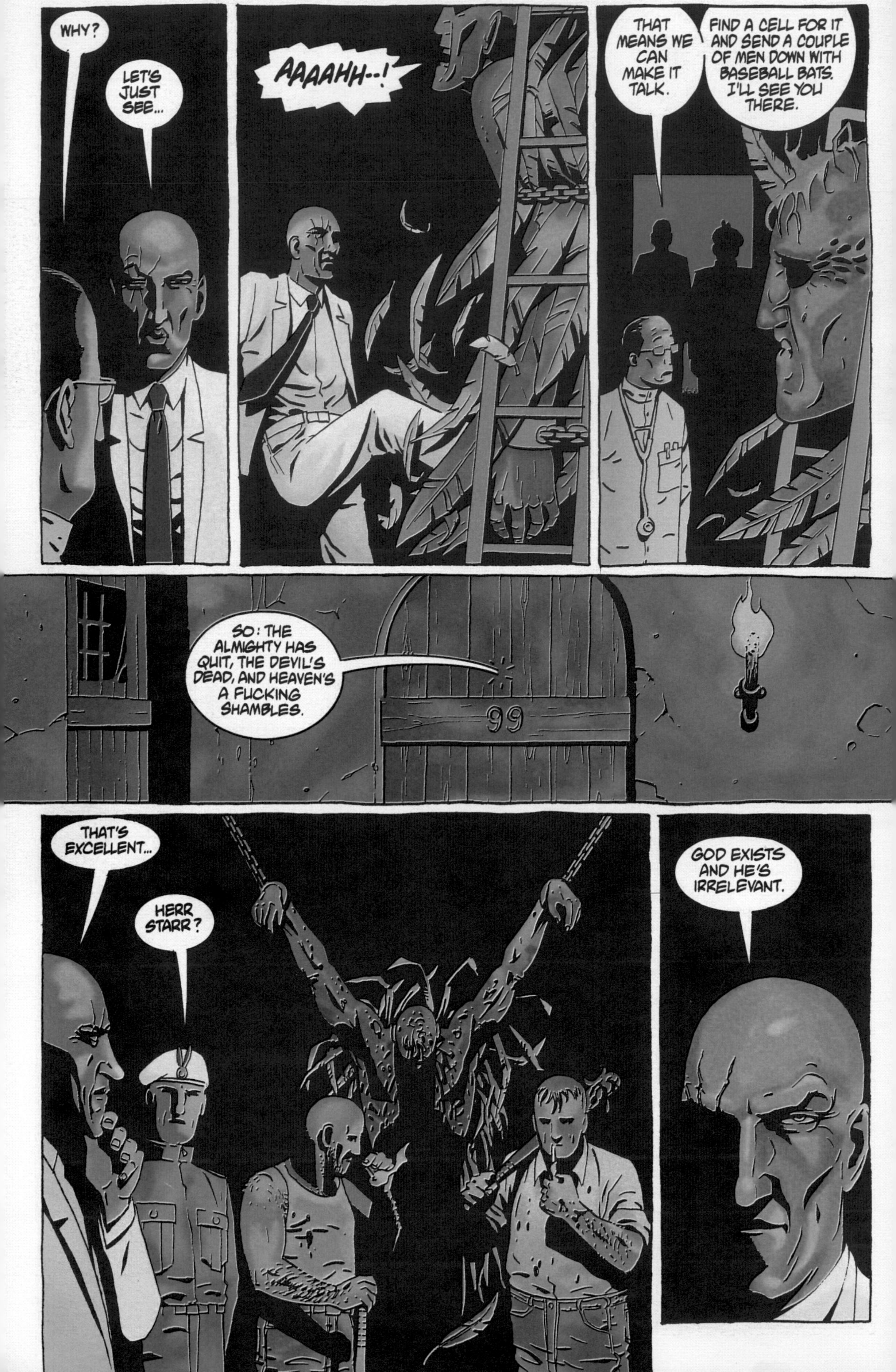
WHY?
LET'S JUST SEE...
AAAAHH--!
THAT MEANS WE CAN MAKE IT TALK.
FIND A CELL FOR IT AND SEND A COUPLE OF MEN DOWN WITH BASEBALL BATS. I'LL SEE YOU THERE.
SO: THE ALMIGHTY HAS QUIT, THE DEVIL'S DEAD, AND HEAVEN'S A FUCKING SHAMBLES.
99
THAT'S EXCELLENT...
HERR STARR?
GOD EXISTS AND HE'S IRRELEVANT.

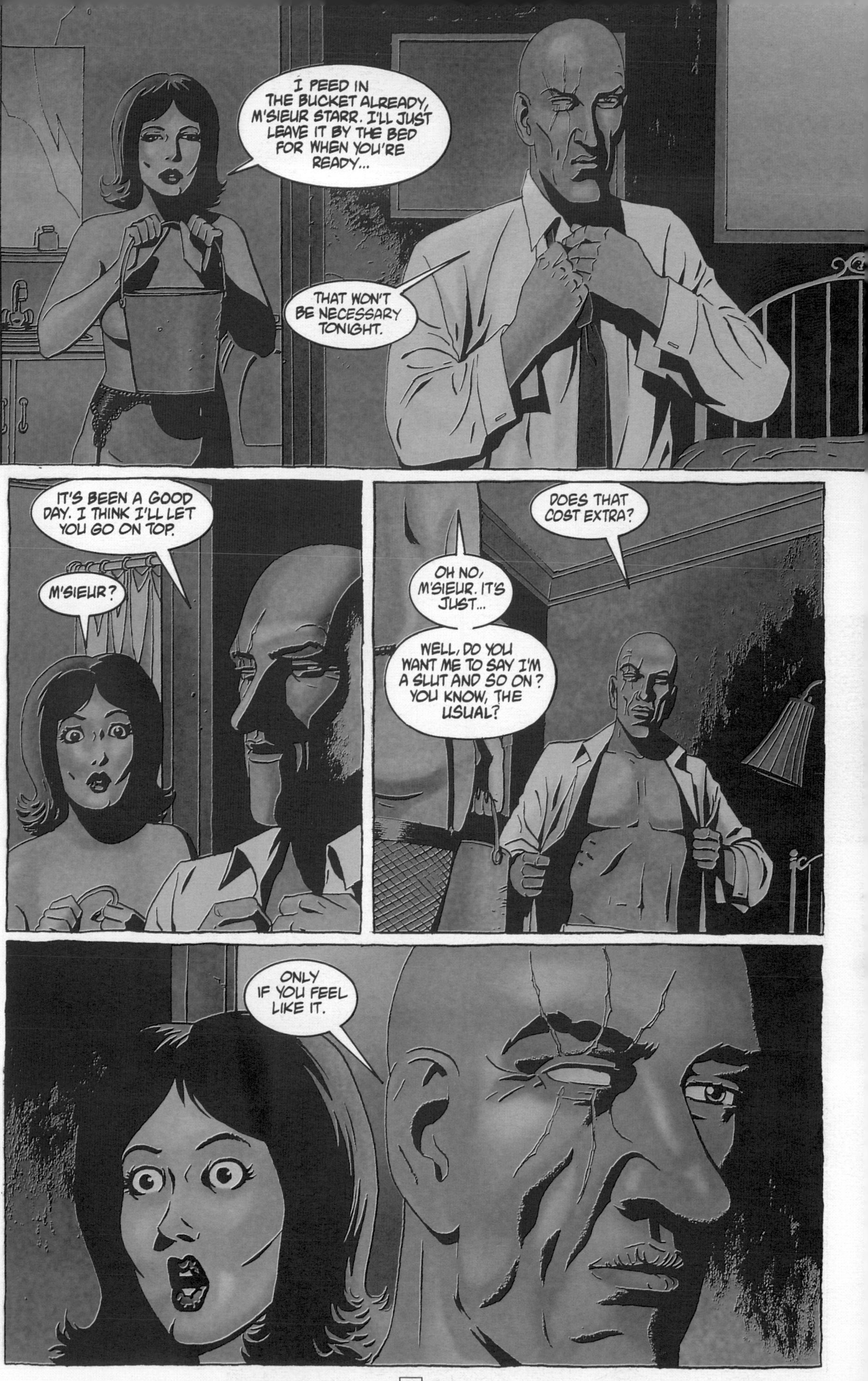
I PEED IN THE BUCKET ALREADY, M'SIEUR STARR. I'LL JUST LEAVE IT BY THE BED FOR WHEN YOU'RE READY...
THAT WON'T BE NECESSARY TONIGHT.
IT'S BEEN A GOOD DAY. I THINK I'LL LET YOU GO ON TOP.
M'SIEUR?
DOES THAT COST EXTRA?
OH NO, M'SIEUR. IT'S JUST...
WELL, DO YOU WANT ME TO SAY I'M A SLUT AND SO ON? YOU KNOW, THE USUAL?
ONLY IF YOU FEEL LIKE IT.

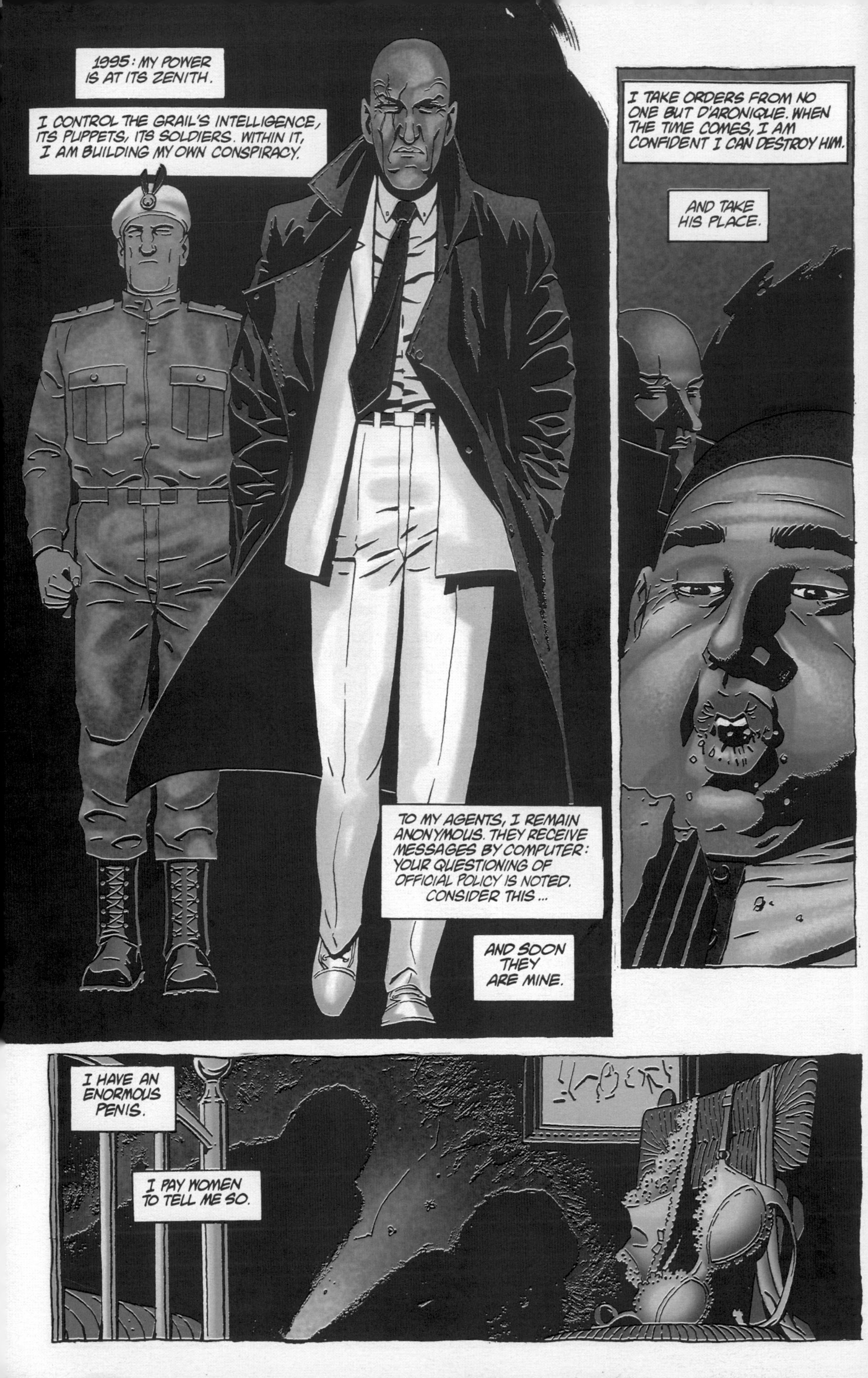
1995: MY POWER IS AT ITS ZENITH.
I CONTROL THE GRAIL'S INTELLIGENCE, ITS PUPPETS, ITS SOLDIERS. WITHIN IT, I AM BUILDING MY OWN CONSPIRACY.
TO MY AGENTS, I REMAIN ANONYMOUS. THEY RECEIVE MESSAGES BY COMPUTER: YOUR QUESTIONING OF OFFICIAL POLICY IS NOTED. CONSIDER THIS ...
AND SOON THEY ARE MINE.
I TAKE ORDERS FROM NO ONE BUT D'ARONIQUE. WHEN THE TIME COMES, I AM CONFIDENT I CAN DESTROY HIM.
AND TAKE HIS PLACE.
I HAVE AN ENORMOUS PENIS.
I PAY WOMEN TO TELL ME SO.

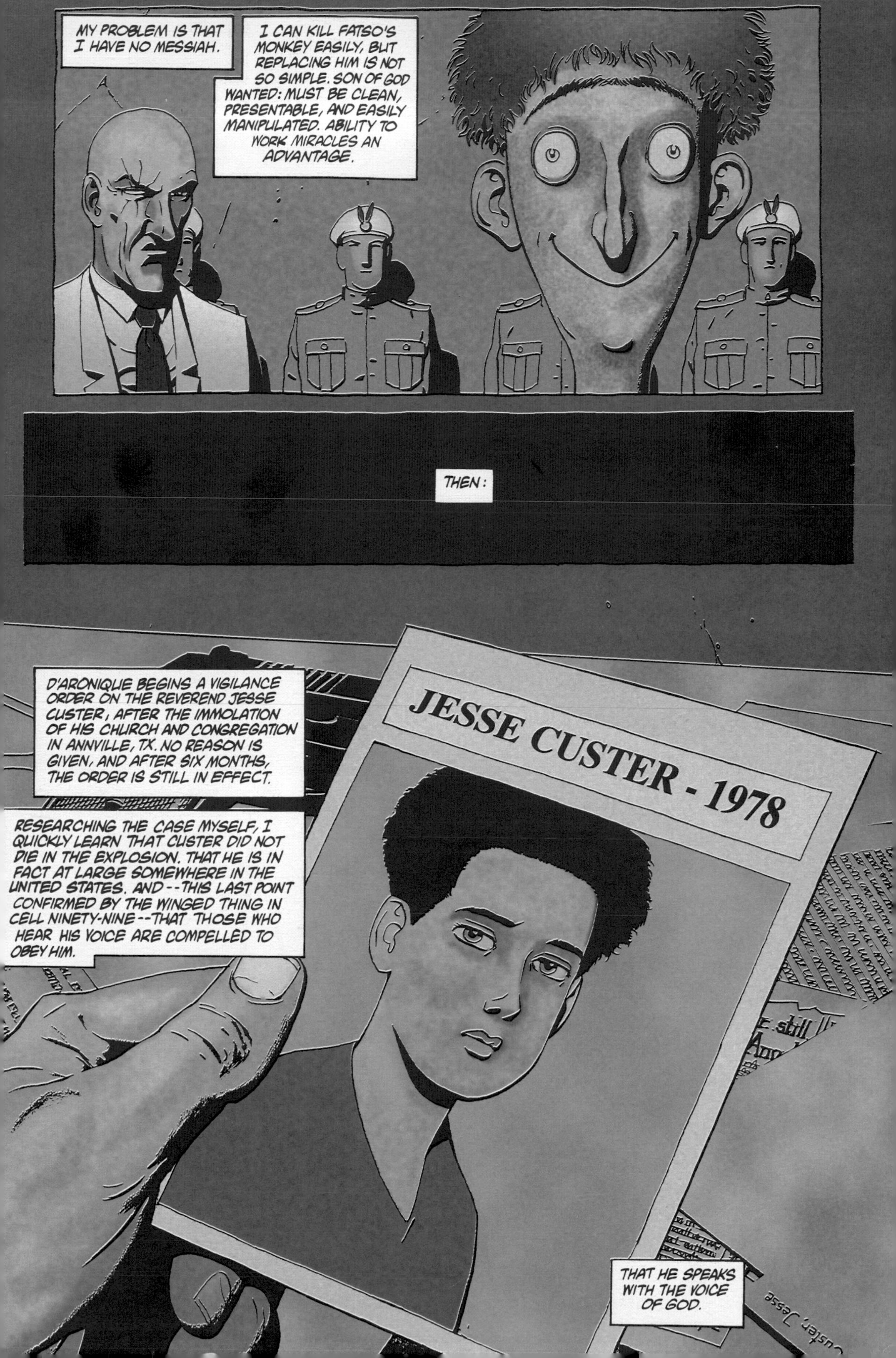
MY PROBLEM IS THAT I HAVE NO MESSIAH.
I CAN KILL FATSO'S MONKEY EASILY, BUT REPLACING HIM IS NOT SO SIMPLE. SON OF GOD WANTED: MUST BE CLEAN, PRESENTABLE, AND EASILY MANIPULATED. ABILITY TO WORK MIRACLES AN ADVANTAGE.
THEN:
JESSE CUSTER - 1978
D'ARONIQUE BEGINS A VIGILANCE ORDER ON THE REVEREND JESSE CUSTER, AFTER THE IMMOLATION OF HIS CHURCH AND CONGREGATION IN ANNVILLE, TX. NO REASON IS GIVEN, AND AFTER SIX MONTHS, THE ORDER IS STILL IN EFFECT.
RESEARCHING THE CASE MYSELF, I QUICKLY LEARN THAT CUSTER DID NOT DIE IN THE EXPLOSION. THAT HE IS IN FACT AT LARGE SOMEWHERE IN THE UNITED STATES. AND--THIS LAST POINT CONFIRMED BY THE WINGED THING IN CELL NINETY-NINE--THAT THOSE WHO HEAR HIS VOICE ARE COMPELLED TO OBEY HIM.
THAT HE SPEAKS WITH THE VOICE OF GOD.
Custer, Jesse

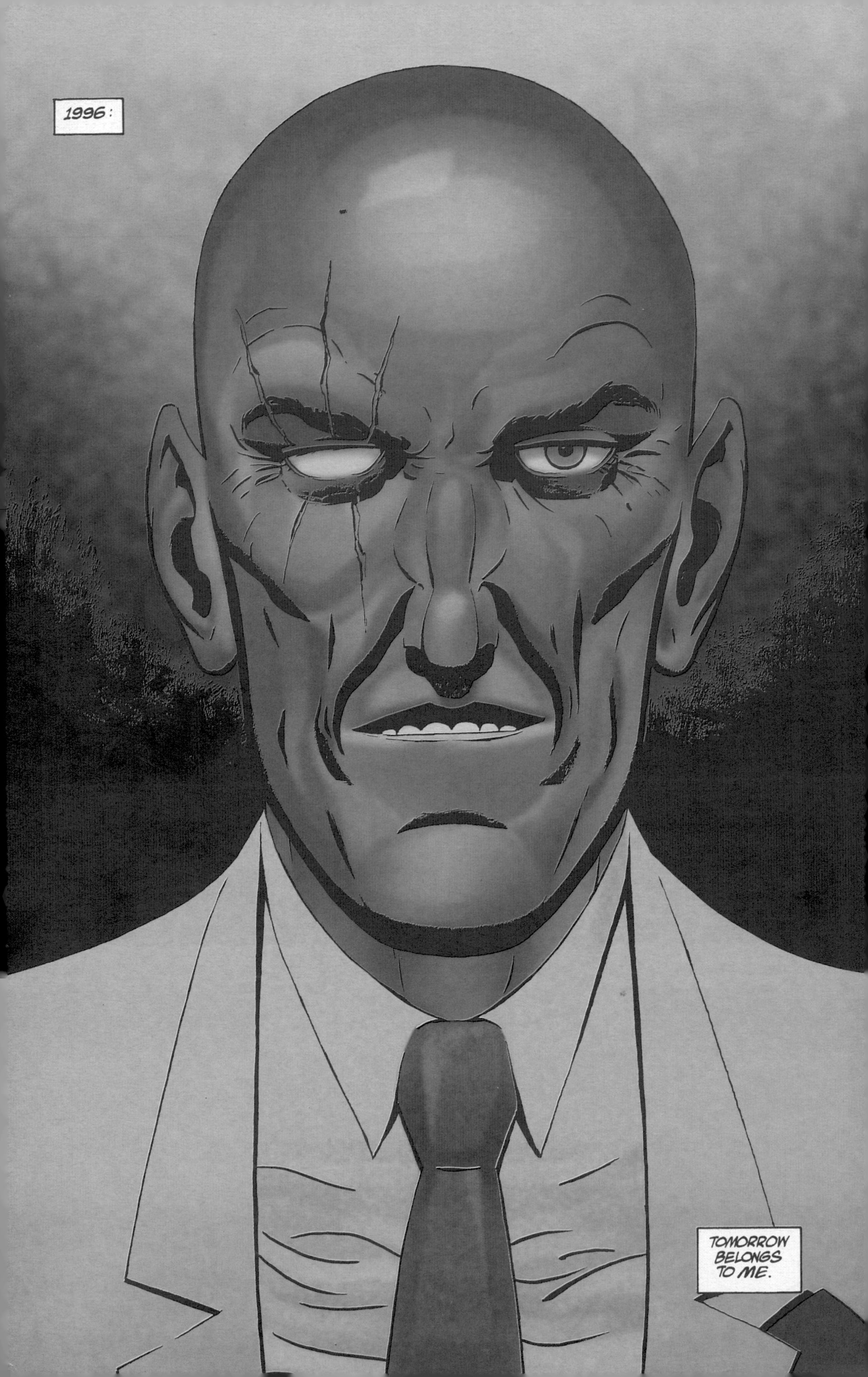
1996:
TOMORROW BELONGS TO ME.

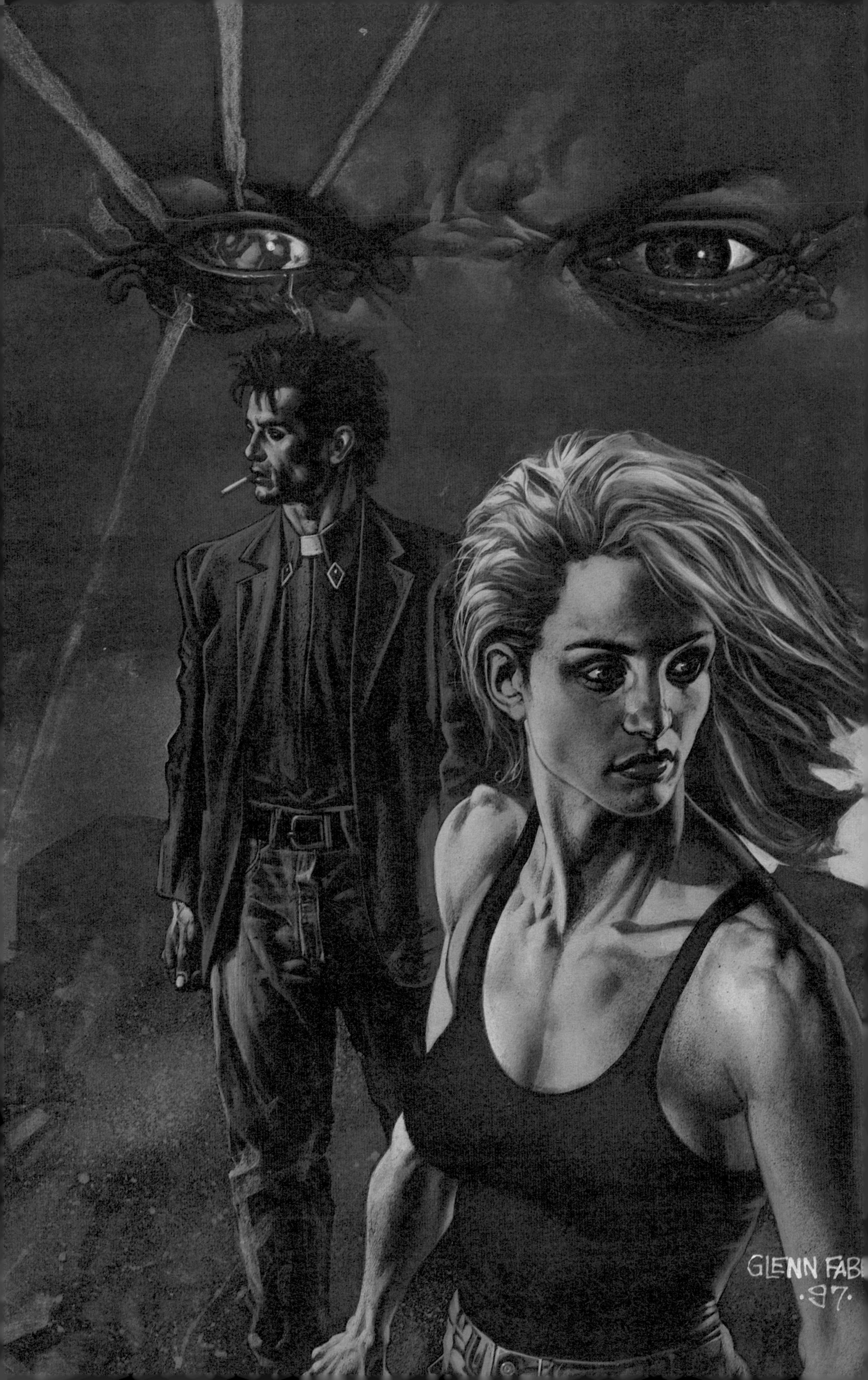
GLENN FABR
·97·

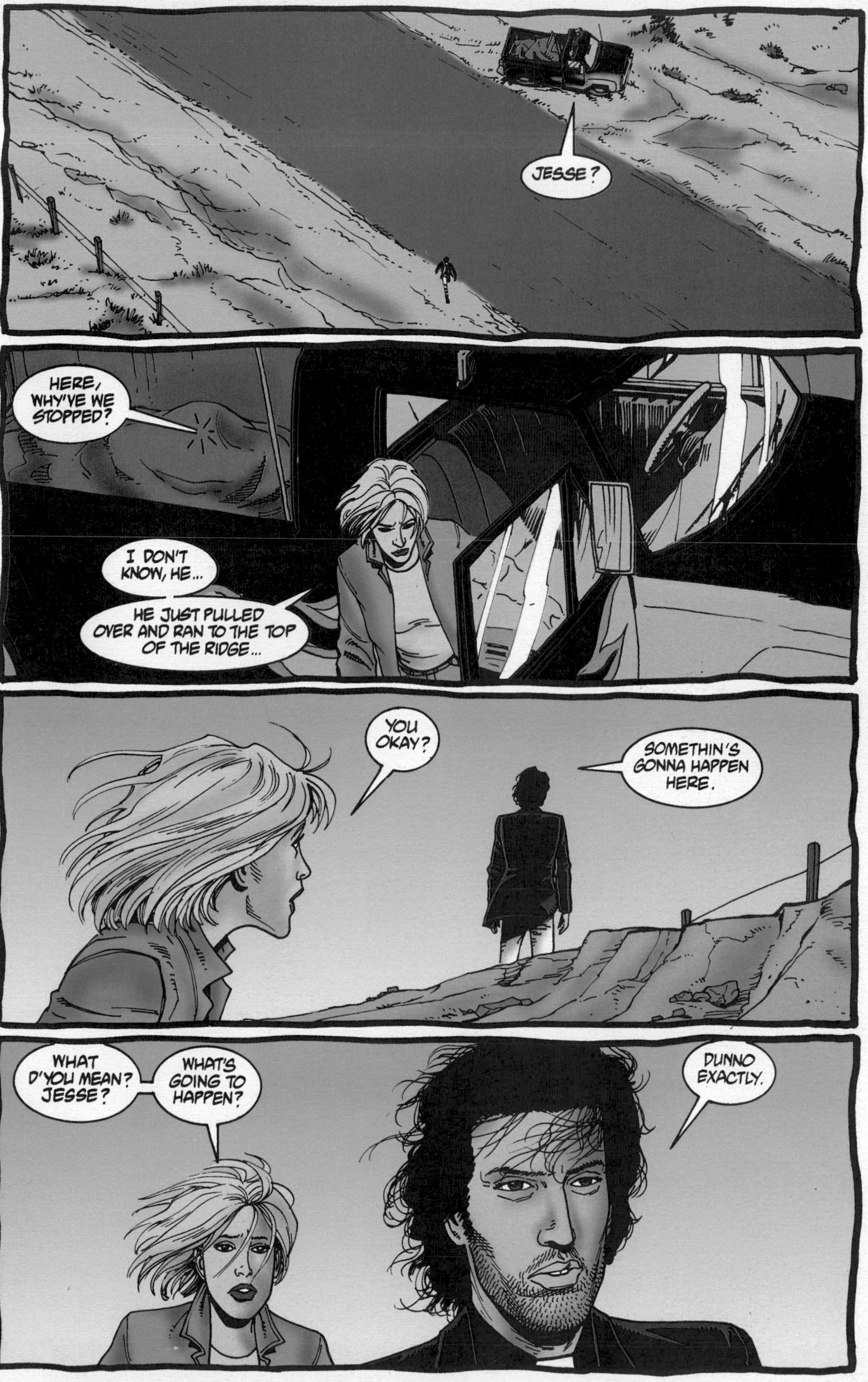
JESSE?
HERE, WHY'VE WE STOPPED?
I DON'T KNOW, HE...
HE JUST PULLED OVER AND RAN TO THE TOP OF THE RIDGE...
YOU OKAY?
SOMETHIN'S GONNA HAPPEN HERE.
WHAT D'YOU MEAN? JESSE?
WHAT'S GOING TO HAPPEN?
DUNNO EXACTLY.

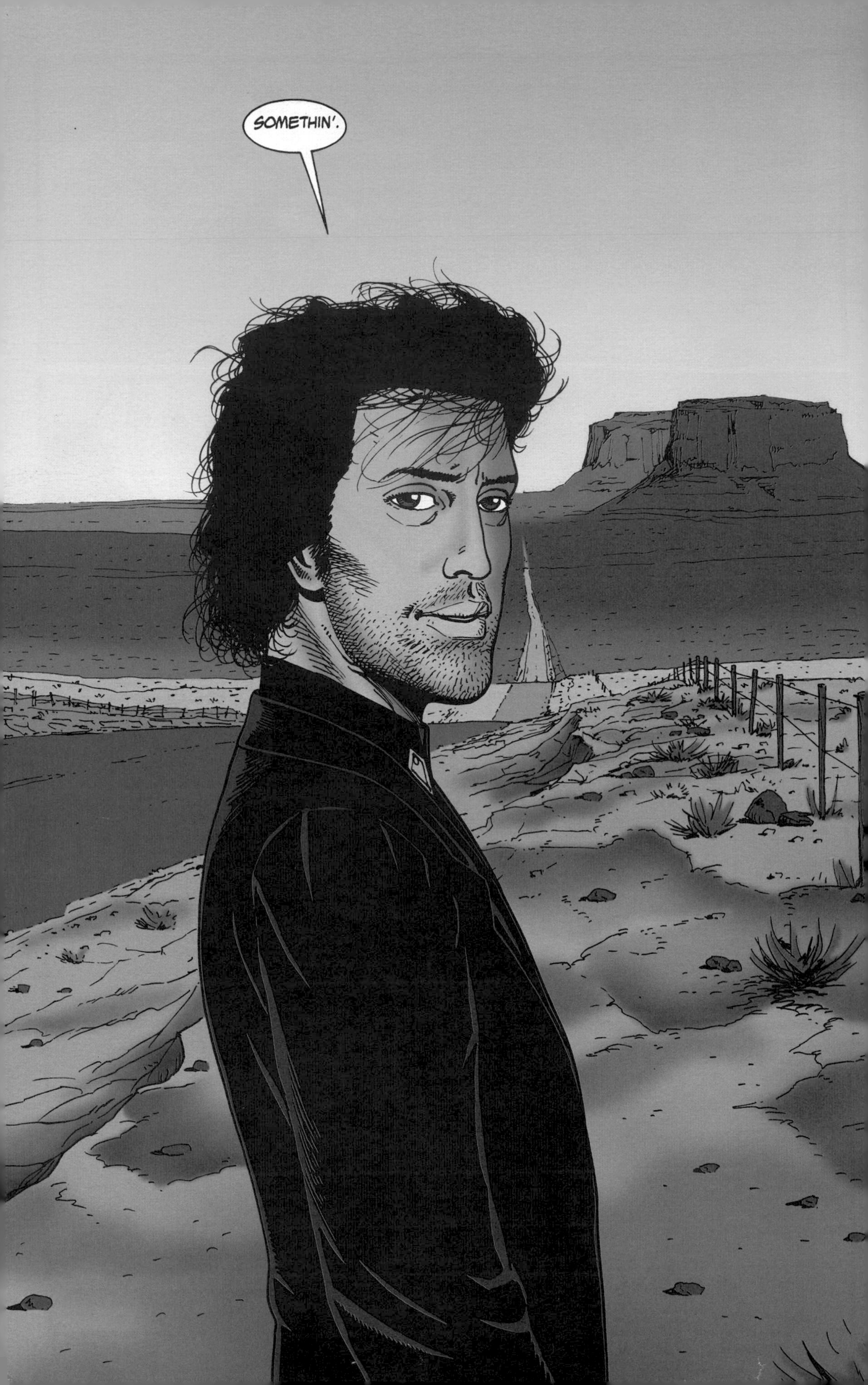
SOMETHIN'.

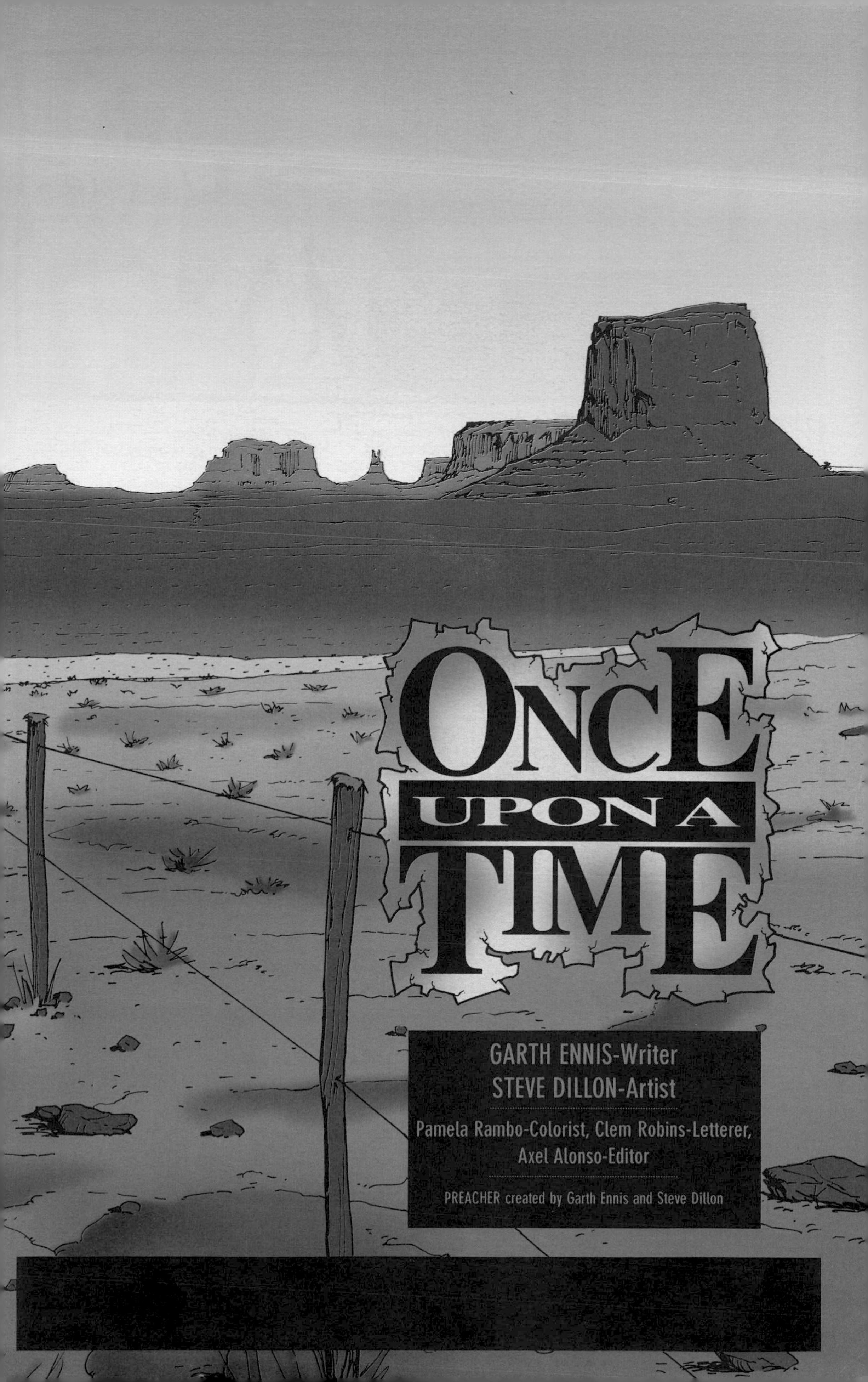
ONCE
UPON A
TIME
GARTH ENNIS-Writer
STEVE DILLON-Artist
Pamela Rambo-Colorist, Clem Robins-Letterer,
Axel Alonso-Editor
PREACHER created by Garth Ennis and Steve Dillon

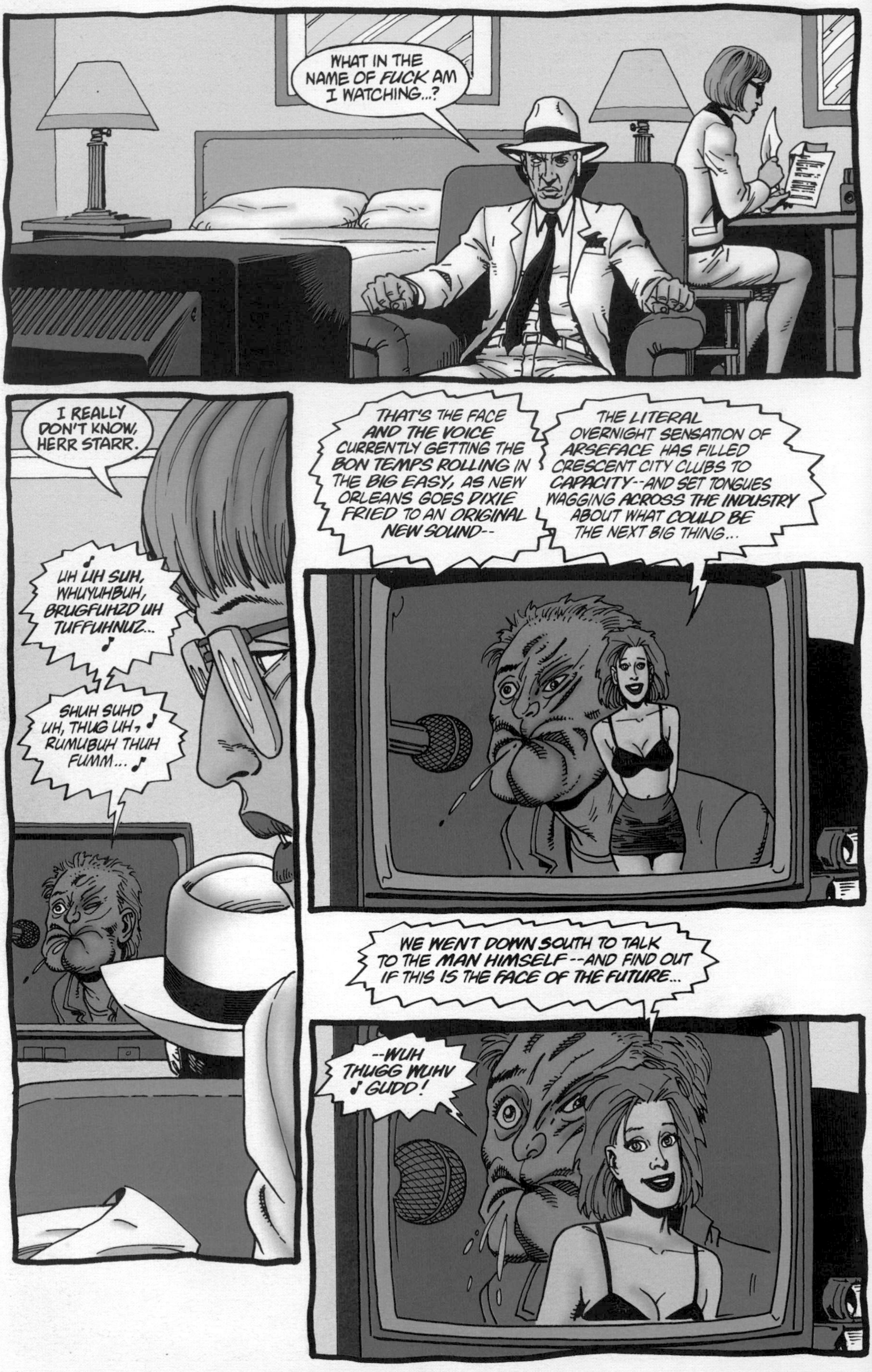
WHAT IN THE NAME OF FUCK AM I WATCHING...?
I REALLY DON'T KNOW, HERR STARR.
UH UH SUH, WHUYUHBUH, BRUGFUHZD UH TUFFUHNUZ...
SHUH SUHD UH, THUG UH, RUMUBUH THUH FUMM...
THAT'S THE FACE AND THE VOICE CURRENTLY GETTING THE BON TEMPS ROLLING IN THE BIG EASY, AS NEW ORLEANS GOES DIXIE FRIED TO AN ORIGINAL NEW SOUND--
THE LITERAL OVERNIGHT SENSATION OF ARSEFACE HAS FILLED CRESCENT CITY CLUBS TO CAPACITY--AND SET TONGUES WAGGING ACROSS THE INDUSTRY ABOUT WHAT COULD BE THE NEXT BIG THING...
WE WENT DOWN SOUTH TO TALK TO THE MAN HIMSELF--AND FIND OUT IF THIS IS THE FACE OF THE FUTURE...
--WUH THUGG WUHV GUDD!

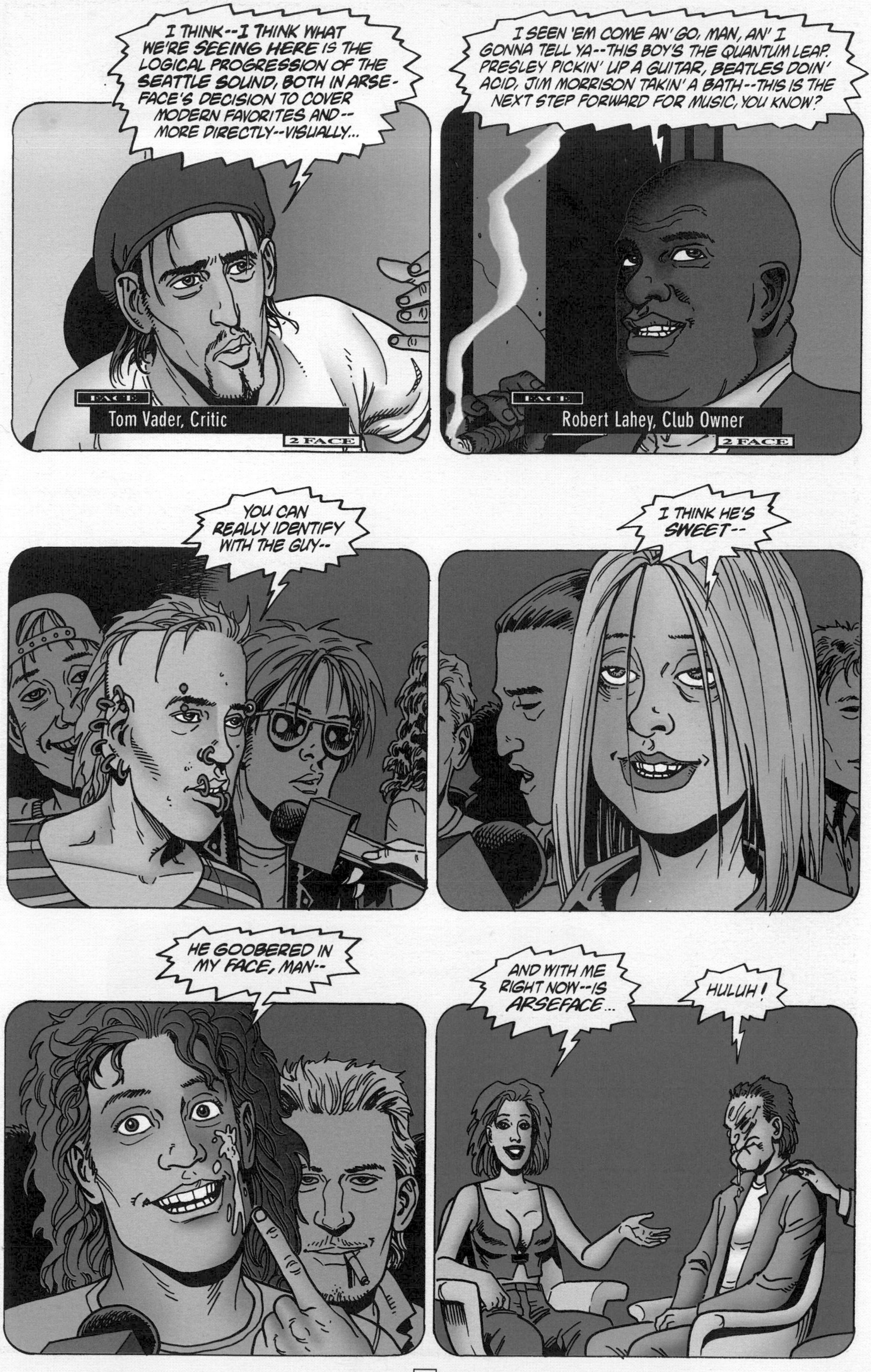
I THINK--I THINK WHAT WE'RE SEEING HERE IS THE LOGICAL PROGRESSION OF THE SEATTLE SOUND, BOTH IN ARSE-FACE'S DECISION TO COVER MODERN FAVORITES AND--MORE DIRECTLY--VISUALLY...
FACE
Tom Vader, Critic
2 FACE
I SEEN 'EM COME AN' GO, MAN, AN' I GONNA TELL YA--THIS BOY'S THE QUANTUM LEAP. PRESLEY PICKIN' UP A GUITAR, BEATLES DOIN' ACID, JIM MORRISON TAKIN' A BATH--THIS IS THE NEXT STEP FORWARD FOR MUSIC, YOU KNOW?
FACE
Robert Lahey, Club Owner
2 FACE
YOU CAN REALLY IDENTIFY WITH THE GUY--
I THINK HE'S SWEET--
HE GOOBERED IN MY FACE, MAN--
AND WITH ME RIGHT NOW--IS ARSEFACE...
HULUH!

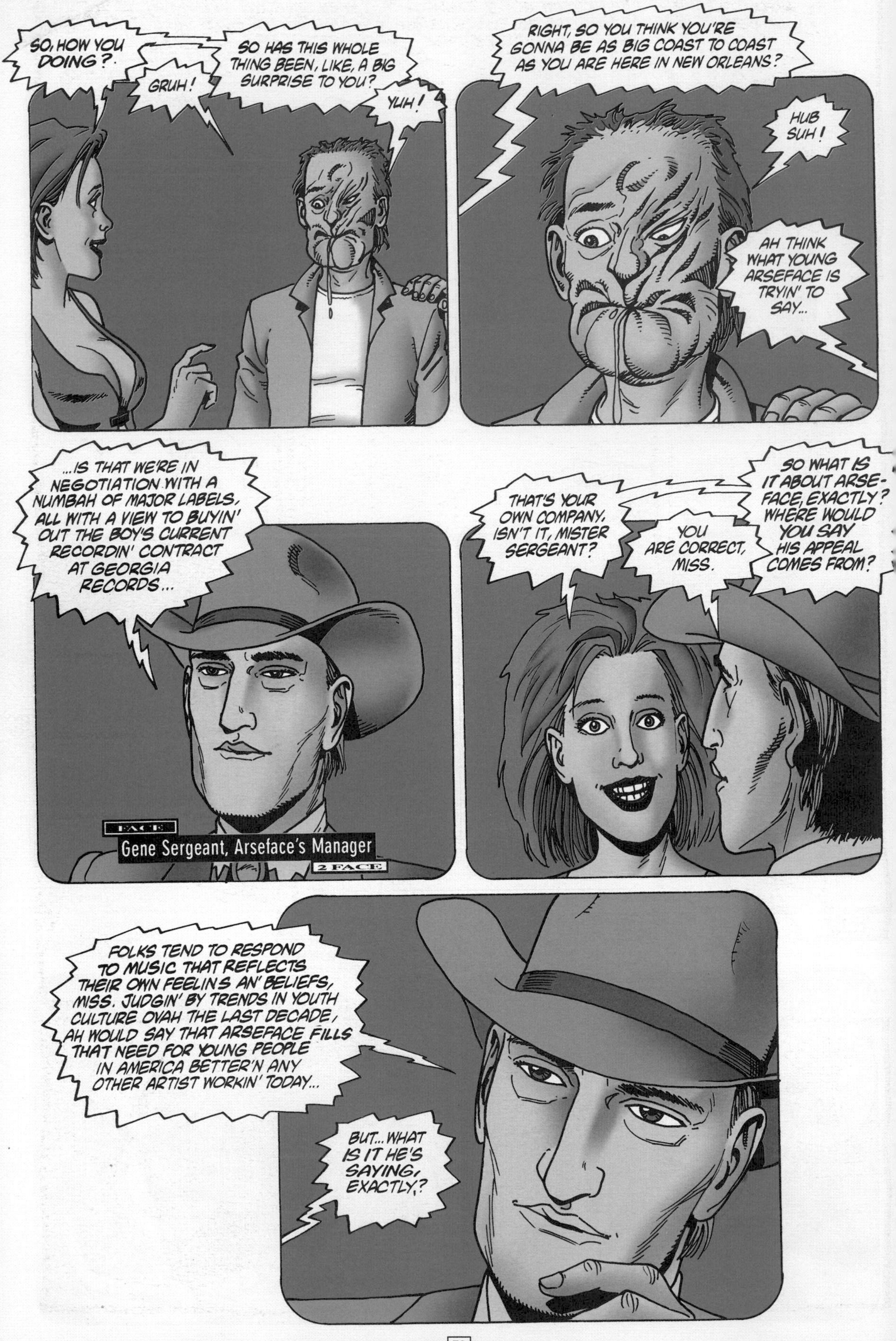
SO, HOW YOU DOING?
GRUH!
SO HAS THIS WHOLE THING BEEN, LIKE, A BIG SURPRISE TO YOU?
YUH!
RIGHT, SO YOU THINK YOU'RE GONNA BE AS BIG COAST TO COAST AS YOU ARE HERE IN NEW ORLEANS?
HUB SUH!
AH THINK WHAT YOUNG ARSEFACE IS TRYIN' TO SAY...
...IS THAT WE'RE IN NEGOTIATION WITH A NUMBAH OF MAJOR LABELS, ALL WITH A VIEW TO BUYIN' OUT THE BOY'S CURRENT RECORDIN' CONTRACT AT GEORGIA RECORDS...
FACE
Gene Sergeant, Arseface's Manager
2 FACE
THAT'S YOUR OWN COMPANY, ISN'T IT, MISTER SERGEANT?
YOU ARE CORRECT, MISS.
SO WHAT IS IT ABOUT ARSE-FACE, EXACTLY? WHERE WOULD YOU SAY HIS APPEAL COMES FROM?
FOLKS TEND TO RESPOND TO MUSIC THAT REFLECTS THEIR OWN FEELIN'S AN' BELIEFS, MISS. JUDGIN' BY TRENDS IN YOUTH CULTURE OVAH THE LAST DECADE, AH WOULD SAY THAT ARSEFACE FILLS THAT NEED FOR YOUNG PEOPLE IN AMERICA BETTER'N ANY OTHER ARTIST WORKIN' TODAY...
BUT... WHAT IS IT HE'S SAYING, EXACTLY?

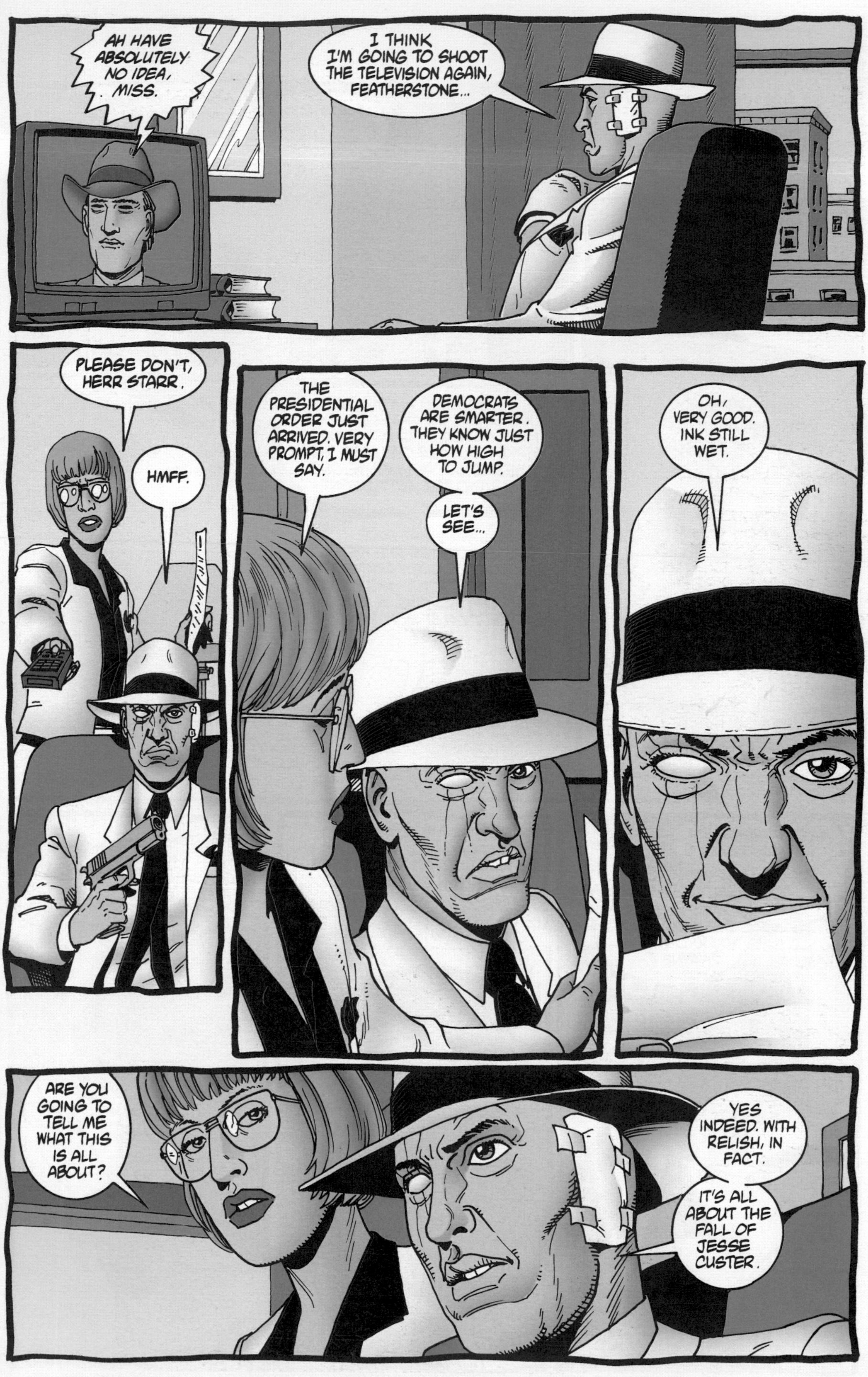
AH HAVE ABSOLUTELY NO IDEA, MISS.
I THINK I'M GOING TO SHOOT THE TELEVISION AGAIN, FEATHERSTONE...
PLEASE DON'T, HERR STARR.
HMFF.
THE PRESIDENTIAL ORDER JUST ARRIVED. VERY PROMPT, I MUST SAY.
DEMOCRATS ARE SMARTER. THEY KNOW JUST HOW HIGH TO JUMP.
LET'S SEE...
OH, VERY GOOD. INK STILL WET.
ARE YOU GOING TO TELL ME WHAT THIS IS ALL ABOUT?
YES INDEED. WITH RELISH, IN FACT.
IT'S ALL ABOUT THE FALL OF JESSE CUSTER.

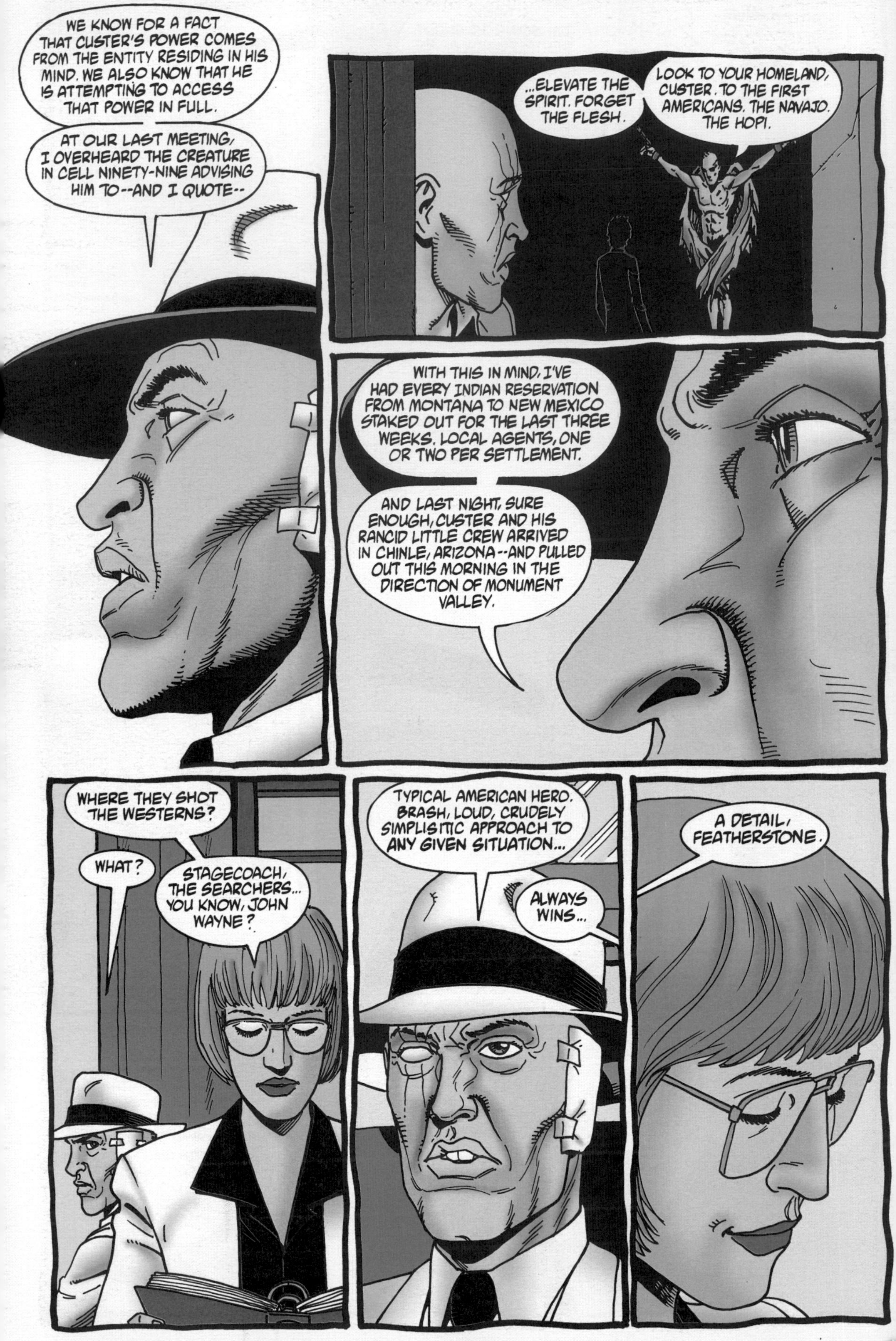
WE KNOW FOR A FACT THAT CUSTER'S POWER COMES FROM THE ENTITY RESIDING IN HIS MIND. WE ALSO KNOW THAT HE IS ATTEMPTING TO ACCESS THAT POWER IN FULL.
AT OUR LAST MEETING, I OVERHEARD THE CREATURE IN CELL NINETY-NINE ADVISING HIM TO--AND I QUOTE--
...ELEVATE THE SPIRIT. FORGET THE FLESH.
LOOK TO YOUR HOMELAND, CUSTER. TO THE FIRST AMERICANS. THE NAVAJO. THE HOPI.
WITH THIS IN MIND, I'VE HAD EVERY INDIAN RESERVATION FROM MONTANA TO NEW MEXICO STAKED OUT FOR THE LAST THREE WEEKS. LOCAL AGENTS, ONE OR TWO PER SETTLEMENT.
AND LAST NIGHT, SURE ENOUGH, CUSTER AND HIS RANCID LITTLE CREW ARRIVED IN CHINLE, ARIZONA--AND PULLED OUT THIS MORNING IN THE DIRECTION OF MONUMENT VALLEY.
WHERE THEY SHOT THE WESTERNS?
WHAT?
STAGECOACH, THE SEARCHERS... YOU KNOW, JOHN WAYNE?
TYPICAL AMERICAN HERO. BRASH, LOUD, CRUDELY SIMPLISITIC APPROACH TO ANY GIVEN SITUATION...
ALWAYS WINS...
A DETAIL, FEATHERSTONE.

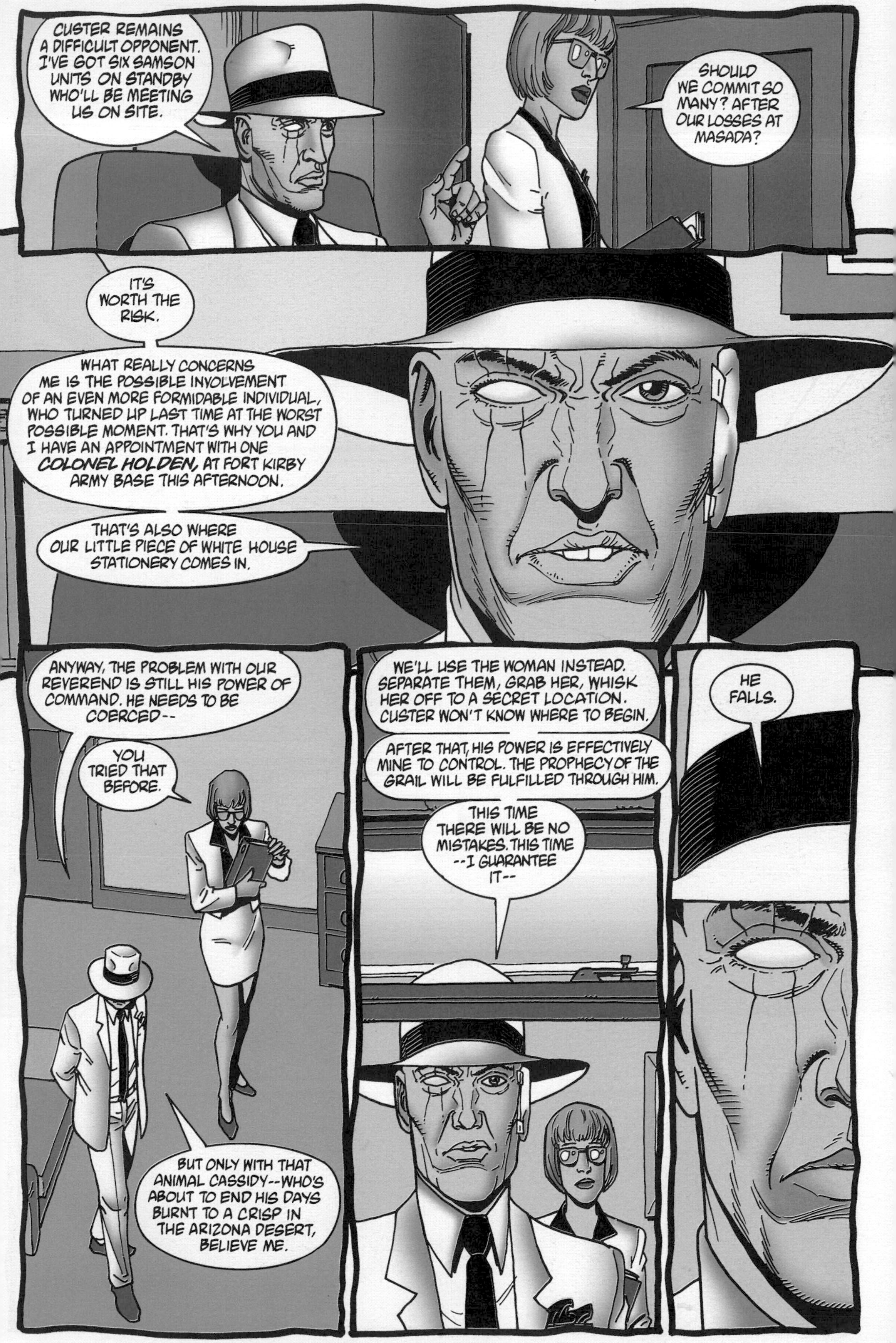
CUSTER REMAINS A DIFFICULT OPPONENT. I'VE GOT SIX SAMSON UNITS ON STANDBY WHO'LL BE MEETING US ON SITE.
SHOULD WE COMMIT SO MANY? AFTER OUR LOSSES AT MASADA?
IT'S WORTH THE RISK.
WHAT REALLY CONCERNS ME IS THE POSSIBLE INVOLVEMENT OF AN EVEN MORE FORMIDABLE INDIVIDUAL, WHO TURNED UP LAST TIME AT THE WORST POSSIBLE MOMENT. THAT'S WHY YOU AND I HAVE AN APPOINTMENT WITH ONE ***COLONEL HOLDEN,*** AT FORT KIRBY ARMY BASE THIS AFTERNOON.
THAT'S ALSO WHERE OUR LITTLE PIECE OF WHITE HOUSE STATIONERY COMES IN.
ANYWAY, THE PROBLEM WITH OUR REVEREND IS STILL HIS POWER OF COMMAND. HE NEEDS TO BE COERCED--
YOU TRIED THAT BEFORE.
BUT ONLY WITH THAT ANIMAL CASSIDY--WHO'S ABOUT TO END HIS DAYS BURNT TO A CRISP IN THE ARIZONA DESERT, BELIEVE ME.
WE'LL USE THE WOMAN INSTEAD. SEPARATE THEM, GRAB HER, WHISK HER OFF TO A SECRET LOCATION. CUSTER WON'T KNOW WHERE TO BEGIN.
AFTER THAT, HIS POWER IS EFFECTIVELY MINE TO CONTROL. THE PROPHECY OF THE GRAIL WILL BE FULFILLED THROUGH HIM.
THIS TIME THERE WILL BE NO MISTAKES. THIS TIME --I GUARANTEE IT--
HE FALLS.

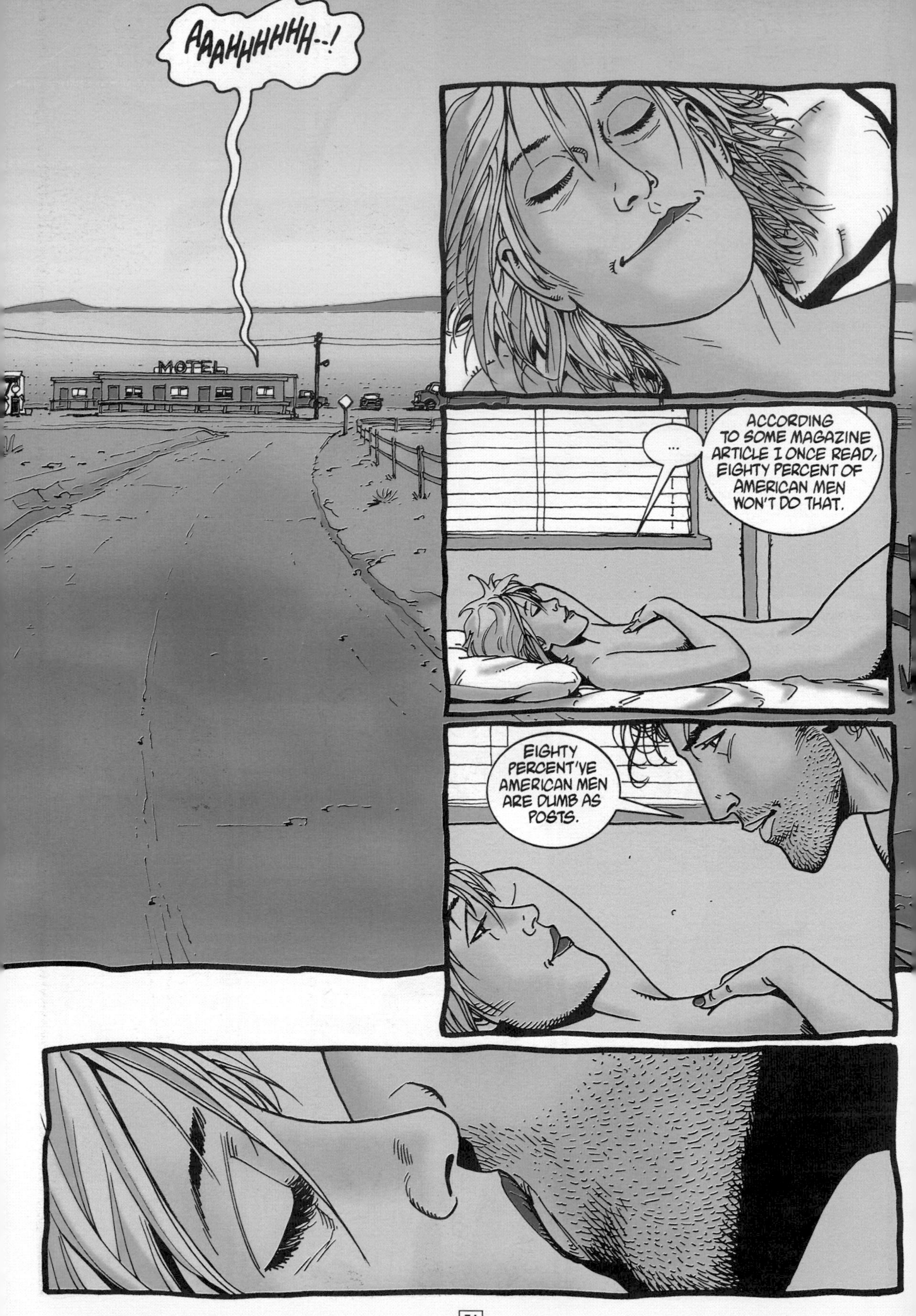
AAAHHHHHH--!
MOTEL
...
ACCORDING TO SOME MAGAZINE ARTICLE I ONCE READ, EIGHTY PERCENT OF AMERICAN MEN WON'T DO THAT.
EIGHTY PERCENT'VE AMERICAN MEN ARE DUMB AS POSTS.

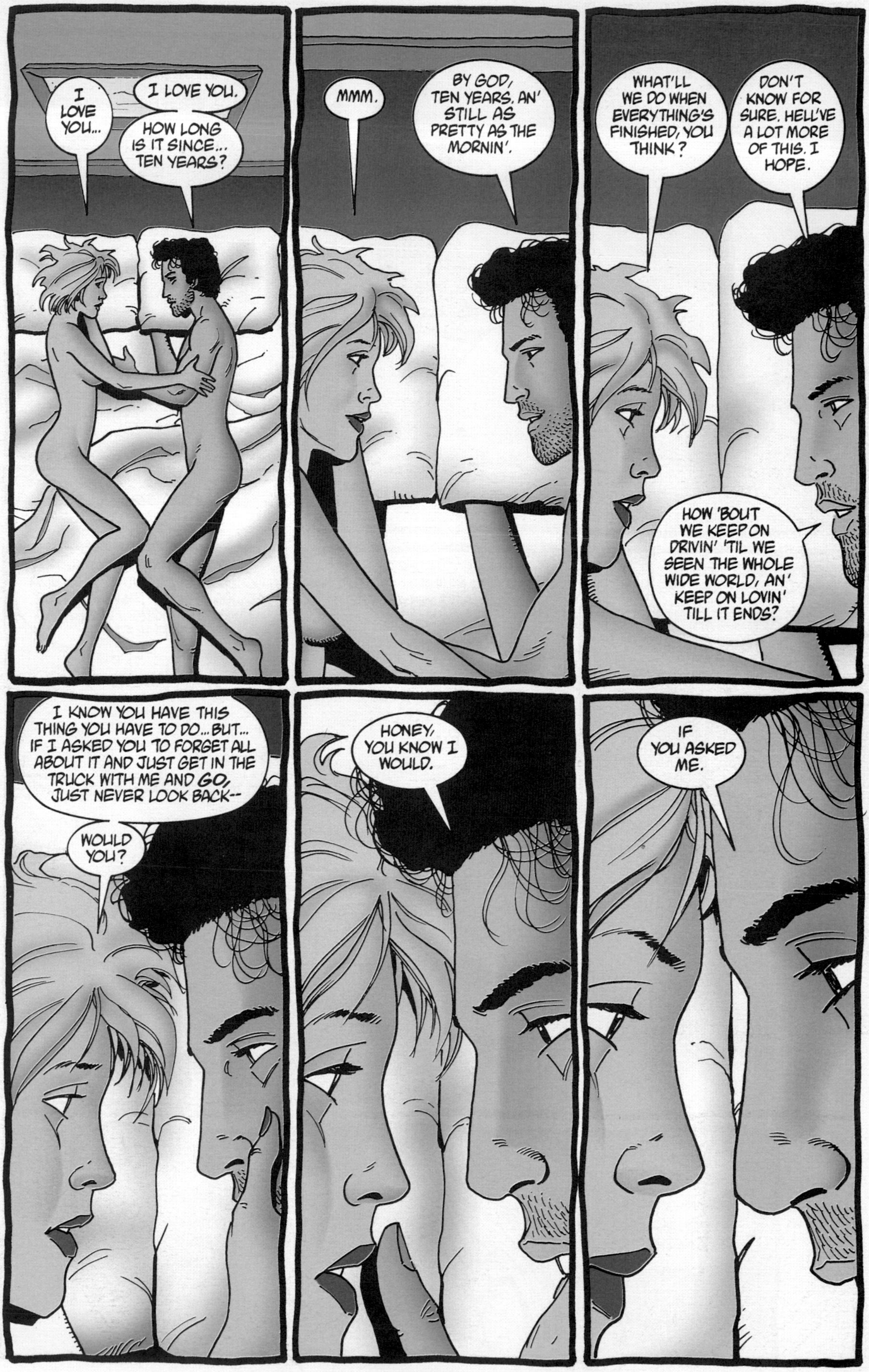
I LOVE YOU...
I LOVE YOU.
HOW LONG IS IT SINCE... TEN YEARS?
MMM.
BY GOD, TEN YEARS, AN' STILL AS PRETTY AS THE MORNIN'.
WHAT'LL WE DO WHEN EVERYTHING'S FINISHED, YOU THINK?
DON'T KNOW FOR SURE. HELL'VE A LOT MORE OF THIS. I HOPE.
HOW 'BOUT WE KEEP ON DRIVIN' 'TIL WE SEEN THE WHOLE WIDE WORLD, AN' KEEP ON LOVIN' TILL IT ENDS?
I KNOW YOU HAVE THIS THING YOU HAVE TO DO... BUT... IF I ASKED YOU TO FORGET ALL ABOUT IT AND JUST GET IN THE TRUCK WITH ME AND GO, JUST NEVER LOOK BACK--
WOULD YOU?
HONEY, YOU KNOW I WOULD.
IF YOU ASKED ME.

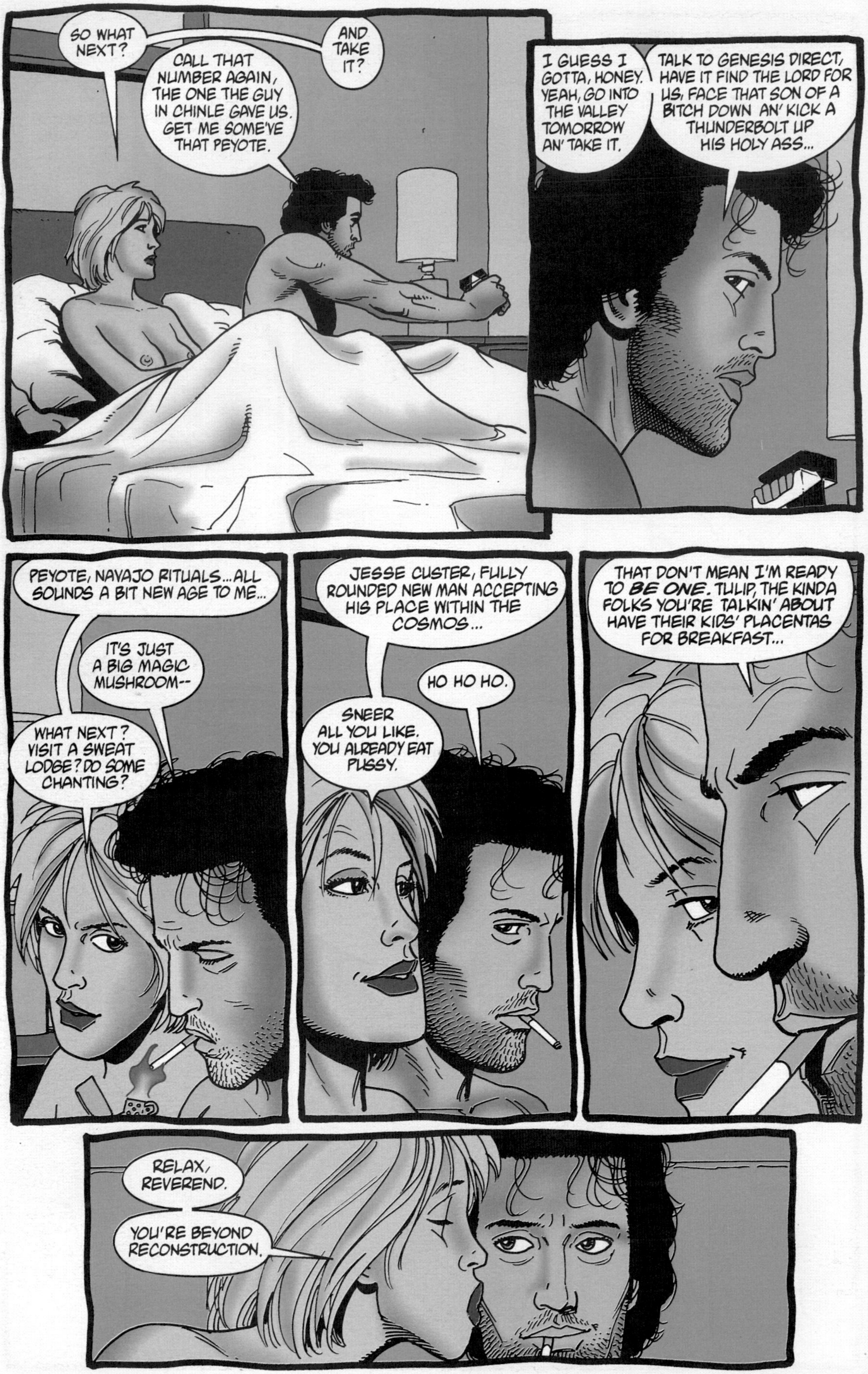
SO WHAT NEXT?
CALL THAT NUMBER AGAIN, THE ONE THE GUY IN CHINLE GAVE US. GET ME SOME'VE THAT PEYOTE.
AND TAKE IT?
I GUESS I GOTTA, HONEY. YEAH, GO INTO THE VALLEY TOMORROW AN' TAKE IT.
TALK TO GENESIS DIRECT, HAVE IT FIND THE LORD FOR US, FACE THAT SON OF A BITCH DOWN AN' KICK A THUNDERBOLT UP HIS HOLY ASS...
PEYOTE, NAVAJO RITUALS...ALL SOUNDS A BIT NEW AGE TO ME...
IT'S JUST A BIG MAGIC MUSHROOM--
WHAT NEXT? VISIT A SWEAT LODGE? DO SOME CHANTING?
JESSE CUSTER, FULLY ROUNDED NEW MAN ACCEPTING HIS PLACE WITHIN THE COSMOS...
HO HO HO.
SNEER ALL YOU LIKE. YOU ALREADY EAT PUSSY.
THAT DON'T MEAN I'M READY TO BE ONE. TULIP, THE KINDA FOLKS YOU'RE TALKIN' ABOUT HAVE THEIR KIDS' PLACENTAS FOR BREAKFAST...
RELAX, REVEREND.
YOU'RE BEYOND RECONSTRUCTION.

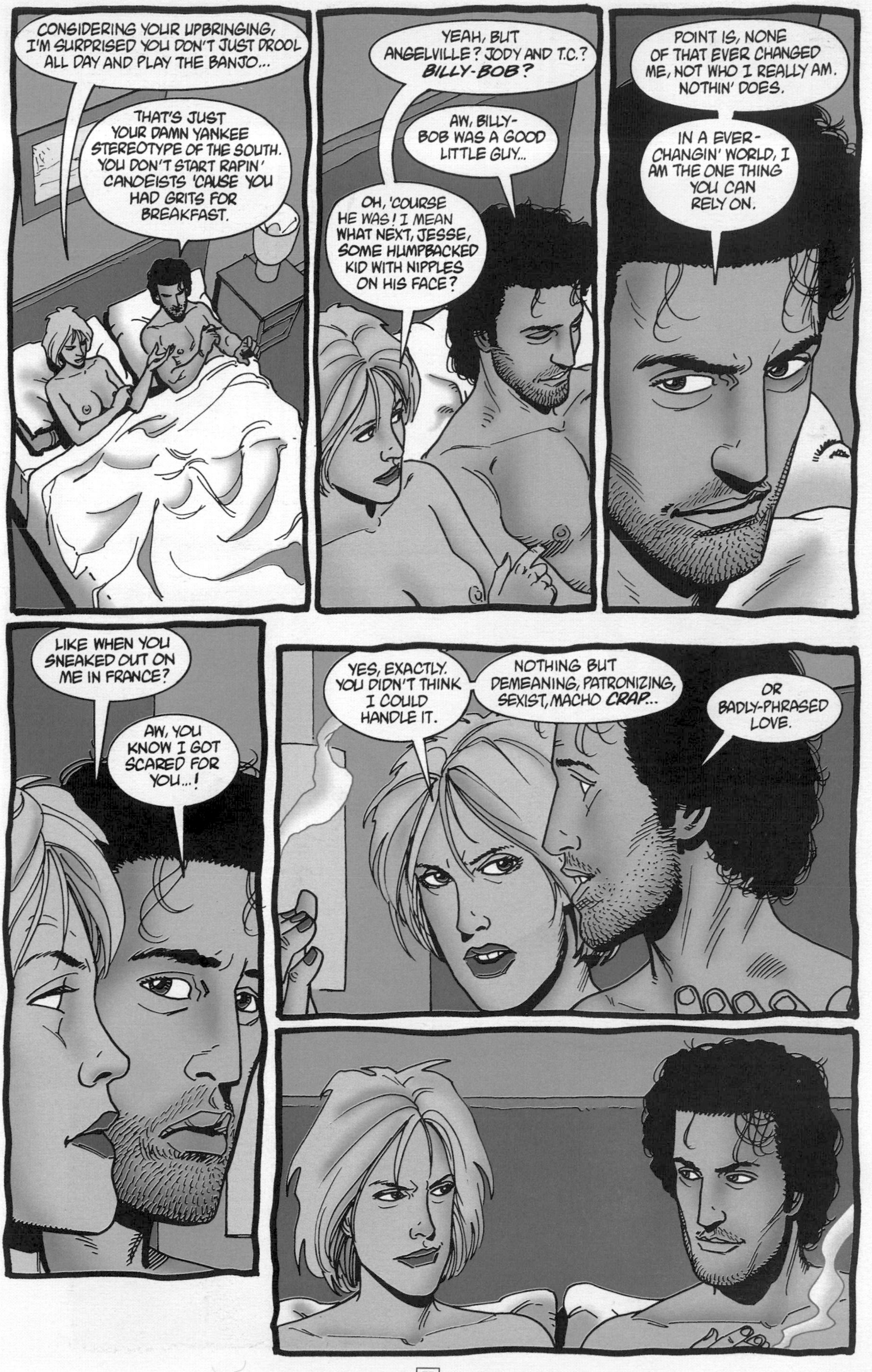
CONSIDERING YOUR UPBRINGING, I'M SURPRISED YOU DON'T JUST DROOL ALL DAY AND PLAY THE BANJO...
THAT'S JUST YOUR DAMN YANKEE STEREOTYPE OF THE SOUTH. YOU DON'T START RAPIN' CANOEISTS 'CAUSE YOU HAD GRITS FOR BREAKFAST.
YEAH, BUT ANGELVILLE? JODY AND T.C.? *BILLY-BOB?*
AW, BILLY-BOB WAS A GOOD LITTLE GUY...
OH, 'COURSE HE WAS! I MEAN WHAT NEXT, JESSE, SOME HUMPBACKED KID WITH NIPPLES ON HIS FACE?
POINT IS, NONE OF THAT EVER CHANGED ME, NOT WHO I REALLY AM. NOTHIN' DOES.
IN A EVER-CHANGIN' WORLD, I AM THE ONE THING YOU CAN RELY ON.
LIKE WHEN YOU SNEAKED OUT ON ME IN FRANCE?
AW, YOU KNOW I GOT SCARED FOR YOU...!
YES, EXACTLY. YOU DIDN'T THINK I COULD HANDLE IT.
NOTHING BUT DEMEANING, PATRONIZING, SEXIST, MACHO *CRAP*...
OR BADLY-PHRASED LOVE.

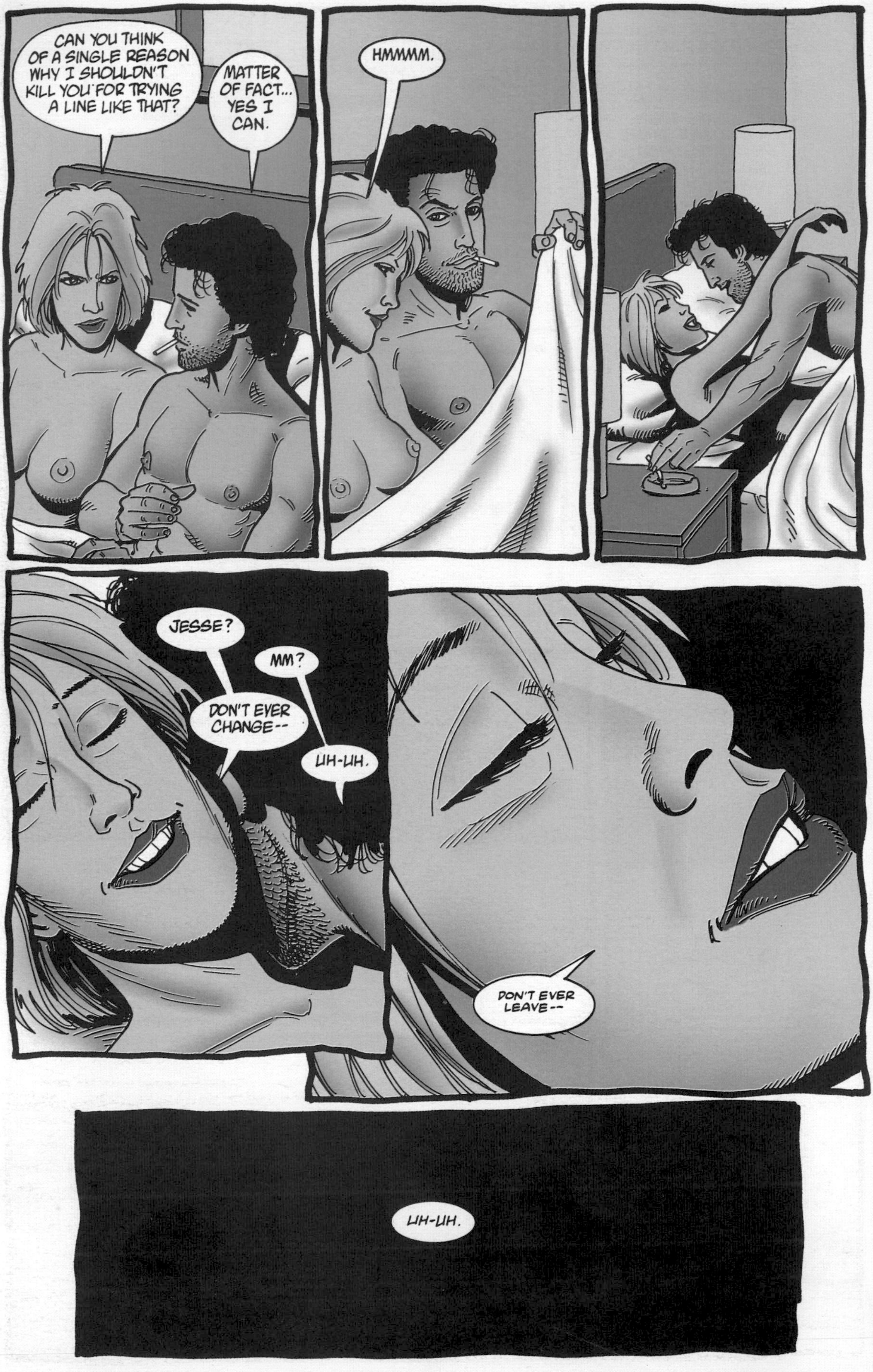
CAN YOU THINK OF A SINGLE REASON WHY I SHOULDN'T KILL YOU FOR TRYING A LINE LIKE THAT?
MATTER OF FACT... YES I CAN.
HMMMM.
JESSE?
MM?
DON'T EVER CHANGE--
UH-UH.
DON'T EVER LEAVE--
UH-UH.

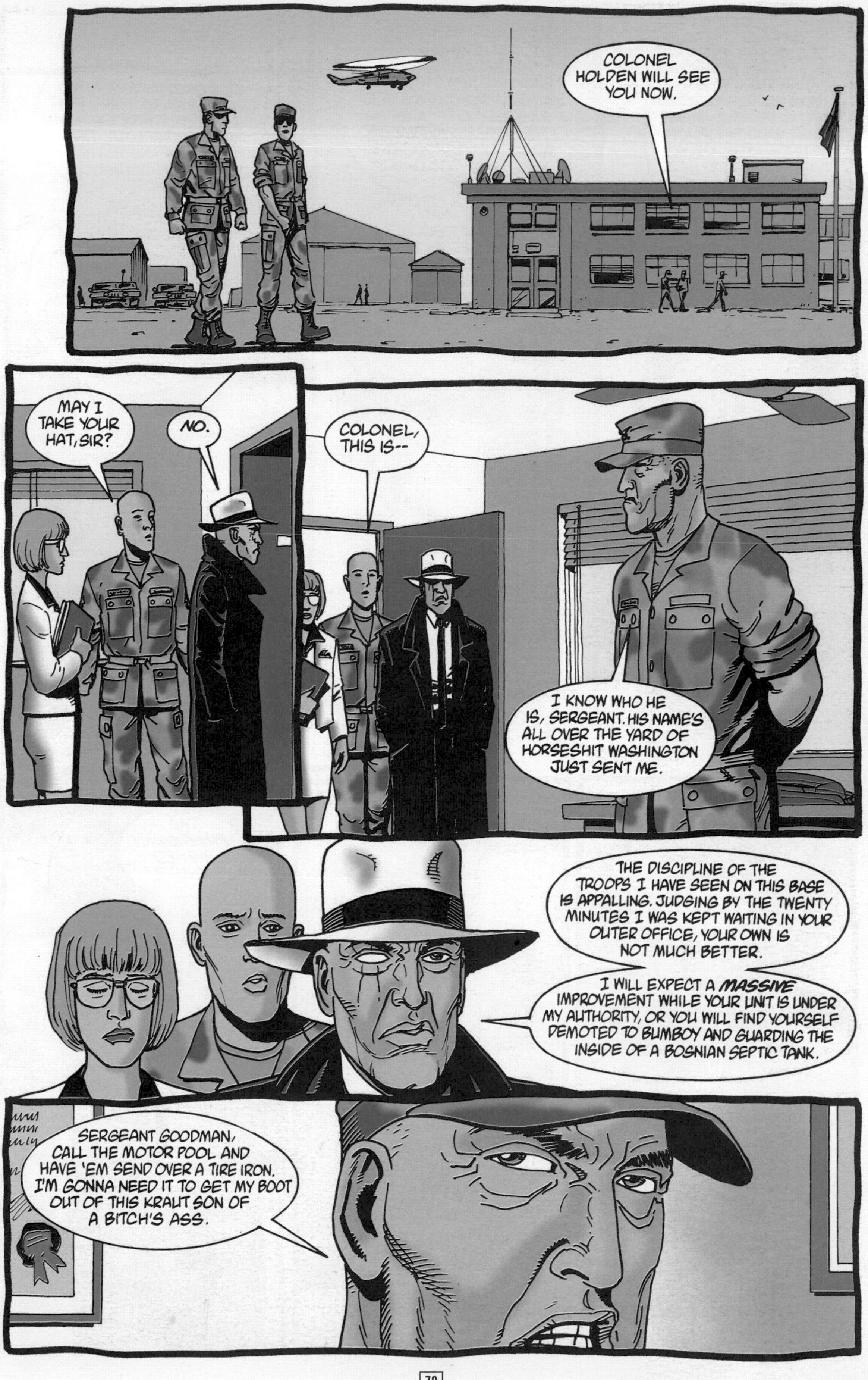
COLONEL HOLDEN WILL SEE YOU NOW.
MAY I TAKE YOUR HAT, SIR?
NO.
COLONEL, THIS IS--
I KNOW WHO HE IS, SERGEANT. HIS NAME'S ALL OVER THE YARD OF HORSESHIT WASHINGTON JUST SENT ME.
THE DISCIPLINE OF THE TROOPS I HAVE SEEN ON THIS BASE IS APPALLING. JUDGING BY THE TWENTY MINUTES I WAS KEPT WAITING IN YOUR OUTER OFFICE, YOUR OWN IS NOT MUCH BETTER.
I WILL EXPECT A MASSIVE IMPROVEMENT WHILE YOUR UNIT IS UNDER MY AUTHORITY, OR YOU WILL FIND YOURSELF DEMOTED TO BUMBOY AND GUARDING THE INSIDE OF A BOSNIAN SEPTIC TANK.
SERGEANT GOODMAN, CALL THE MOTOR POOL AND HAVE 'EM SEND OVER A TIRE IRON. I'M GONNA NEED IT TO GET MY BOOT OUT OF THIS KRAUT SON OF A BITCH'S ASS.

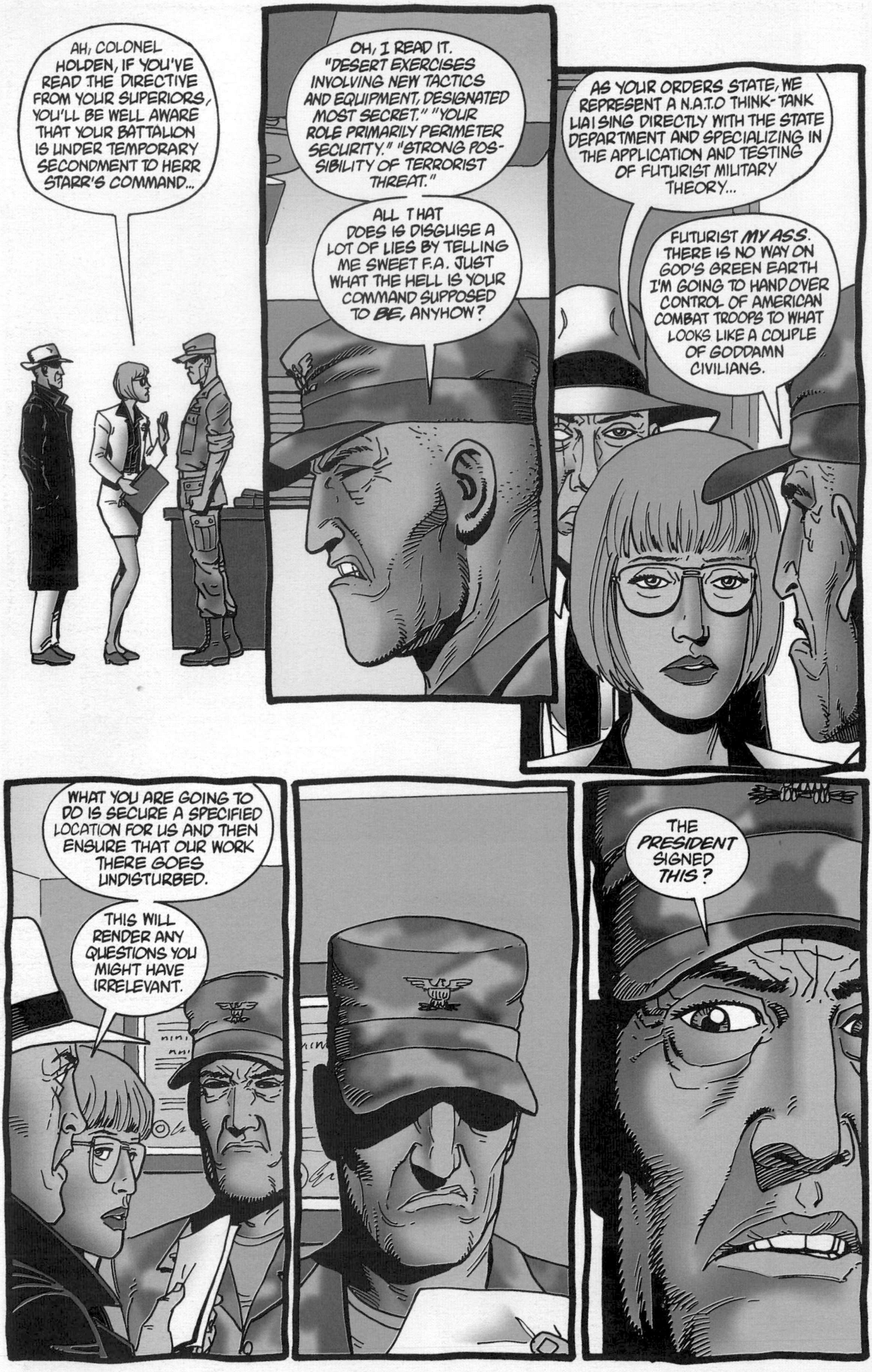
AH, COLONEL HOLDEN, IF YOU'VE READ THE DIRECTIVE FROM YOUR SUPERIORS, YOU'LL BE WELL AWARE THAT YOUR BATTALION IS UNDER TEMPORARY SECONDMENT TO HERR STARR'S COMMAND...
OH, I READ IT. "DESERT EXERCISES INVOLVING NEW TACTICS AND EQUIPMENT, DESIGNATED MOST SECRET." "YOUR ROLE PRIMARILY PERIMETER SECURITY." "STRONG POSSIBILITY OF TERRORIST THREAT."
ALL THAT DOES IS DISGUISE A LOT OF LIES BY TELLING ME SWEET F.A. JUST WHAT THE HELL IS YOUR COMMAND SUPPOSED TO *BE*, ANYHOW?
AS YOUR ORDERS STATE, WE REPRESENT A N.A.T.O THINK-TANK LIAISING DIRECTLY WITH THE STATE DEPARTMENT AND SPECIALIZING IN THE APPLICATION AND TESTING OF FUTURIST MILITARY THEORY...
FUTURIST *MY ASS*. THERE IS NO WAY ON GOD'S GREEN EARTH I'M GOING TO HAND OVER CONTROL OF AMERICAN COMBAT TROOPS TO WHAT LOOKS LIKE A COUPLE OF GODDAMN CIVILIANS.
WHAT YOU ARE GOING TO DO IS SECURE A SPECIFIED LOCATION FOR US AND THEN ENSURE THAT OUR WORK THERE GOES UNDISTURBED.
THIS WILL RENDER ANY QUESTIONS YOU MIGHT HAVE IRRELEVANT.
THE *PRESIDENT* SIGNED *THIS*?

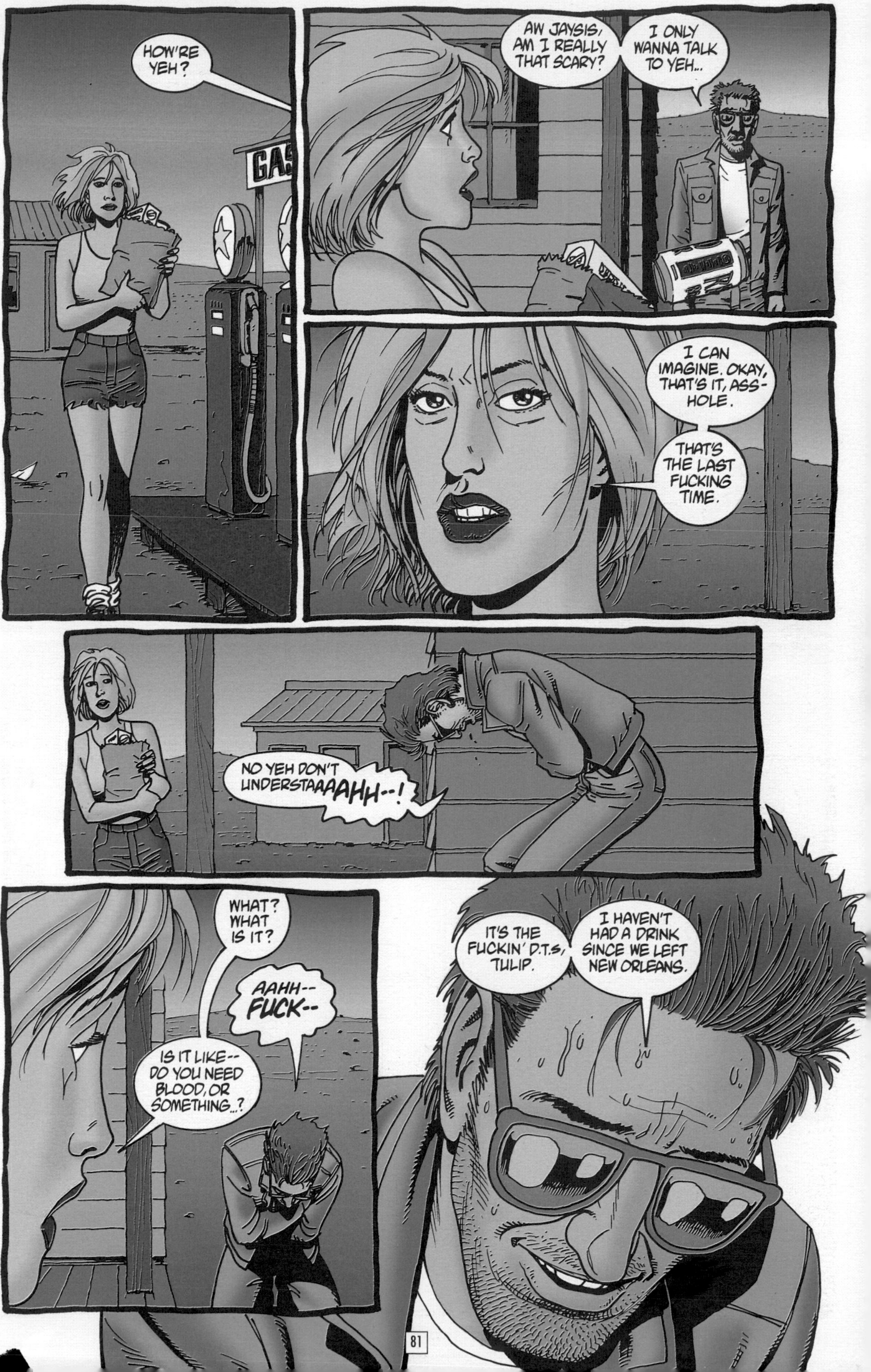
HOW'RE YEH?
AW JAYSIS, AM I REALLY THAT SCARY?
I ONLY WANNA TALK TO YEH...
I CAN IMAGINE. OKAY, THAT'S IT, ASS-HOLE.
THAT'S THE LAST FUCKING TIME.
NO YEH DON'T UNDERSTAAAAHH--!
WHAT? WHAT IS IT?
AAHH-- FUCK--
IS IT LIKE-- DO YOU NEED BLOOD, OR SOMETHING...?
IT'S THE FUCKIN' D.T.s, TULIP.
I HAVEN'T HAD A DRINK SINCE WE LEFT NEW ORLEANS.

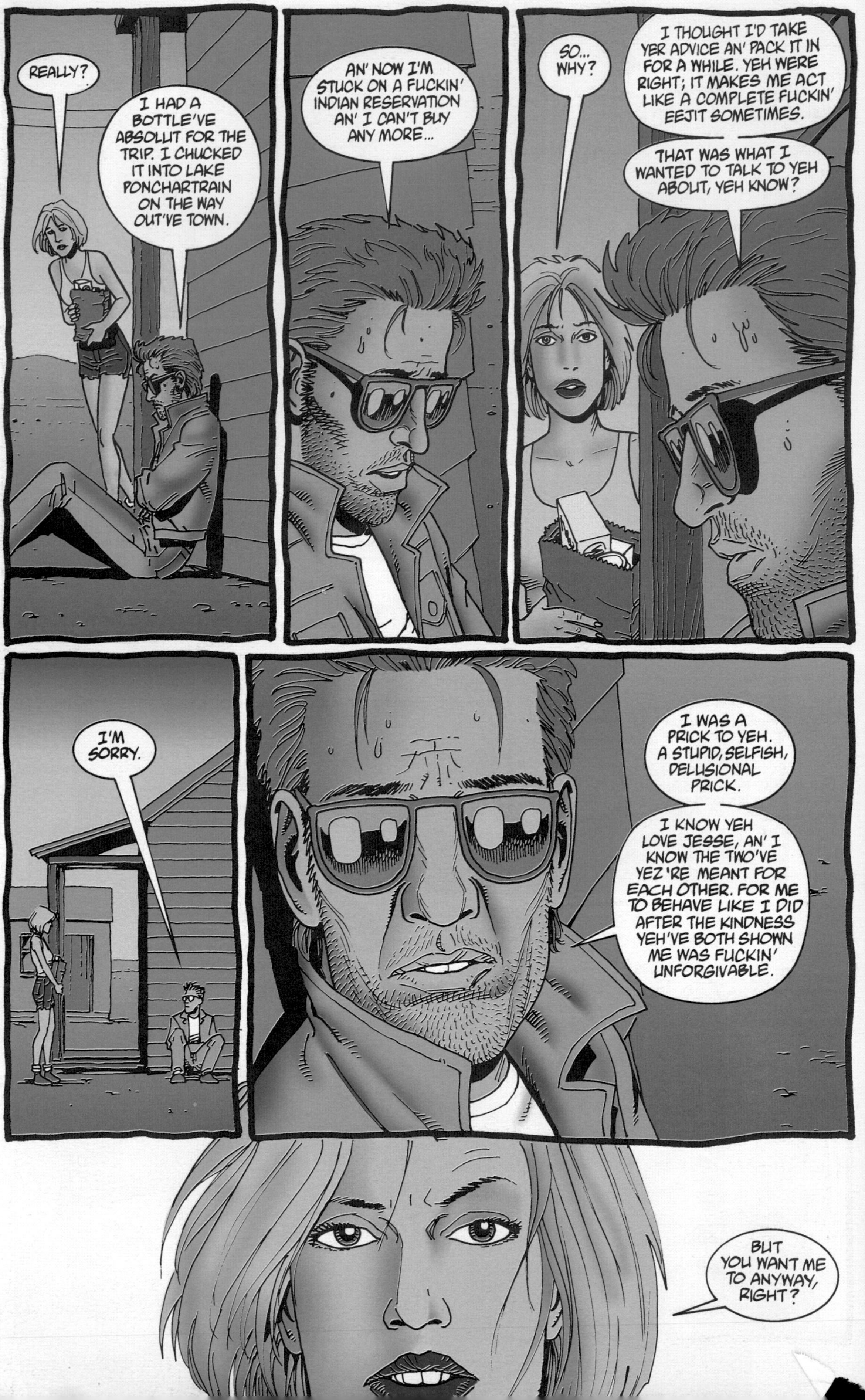
REALLY?
I HAD A BOTTLE'VE ABSOLUT FOR THE TRIP. I CHUCKED IT INTO LAKE PONCHARTRAIN ON THE WAY OUT'VE TOWN.
AN' NOW I'M STUCK ON A FUCKIN' INDIAN RESERVATION AN' I CAN'T BUY ANY MORE...
SO... WHY?
I THOUGHT I'D TAKE YER ADVICE AN' PACK IT IN FOR A WHILE. YEH WERE RIGHT; IT MAKES ME ACT LIKE A COMPLETE FUCKIN' EEJIT SOMETIMES.
THAT WAS WHAT I WANTED TO TALK TO YEH ABOUT, YEH KNOW?
I'M SORRY.
I WAS A PRICK TO YEH. A STUPID, SELFISH, DELUSIONAL PRICK.
I KNOW YEH LOVE JESSE, AN' I KNOW THE TWO'VE YEZ'RE MEANT FOR EACH OTHER. FOR ME TO BEHAVE LIKE I DID AFTER THE KINDNESS YEH'VE BOTH SHOWN ME WAS FUCKIN' UNFORGIVABLE.
BUT YOU WANT ME TO ANYWAY, RIGHT?

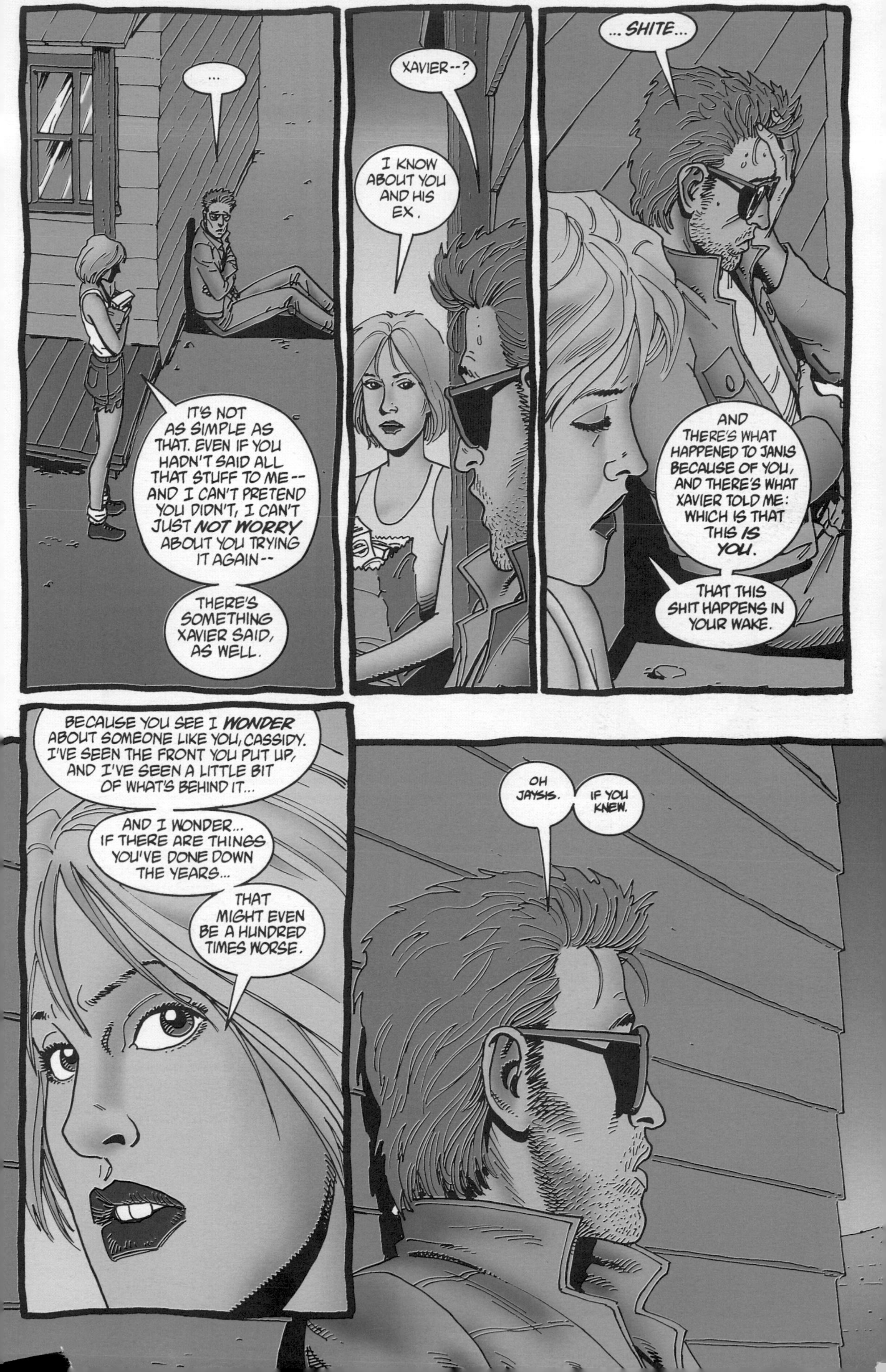
...
IT'S NOT AS SIMPLE AS THAT. EVEN IF YOU HADN'T SAID ALL THAT STUFF TO ME -- AND I CAN'T PRETEND YOU DIDN'T, I CAN'T JUST NOT WORRY ABOUT YOU TRYING IT AGAIN--
THERE'S SOMETHING XAVIER SAID, AS WELL.
XAVIER--?
I KNOW ABOUT YOU AND HIS EX.
... SHITE ...
AND THERE'S WHAT HAPPENED TO JANIS BECAUSE OF YOU, AND THERE'S WHAT XAVIER TOLD ME: WHICH IS THAT THIS IS YOU.
THAT THIS SHIT HAPPENS IN YOUR WAKE.
BECAUSE YOU SEE I WONDER ABOUT SOMEONE LIKE YOU, CASSIDY. I'VE SEEN THE FRONT YOU PUT UP, AND I'VE SEEN A LITTLE BIT OF WHAT'S BEHIND IT...
AND I WONDER... IF THERE ARE THINGS YOU'VE DONE DOWN THE YEARS...
THAT MIGHT EVEN BE A HUNDRED TIMES WORSE.
OH JAYSIS.
IF YOU KNEW.

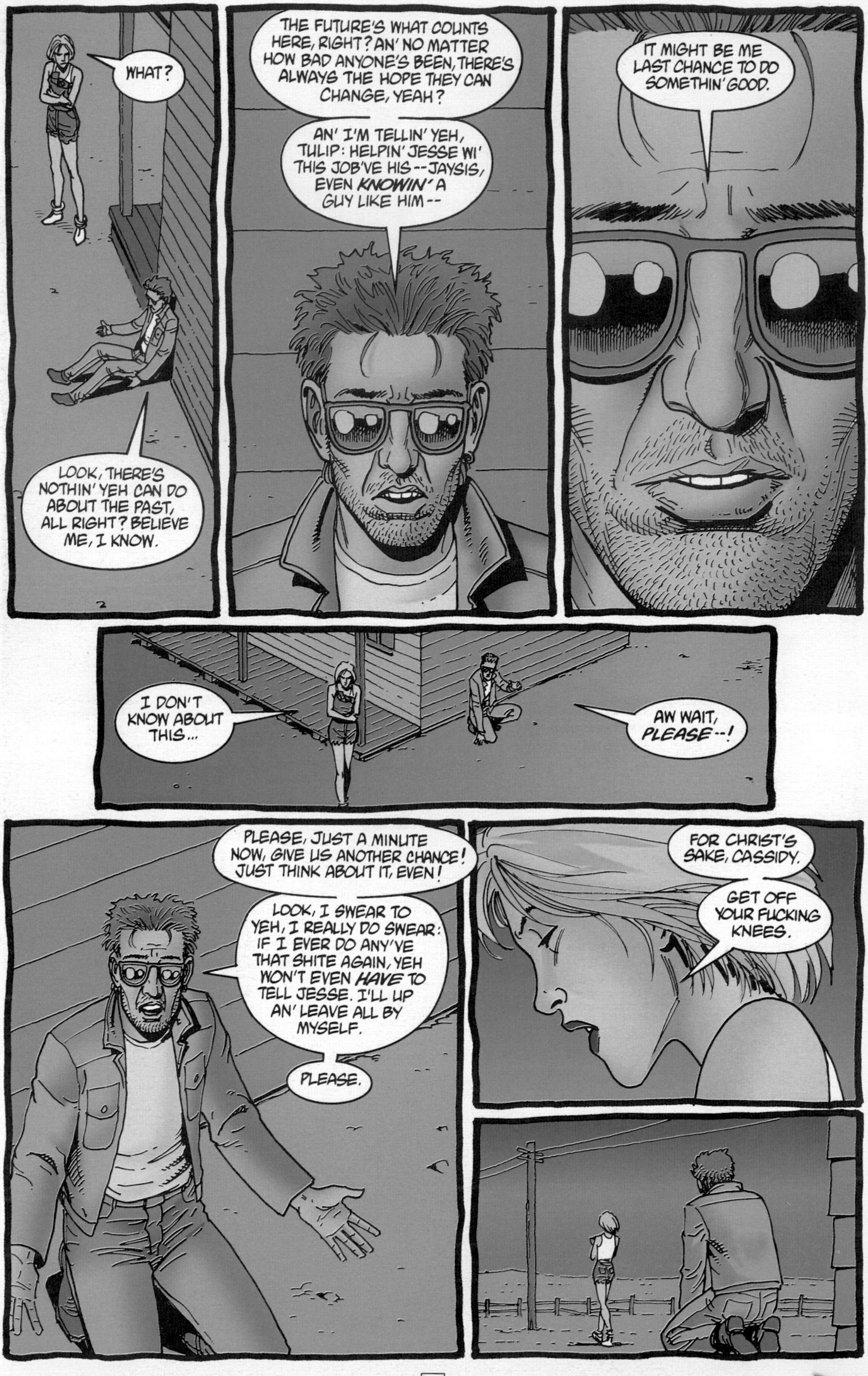

WHAT?
LOOK, THERE'S NOTHIN' YEH CAN DO ABOUT THE PAST, ALL RIGHT? BELIEVE ME, I KNOW.
THE FUTURE'S WHAT COUNTS HERE, RIGHT? AN' NO MATTER HOW BAD ANYONE'S BEEN, THERE'S ALWAYS THE HOPE THEY CAN CHANGE, YEAH?
AN' I'M TELLIN' YEH, TULIP: HELPIN' JESSE WI' THIS JOB'VE HIS--JAYSIS, EVEN KNOWIN' A GUY LIKE HIM--
IT MIGHT BE ME LAST CHANCE TO DO SOMETHIN' GOOD.
I DON'T KNOW ABOUT THIS...
AW WAIT, PLEASE--!
PLEASE, JUST A MINUTE NOW, GIVE US ANOTHER CHANCE! JUST THINK ABOUT IT, EVEN!
LOOK, I SWEAR TO YEH, I REALLY DO SWEAR: IF I EVER DO ANY'VE THAT SHITE AGAIN, YEH WON'T EVEN HAVE TO TELL JESSE. I'LL UP AN' LEAVE ALL BY MYSELF.
PLEASE.
FOR CHRIST'S SAKE, CASSIDY.
GET OFF YOUR FUCKING KNEES.

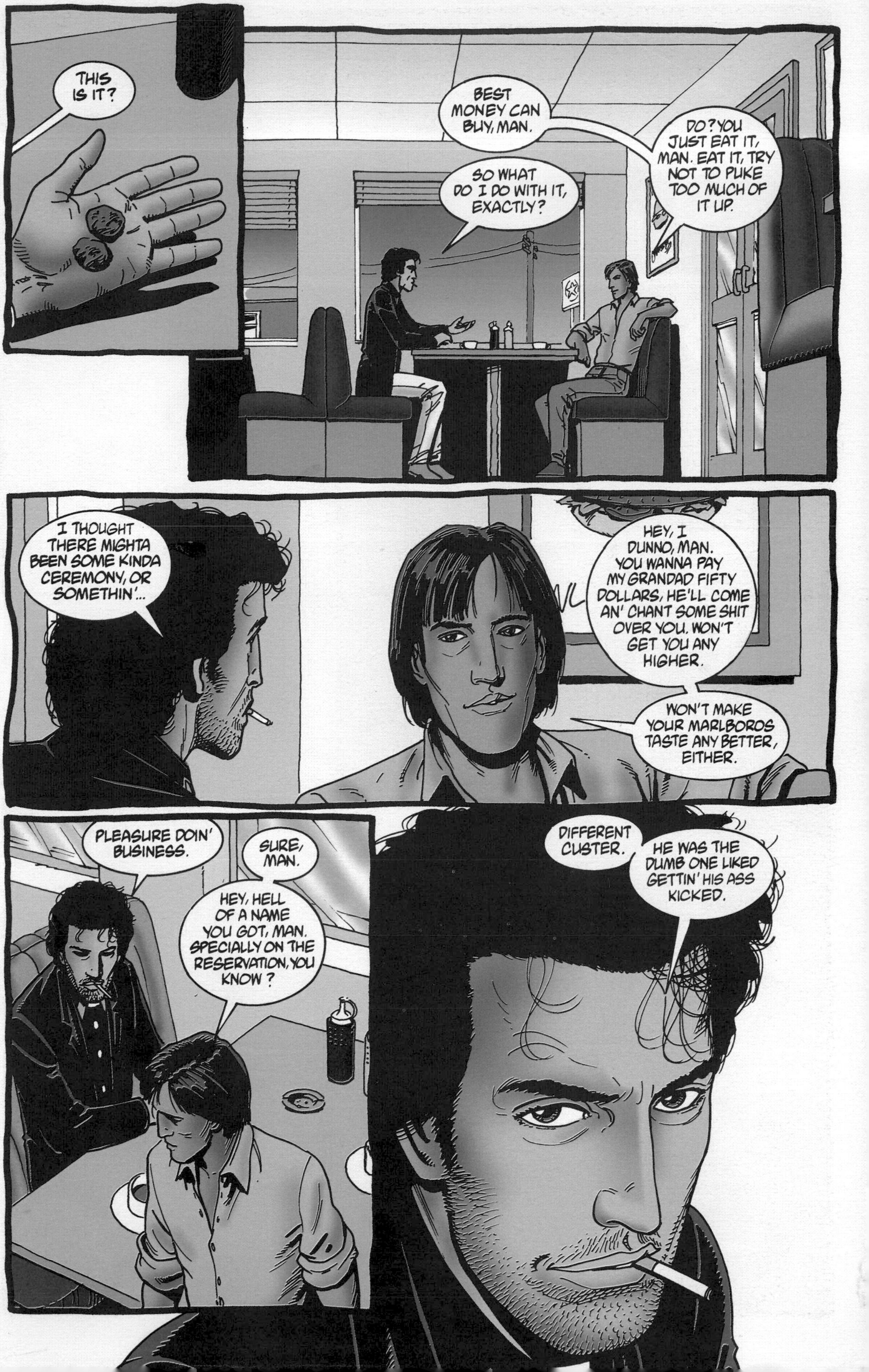
THIS IS IT?
BEST MONEY CAN BUY, MAN.
SO WHAT DO I DO WITH IT, EXACTLY?
DO? YOU JUST EAT IT, MAN. EAT IT, TRY NOT TO PUKE TOO MUCH OF IT UP.
I THOUGHT THERE MIGHTA BEEN SOME KINDA CEREMONY, OR SOMETHIN'...
HEY, I DUNNO, MAN. YOU WANNA PAY MY GRANDAD FIFTY DOLLARS, HE'LL COME AN' CHANT SOME SHIT OVER YOU. WON'T GET YOU ANY HIGHER.
WON'T MAKE YOUR MARLBOROS TASTE ANY BETTER, EITHER.
PLEASURE DOIN' BUSINESS.
SURE, MAN.
HEY, HELL OF A NAME YOU GOT, MAN. SPECIALLY ON THE RESERVATION, YOU KNOW?
DIFFERENT CUSTER.
HE WAS THE DUMB ONE LIKED GETTIN' HIS ASS KICKED.

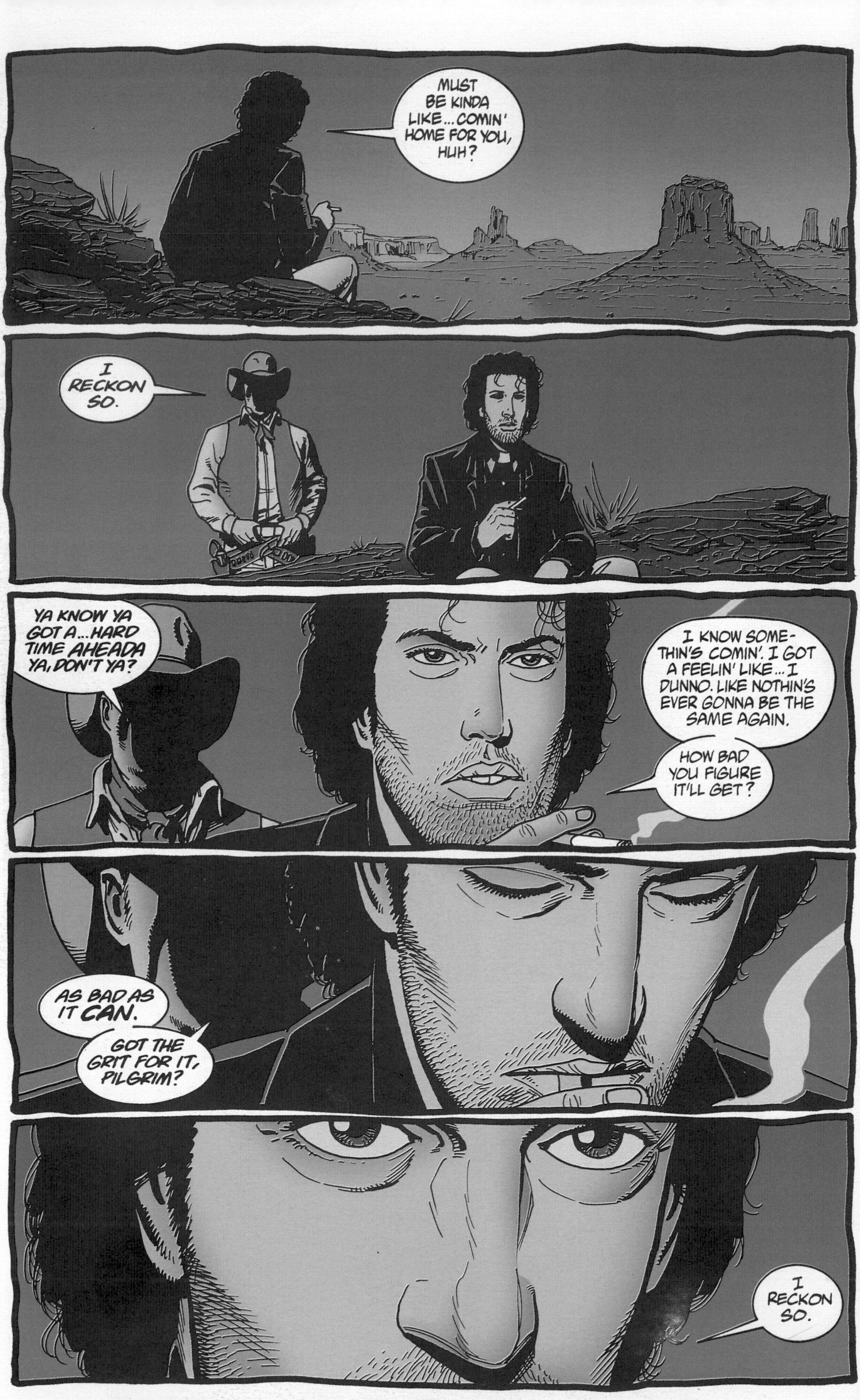
MUST BE KINDA LIKE...COMIN' HOME FOR YOU, HUH?
I RECKON SO.
YA KNOW YA GOT A...HARD TIME AHEADA YA, DON'T YA?
I KNOW SOME-THIN'S COMIN'. I GOT A FEELIN' LIKE... I DUNNO. LIKE NOTHIN'S EVER GONNA BE THE SAME AGAIN.
HOW BAD YOU FIGURE IT'LL GET?
AS BAD AS IT CAN.
GOT THE GRIT FOR IT, PILGRIM?
I RECKON SO.

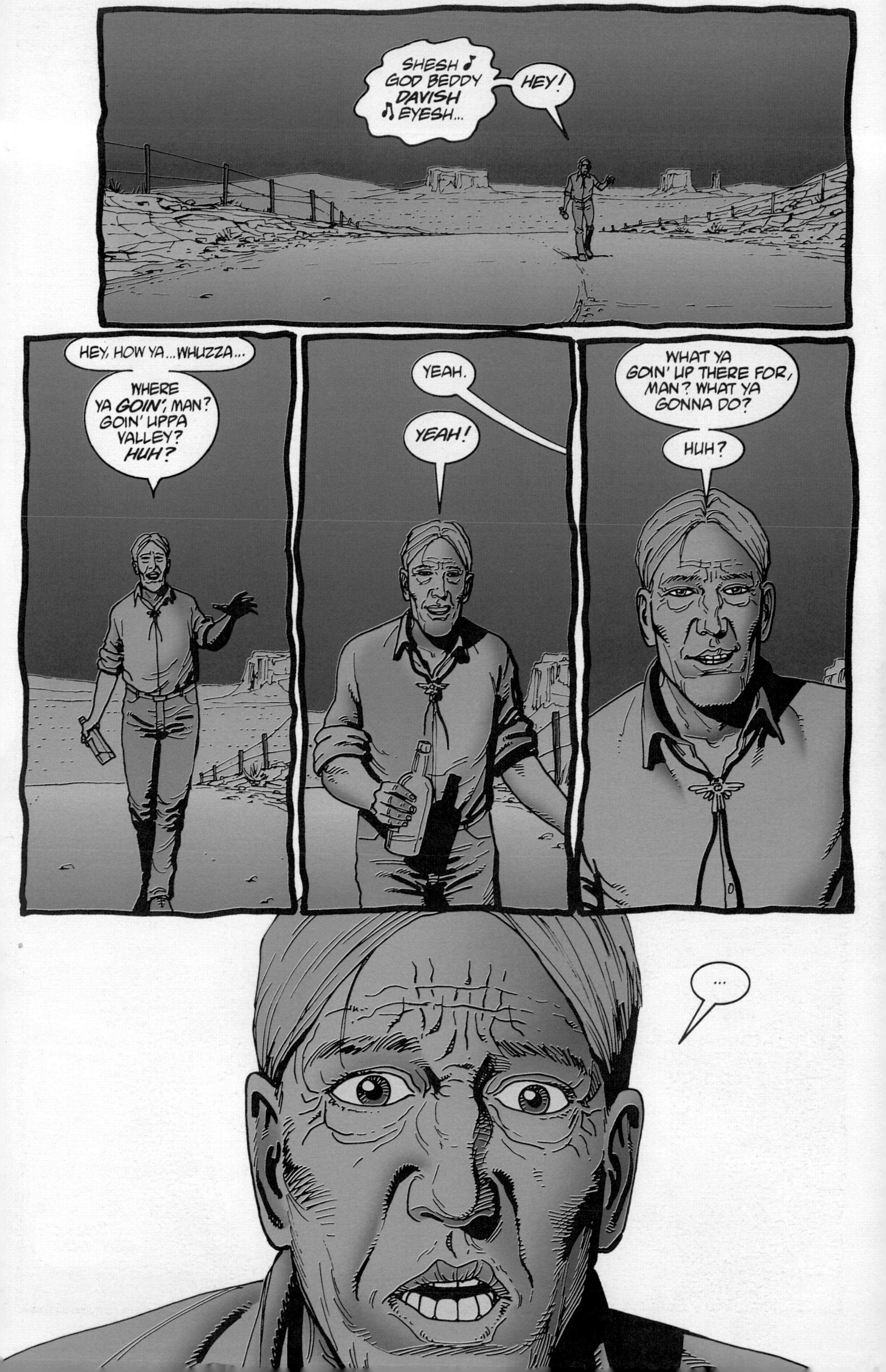
SHESH ♪ GOD BEDDY DAVISH ♫ EYESH...
HEY!
HEY, HOW YA... WHUZZA...
WHERE YA GOIN', MAN? GOIN' UPPA VALLEY? HUH?
YEAH.
YEAH!
WHAT YA GOIN' UP THERE FOR, MAN? WHAT YA GONNA DO?
HUH?
...

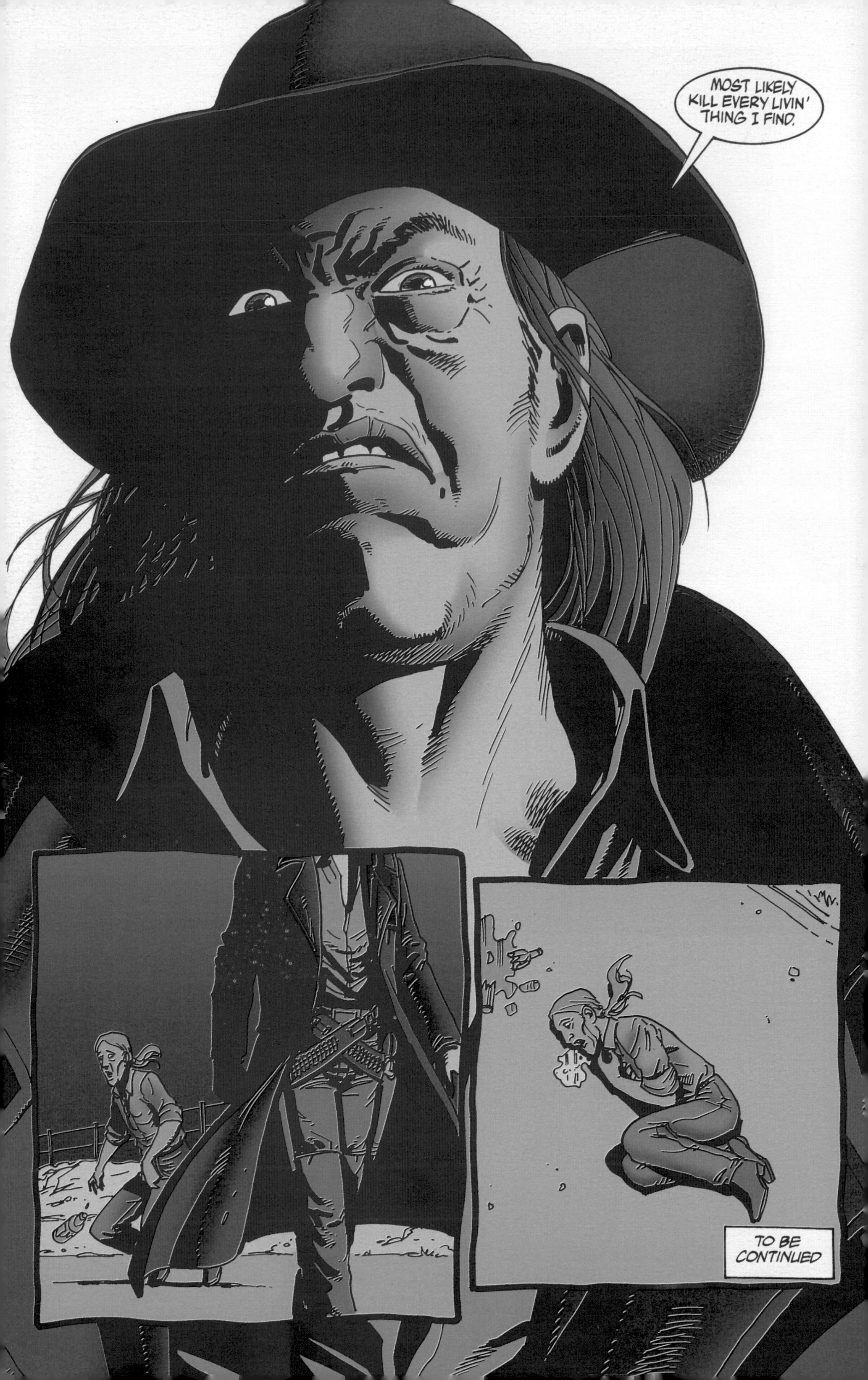
MOST LIKELY KILL EVERY LIVIN' THING I FIND.
TO BE CONTINUED

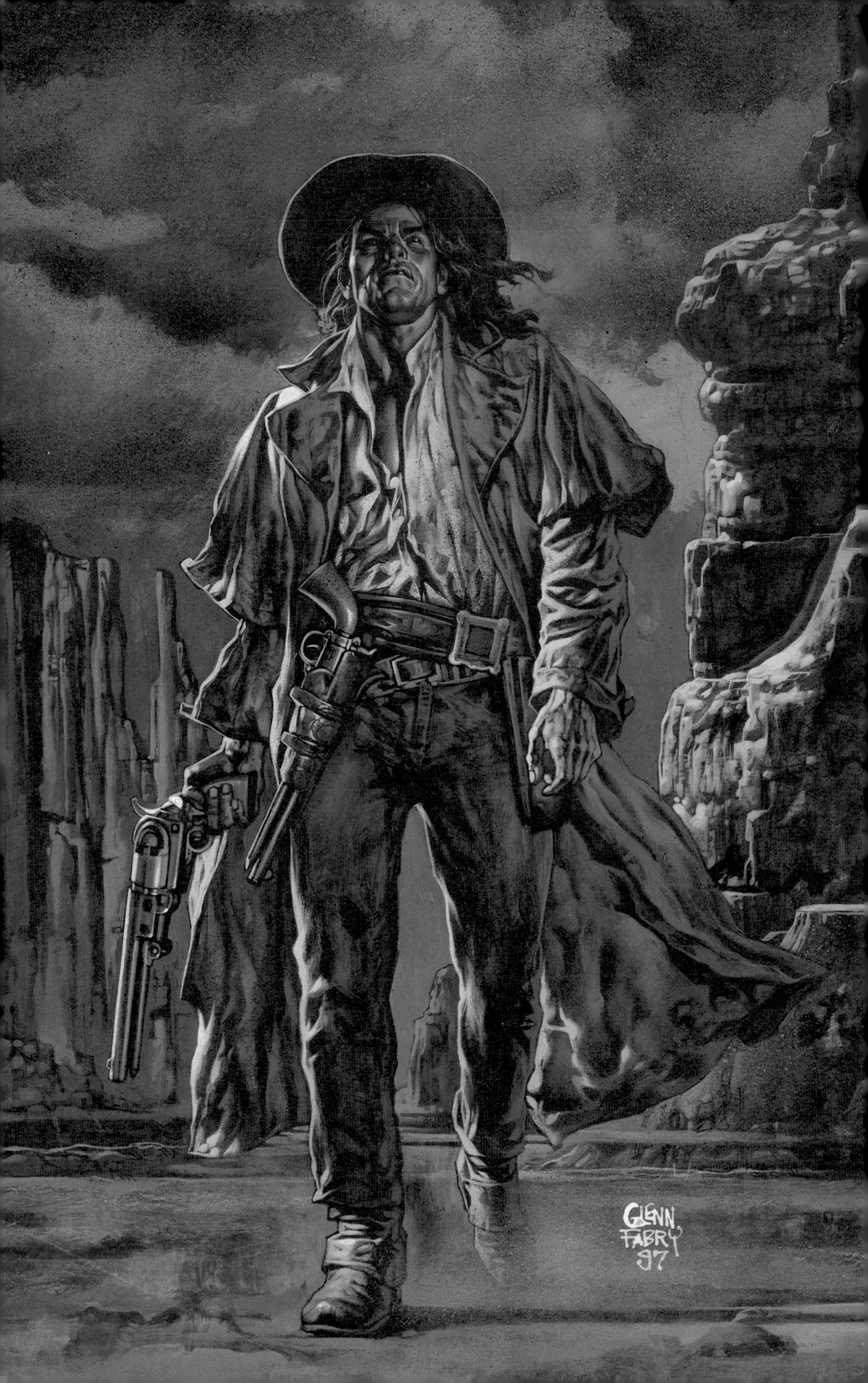
GLENN FABRY 97

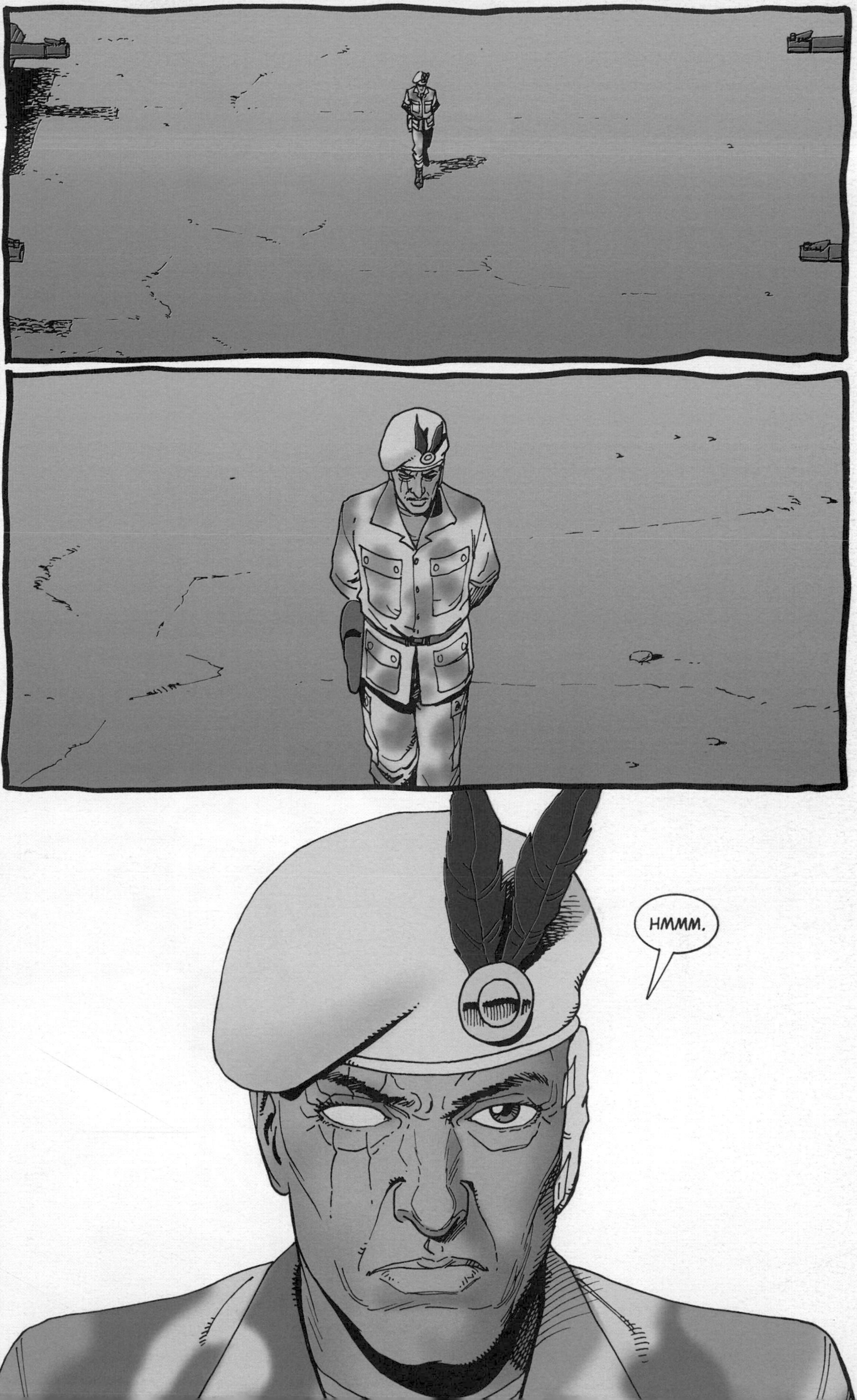
HMMM.

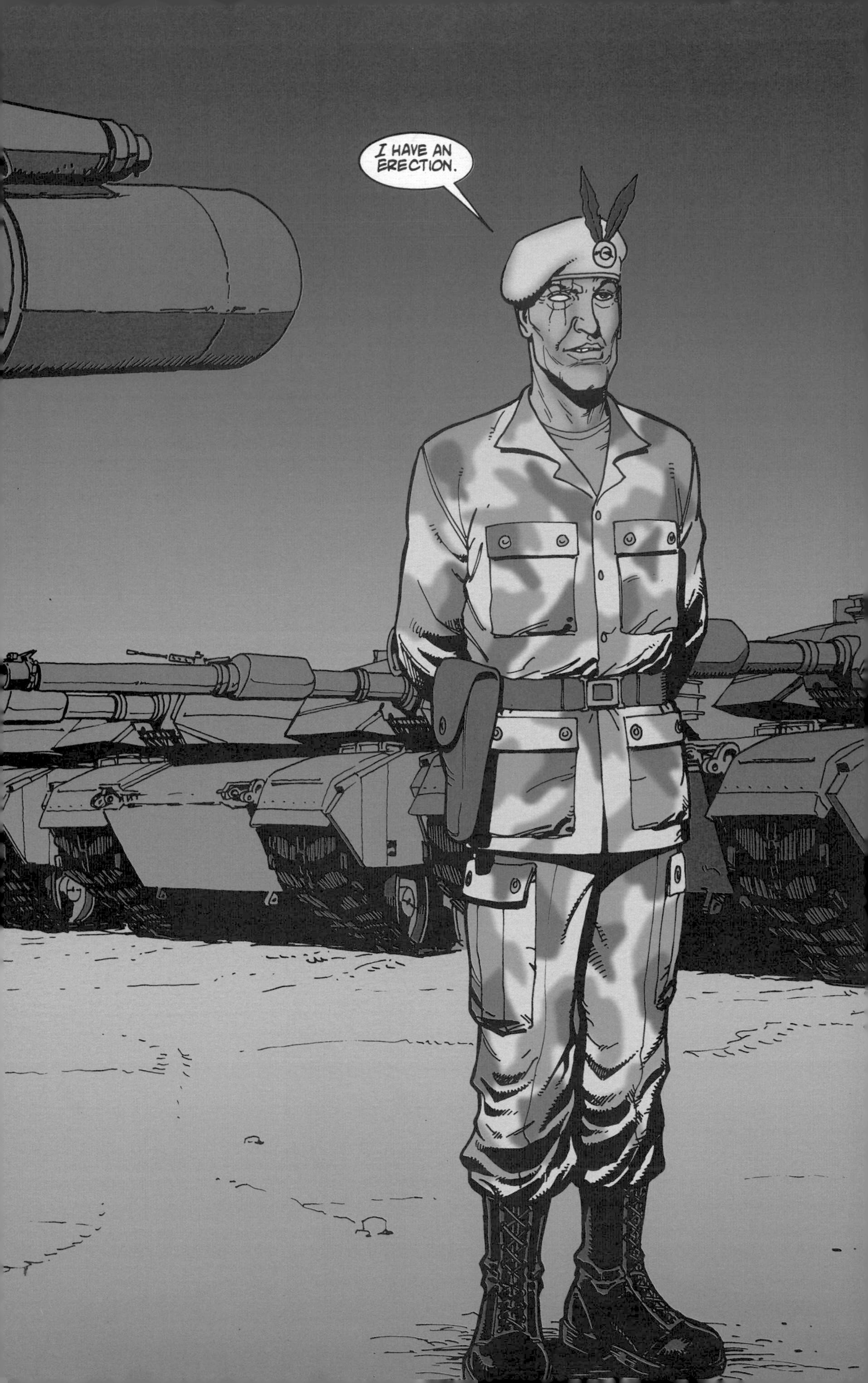
I HAVE AN ERECTION.

You & Me against the WORLD

GARTH ENNIS-Writer
STEVE DILLON-Artist

Pamela Rambo-Colorist, Clem Robins-Letterer,
Axel Alonso-Editor

PREACHER created by Garth Ennis and Steve Dillon

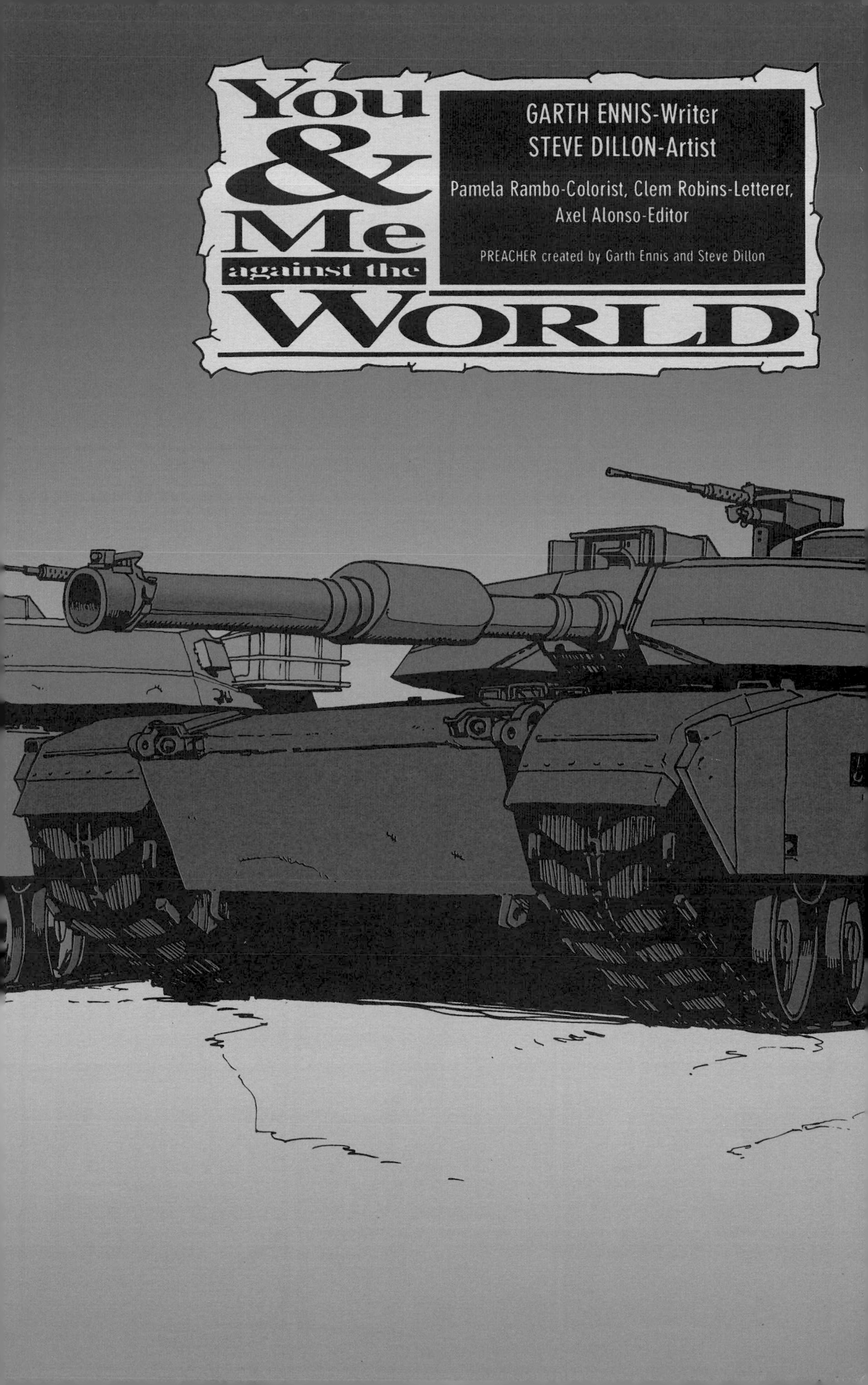

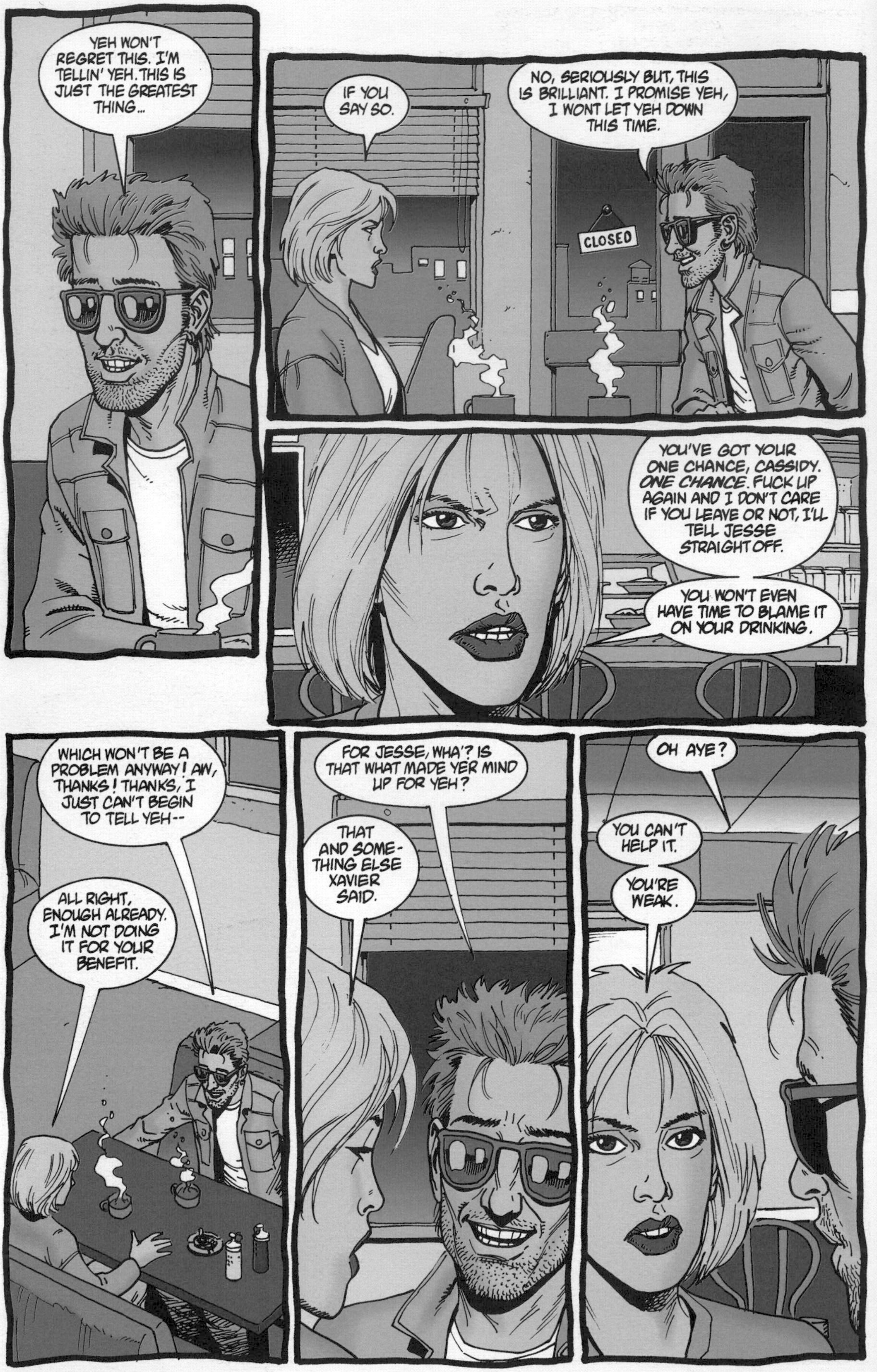
YEH WON'T REGRET THIS. I'M TELLIN' YEH. THIS IS JUST THE GREATEST THING...
IF YOU SAY SO.
NO, SERIOUSLY BUT, THIS IS BRILLIANT. I PROMISE YEH, I WONT LET YEH DOWN THIS TIME.
CLOSED
YOU'VE GOT YOUR ONE CHANCE, CASSIDY. ONE CHANCE. FUCK UP AGAIN AND I DON'T CARE IF YOU LEAVE OR NOT, I'LL TELL JESSE STRAIGHT OFF.
YOU WON'T EVEN HAVE TIME TO BLAME IT ON YOUR DRINKING.
WHICH WON'T BE A PROBLEM ANYWAY! AW, THANKS! THANKS, I JUST CAN'T BEGIN TO TELL YEH--
ALL RIGHT, ENOUGH ALREADY. I'M NOT DOING IT FOR YOUR BENEFIT.
FOR JESSE, WHA'? IS THAT WHAT MADE YER MIND UP FOR YEH?
THAT AND SOME-THING ELSE XAVIER SAID.
OH AYE?
YOU CAN'T HELP IT.
YOU'RE WEAK.

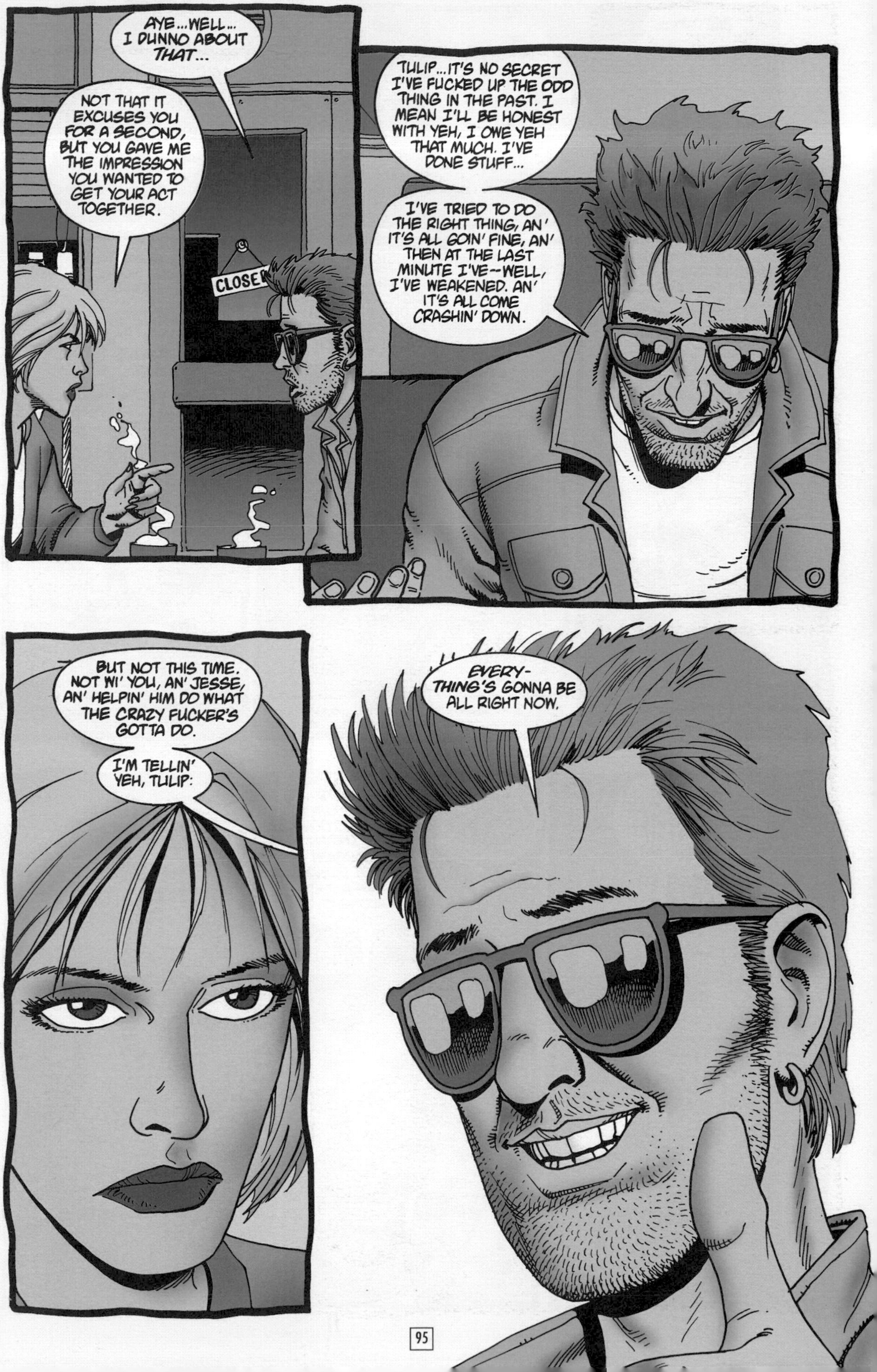
AYE...WELL... I DUNNO ABOUT THAT...
NOT THAT IT EXCUSES YOU FOR A SECOND, BUT YOU GAVE ME THE IMPRESSION YOU WANTED TO GET YOUR ACT TOGETHER.
CLOSE
TULIP...IT'S NO SECRET I'VE FUCKED UP THE ODD THING IN THE PAST. I MEAN I'LL BE HONEST WITH YEH, I OWE YEH THAT MUCH. I'VE DONE STUFF...
I'VE TRIED TO DO THE RIGHT THING, AN' IT'S ALL GOIN' FINE, AN' THEN AT THE LAST MINUTE I'VE--WELL, I'VE WEAKENED. AN' IT'S ALL COME CRASHIN' DOWN.
BUT NOT THIS TIME. NOT WI' YOU, AN' JESSE, AN' HELPIN' HIM DO WHAT THE CRAZY FUCKER'S GOTTA DO.
I'M TELLIN' YEH, TULIP:
EVERY-THING'S GONNA BE ALL RIGHT NOW.

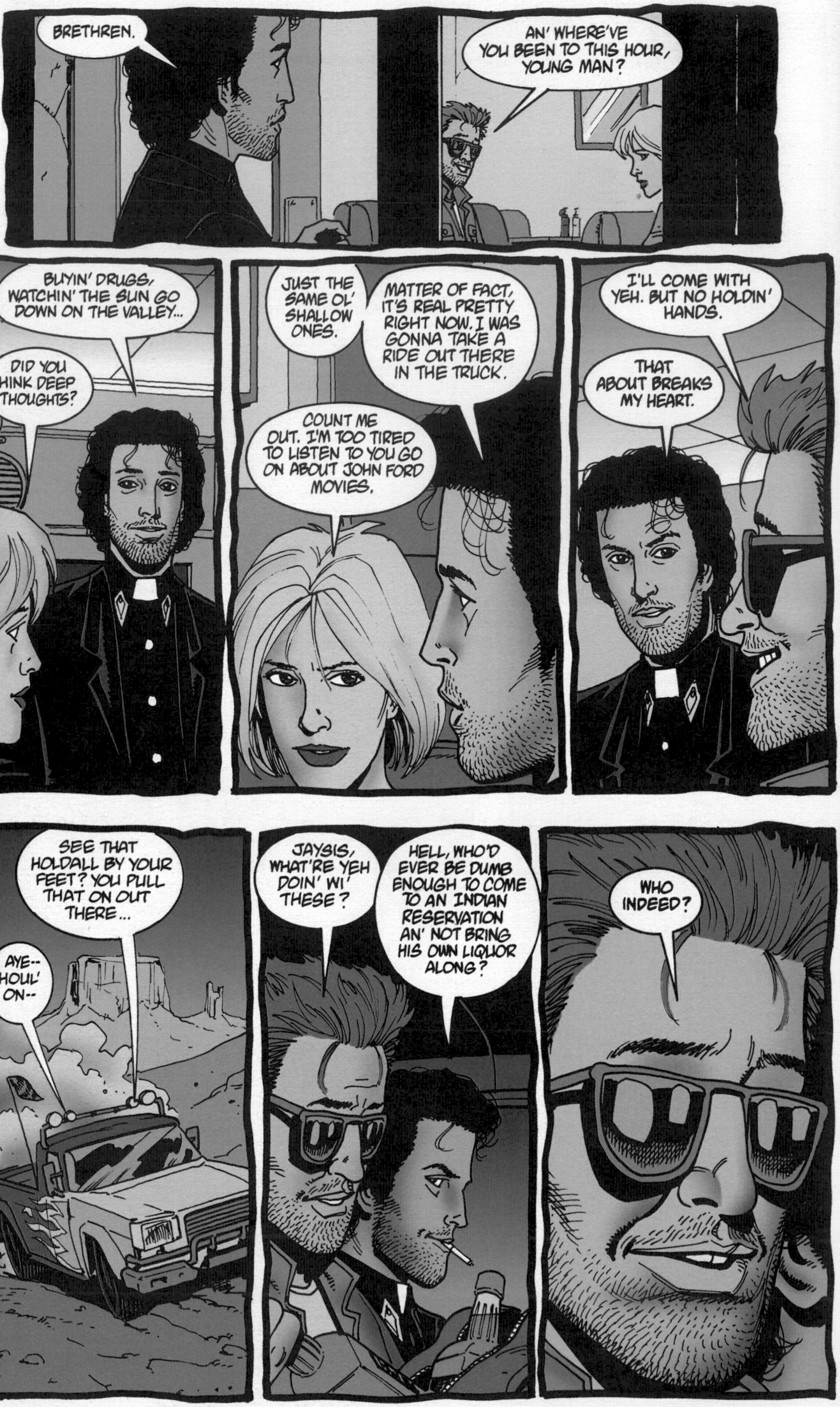
BRETHREN.
AN' WHERE'VE YOU BEEN TO THIS HOUR, YOUNG MAN?
BUYIN' DRUGS, WATCHIN' THE SUN GO DOWN ON THE VALLEY...
DID YOU THINK DEEP THOUGHTS?
JUST THE SAME OL' SHALLOW ONES.
MATTER OF FACT, IT'S REAL PRETTY RIGHT NOW. I WAS GONNA TAKE A RIDE OUT THERE IN THE TRUCK.
COUNT ME OUT. I'M TOO TIRED TO LISTEN TO YOU GO ON ABOUT JOHN FORD MOVIES.
I'LL COME WITH YEH. BUT NO HOLDIN' HANDS.
THAT ABOUT BREAKS MY HEART.
SEE THAT HOLDALL BY YOUR FEET? YOU PULL THAT ON OUT THERE...
AYE-- HOUL' ON--
JAYSIS, WHAT'RE YEH DOIN' WI' THESE?
HELL, WHO'D EVER BE DUMB ENOUGH TO COME TO AN INDIAN RESERVATION AN' NOT BRING HIS OWN LIQUOR ALONG?
WHO INDEED?

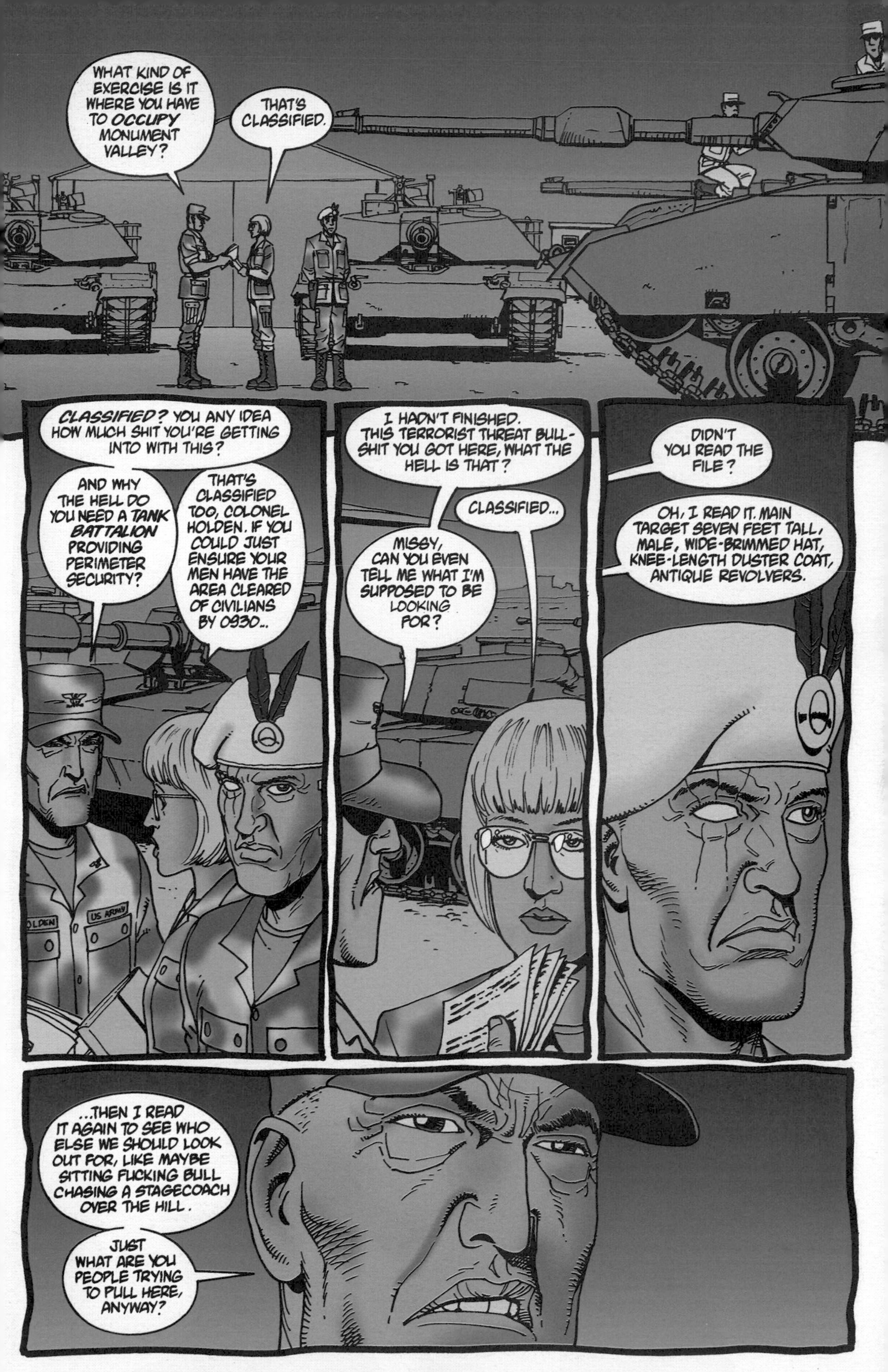

WHAT KIND OF EXERCISE IS IT WHERE YOU HAVE TO OCCUPY MONUMENT VALLEY?
THAT'S CLASSIFIED.
CLASSIFIED? YOU ANY IDEA HOW MUCH SHIT YOU'RE GETTING INTO WITH THIS?
AND WHY THE HELL DO YOU NEED A TANK BATTALION PROVIDING PERIMETER SECURITY?
THAT'S CLASSIFIED TOO, COLONEL HOLDEN. IF YOU COULD JUST ENSURE YOUR MEN HAVE THE AREA CLEARED OF CIVILIANS BY 0930...
HOLDEN
US ARMY
I HADN'T FINISHED. THIS TERRORIST THREAT BULL-SHIT YOU GOT HERE, WHAT THE HELL IS THAT?
CLASSIFIED...
MISSY, CAN YOU EVEN TELL ME WHAT I'M SUPPOSED TO BE LOOKING FOR?
DIDN'T YOU READ THE FILE?
OH, I READ IT. MAIN TARGET SEVEN FEET TALL, MALE, WIDE-BRIMMED HAT, KNEE-LENGTH DUSTER COAT, ANTIQUE REVOLVERS.
...THEN I READ IT AGAIN TO SEE WHO ELSE WE SHOULD LOOK OUT FOR, LIKE MAYBE SITTING FUCKING BULL CHASING A STAGECOACH OVER THE HILL.
JUST WHAT ARE YOU PEOPLE TRYING TO PULL HERE, ANYWAY?

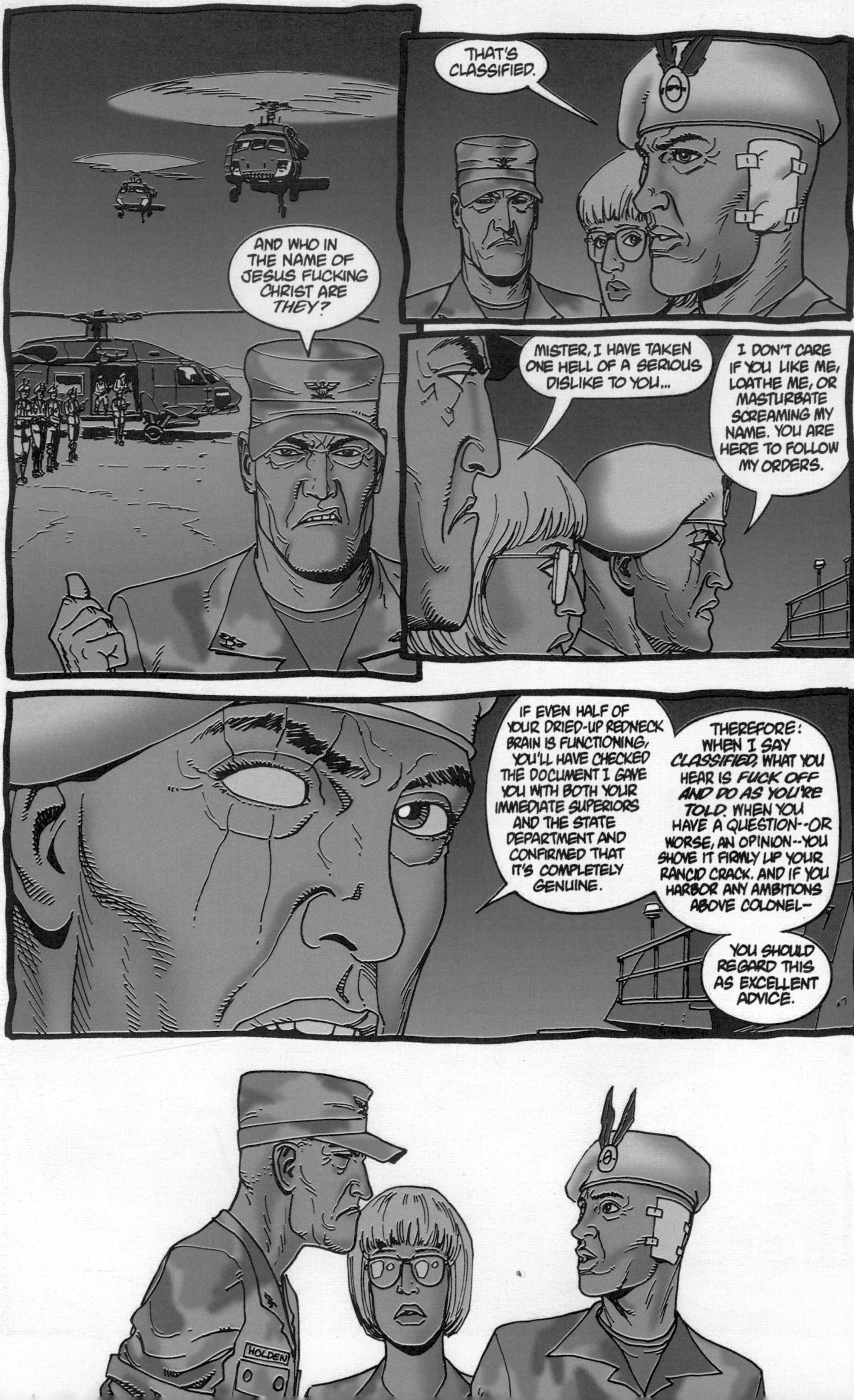
AND WHO IN THE NAME OF JESUS FUCKING CHRIST ARE *THEY?*
THAT'S CLASSIFIED.
MISTER, I HAVE TAKEN ONE HELL OF A SERIOUS DISLIKE TO YOU...
I DON'T CARE IF YOU LIKE ME, LOATHE ME, OR MASTURBATE SCREAMING MY NAME. YOU ARE HERE TO FOLLOW MY ORDERS.
IF EVEN HALF OF YOUR DRIED-UP REDNECK BRAIN IS FUNCTIONING, YOU'LL HAVE CHECKED THE DOCUMENT I GAVE YOU WITH BOTH YOUR IMMEDIATE SUPERIORS AND THE STATE DEPARTMENT AND CONFIRMED THAT IT'S COMPLETELY GENUINE.
THEREFORE: WHEN I SAY *CLASSIFIED,* WHAT YOU HEAR IS *FUCK OFF AND DO AS YOU'RE TOLD.* WHEN YOU HAVE A QUESTION--OR WORSE, AN OPINION--YOU SHOVE IT FIRMLY UP YOUR RANCID CRACK. AND IF YOU HARBOR ANY AMBITIONS ABOVE COLONEL--
YOU SHOULD REGARD THIS AS EXCELLENT ADVICE.
HOLDEN

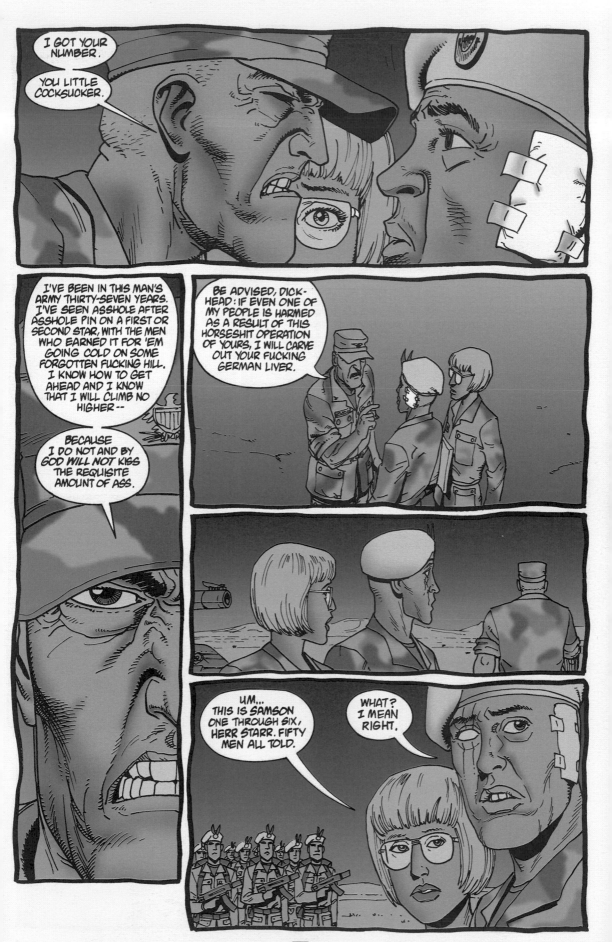

I GOT YOUR NUMBER.

YOU LITTLE COCKSUCKER.

I'VE BEEN IN THIS MAN'S ARMY THIRTY-SEVEN YEARS. I'VE SEEN ASSHOLE AFTER ASSHOLE PIN ON A FIRST OR SECOND STAR, WITH THE MEN WHO EARNED IT FOR 'EM GOING COLD ON SOME FORGOTTEN FUCKING HILL. I KNOW HOW TO GET AHEAD AND I KNOW THAT I WILL CLIMB NO HIGHER --

BECAUSE I DO NOT AND BY GOD WILL NOT KISS THE REQUISITE AMOUNT OF ASS.

BE ADVISED, DICK-HEAD: IF EVEN ONE OF MY PEOPLE IS HARMED AS A RESULT OF THIS HORSESHIT OPERATION OF YOURS, I WILL CARVE OUT YOUR FUCKING GERMAN LIVER.

UM... THIS IS SAMSON ONE THROUGH SIX, HERR STARR. FIFTY MEN ALL TOLD.

WHAT? I MEAN RIGHT.

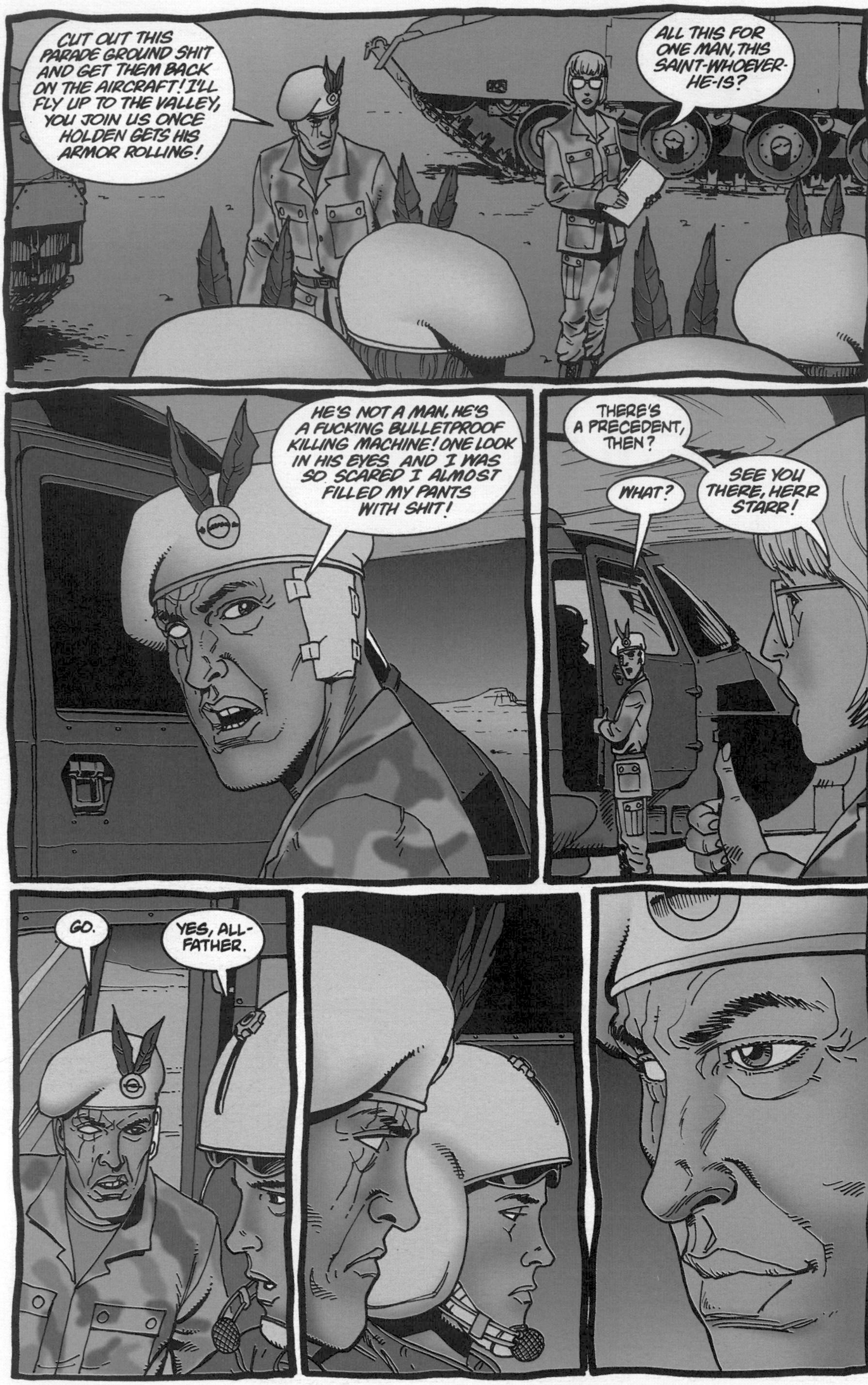
CUT OUT THIS PARADE GROUND SHIT AND GET THEM BACK ON THE AIRCRAFT! I'LL FLY UP TO THE VALLEY, YOU JOIN US ONCE HOLDEN GETS HIS ARMOR ROLLING!
ALL THIS FOR ONE MAN, THIS SAINT-WHOEVER-HE-IS?
HE'S NOT A MAN, HE'S A FUCKING BULLETPROOF KILLING MACHINE! ONE LOOK IN HIS EYES AND I WAS SO SCARED I ALMOST FILLED MY PANTS WITH SHIT!
THERE'S A PRECEDENT, THEN?
WHAT?
SEE YOU THERE, HERR STARR!
GO.
YES, ALL-FATHER.

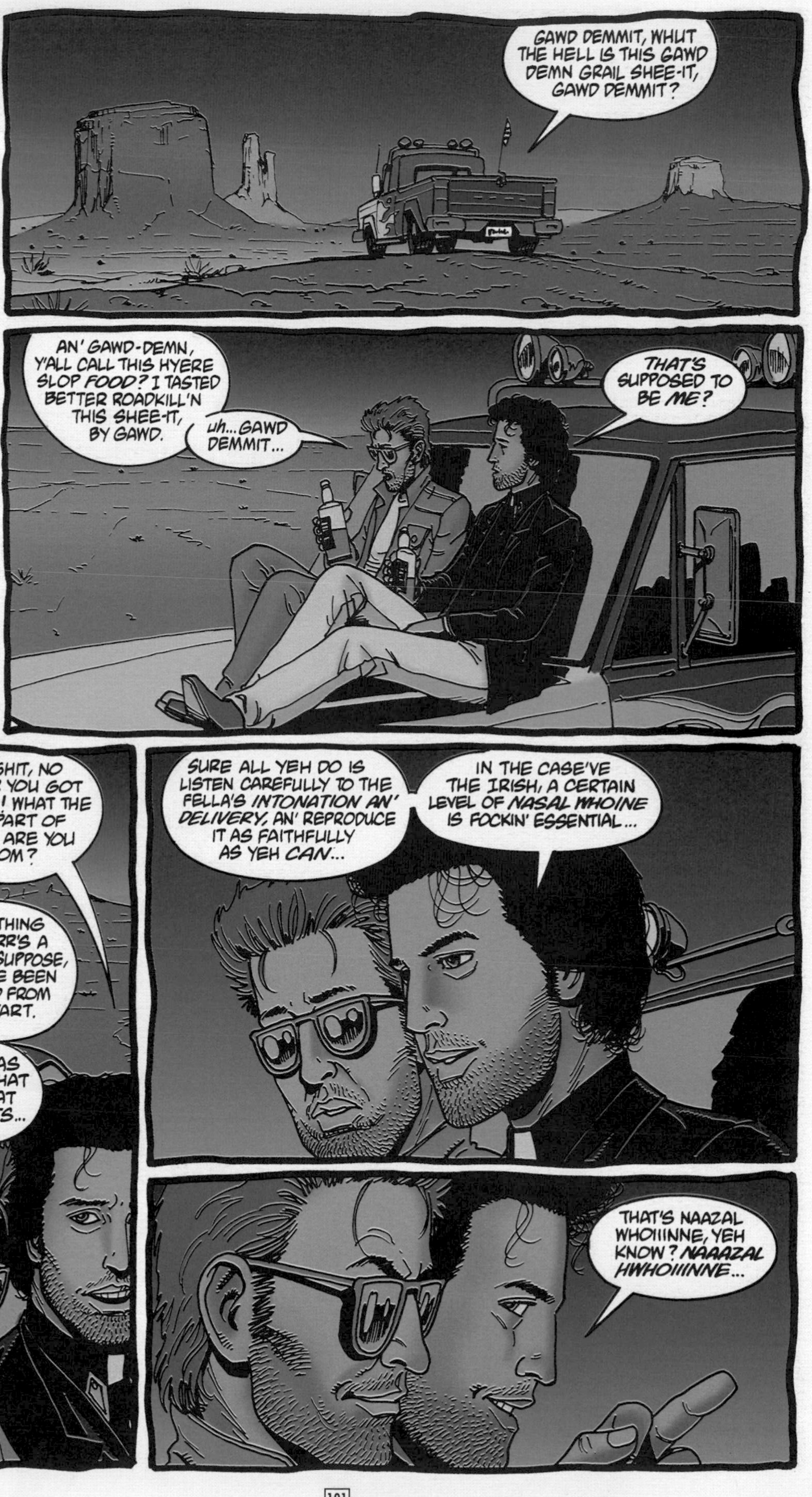
GAWD DEMMIT, WHUT THE HELL IS THIS GAWD DEMN GRAIL SHEE-IT, GAWD DEMMIT?
AN' GAWD-DEMN, Y'ALL CALL THIS HYERE SLOP FOOD? I TASTED BETTER ROADKILL'N THIS SHEE-IT, BY GAWD.
uh...GAWD DEMMIT...
THAT'S SUPPOSED TO BE ME?
HOLY SHIT, NO WONDER YOU GOT CAUGHT! WHAT THE FUCK PART OF TEXAS ARE YOU FROM?
GOOD THING OUL' STARR'S A JERRY, I SUPPOSE, OR I'D'VE BEEN FUCKED FROM THE START.
AH, I WAS NEVER THAT GREAT AT ACCENTS...
SURE ALL YEH DO IS LISTEN CAREFULLY TO THE FELLA'S INTONATION AN' DELIVERY, AN' REPRODUCE IT AS FAITHFULLY AS YEH CAN...
IN THE CASE'VE THE IRISH, A CERTAIN LEVEL OF NASAL WHOINE IS FOCKIN' ESSENTIAL...
THAT'S NAAZAL WHOIIINNE, YEH KNOW? NAAAZAL HWHOIIINNE...

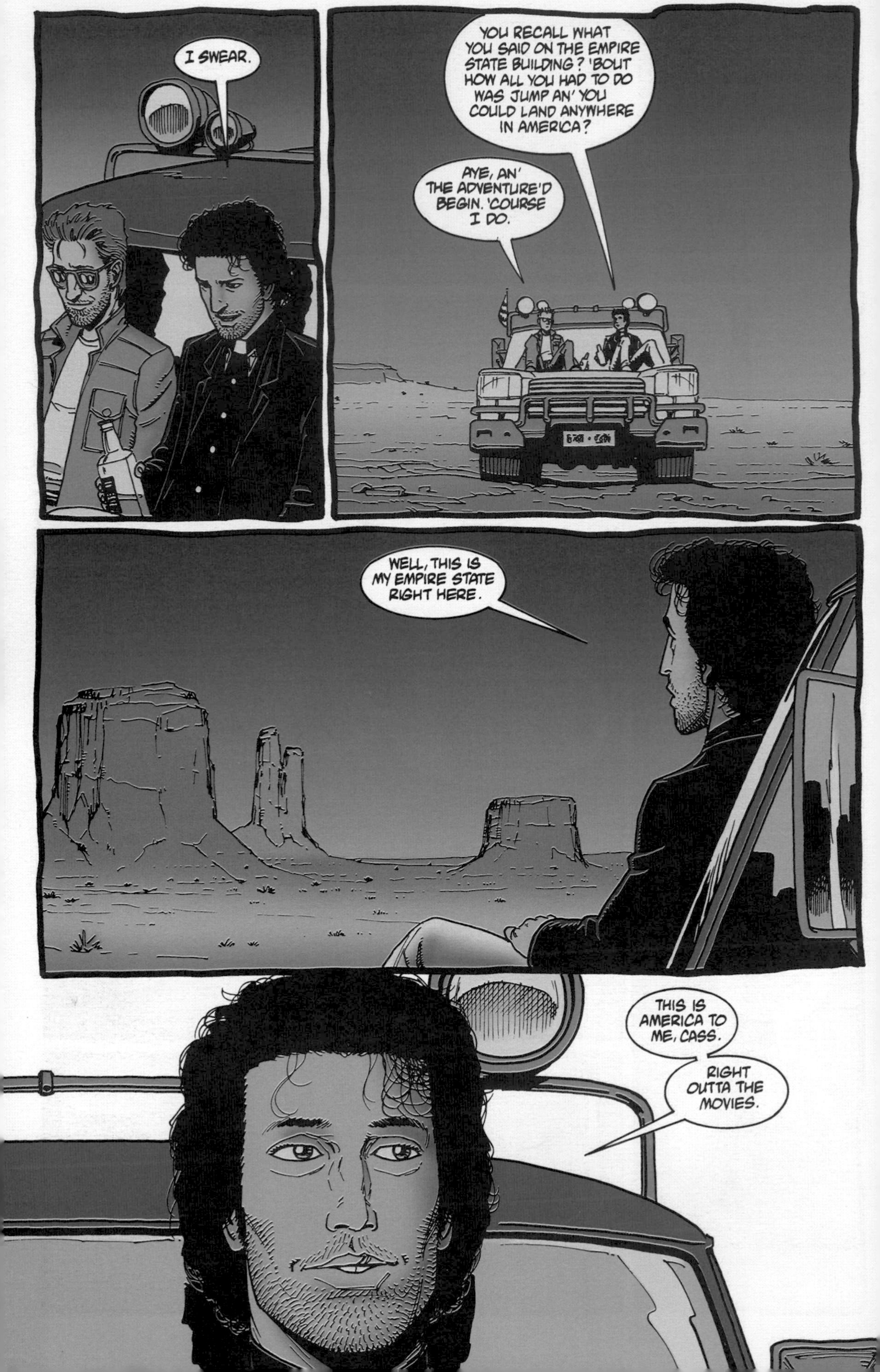
I SWEAR.
YOU RECALL WHAT YOU SAID ON THE EMPIRE STATE BUILDING? 'BOUT HOW ALL YOU HAD TO DO WAS JUMP AN' YOU COULD LAND ANYWHERE IN AMERICA?
AYE, AN' THE ADVENTURE'D BEGIN. 'COURSE I DO.
WELL, THIS IS MY EMPIRE STATE RIGHT HERE.
THIS IS AMERICA TO ME, CASS.
RIGHT OUTTA THE MOVIES.

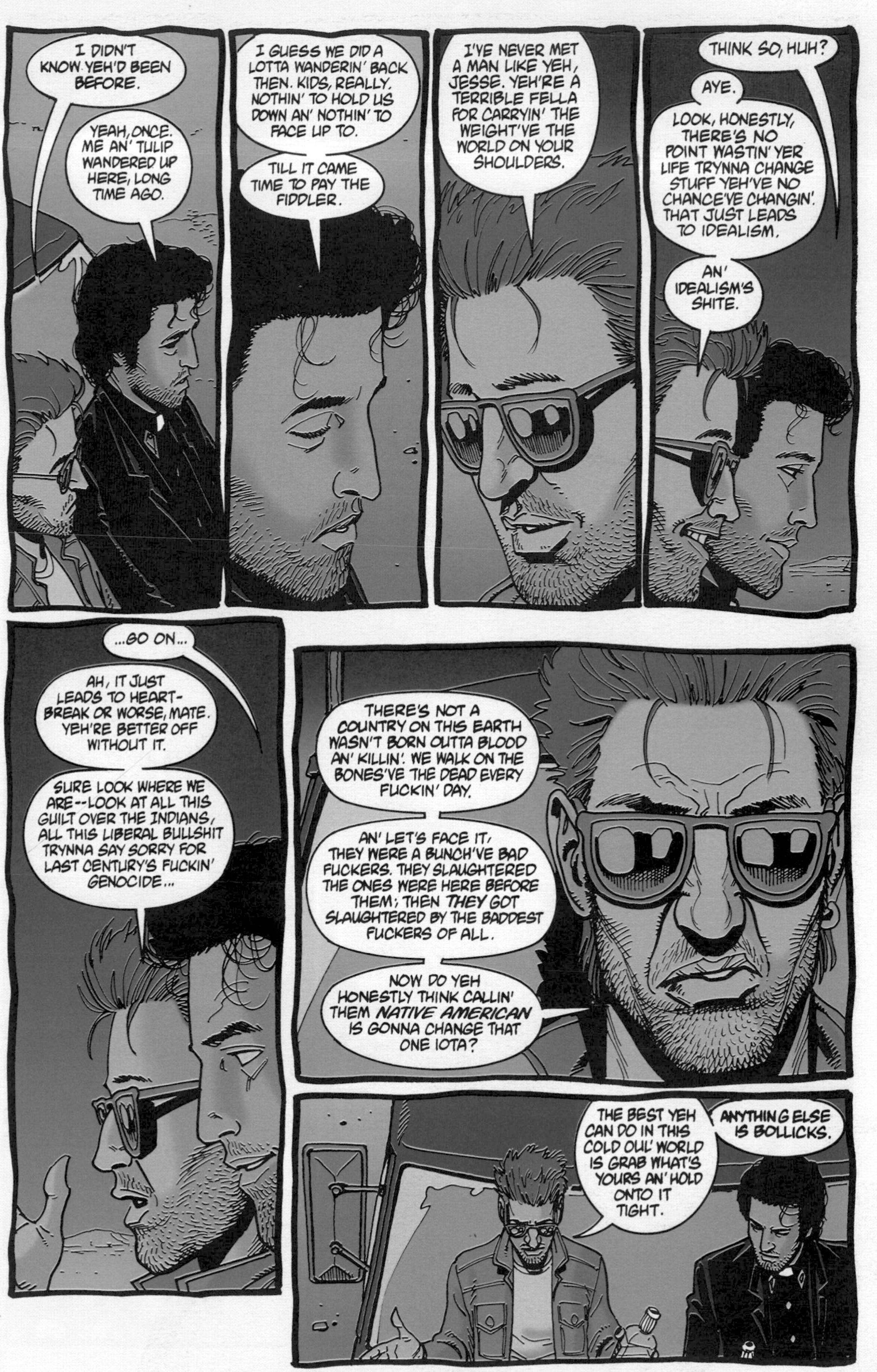
I DIDN'T KNOW YEH'D BEEN BEFORE.
YEAH, ONCE. ME AN' TULIP WANDERED UP HERE, LONG TIME AGO.
I GUESS WE DID A LOTTA WANDERIN' BACK THEN. KIDS, REALLY. NOTHIN' TO HOLD US DOWN AN' NOTHIN' TO FACE UP TO.
TILL IT CAME TIME TO PAY THE FIDDLER.
I'VE NEVER MET A MAN LIKE YEH, JESSE. YEH'RE A TERRIBLE FELLA FOR CARRYIN' THE WEIGHT'VE THE WORLD ON YOUR SHOULDERS.
THINK SO, HUH?
AYE.
LOOK, HONESTLY, THERE'S NO POINT WASTIN' YER LIFE TRYNNA CHANGE STUFF YEH'VE NO CHANCE'VE CHANGIN'. THAT JUST LEADS TO IDEALISM.
AN' IDEALISM'S SHITE.
...GO ON...
AH, IT JUST LEADS TO HEART-BREAK OR WORSE, MATE. YEH'RE BETTER OFF WITHOUT IT.
SURE LOOK WHERE WE ARE--LOOK AT ALL THIS GUILT OVER THE INDIANS, ALL THIS LIBERAL BULLSHIT TRYNNA SAY SORRY FOR LAST CENTURY'S FUCKIN' GENOCIDE...
THERE'S NOT A COUNTRY ON THIS EARTH WASN'T BORN OUTTA BLOOD AN' KILLIN'. WE WALK ON THE BONES'VE THE DEAD EVERY FUCKIN' DAY.
AN' LET'S FACE IT, THEY WERE A BUNCH'VE BAD FUCKERS. THEY SLAUGHTERED THE ONES WERE HERE BEFORE THEM; THEN THEY GOT SLAUGHTERED BY THE BADDEST FUCKERS OF ALL.
NOW DO YEH HONESTLY THINK CALLIN' THEM NATIVE AMERICAN IS GONNA CHANGE THAT ONE IOTA?
THE BEST YEH CAN DO IN THIS COLD OUL' WORLD IS GRAB WHAT'S YOURS AN' HOLD ONTO IT TIGHT.
ANYTHING ELSE IS BOLLICKS.

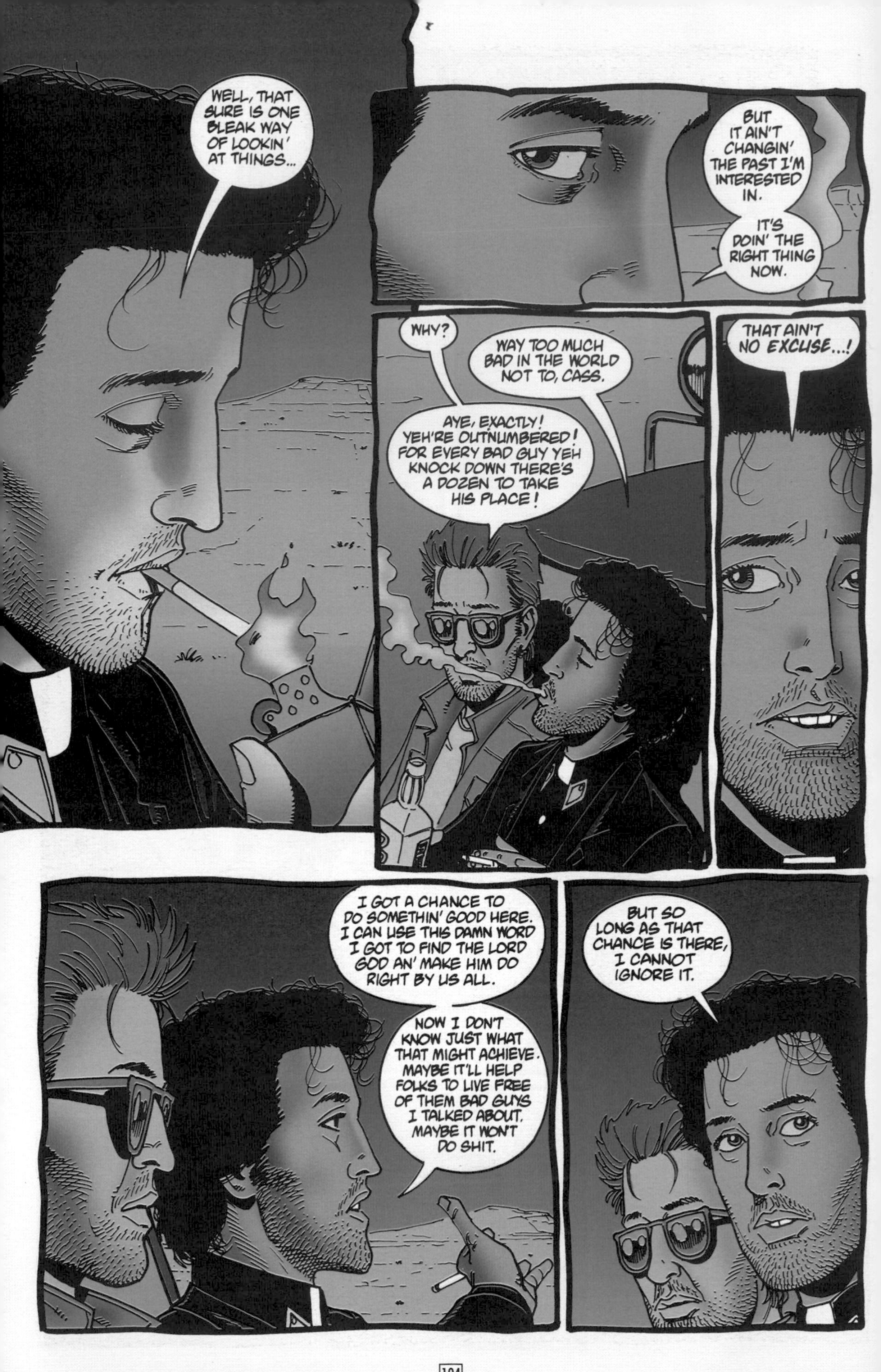
WELL, THAT SURE IS ONE BLEAK WAY OF LOOKIN' AT THINGS...
BUT IT AIN'T CHANGIN' THE PAST I'M INTERESTED IN.
IT'S DOIN' THE RIGHT THING NOW.
WHY?
WAY TOO MUCH BAD IN THE WORLD NOT TO, CASS.
AYE, EXACTLY! YEH'RE OUTNUMBERED! FOR EVERY BAD GUY YEH KNOCK DOWN THERE'S A DOZEN TO TAKE HIS PLACE!
THAT AIN'T NO *EXCUSE*...!
I GOT A CHANCE TO DO SOMETHIN' GOOD HERE. I CAN USE THIS DAMN WORD I GOT TO FIND THE LORD GOD AN' MAKE HIM DO RIGHT BY US ALL.
NOW I DON'T KNOW JUST WHAT THAT MIGHT ACHIEVE. MAYBE IT'LL HELP FOLKS TO LIVE FREE OF THEM BAD GUYS I TALKED ABOUT. MAYBE IT WON'T DO SHIT.
BUT SO LONG AS THAT CHANCE IS THERE, I CANNOT IGNORE IT.

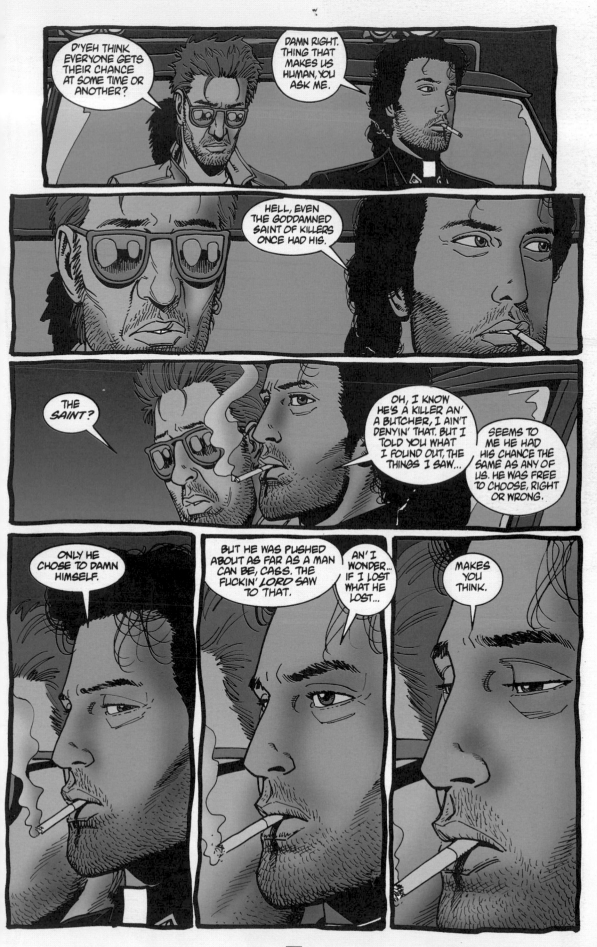

D'YEH THINK EVERYONE GETS THEIR CHANCE AT SOME TIME OR ANOTHER?

DAMN RIGHT. THING THAT MAKES US HUMAN, YOU ASK ME.

HELL, EVEN THE GODDAMNED SAINT OF KILLERS ONCE HAD HIS.

THE SAINT?

OH, I KNOW HE'S A KILLER AN' A BUTCHER, I AIN'T DENYIN' THAT, BUT I TOLD YOU WHAT I FOUND OUT, THE THINGS I SAW...

SEEMS TO ME HE HAD HIS CHANCE THE SAME AS ANY OF US. HE WAS FREE TO CHOOSE, RIGHT OR WRONG.

ONLY HE CHOSE TO DAMN HIMSELF.

BUT HE WAS PUSHED ABOUT AS FAR AS A MAN CAN BE, CASS. THE FUCKIN' LORD SAW TO THAT.

AN' I WONDER... IF I LOST WHAT HE LOST...

MAKES YOU THINK.

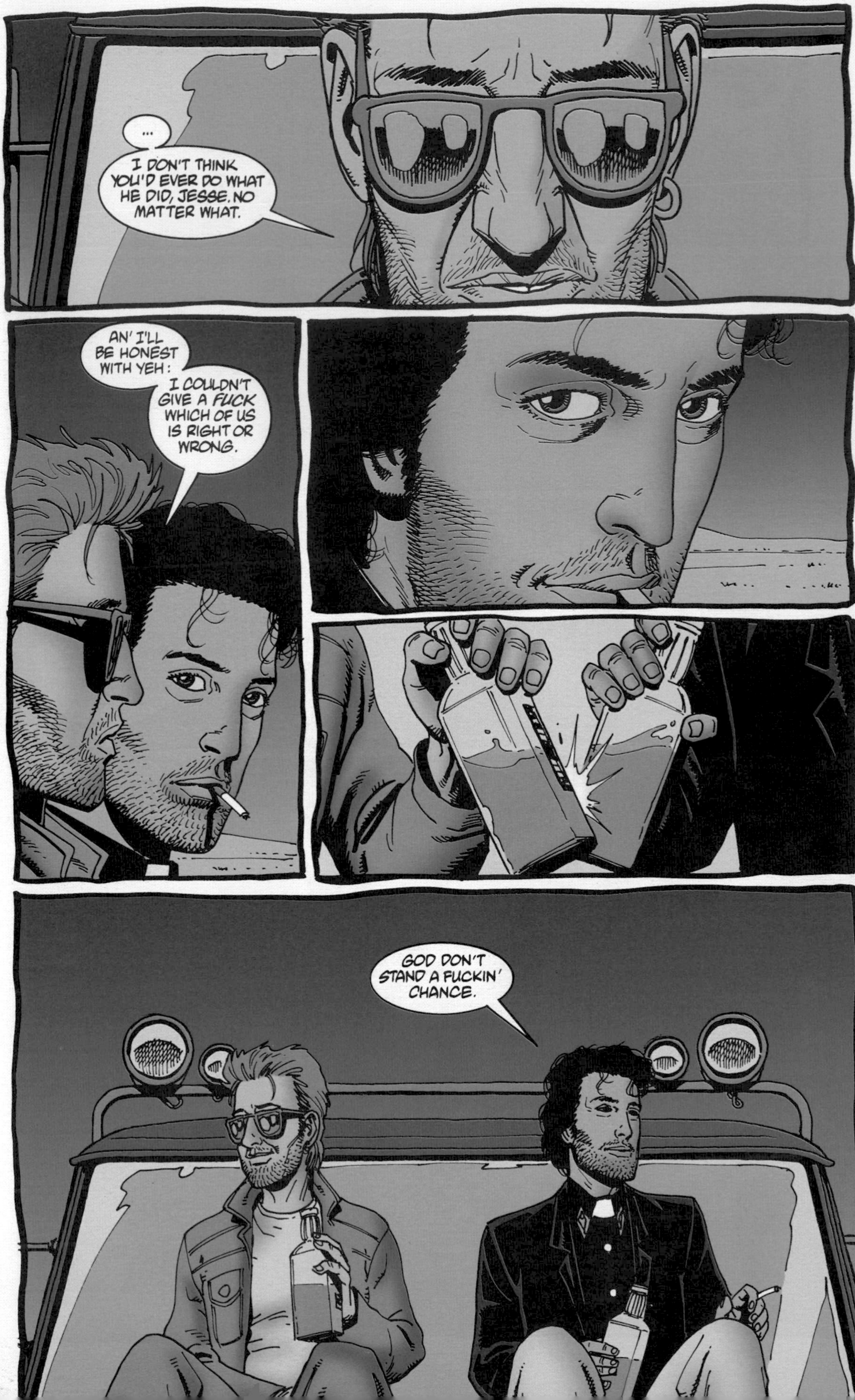
...
I DON'T THINK YOU'D EVER DO WHAT HE DID, JESSE. NO MATTER WHAT.
AN' I'LL BE HONEST WITH YEH: I COULDN'T GIVE A FUCK WHICH OF US IS RIGHT OR WRONG.
GOD DON'T STAND A FUCKIN' CHANCE.

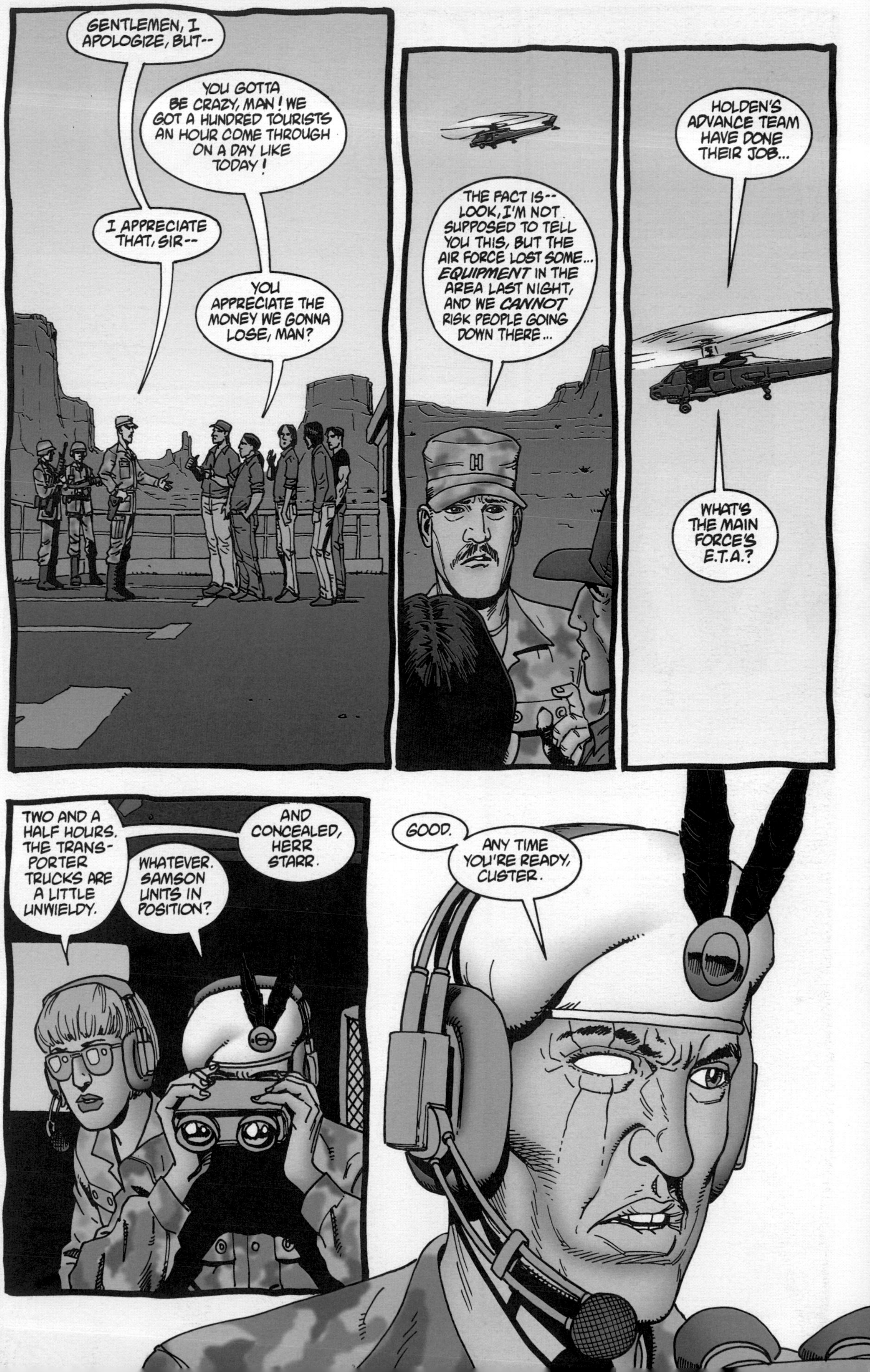
GENTLEMEN, I APOLOGIZE, BUT--
YOU GOTTA BE CRAZY, MAN! WE GOT A HUNDRED TOURISTS AN HOUR COME THROUGH ON A DAY LIKE TODAY!
I APPRECIATE THAT, SIR--
YOU APPRECIATE THE MONEY WE GONNA LOSE, MAN?
THE FACT IS-- LOOK, I'M NOT SUPPOSED TO TELL YOU THIS, BUT THE AIR FORCE LOST SOME... EQUIPMENT IN THE AREA LAST NIGHT, AND WE CANNOT RISK PEOPLE GOING DOWN THERE...
HOLDEN'S ADVANCE TEAM HAVE DONE THEIR JOB...
WHAT'S THE MAIN FORCE'S E.T.A.?
TWO AND A HALF HOURS. THE TRANS-PORTER TRUCKS ARE A LITTLE UNWIELDY.
WHATEVER. SAMSON UNITS IN POSITION?
AND CONCEALED, HERR STARR.
GOOD.
ANY TIME YOU'RE READY, CUSTER.

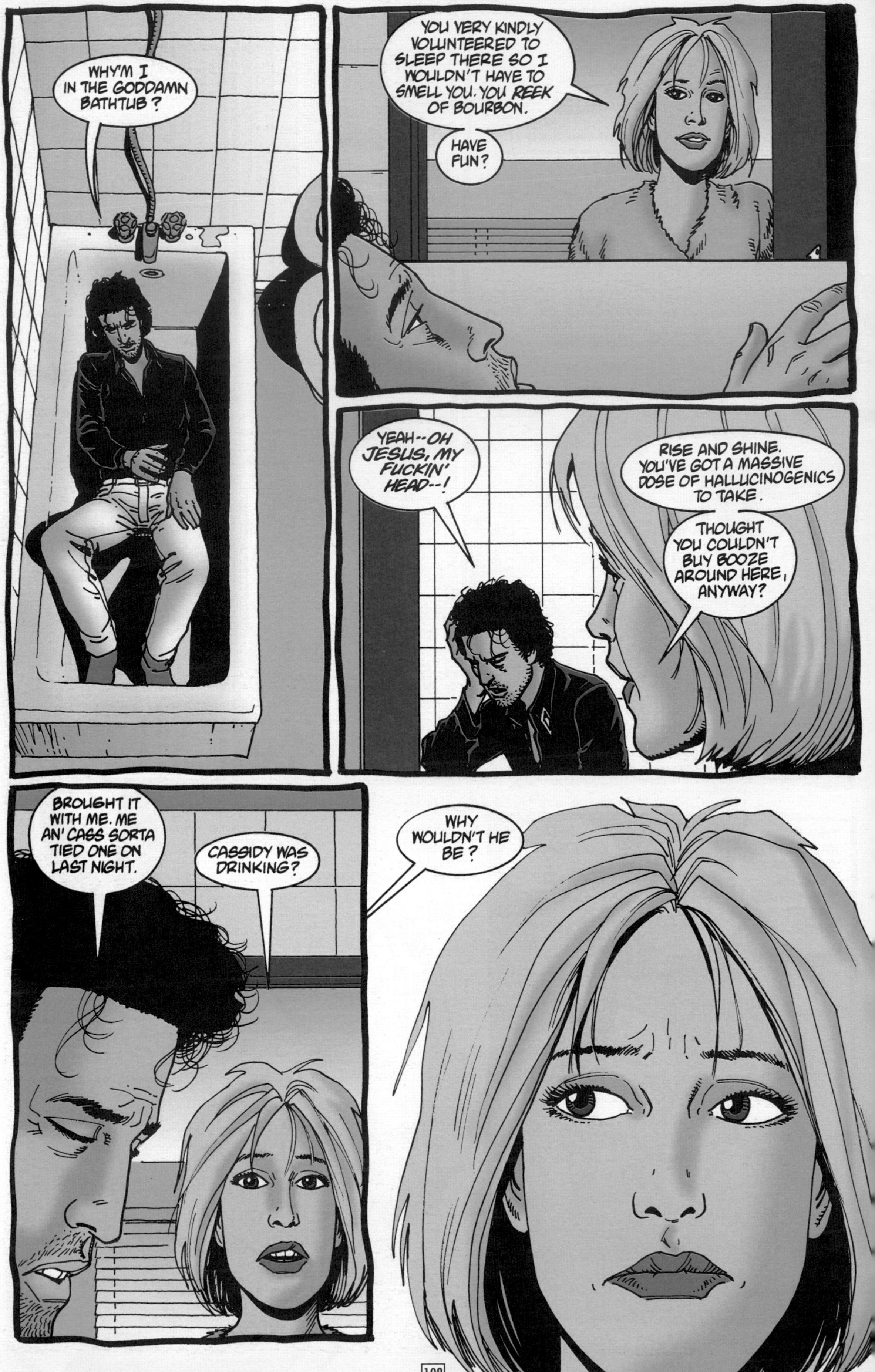
WHY'M I IN THE GODDAMN BATHTUB?
YOU VERY KINDLY VOLUNTEERED TO SLEEP THERE SO I WOULDN'T HAVE TO SMELL YOU. YOU REEK OF BOURBON.
HAVE FUN?
YEAH--OH JESUS, MY FUCKIN' HEAD--!
RISE AND SHINE. YOU'VE GOT A MASSIVE DOSE OF HALLUCINOGENICS TO TAKE.
THOUGHT YOU COULDN'T BUY BOOZE AROUND HERE, ANYWAY?
BROUGHT IT WITH ME. ME AN' CASS SORTA TIED ONE ON LAST NIGHT.
CASSIDY WAS DRINKING?
WHY WOULDN'T HE BE?

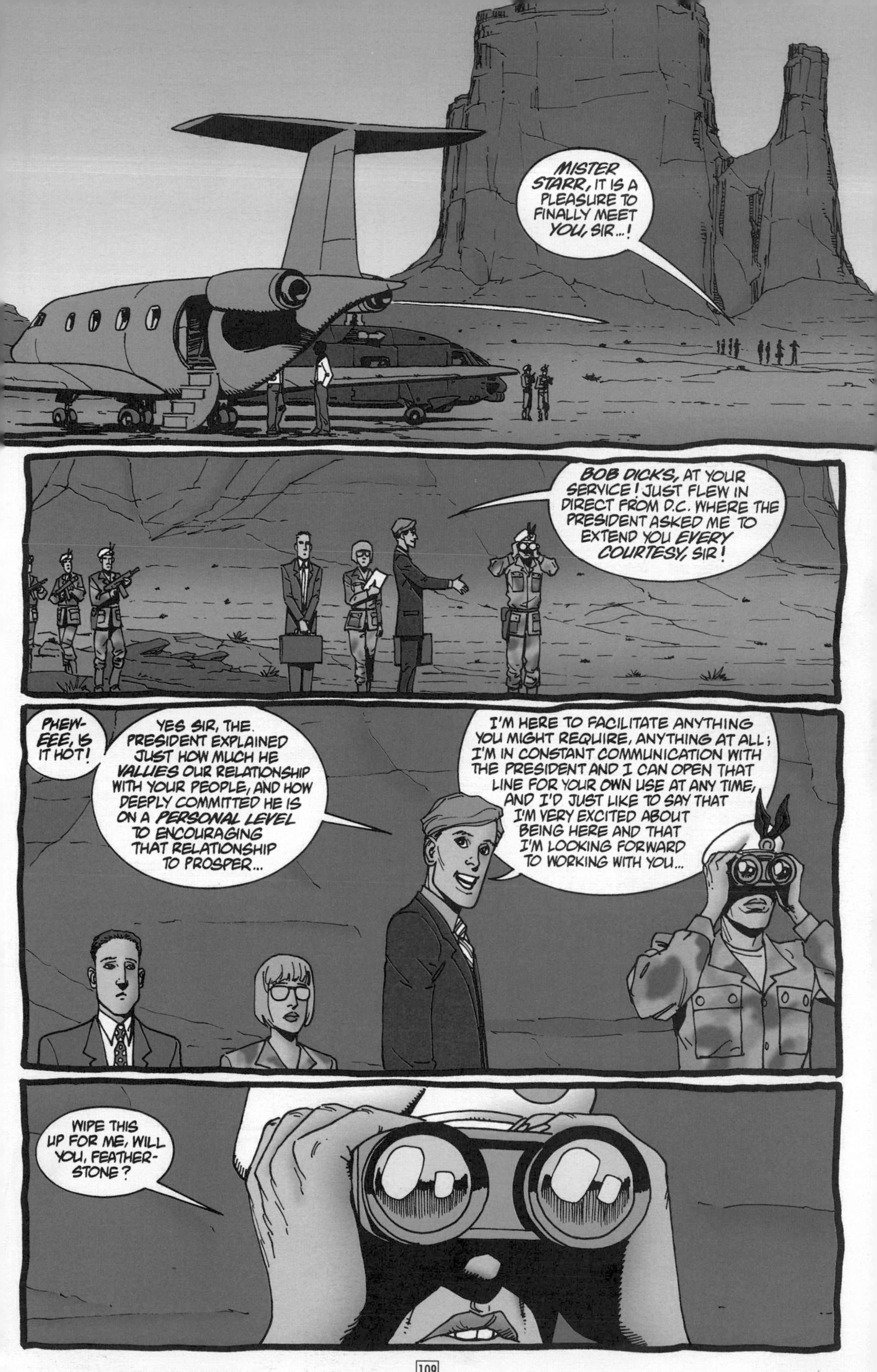
MISTER STARR, IT IS A PLEASURE TO FINALLY MEET YOU, SIR...!
BOB DICKS, AT YOUR SERVICE! JUST FLEW IN DIRECT FROM D.C. WHERE THE PRESIDENT ASKED ME TO EXTEND YOU EVERY COURTESY, SIR!
PHEW-EEE, IS IT HOT!
YES SIR, THE. PRESIDENT EXPLAINED JUST HOW MUCH HE VALUES OUR RELATIONSHIP WITH YOUR PEOPLE, AND HOW DEEPLY COMMITTED HE IS ON A PERSONAL LEVEL TO ENCOURAGING THAT RELATIONSHIP TO PROSPER...
I'M HERE TO FACILITATE ANYTHING YOU MIGHT REQUIRE, ANYTHING AT ALL; I'M IN CONSTANT COMMUNICATION WITH THE PRESIDENT AND I CAN OPEN THAT LINE FOR YOUR OWN USE AT ANY TIME, AND I'D JUST LIKE TO SAY THAT I'M VERY EXCITED ABOUT BEING HERE AND THAT I'M LOOKING FORWARD TO WORKING WITH YOU...
WIPE THIS UP FOR ME, WILL YOU, FEATHER-STONE?

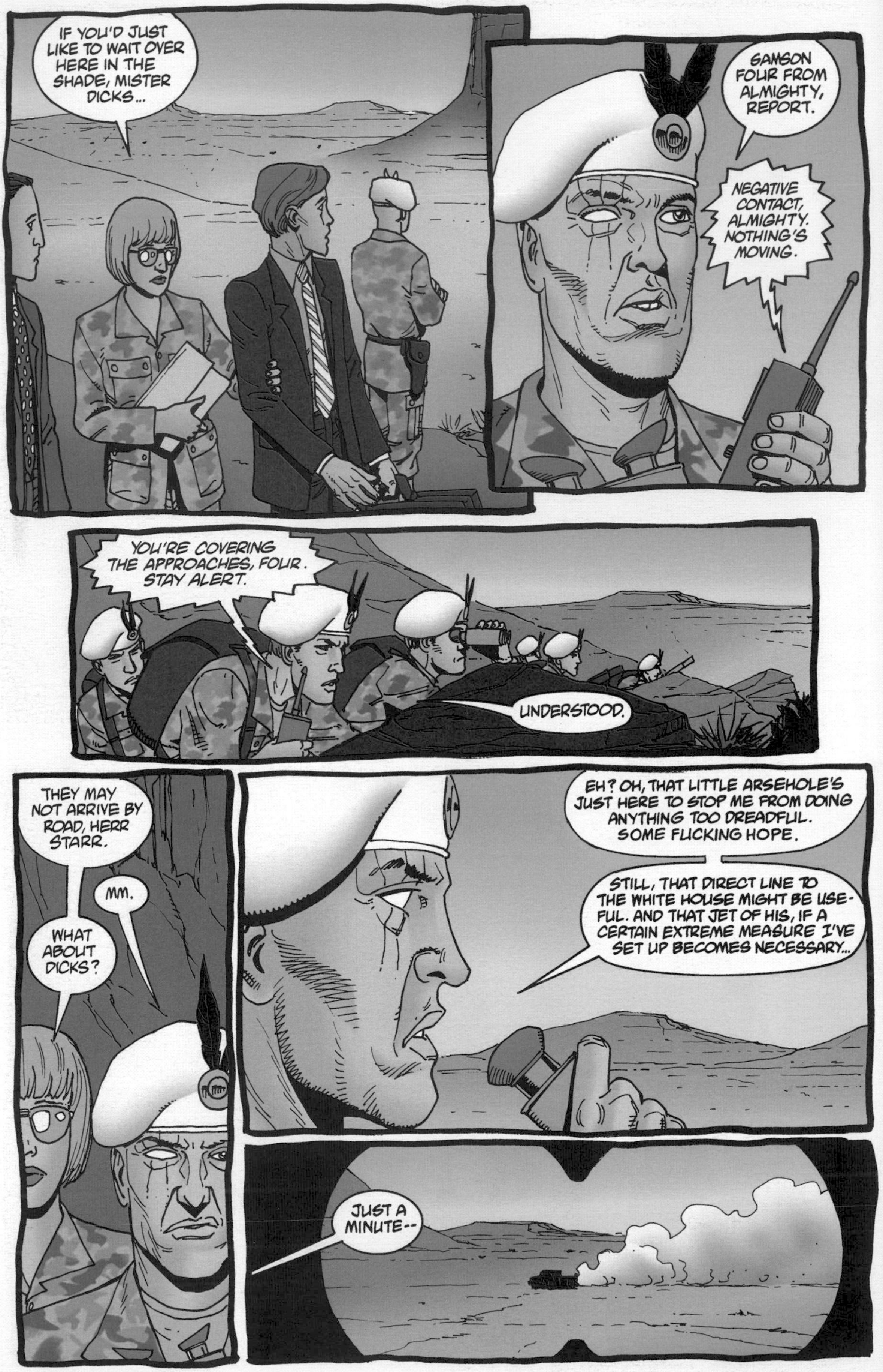
IF YOU'D JUST LIKE TO WAIT OVER HERE IN THE SHADE, MISTER DICKS...
SAMSON FOUR FROM ALMIGHTY, REPORT.
NEGATIVE CONTACT, ALMIGHTY. NOTHING'S MOVING.
YOU'RE COVERING THE APPROACHES, FOUR. STAY ALERT.
UNDERSTOOD.
THEY MAY NOT ARRIVE BY ROAD, HERR STARR.
MM.
WHAT ABOUT DICKS?
EH? OH, THAT LITTLE ARSEHOLE'S JUST HERE TO STOP ME FROM DOING ANYTHING TOO DREADFUL. SOME FUCKING HOPE.
STILL, THAT DIRECT LINE TO THE WHITE HOUSE MIGHT BE USE-FUL. AND THAT JET OF HIS, IF A CERTAIN EXTREME MEASURE I'VE SET UP BECOMES NECESSARY...
JUST A MINUTE--

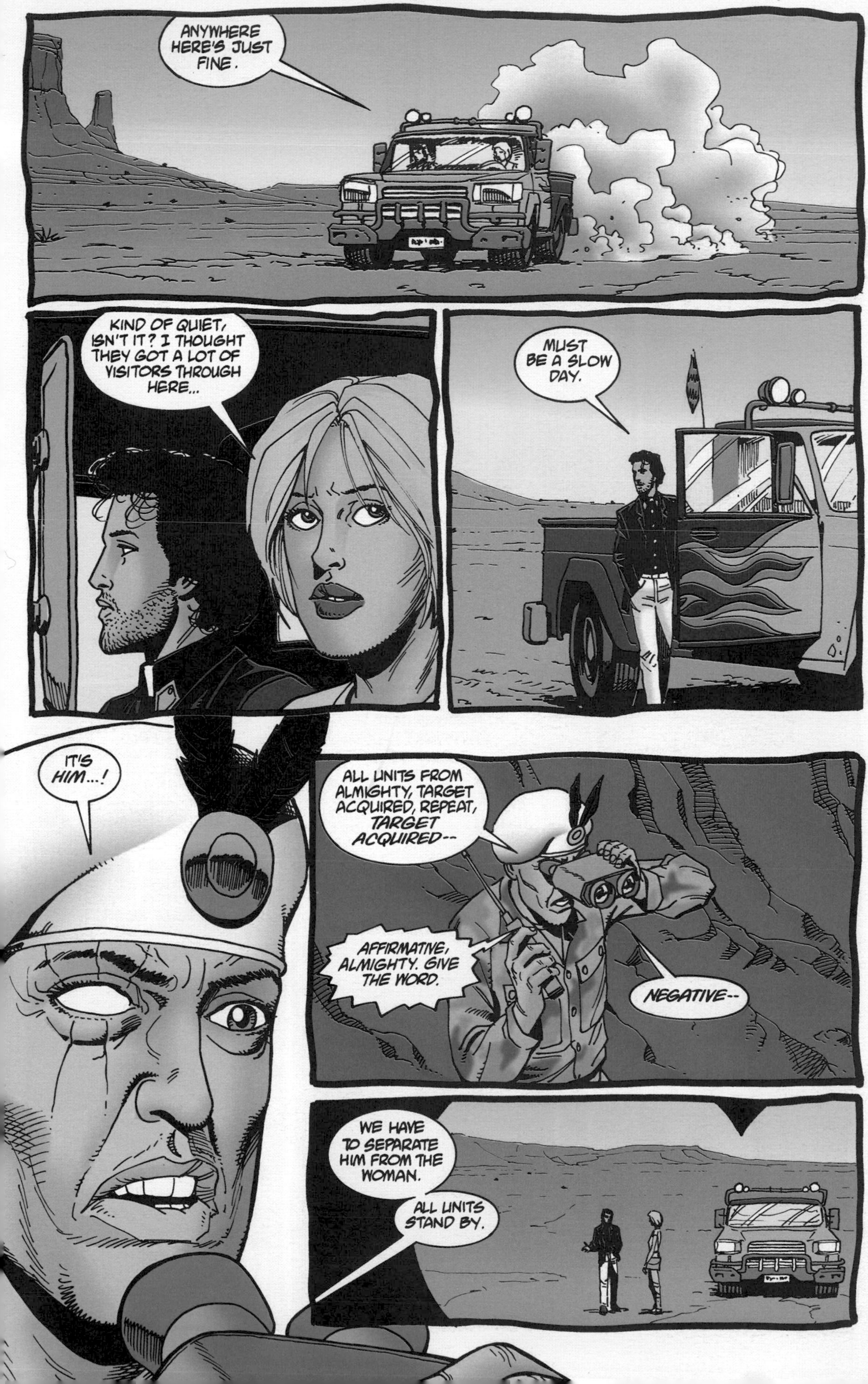
ANYWHERE HERE'S JUST FINE.
KIND OF QUIET, ISN'T IT? I THOUGHT THEY GOT A LOT OF VISITORS THROUGH HERE...
MUST BE A SLOW DAY.
IT'S HIM...!
ALL UNITS FROM ALMIGHTY, TARGET ACQUIRED, REPEAT, TARGET ACQUIRED--
AFFIRMATIVE, ALMIGHTY. GIVE THE WORD.
NEGATIVE--
WE HAVE TO SEPARATE HIM FROM THE WOMAN.
ALL UNITS STAND BY.

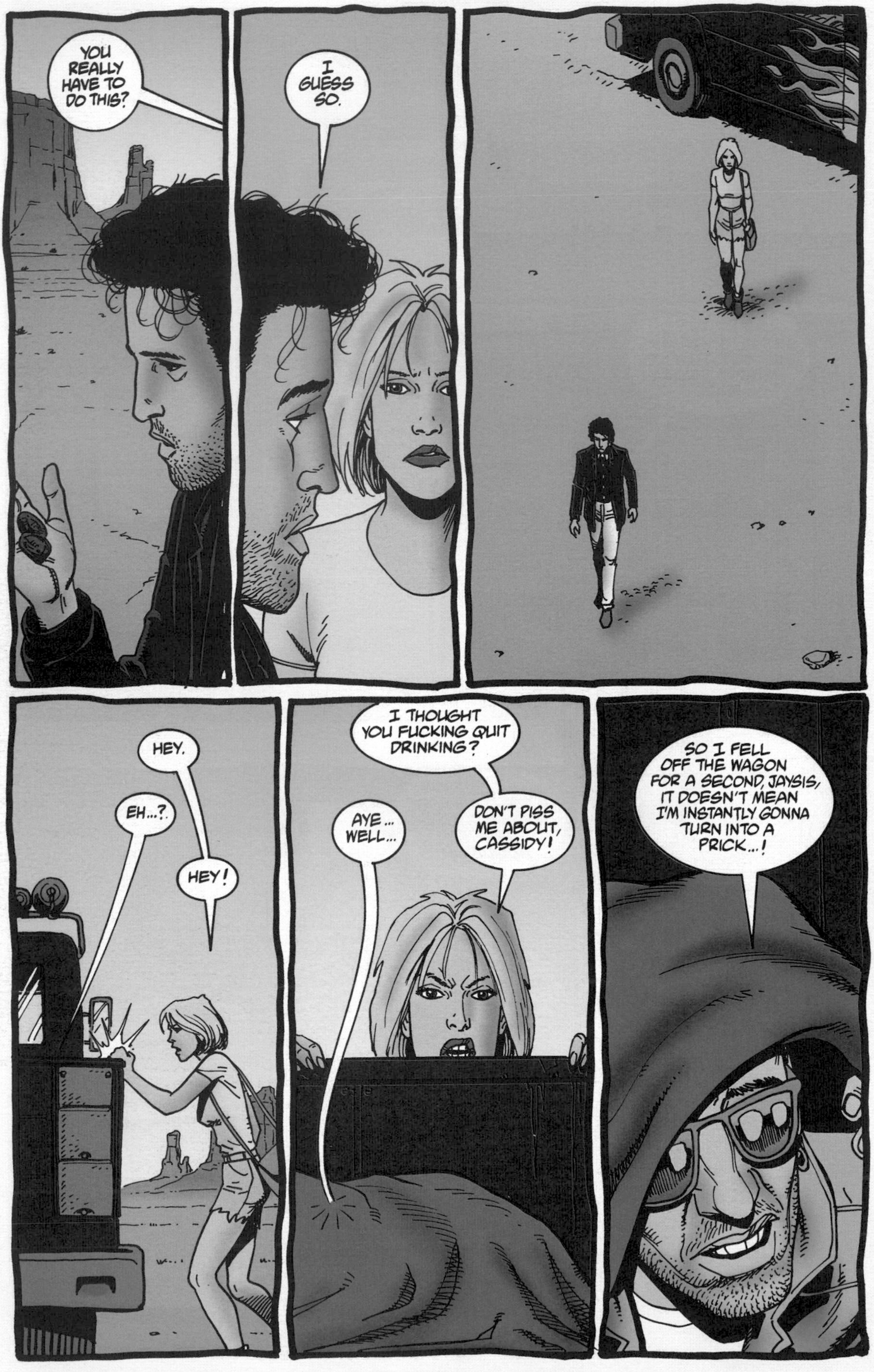
YOU REALLY HAVE TO DO THIS?
I GUESS SO.
HEY.
EH...?
HEY!
I THOUGHT YOU FUCKING QUIT DRINKING?
AYE... WELL...
DON'T PISS ME ABOUT, CASSIDY!
SO I FELL OFF THE WAGON FOR A SECOND, JAYSIS, IT DOESN'T MEAN I'M INSTANTLY GONNA TURN INTO A PRICK...!

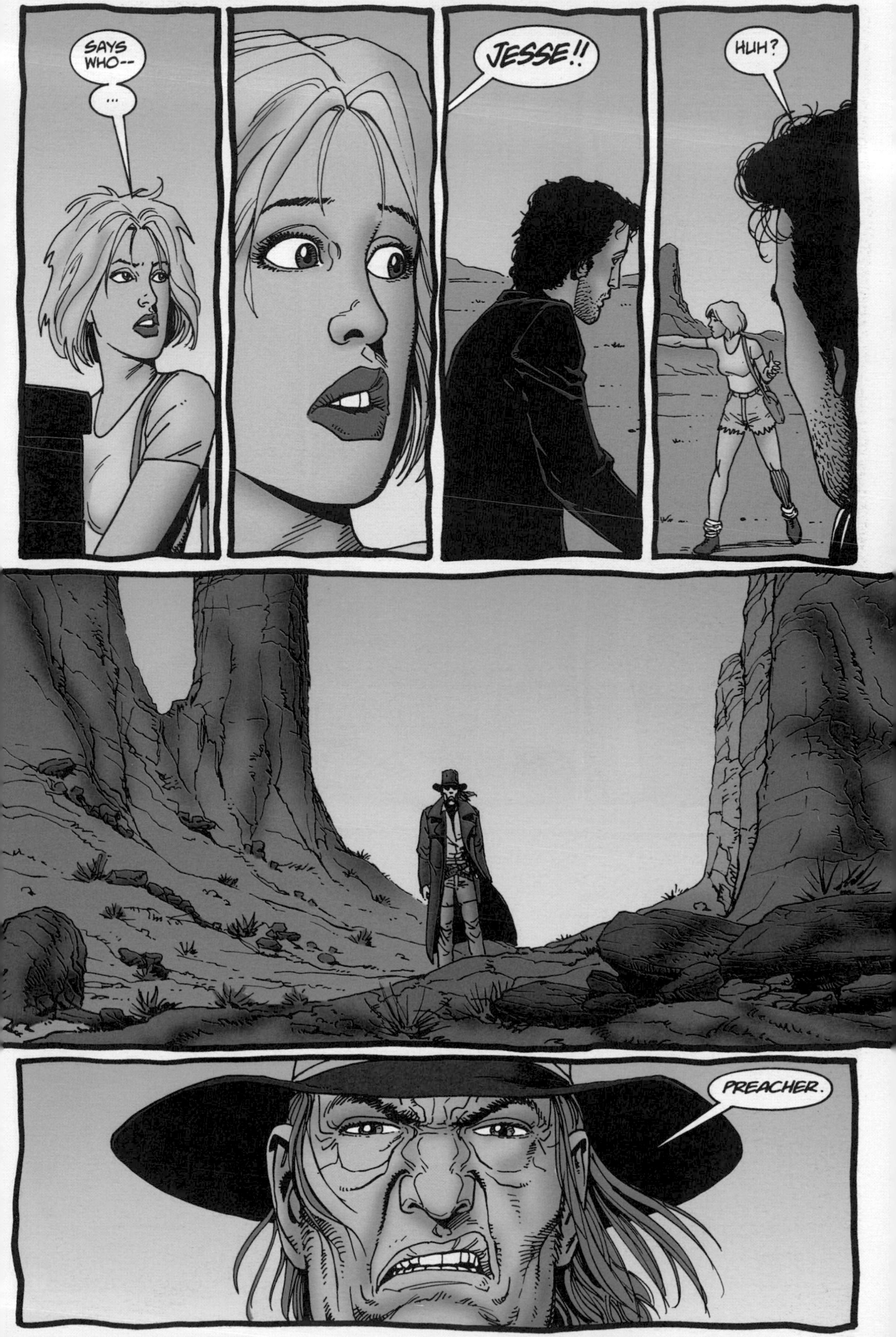
SAYS WHO--
...
JESSE!!
HUH?
PREACHER.

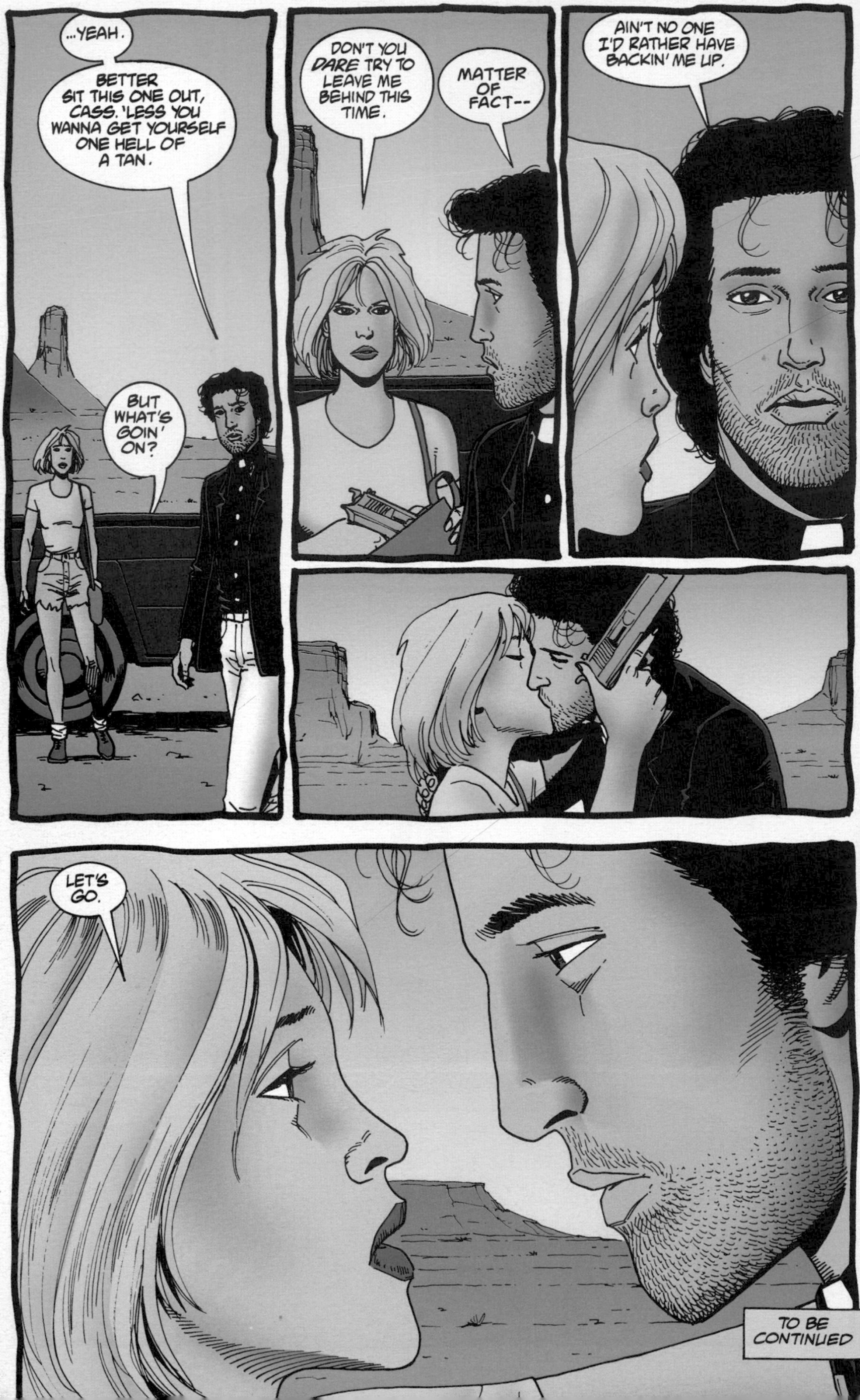
...YEAH.
BETTER SIT THIS ONE OUT, CASS. 'LESS YOU WANNA GET YOURSELF ONE HELL OF A TAN.
BUT WHAT'S GOIN' ON?
DON'T YOU DARE TRY TO LEAVE ME BEHIND THIS TIME.
MATTER OF FACT--
AIN'T NO ONE I'D RATHER HAVE BACKIN' ME UP.
LET'S GO.
TO BE CONTINUED

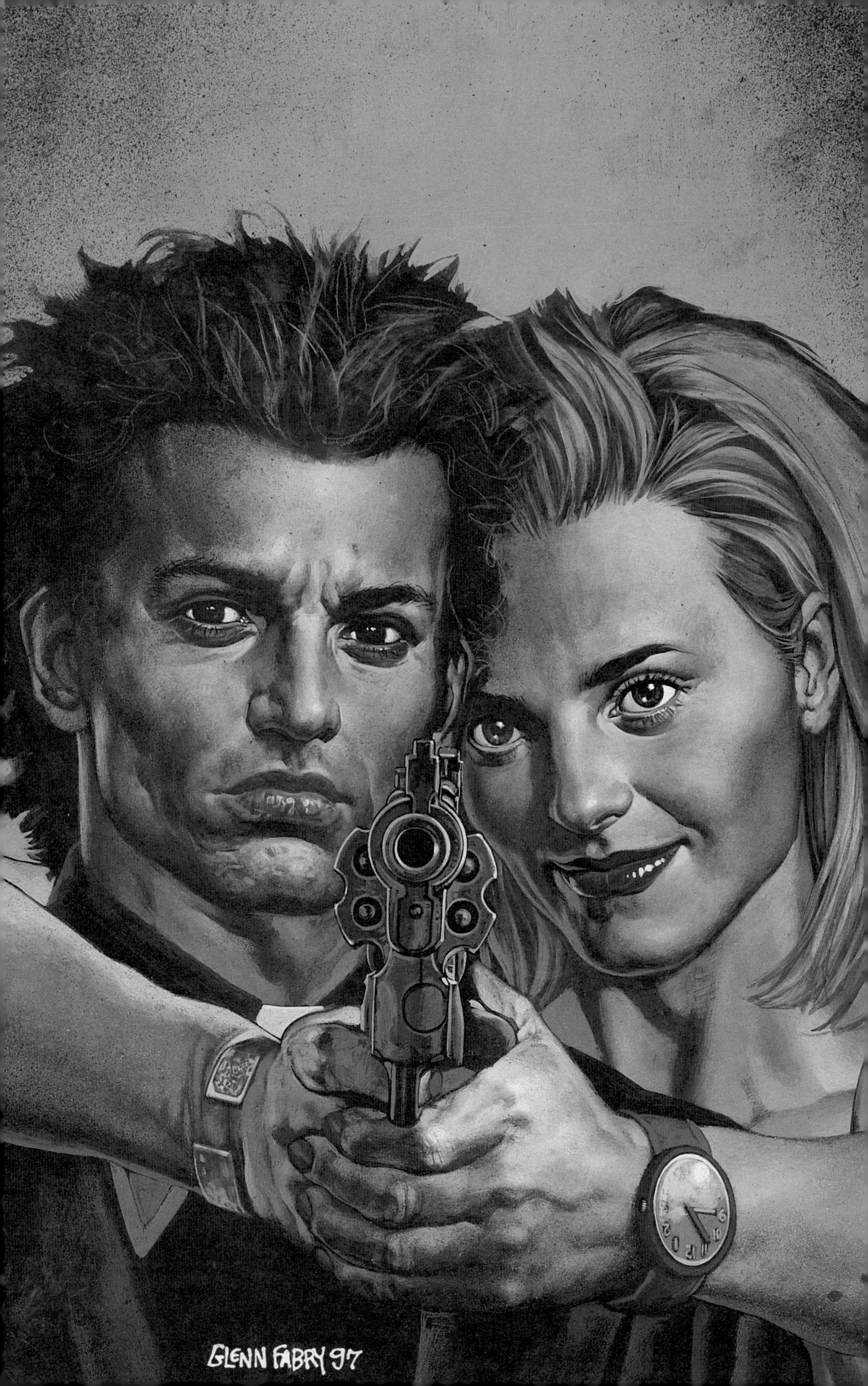
GLENN FABRY 97

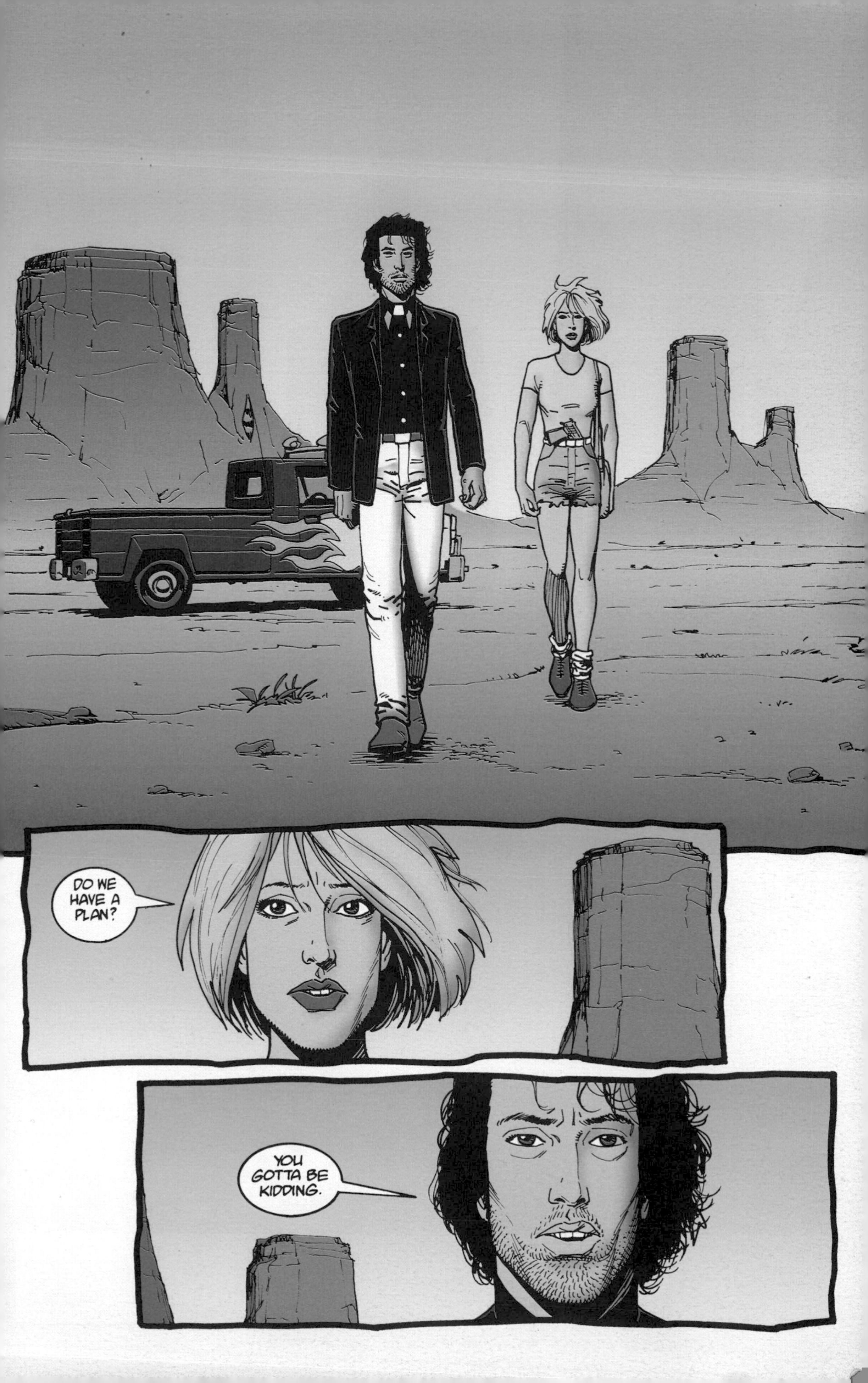
DO WE HAVE A PLAN?
YOU GOTTA BE KIDDING.

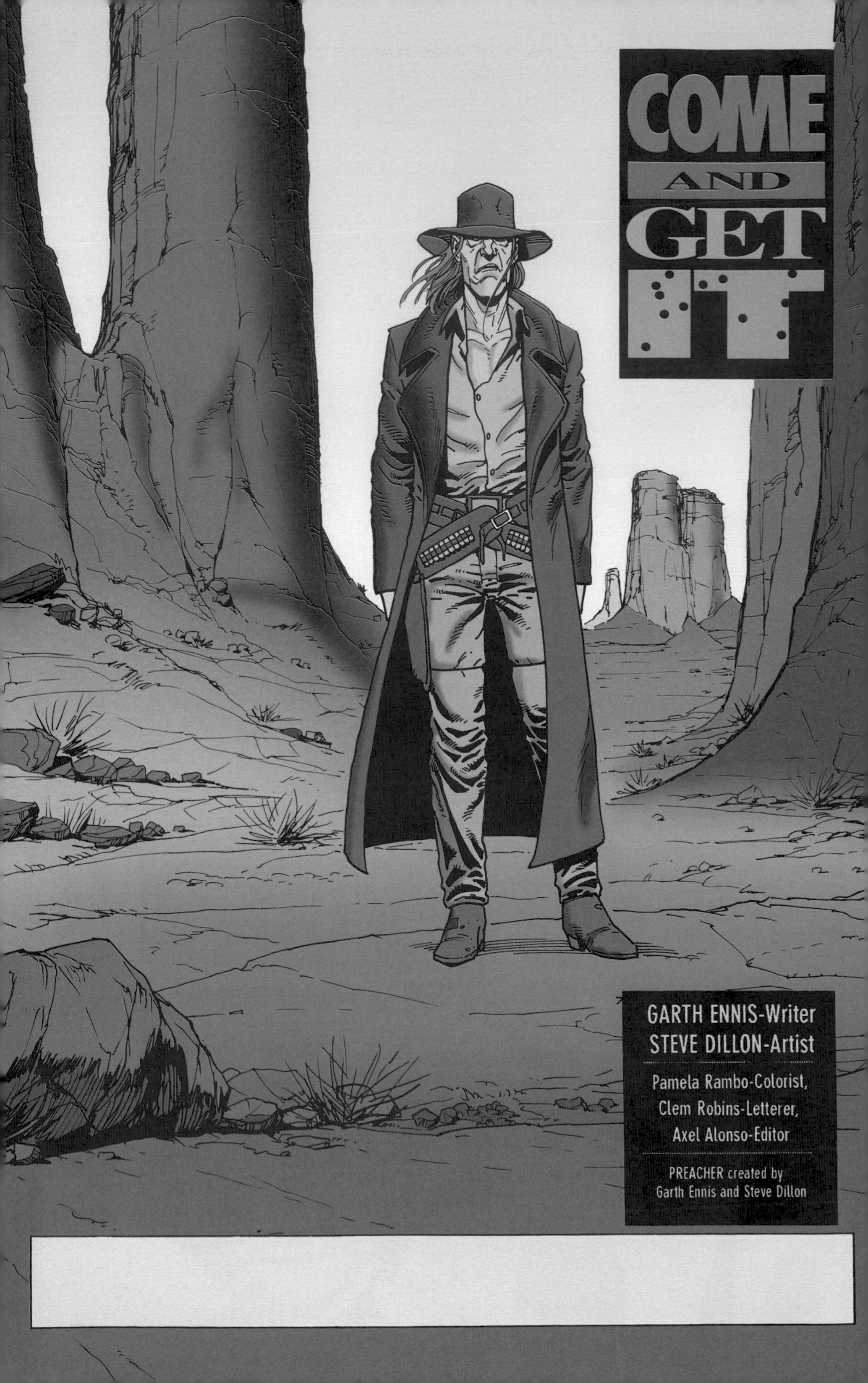

COME AND GET IT
GARTH ENNIS-Writer
STEVE DILLON-Artist
Pamela Rambo-Colorist,
Clem Robins-Letterer,
Axel Alonso-Editor
PREACHER created by
Garth Ennis and Steve Dillon

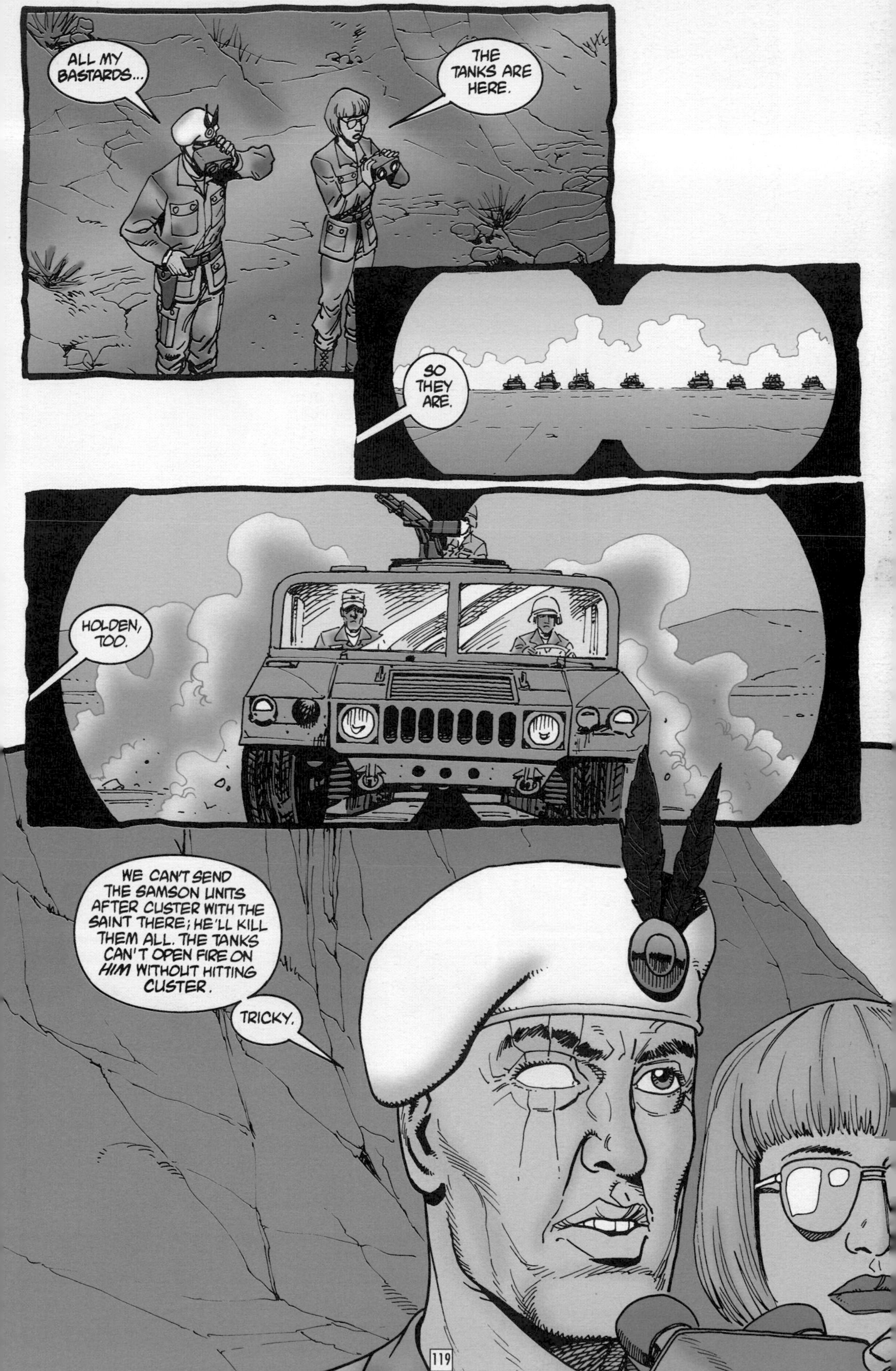
ALL MY BASTARDS...
THE TANKS ARE HERE.
SO THEY ARE.
HOLDEN, TOO.
WE CAN'T SEND THE SAMSON UNITS AFTER CUSTER WITH THE SAINT THERE; HE'LL KILL THEM ALL. THE TANKS CAN'T OPEN FIRE ON *HIM* WITHOUT HITTING CUSTER.
TRICKY.

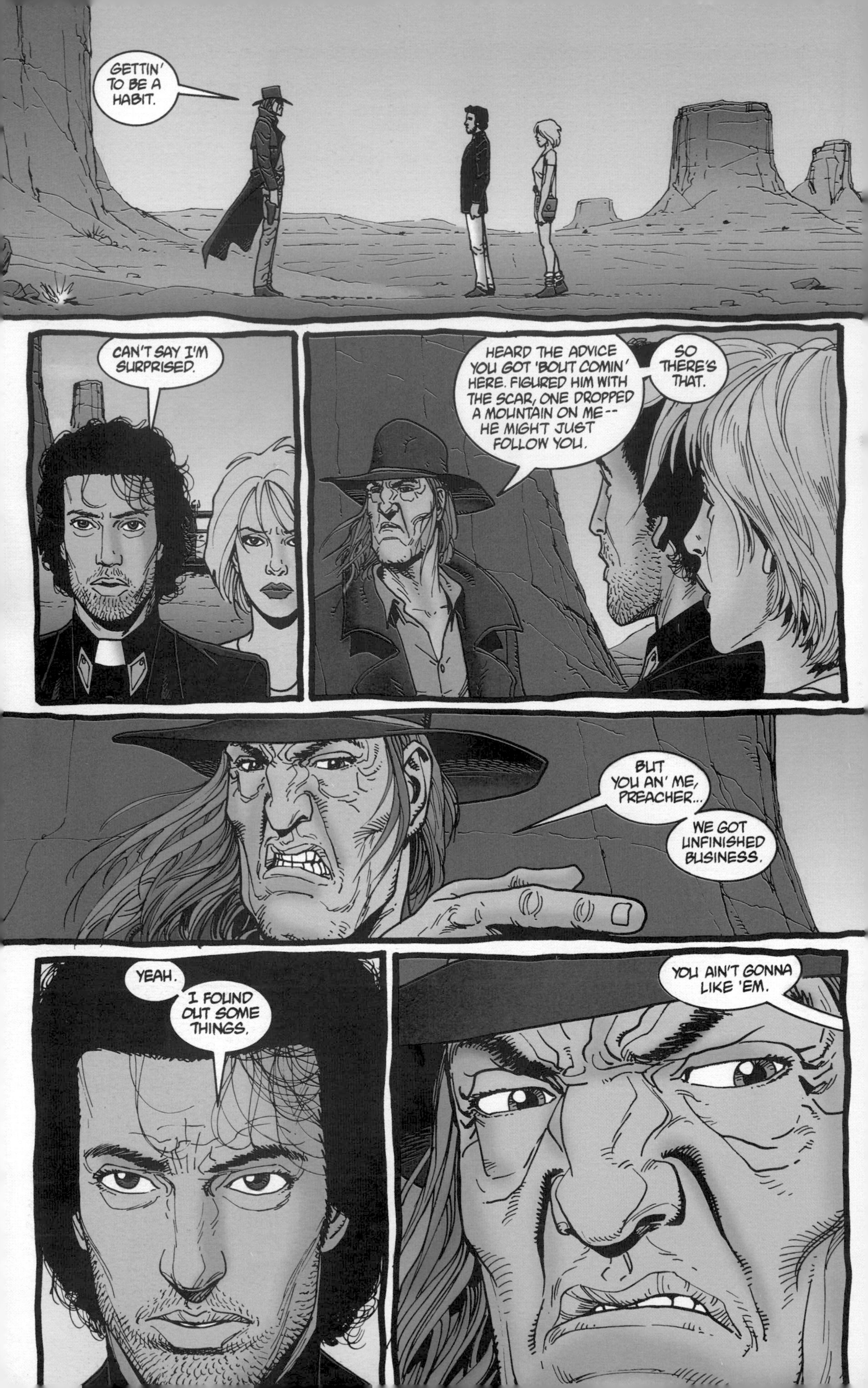
GETTIN' TO BE A HABIT.
CAN'T SAY I'M SURPRISED.
HEARD THE ADVICE YOU GOT 'BOUT COMIN' HERE. FIGURED HIM WITH THE SCAR, ONE DROPPED A MOUNTAIN ON ME-- HE MIGHT JUST FOLLOW YOU.
SO THERE'S THAT.
BUT YOU AN' ME, PREACHER...
WE GOT UNFINISHED BUSINESS.
YEAH.
I FOUND OUT SOME THINGS.
YOU AIN'T GONNA LIKE 'EM.

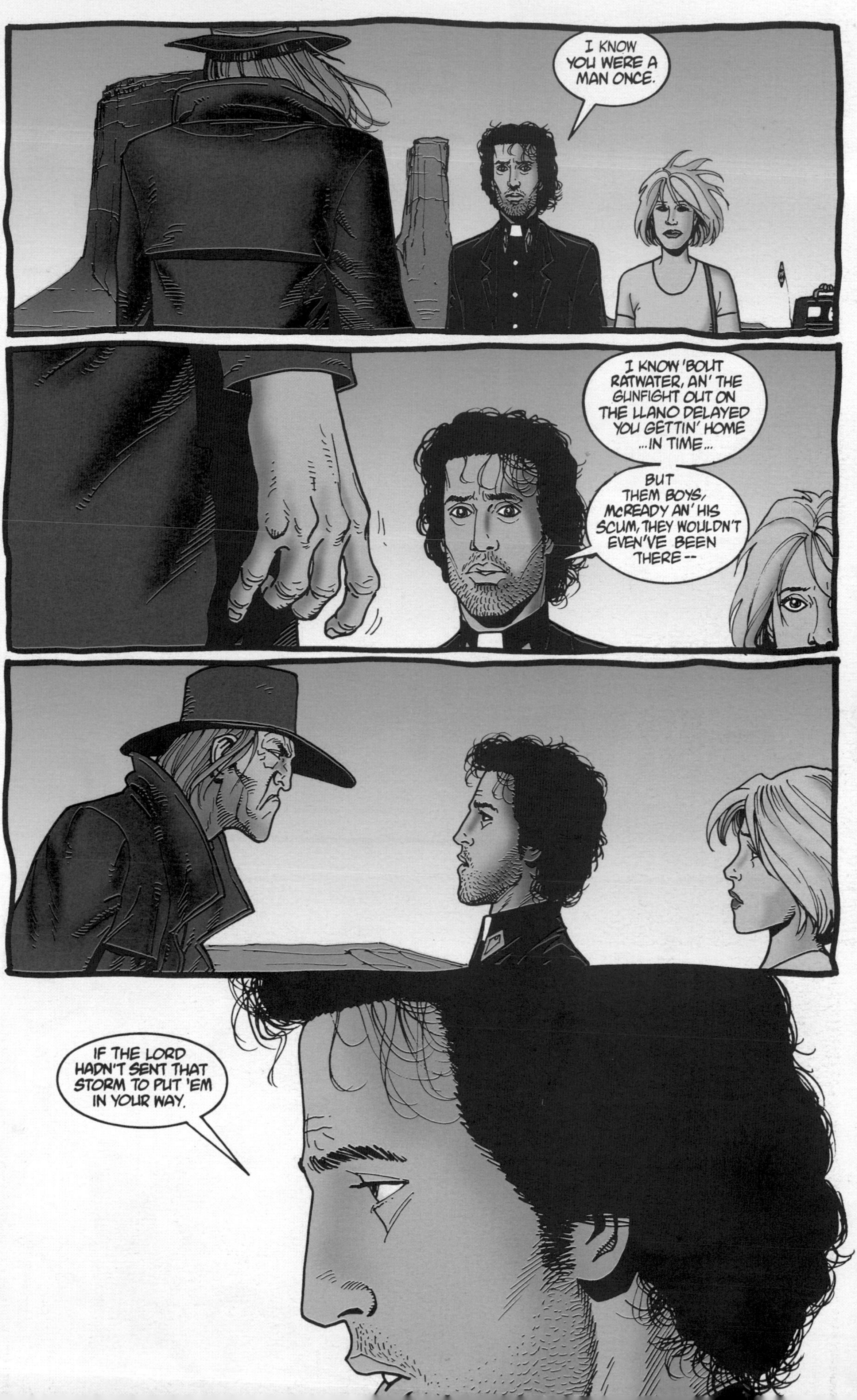
I KNOW YOU WERE A MAN ONCE.
I KNOW 'BOUT RATWATER, AN' THE GUNFIGHT OUT ON THE LLANO DELAYED YOU GETTIN' HOME ...IN TIME...
BUT THEM BOYS, McCREADY AN' HIS SCUM, THEY WOULDN'T EVEN'VE BEEN THERE --
IF THE LORD HADN'T SENT THAT STORM TO PUT 'EM IN YOUR WAY.

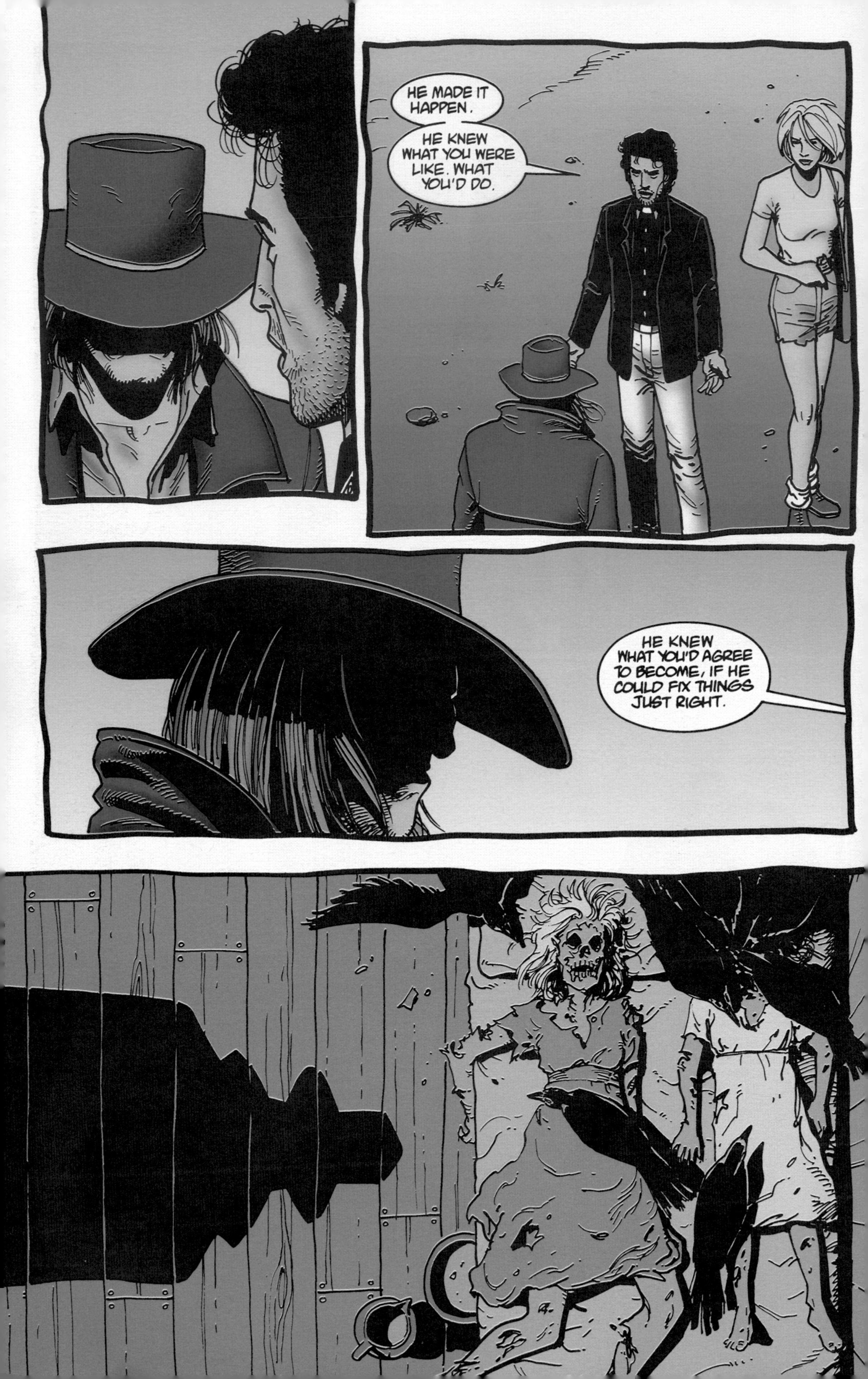
HE MADE IT HAPPEN.
HE KNEW WHAT YOU WERE LIKE. WHAT YOU'D DO.
HE KNEW WHAT YOU'D AGREE TO BECOME, IF HE COULD FIX THINGS JUST RIGHT.

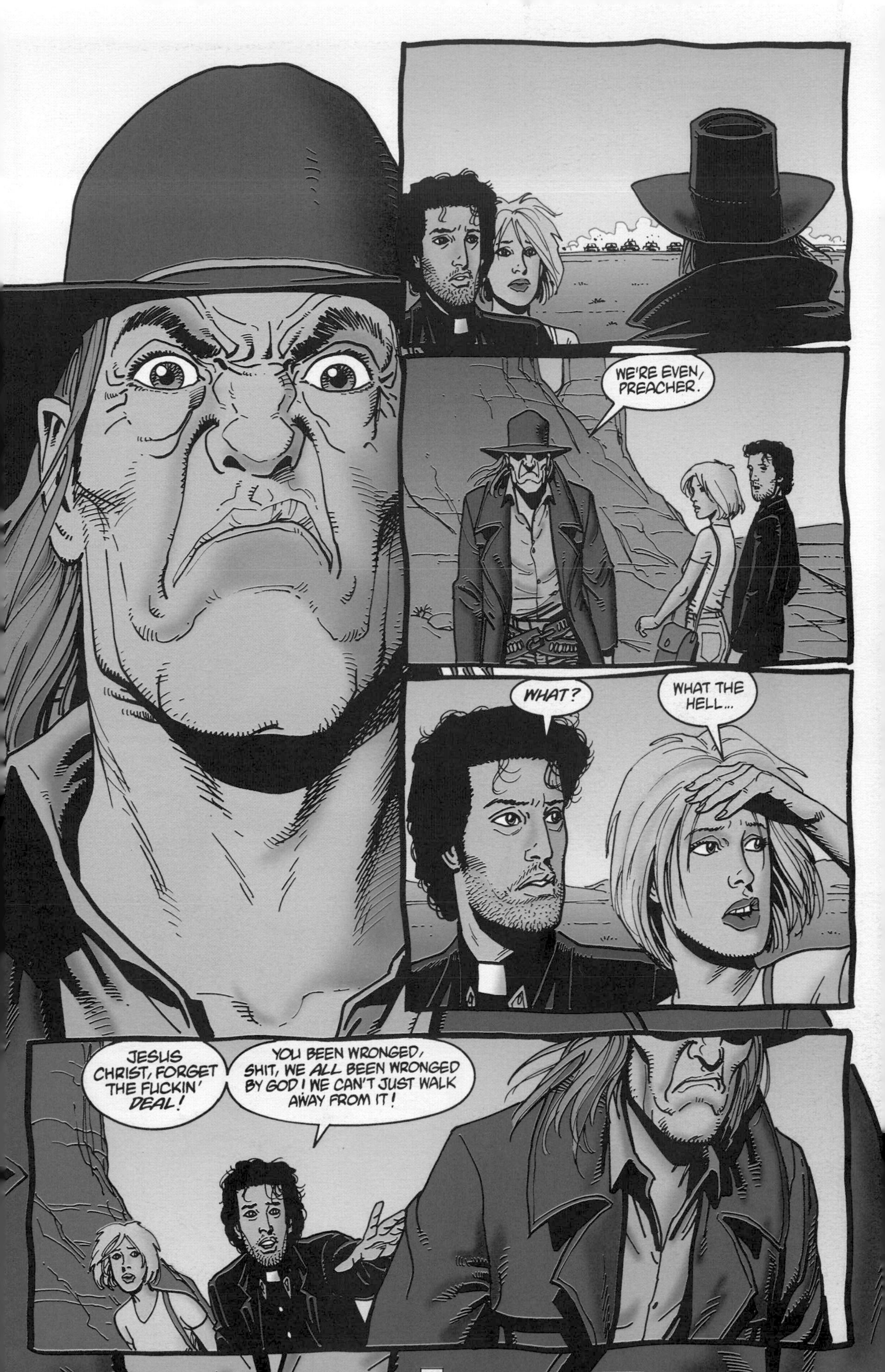
WE'RE EVEN, PREACHER.
WHAT?
WHAT THE HELL...
JESUS CHRIST, FORGET THE FUCKIN' DEAL!
YOU BEEN WRONGED, SHIT, WE ALL BEEN WRONGED BY GOD! WE CAN'T JUST WALK AWAY FROM IT!

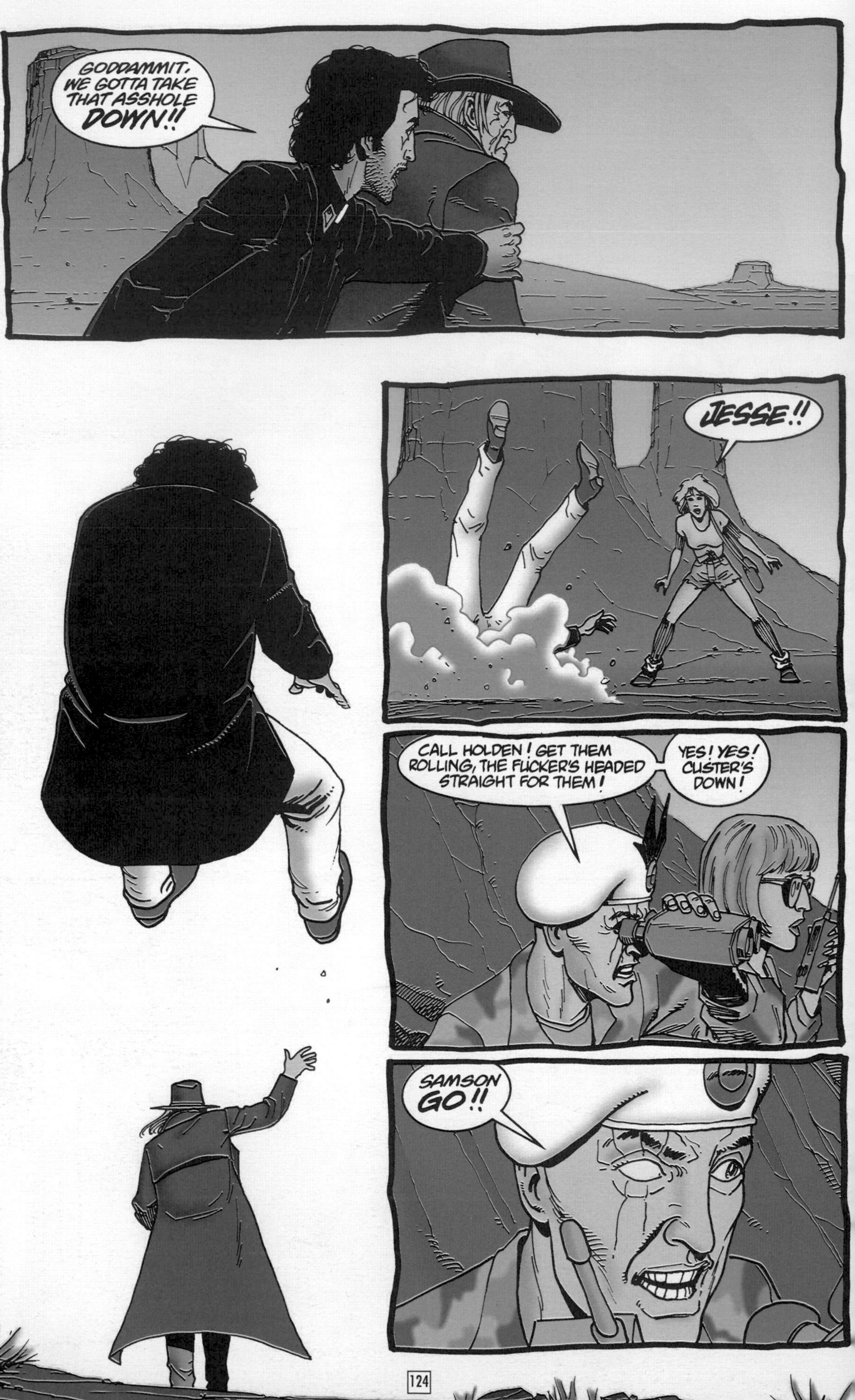
GODDAMMIT, WE GOTTA TAKE THAT ASSHOLE DOWN!!
¡JESSE!!
CALL HOLDEN! GET THEM ROLLING, THE FUCKER'S HEADED STRAIGHT FOR THEM!
YES! YES! CUSTER'S DOWN!
SAMSON GO!!

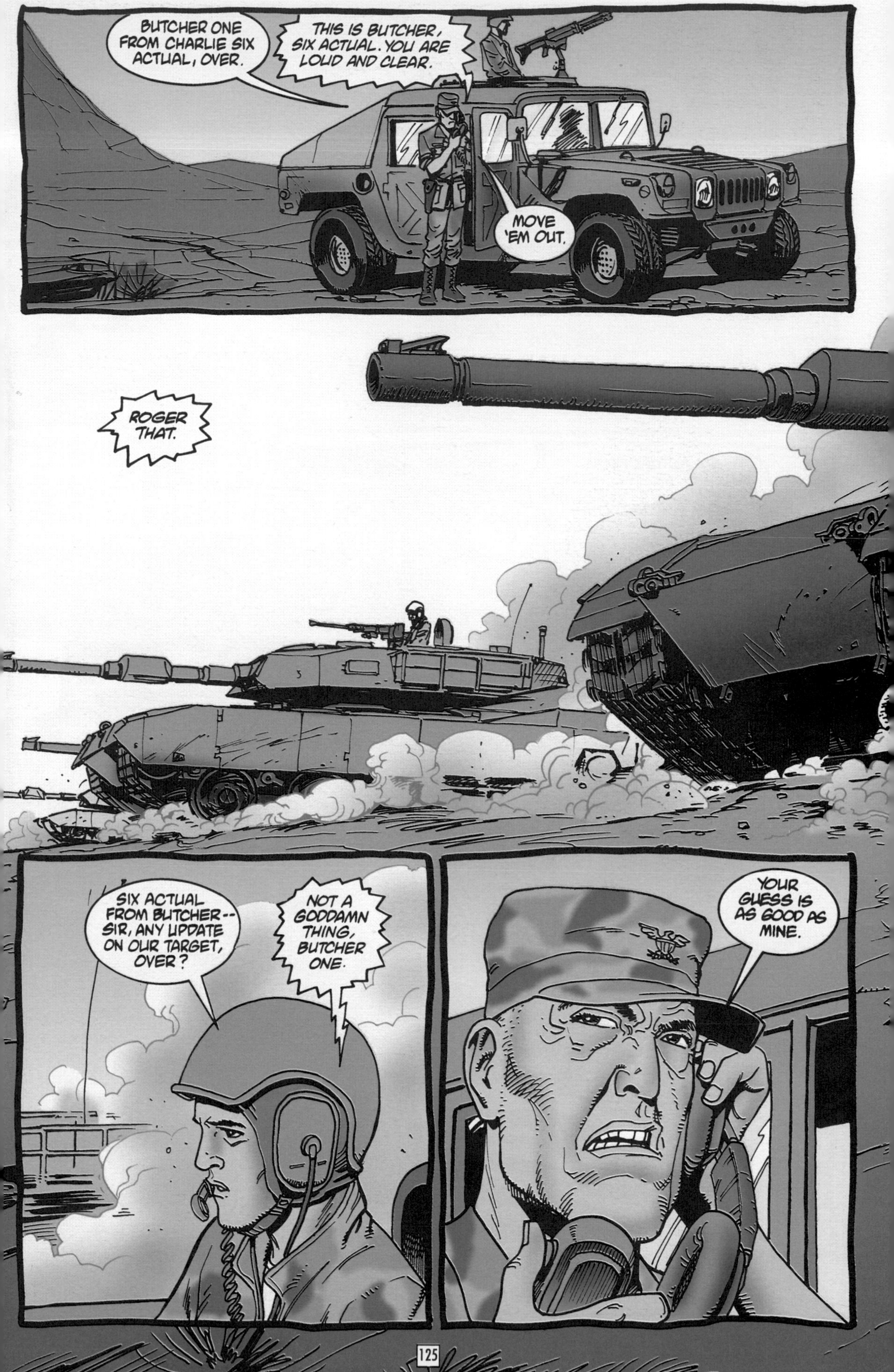
BUTCHER ONE FROM CHARLIE SIX ACTUAL, OVER.
THIS IS BUTCHER, SIX ACTUAL. YOU ARE LOUD AND CLEAR.
MOVE 'EM OUT.
ROGER THAT.
SIX ACTUAL FROM BUTCHER-- SIR, ANY UPDATE ON OUR TARGET, OVER?
NOT A GODDAMN THING, BUTCHER ONE.
YOUR GUESS IS AS GOOD AS MINE.

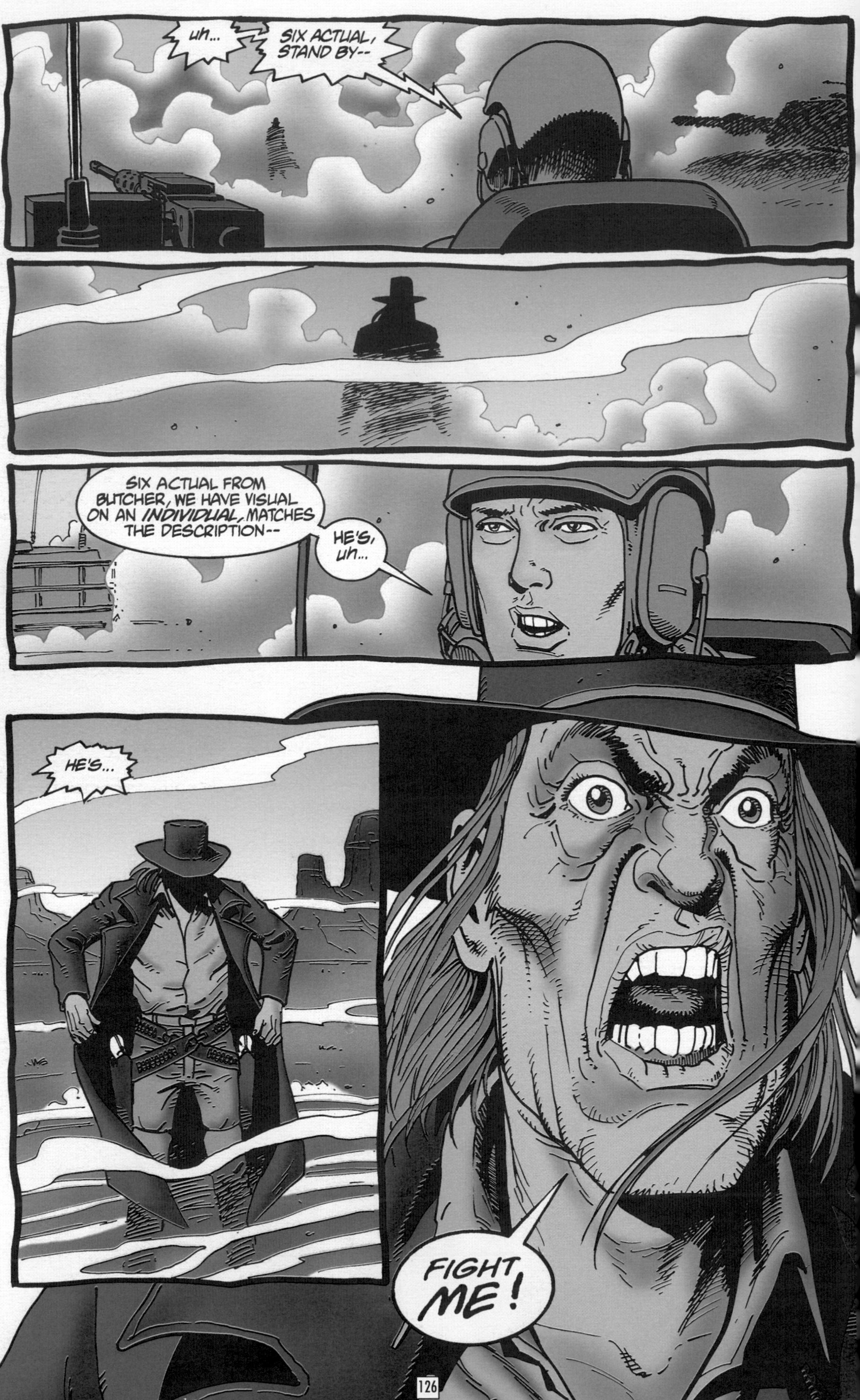
uh...
SIX ACTUAL, STAND BY--
SIX ACTUAL FROM BUTCHER, WE HAVE VISUAL ON AN INDIVIDUAL, MATCHES THE DESCRIPTION--
HE'S, uh...
HE'S...
FIGHT ME!

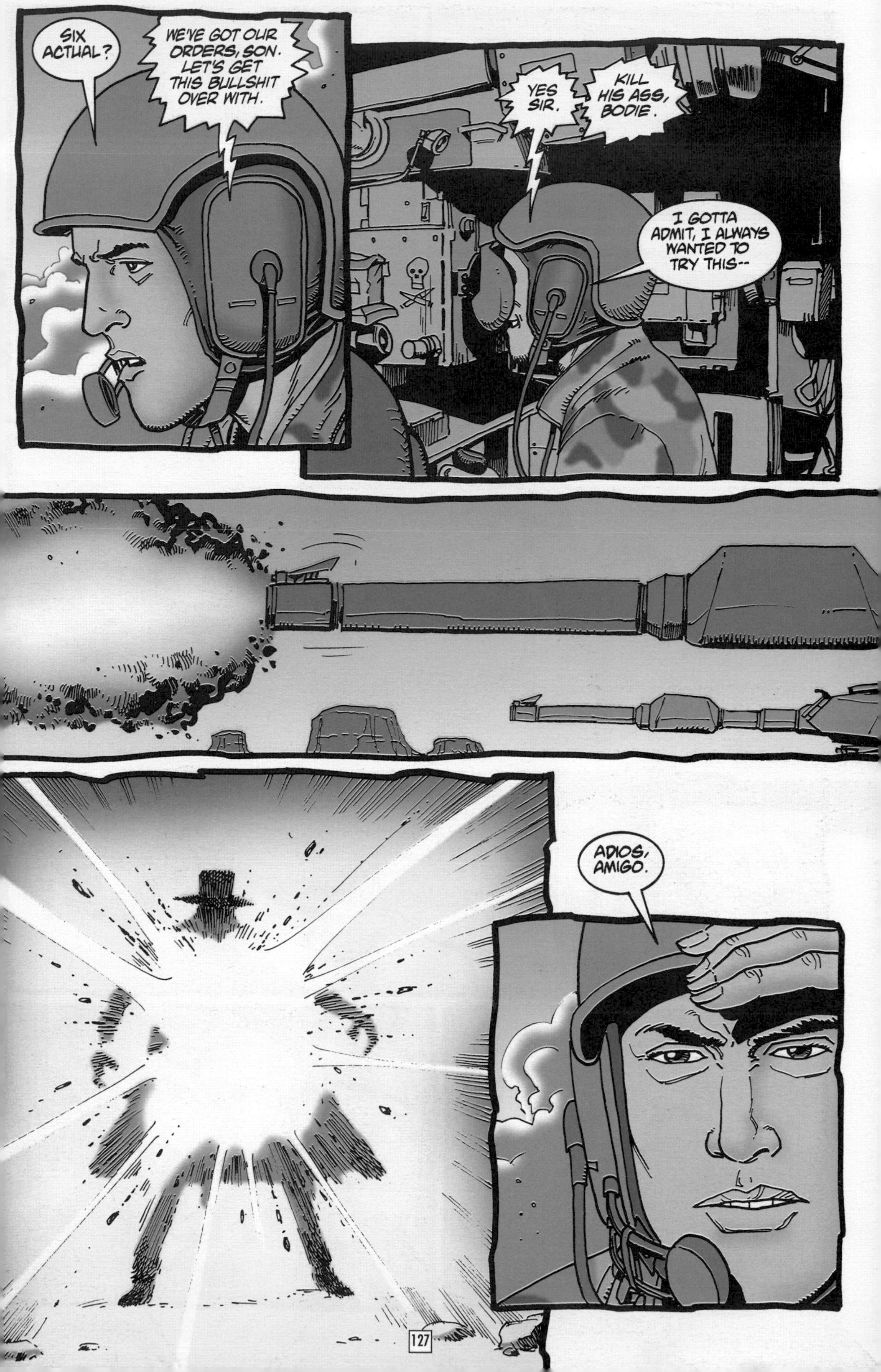
SIX ACTUAL?
WE'VE GOT OUR ORDERS, SON. LET'S GET THIS BULLSHIT OVER WITH.
YES SIR.
KILL HIS ASS, BODIE.
I GOTTA ADMIT, I ALWAYS WANTED TO TRY THIS--
ADIOS, AMIGO.

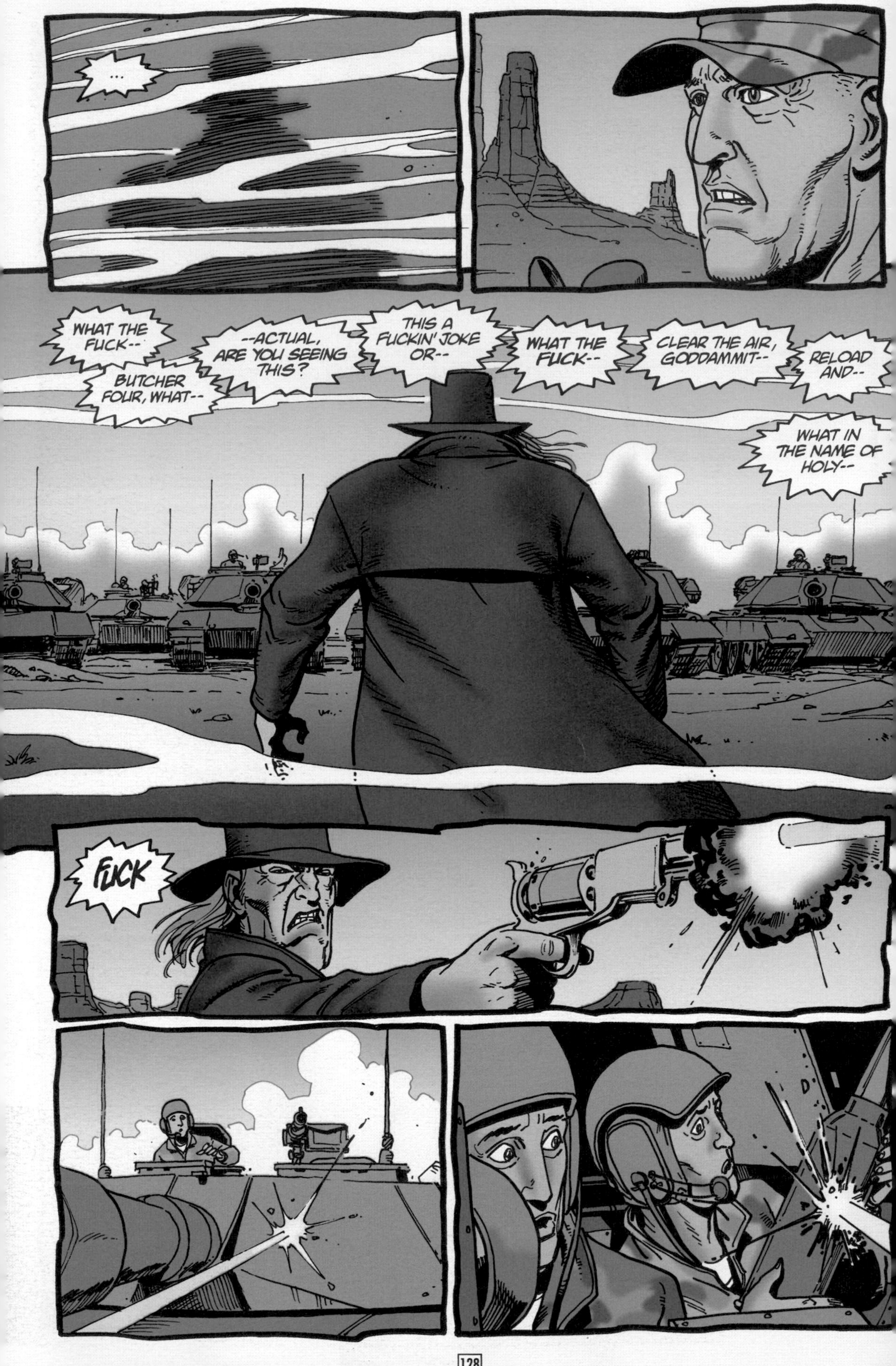
...
WHAT THE FUCK--
BUTCHER FOUR, WHAT--
--ACTUAL, ARE YOU SEEING THIS?
THIS A FUCKIN' JOKE OR--
WHAT THE FUCK--
CLEAR THE AIR, GODDAMMIT--
RELOAD AND--
WHAT IN THE NAME OF HOLY--
FUCK

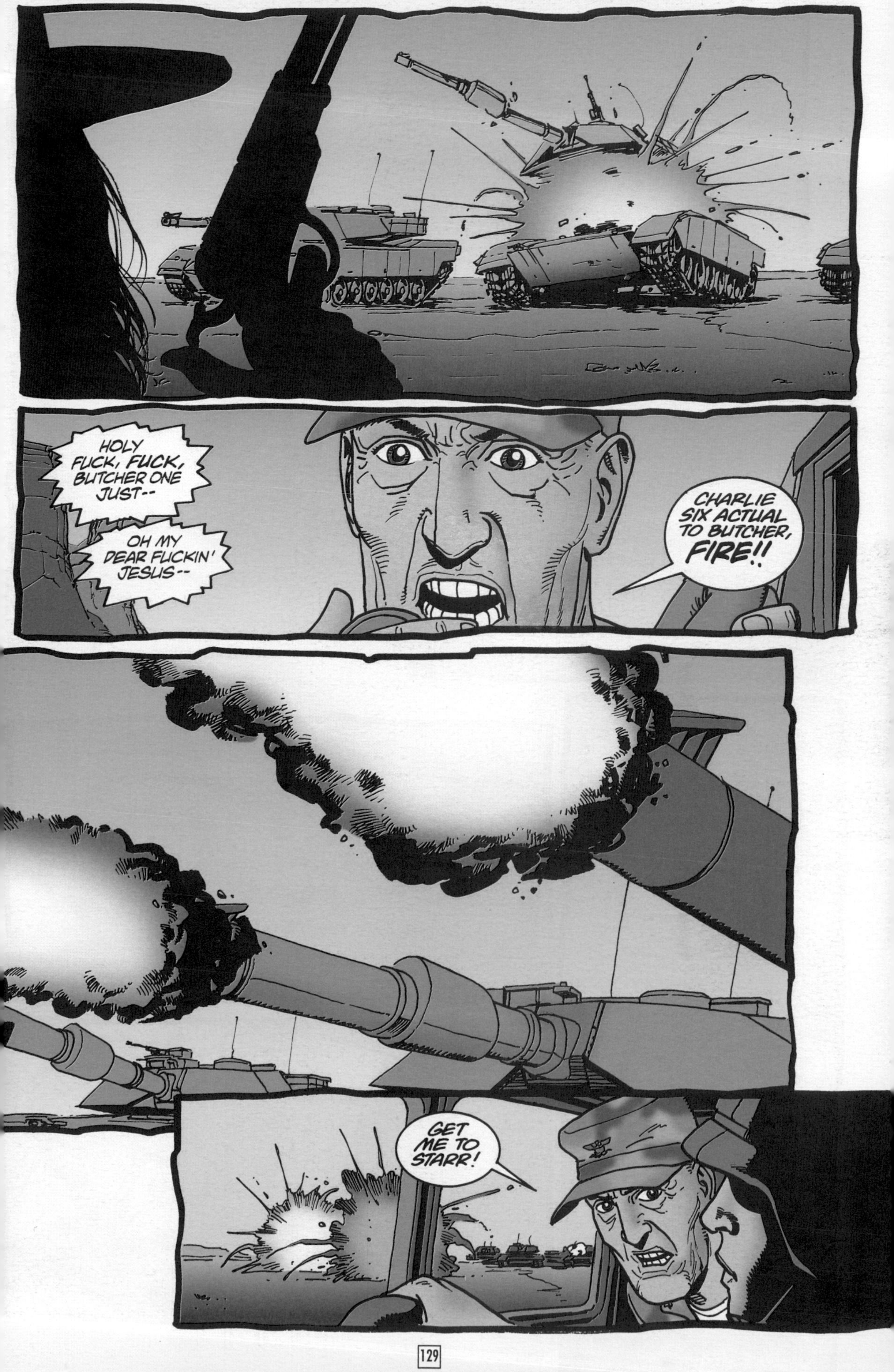
HOLY FUCK, FUCK, BUTCHER ONE JUST--
OH MY DEAR FUCKIN' JESUS--
CHARLIE SIX ACTUAL TO BUTCHER, FIRE!!
GET ME TO STARR!

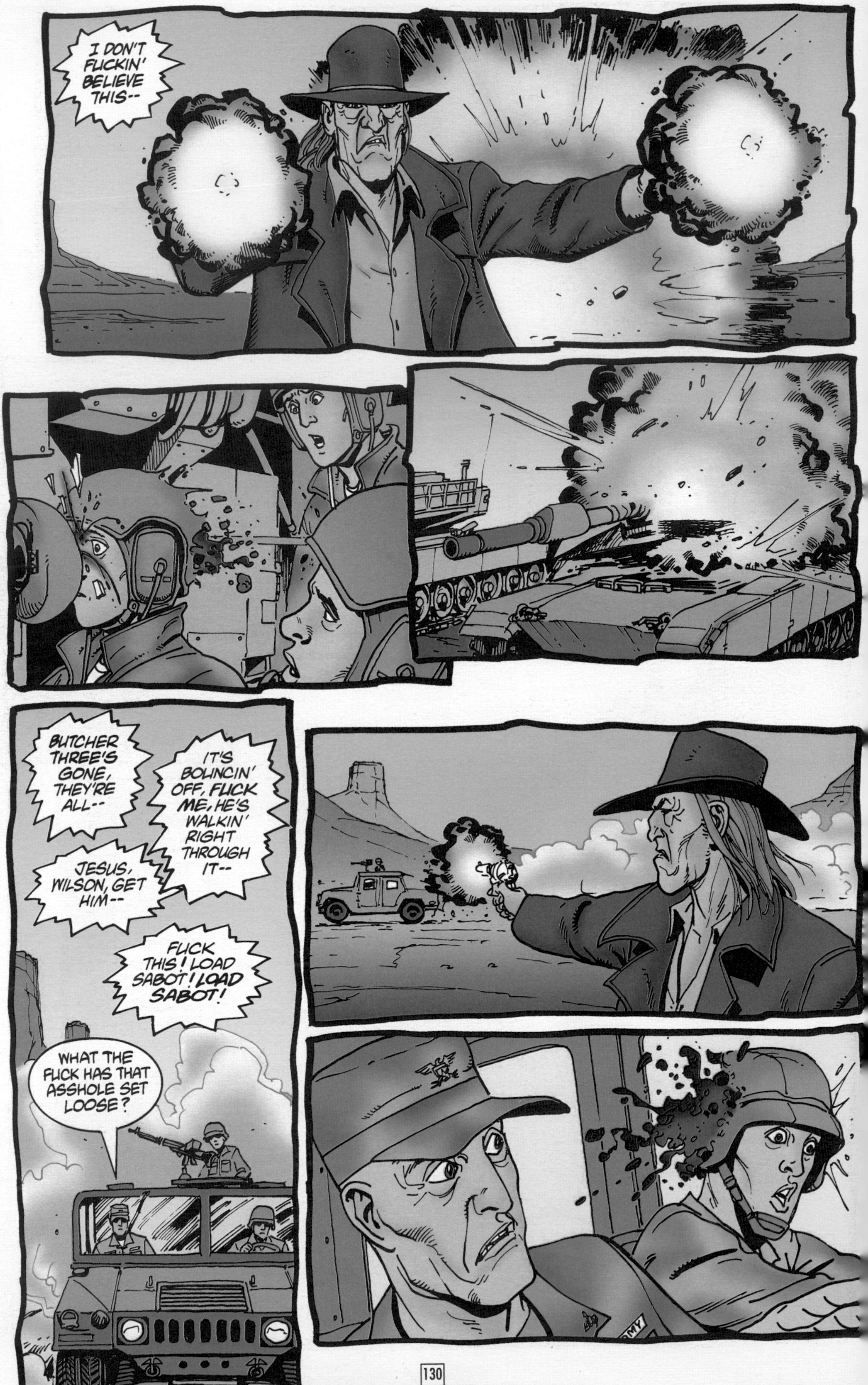
I DON'T FUCKIN' BELIEVE THIS--
BUTCHER THREE'S GONE, THEY'RE ALL--
IT'S BOUNCIN' OFF. FUCK ME, HE'S WALKIN' RIGHT THROUGH IT--
JESUS, WILSON, GET HIM--
FUCK THIS! LOAD SABOT! LOAD SABOT!
WHAT THE FUCK HAS THAT ASSHOLE SET LOOSE?

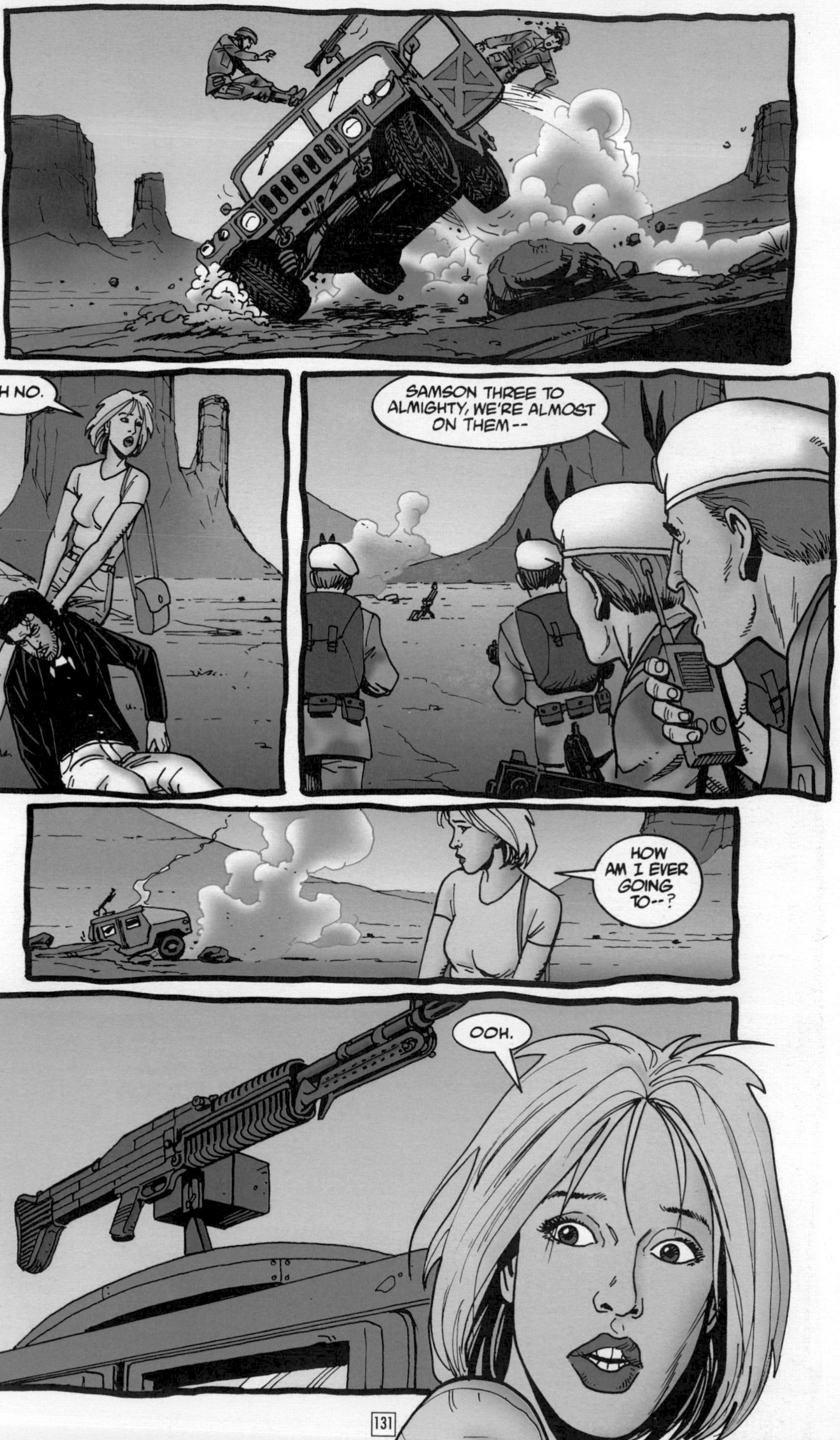
OH NO.
SAMSON THREE TO ALMIGHTY, WE'RE ALMOST ON THEM--
HOW AM I EVER GOING TO--?
OOH.

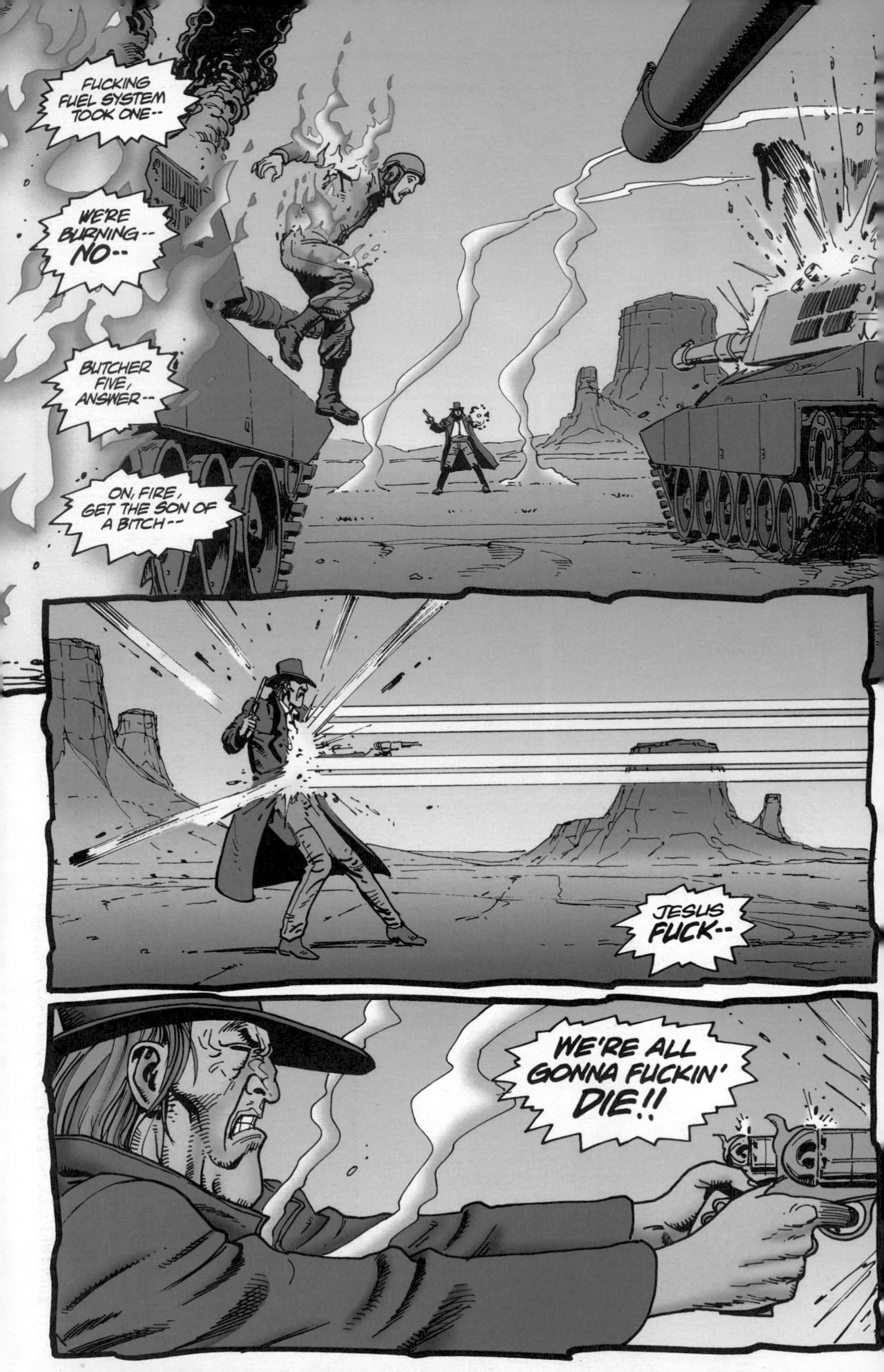
FUCKING FUEL SYSTEM TOOK ONE--
WE'RE BURNING-- NO--
BUTCHER FIVE, ANSWER--
ON, FIRE, GET THE SON OF A BITCH--
JESUS FUCK--
WE'RE ALL GONNA FUCKIN' DIE!!

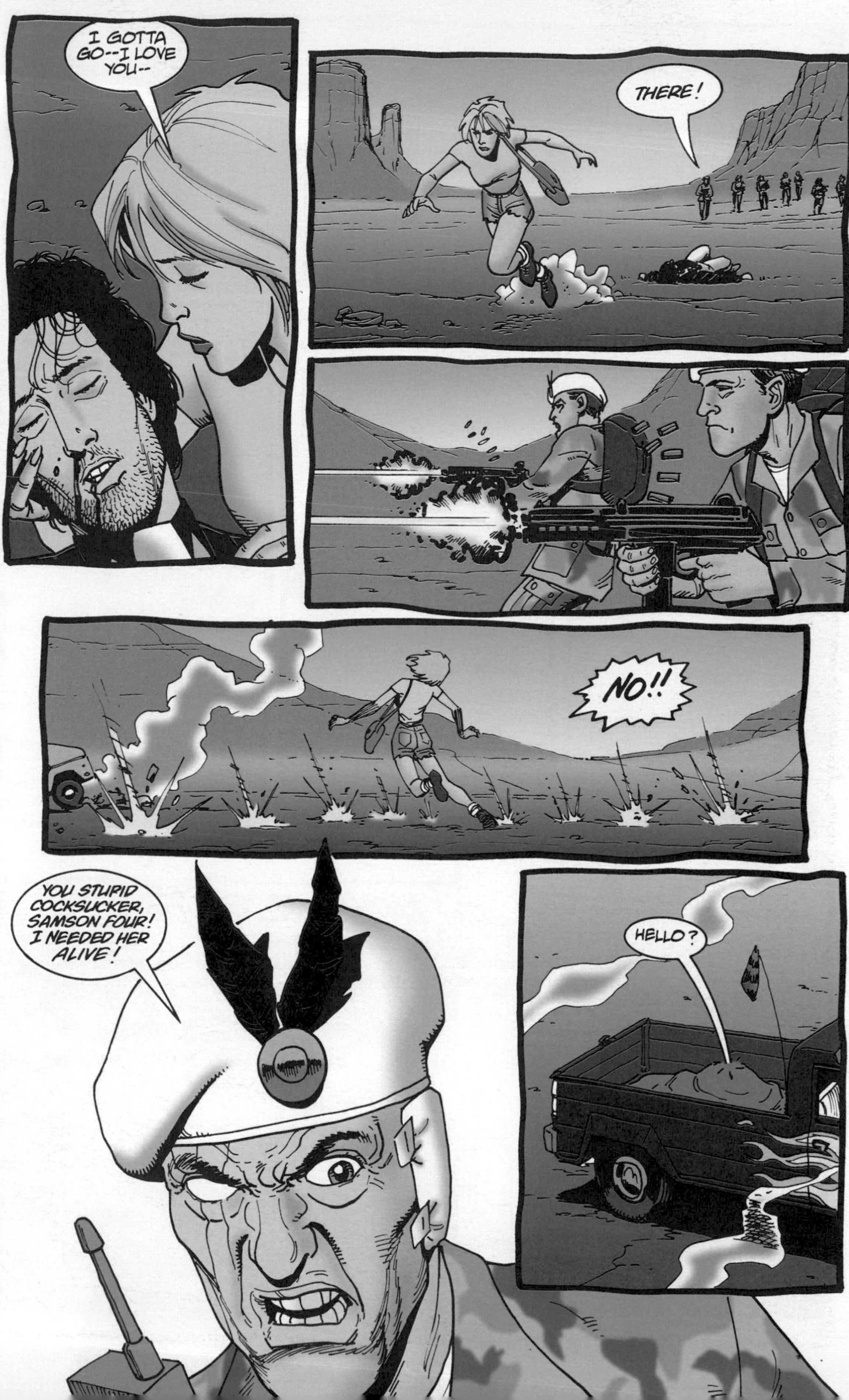
I GOTTA GO--I LOVE YOU--
THERE!
NO!!
YOU STUPID COCKSUCKER, SAMSON FOUR! I NEEDED HER ALIVE!
HELLO?

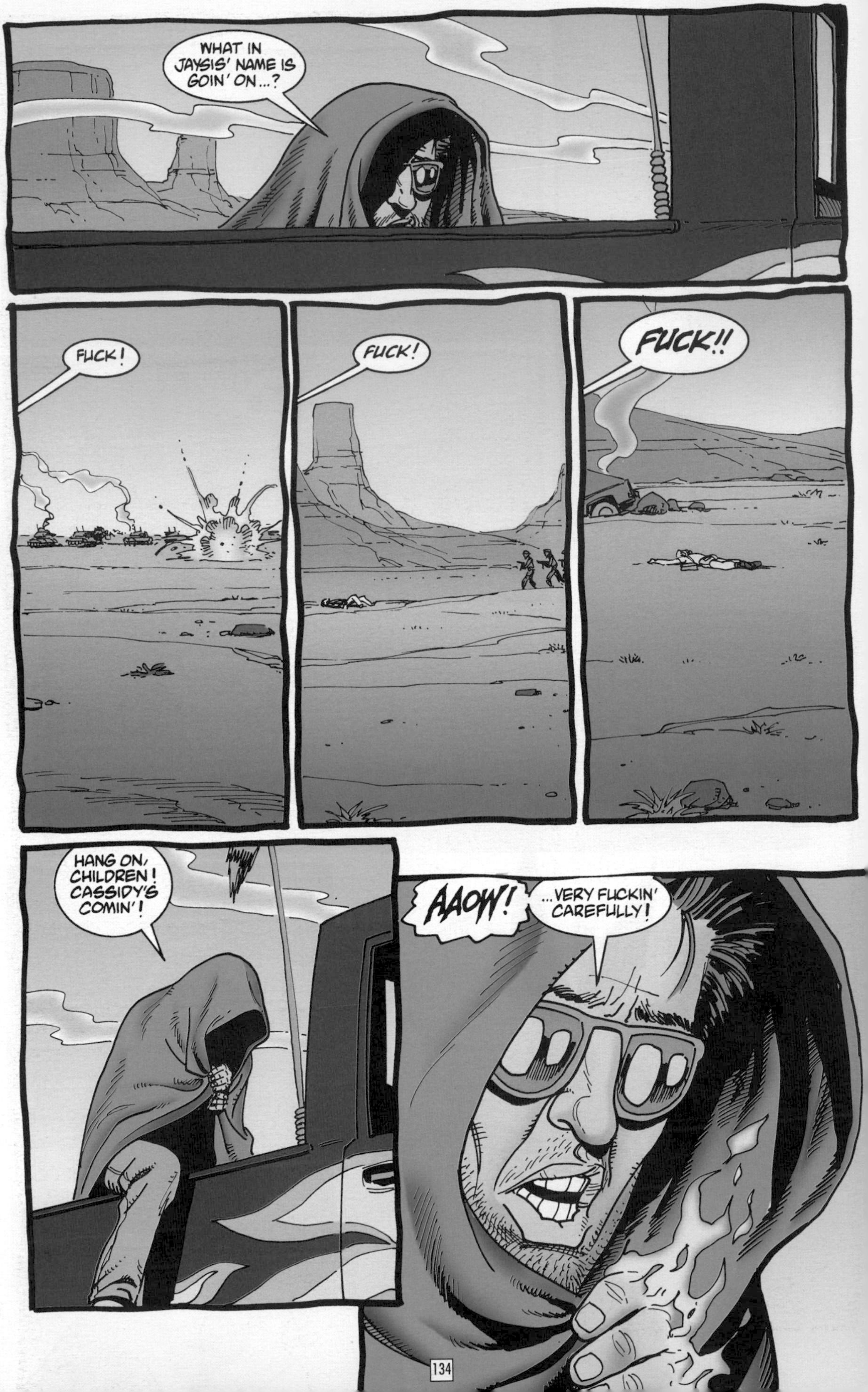
WHAT IN JAYSIS' NAME IS GOIN' ON...?
FUCK!
FUCK!
FUCK!!
HANG ON, CHILDREN! CASSIDY'S COMIN'!
AAOW!
...VERY FUCKIN' CAREFULLY!

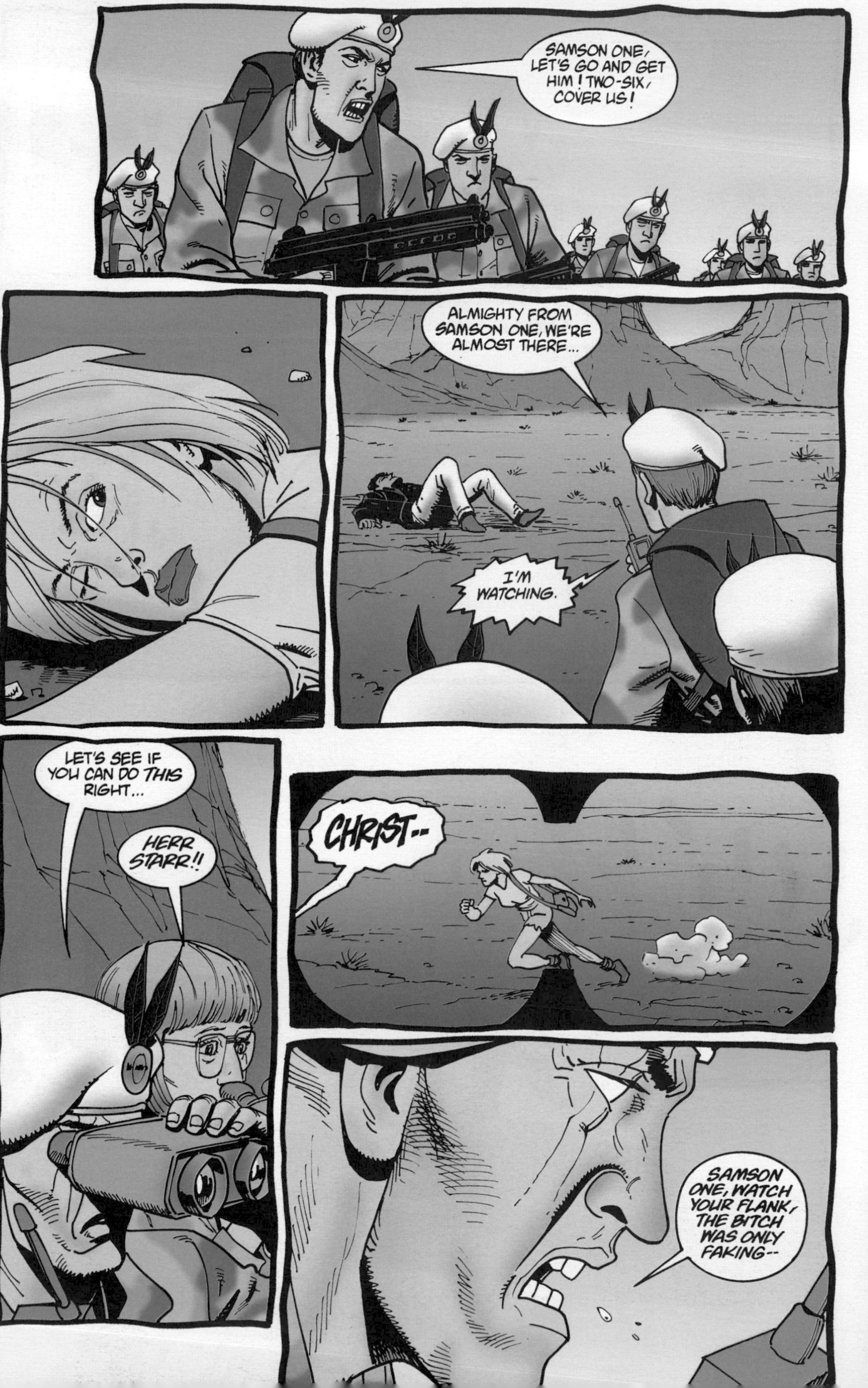
SAMSON ONE, LET'S GO AND GET HIM! TWO-SIX, COVER US!
ALMIGHTY FROM SAMSON ONE, WE'RE ALMOST THERE...
I'M WATCHING.
LET'S SEE IF YOU CAN DO THIS RIGHT...
HERR STARR!!
CHRIST--
SAMSON ONE, WATCH YOUR FLANK, THE BITCH WAS ONLY FAKING--

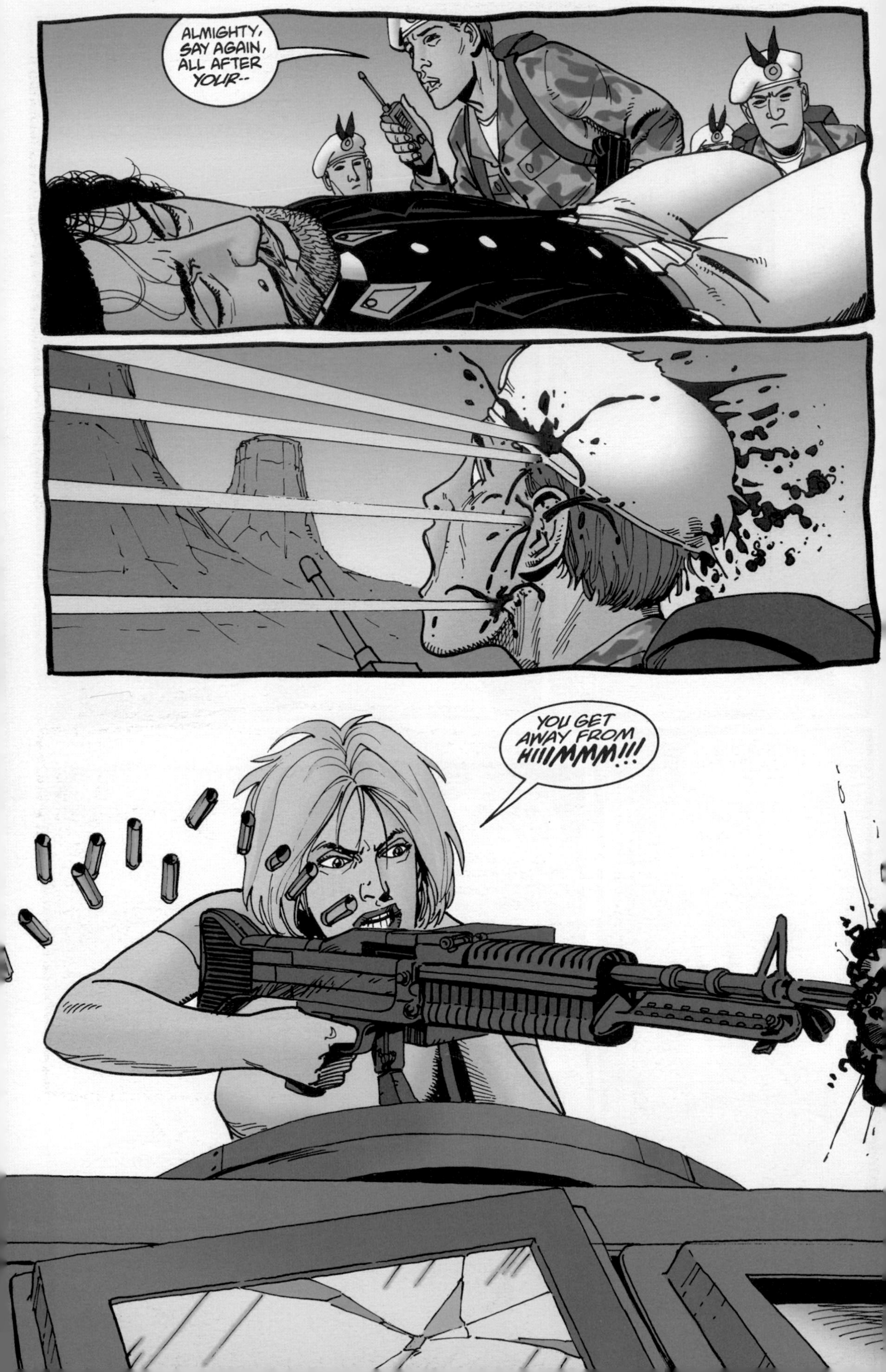
ALMIGHTY, SAY AGAIN, ALL AFTER YOUR--
YOU GET AWAY FROM HIIIMMM!!!

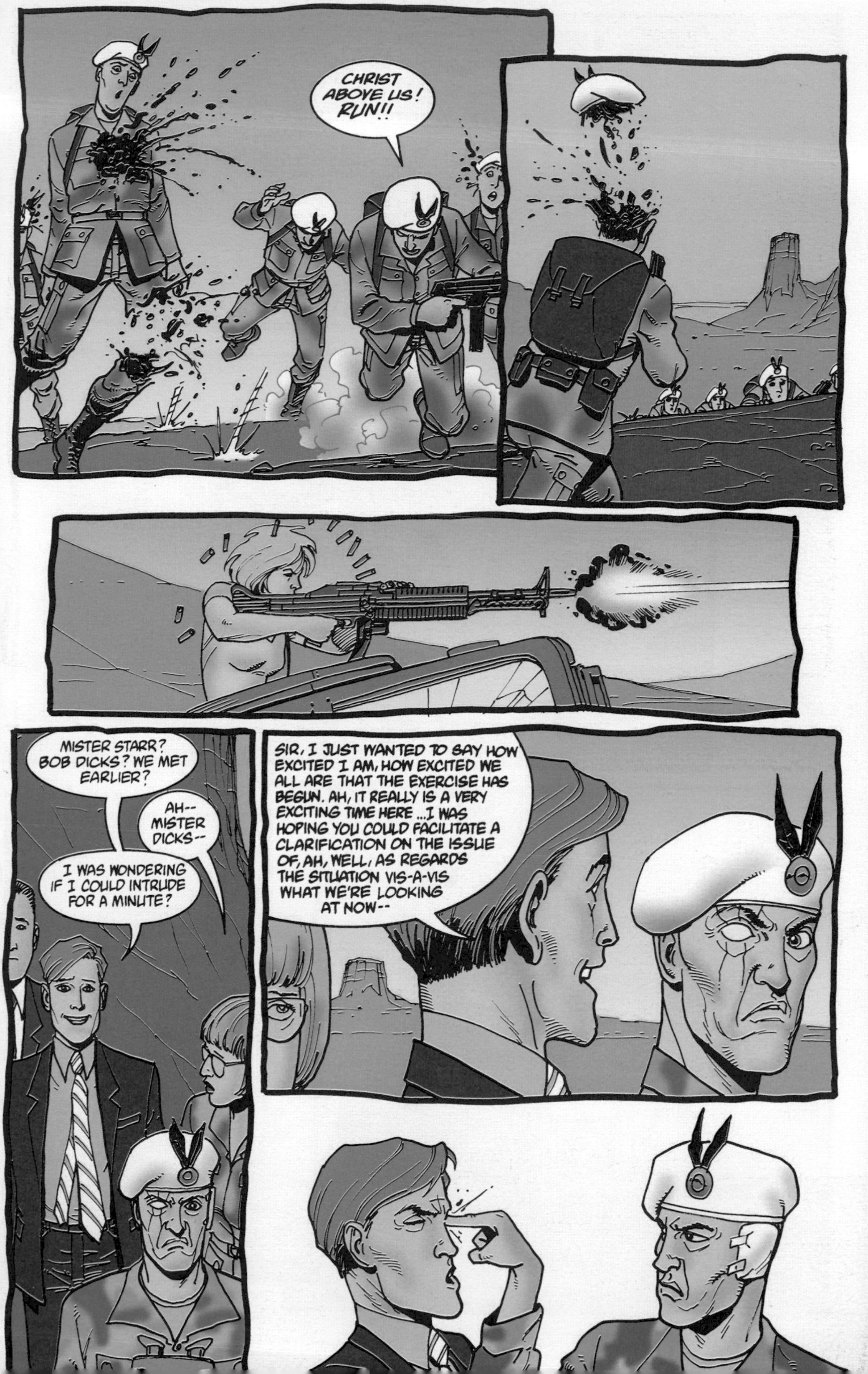
CHRIST ABOVE US! RUN!!
MISTER STARR? BOB DICKS? WE MET EARLIER?
AH-- MISTER DICKS--
I WAS WONDERING IF I COULD INTRUDE FOR A MINUTE?
SIR, I JUST WANTED TO SAY HOW EXCITED I AM, HOW EXCITED WE ALL ARE THAT THE EXERCISE HAS BEGUN. AH, IT REALLY IS A VERY EXCITING TIME HERE ...I WAS HOPING YOU COULD FACILITATE A CLARIFICATION ON THE ISSUE OF, AH, WELL, AS REGARDS THE SITUATION VIS-A-VIS WHAT WE'RE LOOKING AT NOW--

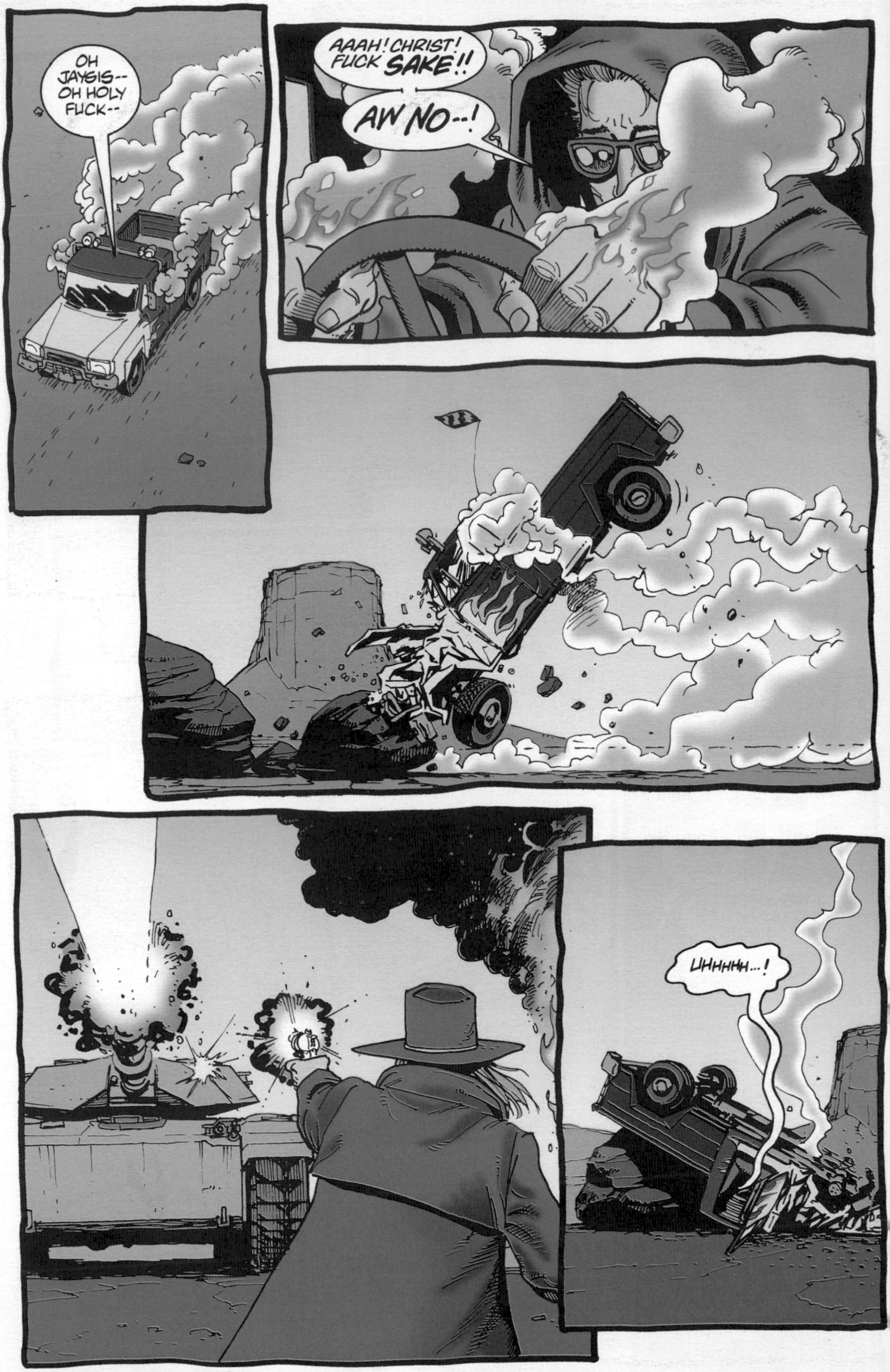
OH JAYSIS-- OH HOLY FUCK--
AAAH! CHRIST! FUCK SAKE!!
AW NO--!
UHHHHH...!

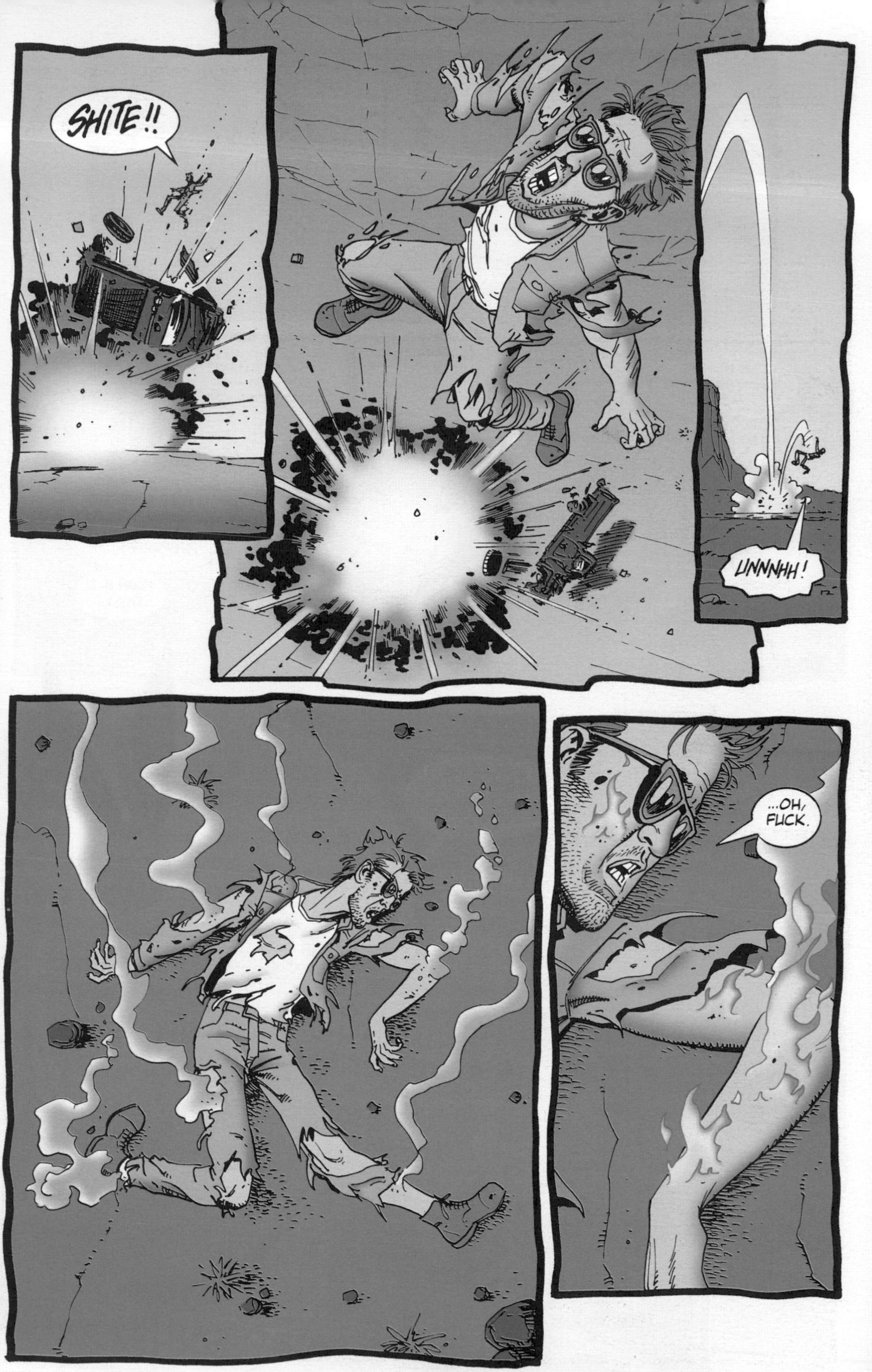
SHITE!!
UNNNHH!
...OH, FUCK.

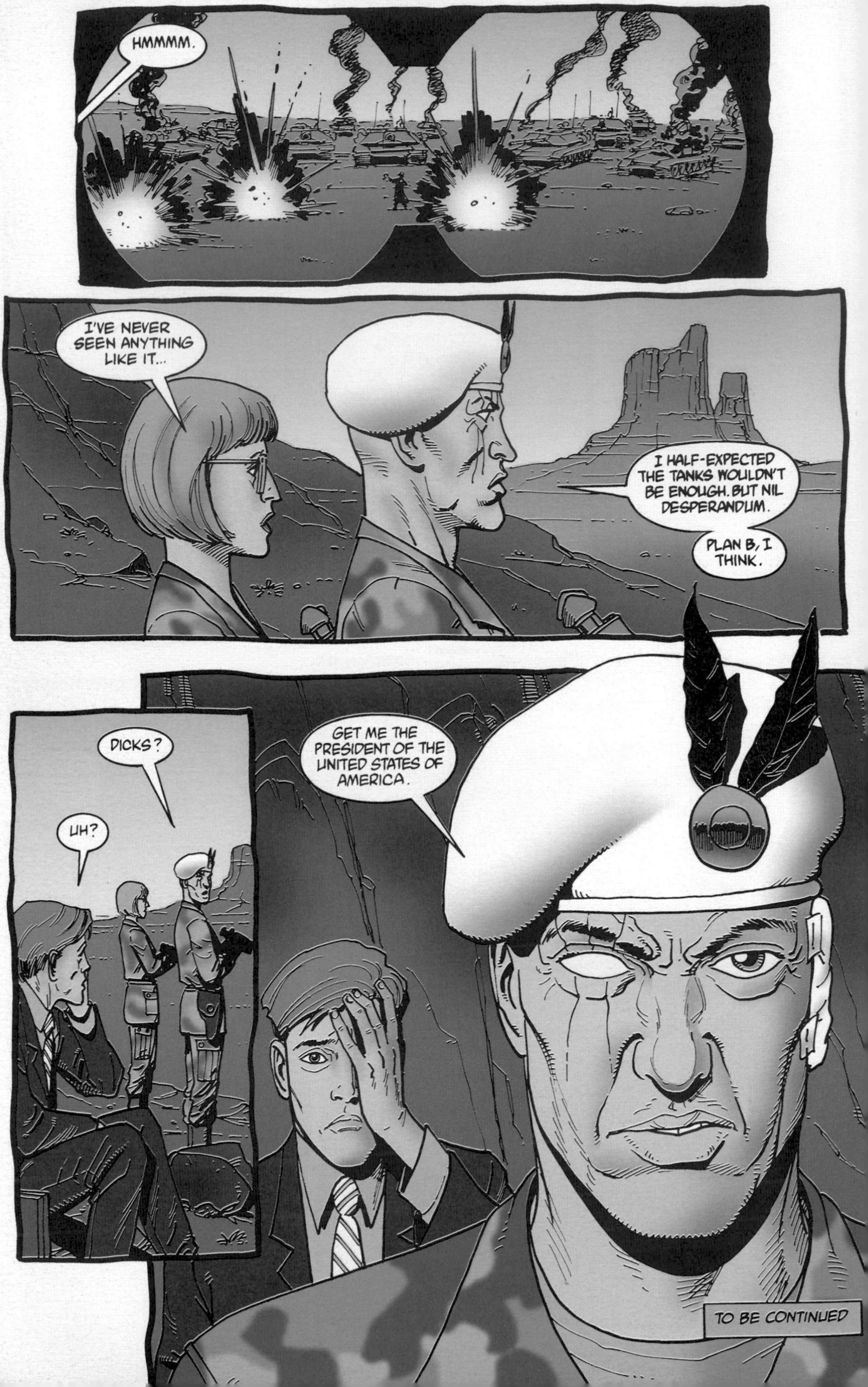
HMMMM.
I'VE NEVER SEEN ANYTHING LIKE IT...
I HALF-EXPECTED THE TANKS WOULDN'T BE ENOUGH. BUT NIL DESPERANDUM.
PLAN B, I THINK.
DICKS?
UH?
GET ME THE PRESIDENT OF THE UNITED STATES OF AMERICA.
TO BE CONTINUED

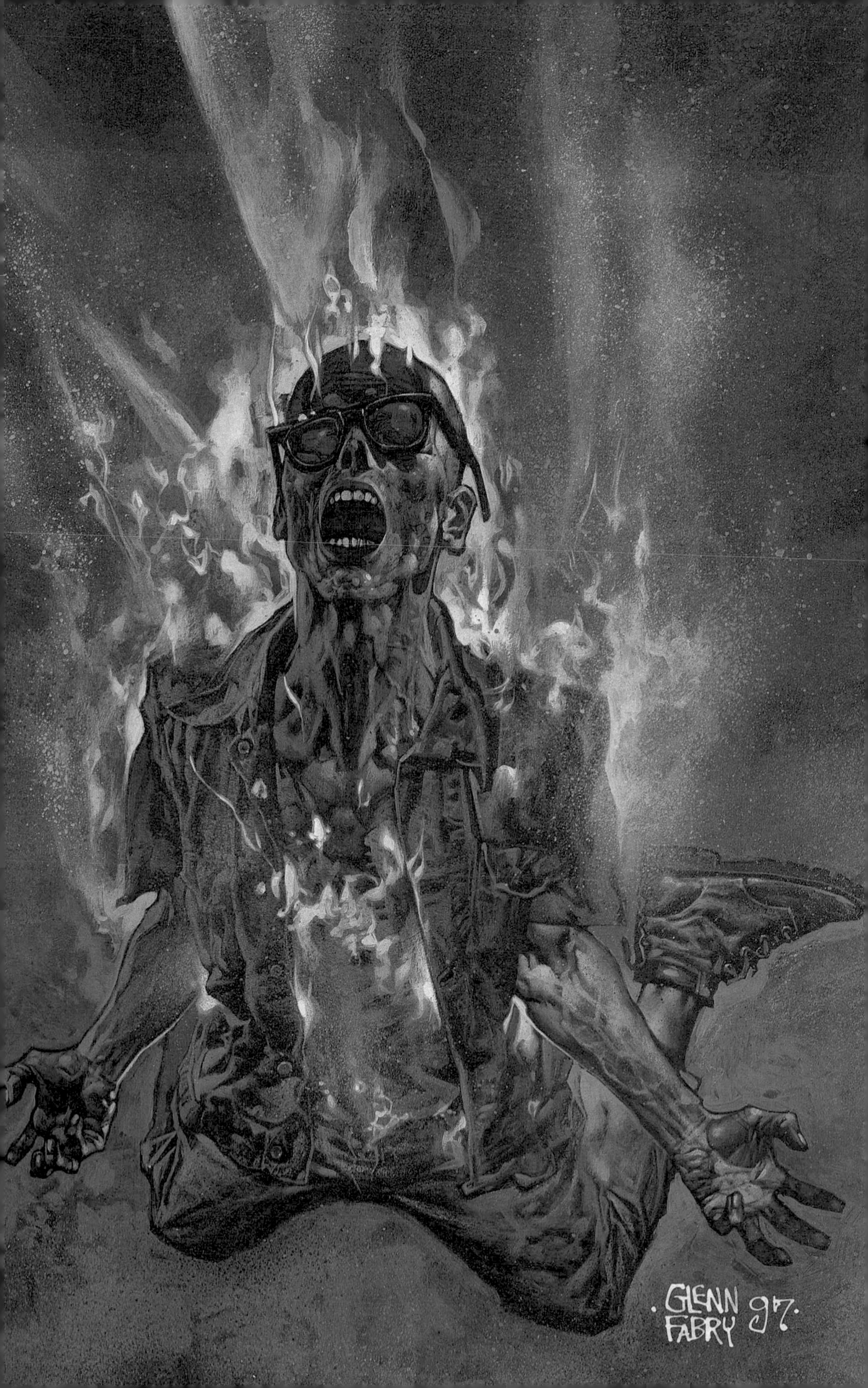
GLENN FABRY 97

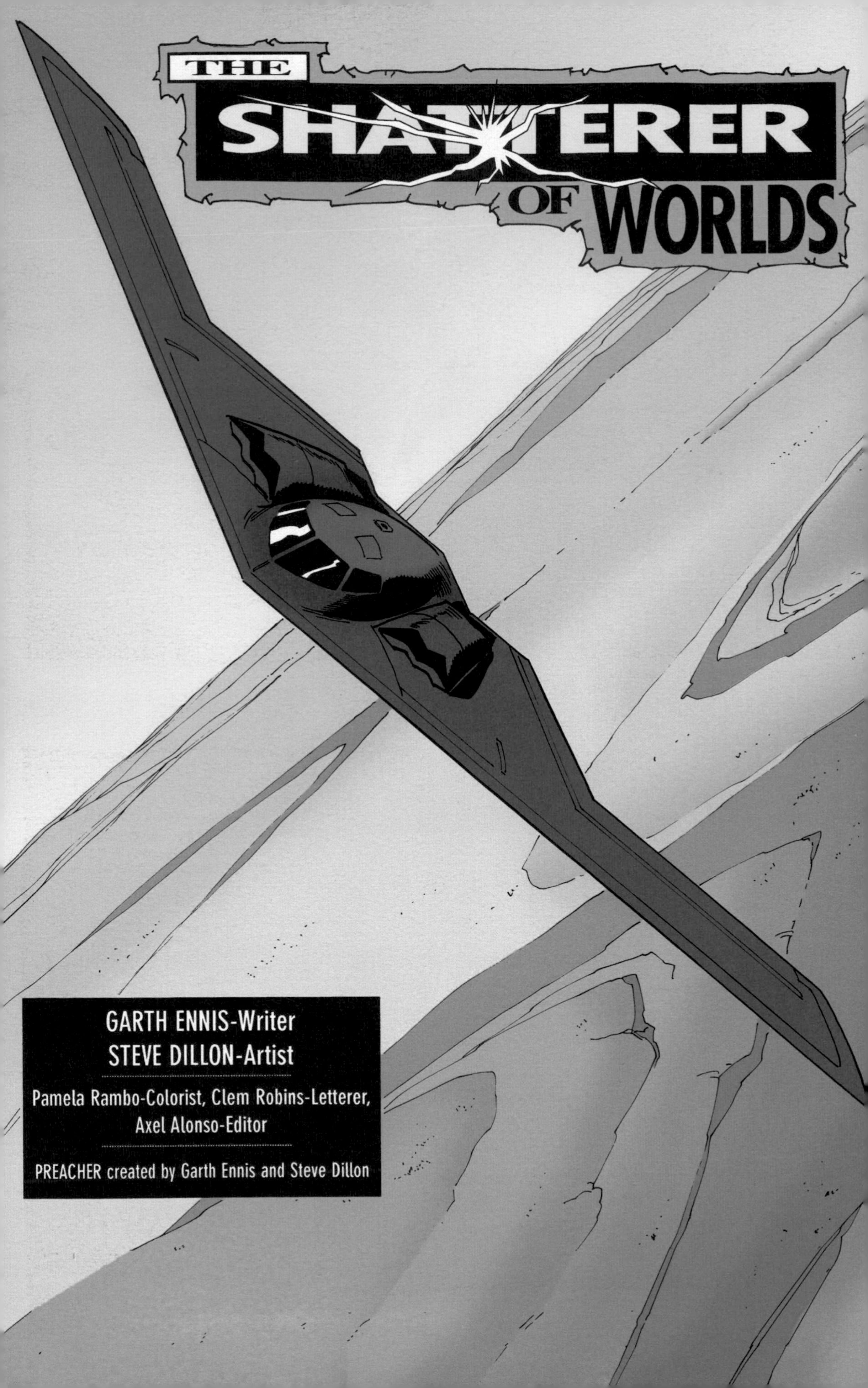
THE SHATTERER OF WORLDS
GARTH ENNIS-Writer
STEVE DILLON-Artist
Pamela Rambo-Colorist, Clem Robins-Letterer,
Axel Alonso-Editor
PREACHER created by Garth Ennis and Steve Dillon

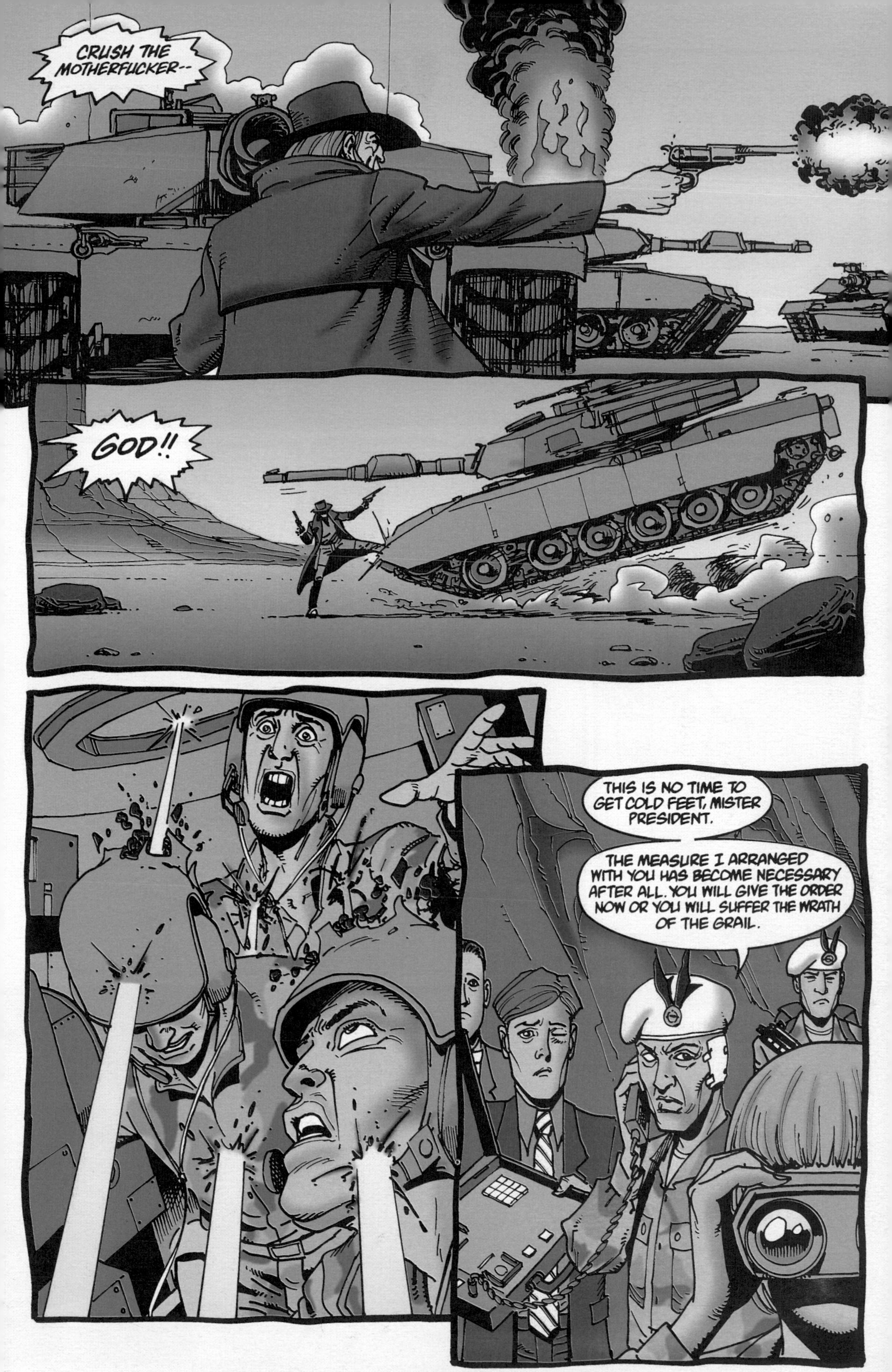
CRUSH THE MOTHERFUCKER--
GOD!!
THIS IS NO TIME TO GET COLD FEET, MISTER PRESIDENT.
THE MEASURE I ARRANGED WITH YOU HAS BECOME NECESSARY AFTER ALL. YOU WILL GIVE THE ORDER NOW OR YOU WILL SUFFER THE WRATH OF THE GRAIL.

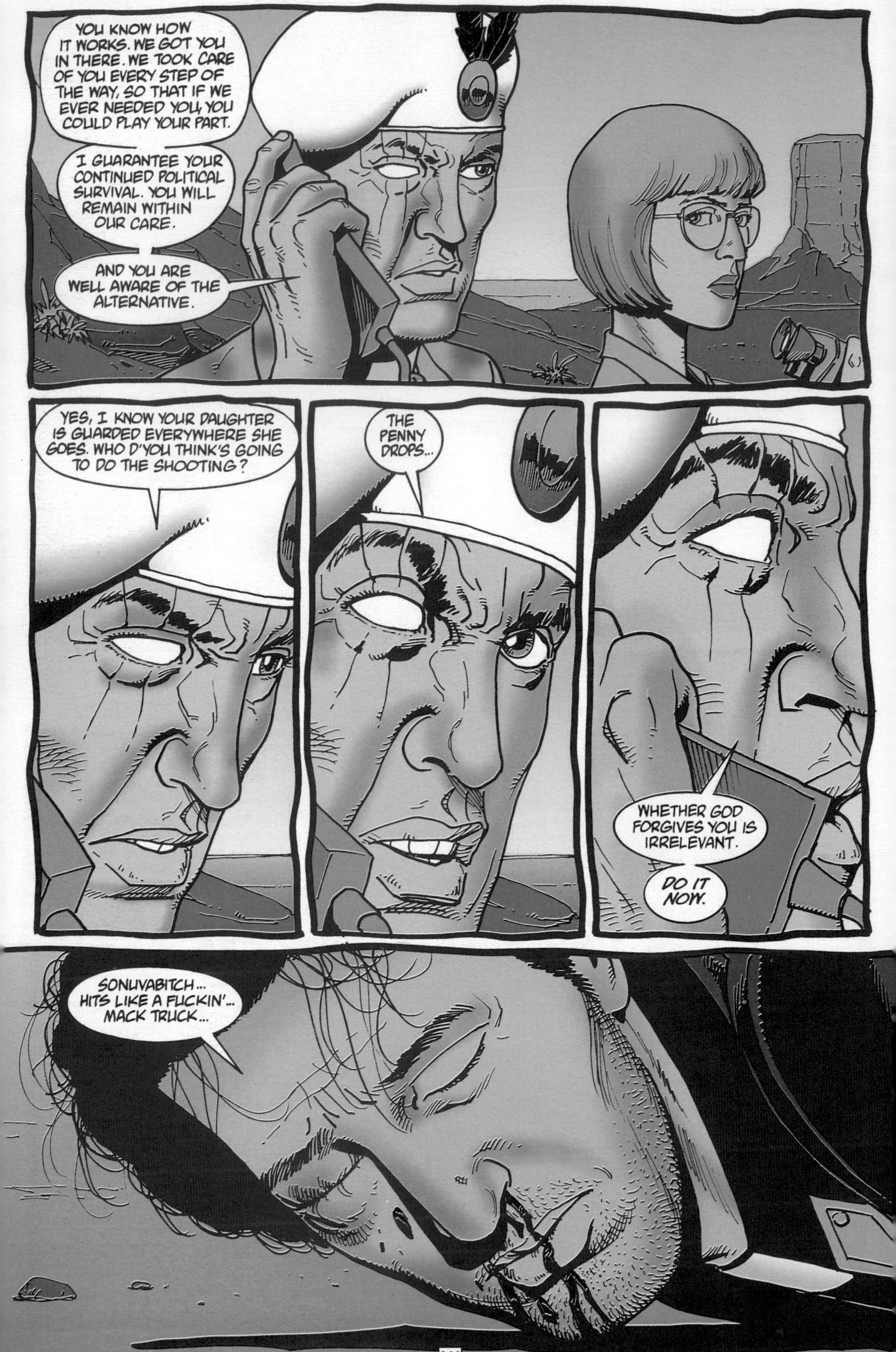
YOU KNOW HOW IT WORKS. WE GOT YOU IN THERE. WE TOOK CARE OF YOU EVERY STEP OF THE WAY, SO THAT IF WE EVER NEEDED YOU, YOU COULD PLAY YOUR PART.
I GUARANTEE YOUR CONTINUED POLITICAL SURVIVAL. YOU WILL REMAIN WITHIN OUR CARE.
AND YOU ARE WELL AWARE OF THE ALTERNATIVE.
YES, I KNOW YOUR DAUGHTER IS GUARDED EVERYWHERE SHE GOES. WHO D'YOU THINK'S GOING TO DO THE SHOOTING?
THE PENNY DROPS...
WHETHER GOD FORGIVES YOU IS IRRELEVANT.
DO IT NOW.
SONUVABITCH... HITS LIKE A FUCKIN'... MACK TRUCK...

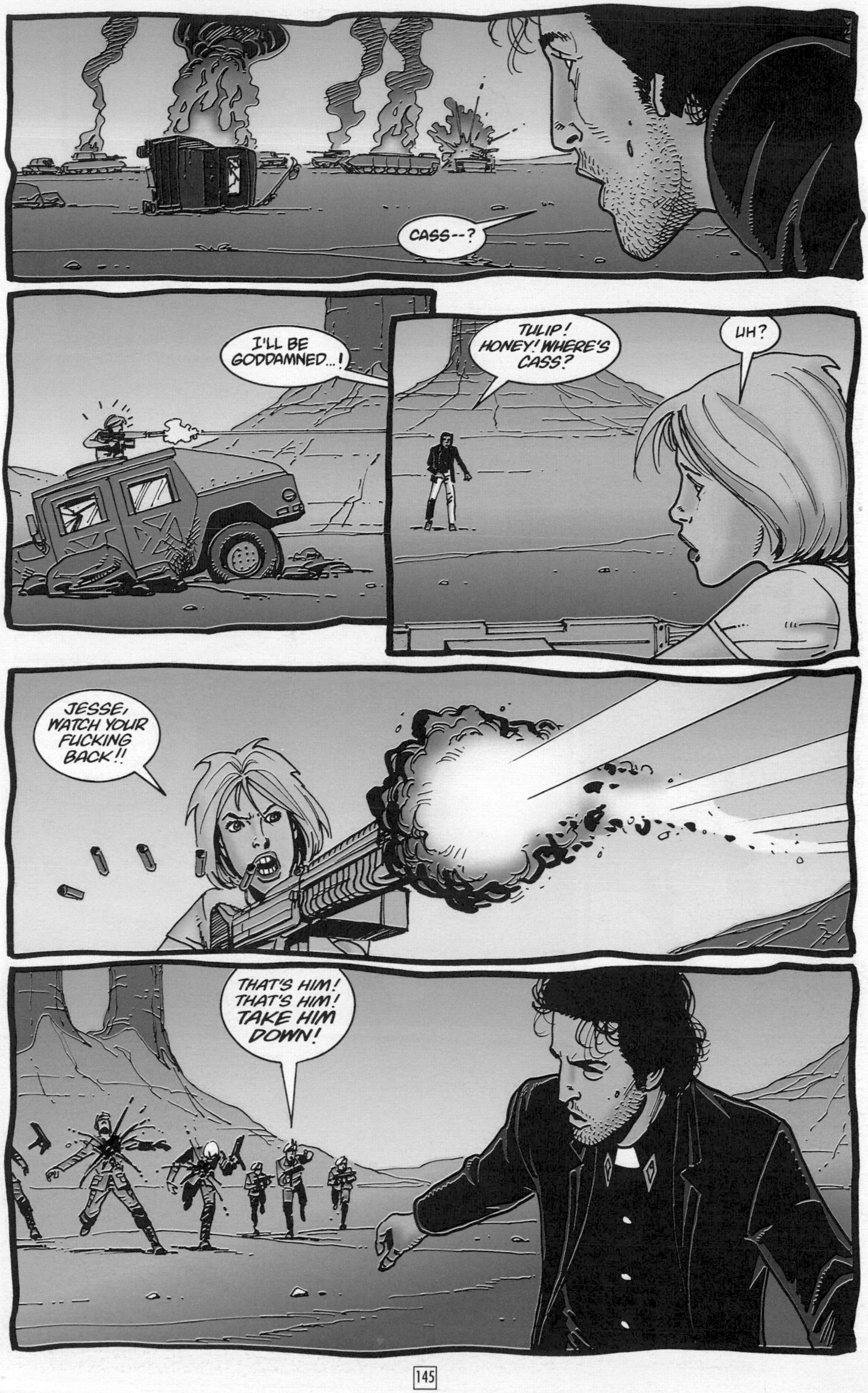
CASS--?
I'LL BE GODDAMNED...!
TULIP! HONEY! WHERE'S CASS?
UH?
JESSE, WATCH YOUR FUCKING BACK!!
THAT'S HIM! THAT'S HIM! TAKE HIM DOWN!

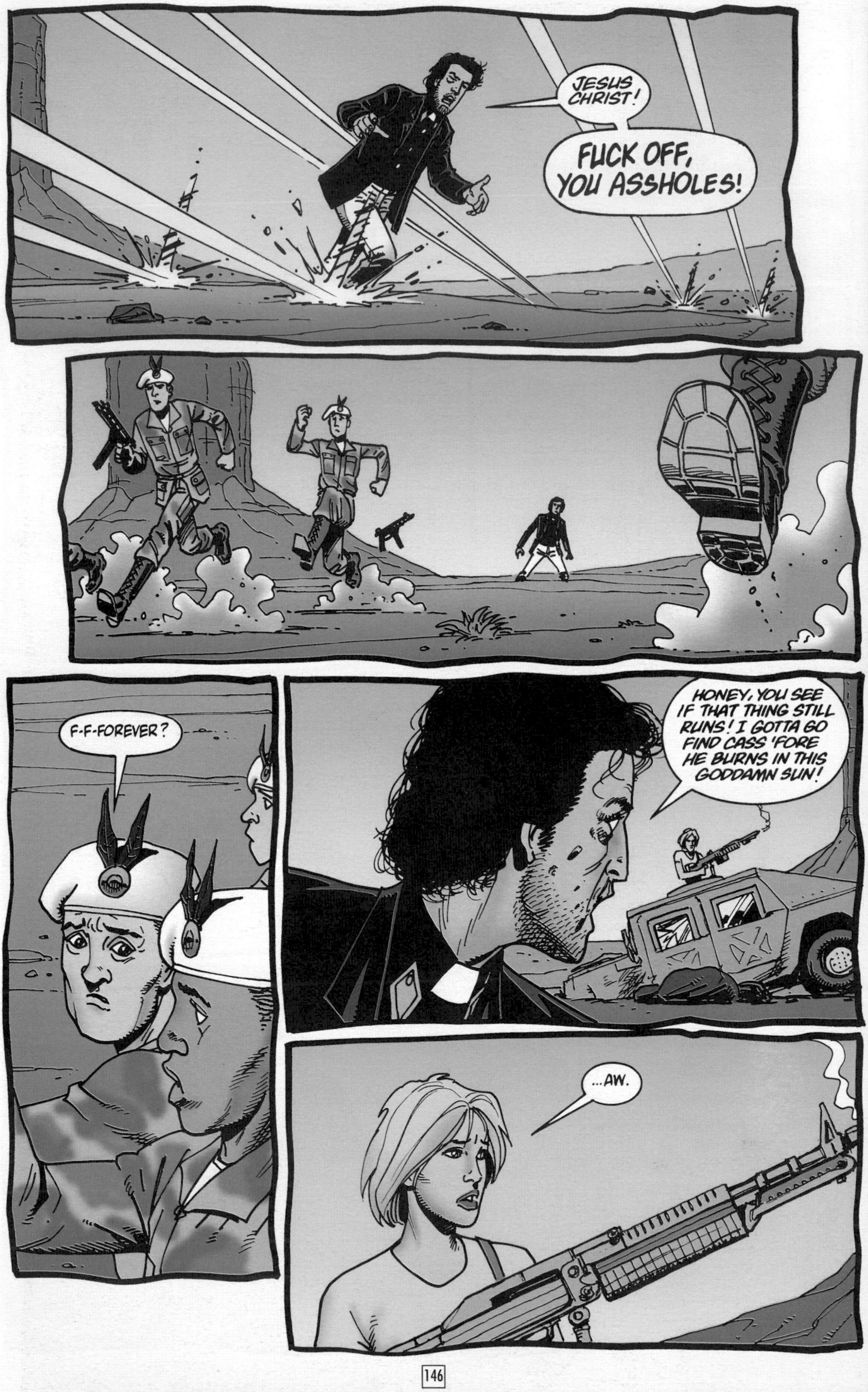
JESUS CHRIST!
FUCK OFF, YOU ASSHOLES!
F-F-FOREVER?
HONEY, YOU SEE IF THAT THING STILL RUNS! I GOTTA GO FIND CASS 'FORE HE BURNS IN THIS GODDAMN SUN!
...AW.

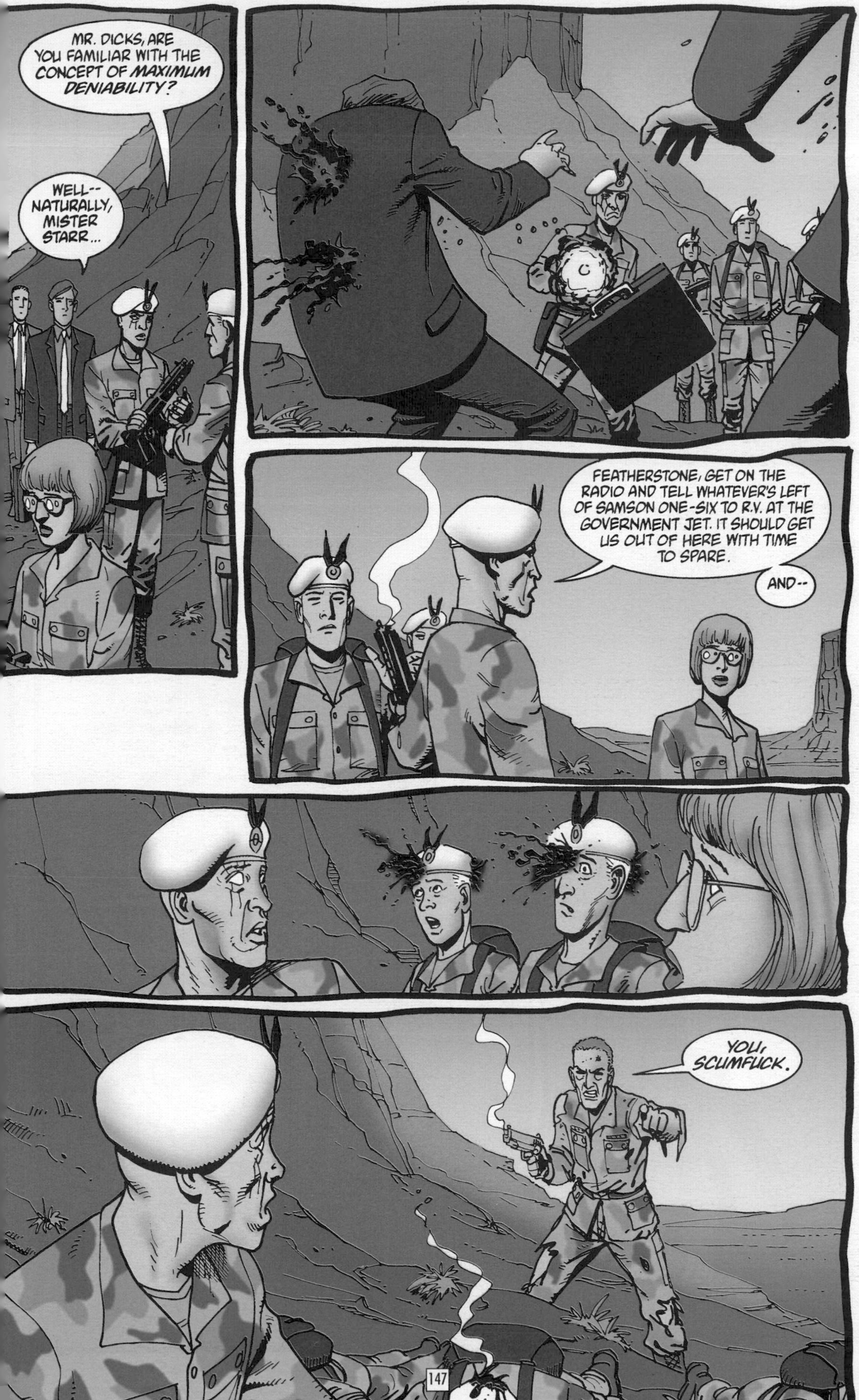
MR. DICKS, ARE YOU FAMILIAR WITH THE CONCEPT OF MAXIMUM DENIABILITY?
WELL-- NATURALLY, MISTER STARR...
FEATHERSTONE, GET ON THE RADIO AND TELL WHATEVER'S LEFT OF SAMSON ONE-SIX TO R.V. AT THE GOVERNMENT JET. IT SHOULD GET US OUT OF HERE WITH TIME TO SPARE.
AND--
YOU, SCUMFUCK.

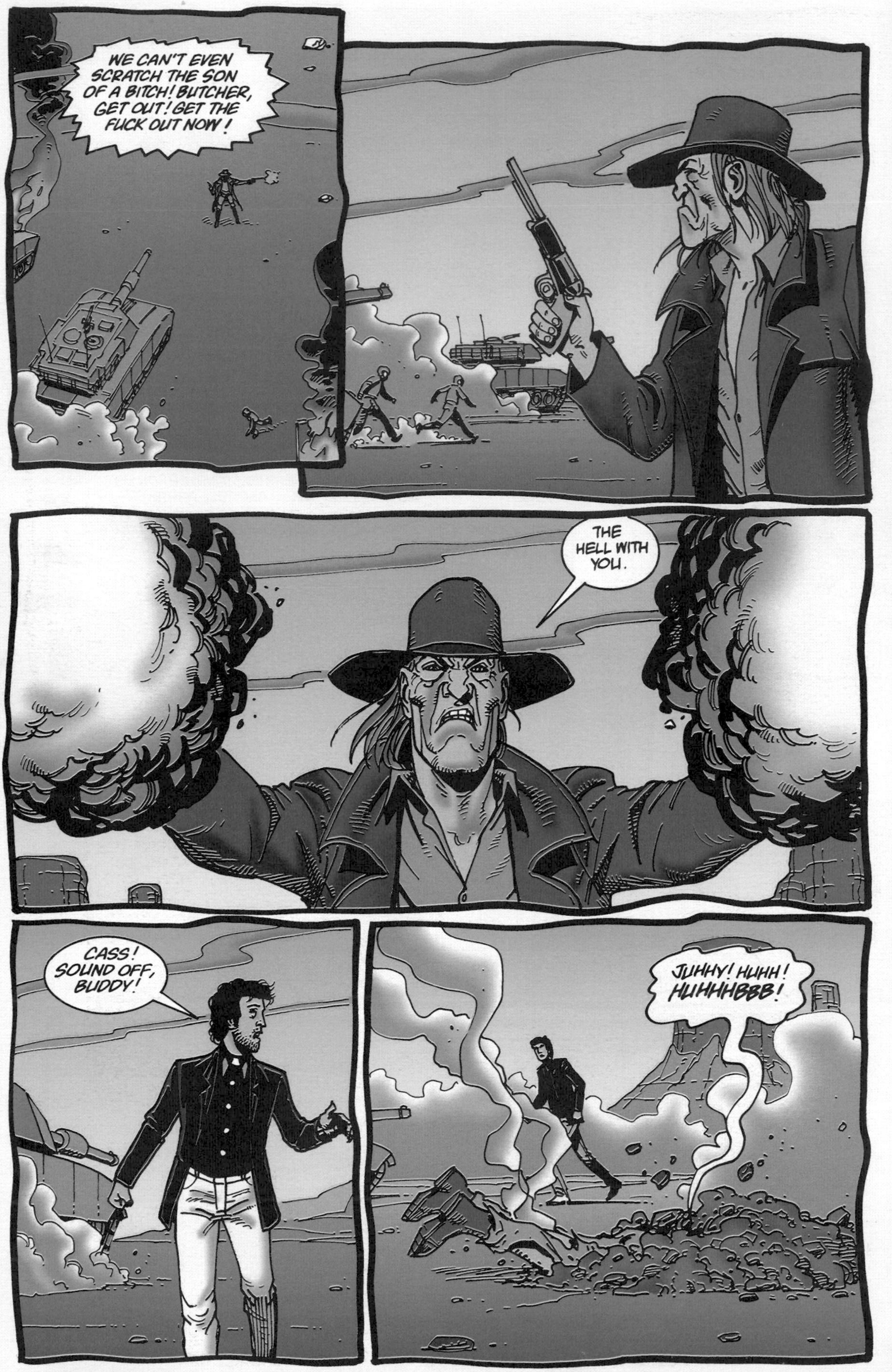
WE CAN'T EVEN SCRATCH THE SON OF A BITCH! BUTCHER, GET OUT! GET THE FUCK OUT NOW!
THE HELL WITH YOU.
CASS! SOUND OFF, BUDDY!
JUHHY! HUHH! HUHHHBBB!

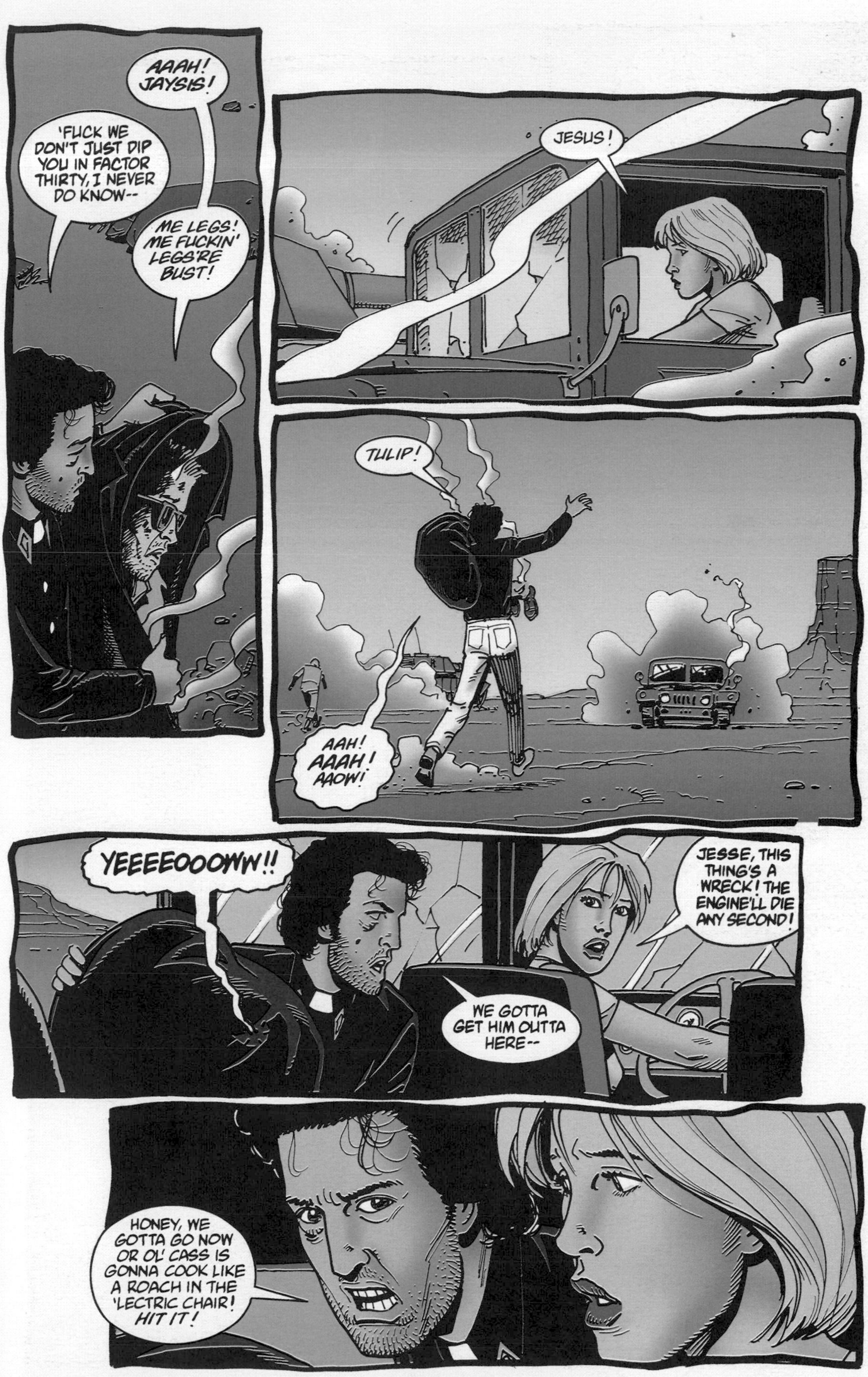
AAAH! JAYSIS!
'FUCK WE DON'T JUST DIP YOU IN FACTOR THIRTY, I NEVER DO KNOW--
ME LEGS! ME FUCKIN' LEGS'RE BUST!
JESUS!
TULIP!
AAH! AAAH! AAOW!
YEEEEOOOWW!!
JESSE, THIS THING'S A WRECK! THE ENGINE'LL DIE ANY SECOND!
WE GOTTA GET HIM OUTTA HERE--
HONEY, WE GOTTA GO NOW OR OL' CASS IS GONNA COOK LIKE A ROACH IN THE 'LECTRIC CHAIR! HIT IT!

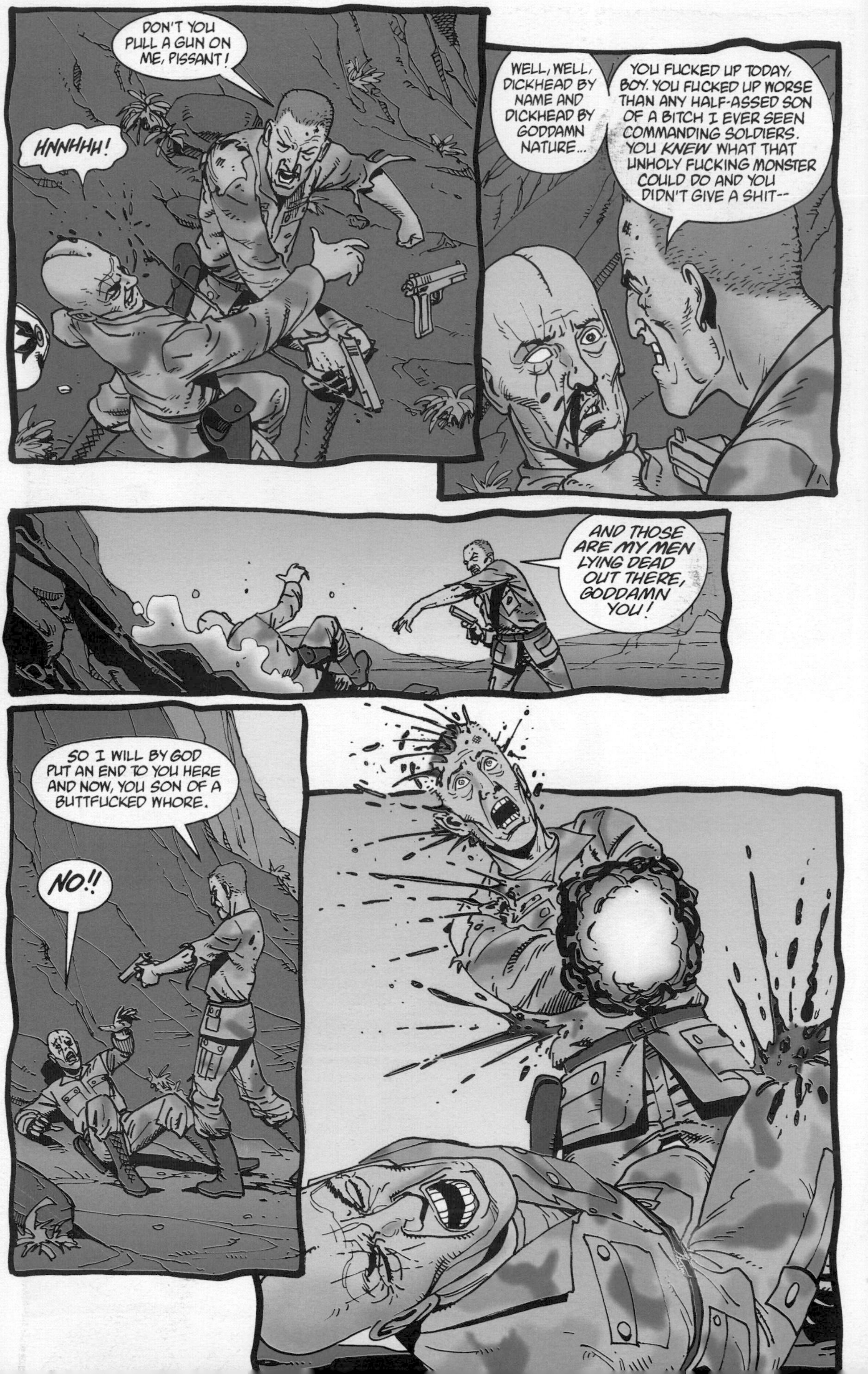
DON'T YOU PULL A GUN ON ME, PISSANT!
HNNHHH!
WELL, WELL, DICKHEAD BY NAME AND DICKHEAD BY GODDAMN NATURE...
YOU FUCKED UP TODAY, BOY. YOU FUCKED UP WORSE THAN ANY HALF-ASSED SON OF A BITCH I EVER SEEN COMMANDING SOLDIERS. YOU KNEW WHAT THAT UNHOLY FUCKING MONSTER COULD DO AND YOU DIDN'T GIVE A SHIT--
AND THOSE ARE MY MEN LYING DEAD OUT THERE, GODDAMN YOU!
SO I WILL BY GOD PUT AN END TO YOU HERE AND NOW, YOU SON OF A BUTTFUCKED WHORE.
NO!!

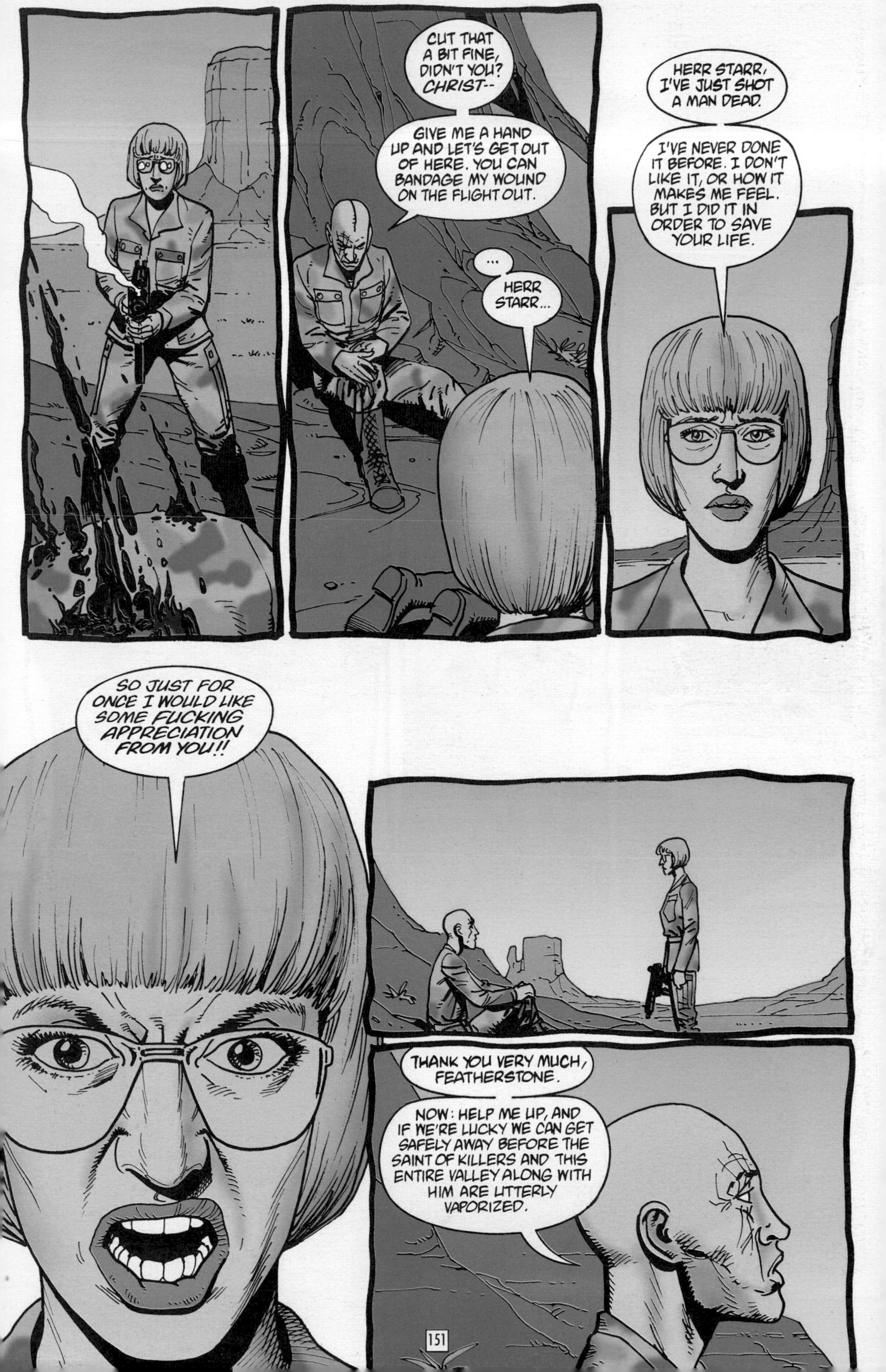
CUT THAT A BIT FINE, DIDN'T YOU? CHRIST--
GIVE ME A HAND UP AND LET'S GET OUT OF HERE. YOU CAN BANDAGE MY WOUND ON THE FLIGHT OUT.
...
HERR STARR...
HERR STARR, I'VE JUST SHOT A MAN DEAD.
I'VE NEVER DONE IT BEFORE. I DON'T LIKE IT, OR HOW IT MAKES ME FEEL. BUT I DID IT IN ORDER TO SAVE YOUR LIFE.
SO JUST FOR ONCE I WOULD LIKE SOME FUCKING APPRECIATION FROM YOU!!
THANK YOU VERY MUCH, FEATHERSTONE.
NOW: HELP ME UP, AND IF WE'RE LUCKY WE CAN GET SAFELY AWAY BEFORE THE SAINT OF KILLERS AND THIS ENTIRE VALLEY ALONG WITH HIM ARE UTTERLY VAPORIZED.

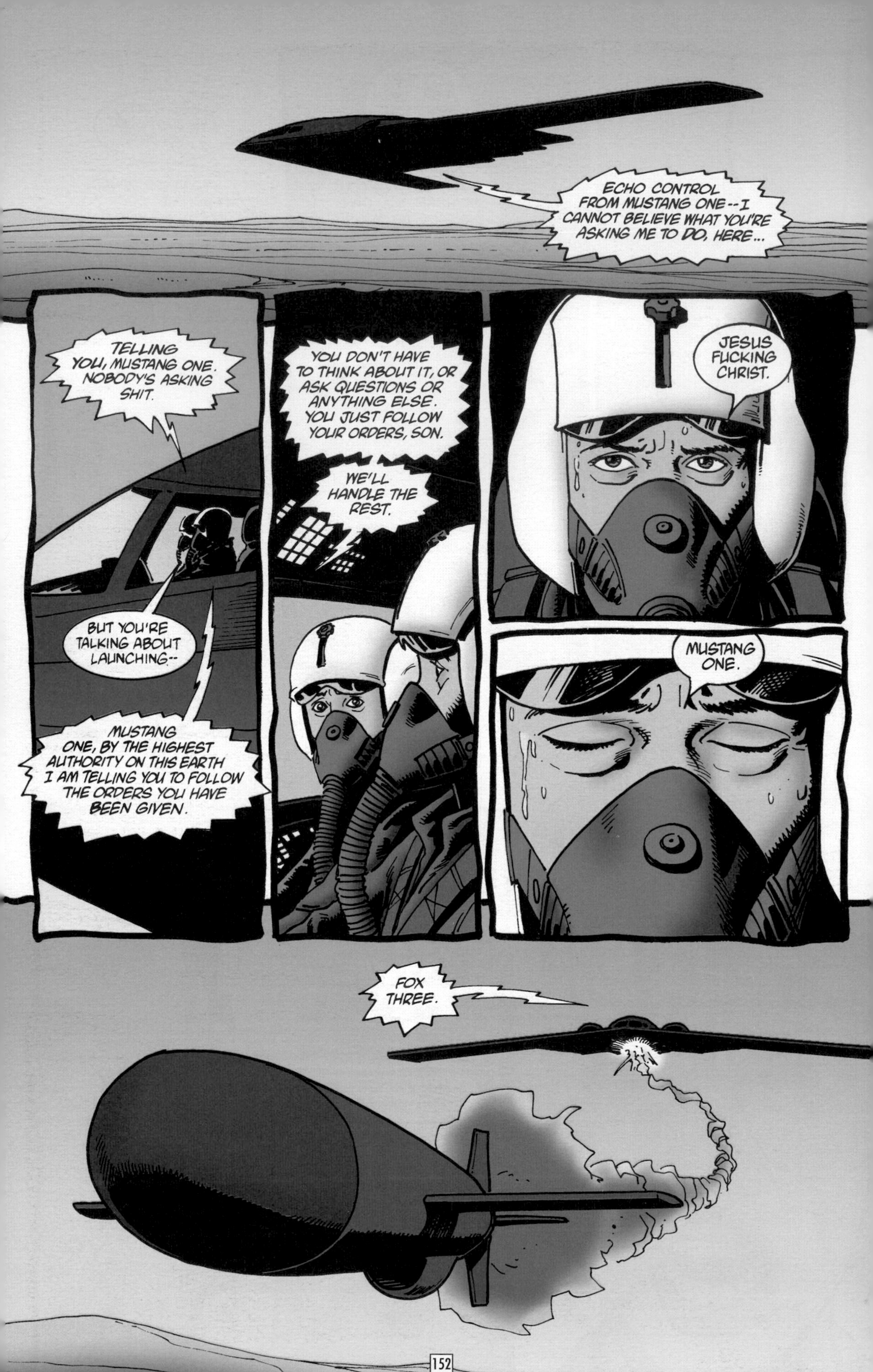
ECHO CONTROL FROM MUSTANG ONE--I CANNOT BELIEVE WHAT YOU'RE ASKING ME TO DO, HERE...
TELLING YOU, MUSTANG ONE. NOBODY'S ASKING SHIT.
BUT YOU'RE TALKING ABOUT LAUNCHING--
MUSTANG ONE, BY THE HIGHEST AUTHORITY ON THIS EARTH I AM TELLING YOU TO FOLLOW THE ORDERS YOU HAVE BEEN GIVEN.
YOU DON'T HAVE TO THINK ABOUT IT, OR ASK QUESTIONS OR ANYTHING ELSE. YOU JUST FOLLOW YOUR ORDERS, SON.
WE'LL HANDLE THE REST.
JESUS FUCKING CHRIST.
MUSTANG ONE.
FOX THREE.

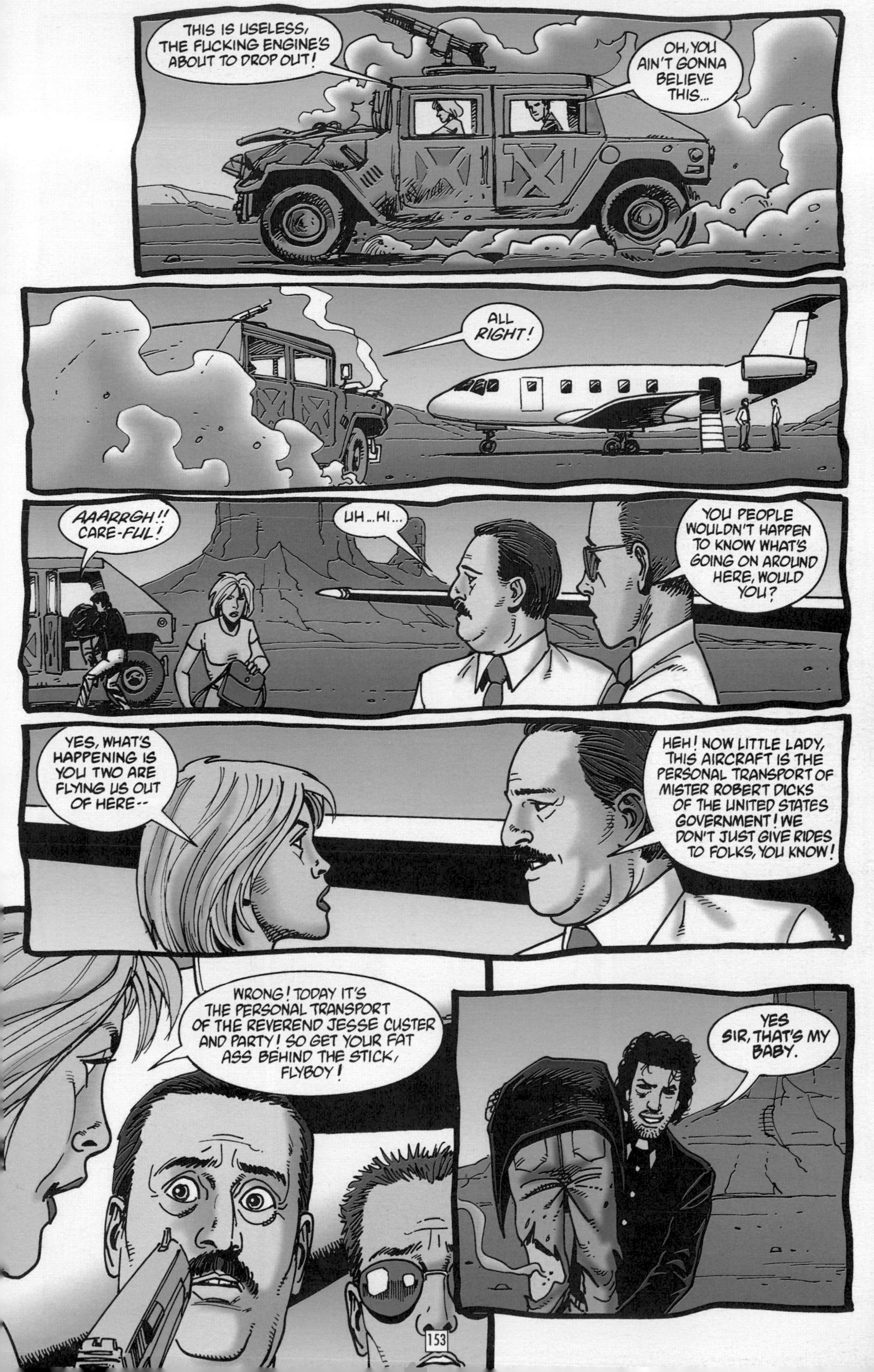
THIS IS USELESS, THE FUCKING ENGINE'S ABOUT TO DROP OUT!
OH, YOU AIN'T GONNA BELIEVE THIS...
ALL RIGHT!
AAARRGH!! CARE-FUL!
UH...HI...
YOU PEOPLE WOULDN'T HAPPEN TO KNOW WHAT'S GOING ON AROUND HERE, WOULD YOU?
YES, WHAT'S HAPPENING IS YOU TWO ARE FLYING US OUT OF HERE--
HEH! NOW LITTLE LADY, THIS AIRCRAFT IS THE PERSONAL TRANSPORT OF MISTER ROBERT DICKS OF THE UNITED STATES GOVERNMENT! WE DON'T JUST GIVE RIDES TO FOLKS, YOU KNOW!
WRONG! TODAY IT'S THE PERSONAL TRANSPORT OF THE REVEREND JESSE CUSTER AND PARTY! SO GET YOUR FAT ASS BEHIND THE STICK, FLYBOY!
YES SIR, THAT'S MY BABY.

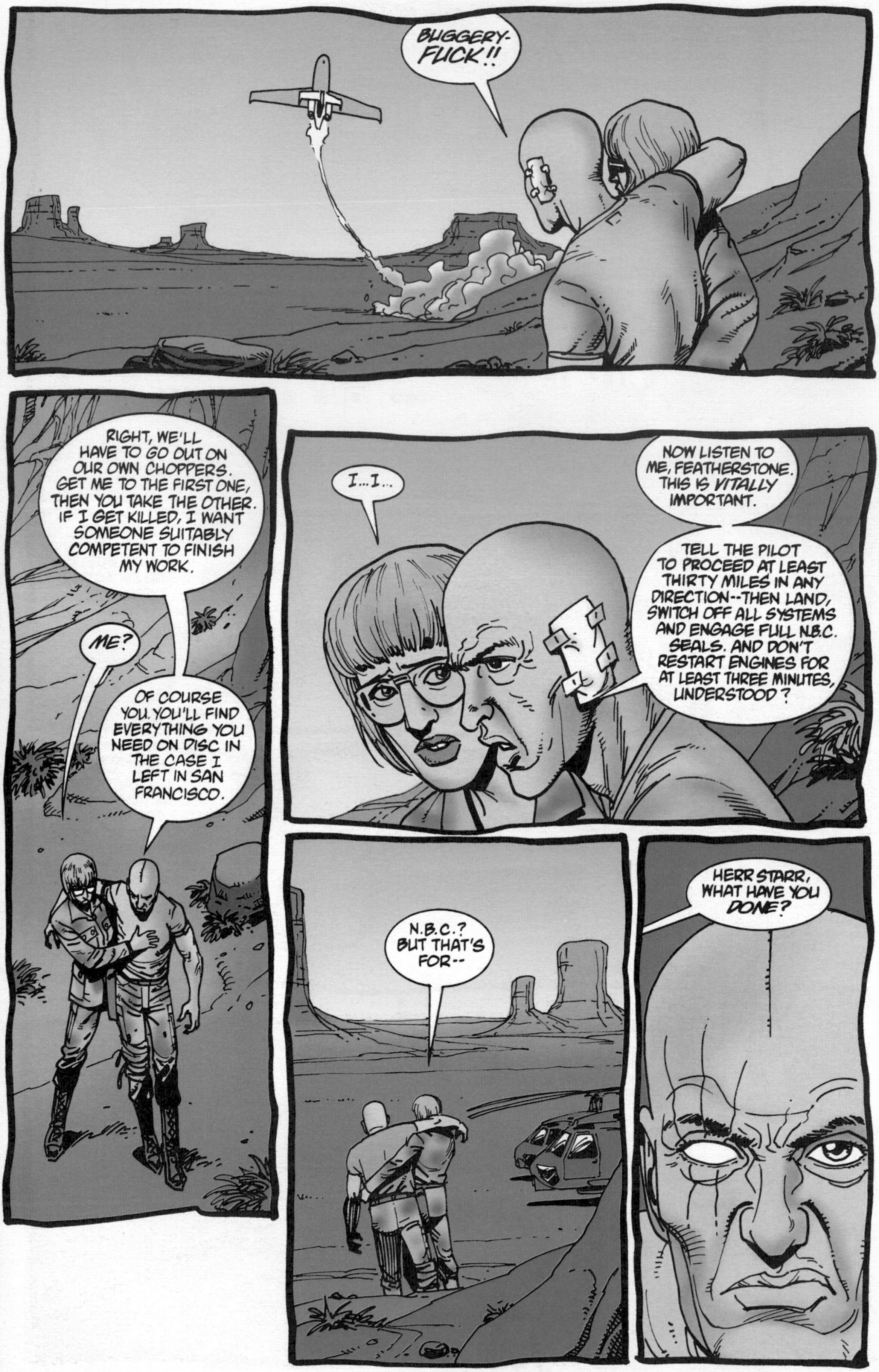

BUGGERY-FUCK!!
RIGHT, WE'LL HAVE TO GO OUT ON OUR OWN CHOPPERS. GET ME TO THE FIRST ONE, THEN YOU TAKE THE OTHER. IF I GET KILLED, I WANT SOMEONE SUITABLY COMPETENT TO FINISH MY WORK.
ME?
OF COURSE YOU. YOU'LL FIND EVERYTHING YOU NEED ON DISC IN THE CASE I LEFT IN SAN FRANCISCO.
I...I...
NOW LISTEN TO ME, FEATHERSTONE. THIS IS VITALLY IMPORTANT.
TELL THE PILOT TO PROCEED AT LEAST THIRTY MILES IN ANY DIRECTION--THEN LAND, SWITCH OFF ALL SYSTEMS AND ENGAGE FULL N.B.C. SEALS. AND DON'T RESTART ENGINES FOR AT LEAST THREE MINUTES, UNDERSTOOD?
N.B.C.? BUT THAT'S FOR--
HERR STARR, WHAT HAVE YOU DONE?

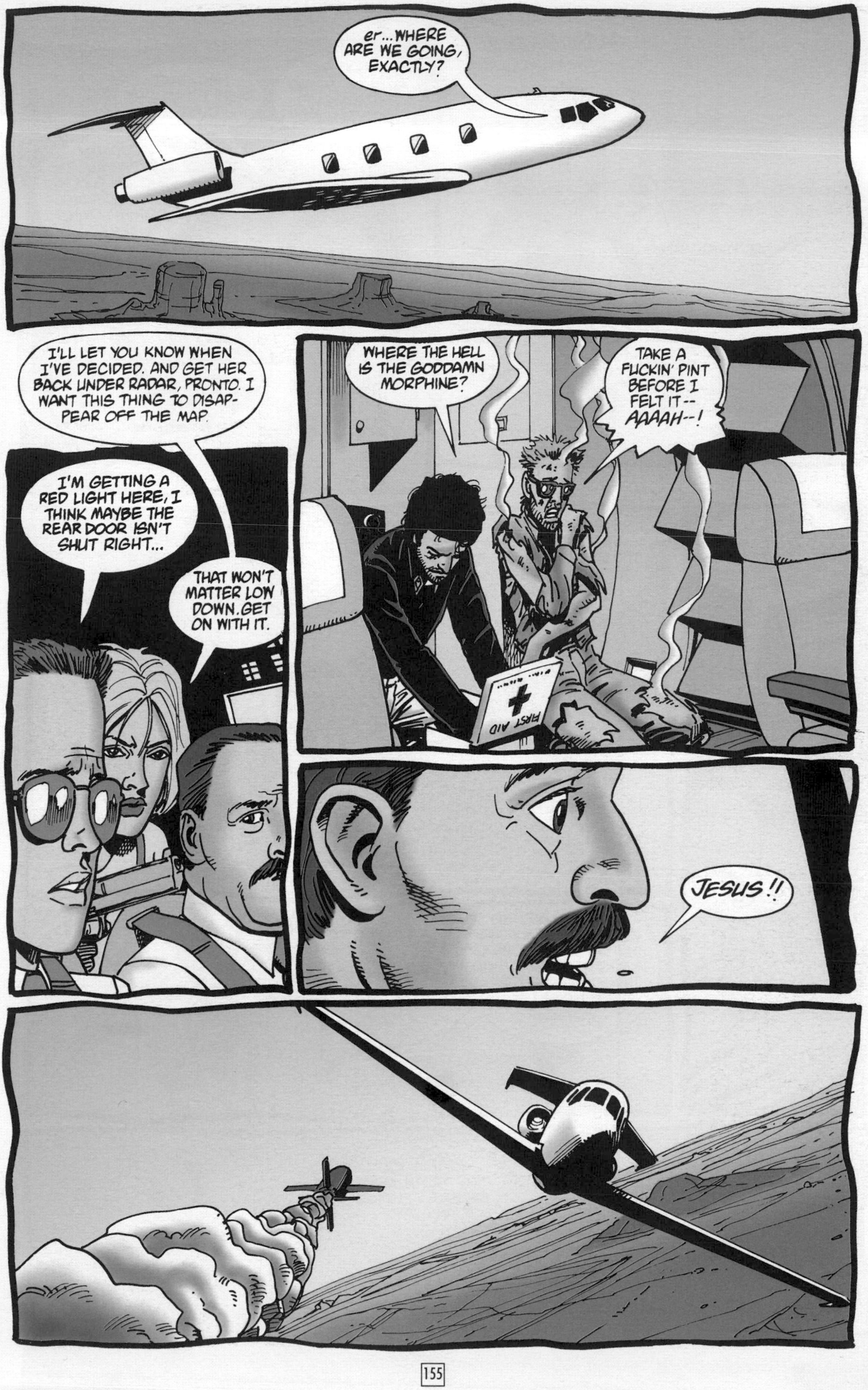
er... WHERE ARE WE GOING, EXACTLY?
I'LL LET YOU KNOW WHEN I'VE DECIDED. AND GET HER BACK UNDER RADAR, PRONTO. I WANT THIS THING TO DISAPPEAR OFF THE MAP.
WHERE THE HELL IS THE GODDAMN MORPHINE?
TAKE A FUCKIN' PINT BEFORE I FELT IT -- AAAAH--!
FIRST AID
I'M GETTING A RED LIGHT HERE, I THINK MAYBE THE REAR DOOR ISN'T SHUT RIGHT...
THAT WON'T MATTER LOW DOWN. GET ON WITH IT.
JESUS!!

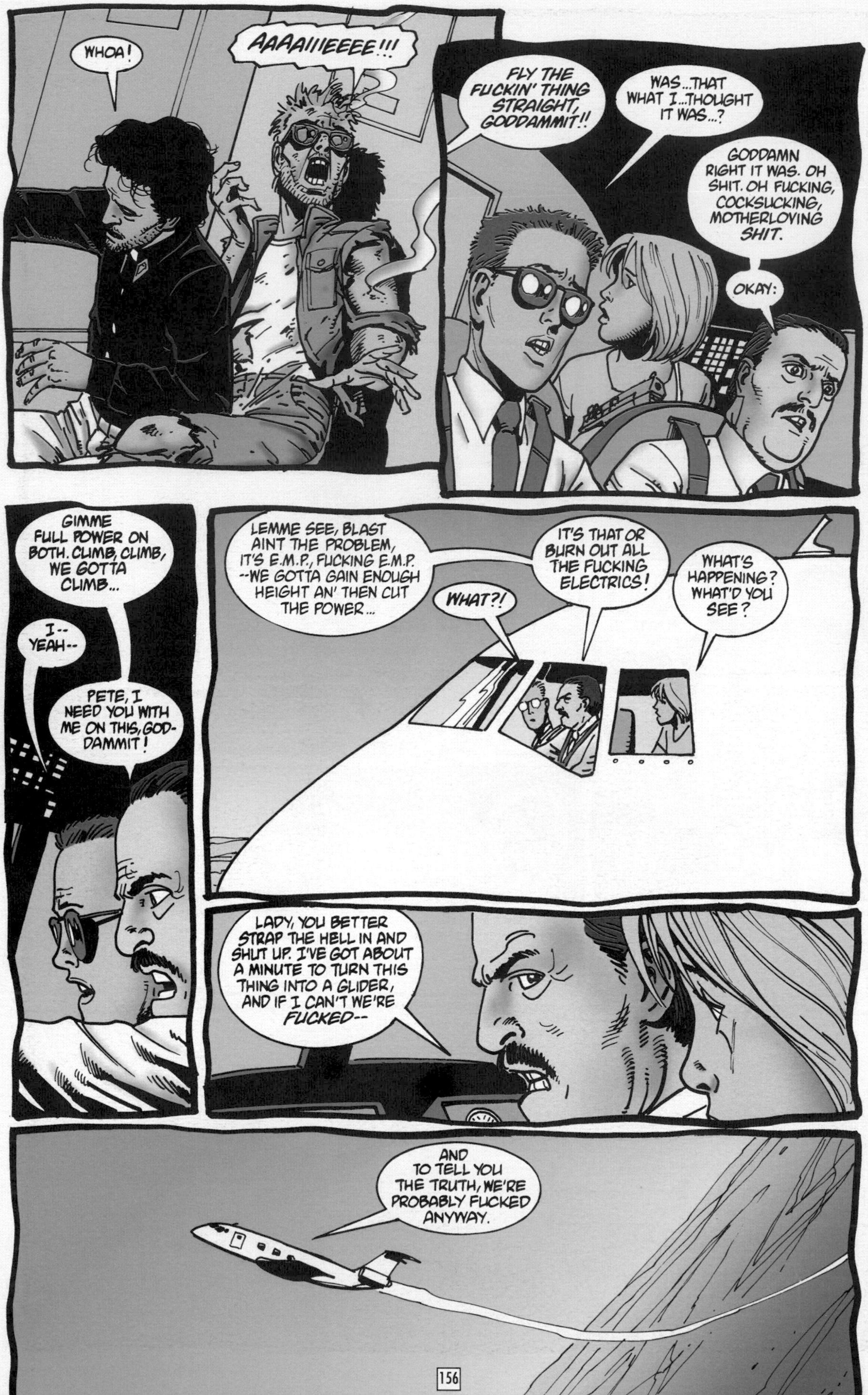
WHOA!
AAAAIIIEEEE!!!
FLY THE FUCKIN' THING STRAIGHT, GODDAMMIT!!
WAS...THAT WHAT I...THOUGHT IT WAS...?
GODDAMN RIGHT IT WAS. OH SHIT. OH FUCKING, COCKSUCKING, MOTHERLOVING SHIT.
OKAY:
GIMME FULL POWER ON BOTH. CLIMB, CLIMB, WE GOTTA CLIMB...
I-- YEAH--
PETE, I NEED YOU WITH ME ON THIS, GOD-DAMMIT!
LEMME SEE, BLAST AINT THE PROBLEM, IT'S E.M.P., FUCKING E.M.P. --WE GOTTA GAIN ENOUGH HEIGHT AN' THEN CUT THE POWER...
WHAT?!
IT'S THAT OR BURN OUT ALL THE FUCKING ELECTRICS!
WHAT'S HAPPENING? WHAT'D YOU SEE?
LADY, YOU BETTER STRAP THE HELL IN AND SHUT UP. I'VE GOT ABOUT A MINUTE TO TURN THIS THING INTO A GLIDER, AND IF I CAN'T WE'RE FUCKED--
AND TO TELL YOU THE TRUTH, WE'RE PROBABLY FUCKED ANYWAY.

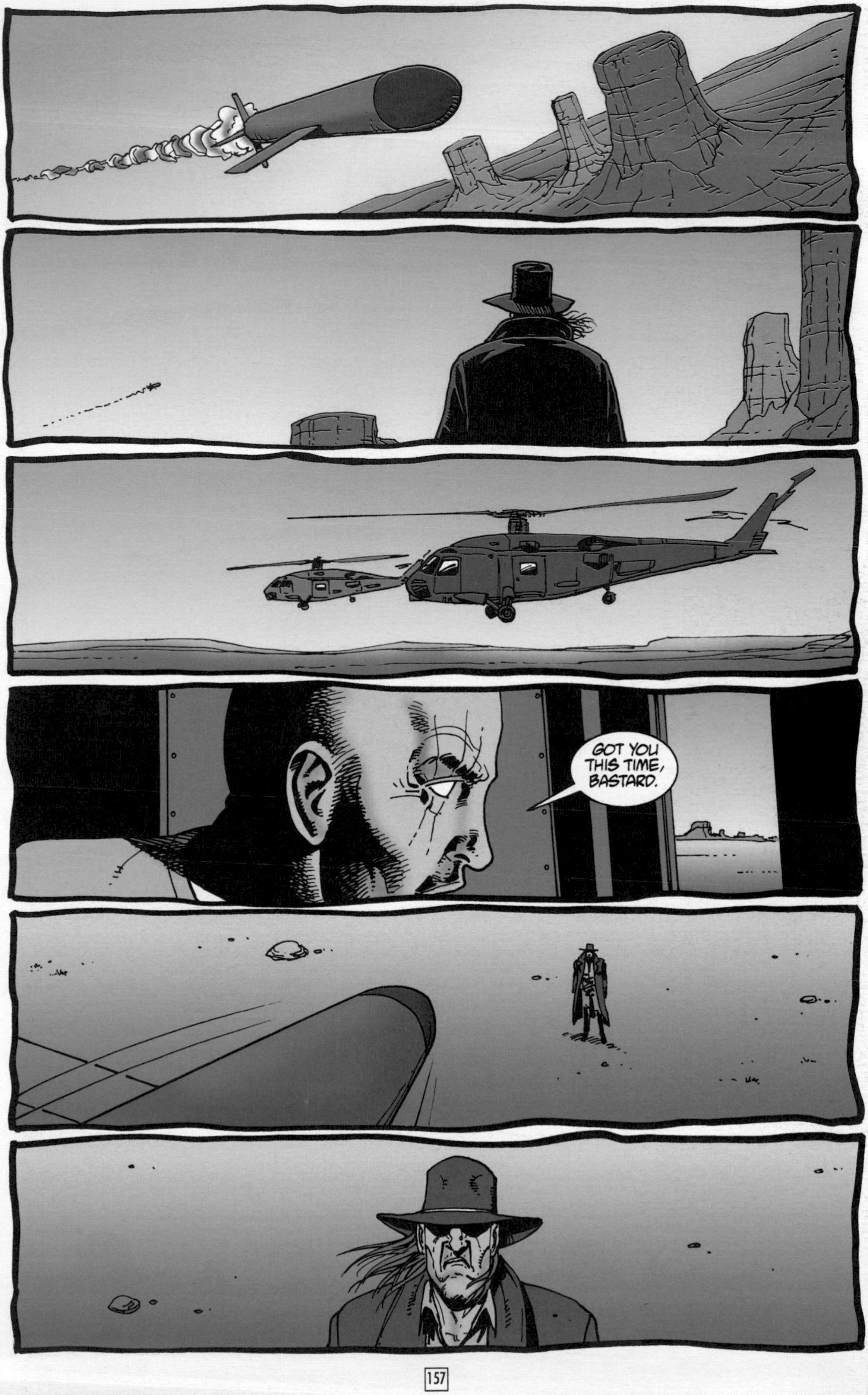
GOT YOU THIS TIME, BASTARD.

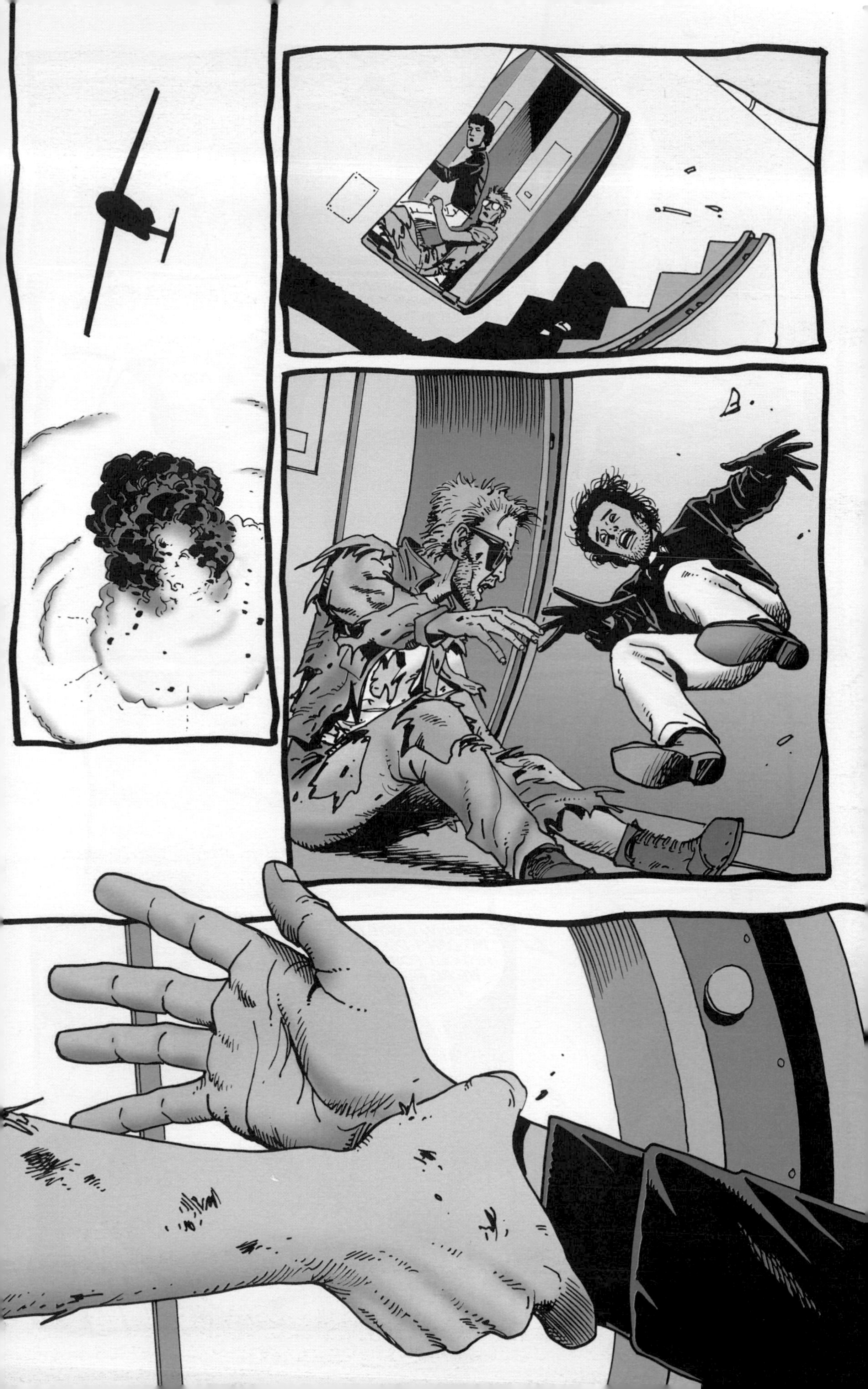

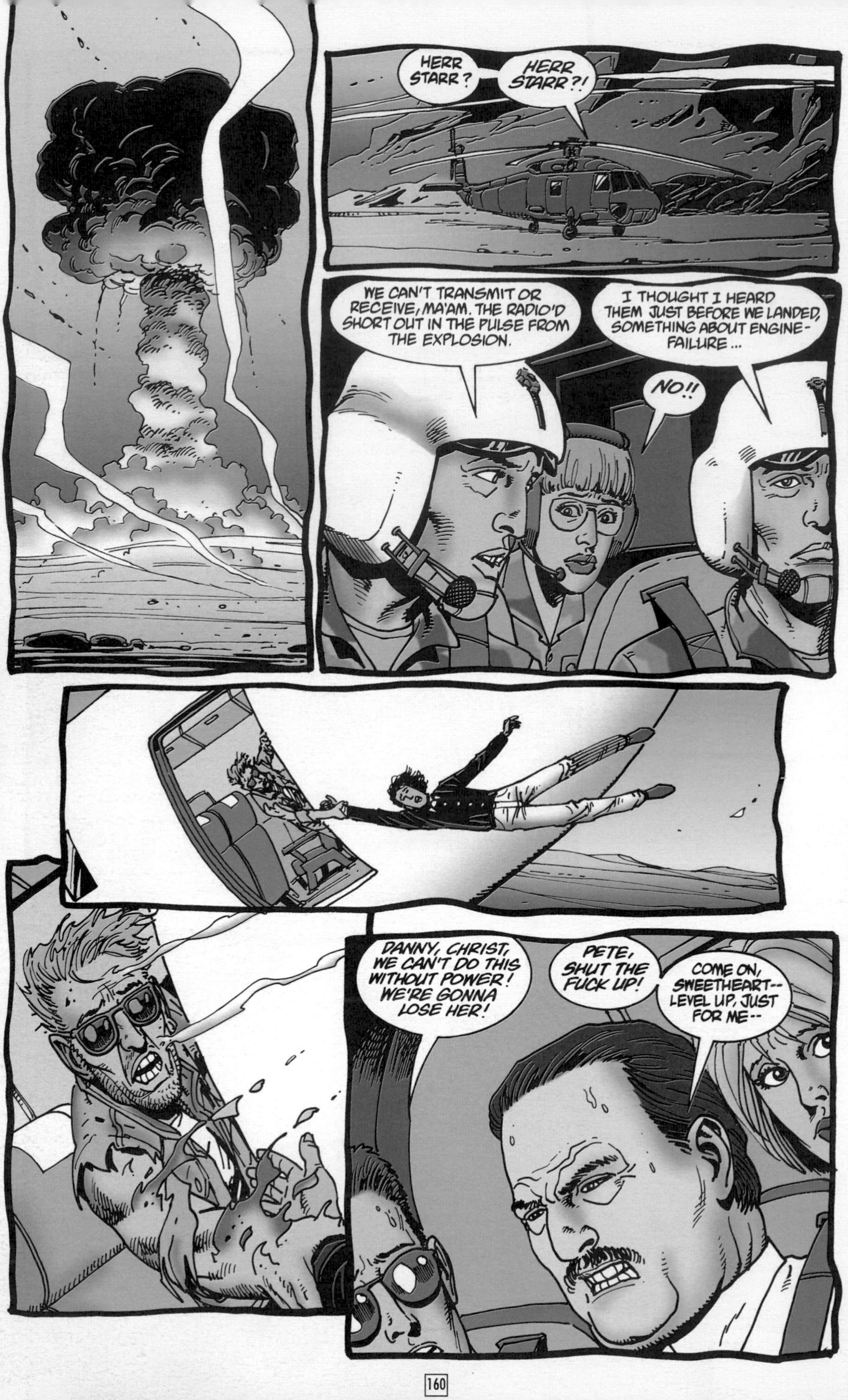
HERR STARR?
HERR STARR?!
WE CAN'T TRANSMIT OR RECEIVE, MA'AM. THE RADIO'D SHORT OUT IN THE PULSE FROM THE EXPLOSION.
NO!!
I THOUGHT I HEARD THEM JUST BEFORE WE LANDED, SOMETHING ABOUT ENGINE-FAILURE ...
DANNY, CHRIST, WE CAN'T DO THIS WITHOUT POWER! WE'RE GONNA LOSE HER!
PETE, SHUT THE FUCK UP!
COME ON, SWEETHEART-- LEVEL UP, JUST FOR ME--

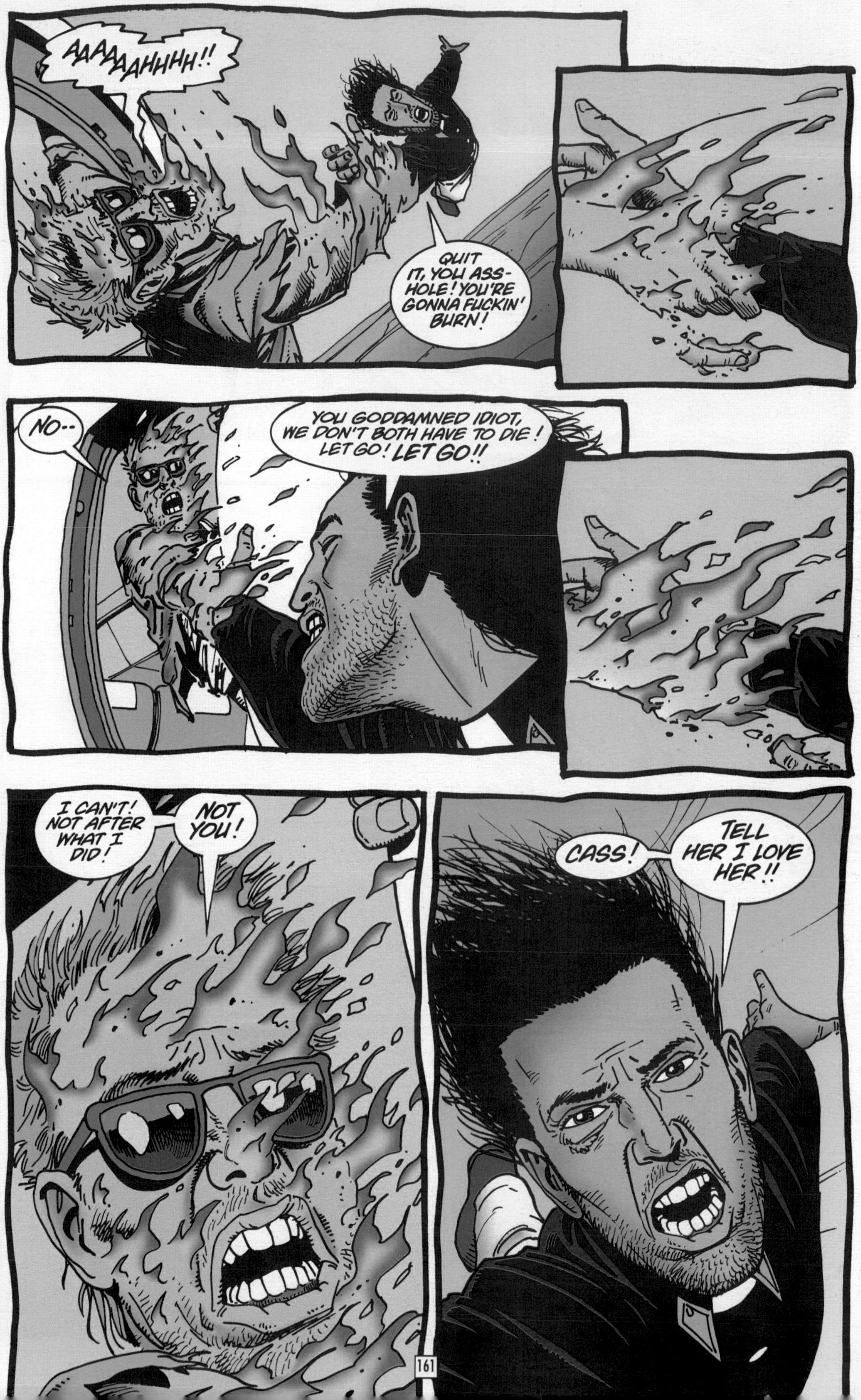
AAAAAAHHHH!!
QUIT IT, YOU ASS-HOLE! YOU'RE GONNA FUCKIN' BURN!
NO--
YOU GODDAMNED IDIOT, WE DON'T BOTH HAVE TO DIE! LET GO! LET GO!!
I CAN'T! NOT AFTER WHAT I DID!
NOT YOU!
CASS!
TELL HER I LOVE HER!!

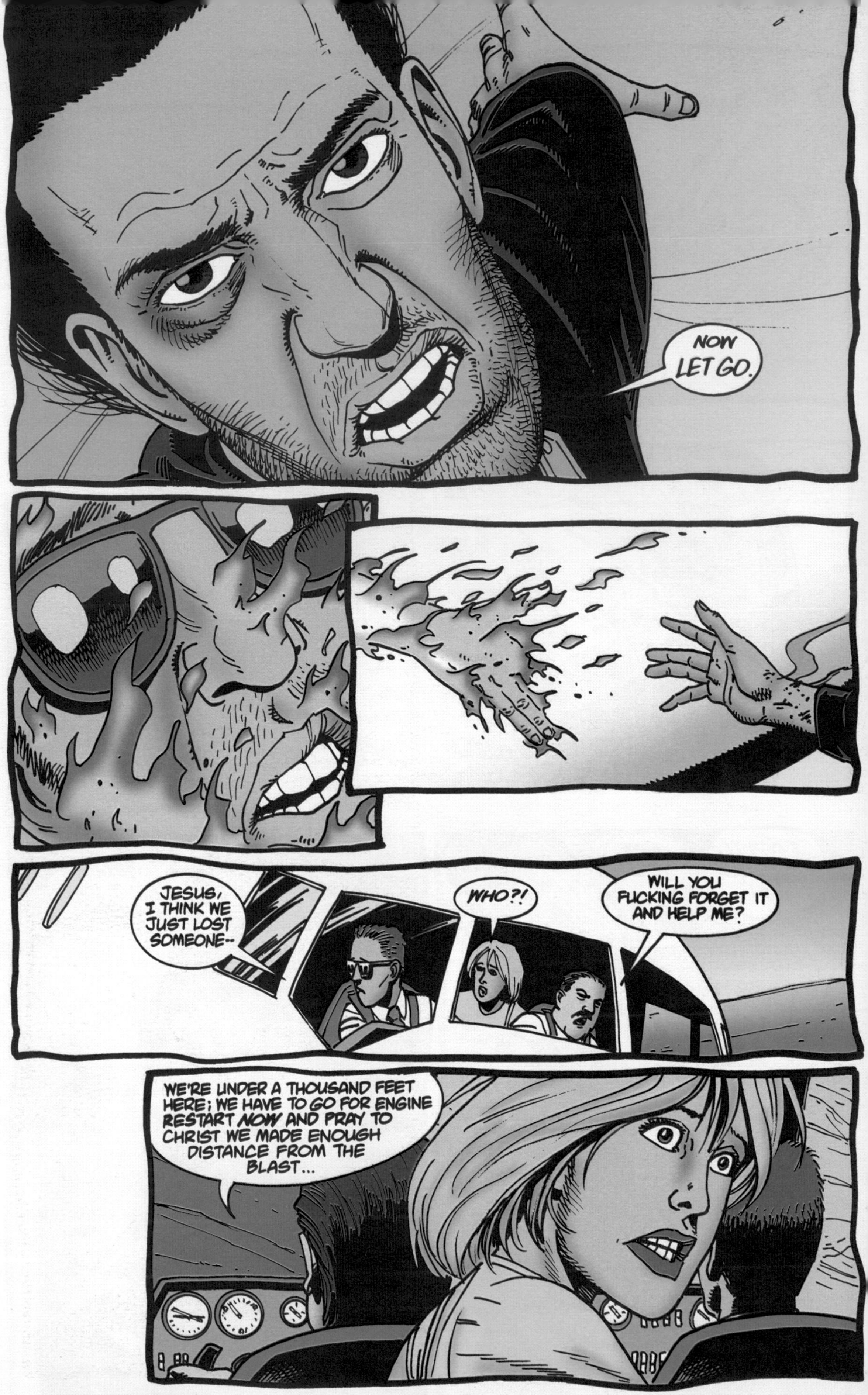
NOW LET GO.
JESUS, I THINK WE JUST LOST SOMEONE--
WHO?!
WILL YOU FUCKING FORGET IT AND HELP ME?
WE'RE UNDER A THOUSAND FEET HERE; WE HAVE TO GO FOR ENGINE RESTART NOW AND PRAY TO CHRIST WE MADE ENOUGH DISTANCE FROM THE BLAST...

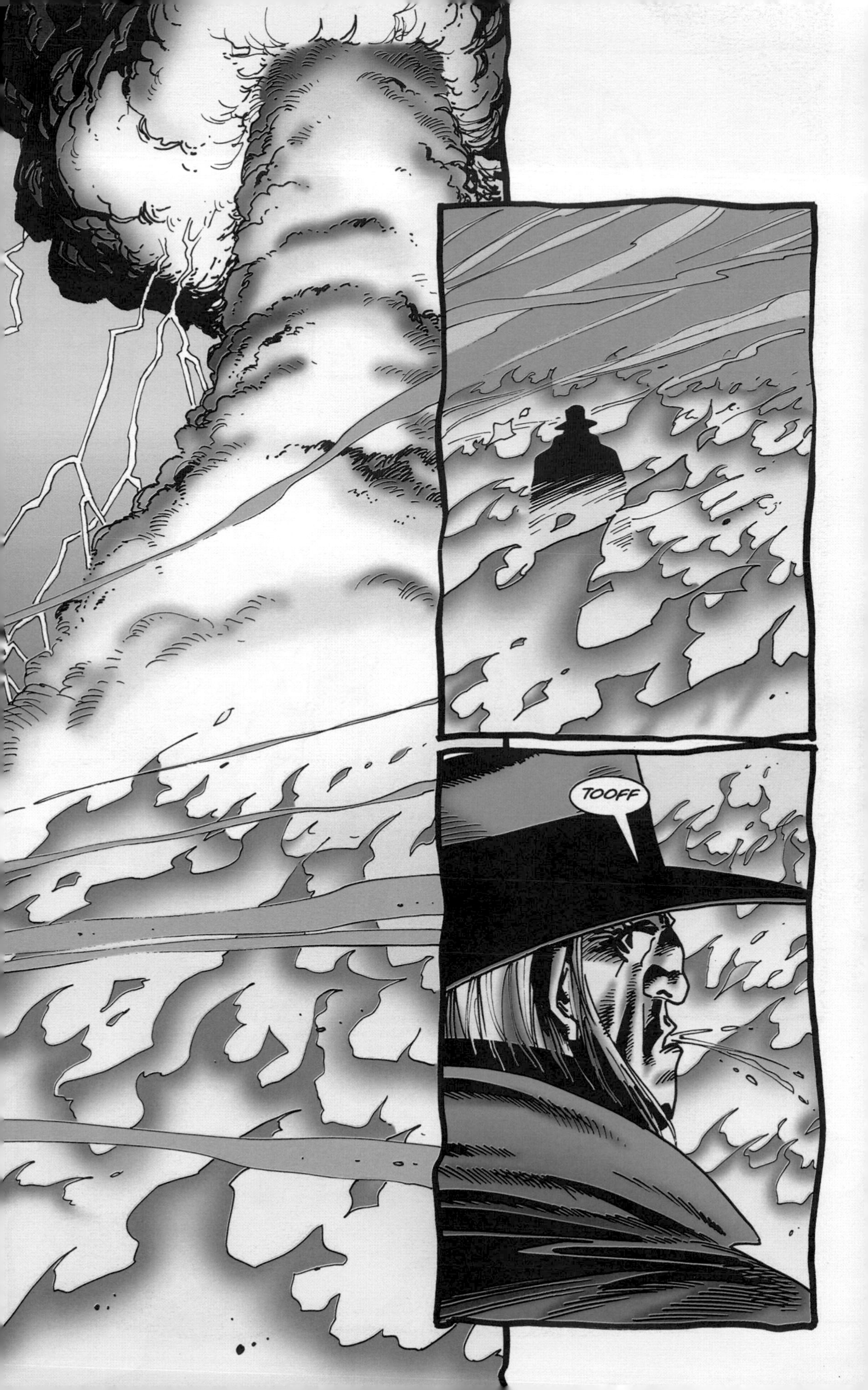
TOOFF

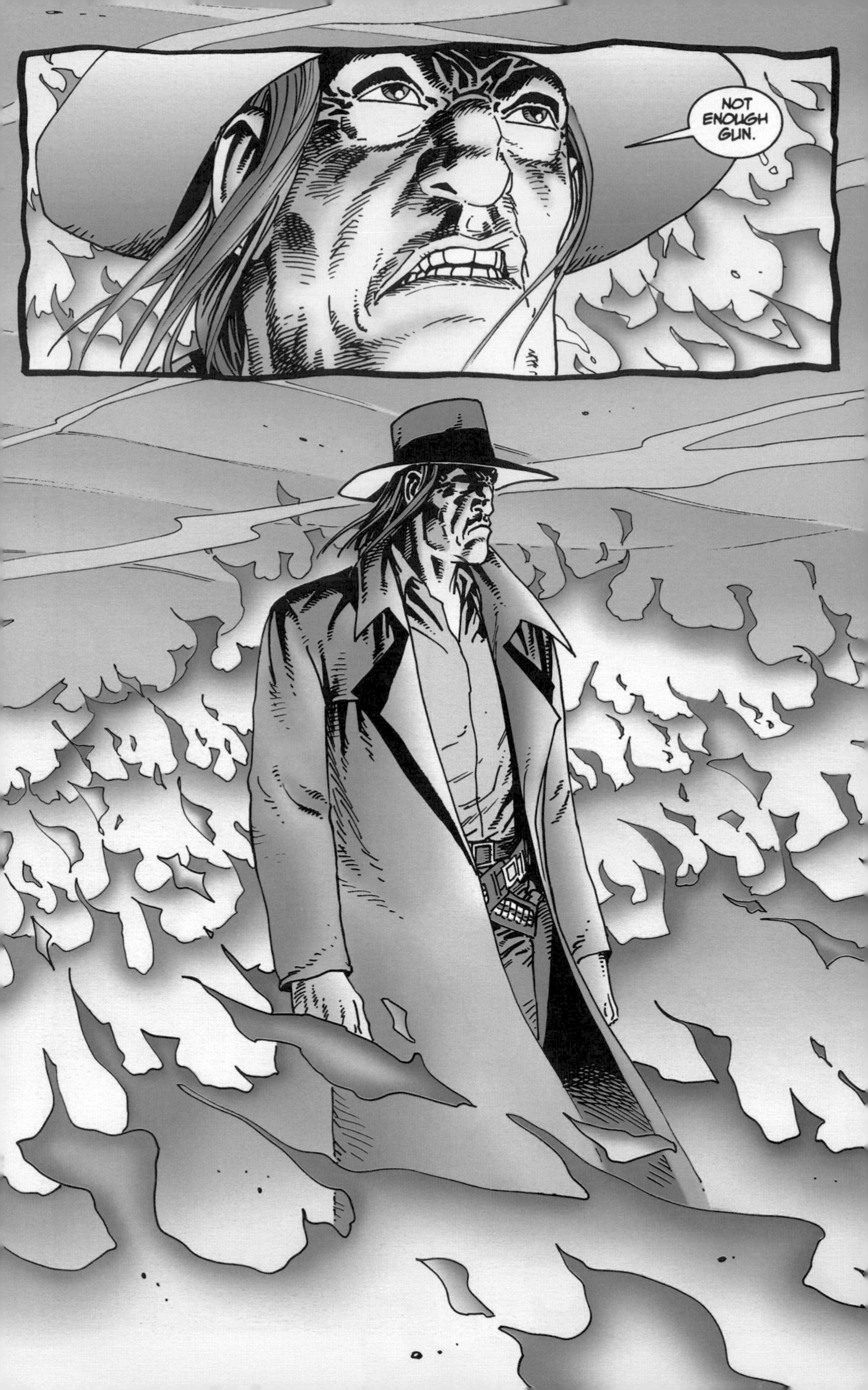
NOT ENOUGH GUN.

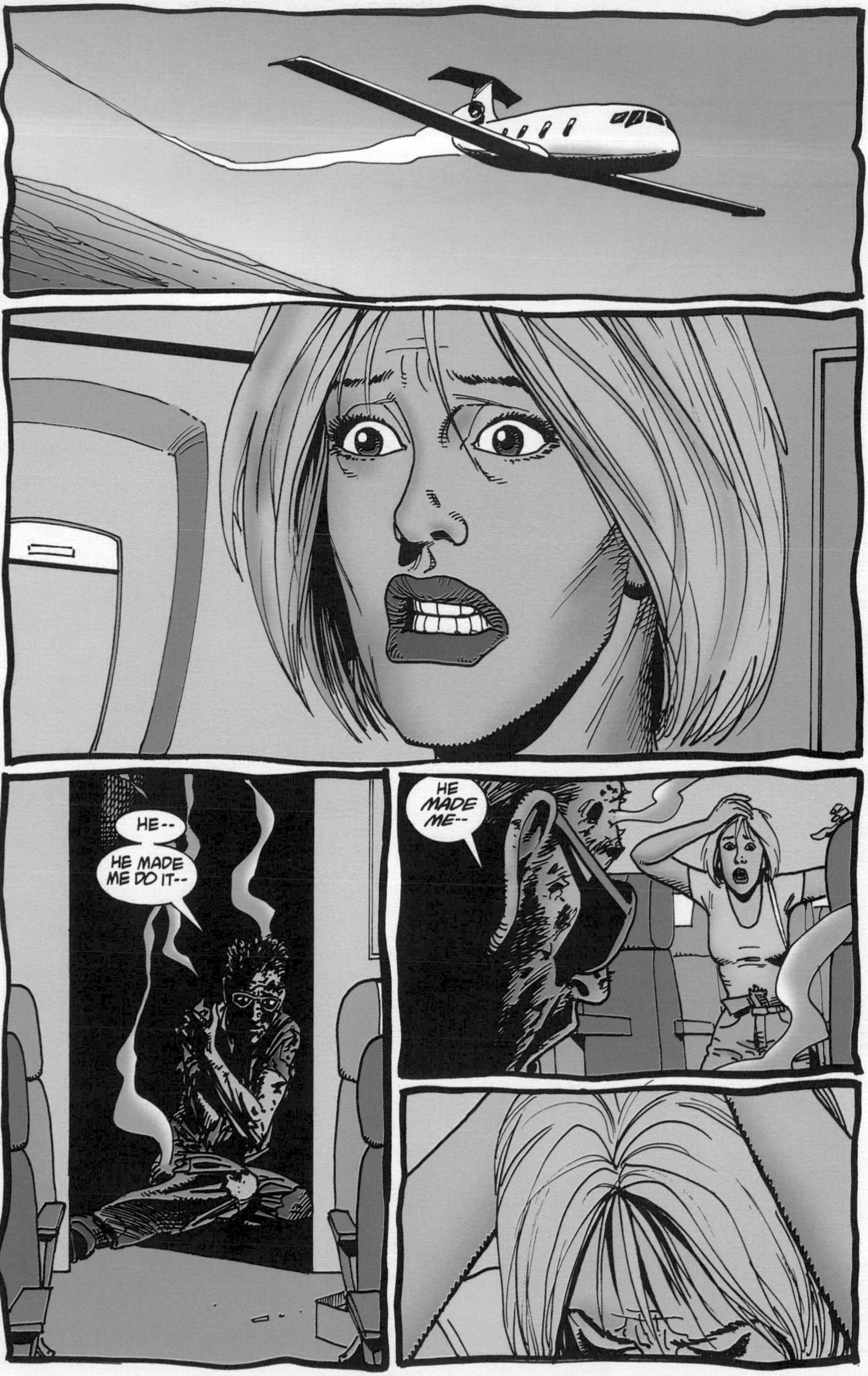
HE--
HE MADE ME DO IT--
HE MADE ME--

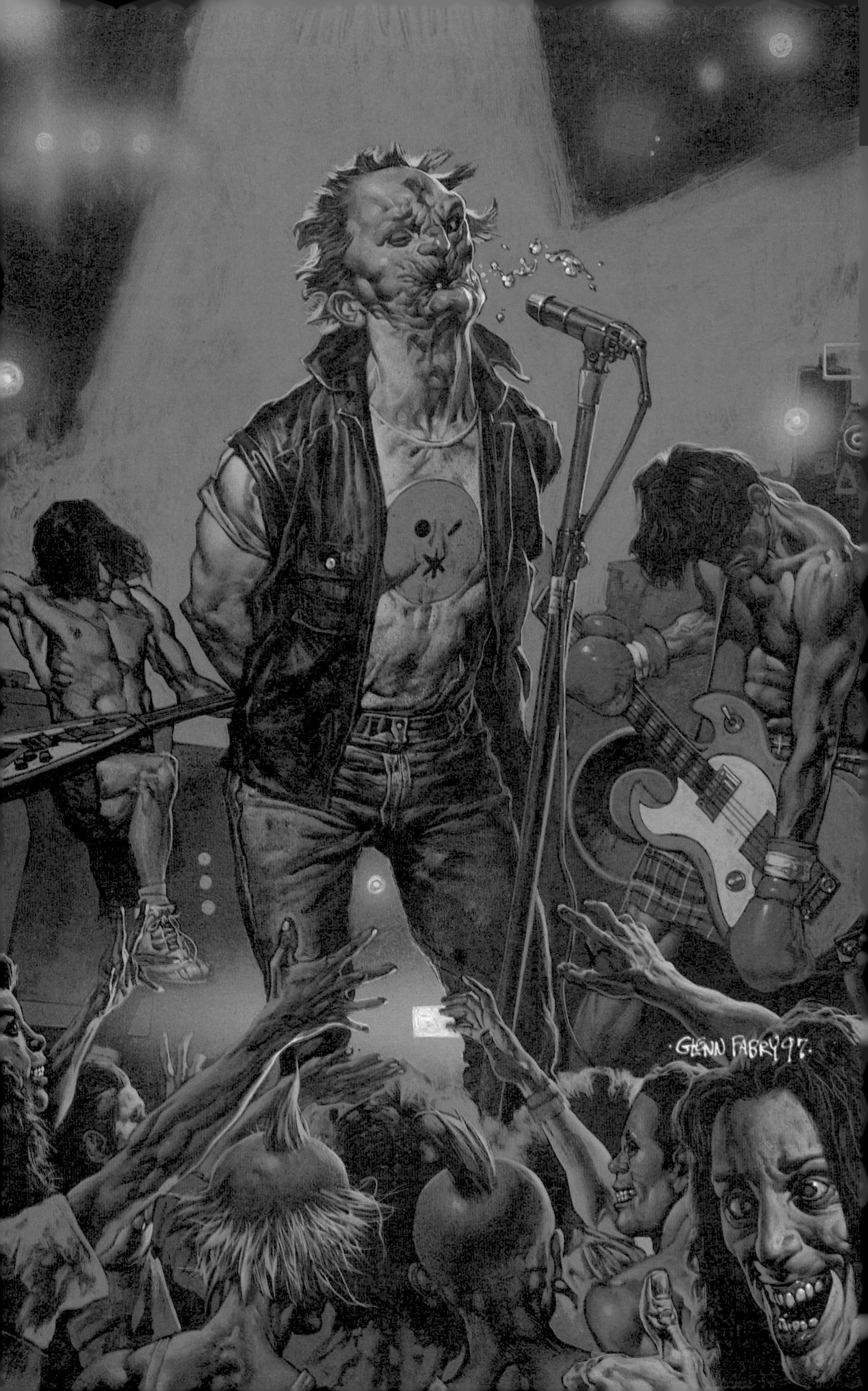
·GLENN FABRY 97·

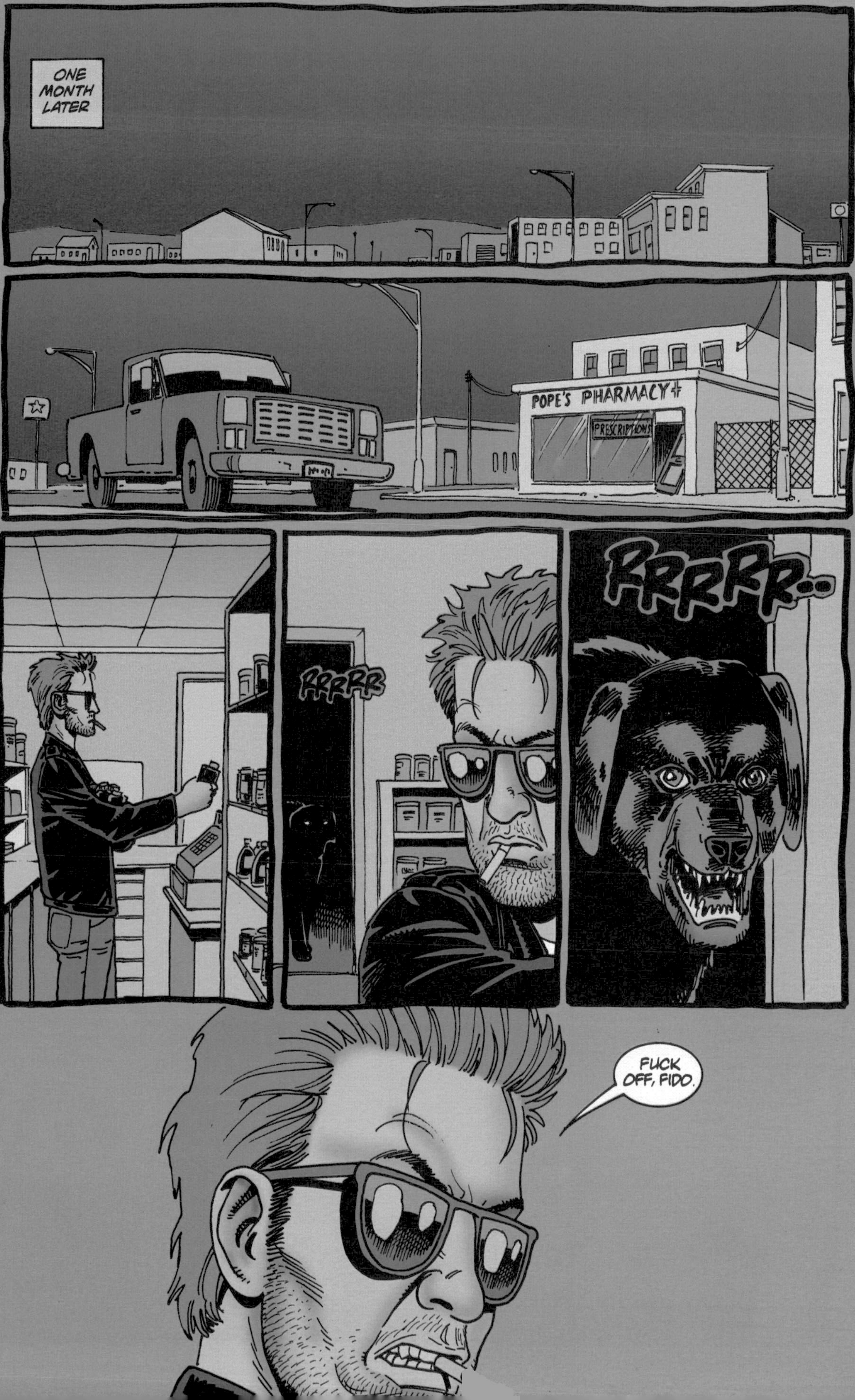
ONE MONTH LATER
POPE'S PHARMACY
PRESCRIPTIONS
RRRRR
RRRRR..
FUCK OFF, FIDO.

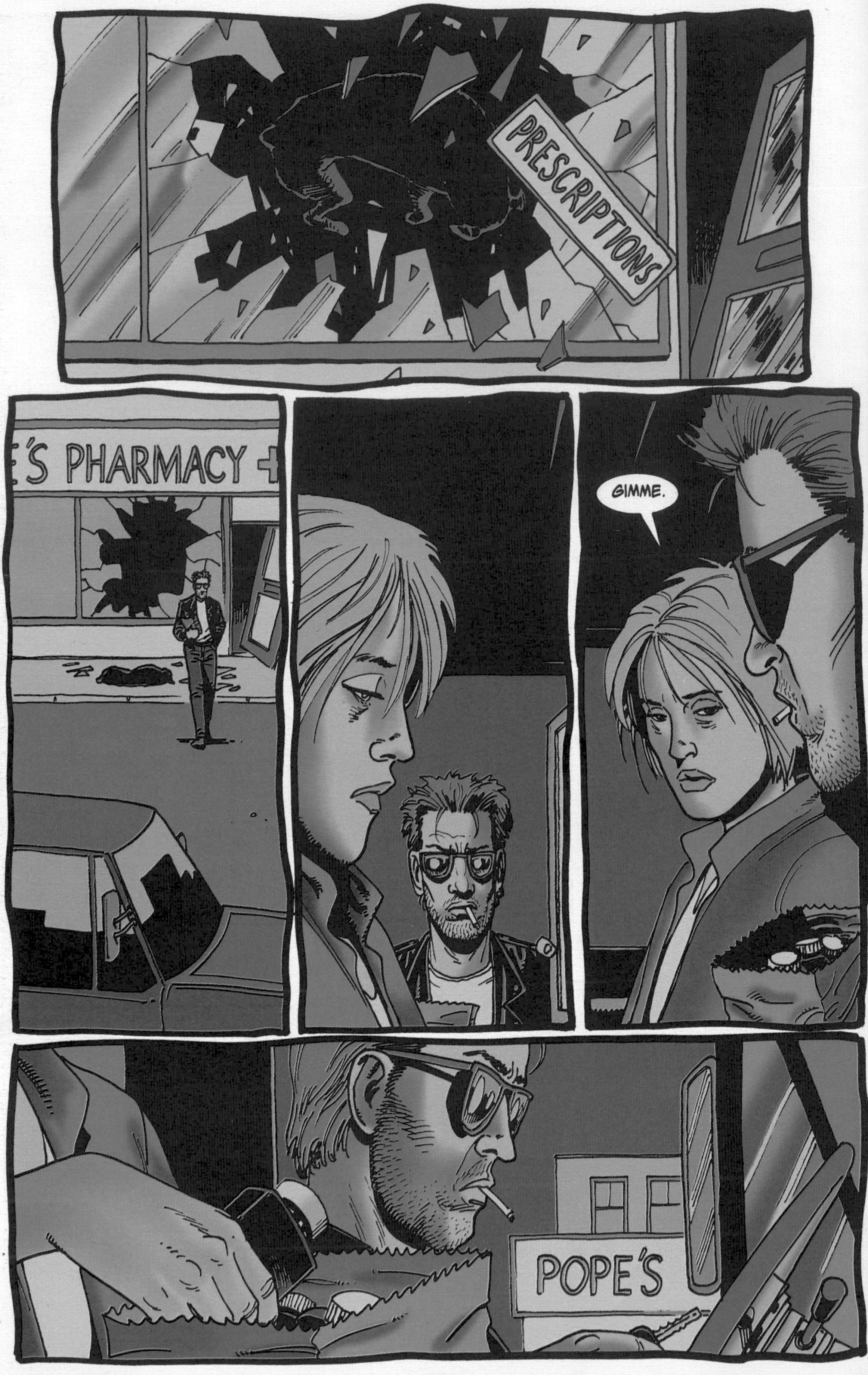
PRESCRIPTIONS
'S PHARMACY
GIMME.
POPE'S

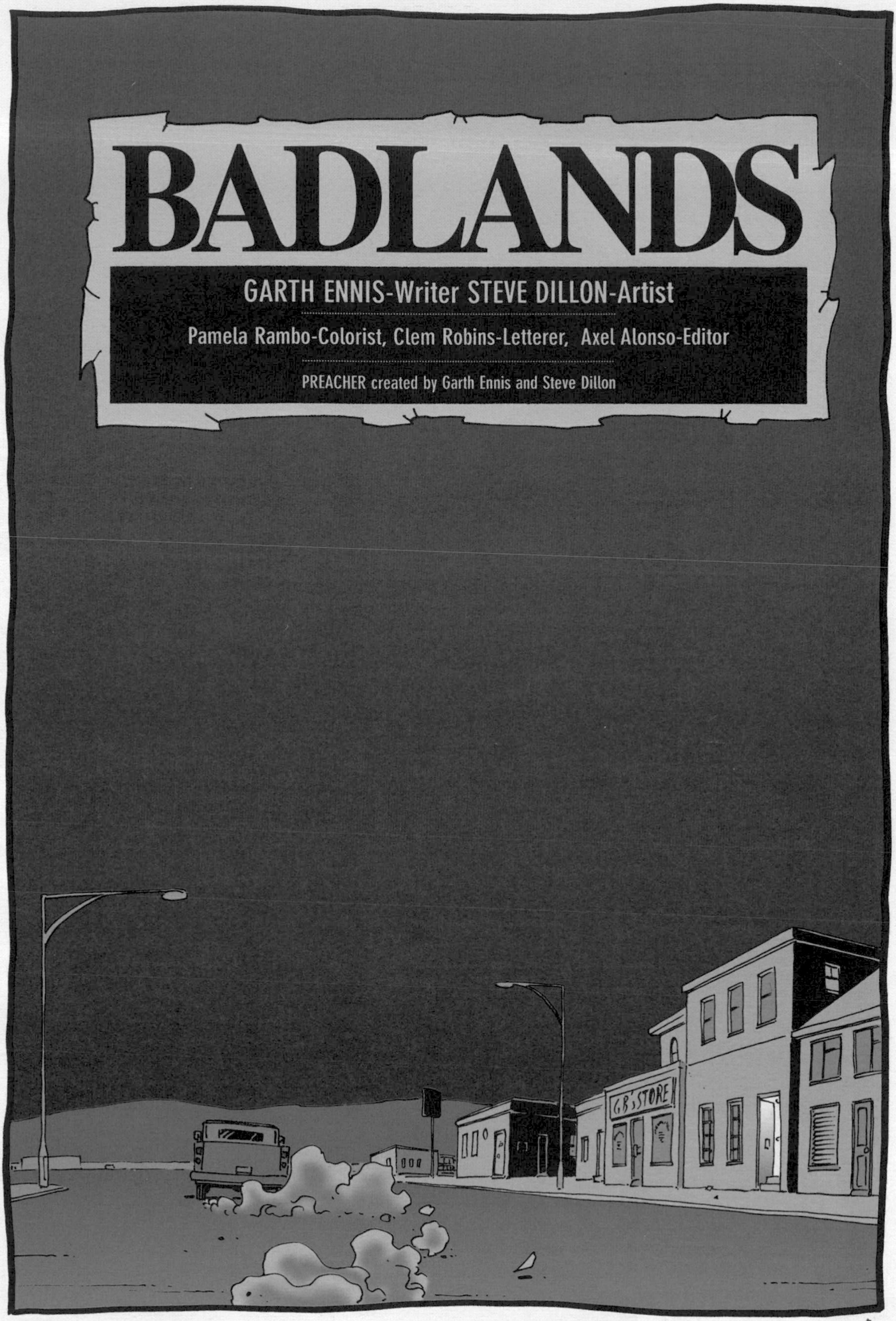
BADLANDS
GARTH ENNIS-Writer STEVE DILLON-Artist
Pamela Rambo-Colorist, Clem Robins-Letterer, Axel Alonso-Editor
PREACHER created by Garth Ennis and Steve Dillon
G.B.'s STORE

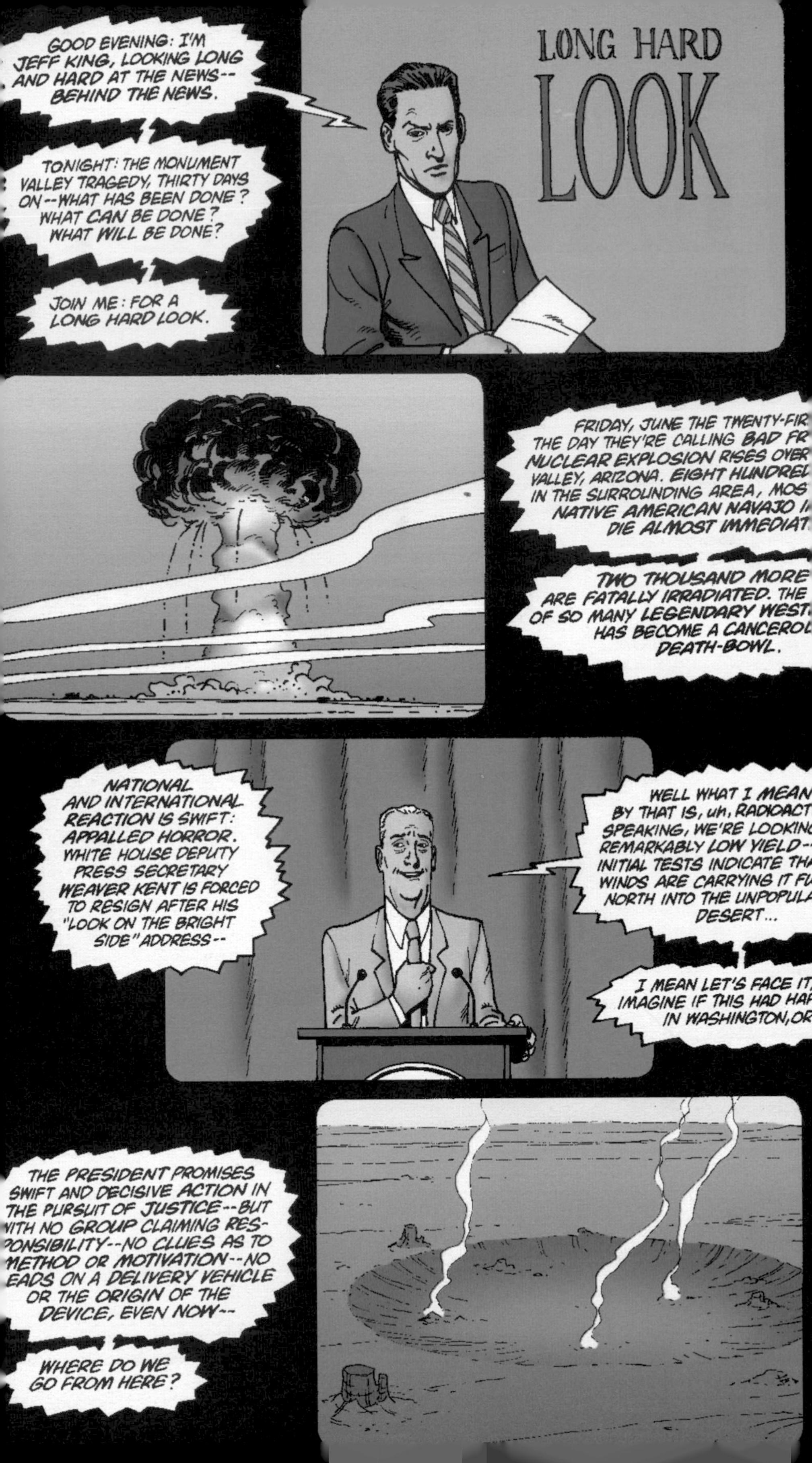
LONG HARD LOOK
GOOD EVENING: I'M JEFF KING, LOOKING LONG AND HARD AT THE NEWS-- BEHIND THE NEWS.
TONIGHT: THE MONUMENT VALLEY TRAGEDY, THIRTY DAYS ON--WHAT HAS BEEN DONE? WHAT CAN BE DONE? WHAT WILL BE DONE?
JOIN ME: FOR A LONG HARD LOOK.
FRIDAY, JUNE THE TWENTY-FIR THE DAY THEY'RE CALLING BAD FR NUCLEAR EXPLOSION RISES OVER VALLEY, ARIZONA. EIGHT HUNDREL IN THE SURROUNDING AREA, MOS NATIVE AMERICAN NAVAJO I DIE ALMOST IMMEDIAT
TWO THOUSAND MORE ARE FATALLY IRRADIATED. THE OF SO MANY LEGENDARY WEST HAS BECOME A CANCEROL DEATH-BOWL.
NATIONAL AND INTERNATIONAL REACTION IS SWIFT: APPALLED HORROR. WHITE HOUSE DEPUTY PRESS SECRETARY WEAVER KENT IS FORCED TO RESIGN AFTER HIS "LOOK ON THE BRIGHT SIDE" ADDRESS--
WELL WHAT I MEAN BY THAT IS, uh, RADIOACT SPEAKING, WE'RE LOOKING REMARKABLY LOW YIELD-- INITIAL TESTS INDICATE THA WINDS ARE CARRYING IT FU NORTH INTO THE UNPOPULA DESERT...
I MEAN LET'S FACE IT, IMAGINE IF THIS HAD HAP IN WASHINGTON, OR
THE PRESIDENT PROMISES SWIFT AND DECISIVE ACTION IN THE PURSUIT OF JUSTICE--BUT WITH NO GROUP CLAIMING RES-PONSIBILITY--NO CLUES AS TO METHOD OR MOTIVATION--NO LEADS ON A DELIVERY VEHICLE OR THE ORIGIN OF THE DEVICE, EVEN NOW--
WHERE DO WE GO FROM HERE?

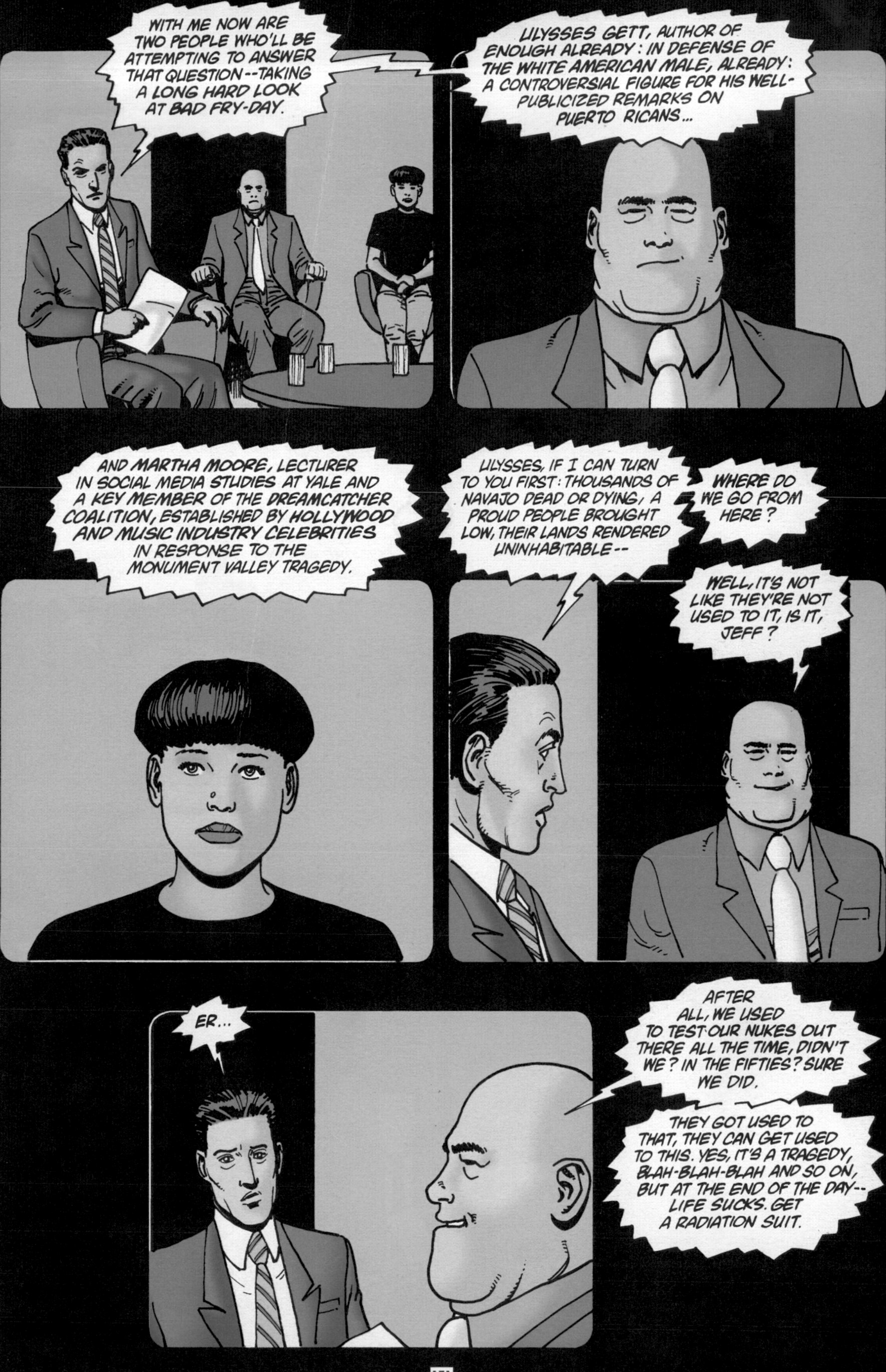
WITH ME NOW ARE TWO PEOPLE WHO'LL BE ATTEMPTING TO ANSWER THAT QUESTION--TAKING A LONG HARD LOOK AT BAD FRY-DAY.
ULYSSES GETT, AUTHOR OF ENOUGH ALREADY: IN DEFENSE OF THE WHITE AMERICAN MALE, ALREADY: A CONTROVERSIAL FIGURE FOR HIS WELL-PUBLICIZED REMARKS ON PUERTO RICANS...
AND MARTHA MOORE, LECTURER IN SOCIAL MEDIA STUDIES AT YALE AND A KEY MEMBER OF THE DREAMCATCHER COALITION, ESTABLISHED BY HOLLYWOOD AND MUSIC INDUSTRY CELEBRITIES IN RESPONSE TO THE MONUMENT VALLEY TRAGEDY.
ULYSSES, IF I CAN TURN TO YOU FIRST: THOUSANDS OF NAVAJO DEAD OR DYING, A PROUD PEOPLE BROUGHT LOW, THEIR LANDS RENDERED UNINHABITABLE--
WHERE DO WE GO FROM HERE?
WELL, IT'S NOT LIKE THEY'RE NOT USED TO IT, IS IT, JEFF?
ER...
AFTER ALL, WE USED TO TEST OUR NUKES OUT THERE ALL THE TIME, DIDN'T WE? IN THE FIFTIES? SURE WE DID.
THEY GOT USED TO THAT, THEY CAN GET USED TO THIS. YES, IT'S A TRAGEDY, BLAH-BLAH-BLAH AND SO ON, BUT AT THE END OF THE DAY--LIFE SUCKS. GET A RADIATION SUIT.

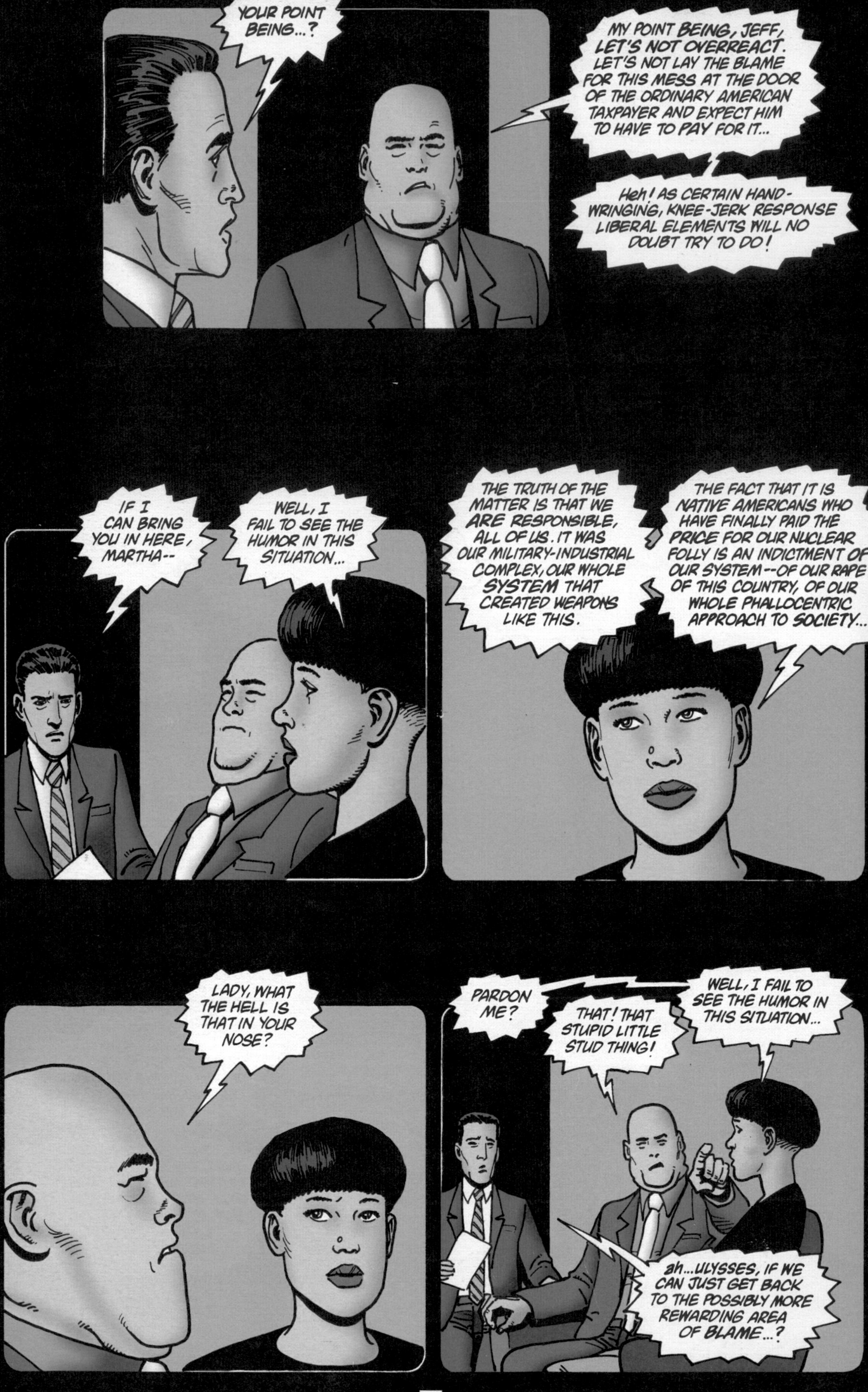
YOUR POINT BEING...?
MY POINT BEING, JEFF, LET'S NOT OVERREACT. LET'S NOT LAY THE BLAME FOR THIS MESS AT THE DOOR OF THE ORDINARY AMERICAN TAXPAYER AND EXPECT HIM TO HAVE TO PAY FOR IT...
Heh! AS CERTAIN HAND-WRINGING, KNEE-JERK RESPONSE LIBERAL ELEMENTS WILL NO DOUBT TRY TO DO!
IF I CAN BRING YOU IN HERE, MARTHA--
WELL, I FAIL TO SEE THE HUMOR IN THIS SITUATION...
THE TRUTH OF THE MATTER IS THAT WE ARE RESPONSIBLE, ALL OF US. IT WAS OUR MILITARY-INDUSTRIAL COMPLEX, OUR WHOLE SYSTEM THAT CREATED WEAPONS LIKE THIS.
THE FACT THAT IT IS NATIVE AMERICANS WHO HAVE FINALLY PAID THE PRICE FOR OUR NUCLEAR FOLLY IS AN INDICTMENT OF OUR SYSTEM--OF OUR RAPE OF THIS COUNTRY, OF OUR WHOLE PHALLOCENTRIC APPROACH TO SOCIETY...
LADY, WHAT THE HELL IS THAT IN YOUR NOSE?
PARDON ME?
WELL, I FAIL TO SEE THE HUMOR IN THIS SITUATION...
THAT! THAT STUPID LITTLE STUD THING!
ah...ULYSSES, IF WE CAN JUST GET BACK TO THE POSSIBLY MORE REWARDING AREA OF BLAME...?

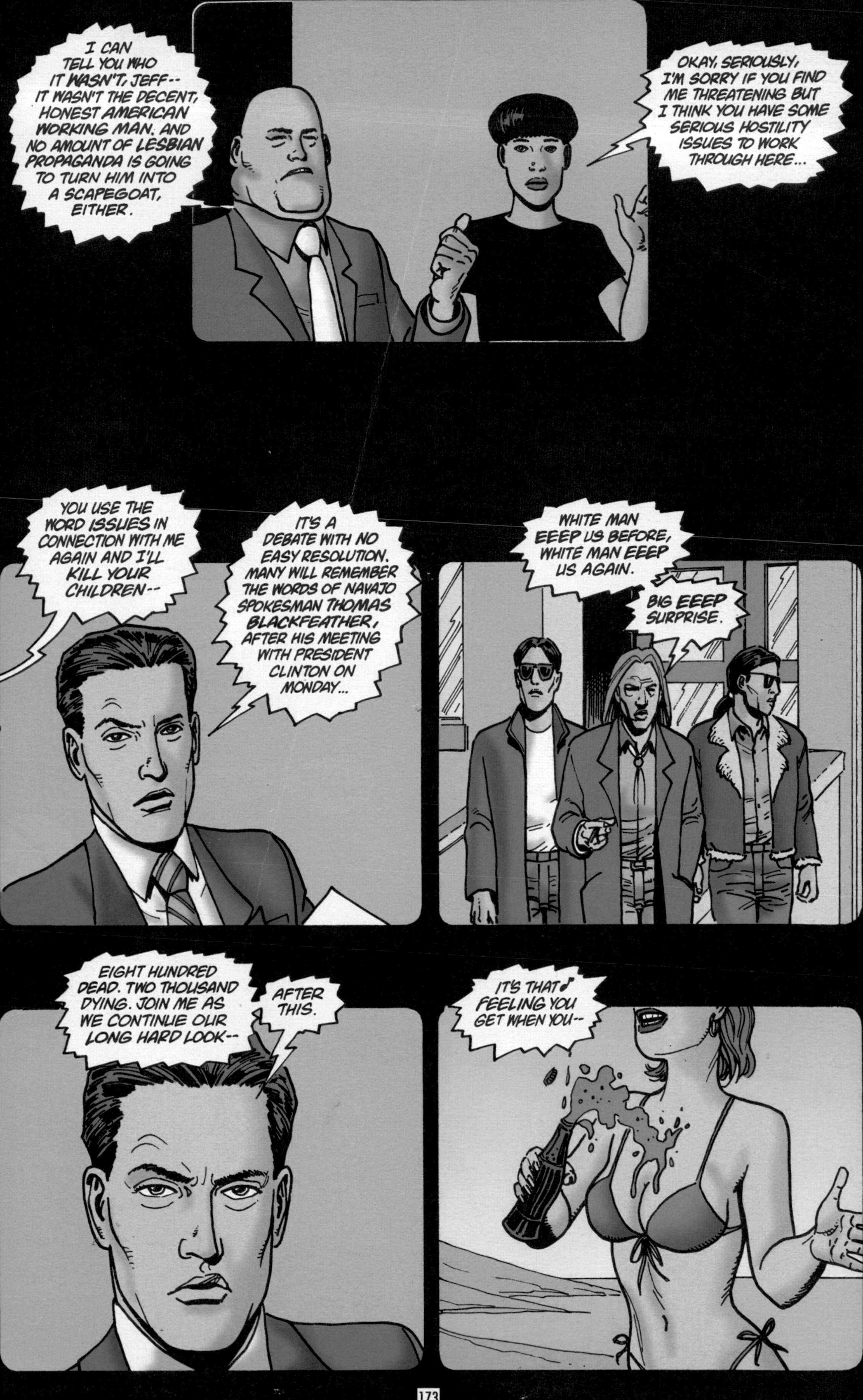
I CAN TELL YOU WHO IT WASN'T, JEFF-- IT WASN'T THE DECENT, HONEST AMERICAN WORKING MAN. AND NO AMOUNT OF LESBIAN PROPAGANDA IS GOING TO TURN HIM INTO A SCAPEGOAT, EITHER.
OKAY, SERIOUSLY, I'M SORRY IF YOU FIND ME THREATENING BUT I THINK YOU HAVE SOME SERIOUS HOSTILITY ISSUES TO WORK THROUGH HERE...
YOU USE THE WORD ISSUES IN CONNECTION WITH ME AGAIN AND I'LL KILL YOUR CHILDREN--
IT'S A DEBATE WITH NO EASY RESOLUTION. MANY WILL REMEMBER THE WORDS OF NAVAJO SPOKESMAN THOMAS BLACKFEATHER, AFTER HIS MEETING WITH PRESIDENT CLINTON ON MONDAY...
WHITE MAN EEEP US BEFORE, WHITE MAN EEEP US AGAIN.
BIG EEEP SURPRISE.
EIGHT HUNDRED DEAD. TWO THOUSAND DYING. JOIN ME AS WE CONTINUE OUR LONG HARD LOOK--
AFTER THIS.
IT'S THAT♪ FEELING YOU GET WHEN YOU--

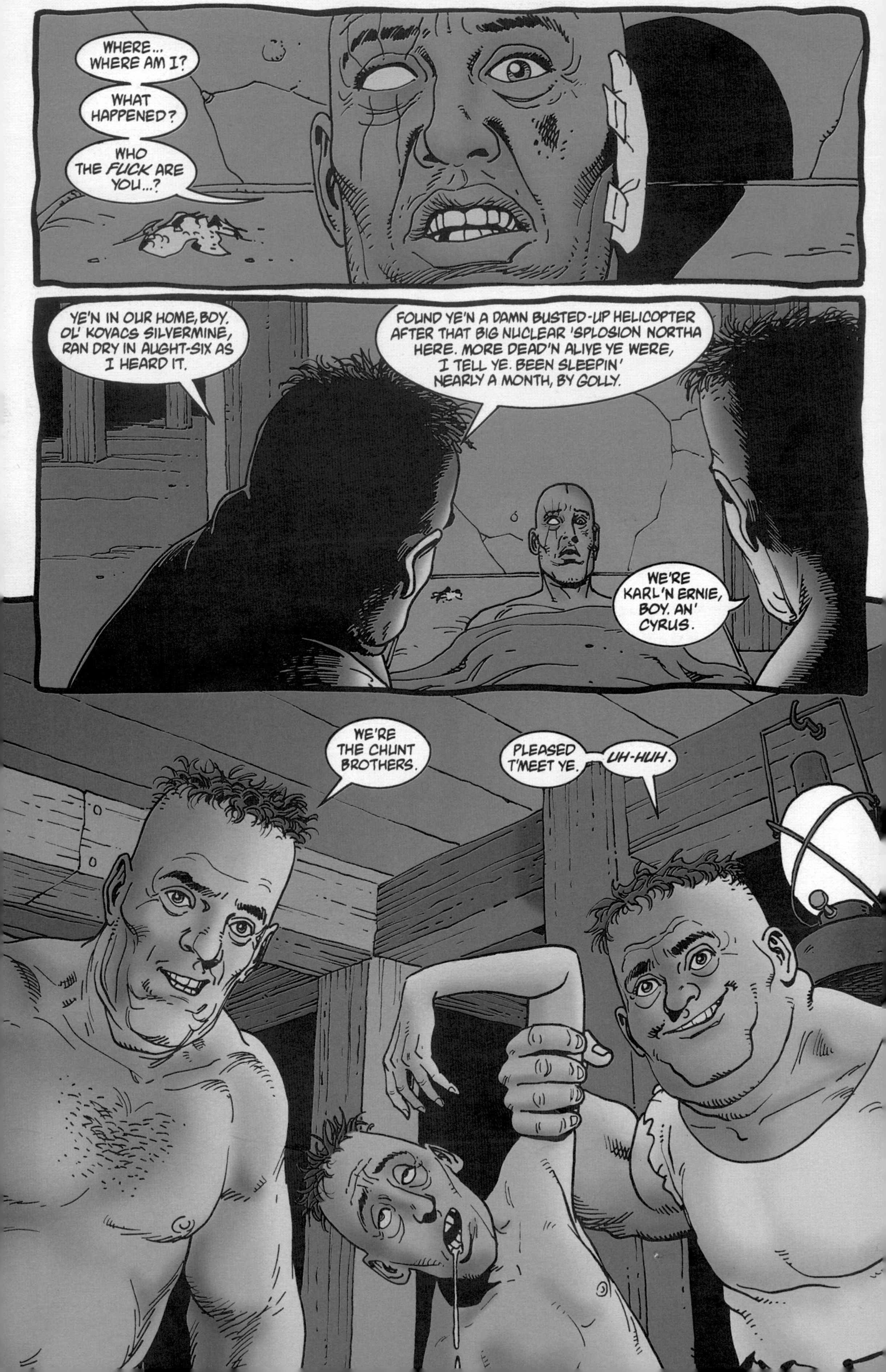
WHERE... WHERE AM I?
WHAT HAPPENED?
WHO THE *FUCK* ARE YOU...?
YE'N IN OUR HOME, BOY. OL' KOVACS SILVERMINE, RAN DRY IN AUGHT-SIX AS I HEARD IT.
FOUND YE'N A DAMN BUSTED-UP HELICOPTER AFTER THAT BIG NUCLEAR 'SPLOSION NORTHA HERE. MORE DEAD'N ALIVE YE WERE, I TELL YE. BEEN SLEEPIN' NEARLY A MONTH, BY GOLLY.
WE'RE KARL'N ERNIE, BOY. AN' CYRUS.
WE'RE THE CHUNT BROTHERS.
PLEASED T'MEET YE.
UH-HUH.

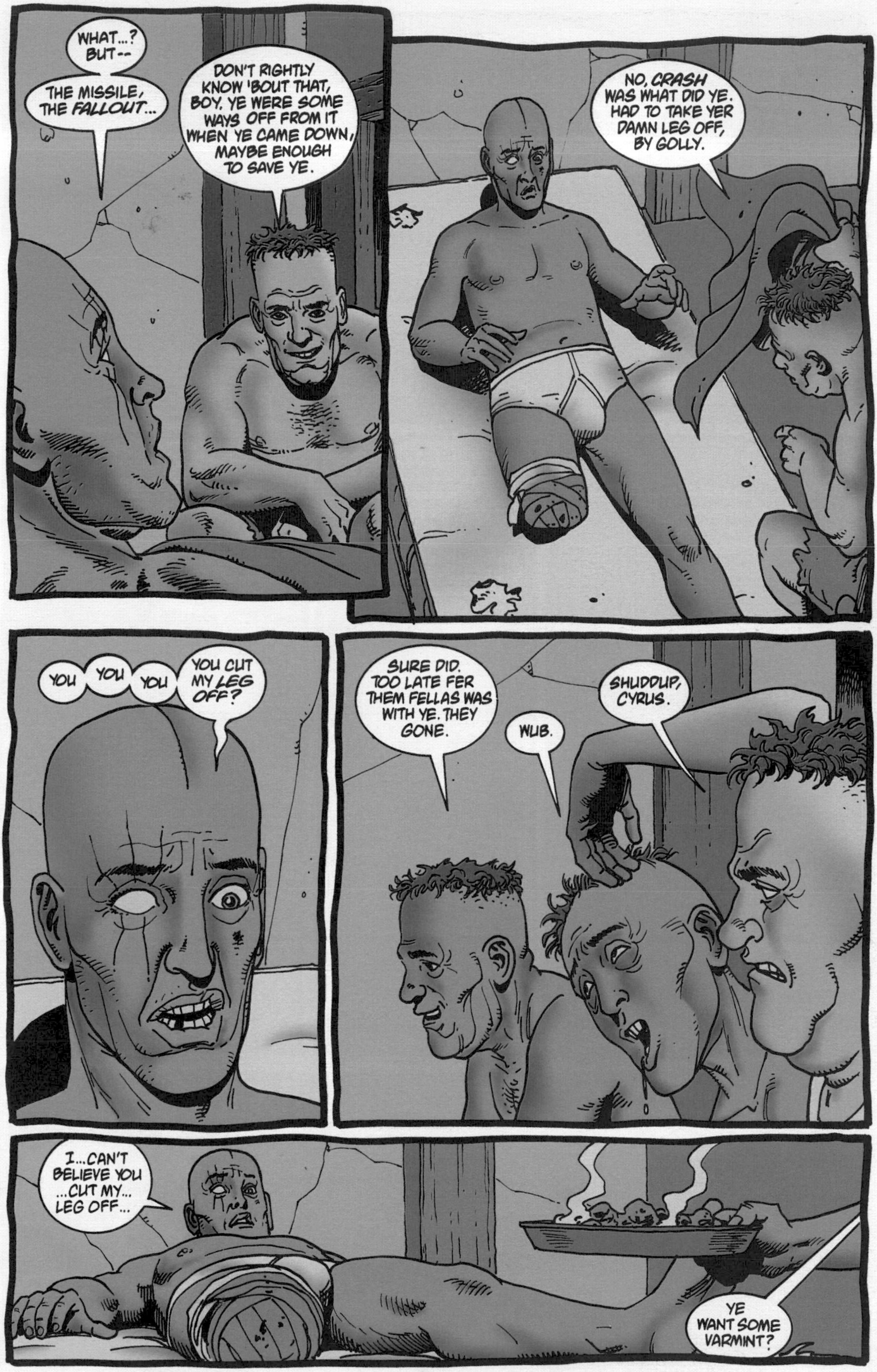
WHAT...? BUT--
THE MISSILE, THE FALLOUT...
DON'T RIGHTLY KNOW 'BOUT THAT, BOY. YE WERE SOME WAYS OFF FROM IT WHEN YE CAME DOWN, MAYBE ENOUGH TO SAVE YE.
NO, CRASH WAS WHAT DID YE. HAD TO TAKE YER DAMN LEG OFF, BY GOLLY.
YOU
YOU
YOU
YOU CUT MY LEG OFF?
SURE DID. TOO LATE FER THEM FELLAS WAS WITH YE. THEY GONE.
WUB.
SHUDDUP, CYRUS.
I...CAN'T BELIEVE YOU ...CUT MY... LEG OFF...
YE WANT SOME VARMINT?

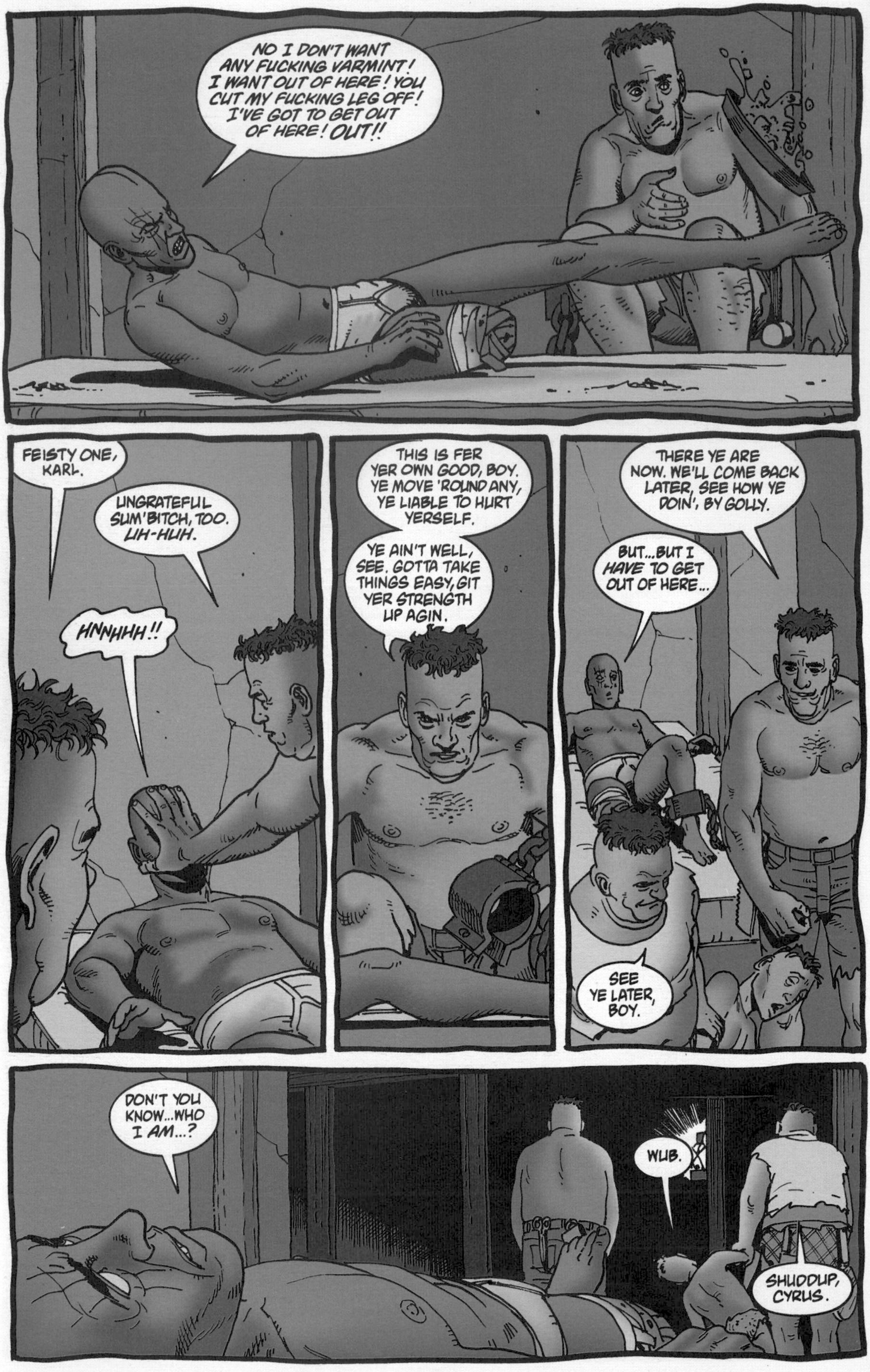
NO I DON'T WANT ANY FUCKING VARMINT! I WANT OUT OF HERE! YOU CUT MY FUCKING LEG OFF! I'VE GOT TO GET OUT OF HERE! OUT!!
FEISTY ONE, KARL.
UNGRATEFUL SUM'BITCH, TOO. UH-HUH.
HNNHHH!!
THIS IS FER YER OWN GOOD, BOY. YE MOVE 'ROUND ANY, YE LIABLE TO HURT YERSELF.
YE AIN'T WELL, SEE. GOTTA TAKE THINGS EASY, GIT YER STRENGTH UP AGIN.
THERE YE ARE NOW. WE'LL COME BACK LATER, SEE HOW YE DOIN', BY GOLLY.
BUT...BUT I HAVE TO GET OUT OF HERE...
SEE YE LATER, BOY.
DON'T YOU KNOW...WHO I AM...?
WUB.
SHUDDUP, CYRUS.

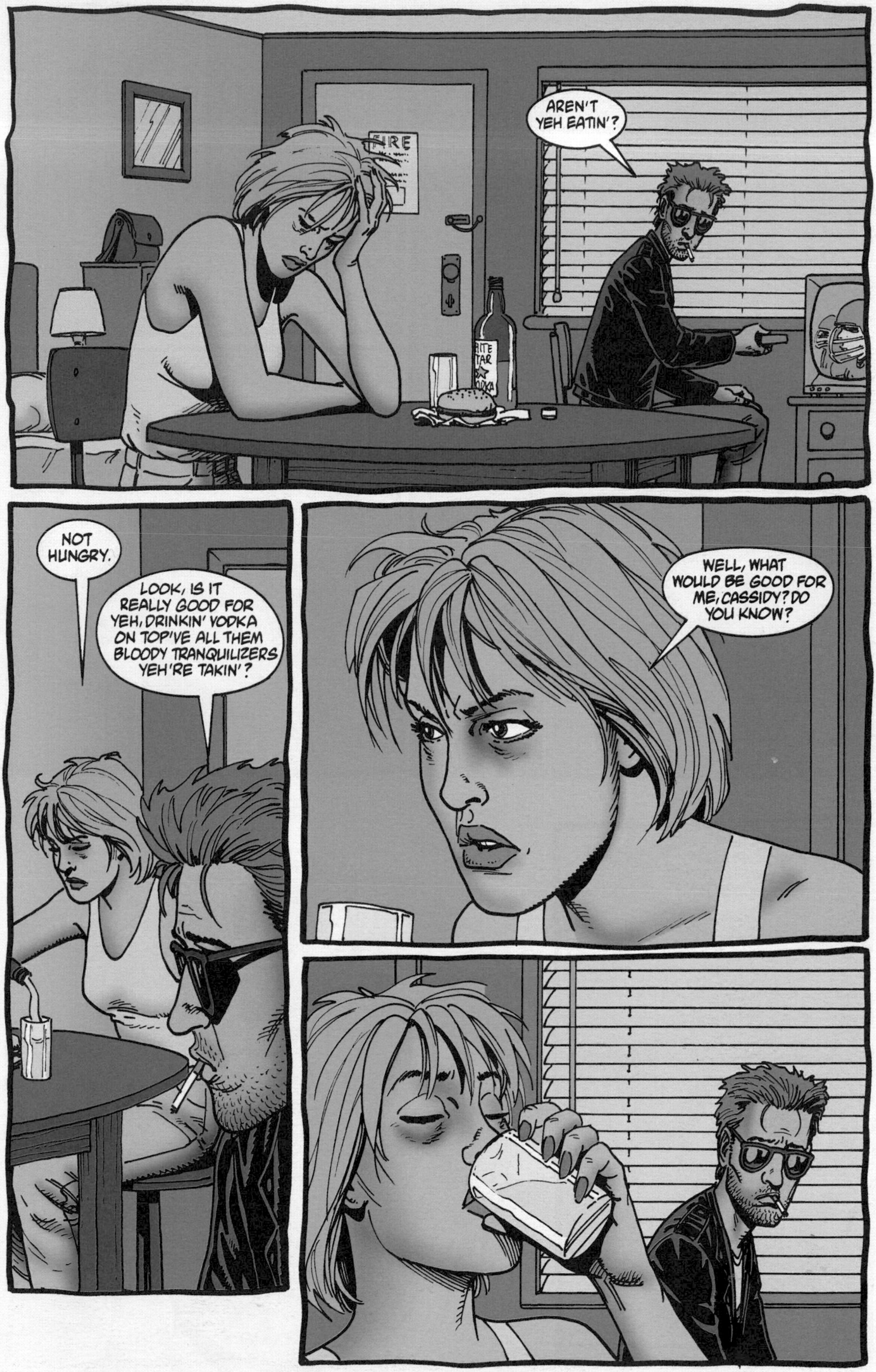
AREN'T YEH EATIN'?
NOT HUNGRY.
LOOK, IS IT REALLY GOOD FOR YEH, DRINKIN' VODKA ON TOP'VE ALL THEM BLOODY TRANQUILIZERS YEH'RE TAKIN'?
WELL, WHAT WOULD BE GOOD FOR ME, CASSIDY? DO YOU KNOW?

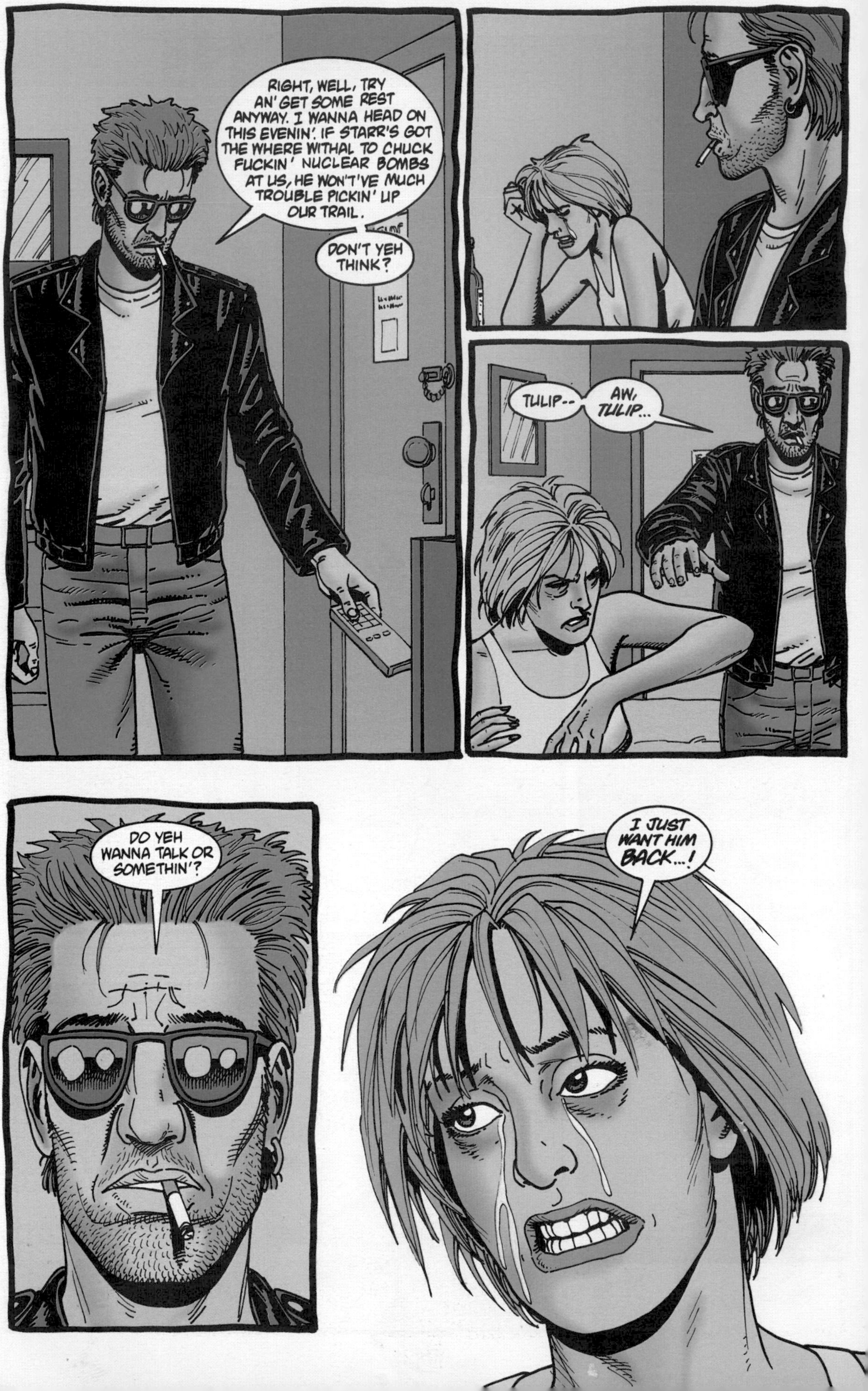
RIGHT, WELL, TRY AN' GET SOME REST ANYWAY. I WANNA HEAD ON THIS EVENIN'. IF STARR'S GOT THE WHERE WITHAL TO CHUCK FUCKIN' NUCLEAR BOMBS AT US, HE WON'T'VE MUCH TROUBLE PICKIN' UP OUR TRAIL.
DON'T YEH THINK?
TULIP--
AW, TULIP...
DO YEH WANNA TALK OR SOMETHIN'?
I JUST WANT HIM BACK...!

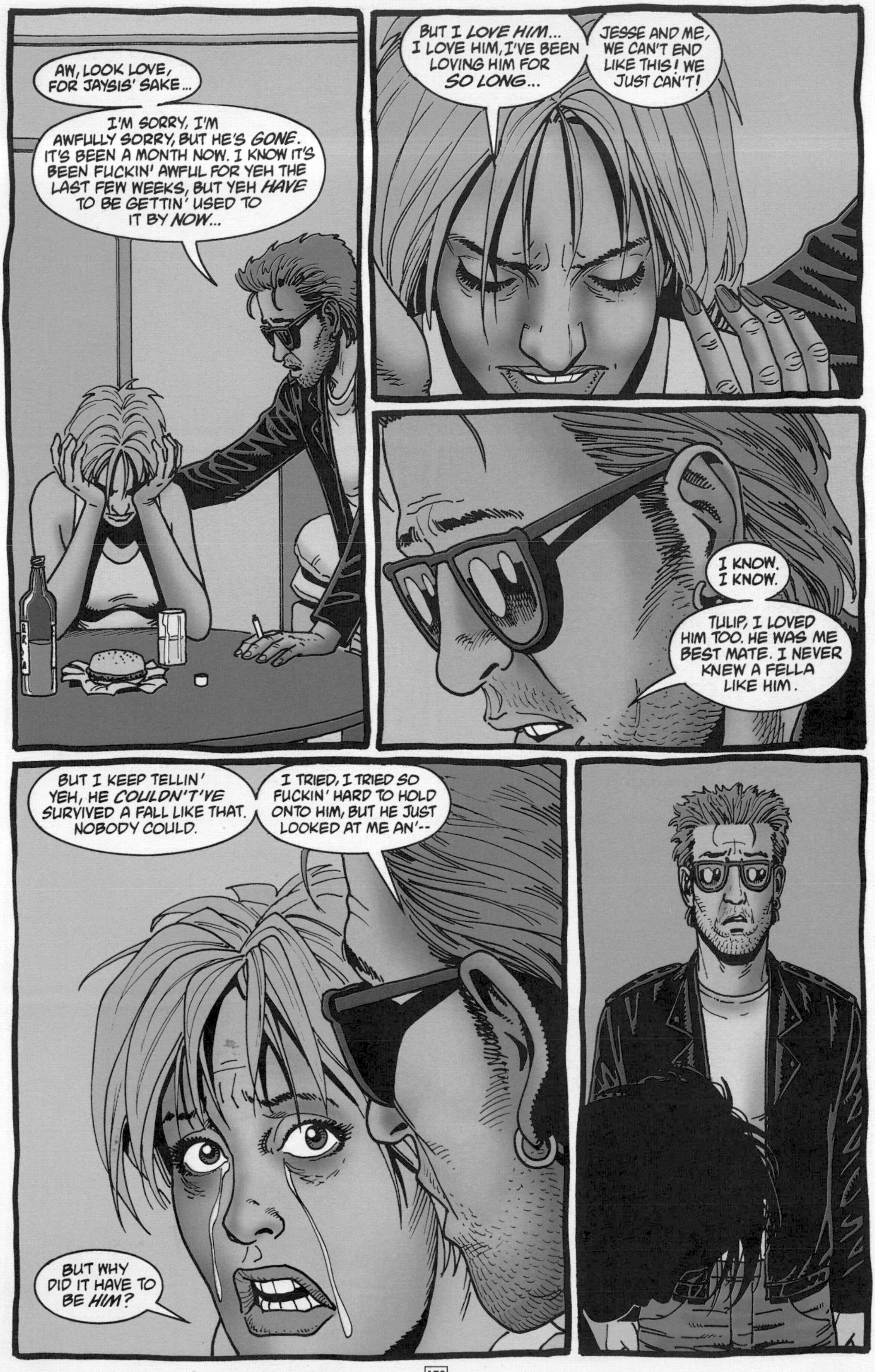
AW, LOOK LOVE, FOR JAYSIS' SAKE...
I'M SORRY, I'M AWFULLY SORRY, BUT HE'S GONE. IT'S BEEN A MONTH NOW. I KNOW IT'S BEEN FUCKIN' AWFUL FOR YEH THE LAST FEW WEEKS, BUT YEH HAVE TO BE GETTIN' USED TO IT BY NOW...
BUT I LOVE HIM... I LOVE HIM, I'VE BEEN LOVING HIM FOR SO LONG...
JESSE AND ME, WE CAN'T END LIKE THIS! WE JUST CAN'T!
I KNOW. I KNOW.
TULIP, I LOVED HIM TOO. HE WAS ME BEST MATE. I NEVER KNEW A FELLA LIKE HIM.
BUT I KEEP TELLIN' YEH, HE COULDN'T'VE SURVIVED A FALL LIKE THAT. NOBODY COULD.
I TRIED, I TRIED SO FUCKIN' HARD TO HOLD ONTO HIM, BUT HE JUST LOOKED AT ME AN'--
BUT WHY DID IT HAVE TO BE HIM?

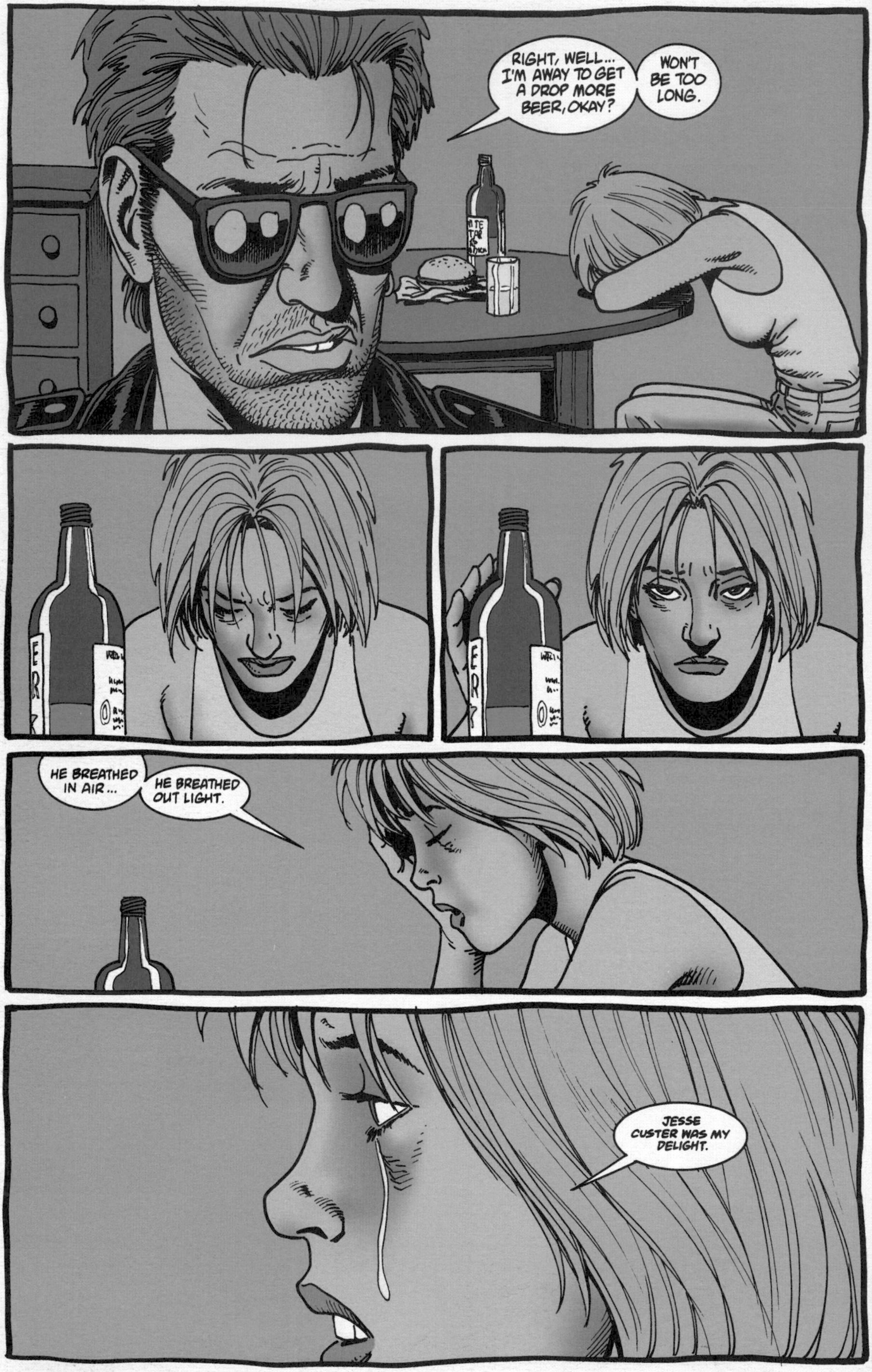
RIGHT, WELL... I'M AWAY TO GET A DROP MORE BEER, OKAY?
WON'T BE TOO LONG.
HE BREATHED IN AIR...
HE BREATHED OUT LIGHT.
JESSE CUSTER WAS MY DELIGHT.

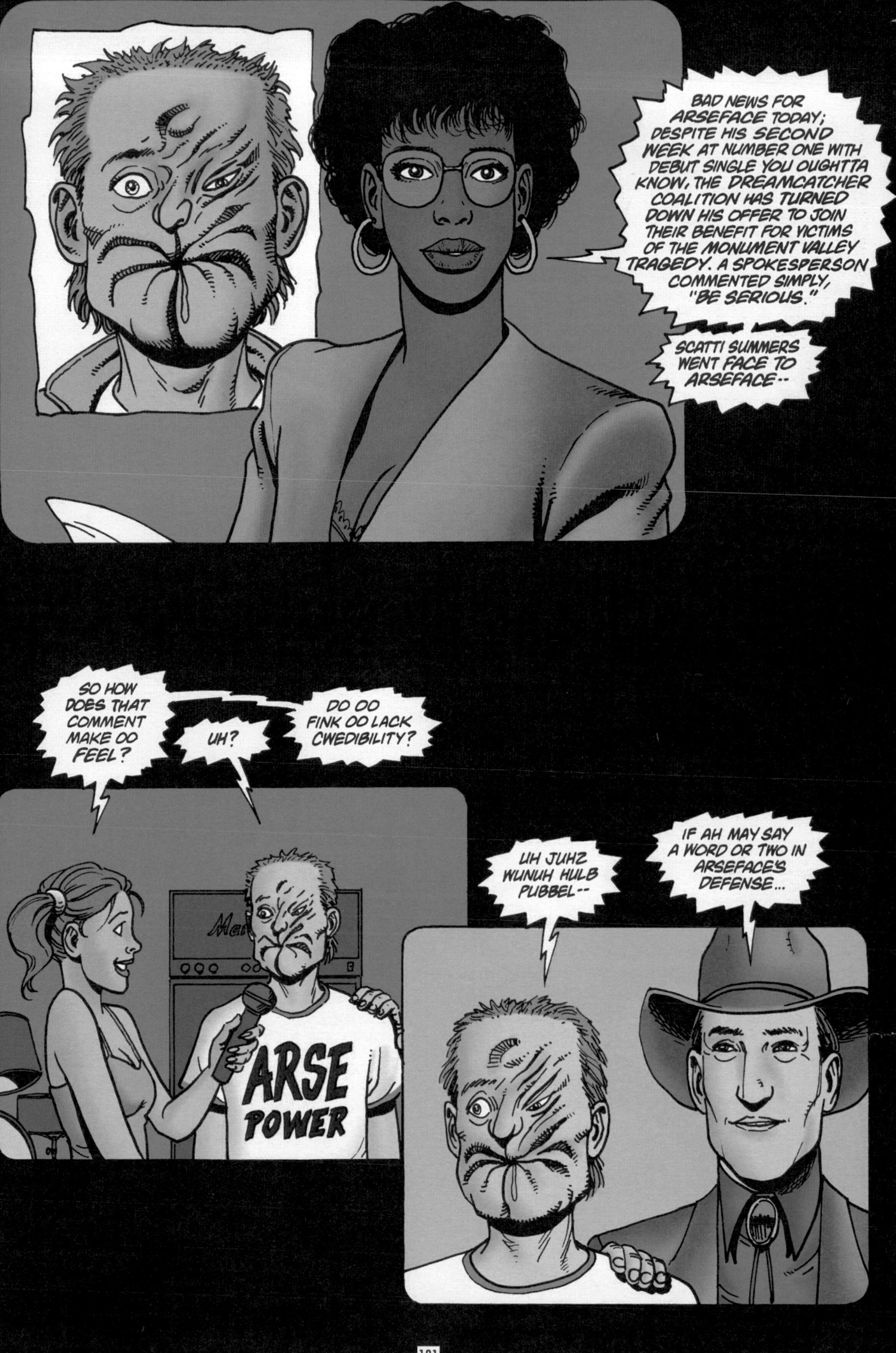
BAD NEWS FOR ARSEFACE TODAY; DESPITE HIS SECOND WEEK AT NUMBER ONE WITH DEBUT SINGLE YOU OUGHTTA KNOW, THE DREAMCATCHER COALITION HAS TURNED DOWN HIS OFFER TO JOIN THEIR BENEFIT FOR VICTIMS OF THE MONUMENT VALLEY TRAGEDY. A SPOKESPERSON COMMENTED SIMPLY, "BE SERIOUS."
SCATTI SUMMERS WENT FACE TO ARSEFACE--
SO HOW DOES THAT COMMENT MAKE OO FEEL?
UH?
DO OO FINK OO LACK CWEDIBILITY?
ARSE POWER
UH JUHZ WUNUH HULB PUBBEL--
IF AH MAY SAY A WORD OR TWO IN ARSEFACE'S DEFENSE...

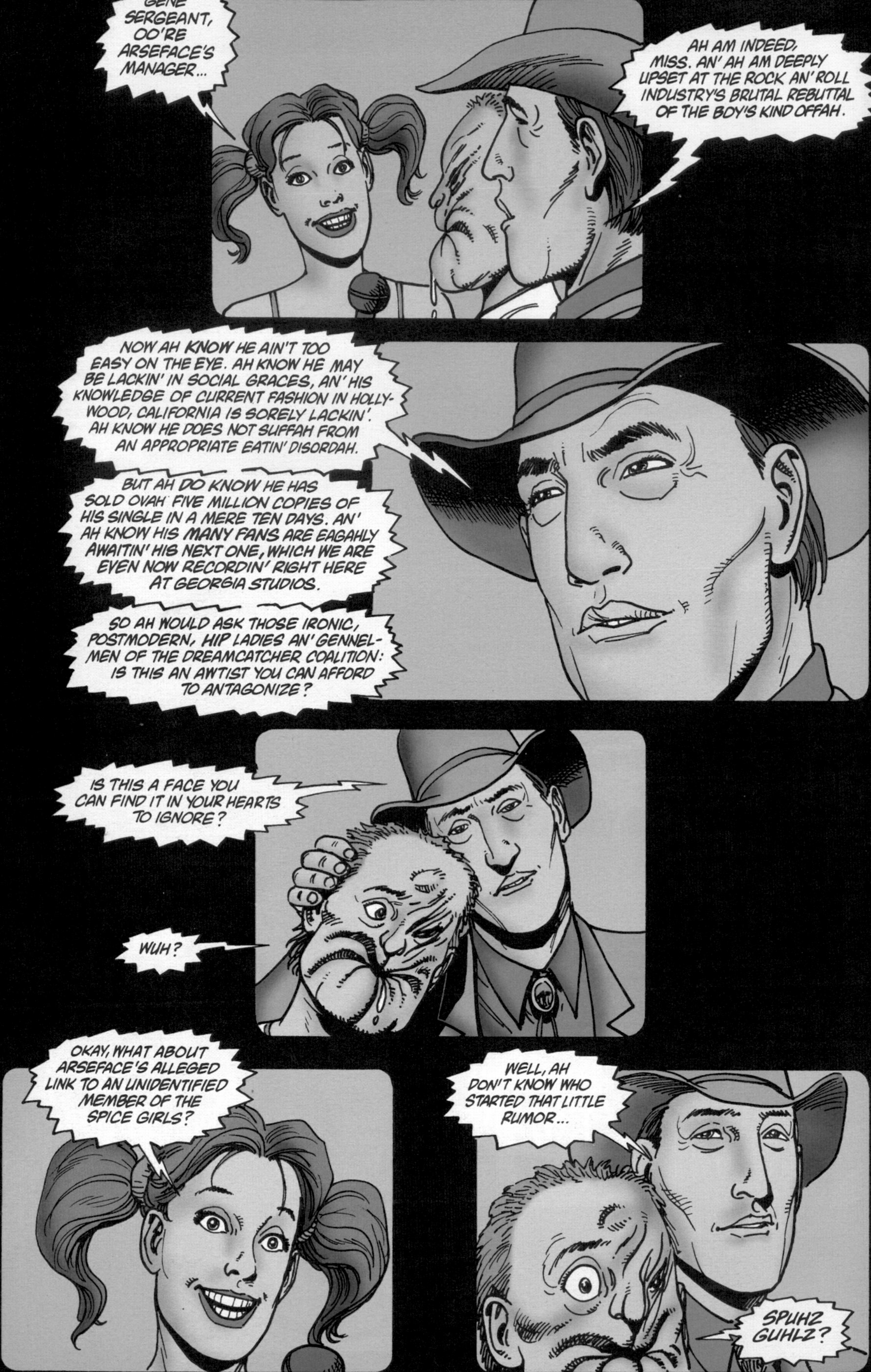
GENE SERGEANT, OO'RE ARSEFACE'S MANAGER...
AH AM INDEED, MISS. AN' AH AM DEEPLY UPSET AT THE ROCK AN' ROLL INDUSTRY'S BRUTAL REBUTTAL OF THE BOY'S KIND OFFAH.
NOW AH KNOW HE AIN'T TOO EASY ON THE EYE. AH KNOW HE MAY BE LACKIN' IN SOCIAL GRACES, AN' HIS KNOWLEDGE OF CURRENT FASHION IN HOLLY-WOOD, CALIFORNIA IS SORELY LACKIN'. AH KNOW HE DOES NOT SUFFAH FROM AN APPROPRIATE EATIN' DISORDAH.
BUT AH DO KNOW HE HAS SOLD OVAH FIVE MILLION COPIES OF HIS SINGLE IN A MERE TEN DAYS. AN' AH KNOW HIS MANY FANS ARE EAGAHLY AWAITIN' HIS NEXT ONE, WHICH WE ARE EVEN NOW RECORDIN' RIGHT HERE AT GEORGIA STUDIOS.
SO AH WOULD ASK THOSE IRONIC, POSTMODERN, HIP LADIES AN' GENNEL-MEN OF THE DREAMCATCHER COALITION: IS THIS AN AWTIST YOU CAN AFFORD TO ANTAGONIZE?
IS THIS A FACE YOU CAN FIND IT IN YOUR HEARTS TO IGNORE?
WUH?
OKAY, WHAT ABOUT ARSEFACE'S ALLEGED LINK TO AN UNIDENTIFIED MEMBER OF THE SPICE GIRLS?
WELL, AH DON'T KNOW WHO STARTED THAT LITTLE RUMOR...
SPUHZ GUHLZ?

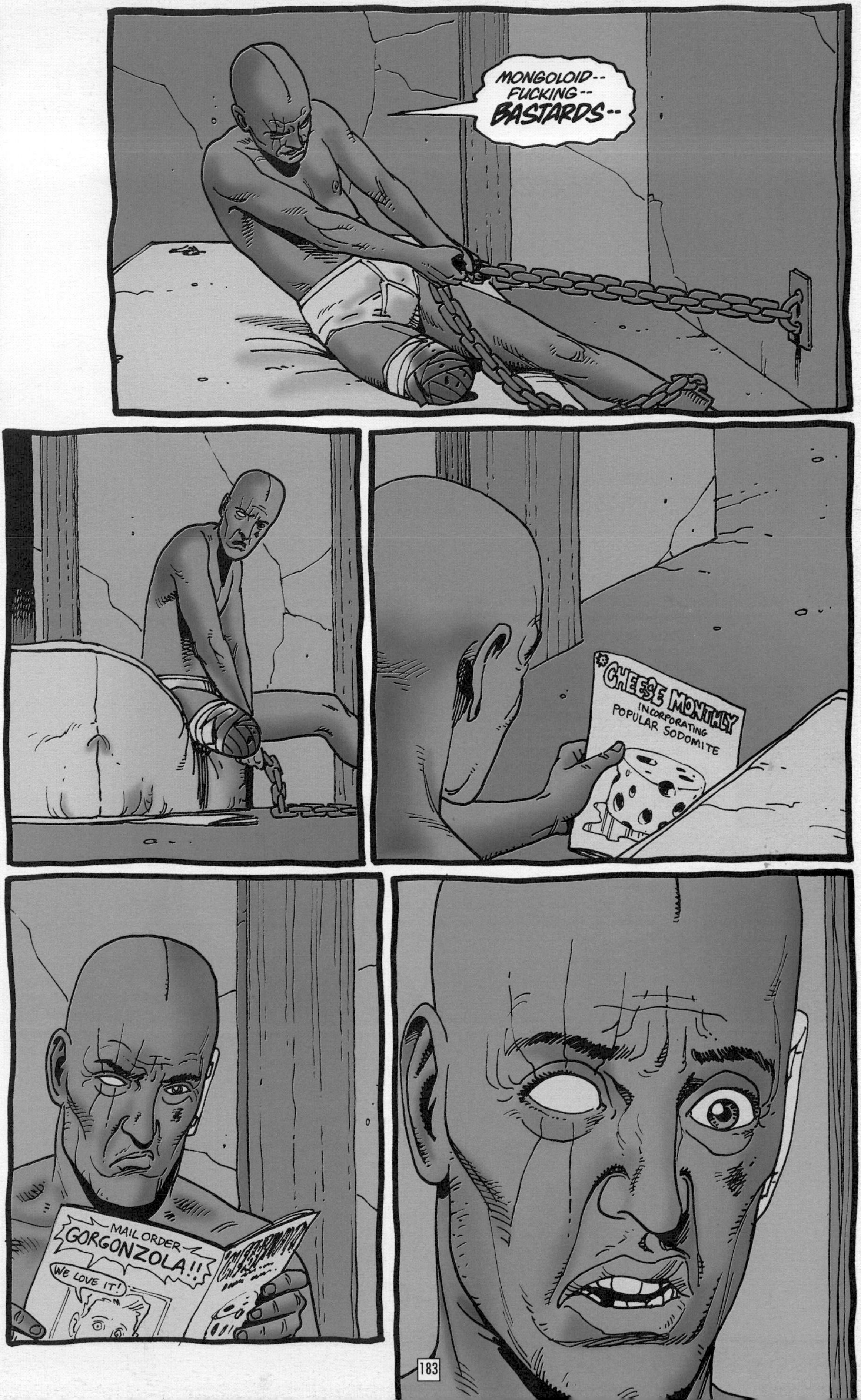
MONGOLOID-- FUCKING-- BASTARDS--
CHEESE MONTHLY
INCORPORATING POPULAR SODOMITE
MAIL ORDER
GORGONZOLA!!
WE LOVE IT!

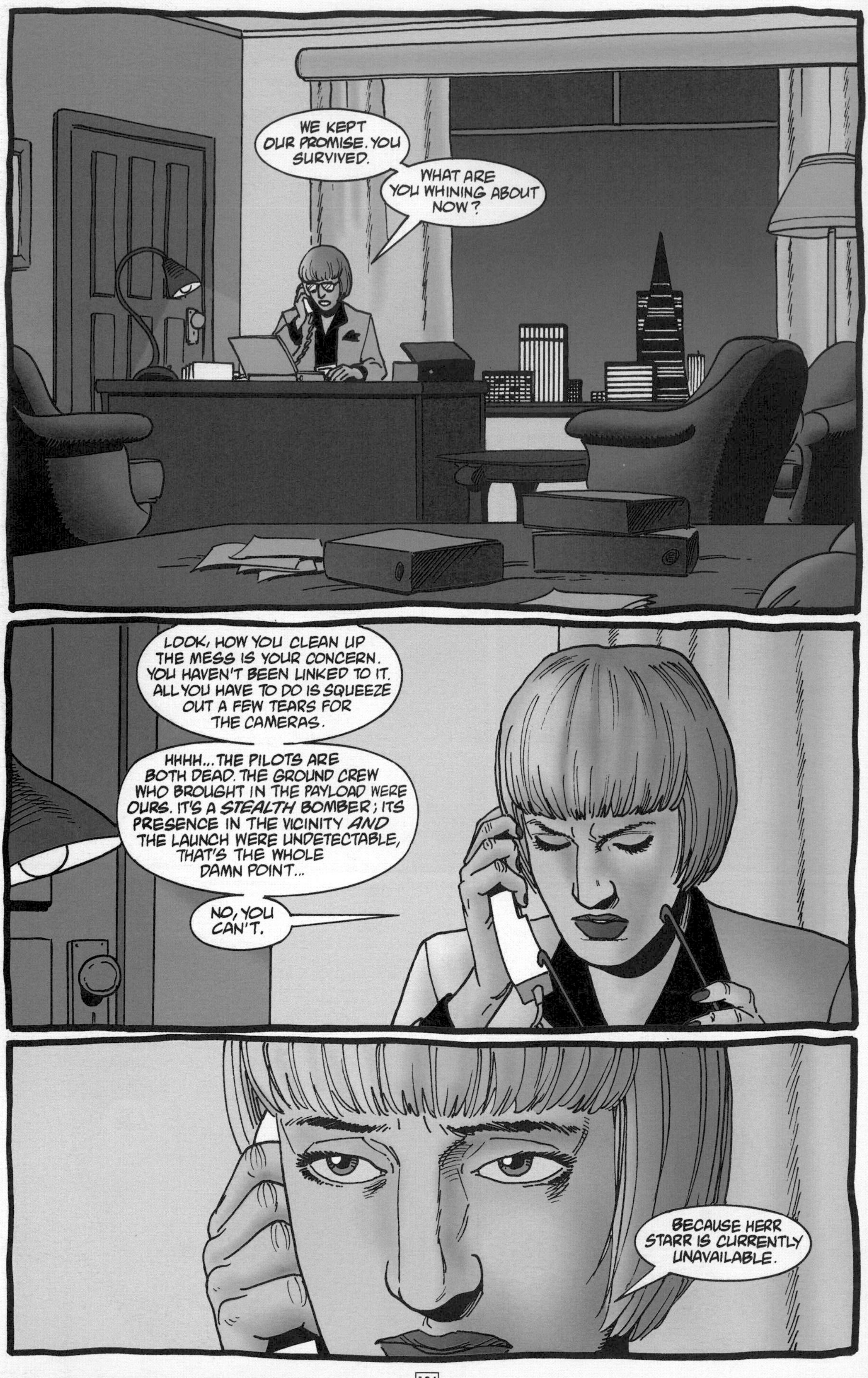
WE KEPT OUR PROMISE. YOU SURVIVED.
WHAT ARE YOU WHINING ABOUT NOW?
LOOK, HOW YOU CLEAN UP THE MESS IS YOUR CONCERN. YOU HAVEN'T BEEN LINKED TO IT. ALL YOU HAVE TO DO IS SQUEEZE OUT A FEW TEARS FOR THE CAMERAS.
HHHH... THE PILOTS ARE BOTH DEAD. THE GROUND CREW WHO BROUGHT IN THE PAYLOAD WERE OURS. IT'S A *STEALTH* BOMBER; ITS PRESENCE IN THE VICINITY *AND* THE LAUNCH WERE UNDETECTABLE, THAT'S THE WHOLE DAMN POINT...
NO, YOU CAN'T.
BECAUSE HERR STARR IS CURRENTLY UNAVAILABLE.

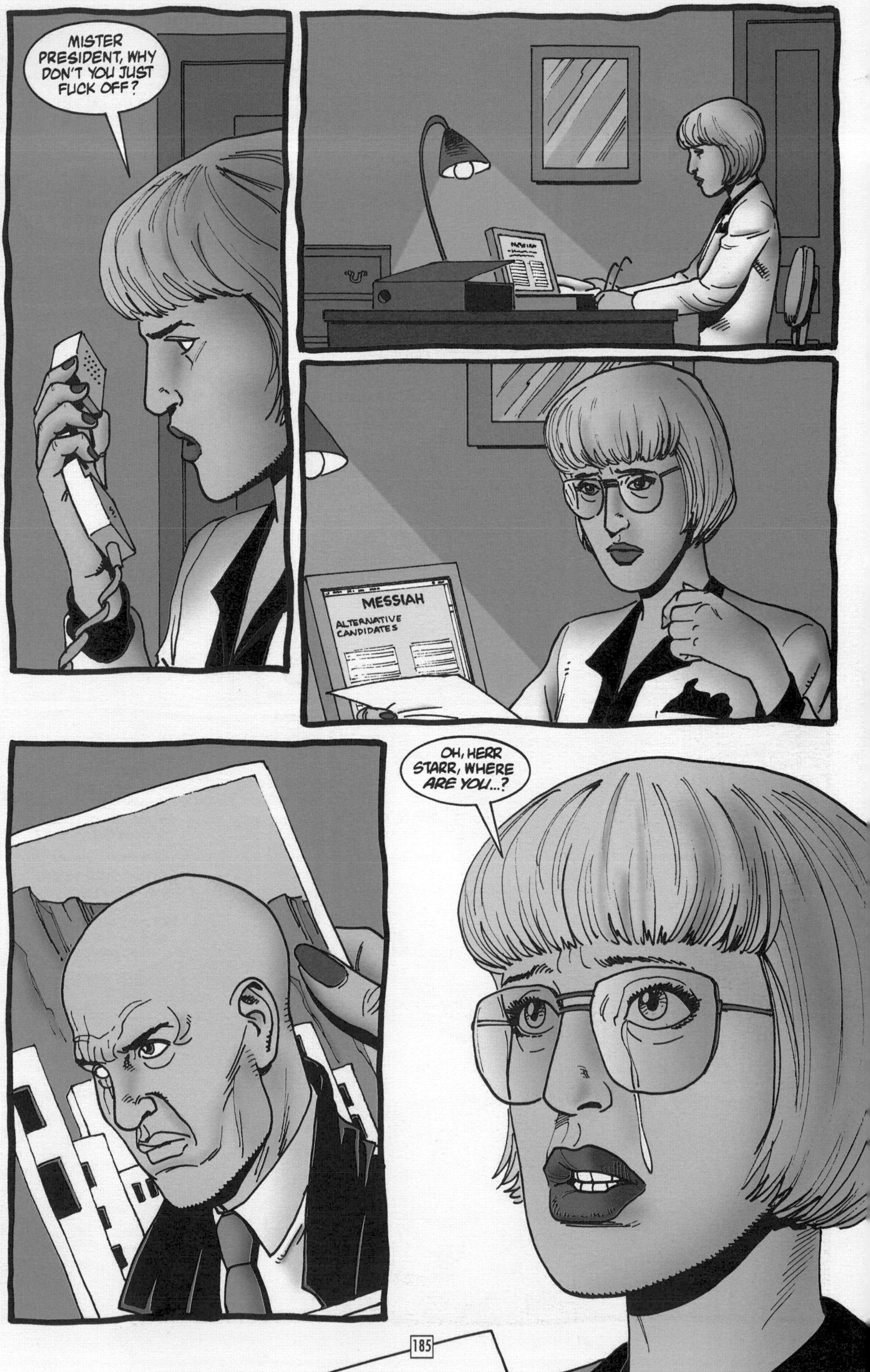
MISTER PRESIDENT, WHY DON'T YOU JUST FUCK OFF?
MESSIAH
ALTERNATIVE CANDIDATES
OH, HERR STARR, WHERE ARE YOU...?

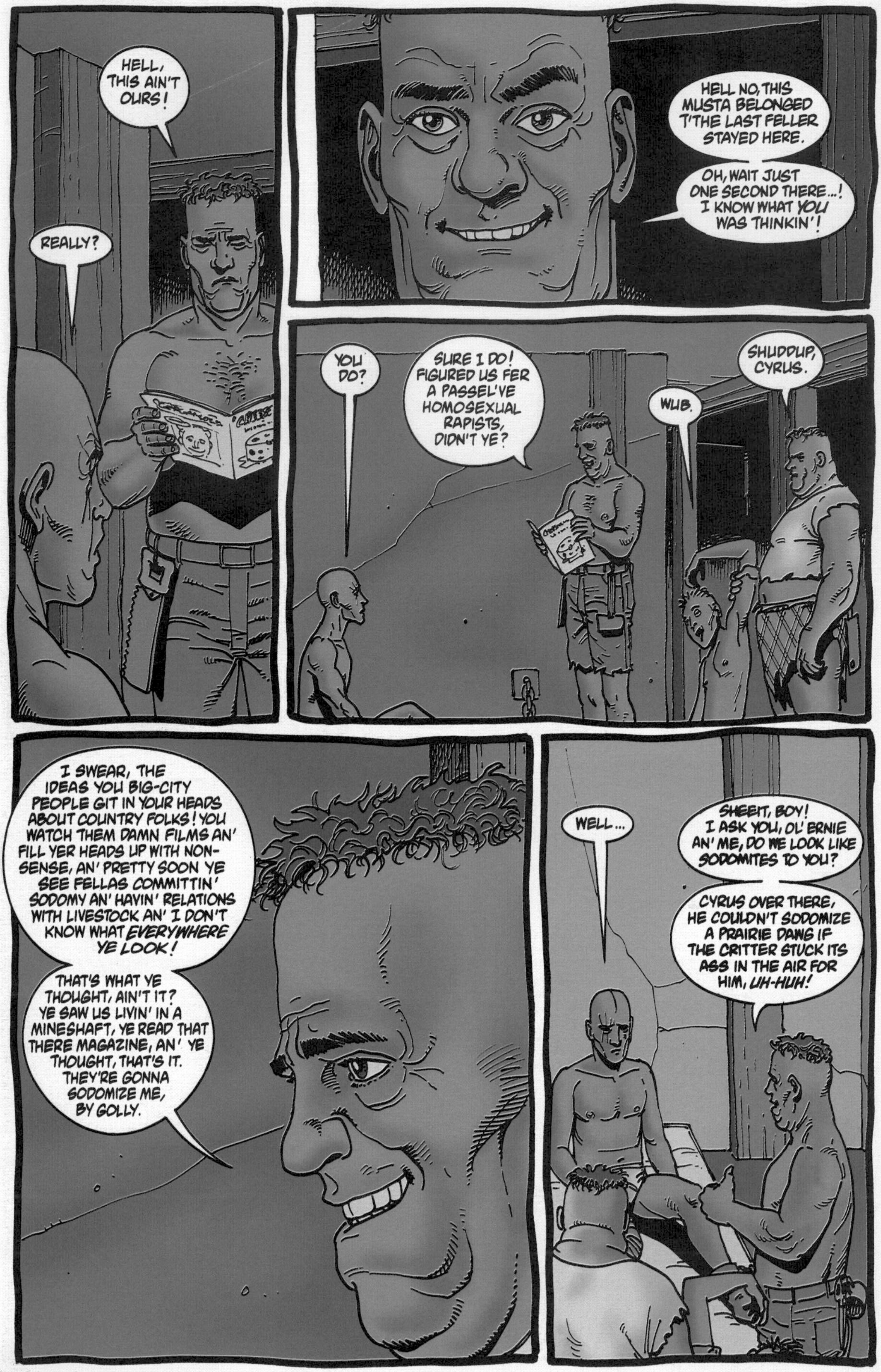
HELL, THIS AIN'T OURS!
REALLY?
HELL NO, THIS MUSTA BELONGED T'THE LAST FELLER STAYED HERE.
OH, WAIT JUST ONE SECOND THERE...! I KNOW WHAT YOU WAS THINKIN'!
YOU DO?
SURE I DO! FIGURED US FER A PASSEL'VE HOMOSEXUAL RAPISTS, DIDN'T YE?
WUB.
SHUDDUP, CYRUS.
I SWEAR, THE IDEAS YOU BIG-CITY PEOPLE GIT IN YOUR HEADS ABOUT COUNTRY FOLKS! YOU WATCH THEM DAMN FILMS AN' FILL YER HEADS UP WITH NON-SENSE, AN' PRETTY SOON YE SEE FELLAS COMMITTIN' SODOMY AN' HAVIN' RELATIONS WITH LIVESTOCK AN' I DON'T KNOW WHAT EVERYWHERE YE LOOK!
THAT'S WHAT YE THOUGHT, AIN'T IT? YE SAW US LIVIN' IN A MINESHAFT, YE READ THAT THERE MAGAZINE, AN' YE THOUGHT, THAT'S IT. THEY'RE GONNA SODOMIZE ME, BY GOLLY.
WELL...
SHEEIT, BOY! I ASK YOU, OL' ERNIE AN' ME, DO WE LOOK LIKE SODOMITES TO YOU?
CYRUS OVER THERE, HE COULDN'T SODOMIZE A PRAIRIE DAWG IF THE CRITTER STUCK ITS ASS IN THE AIR FOR HIM, UH-HUH!

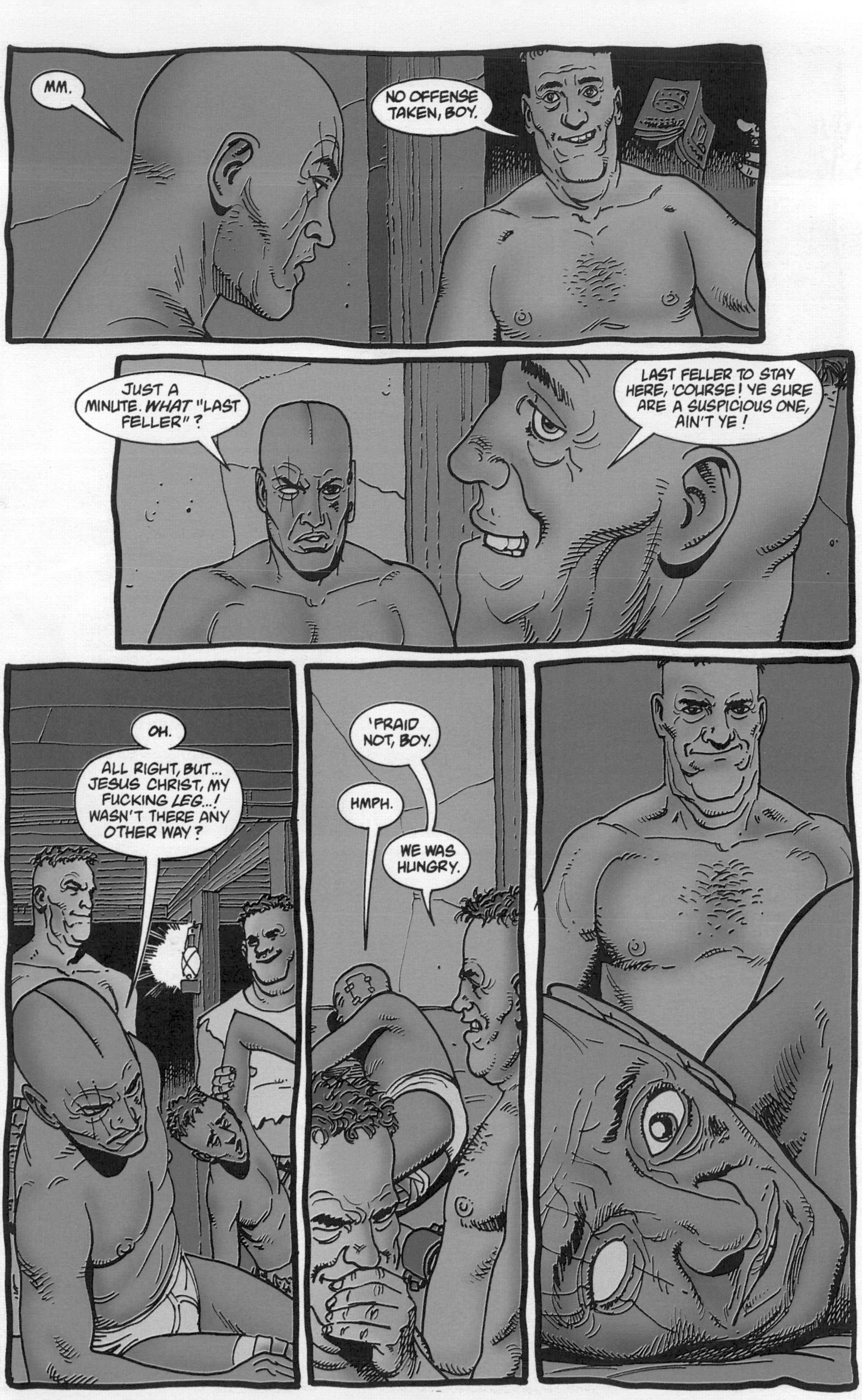
MM.
NO OFFENSE TAKEN, BOY.
JUST A MINUTE. WHAT "LAST FELLER"?
LAST FELLER TO STAY HERE, 'COURSE! YE SURE ARE A SUSPICIOUS ONE, AIN'T YE!
OH.
ALL RIGHT, BUT... JESUS CHRIST, MY FUCKING LEG...! WASN'T THERE ANY OTHER WAY?
'FRAID NOT, BOY.
HMPH.
WE WAS HUNGRY.

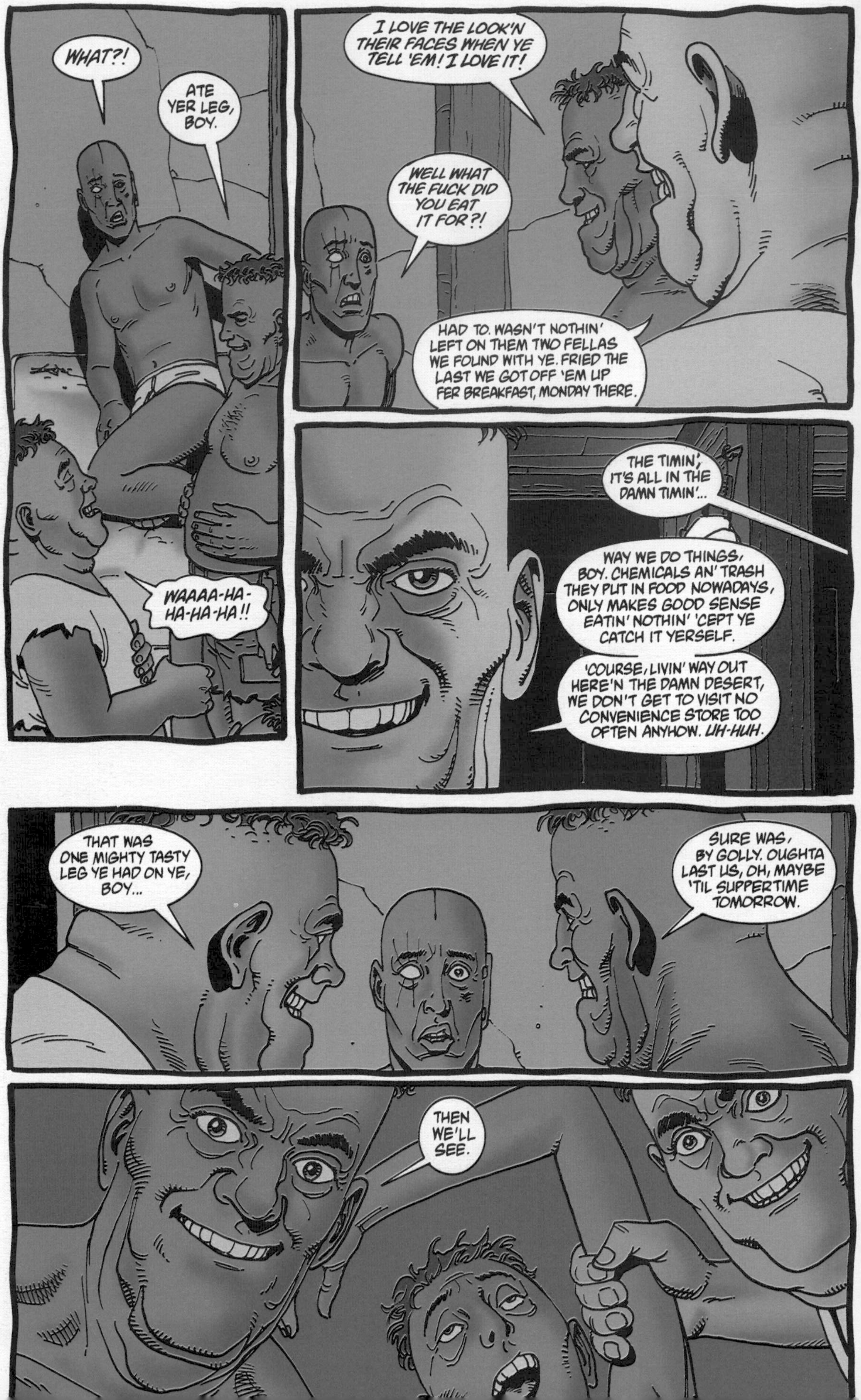
WHAT?!
ATE YER LEG, BOY.
WAAAA-HA-HA-HA-HA!!
I LOVE THE LOOK'N THEIR FACES WHEN YE TELL 'EM! I LOVE IT!
WELL WHAT THE FUCK DID YOU EAT IT FOR?!
HAD TO. WASN'T NOTHIN' LEFT ON THEM TWO FELLAS WE FOUND WITH YE. FRIED THE LAST WE GOT OFF 'EM UP FER BREAKFAST, MONDAY THERE.
THE TIMIN', IT'S ALL IN THE DAMN TIMIN'...
WAY WE DO THINGS, BOY. CHEMICALS AN' TRASH THEY PUT IN FOOD NOWADAYS, ONLY MAKES GOOD SENSE EATIN' NOTHIN' 'CEPT YE CATCH IT YERSELF.
'COURSE, LIVIN' WAY OUT HERE'N THE DAMN DESERT, WE DON'T GET TO VISIT NO CONVENIENCE STORE TOO OFTEN ANYHOW. UH-HUH.
THAT WAS ONE MIGHTY TASTY LEG YE HAD ON YE, BOY...
SURE WAS, BY GOLLY. OUGHTA LAST US, OH, MAYBE 'TIL SUPPERTIME TOMORROW.
THEN WE'LL SEE.

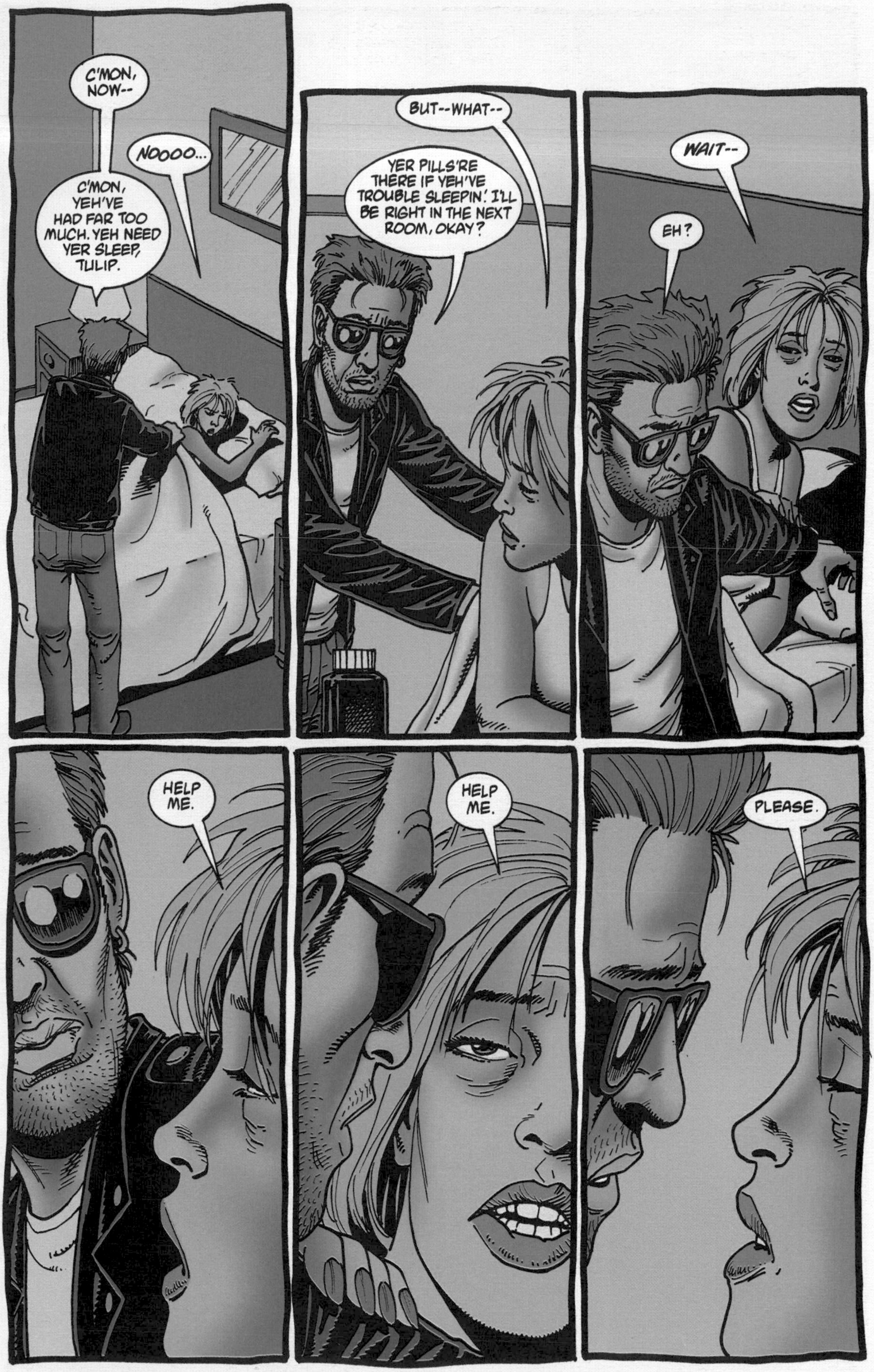
C'MON, NOW--
NOOOO...
C'MON, YEH'VE HAD FAR TOO MUCH. YEH NEED YER SLEEP, TULIP.
BUT--WHAT--
YER PILLS'RE THERE IF YEH'VE TROUBLE SLEEPIN.' I'LL BE RIGHT IN THE NEXT ROOM, OKAY?
WAIT--
EH?
HELP ME.
HELP ME.
PLEASE.

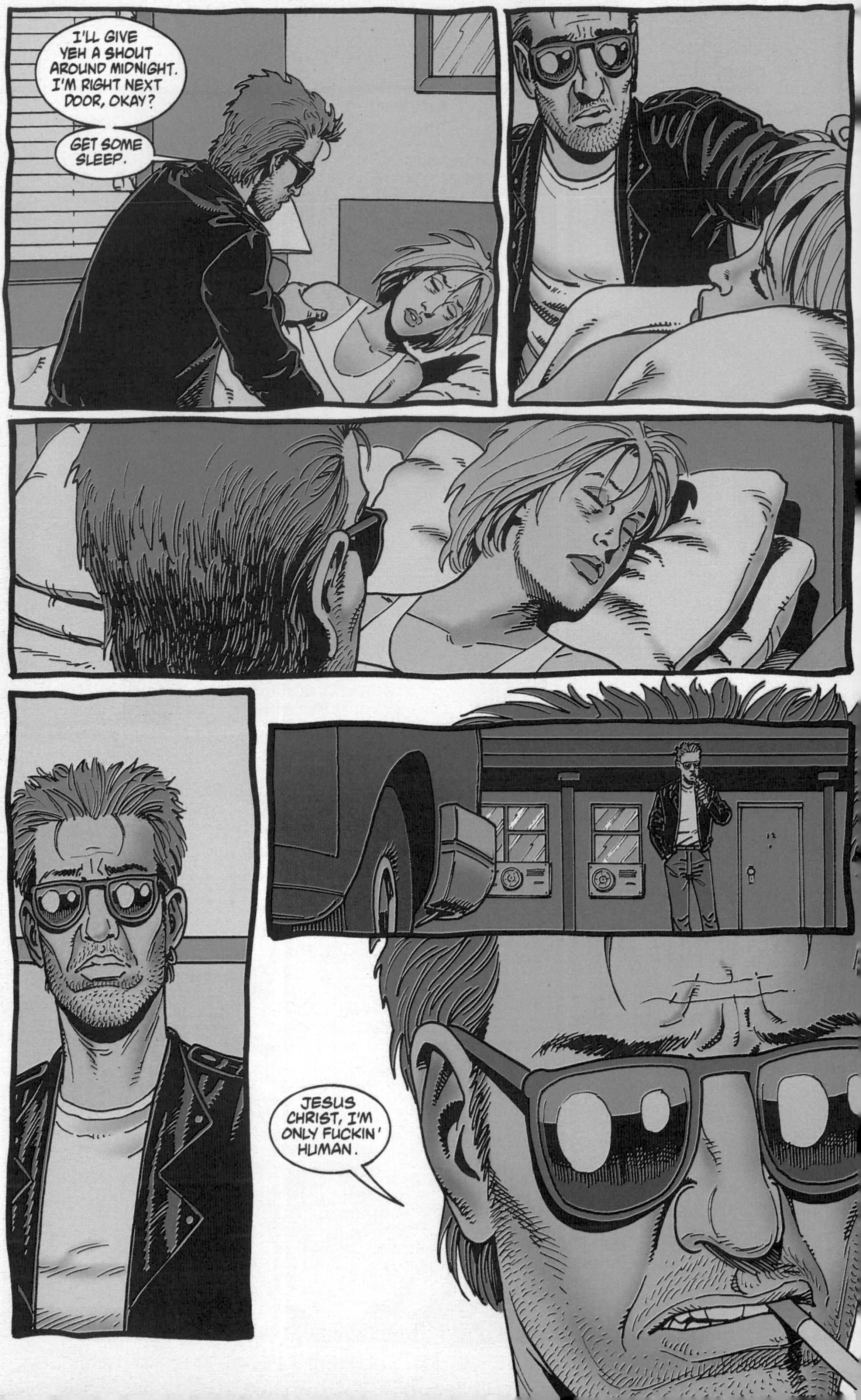
I'LL GIVE YEH A SHOUT AROUND MIDNIGHT. I'M RIGHT NEXT DOOR, OKAY?
GET SOME SLEEP.
JESUS CHRIST, I'M ONLY FUCKIN' HUMAN.

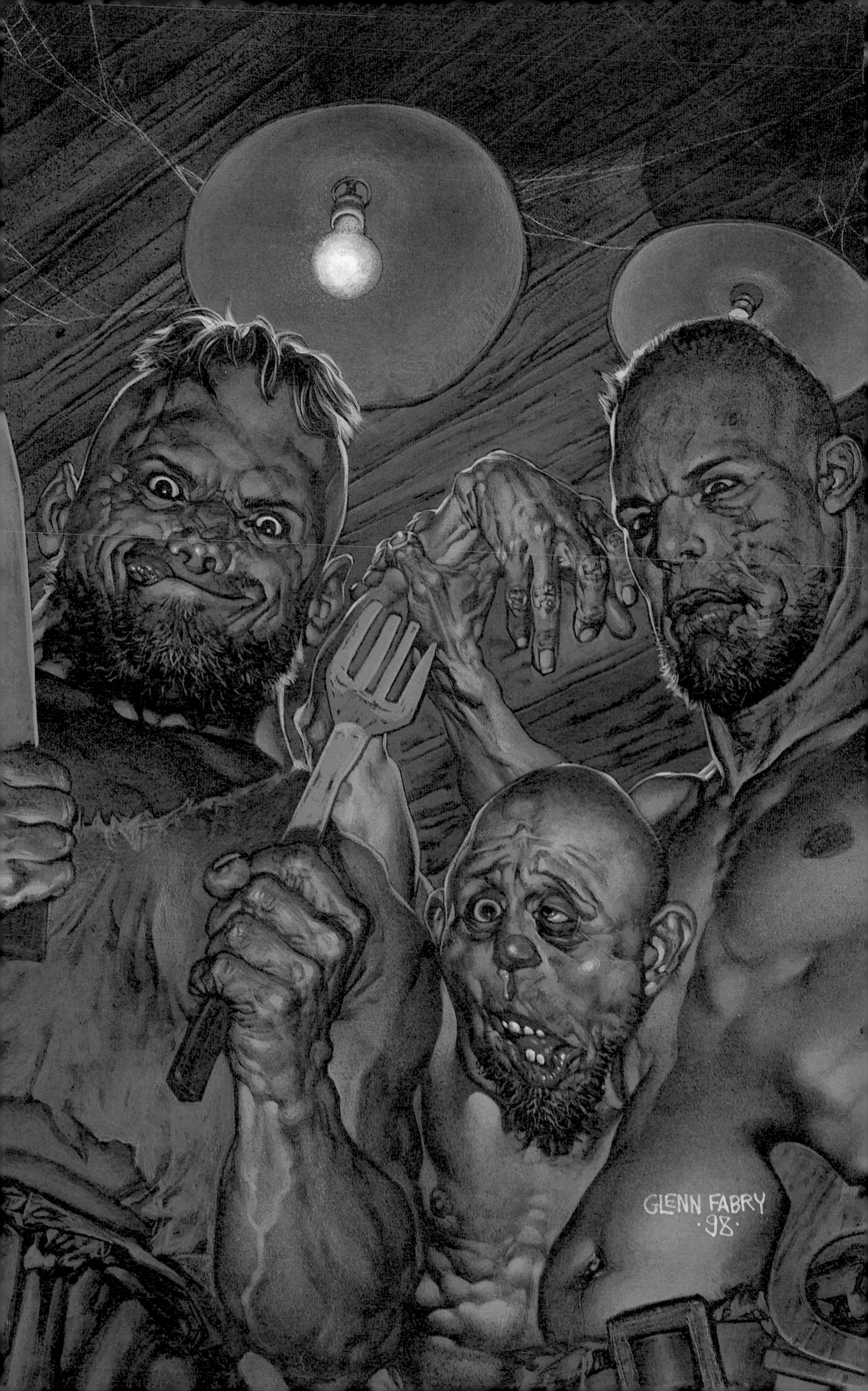
GLENN FABRY
·98·

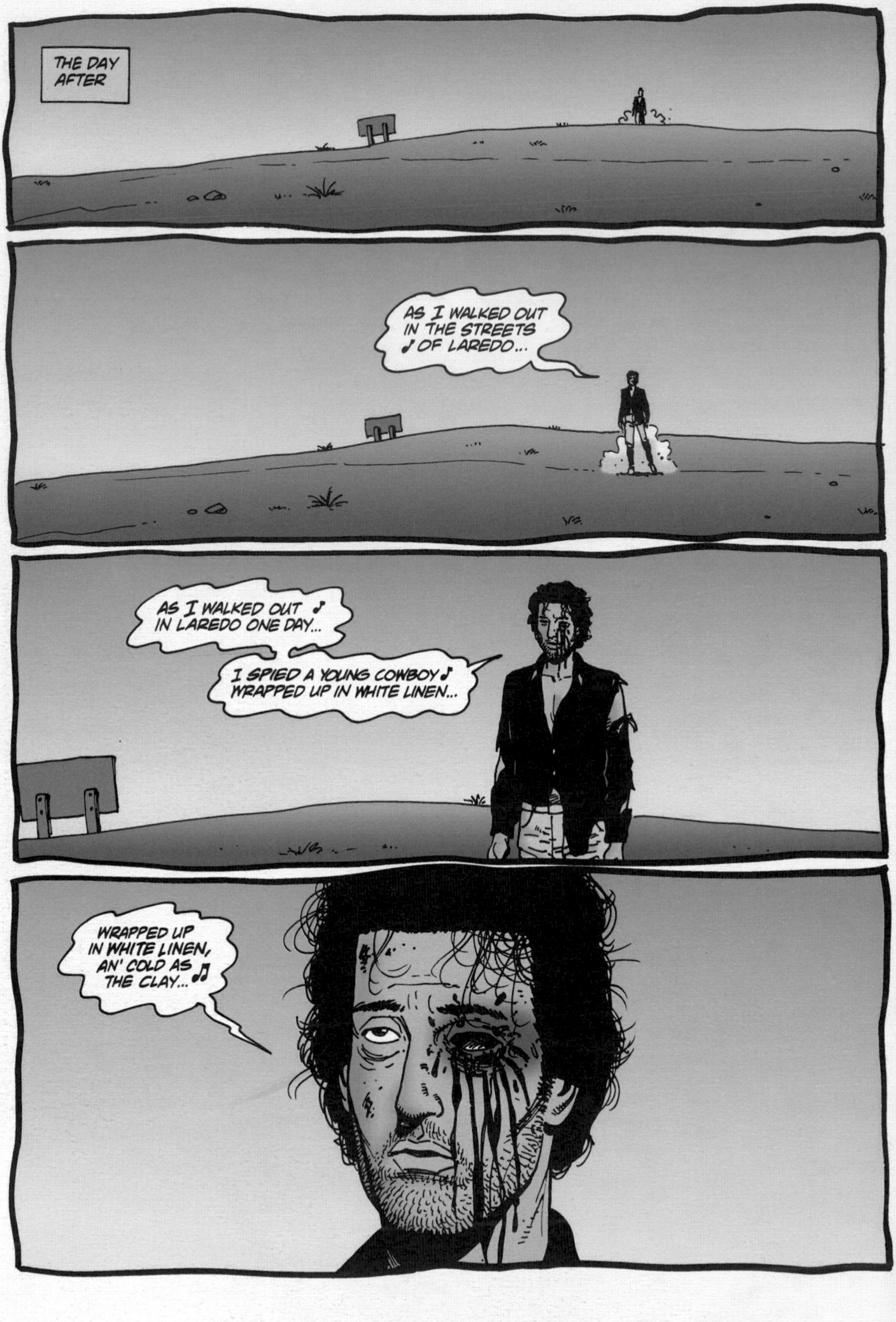
THE DAY AFTER
AS I WALKED OUT IN THE STREETS ♪ OF LAREDO...
AS I WALKED OUT ♪ IN LAREDO ONE DAY...
I SPIED A YOUNG COWBOY ♪ WRAPPED UP IN WHITE LINEN...
WRAPPED UP IN WHITE LINEN, AN' COLD AS THE CLAY... ♫

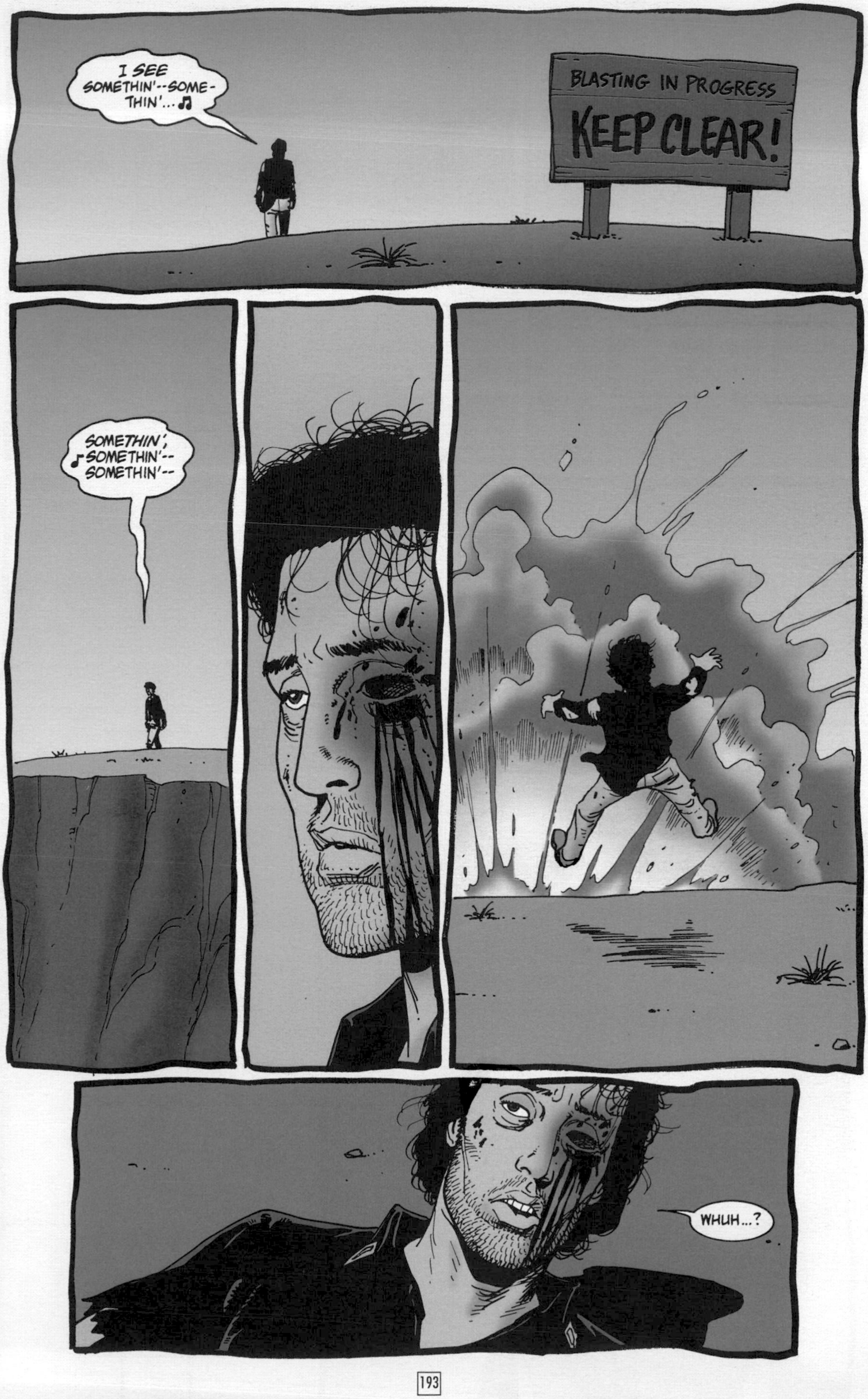

I SEE SOMETHIN'--SOME-THIN'...
BLASTING IN PROGRESS
KEEP CLEAR!
SOMETHIN', SOMETHIN'-- SOMETHIN'--
WHUH...?

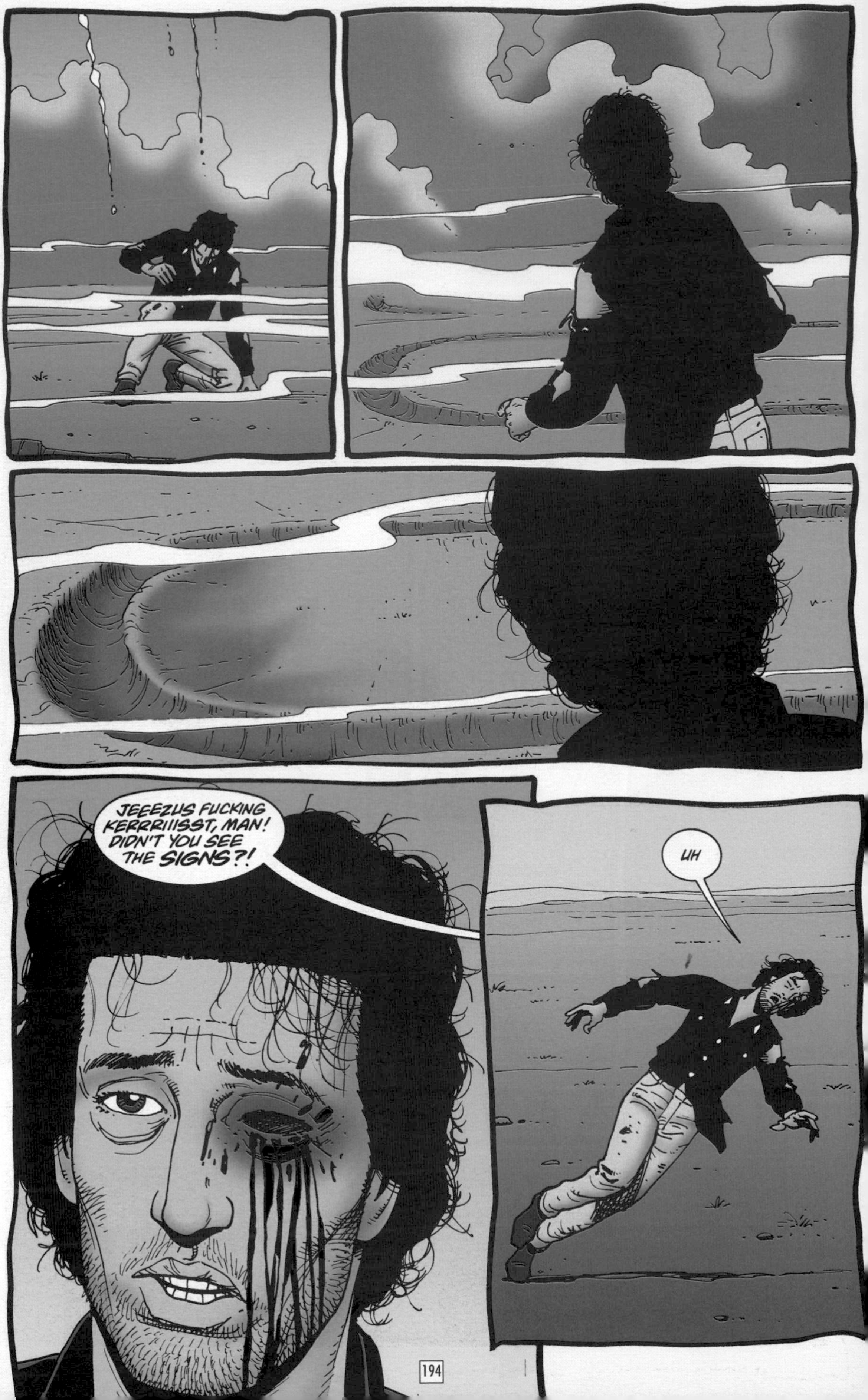
JEEEZUS FUCKING KERRRIIISST, MAN! DIDN'T YOU SEE THE SIGNS?!
UH

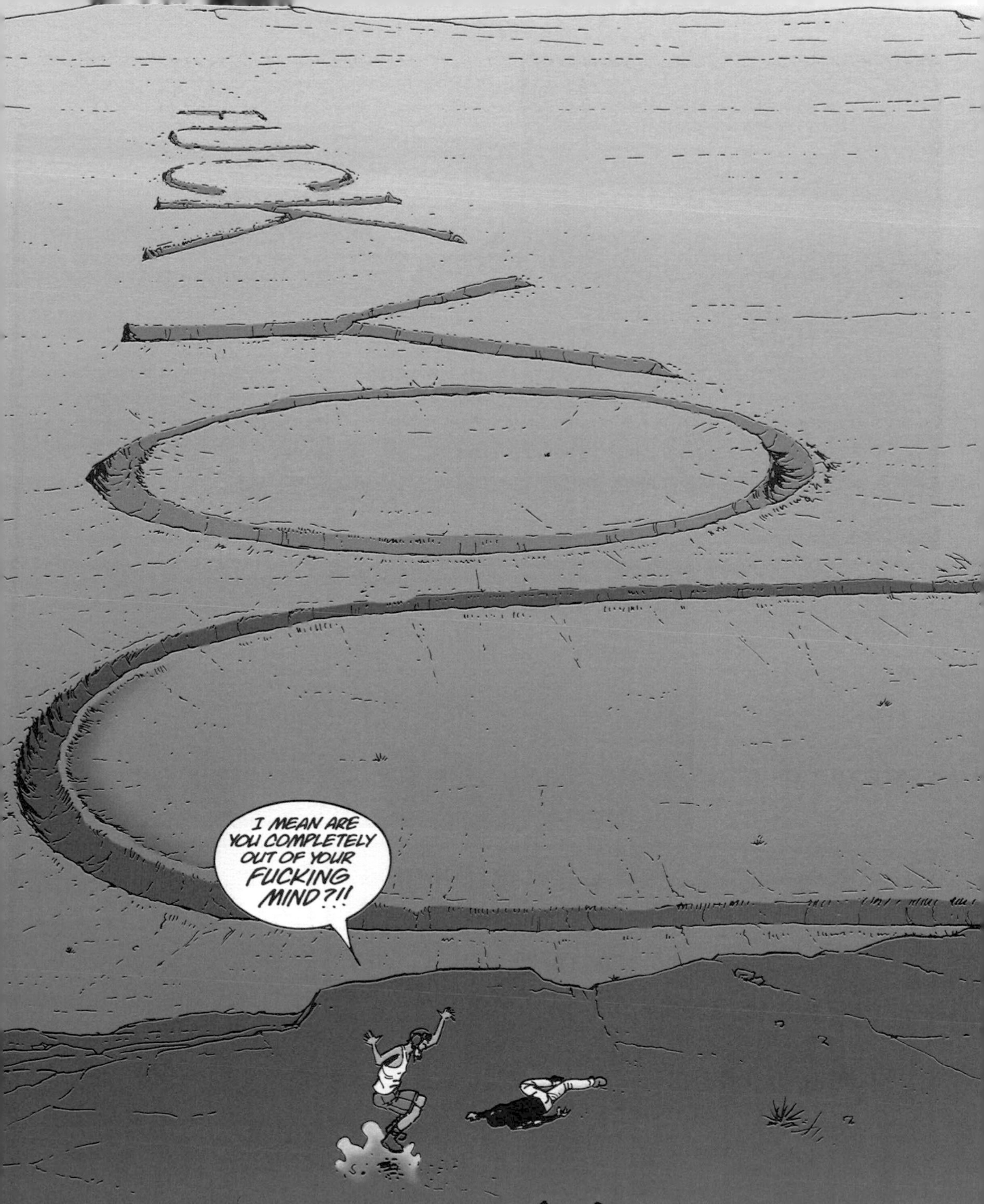
I MEAN ARE YOU COMPLETELY OUT OF YOUR FUCKING MIND?!!

FOR ALL MANKIND

GARTH ENNIS-Writer STEVE DILLON-Artist

Pamela Rambo-Colorist, Clem Robins-Letterer, Axel Alonso-Editor

PREACHER created by Garth Ennis and Steve Dillon

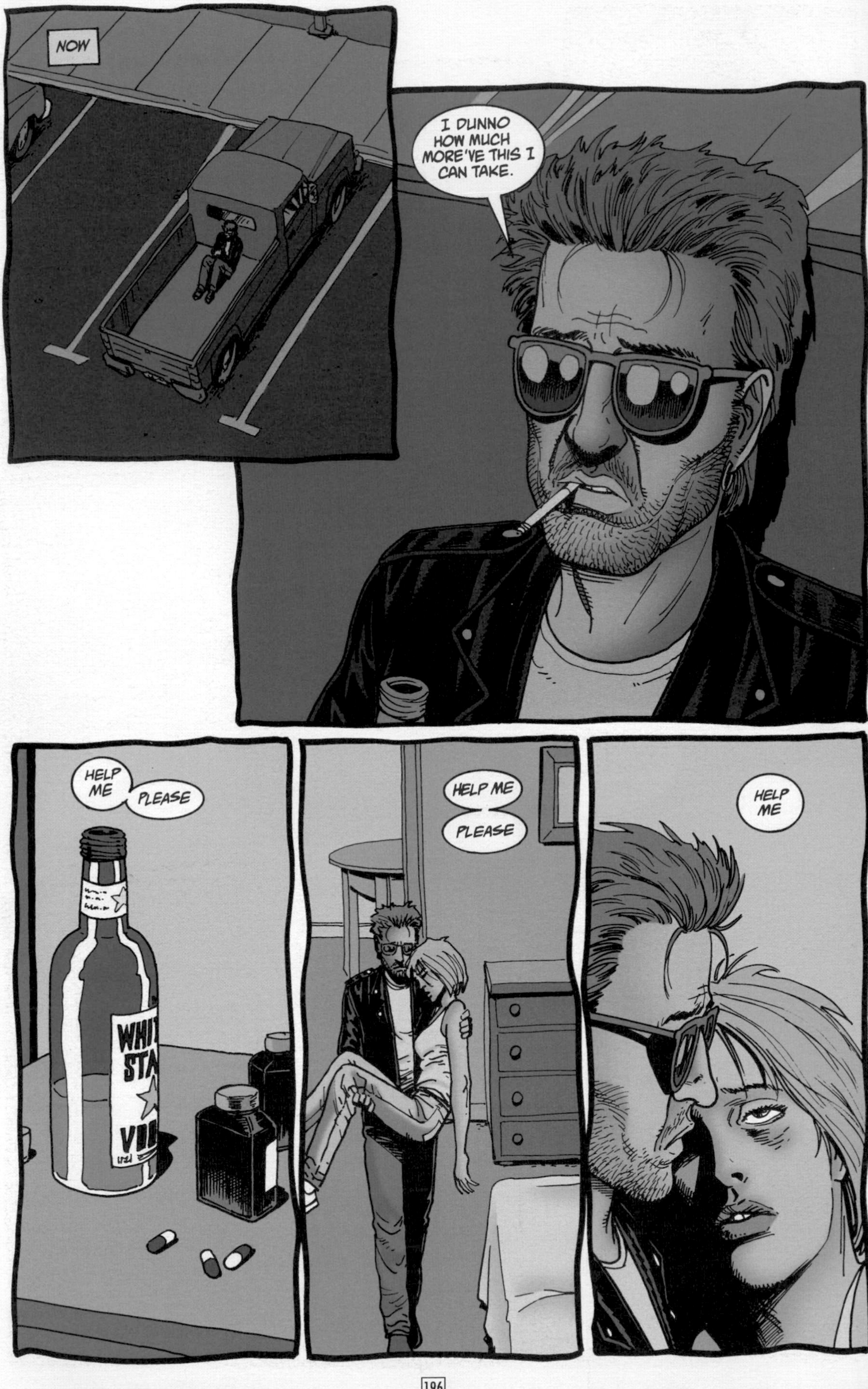
NOW
I DUNNO HOW MUCH MORE'VE THIS I CAN TAKE.
HELP ME
PLEASE
WHITE STAR VODKA
HELP ME
PLEASE
HELP ME

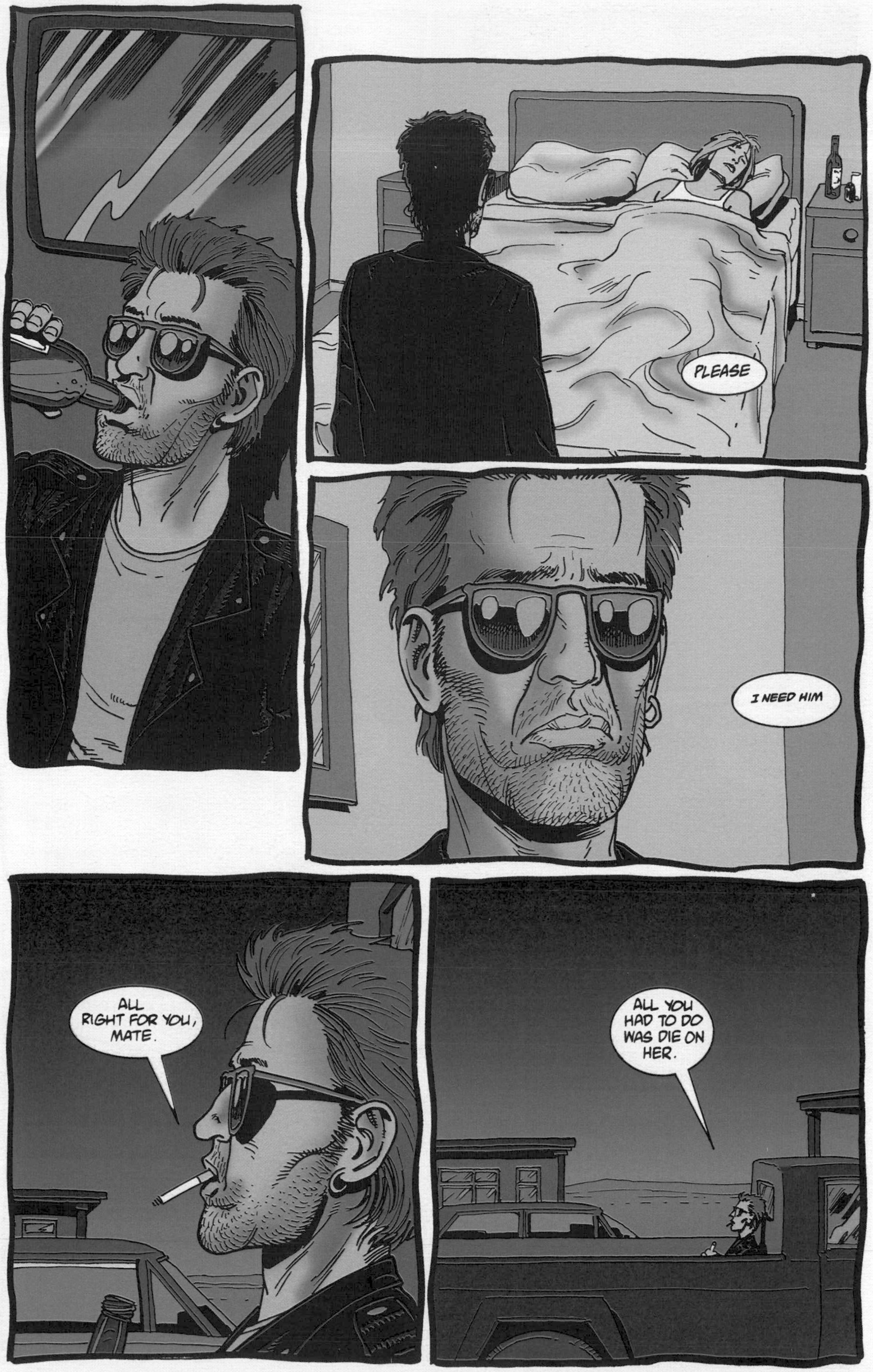
PLEASE
I NEED HIM
ALL RIGHT FOR YOU, MATE.
ALL YOU HAD TO DO WAS DIE ON HER.

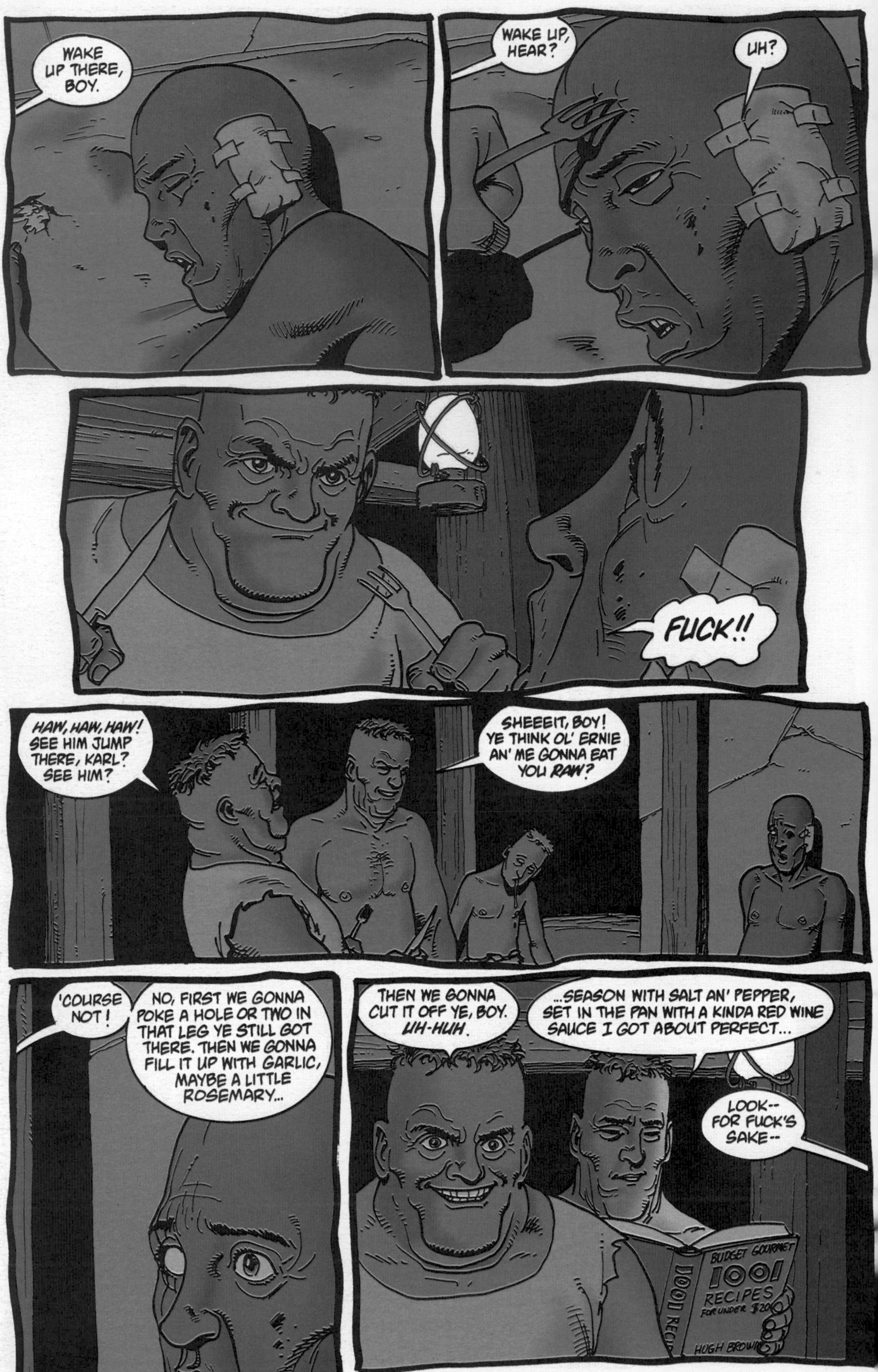
WAKE UP THERE, BOY.
WAKE UP, HEAR?
UH?
FUCK!!
HAW, HAW, HAW! SEE HIM JUMP THERE, KARL? SEE HIM?
SHEEEIT, BOY! YE THINK OL' ERNIE AN' ME GONNA EAT YOU RAW?
'COURSE NOT!
NO, FIRST WE GONNA POKE A HOLE OR TWO IN THAT LEG YE STILL GOT THERE. THEN WE GONNA FILL IT UP WITH GARLIC, MAYBE A LITTLE ROSEMARY...
THEN WE GONNA CUT IT OFF YE, BOY. UH-HUH.
...SEASON WITH SALT AN' PEPPER, SET IN THE PAN WITH A KINDA RED WINE SAUCE I GOT ABOUT PERFECT...
LOOK-- FOR FUCK'S SAKE--
BUDGET GOURMET 1001 RECIPES FOR UNDER $20
HUGH BROWN

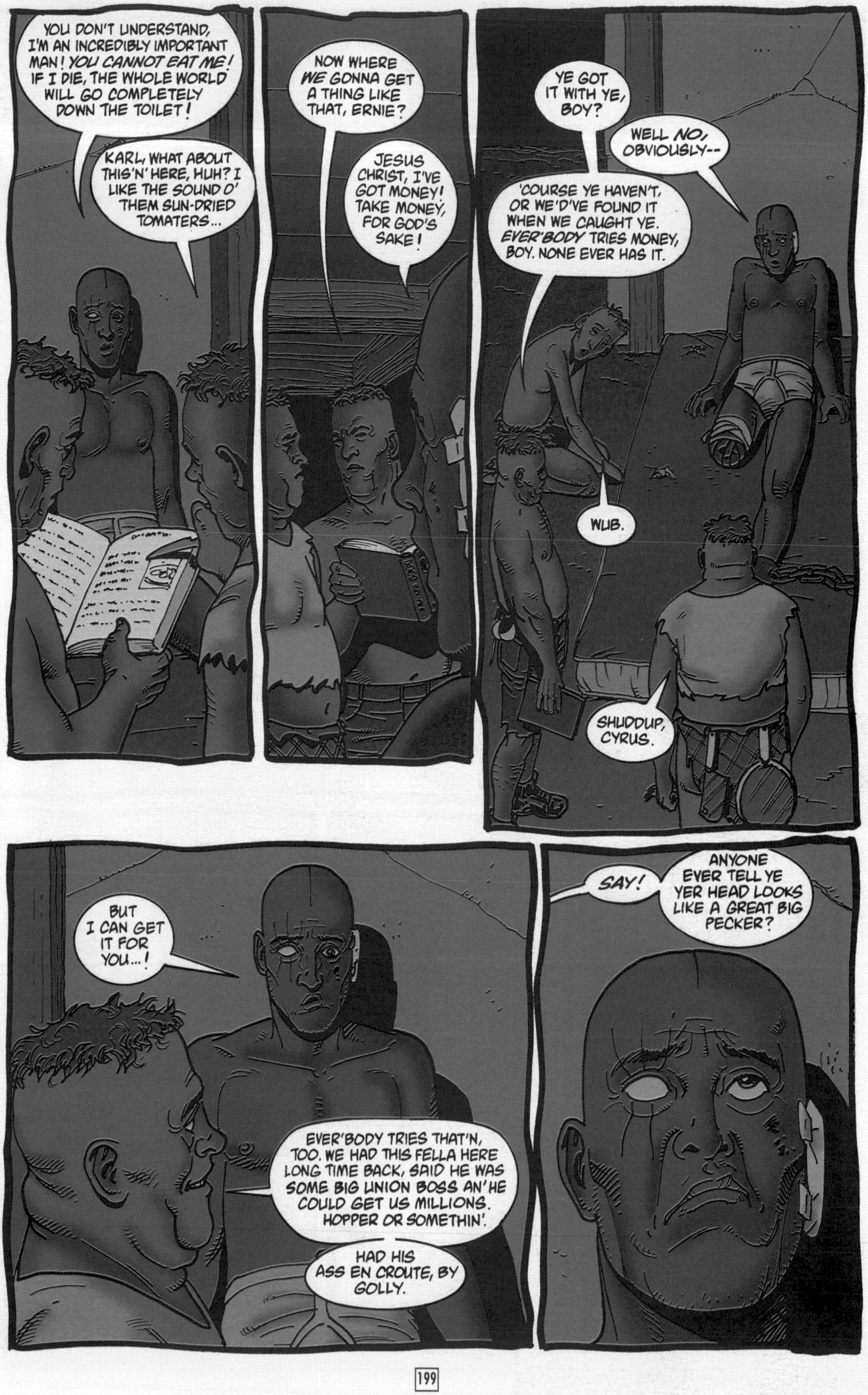
YOU DON'T UNDERSTAND, I'M AN INCREDIBLY IMPORTANT MAN! YOU CANNOT EAT ME! IF I DIE, THE WHOLE WORLD WILL GO COMPLETELY DOWN THE TOILET!
KARL, WHAT ABOUT THIS'N' HERE, HUH? I LIKE THE SOUND O' THEM SUN-DRIED TOMATERS...
NOW WHERE WE GONNA GET A THING LIKE THAT, ERNIE?
JESUS CHRIST, I'VE GOT MONEY! TAKE MONEY, FOR GOD'S SAKE!
YE GOT IT WITH YE, BOY?
WELL NO, OBVIOUSLY--
'COURSE YE HAVEN'T, OR WE'D'VE FOUND IT WHEN WE CAUGHT YE. EVER'BODY TRIES MONEY, BOY. NONE EVER HAS IT.
WUB.
SHUDDUP, CYRUS.
BUT I CAN GET IT FOR YOU...!
EVER'BODY TRIES THAT'N, TOO. WE HAD THIS FELLA HERE LONG TIME BACK, SAID HE WAS SOME BIG UNION BOSS AN' HE COULD GET US MILLIONS. HOPPER OR SOMETHIN'.
HAD HIS ASS EN CROUTE, BY GOLLY.
SAY!
ANYONE EVER TELL YE YER HEAD LOOKS LIKE A GREAT BIG PECKER?

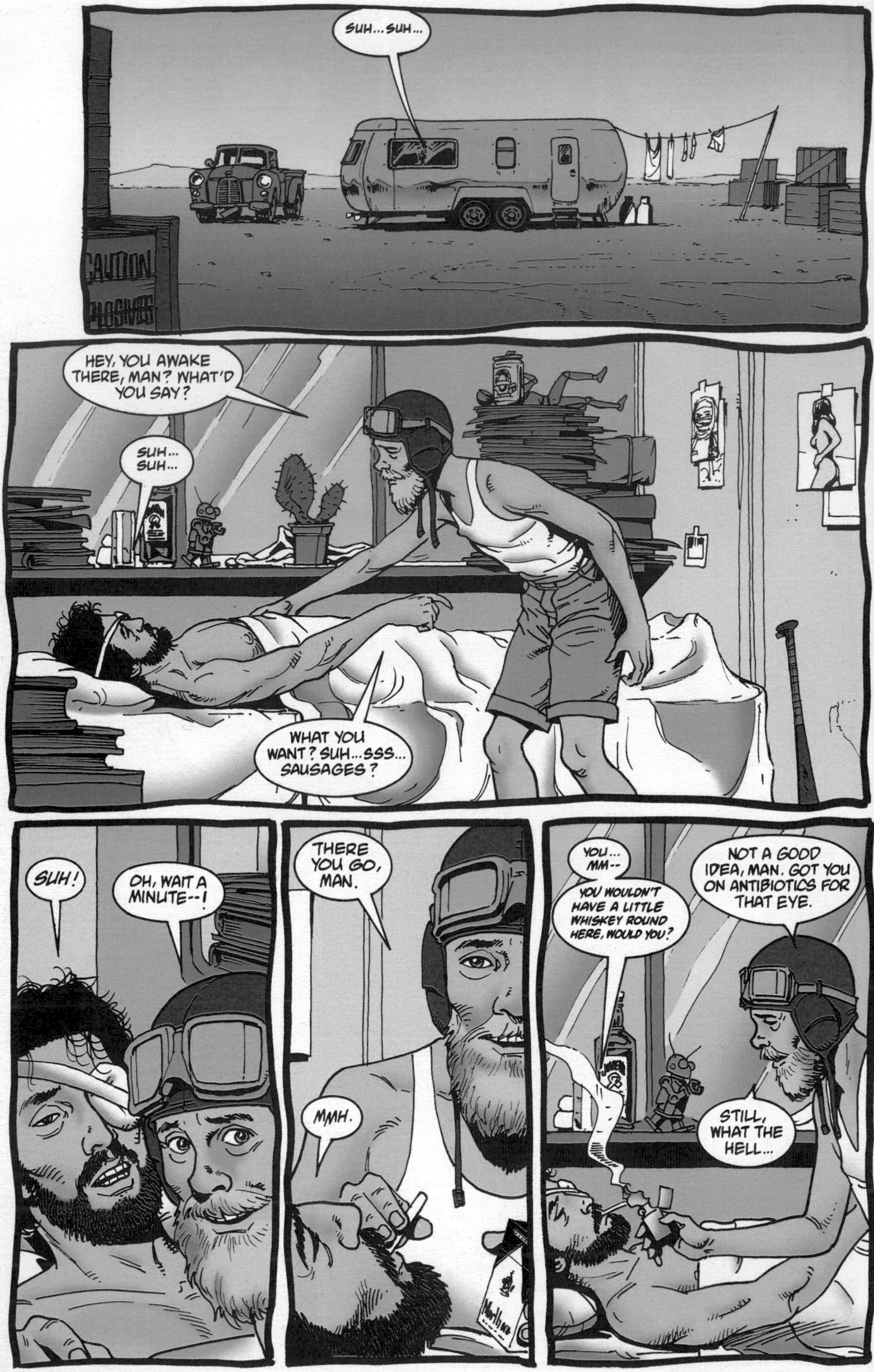
SUH... SUH...
CAUTION
HEY, YOU AWAKE THERE, MAN? WHAT'D YOU SAY?
SUH... SUH...
WHAT YOU WANT? SUH...SSS... SAUSAGES?
SUH!
OH, WAIT A MINUTE--!
THERE YOU GO, MAN.
MMH.
YOU... MM--
YOU WOULDN'T HAVE A LITTLE WHISKEY ROUND HERE, WOULD YOU?
NOT A GOOD IDEA, MAN. GOT YOU ON ANTIBIOTICS FOR THAT EYE.
STILL, WHAT THE HELL...

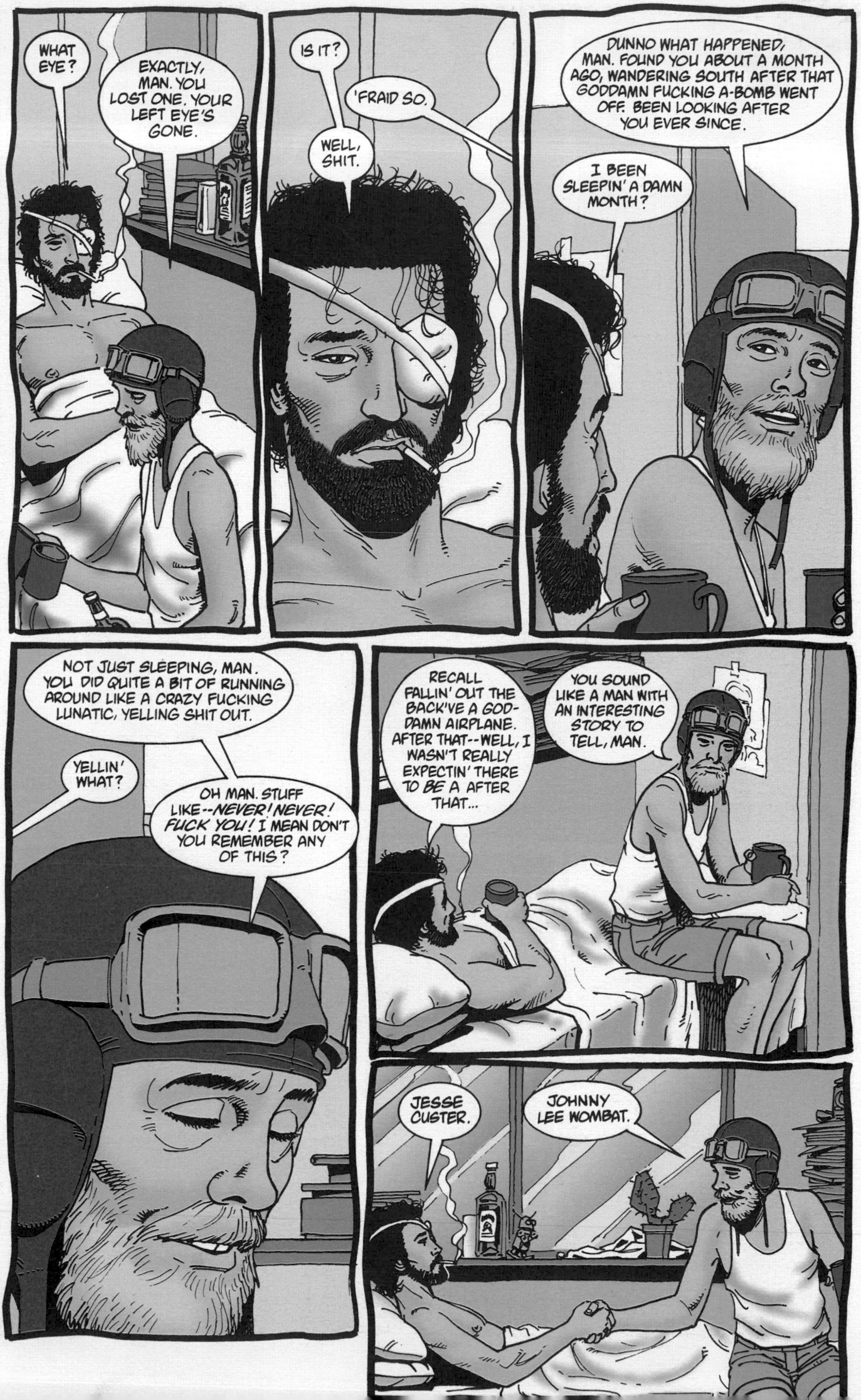

WHAT EYE?
EXACTLY, MAN. YOU LOST ONE. YOUR LEFT EYE'S GONE.
IS IT?
'FRAID SO.
WELL, SHIT.
DUNNO WHAT HAPPENED, MAN. FOUND YOU ABOUT A MONTH AGO, WANDERING SOUTH AFTER THAT GODDAMN FUCKING A-BOMB WENT OFF. BEEN LOOKING AFTER YOU EVER SINCE.
I BEEN SLEEPIN' A DAMN MONTH?
NOT JUST SLEEPING, MAN. YOU DID QUITE A BIT OF RUNNING AROUND LIKE A CRAZY FUCKING LUNATIC, YELLING SHIT OUT.
YELLIN' WHAT?
OH MAN. STUFF LIKE--*NEVER! NEVER! FUCK YOU!* I MEAN DON'T YOU REMEMBER ANY OF THIS?
RECALL FALLIN' OUT THE BACK'VE A GOD-DAMN AIRPLANE. AFTER THAT--WELL, I WASN'T REALLY EXPECTIN' THERE TO *BE* A AFTER THAT...
YOU SOUND LIKE A MAN WITH AN INTERESTING STORY TO TELL, MAN.
JESSE CUSTER.
JOHNNY LEE WOMBAT.

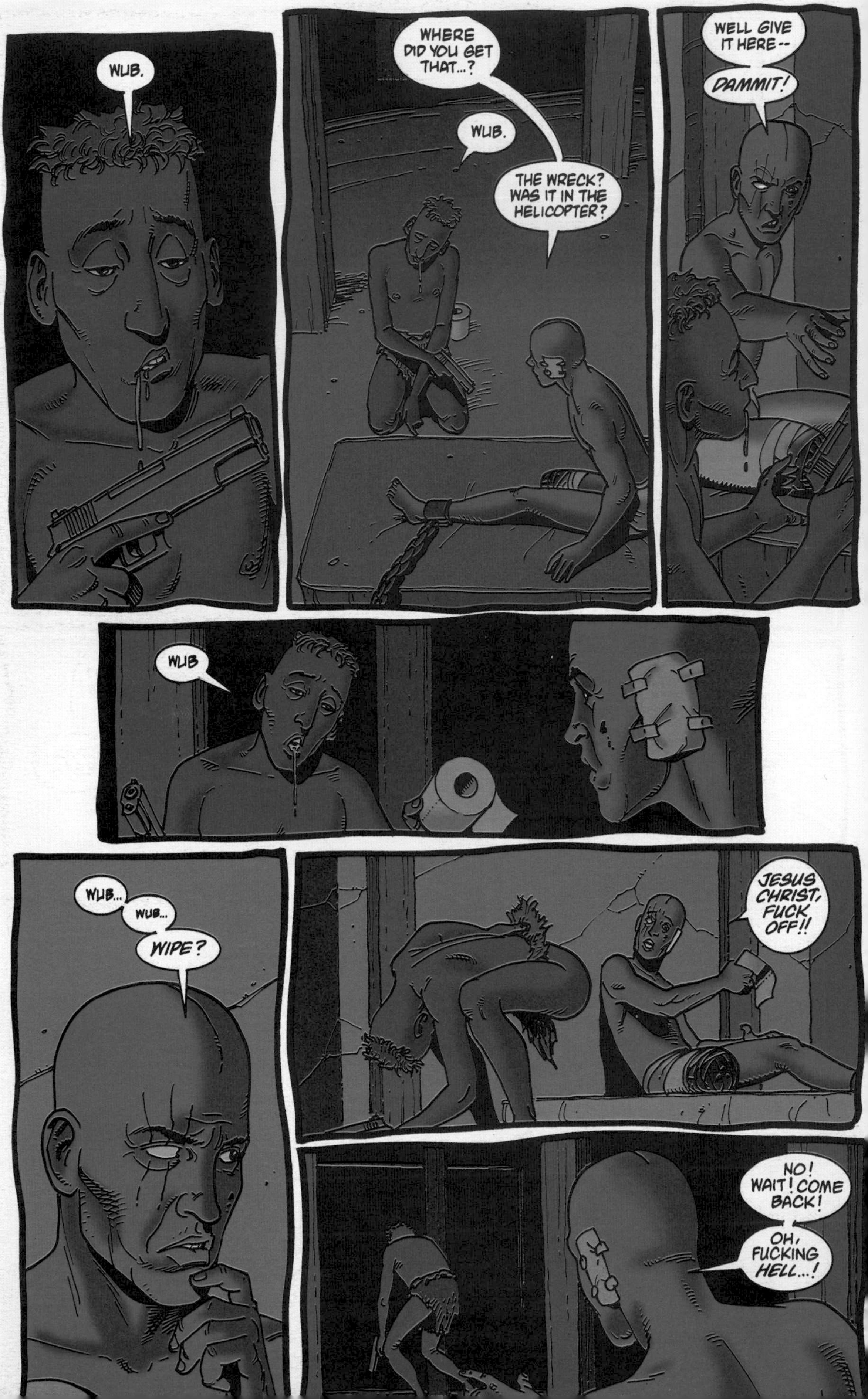
WUB.
WHERE DID YOU GET THAT...?
WUB.
THE WRECK? WAS IT IN THE HELICOPTER?
WELL GIVE IT HERE --
DAMMIT!
WUB
WUB...
WUB...
WIPE?
JESUS CHRIST, FUCK OFF!!
NO! WAIT! COME BACK!
OH, FUCKING HELL...!

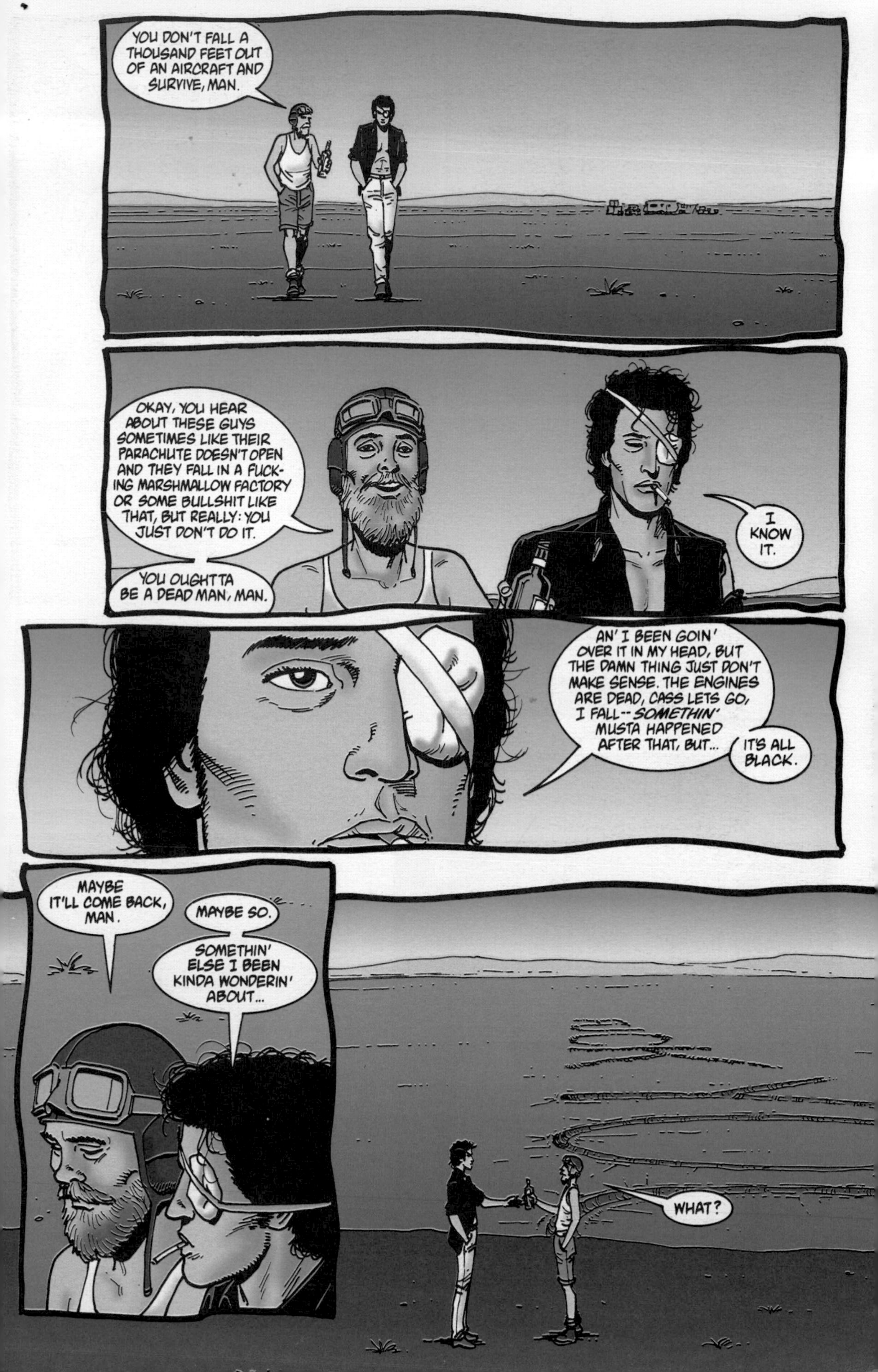
YOU DON'T FALL A THOUSAND FEET OUT OF AN AIRCRAFT AND SURVIVE, MAN.
OKAY, YOU HEAR ABOUT THESE GUYS SOMETIMES LIKE THEIR PARACHUTE DOESN'T OPEN AND THEY FALL IN A FUCKING MARSHMALLOW FACTORY OR SOME BULLSHIT LIKE THAT, BUT REALLY: YOU JUST DON'T DO IT.
YOU OUGHTTA BE A DEAD MAN, MAN.
I KNOW IT.
AN' I BEEN GOIN' OVER IT IN MY HEAD, BUT THE DAMN THING JUST DON'T MAKE SENSE. THE ENGINES ARE DEAD, CASS LETS GO, I FALL-- SOMETHIN' MUSTA HAPPENED AFTER THAT, BUT...
IT'S ALL BLACK.
MAYBE IT'LL COME BACK, MAN.
MAYBE SO.
SOMETHIN' ELSE I BEEN KINDA WONDERIN' ABOUT...
WHAT?

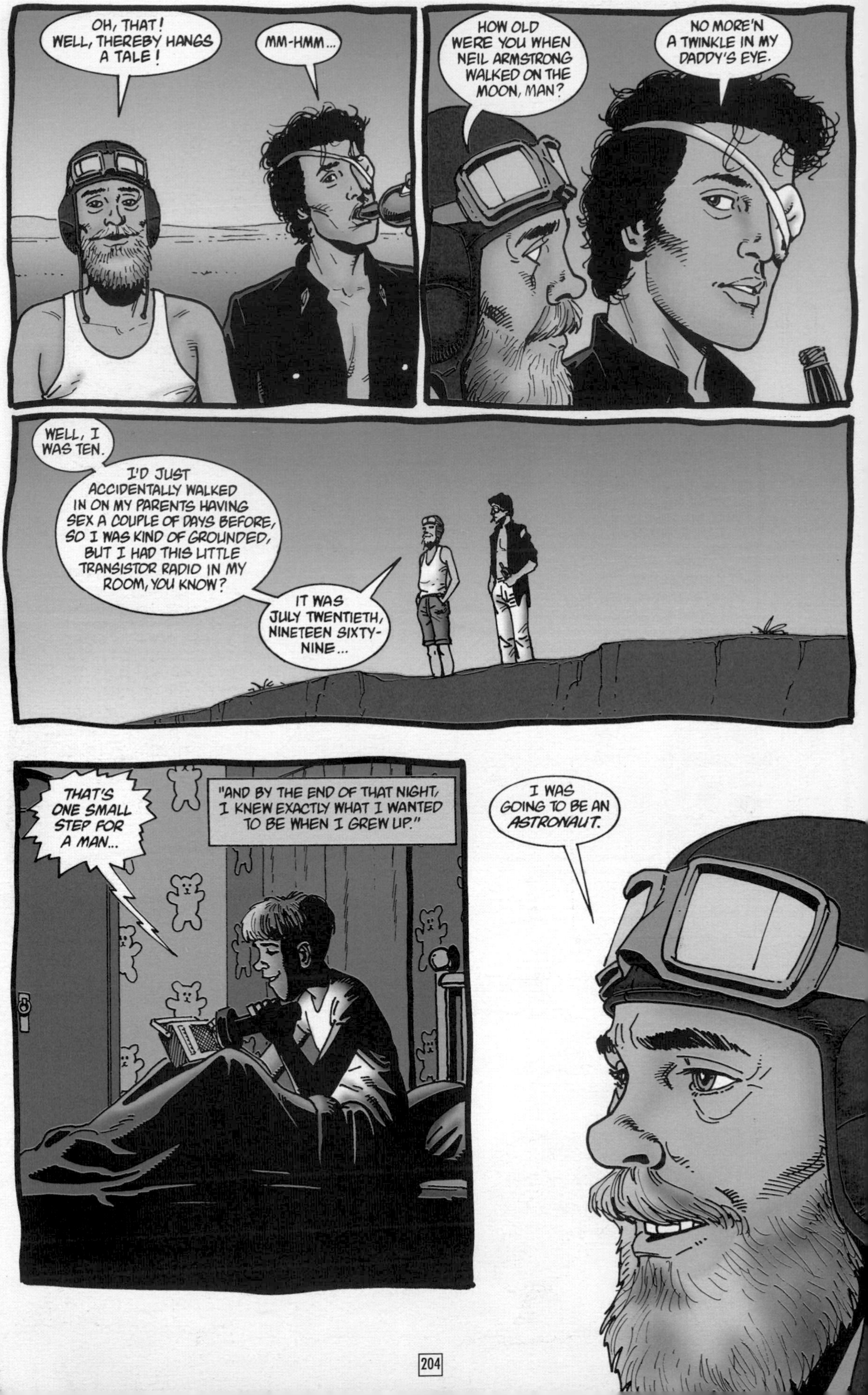
OH, THAT! WELL, THEREBY HANGS A TALE!
MM-HMM...
HOW OLD WERE YOU WHEN NEIL ARMSTRONG WALKED ON THE MOON, MAN?
NO MORE'N A TWINKLE IN MY DADDY'S EYE.
WELL, I WAS TEN.
I'D JUST ACCIDENTALLY WALKED IN ON MY PARENTS HAVING SEX A COUPLE OF DAYS BEFORE, SO I WAS KIND OF GROUNDED, BUT I HAD THIS LITTLE TRANSISTOR RADIO IN MY ROOM, YOU KNOW?
IT WAS JULY TWENTIETH, NINETEEN SIXTY-NINE...
THAT'S ONE SMALL STEP FOR A MAN...
"AND BY THE END OF THAT NIGHT, I KNEW EXACTLY WHAT I WANTED TO BE WHEN I GREW UP."
I WAS GOING TO BE AN *ASTRONAUT*.

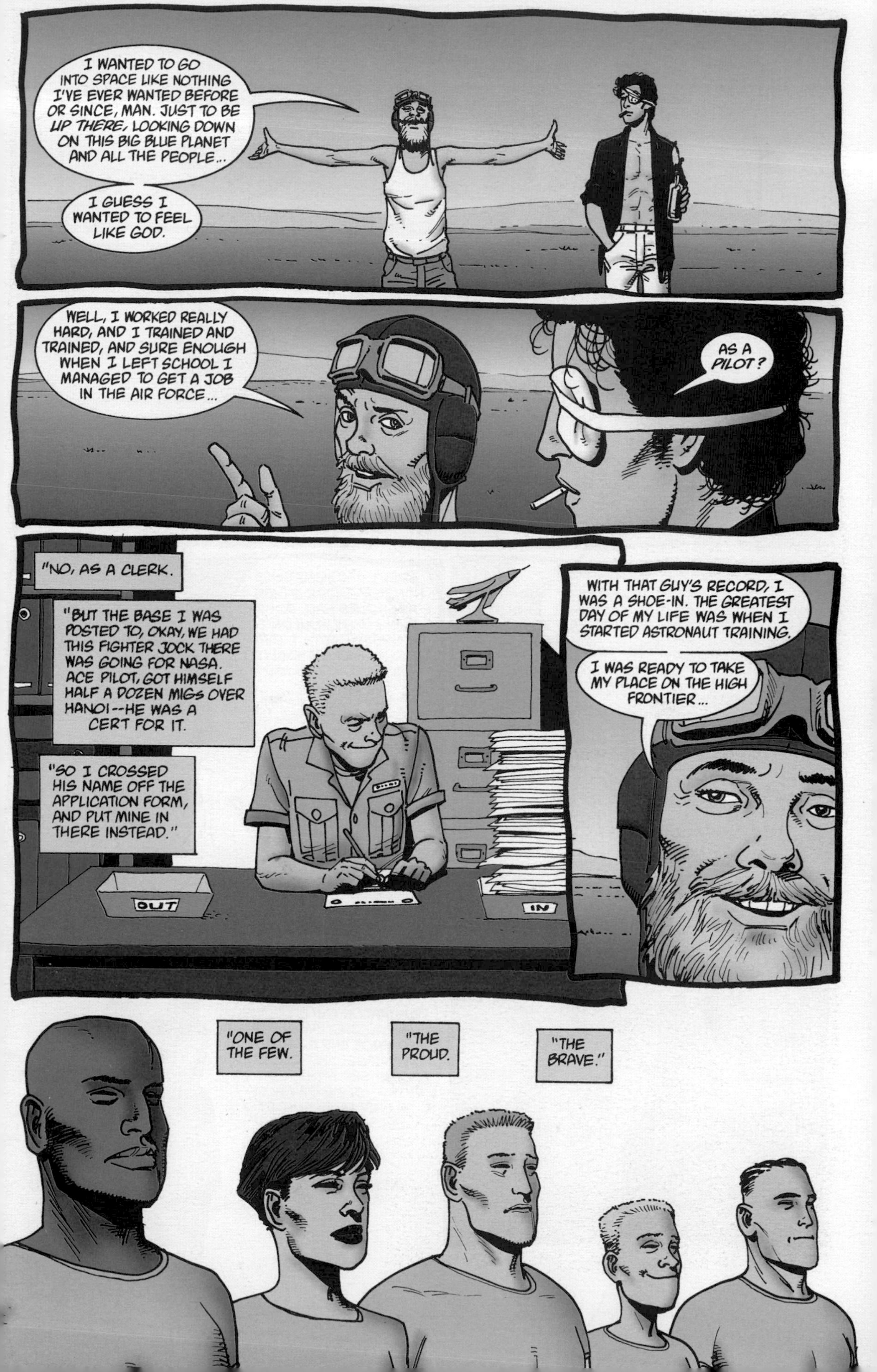
I WANTED TO GO INTO SPACE LIKE NOTHING I'VE EVER WANTED BEFORE OR SINCE, MAN. JUST TO BE UP THERE, LOOKING DOWN ON THIS BIG BLUE PLANET AND ALL THE PEOPLE...
I GUESS I WANTED TO FEEL LIKE GOD.
WELL, I WORKED REALLY HARD, AND I TRAINED AND TRAINED, AND SURE ENOUGH WHEN I LEFT SCHOOL I MANAGED TO GET A JOB IN THE AIR FORCE...
AS A PILOT?
"NO, AS A CLERK.
"BUT THE BASE I WAS POSTED TO, OKAY, WE HAD THIS FIGHTER JOCK THERE WAS GOING FOR NASA. ACE PILOT, GOT HIMSELF HALF A DOZEN MIGS OVER HANOI--HE WAS A CERT FOR IT.
"SO I CROSSED HIS NAME OFF THE APPLICATION FORM, AND PUT MINE IN THERE INSTEAD."
OUT
IN
WITH THAT GUY'S RECORD, I WAS A SHOE-IN. THE GREATEST DAY OF MY LIFE WAS WHEN I STARTED ASTRONAUT TRAINING.
I WAS READY TO TAKE MY PLACE ON THE HIGH FRONTIER...
"ONE OF THE FEW.
"THE PROUD.
"THE BRAVE."

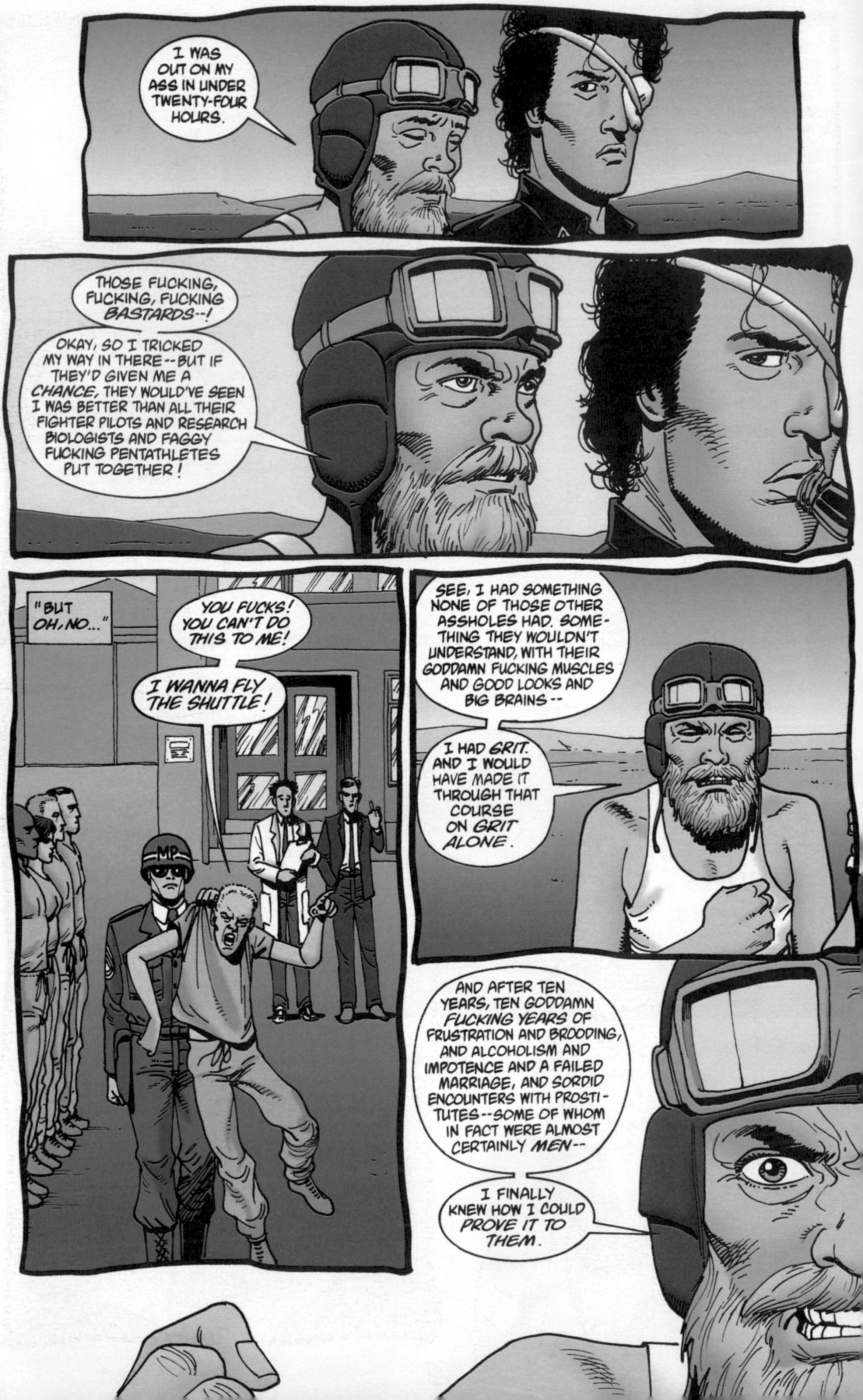
I WAS OUT ON MY ASS IN UNDER TWENTY-FOUR HOURS.
THOSE FUCKING, FUCKING, FUCKING BASTARDS--!
OKAY, SO I TRICKED MY WAY IN THERE--BUT IF THEY'D GIVEN ME A CHANCE, THEY WOULD'VE SEEN I WAS BETTER THAN ALL THEIR FIGHTER PILOTS AND RESEARCH BIOLOGISTS AND FAGGY FUCKING PENTATHLETES PUT TOGETHER!
"BUT OH, NO..."
YOU FUCKS! YOU CAN'T DO THIS TO ME!
I WANNA FLY THE SHUTTLE!
MP
SEE, I HAD SOMETHING NONE OF THOSE OTHER ASSHOLES HAD. SOMETHING THEY WOULDN'T UNDERSTAND, WITH THEIR GODDAMN FUCKING MUSCLES AND GOOD LOOKS AND BIG BRAINS--
I HAD GRIT. AND I WOULD HAVE MADE IT THROUGH THAT COURSE ON GRIT ALONE.
AND AFTER TEN YEARS, TEN GODDAMN FUCKING YEARS OF FRUSTRATION AND BROODING, AND ALCOHOLISM AND IMPOTENCE AND A FAILED MARRIAGE, AND SORDID ENCOUNTERS WITH PROSTITUTES--SOME OF WHOM IN FACT WERE ALMOST CERTAINLY MEN--
I FINALLY KNEW HOW I COULD PROVE IT TO THEM.

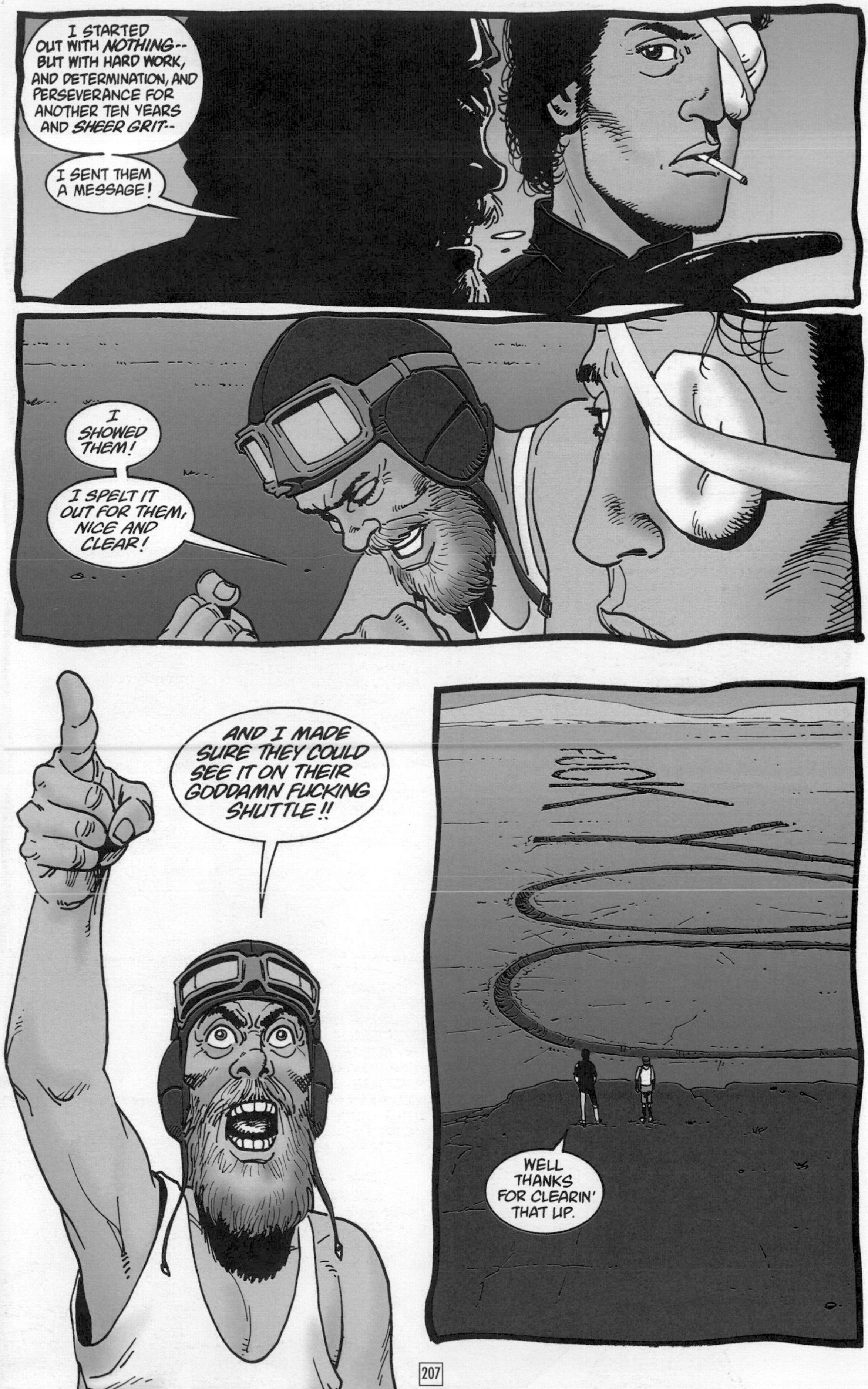
I STARTED OUT WITH NOTHING-- BUT WITH HARD WORK, AND DETERMINATION, AND PERSEVERANCE FOR ANOTHER TEN YEARS AND SHEER GRIT--
I SENT THEM A MESSAGE!
I SHOWED THEM!
I SPELT IT OUT FOR THEM, NICE AND CLEAR!
AND I MADE SURE THEY COULD SEE IT ON THEIR GODDAMN FUCKING SHUTTLE!!
WELL THANKS FOR CLEARIN' THAT UP.

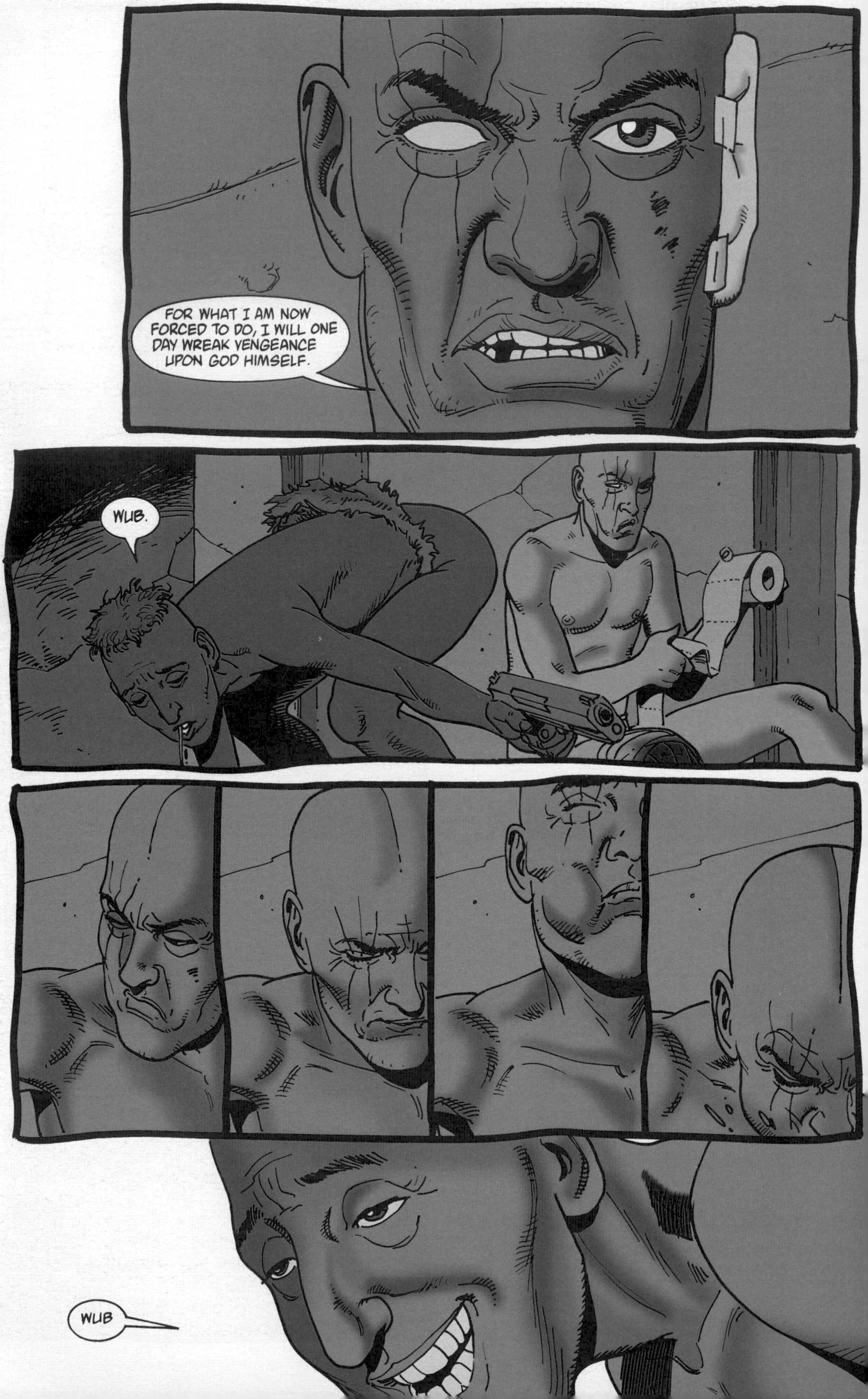
FOR WHAT I AM NOW FORCED TO DO, I WILL ONE DAY WREAK VENGEANCE UPON GOD HIMSELF.
WUB.
WUB

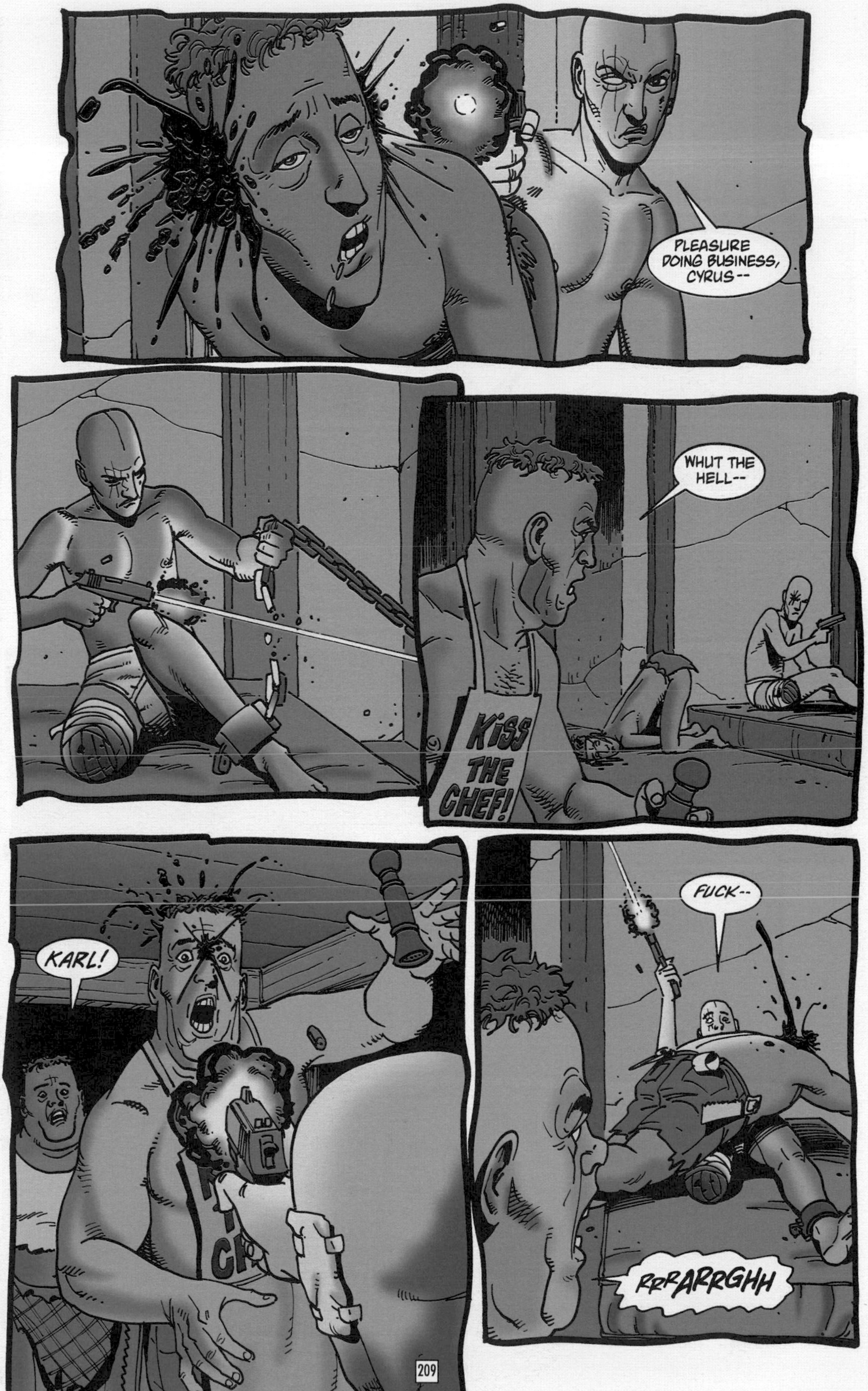
PLEASURE DOING BUSINESS, CYRUS--
WHUT THE HELL--
KISS THE CHEF!
KARL!
FUCK--
RRRARRGHH

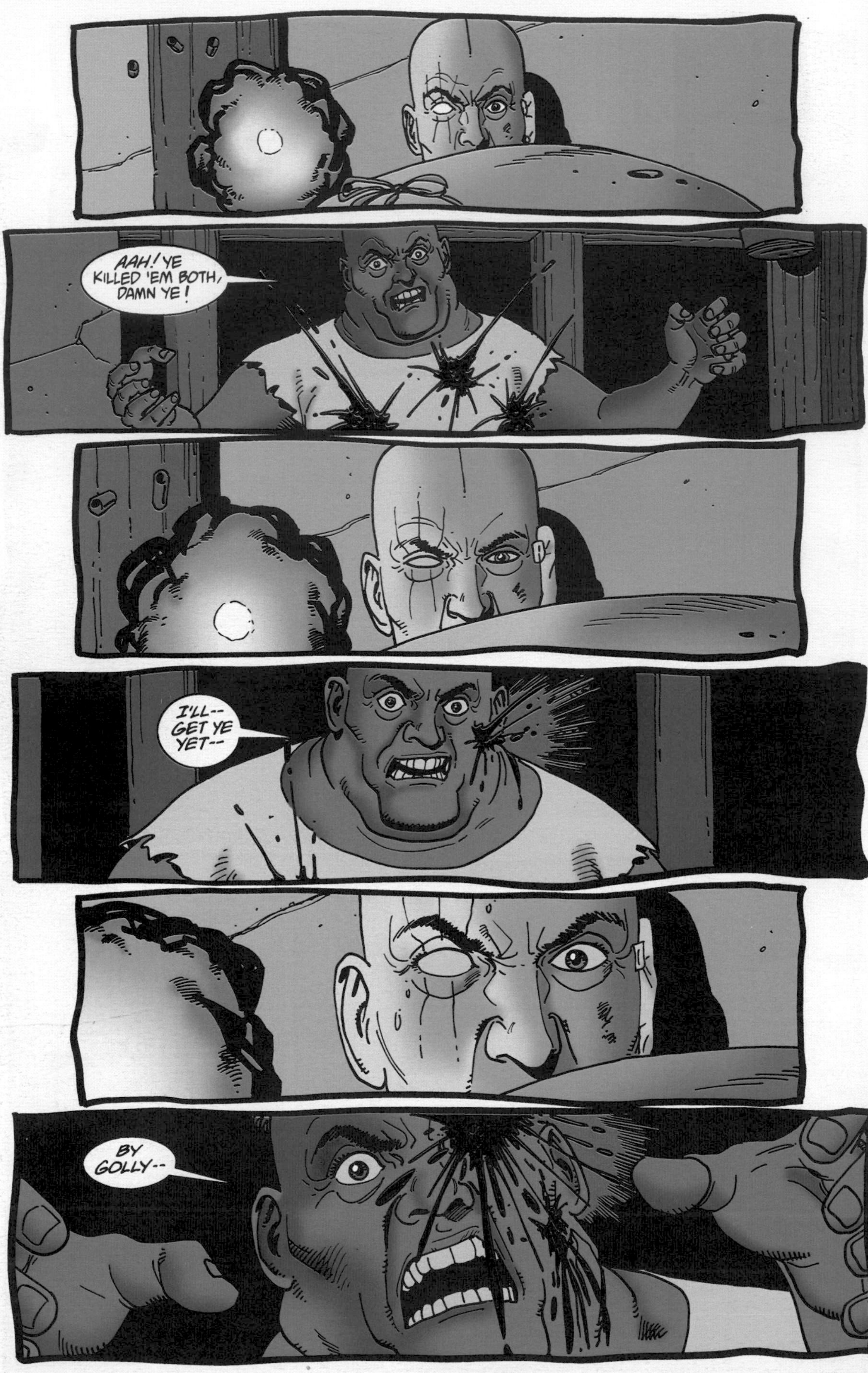
AAH! YE KILLED 'EM BOTH, DAMN YE!
I'LL-- GET YE YET--
BY GOLLY--

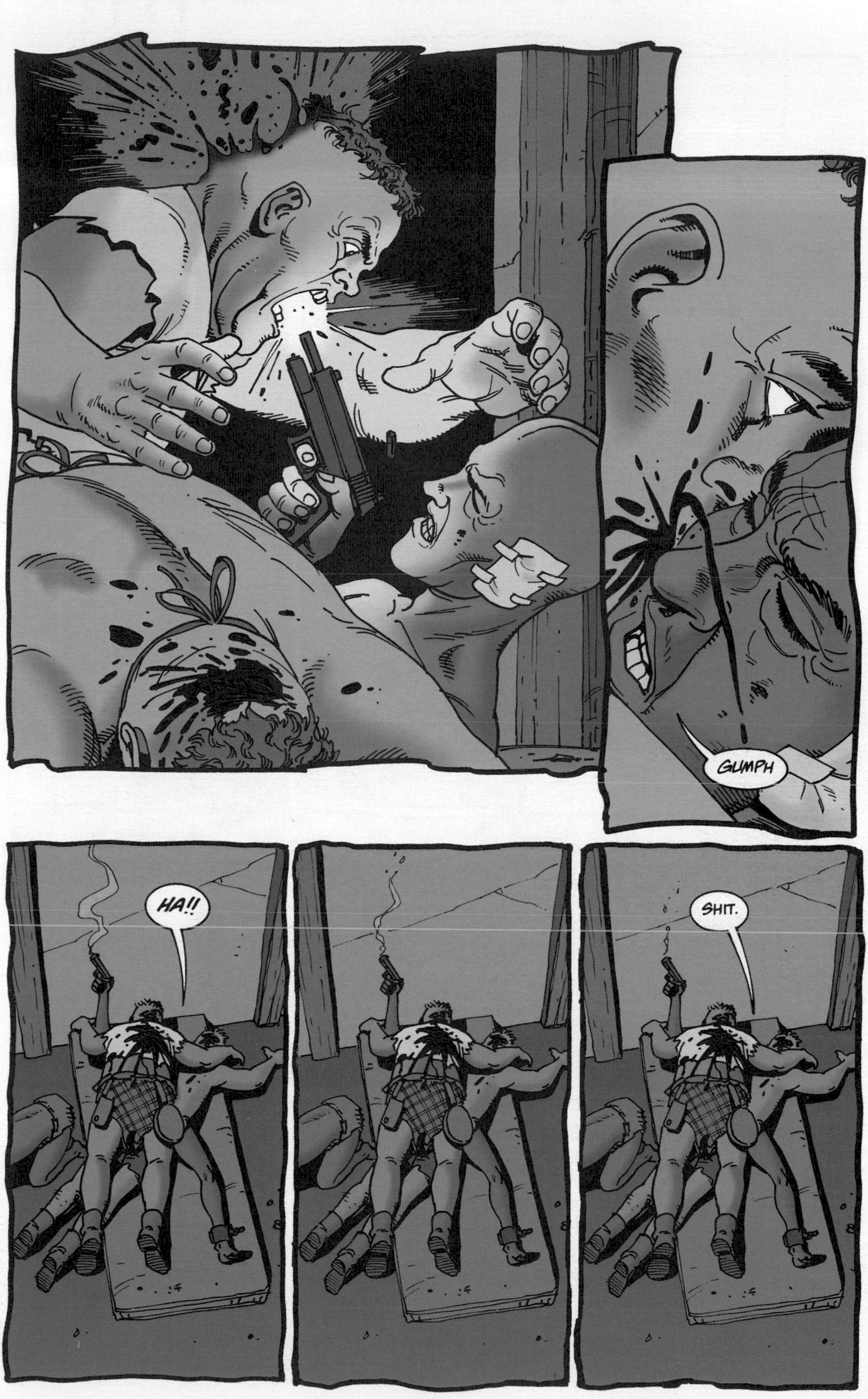
GUMPH
HA!!
SHIT.

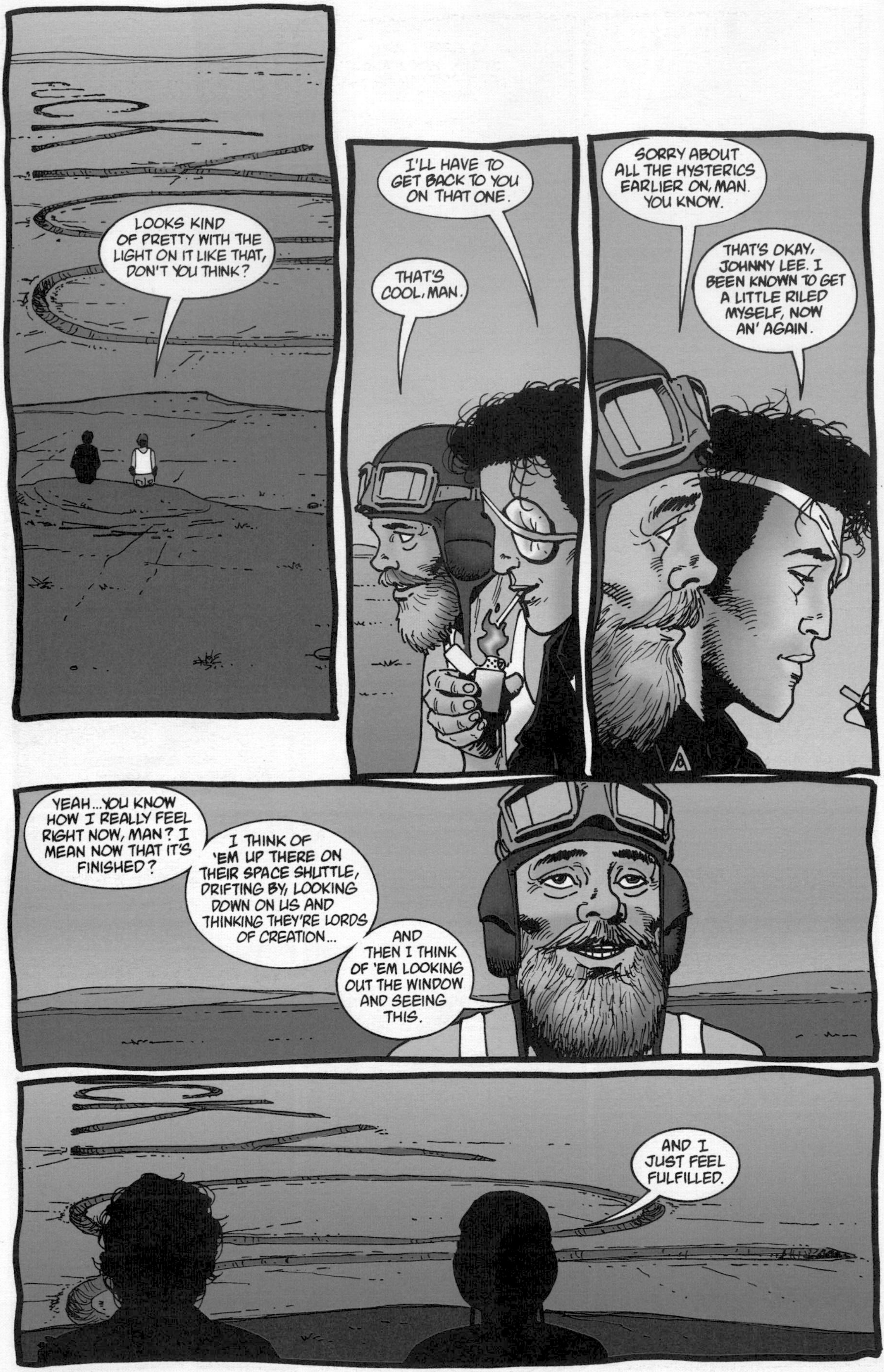
LOOKS KIND OF PRETTY WITH THE LIGHT ON IT LIKE THAT, DON'T YOU THINK?
I'LL HAVE TO GET BACK TO YOU ON THAT ONE.
THAT'S COOL, MAN.
SORRY ABOUT ALL THE HYSTERICS EARLIER ON, MAN. YOU KNOW.
THAT'S OKAY, JOHNNY LEE. I BEEN KNOWN TO GET A LITTLE RILED MYSELF, NOW AN' AGAIN.
YEAH...YOU KNOW HOW I REALLY FEEL RIGHT NOW, MAN? I MEAN NOW THAT IT'S FINISHED?
I THINK OF 'EM UP THERE ON THEIR SPACE SHUTTLE, DRIFTING BY, LOOKING DOWN ON US AND THINKING THEY'RE LORDS OF CREATION...
AND THEN I THINK OF 'EM LOOKING OUT THE WINDOW AND SEEING THIS.
AND I JUST FEEL FULFILLED.

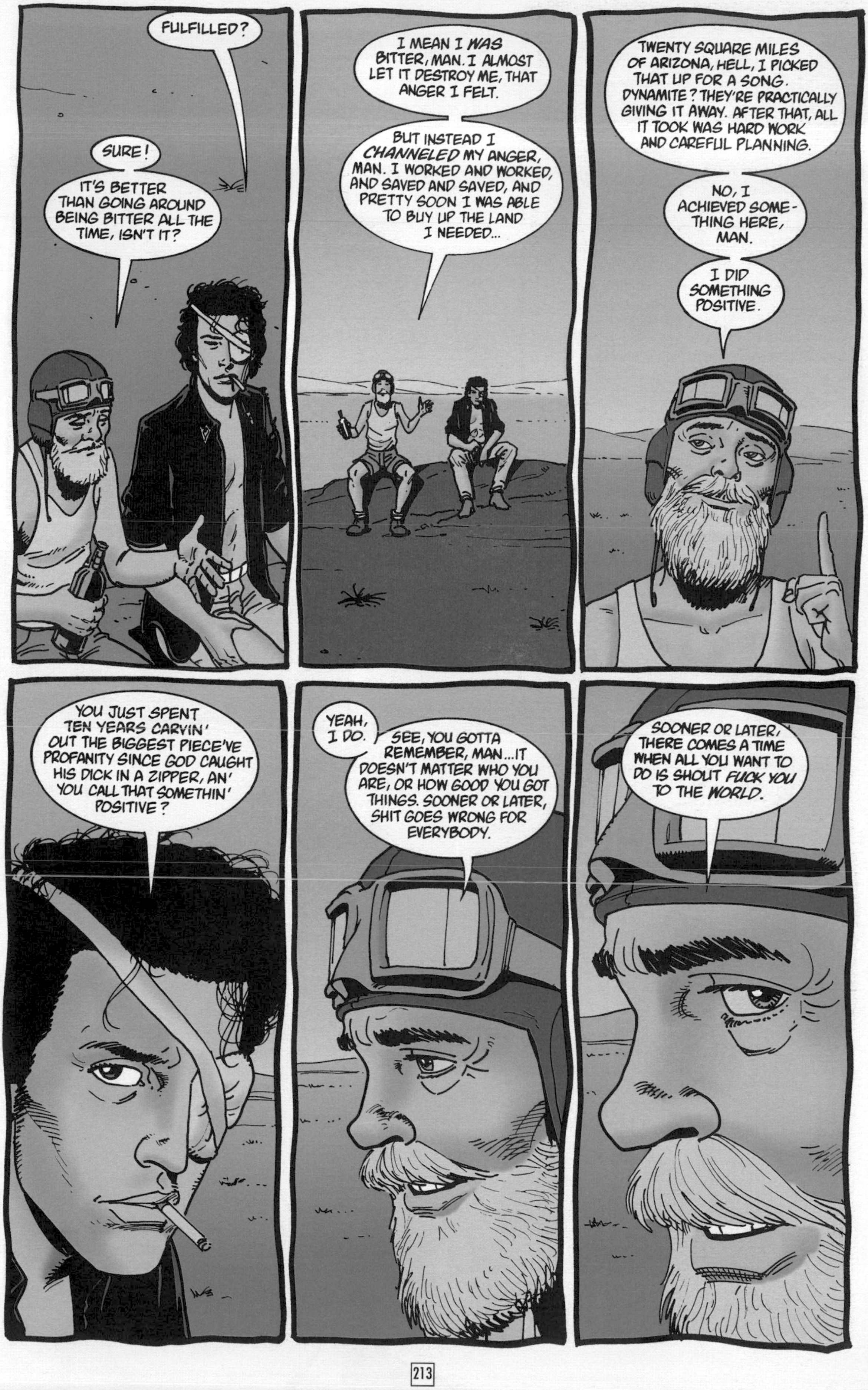

FULFILLED?
SURE!
IT'S BETTER THAN GOING AROUND BEING BITTER ALL THE TIME, ISN'T IT?
I MEAN I *WAS* BITTER, MAN. I ALMOST LET IT DESTROY ME, THAT ANGER I FELT.
BUT INSTEAD I *CHANNELED* MY ANGER, MAN. I WORKED AND WORKED, AND SAVED AND SAVED, AND PRETTY SOON I WAS ABLE TO BUY UP THE LAND I NEEDED...
TWENTY SQUARE MILES OF ARIZONA, HELL, I PICKED THAT UP FOR A SONG. DYNAMITE? THEY'RE PRACTICALLY GIVING IT AWAY. AFTER THAT, ALL IT TOOK WAS HARD WORK AND CAREFUL PLANNING.
NO, I ACHIEVED SOMETHING HERE, MAN.
I DID SOMETHING POSITIVE.
YOU JUST SPENT TEN YEARS CARVIN' OUT THE BIGGEST PIECE'VE PROFANITY SINCE GOD CAUGHT HIS DICK IN A ZIPPER, AN' YOU CALL THAT SOMETHIN' POSITIVE?
YEAH, I DO.
SEE, YOU GOTTA REMEMBER, MAN... IT DOESN'T MATTER WHO YOU ARE, OR HOW GOOD YOU GOT THINGS. SOONER OR LATER, SHIT GOES WRONG FOR EVERYBODY.
SOONER OR LATER, THERE COMES A TIME WHEN ALL YOU WANT TO DO IS SHOUT *FUCK YOU* TO THE *WORLD*.

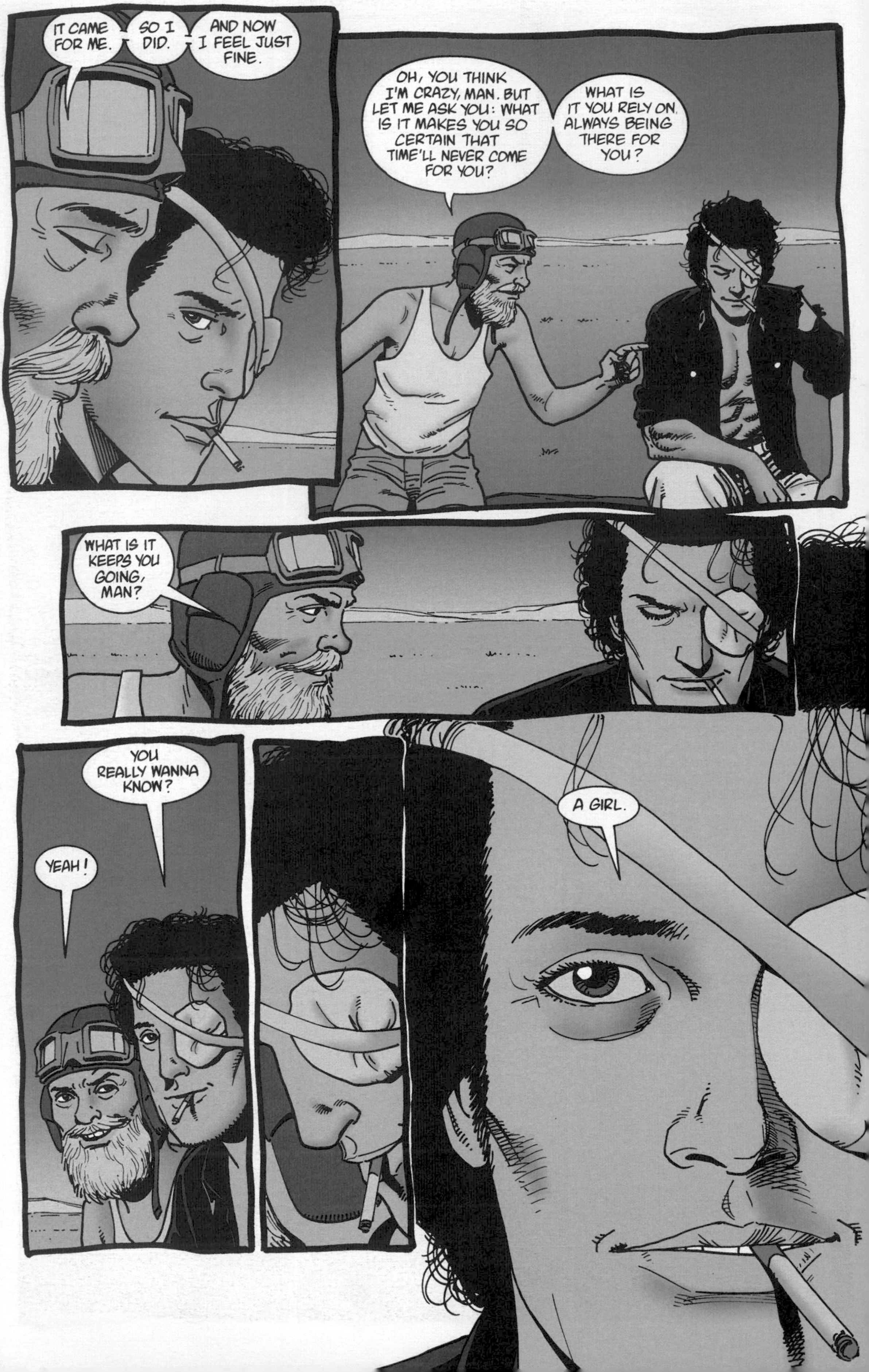
IT CAME FOR ME.
SO I DID.
AND NOW I FEEL JUST FINE.
OH, YOU THINK I'M CRAZY, MAN. BUT LET ME ASK YOU: WHAT IS IT MAKES YOU SO CERTAIN THAT TIME'LL NEVER COME FOR YOU?
WHAT IS IT YOU RELY ON, ALWAYS BEING THERE FOR YOU?
WHAT IS IT KEEPS YOU GOING, MAN?
YOU REALLY WANNA KNOW?
YEAH!
A GIRL.

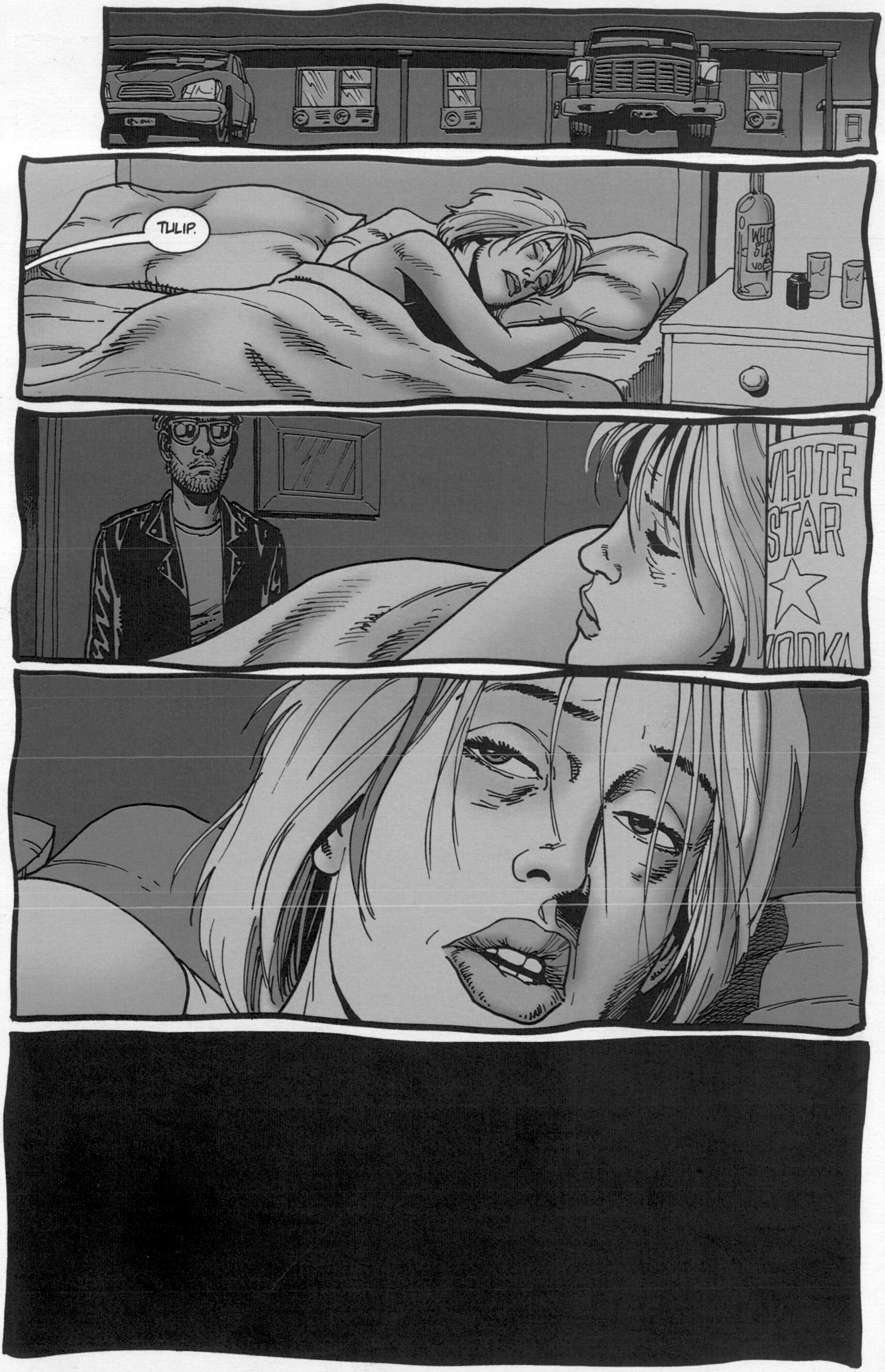
TULIP.
WHITE STAR

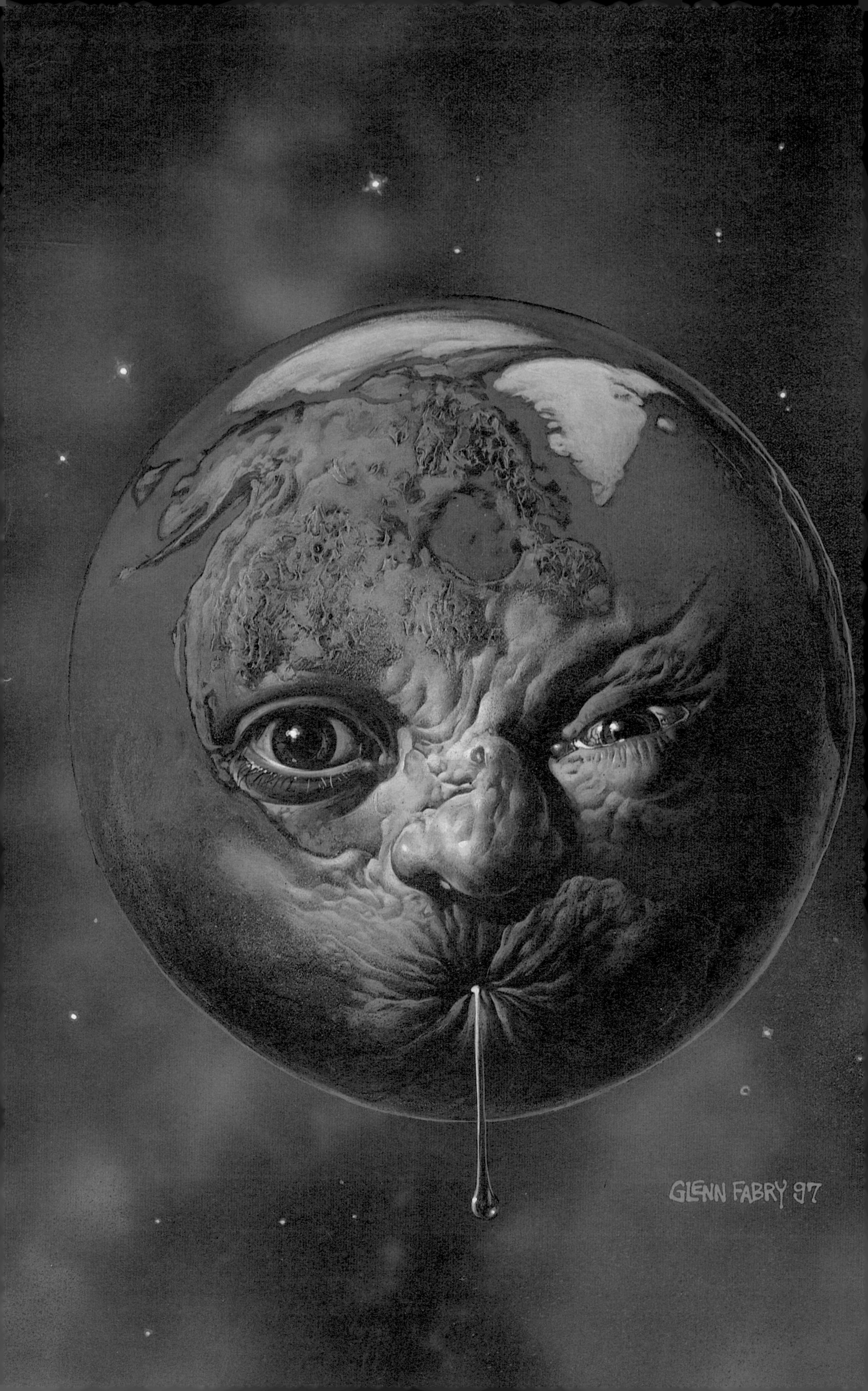
GLENN FABRY 97

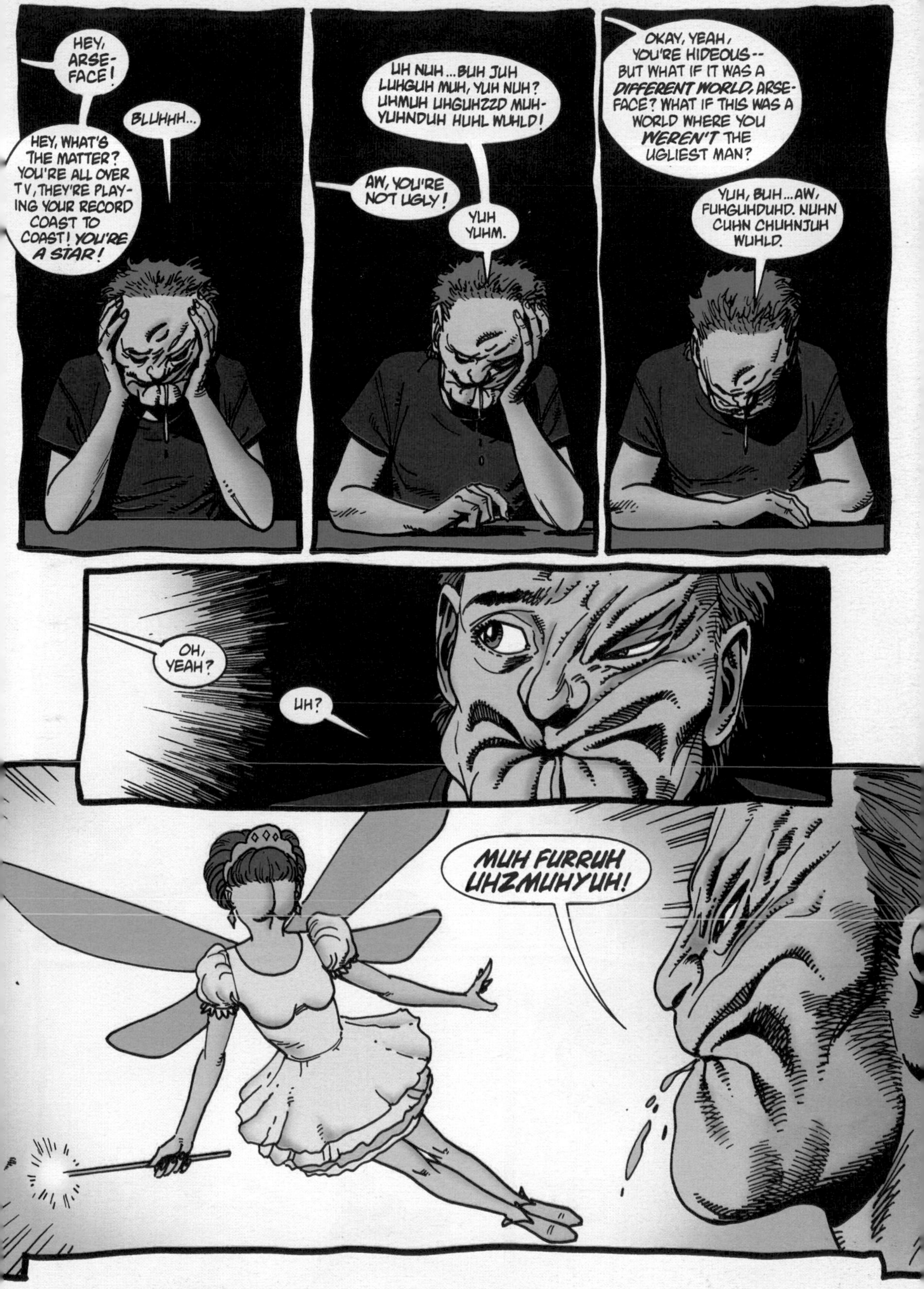
HEY, ARSE-FACE!
BLUHHH...
HEY, WHAT'S THE MATTER? YOU'RE ALL OVER TV, THEY'RE PLAYING YOUR RECORD COAST TO COAST! YOU'RE A STAR!
UH NUH ...BUH JUH LUHGUH MUH, YUH NUH? UHMUH UHGUHZZD MUH-YUHNDUH HUHL WUHLD!
AW, YOU'RE NOT UGLY!
YUH YUHM.
OKAY, YEAH, YOU'RE HIDEOUS -- BUT WHAT IF IT WAS A DIFFERENT WORLD, ARSE-FACE? WHAT IF THIS WAS A WORLD WHERE YOU WEREN'T THE UGLIEST MAN?
YUH, BUH ...AW, FUHGUHDUHD. NUHN CUHN CHUHNJUH WUHLD.
OH, YEAH?
UH?
MUH FURRUH UHZMUHYUH!

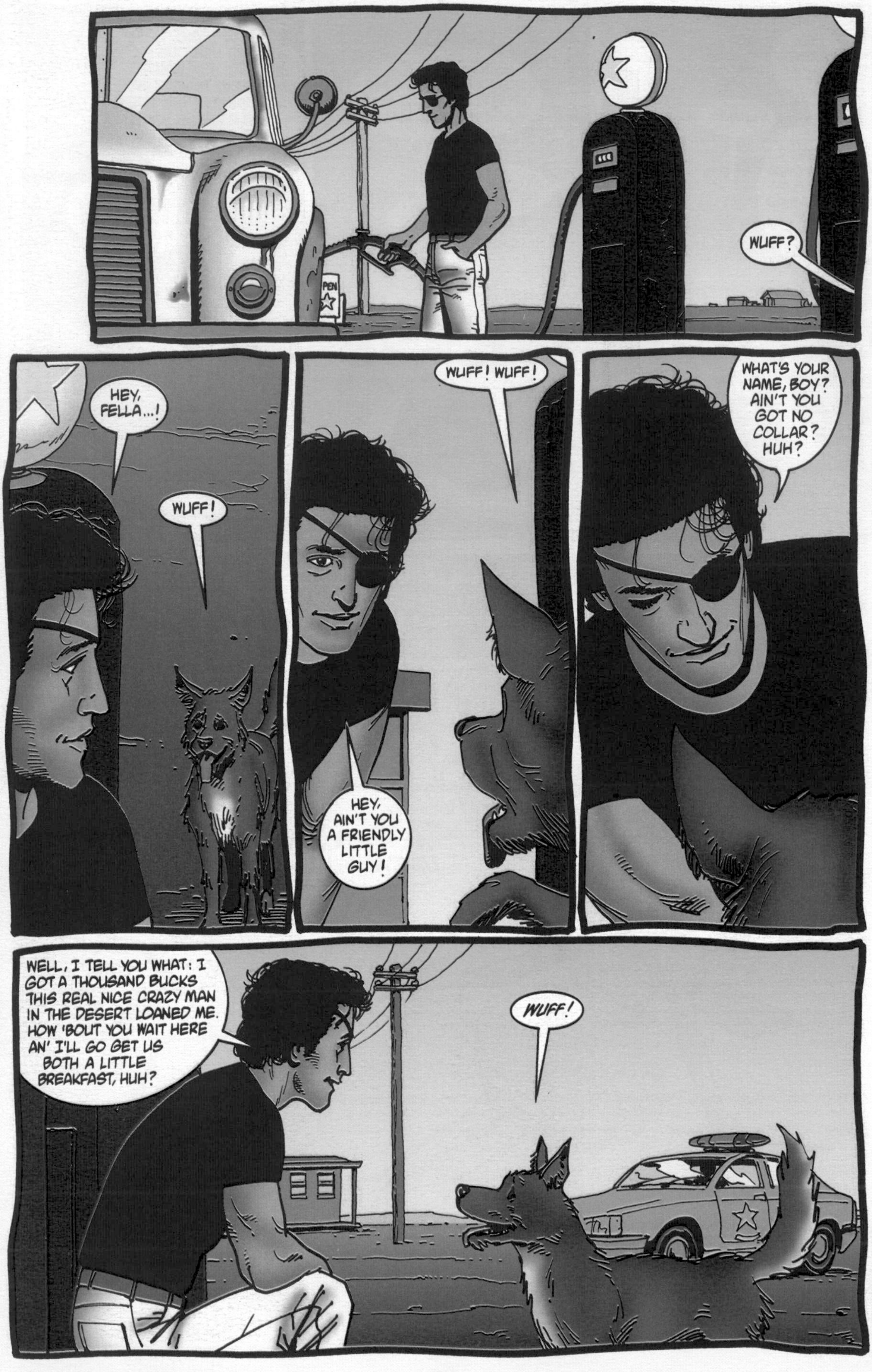

WUFF?
HEY, FELLA...!
WUFF!
WUFF! WUFF!
HEY, AIN'T YOU A FRIENDLY LITTLE GUY!
WHAT'S YOUR NAME, BOY? AIN'T YOU GOT NO COLLAR? HUH?
WELL, I TELL YOU WHAT: I GOT A THOUSAND BUCKS THIS REAL NICE CRAZY MAN IN THE DESERT LOANED ME. HOW 'BOUT YOU WAIT HERE AN' I'LL GO GET US BOTH A LITTLE BREAKFAST, HUH?
WUFF!

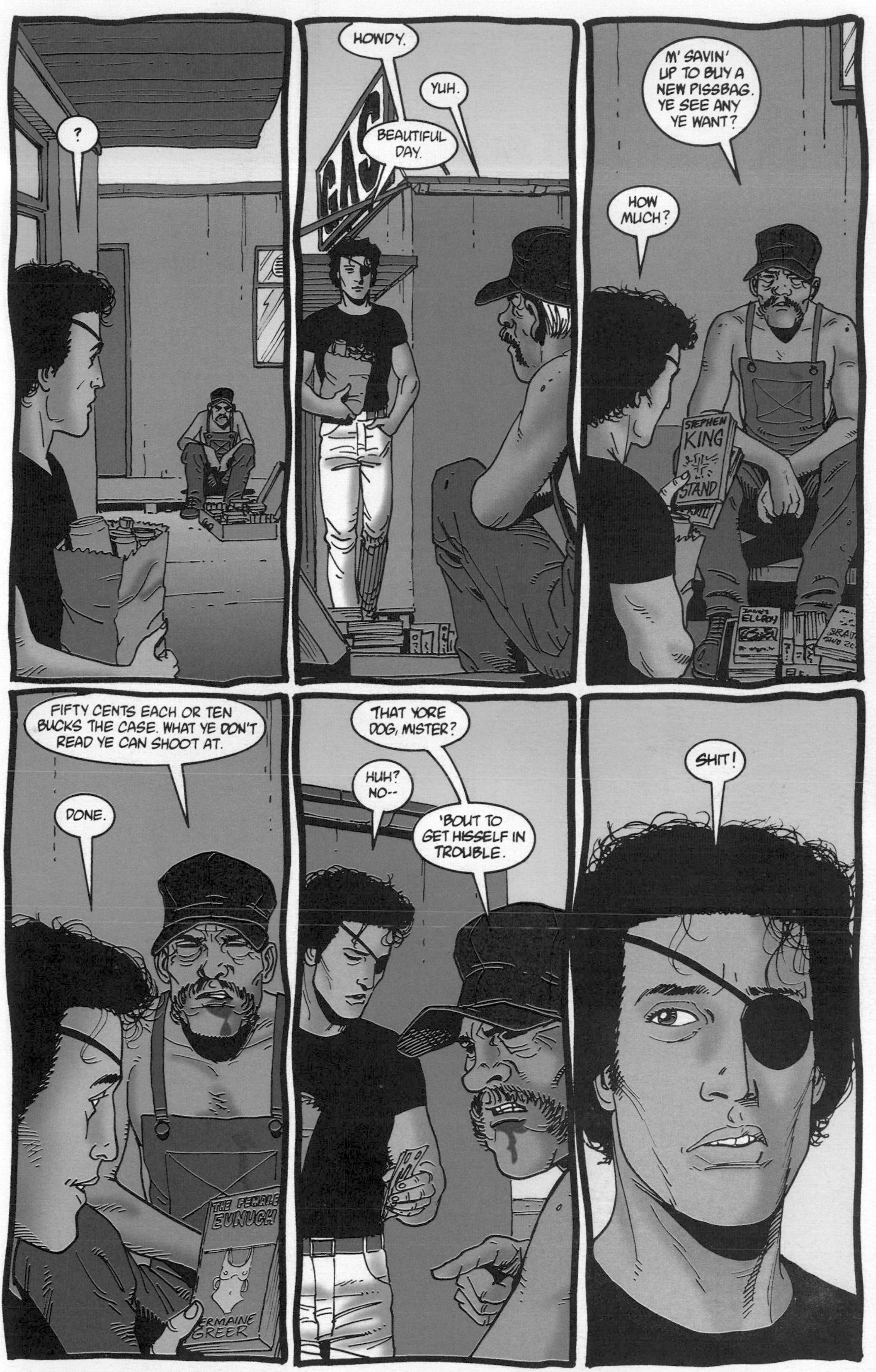
?
HOWDY.
YUH.
BEAUTIFUL DAY.
GAS
M' SAVIN' UP TO BUY A NEW PISSBAG. YE SEE ANY YE WANT?
HOW MUCH?
STEPHEN KING
STAND
ELLROY
FIFTY CENTS EACH OR TEN BUCKS THE CASE. WHAT YE DON'T READ YE CAN SHOOT AT.
DONE.
THE FEMALE EUNUCH
GERMAINE GREER
THAT YORE DOG, MISTER?
HUH? NO--
'BOUT TO GET HISSELF IN TROUBLE.
SHIT!

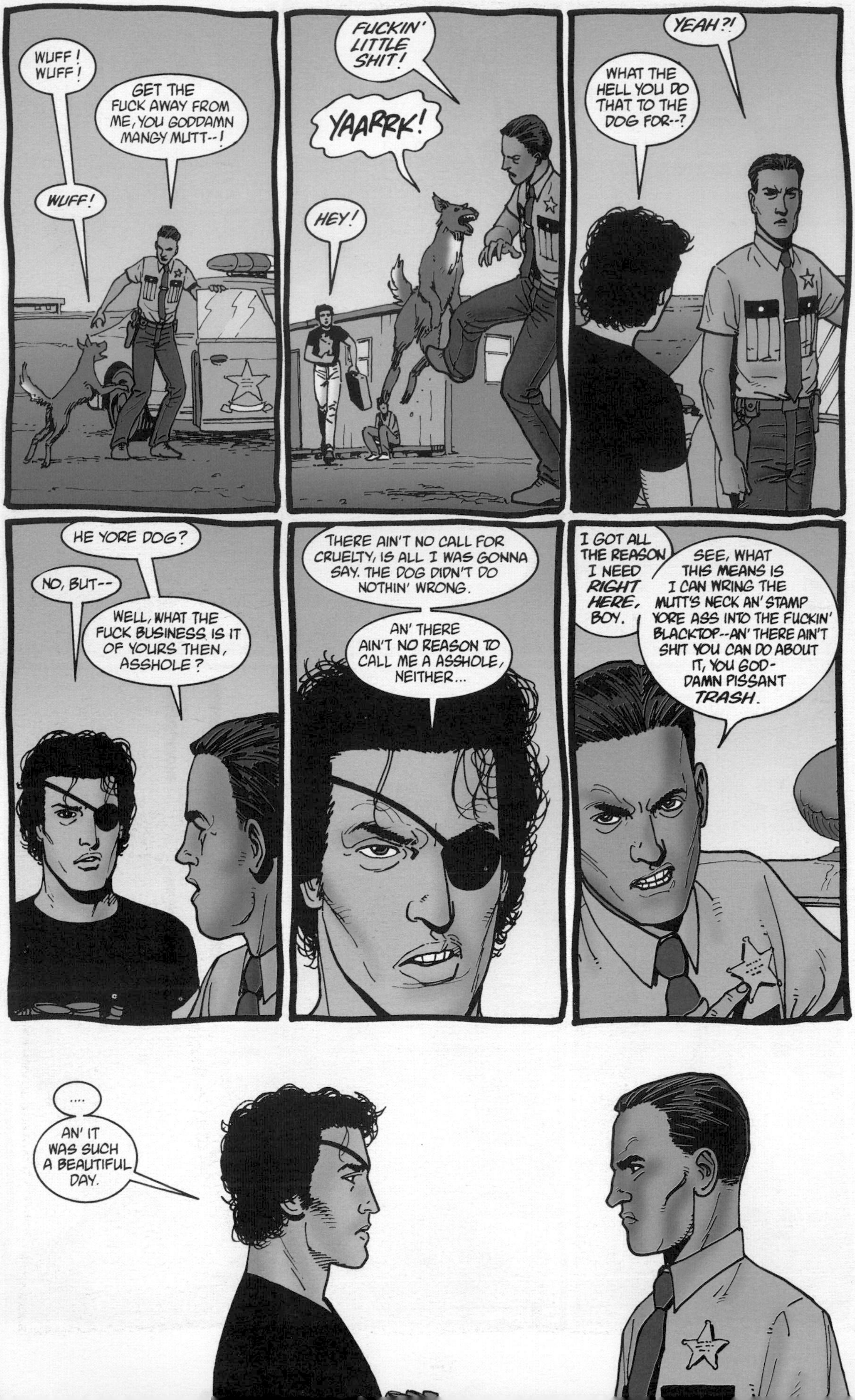
WUFF! WUFF!
GET THE FUCK AWAY FROM ME, YOU GODDAMN MANGY MUTT--!
WUFF!
FUCKIN' LITTLE SHIT!
YAARRK!
HEY!
YEAH?!
WHAT THE HELL YOU DO THAT TO THE DOG FOR--?
HE YORE DOG?
NO, BUT--
WELL, WHAT THE FUCK BUSINESS IS IT OF YOURS THEN, ASSHOLE?
THERE AIN'T NO CALL FOR CRUELTY, IS ALL I WAS GONNA SAY. THE DOG DIDN'T DO NOTHIN' WRONG.
AN' THERE AIN'T NO REASON TO CALL ME A ASSHOLE, NEITHER...
I GOT ALL THE REASON I NEED RIGHT HERE, BOY.
SEE, WHAT THIS MEANS IS I CAN WRING THE MUTT'S NECK AN' STAMP YORE ASS INTO THE FUCKIN' BLACKTOP--AN' THERE AIN'T SHIT YOU CAN DO ABOUT IT, YOU GOD-DAMN PISSANT TRASH.
....
AN' IT WAS SUCH A BEAUTIFUL DAY.

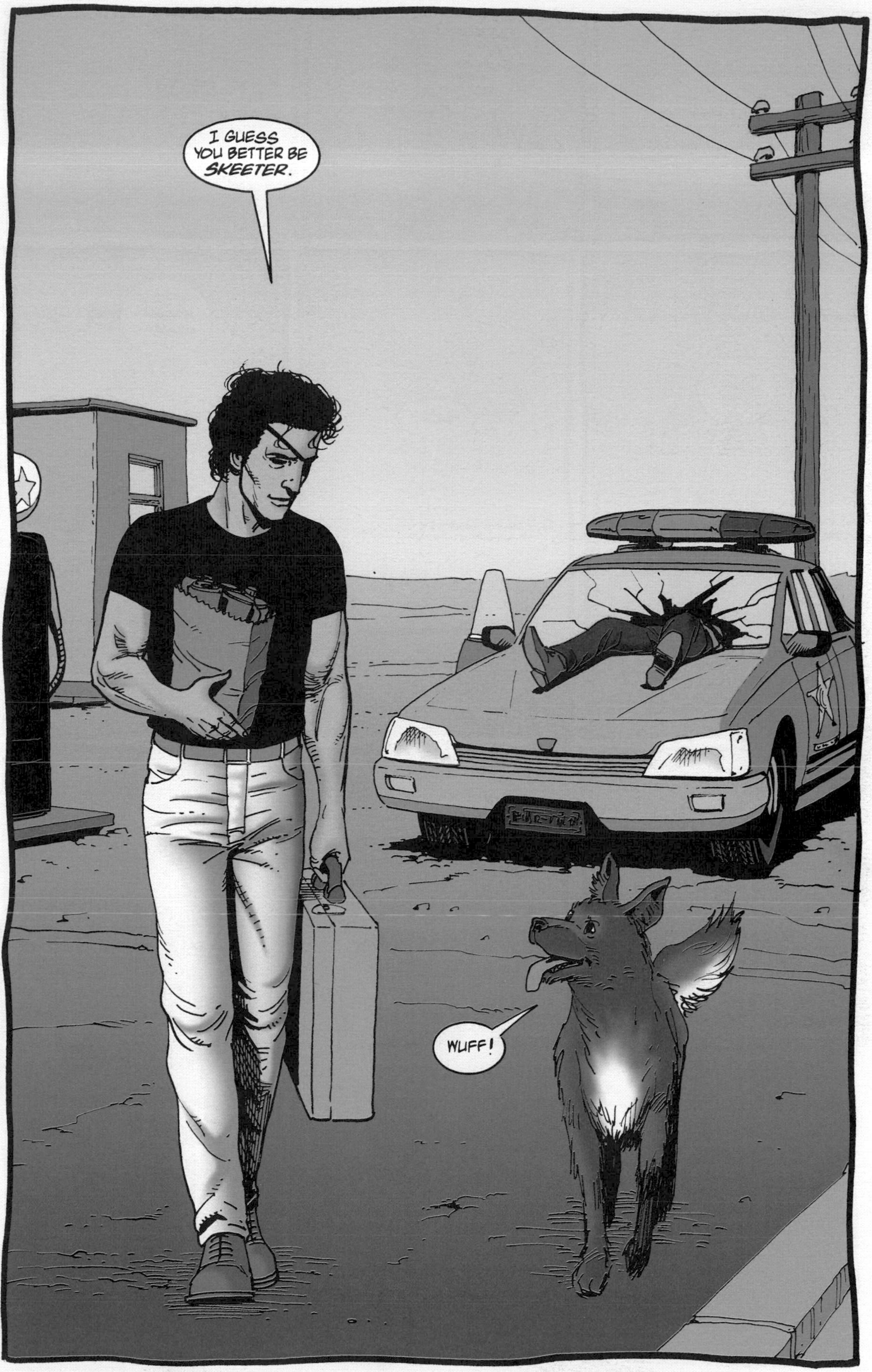
I GUESS YOU BETTER BE SKEETER.
WUFF!

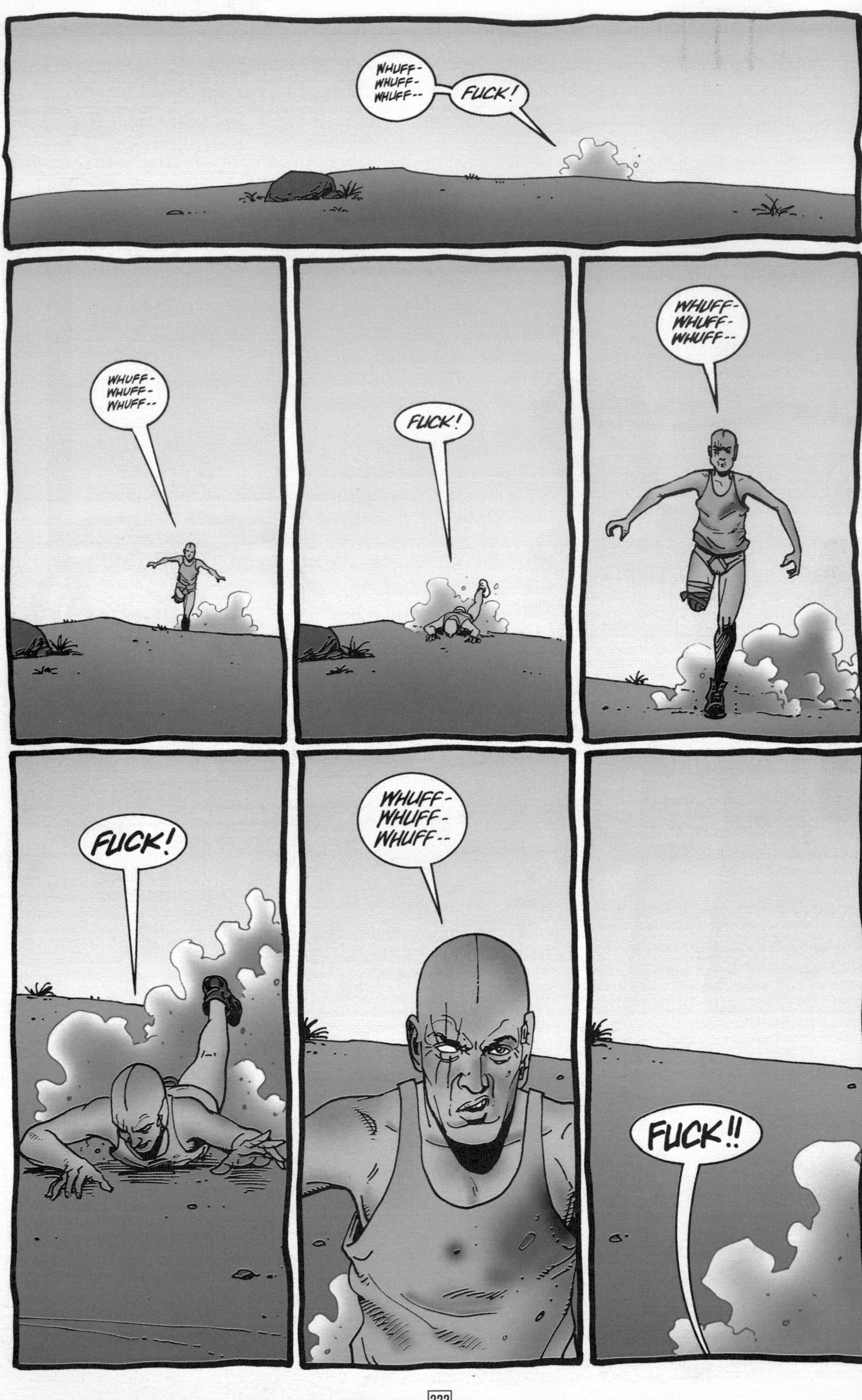
WHUFF-
WHUFF-
WHUFF--
FUCK!
WHUFF-
WHUFF-
WHUFF--
FUCK!
WHUFF-
WHUFF-
WHUFF--
FUCK!
WHUFF-
WHUFF-
WHUFF--
FUCK!!

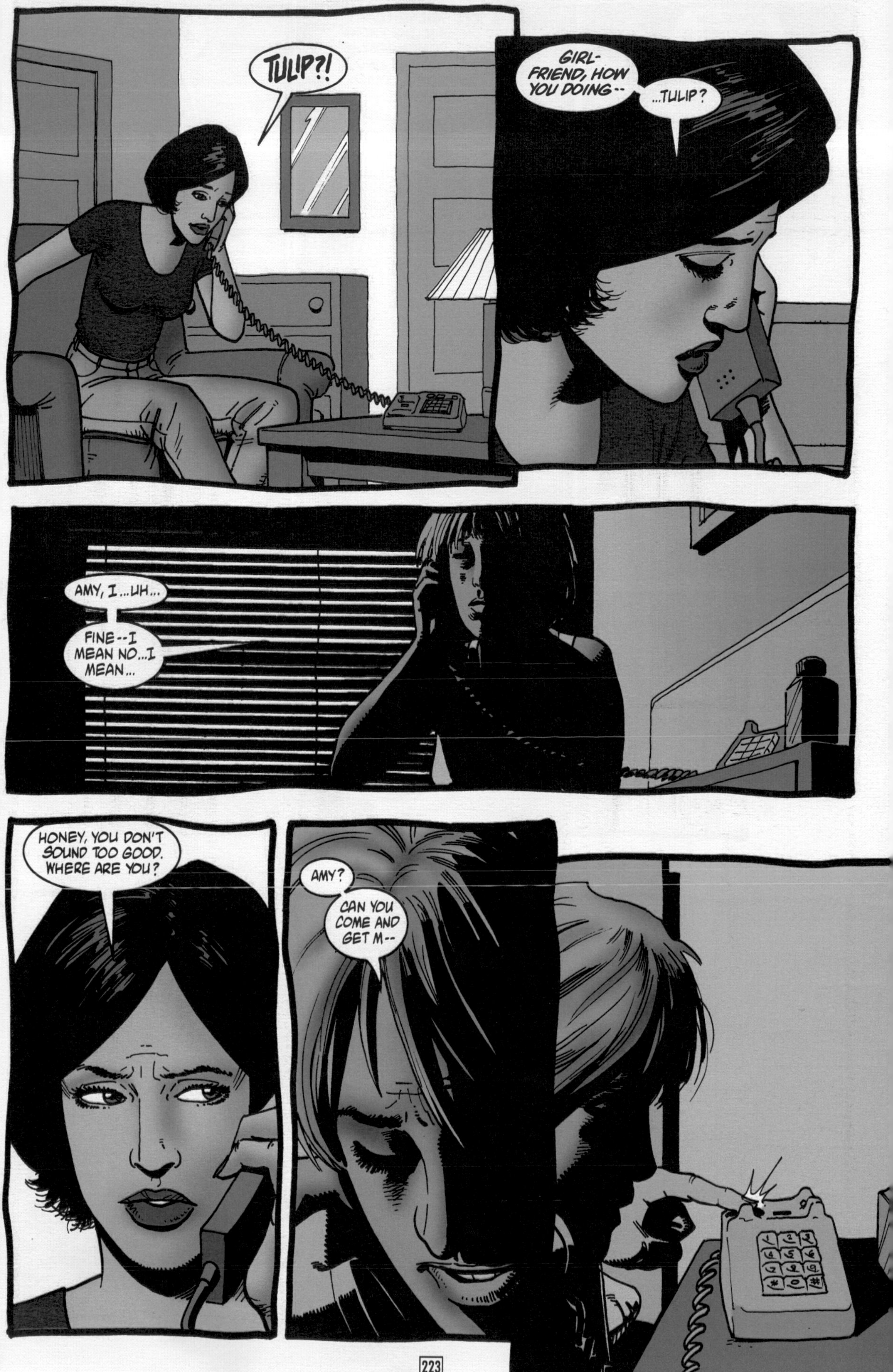
TULIP?!
GIRL-FRIEND, HOW YOU DOING--
...TULIP?
AMY, I...UH...
FINE--I MEAN NO...I MEAN...
HONEY, YOU DON'T SOUND TOO GOOD. WHERE ARE YOU?
AMY?
CAN YOU COME AND GET M--

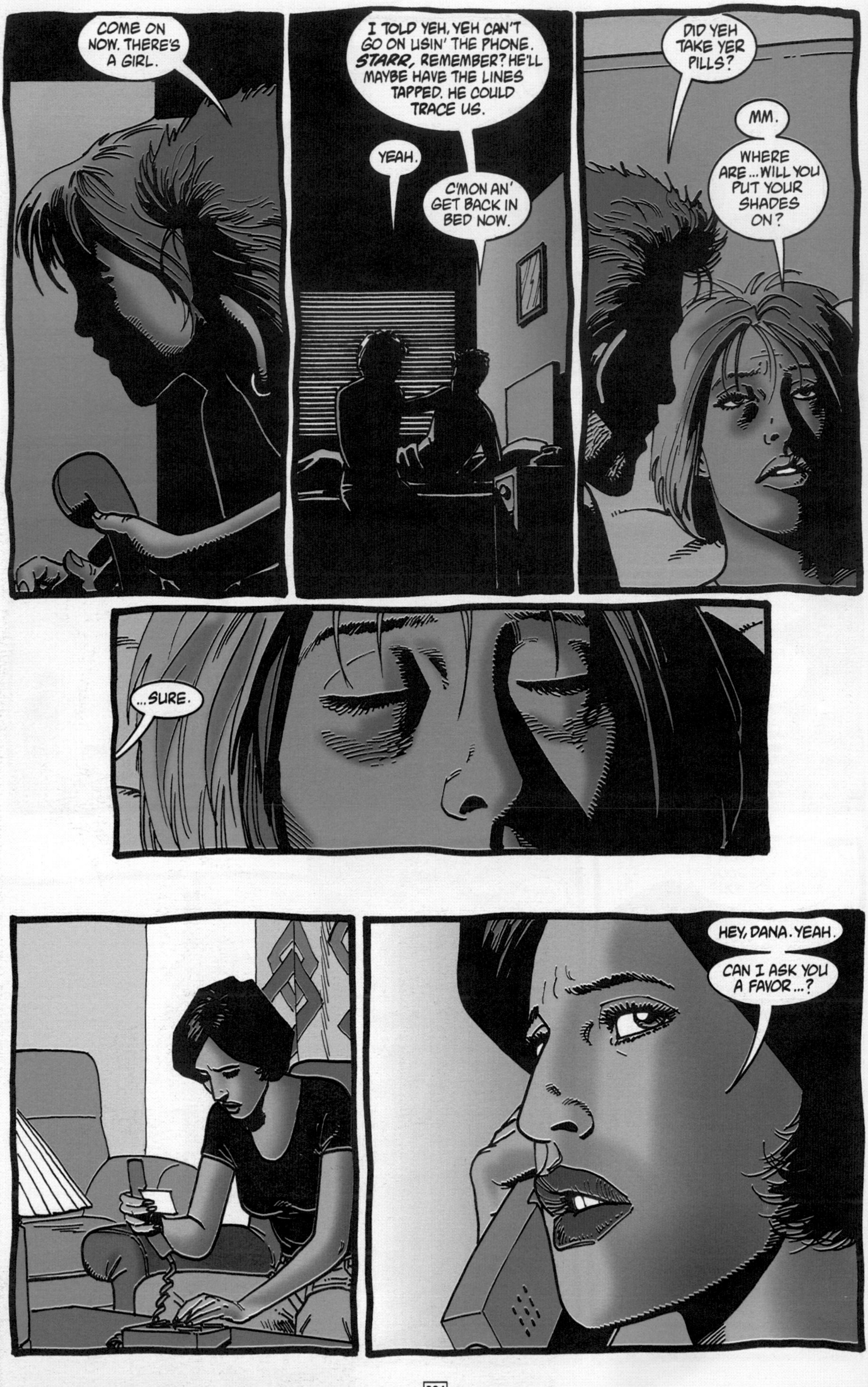
COME ON NOW. THERE'S A GIRL.
I TOLD YEH, YEH CAN'T GO ON USIN' THE PHONE. STARR, REMEMBER? HE'LL MAYBE HAVE THE LINES TAPPED. HE COULD TRACE US.
YEAH.
C'MON AN' GET BACK IN BED NOW.
DID YEH TAKE YER PILLS?
MM.
WHERE ARE...WILL YOU PUT YOUR SHADES ON?
...SURE.
HEY, DANA. YEAH.
CAN I ASK YOU A FAVOR...?

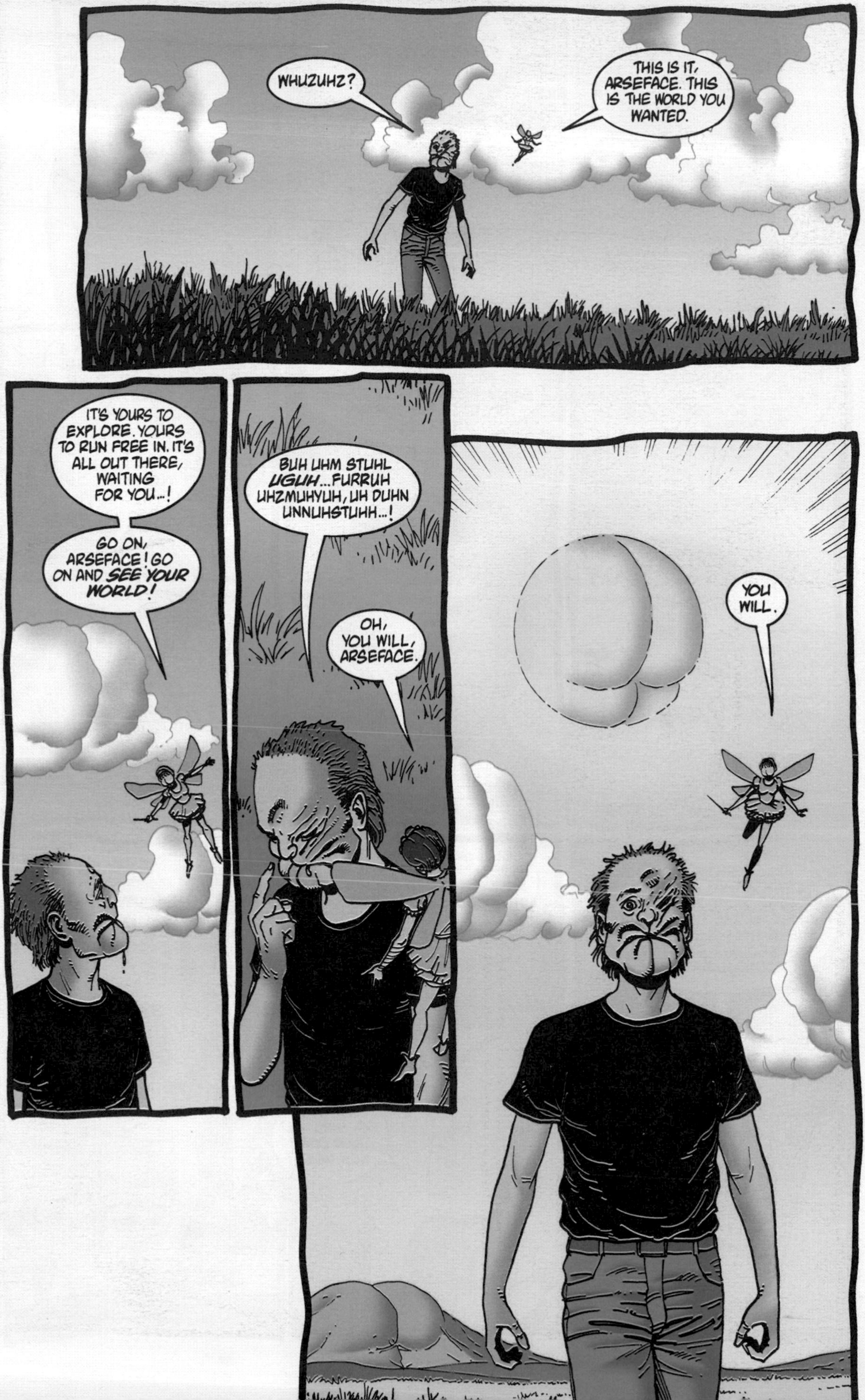
WHUZUHZ?
THIS IS IT, ARSEFACE. THIS IS THE WORLD YOU WANTED.
IT'S YOURS TO EXPLORE. YOURS TO RUN FREE IN. IT'S ALL OUT THERE, WAITING FOR YOU...!
GO ON, ARSEFACE! GO ON AND SEE YOUR WORLD!
BUH UHM STUHL UGUH...FURRUH UHZMUHYUH, UH DUHN UNNUHSTUHH...!
OH, YOU WILL, ARSEFACE.
YOU WILL.

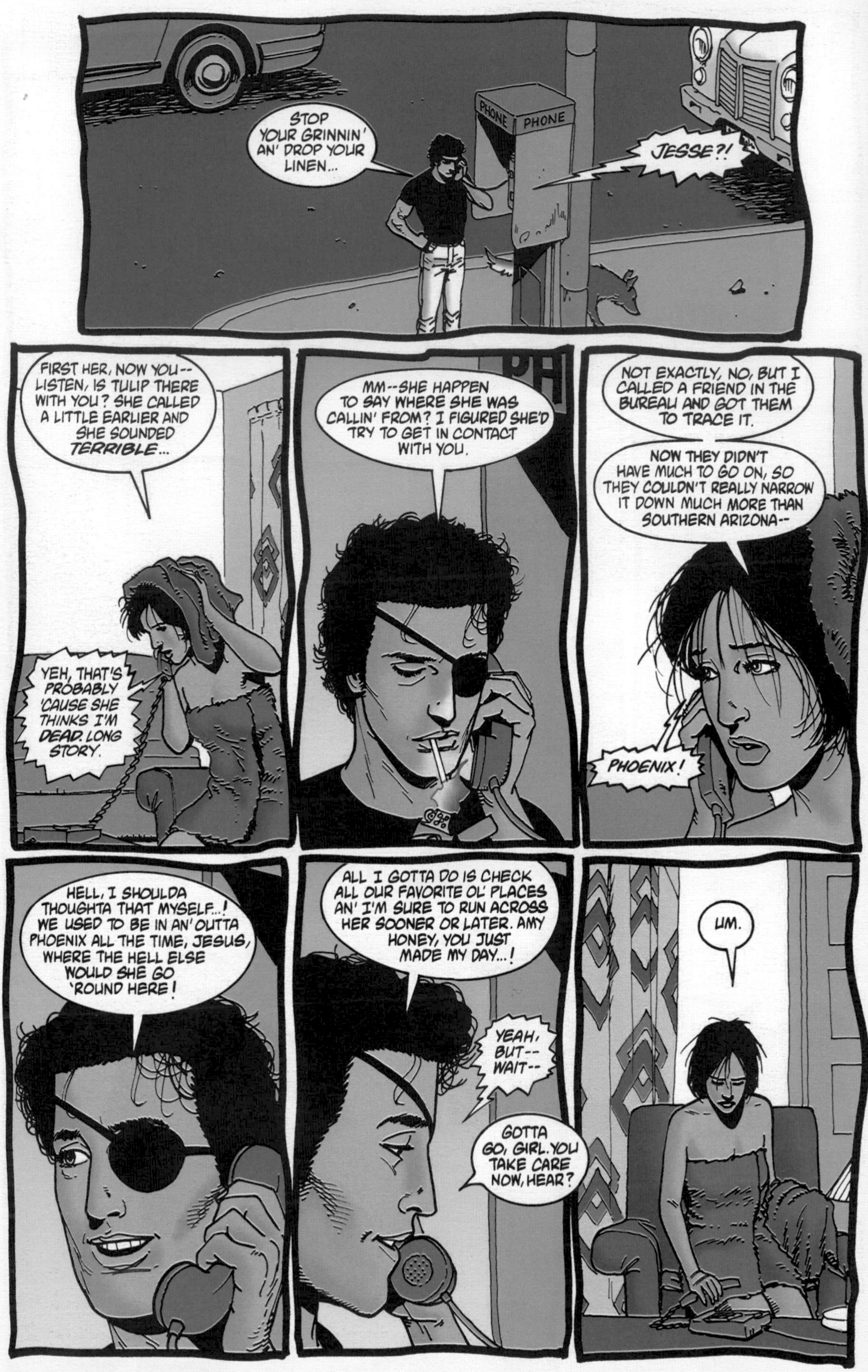
PHONE
PHONE
STOP YOUR GRINNIN' AN' DROP YOUR LINEN...
JESSE?!
FIRST HER, NOW YOU-- LISTEN, IS TULIP THERE WITH YOU? SHE CALLED A LITTLE EARLIER AND SHE SOUNDED TERRIBLE...
YEH, THAT'S PROBABLY 'CAUSE SHE THINKS I'M DEAD. LONG STORY.
MM--SHE HAPPEN TO SAY WHERE SHE WAS CALLIN' FROM? I FIGURED SHE'D TRY TO GET IN CONTACT WITH YOU.
NOT EXACTLY, NO, BUT I CALLED A FRIEND IN THE BUREAU AND GOT THEM TO TRACE IT.
NOW THEY DIDN'T HAVE MUCH TO GO ON, SO THEY COULDN'T REALLY NARROW IT DOWN MUCH MORE THAN SOUTHERN ARIZONA--
PHOENIX!
HELL, I SHOULDA THOUGHTA THAT MYSELF...! WE USED TO BE IN AN' OUTTA PHOENIX ALL THE TIME, JESUS, WHERE THE HELL ELSE WOULD SHE GO 'ROUND HERE!
ALL I GOTTA DO IS CHECK ALL OUR FAVORITE OL' PLACES AN' I'M SURE TO RUN ACROSS HER SOONER OR LATER. AMY HONEY, YOU JUST MADE MY DAY...!
YEAH, BUT-- WAIT--
GOTTA GO, GIRL. YOU TAKE CARE NOW, HEAR?
UM.

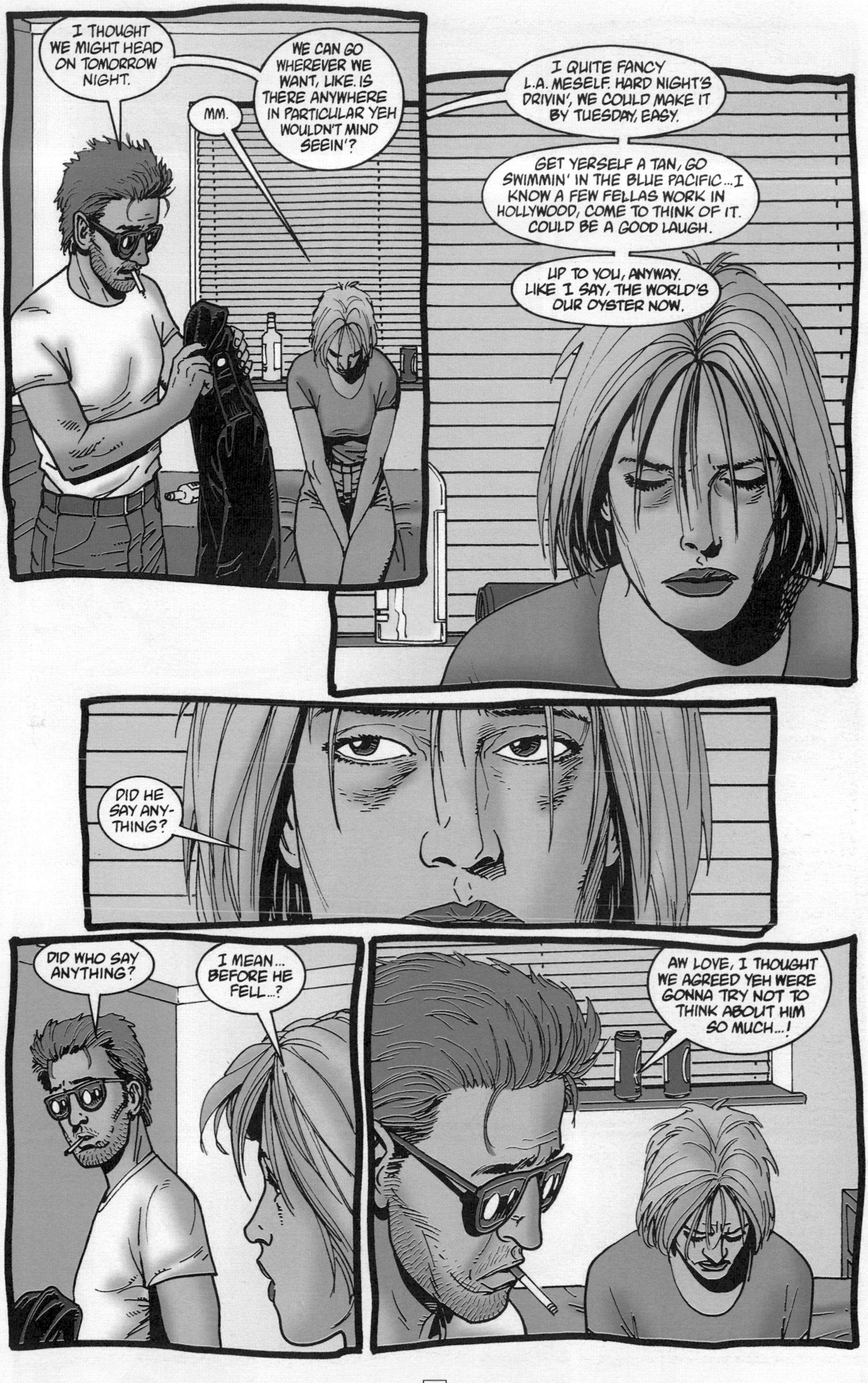
I THOUGHT WE MIGHT HEAD ON TOMORROW NIGHT.
MM.
WE CAN GO WHEREVER WE WANT, LIKE. IS THERE ANYWHERE IN PARTICULAR YEH WOULDN'T MIND SEEIN'?
I QUITE FANCY L.A. MESELF. HARD NIGHT'S DRIVIN', WE COULD MAKE IT BY TUESDAY, EASY.
GET YERSELF A TAN, GO SWIMMIN' IN THE BLUE PACIFIC... I KNOW A FEW FELLAS WORK IN HOLLYWOOD, COME TO THINK OF IT. COULD BE A GOOD LAUGH.
UP TO YOU, ANYWAY. LIKE I SAY, THE WORLD'S OUR OYSTER NOW.
DID HE SAY ANY-THING?
DID WHO SAY ANYTHING?
I MEAN... BEFORE HE FELL...?
AW LOVE, I THOUGHT WE AGREED YEH WERE GONNA TRY NOT TO THINK ABOUT HIM SO MUCH...!

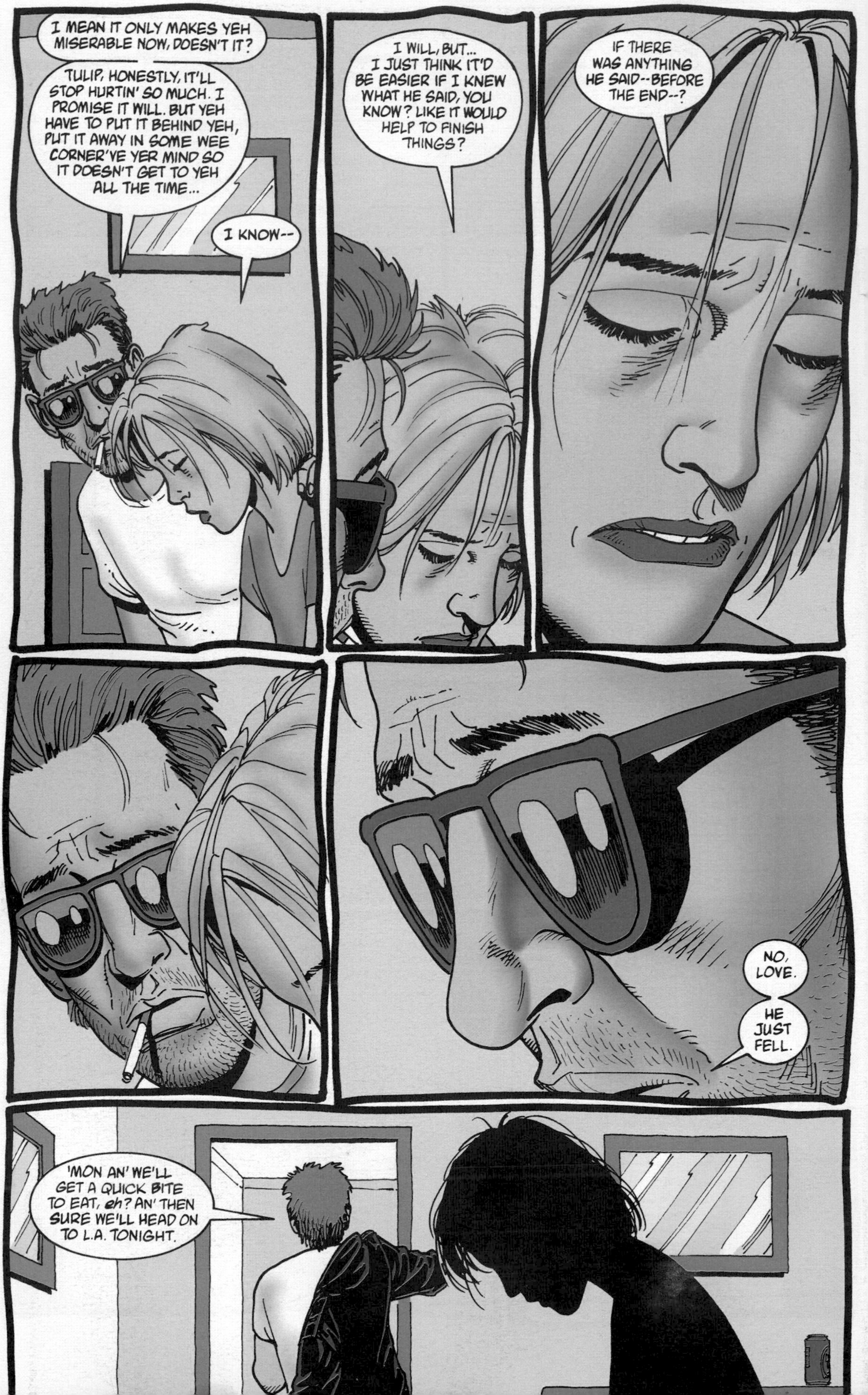
I MEAN IT ONLY MAKES YEH MISERABLE NOW, DOESN'T IT?
TULIP, HONESTLY, IT'LL STOP HURTIN' SO MUCH. I PROMISE IT WILL. BUT YEH HAVE TO PUT IT BEHIND YEH, PUT IT AWAY IN SOME WEE CORNER'VE YER MIND SO IT DOESN'T GET TO YEH ALL THE TIME...
I KNOW--
I WILL, BUT... I JUST THINK IT'D BE EASIER IF I KNEW WHAT HE SAID, YOU KNOW? LIKE IT WOULD HELP TO FINISH THINGS?
IF THERE WAS ANYTHING HE SAID--BEFORE THE END--?
NO, LOVE.
HE JUST FELL.
'MON AN' WE'LL GET A QUICK BITE TO EAT, *eh*? AN' THEN SURE WE'LL HEAD ON TO L.A. TONIGHT.

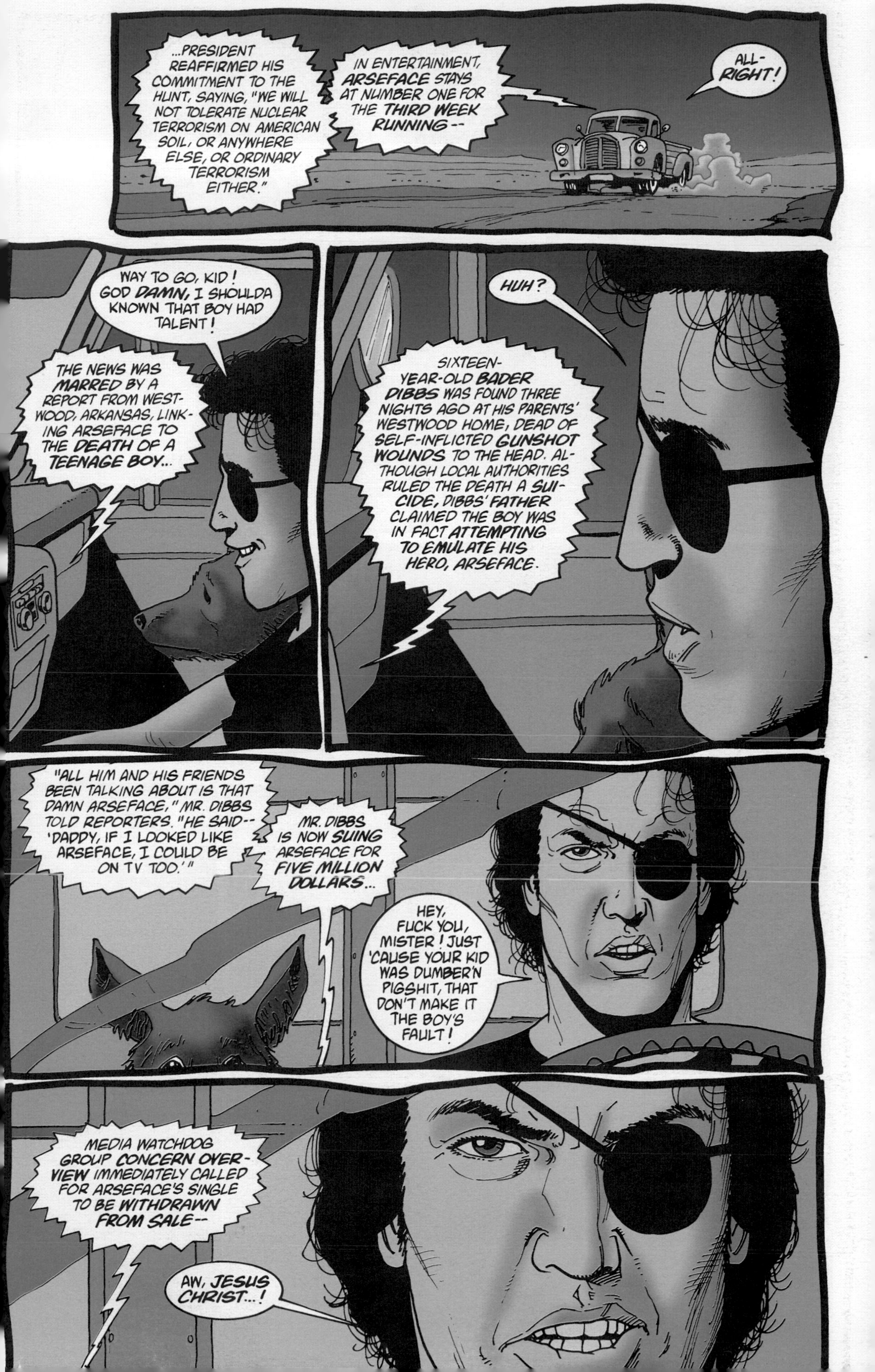
...PRESIDENT REAFFIRMED HIS COMMITMENT TO THE HUNT, SAYING, "WE WILL NOT TOLERATE NUCLEAR TERRORISM ON AMERICAN SOIL, OR ANYWHERE ELSE, OR ORDINARY TERRORISM EITHER."
IN ENTERTAINMENT, ARSEFACE STAYS AT NUMBER ONE FOR THE THIRD WEEK RUNNING--
ALL-RIGHT!
WAY TO GO, KID! GOD DAMN, I SHOULDA KNOWN THAT BOY HAD TALENT!
THE NEWS WAS MARRED BY A REPORT FROM WEST-WOOD, ARKANSAS, LINK-ING ARSEFACE TO THE DEATH OF A TEENAGE BOY...
HUH?
SIXTEEN-YEAR-OLD BADER DIBBS WAS FOUND THREE NIGHTS AGO AT HIS PARENTS' WESTWOOD HOME, DEAD OF SELF-INFLICTED GUNSHOT WOUNDS TO THE HEAD. AL-THOUGH LOCAL AUTHORITIES RULED THE DEATH A SUI-CIDE, DIBBS' FATHER CLAIMED THE BOY WAS IN FACT ATTEMPTING TO EMULATE HIS HERO, ARSEFACE.
"ALL HIM AND HIS FRIENDS BEEN TALKING ABOUT IS THAT DAMN ARSEFACE," MR. DIBBS TOLD REPORTERS. "HE SAID-- 'DADDY, IF I LOOKED LIKE ARSEFACE, I COULD BE ON TV TOO.'"
MR. DIBBS IS NOW SUING ARSEFACE FOR FIVE MILLION DOLLARS...
HEY, FUCK YOU, MISTER! JUST 'CAUSE YOUR KID WAS DUMBER'N PIGSHIT, THAT DON'T MAKE IT THE BOY'S FAULT!
MEDIA WATCHDOG GROUP CONCERN OVER-VIEW IMMEDIATELY CALLED FOR ARSEFACE'S SINGLE TO BE WITHDRAWN FROM SALE--
AW, JESUS CHRIST...!

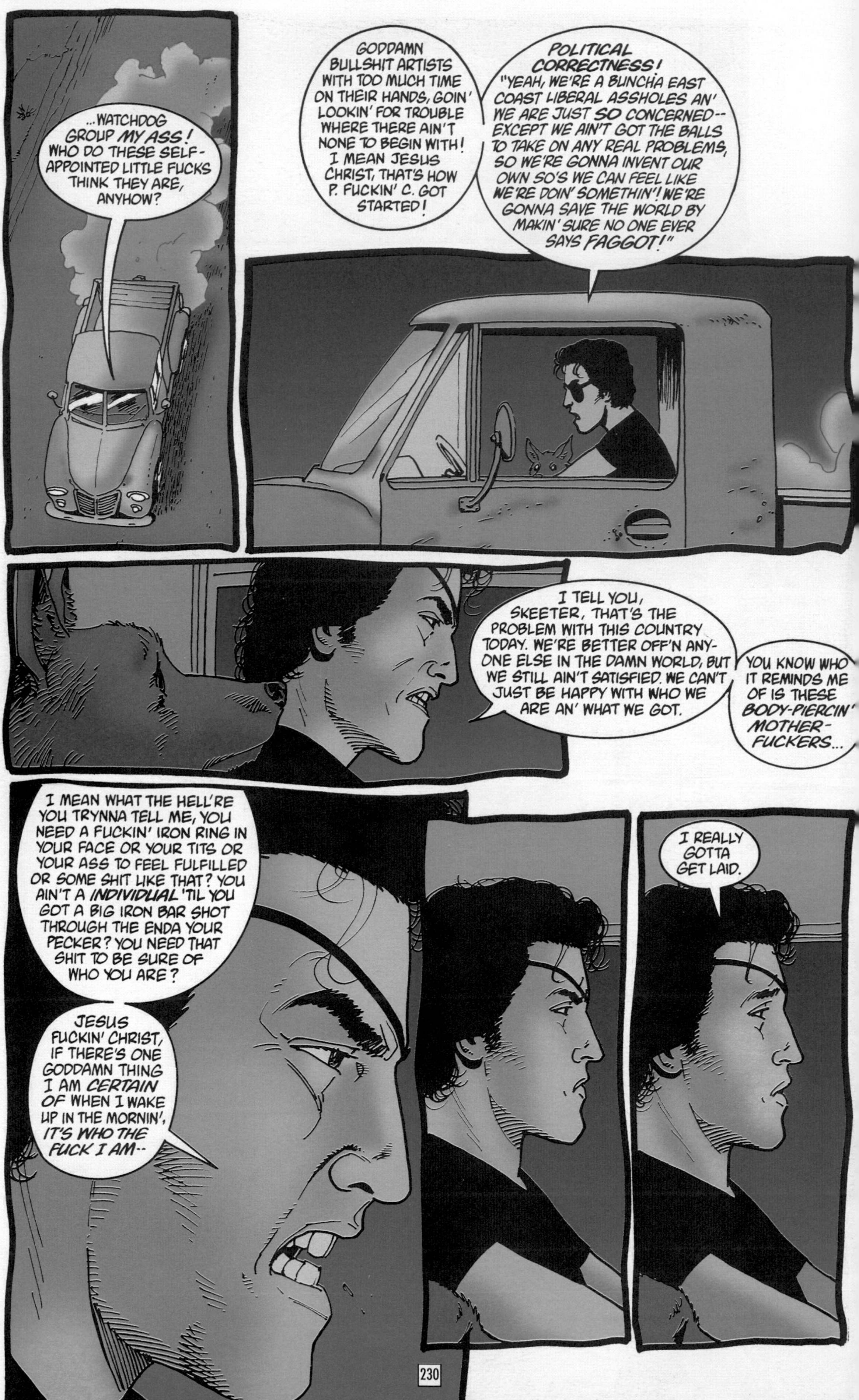
...WATCHDOG GROUP MY ASS! WHO DO THESE SELF-APPOINTED LITTLE FUCKS THINK THEY ARE, ANYHOW?
GODDAMN BULLSHIT ARTISTS WITH TOO MUCH TIME ON THEIR HANDS, GOIN' LOOKIN' FOR TROUBLE WHERE THERE AIN'T NONE TO BEGIN WITH! I MEAN JESUS CHRIST, THAT'S HOW P. FUCKIN' C. GOT STARTED!
POLITICAL CORRECTNESS! "YEAH, WE'RE A BUNCHA EAST COAST LIBERAL ASSHOLES AN' WE ARE JUST SO CONCERNED-- EXCEPT WE AIN'T GOT THE BALLS TO TAKE ON ANY REAL PROBLEMS, SO WE'RE GONNA INVENT OUR OWN SO'S WE CAN FEEL LIKE WE'RE DOIN' SOMETHIN'! WE'RE GONNA SAVE THE WORLD BY MAKIN' SURE NO ONE EVER SAYS FAGGOT!"
I TELL YOU, SKEETER, THAT'S THE PROBLEM WITH THIS COUNTRY TODAY. WE'RE BETTER OFF'N ANY-ONE ELSE IN THE DAMN WORLD, BUT WE STILL AIN'T SATISFIED. WE CAN'T JUST BE HAPPY WITH WHO WE ARE AN' WHAT WE GOT.
YOU KNOW WHO IT REMINDS ME OF IS THESE BODY-PIERCIN' MOTHER-FUCKERS...
I MEAN WHAT THE HELL'RE YOU TRYNNA TELL ME, YOU NEED A FUCKIN' IRON RING IN YOUR FACE OR YOUR TITS OR YOUR ASS TO FEEL FULFILLED OR SOME SHIT LIKE THAT? YOU AIN'T A INDIVIDUAL 'TIL YOU GOT A BIG IRON BAR SHOT THROUGH THE ENDA YOUR PECKER? YOU NEED THAT SHIT TO BE SURE OF WHO YOU ARE?
JESUS FUCKIN' CHRIST, IF THERE'S ONE GODDAMN THING I AM CERTAIN OF WHEN I WAKE UP IN THE MORNIN', IT'S WHO THE FUCK I AM--
I REALLY GOTTA GET LAID.

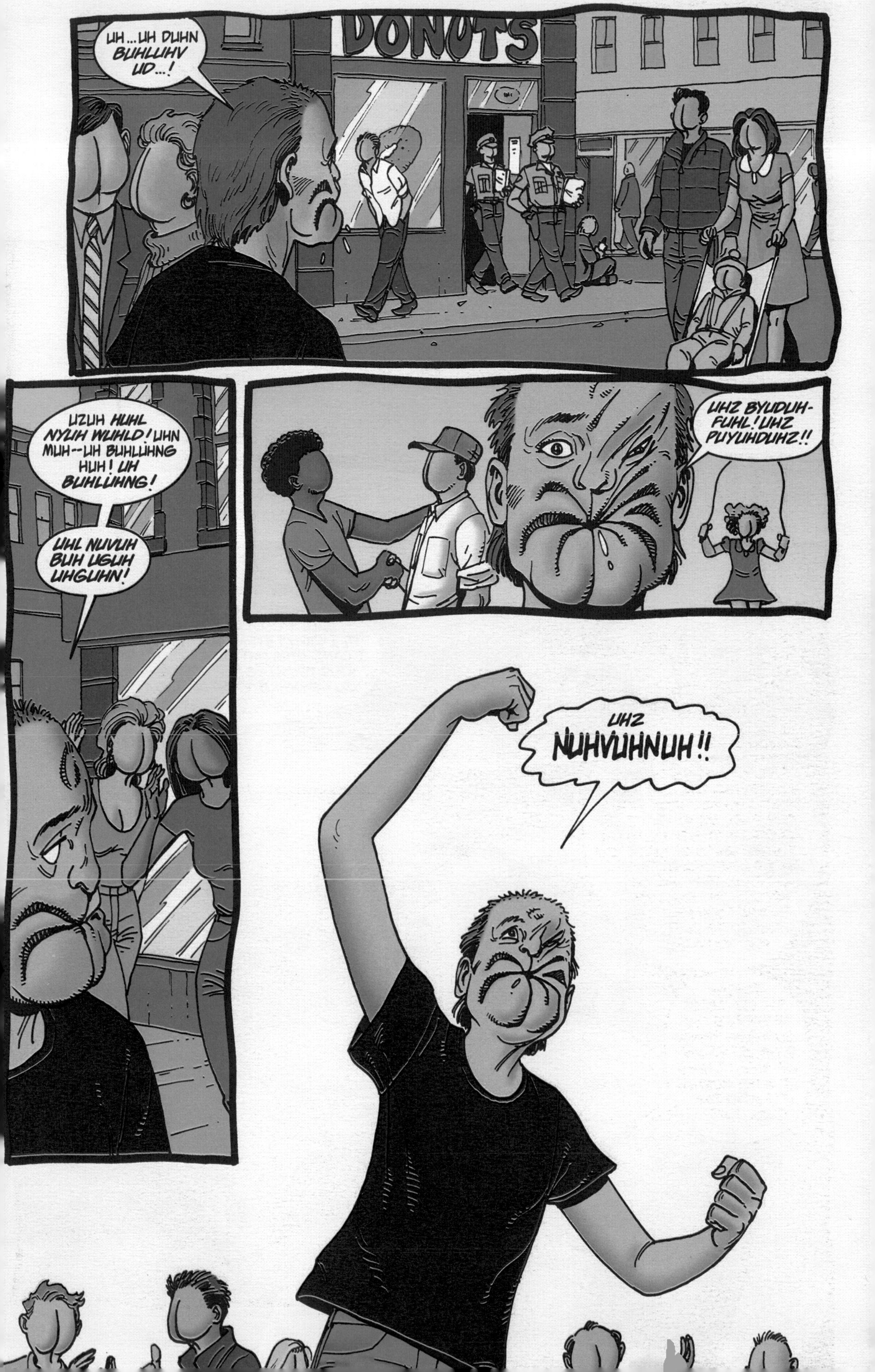

DONUTS
UH...UH DUHN BUHLUHV UD...!
UZUH HUHL NYUH WUHLD! UHN MUH--UH BUHLUHNG HUH! UH BUHLUHNG!
UHL NUVUH BUH UGUH UHGUHN!
UHZ BYUDUH-FUHL! UHZ PUYUHDUHZ!!
UHZ NUHVUHNUH!!

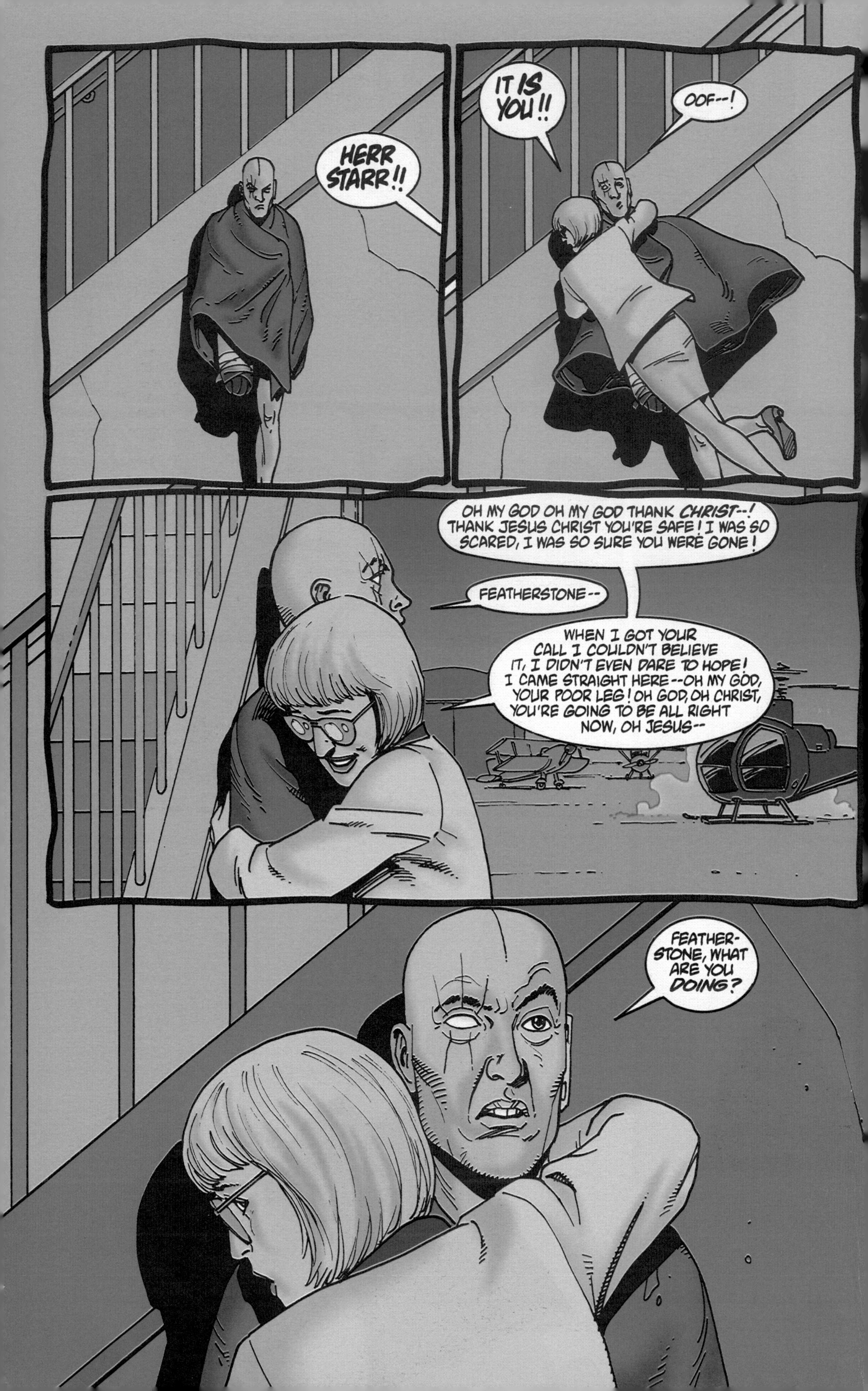
HERR STARR!!
IT IS YOU!!
OOF--!
OH MY GOD OH MY GOD THANK CHRIST--! THANK JESUS CHRIST YOU'RE SAFE! I WAS SO SCARED, I WAS SO SURE YOU WERE GONE!
FEATHERSTONE--
WHEN I GOT YOUR CALL I COULDN'T BELIEVE IT, I DIDN'T EVEN DARE TO HOPE! I CAME STRAIGHT HERE--OH MY GOD, YOUR POOR LEG! OH GOD, OH CHRIST, YOU'RE GOING TO BE ALL RIGHT NOW, OH JESUS--
FEATHERSTONE, WHAT ARE YOU DOING?

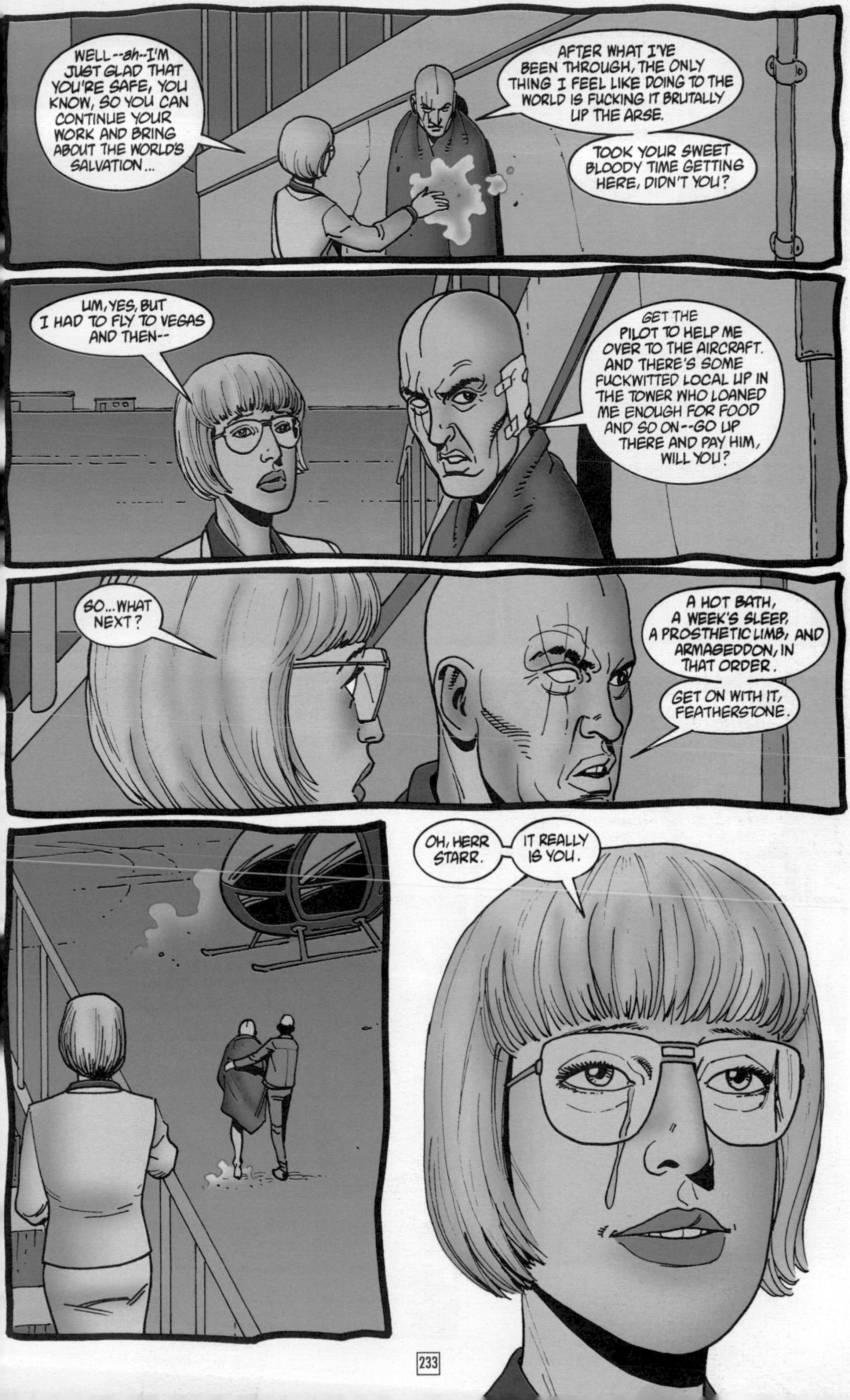
WELL--ah--I'M JUST GLAD THAT YOU'RE SAFE, YOU KNOW, SO YOU CAN CONTINUE YOUR WORK AND BRING ABOUT THE WORLD'S SALVATION...
AFTER WHAT I'VE BEEN THROUGH, THE ONLY THING I FEEL LIKE DOING TO THE WORLD IS FUCKING IT BRUTALLY UP THE ARSE.
TOOK YOUR SWEET BLOODY TIME GETTING HERE, DIDN'T YOU?
UM, YES, BUT I HAD TO FLY TO VEGAS AND THEN--
GET THE PILOT TO HELP ME OVER TO THE AIRCRAFT. AND THERE'S SOME FUCKWITTED LOCAL UP IN THE TOWER WHO LOANED ME ENOUGH FOR FOOD AND SO ON--GO UP THERE AND PAY HIM, WILL YOU?
SO...WHAT NEXT?
A HOT BATH, A WEEK'S SLEEP, A PROSTHETIC LIMB, AND ARMAGEDDON, IN THAT ORDER.
GET ON WITH IT, FEATHERSTONE.
OH, HERR STARR.
IT REALLY IS YOU.

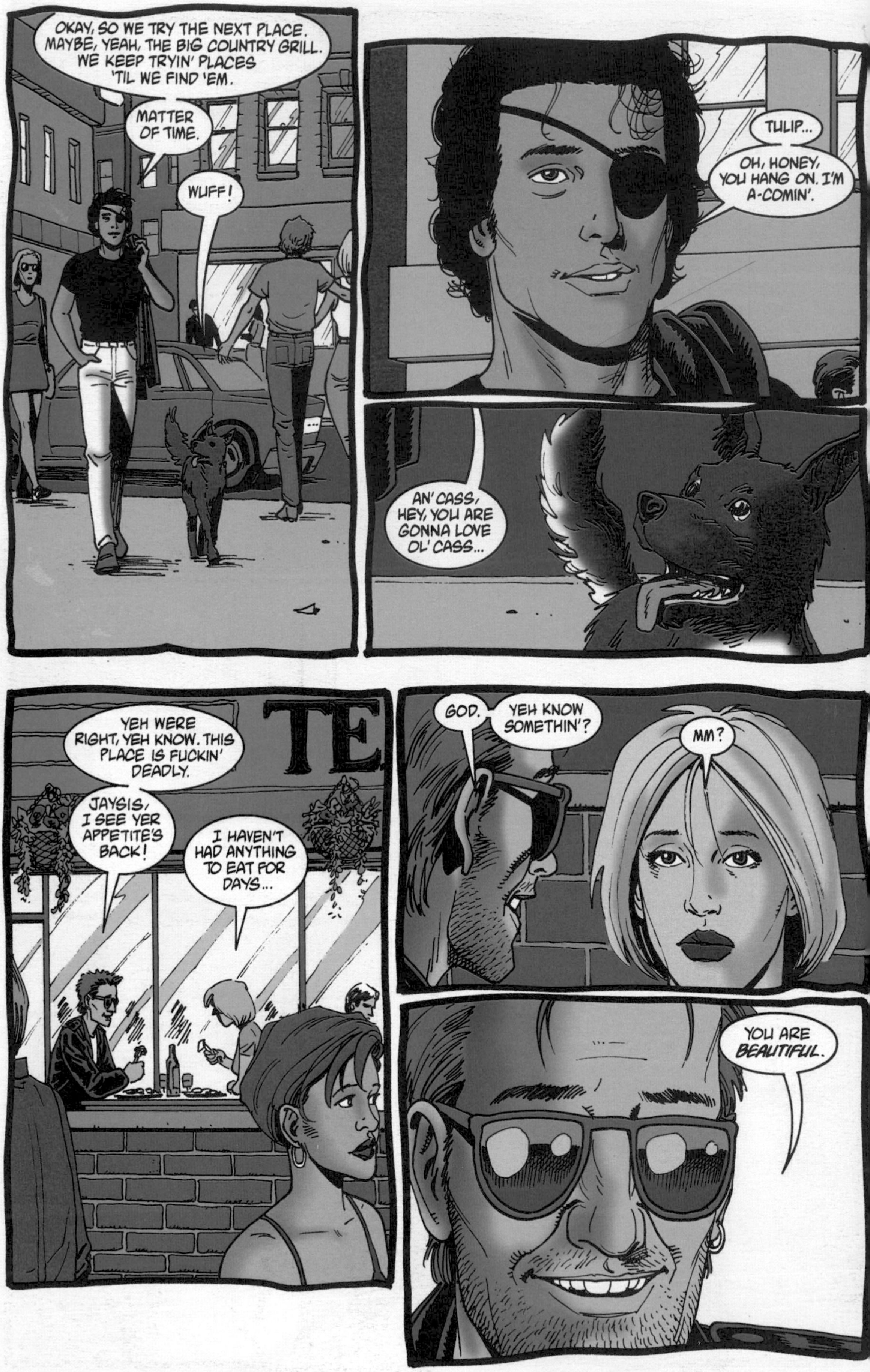
OKAY, SO WE TRY THE NEXT PLACE. MAYBE, YEAH, THE BIG COUNTRY GRILL. WE KEEP TRYIN' PLACES 'TIL WE FIND 'EM.
MATTER OF TIME.
WUFF!
TULIP...
OH, HONEY, YOU HANG ON. I'M A-COMIN'.
AN' CASS, HEY, YOU ARE GONNA LOVE OL' CASS...
TE
YEH WERE RIGHT, YEH KNOW. THIS PLACE IS FUCKIN' DEADLY.
JAYSIS, I SEE YER APPETITE'S BACK!
I HAVEN'T HAD ANYTHING TO EAT FOR DAYS...
GOD.
YEH KNOW SOMETHIN'?
MM?
YOU ARE *BEAUTIFUL*.

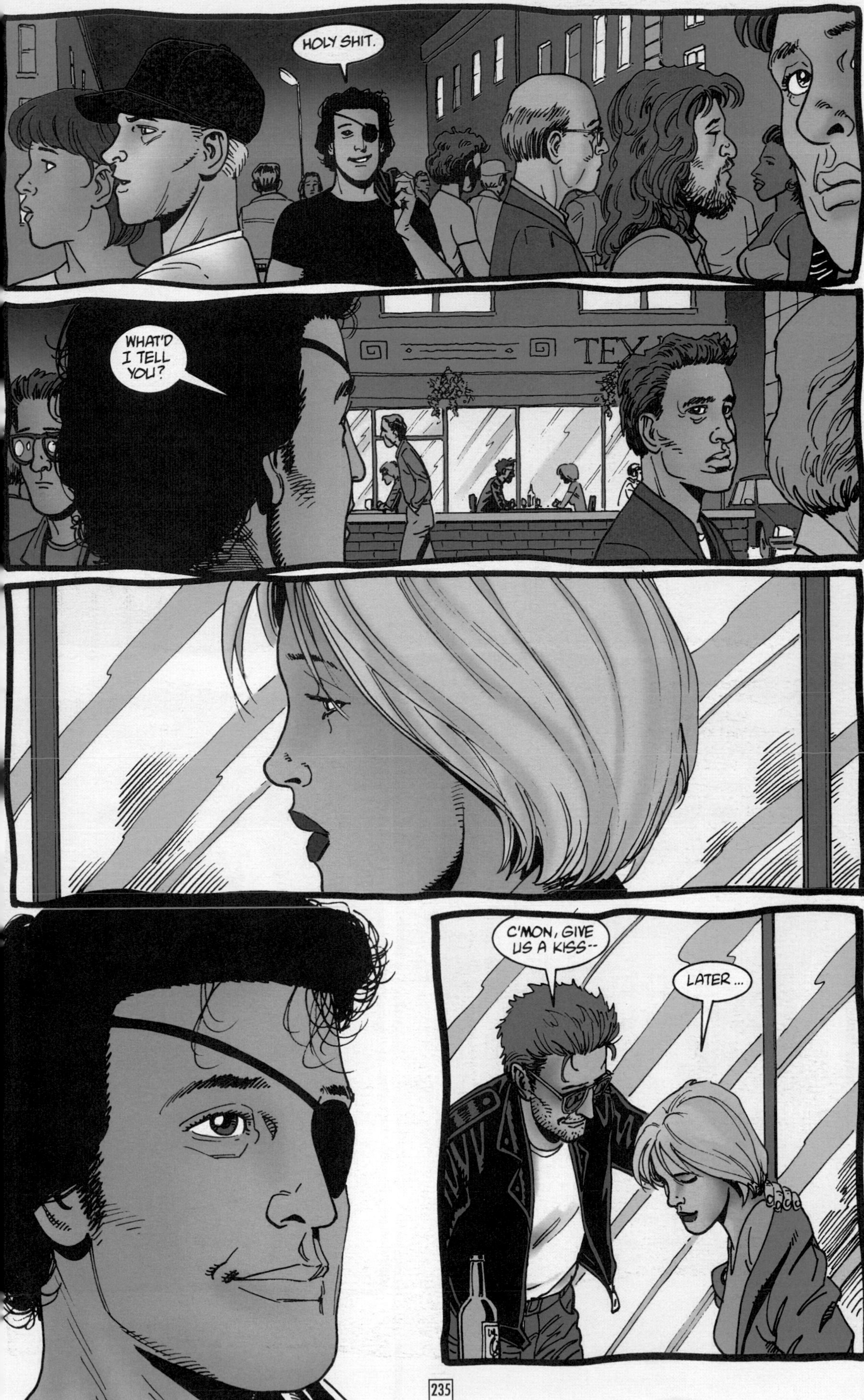
HOLY SHIT.
WHAT'D I TELL YOU?
C'MON, GIVE US A KISS--
LATER...

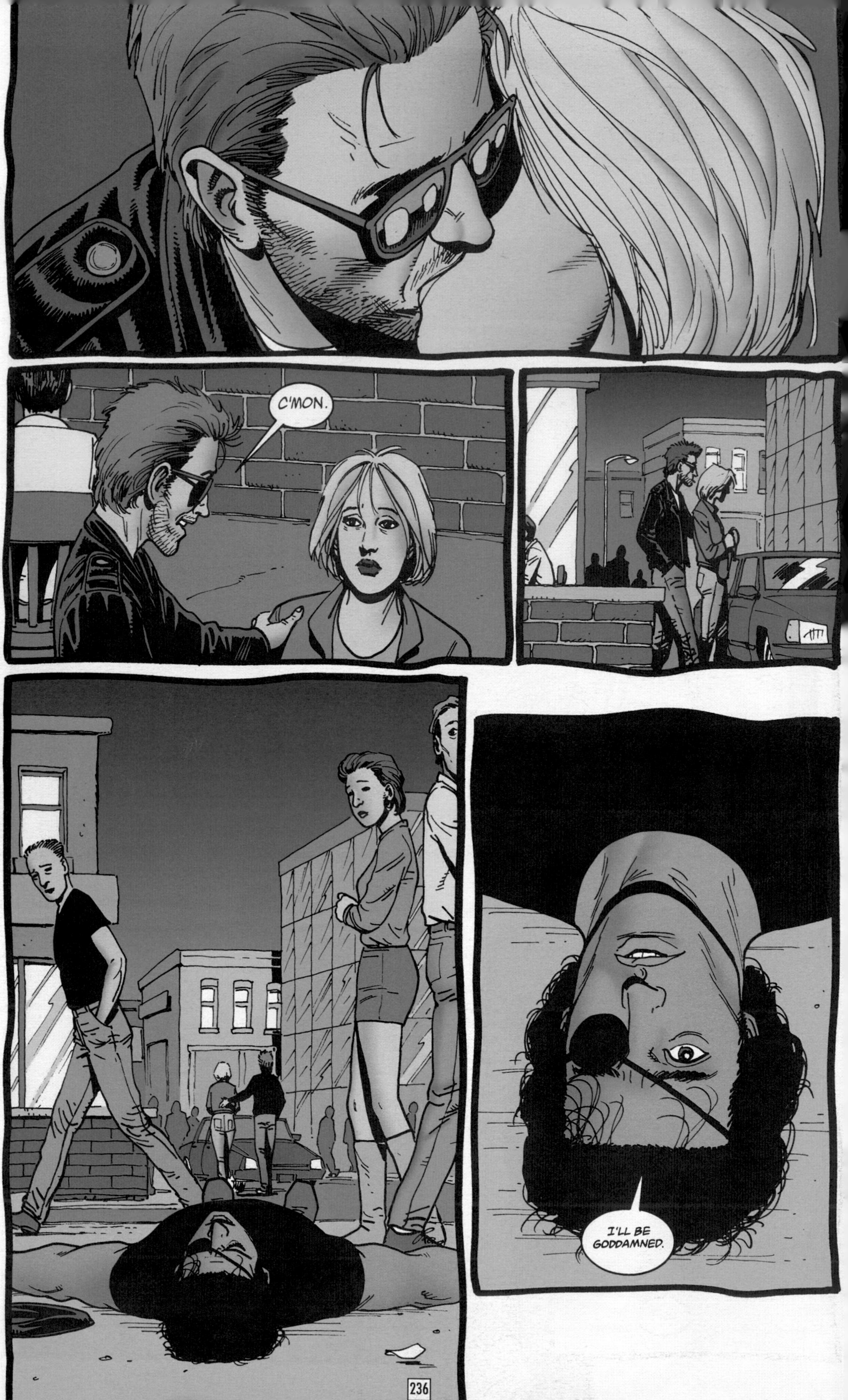
C'MON.
I'LL BE GODDAMNED.

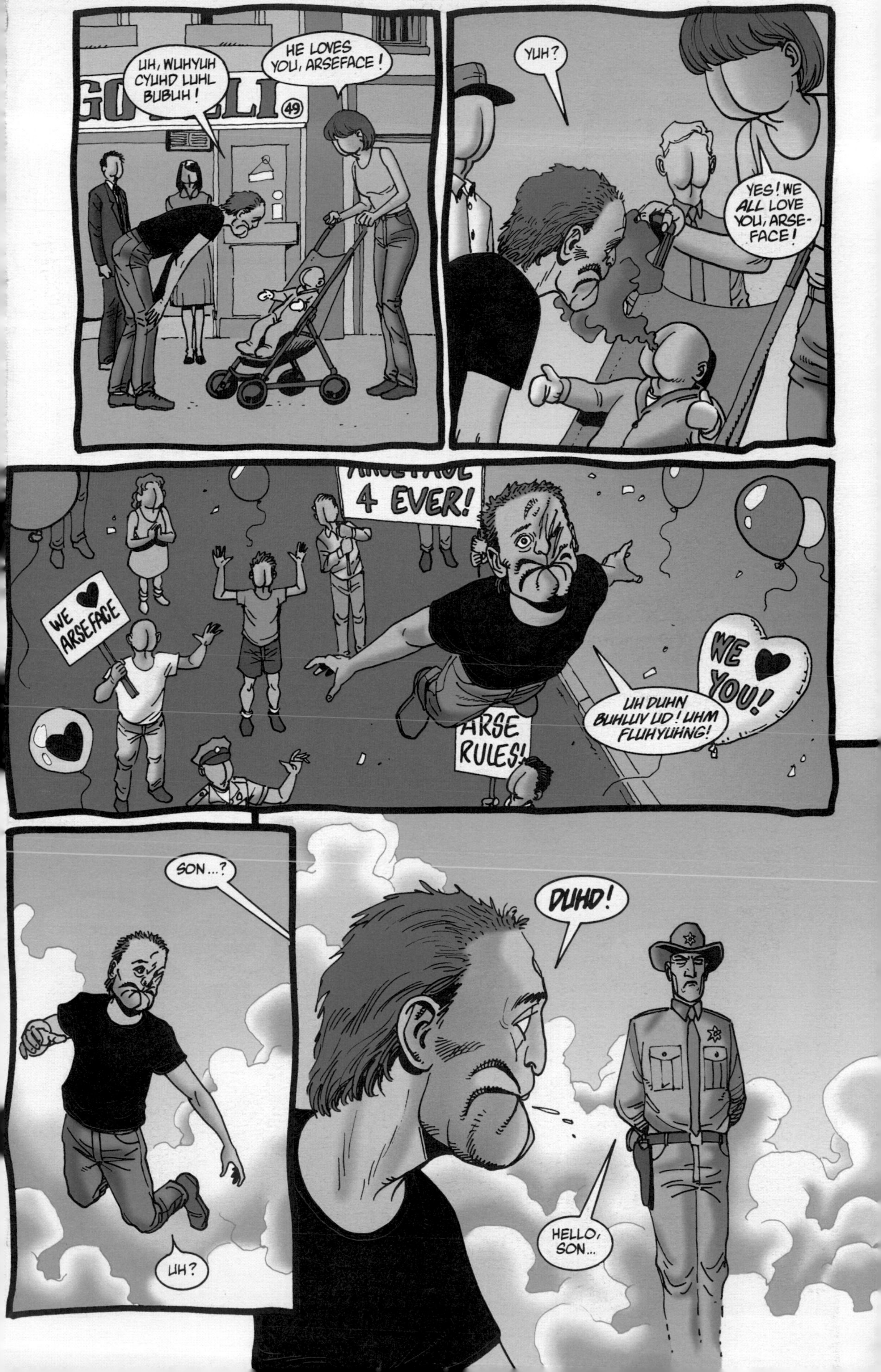
UH, WUHYUH CYUHD LUHL BUBUH!
HE LOVES YOU, ARSEFACE!
YUH?
YES! WE ALL LOVE YOU, ARSEFACE!
4 EVER!
WE ♥ ARSEFACE
ARSE RULES!
WE ♥ YOU!
UH DUHN BUHLUV UD! UHM FLUHYUHNG!
SON...?
UH?
DUHD!
HELLO, SON...

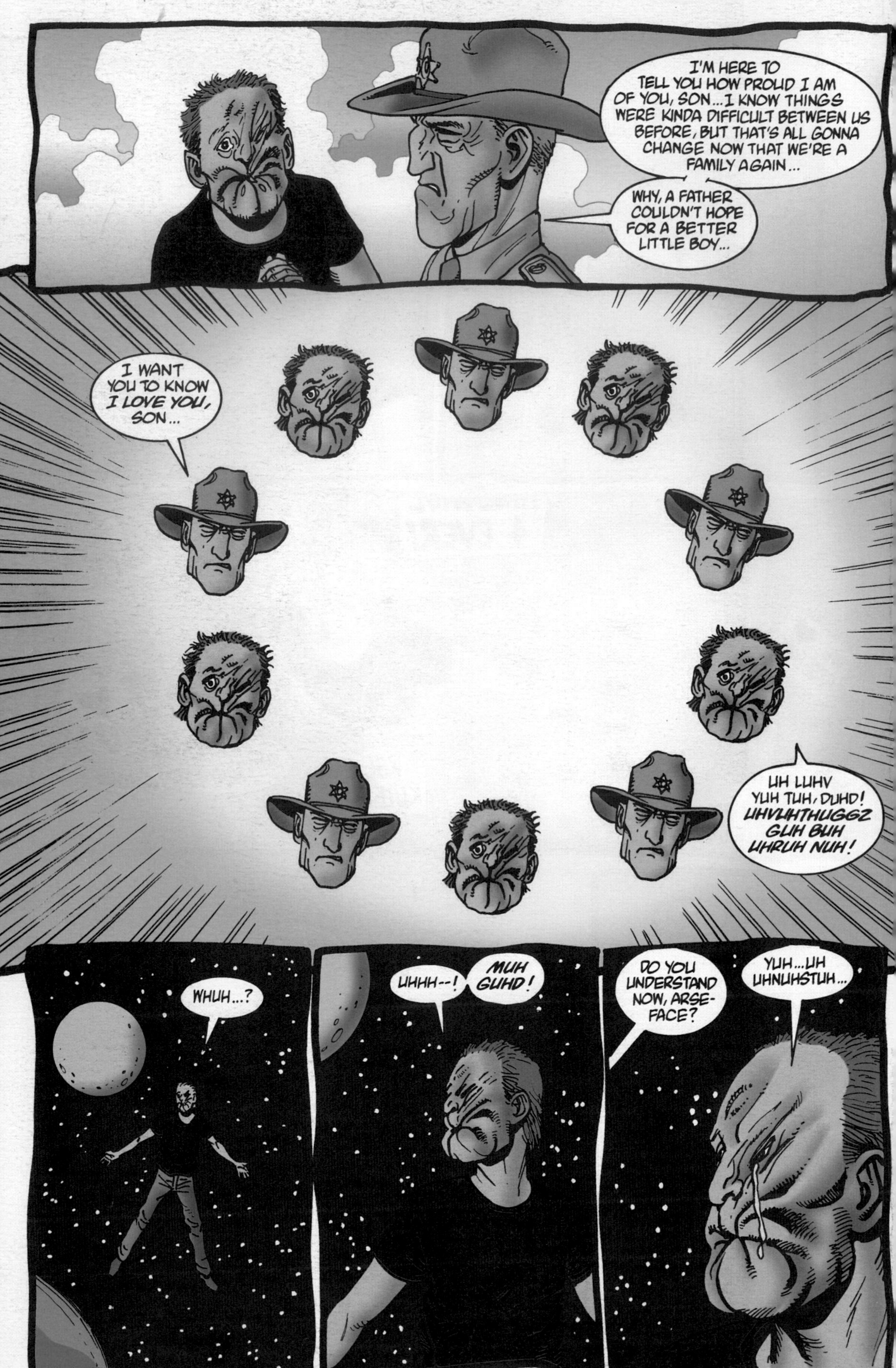
I'M HERE TO TELL YOU HOW PROUD I AM OF YOU, SON... I KNOW THINGS WERE KINDA DIFFICULT BETWEEN US BEFORE, BUT THAT'S ALL GONNA CHANGE NOW THAT WE'RE A FAMILY AGAIN...
WHY, A FATHER COULDN'T HOPE FOR A BETTER LITTLE BOY...
I WANT YOU TO KNOW *I LOVE YOU*, SON...
UH LUHV YUH TUH, DUHD! *UHVUHTHUGGZ GUH BUH UHRUH NUH!*
WHUH...?
UHHH--!
MUH GUHD!
DO YOU UNDERSTAND NOW, ARSE-FACE?
YUH...UH UHNUHSTUH...

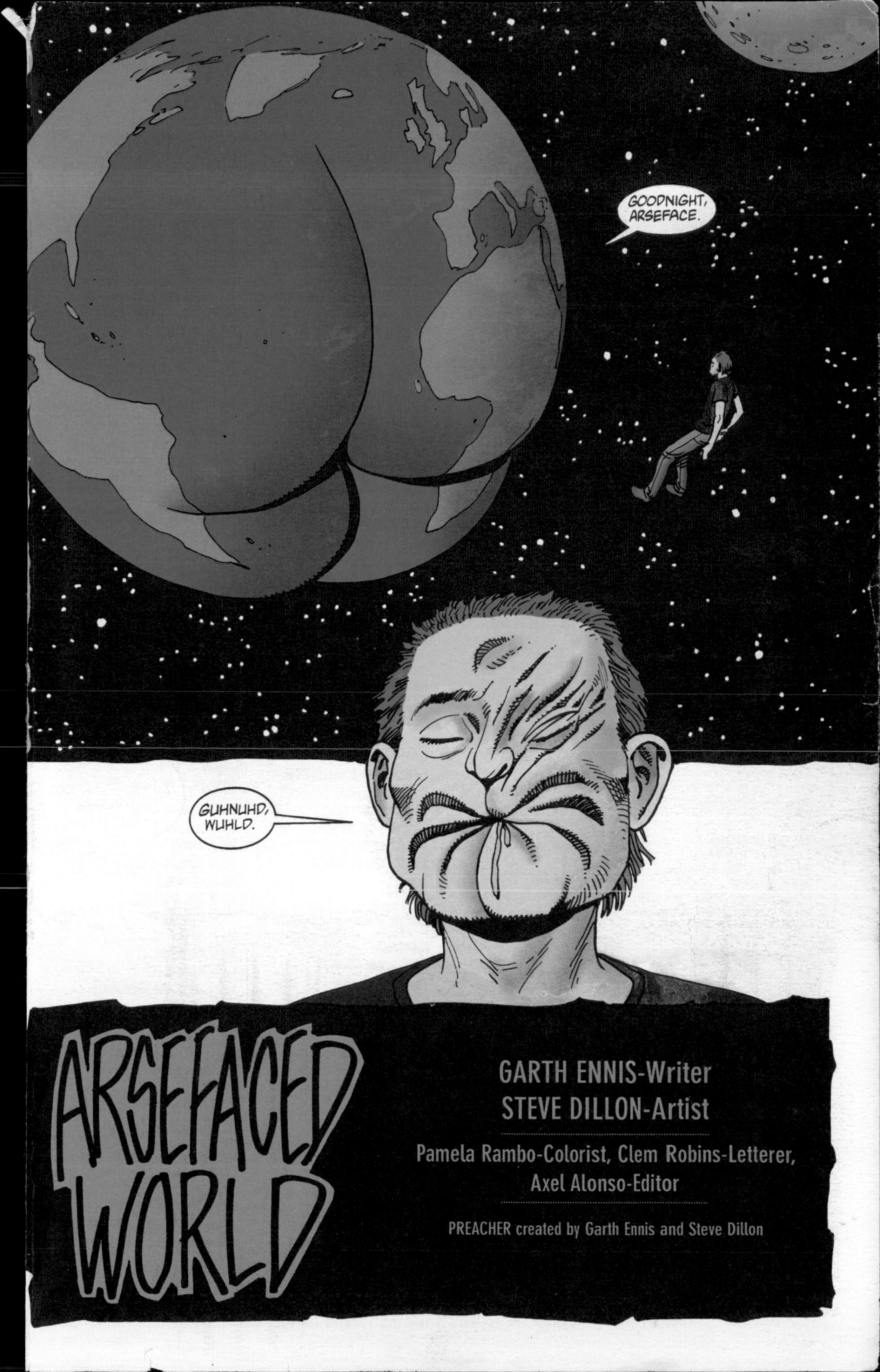
GOODNIGHT, ARSEFACE.
GUHNUHD, WUHLD.

ARSEFACED WORLD

GARTH ENNIS-Writer
STEVE DILLON-Artist

Pamela Rambo-Colorist, Clem Robins-Letterer,
Axel Alonso-Editor

PREACHER created by Garth Ennis and Steve Dillon

Look for these other Titan books:

All titles are Suggested for Mature Readers

100 BULLETS
Brian Azzarello/Eduardo Risso
With one special briefcase, Agent Graves gives you the chance to kill without retribution. But what is the real price for this chance — and who is setting it?
Vol 1: FIRST SHOT, LAST CALL
Vol 2: SPLIT SECOND CHANCE
Vol 3: HANG UP ON THE HANG LOW
Vol 4: A FOREGONE TOMORROW
Vol 5: THE COUNTERFIFTH DETECTIVE
Vol 6: SIX FEET UNDER THE GUN
Vol 7: SAMURAI
Vol 8: THE HARD WAY
Vol 9: STRYCHNINE LIVES
Vol 10: ONCE UPON A CRIME
Vol 11: DECAYED

THE BOOKS OF MAGIC
Neil Gaiman/various
A quartet of fallen mystics introduce the world of magic to young Tim Hunter, who is destined to become the world's most powerful magician.

DEATH: AT DEATH'S DOOR
Jill Thompson
Part fanciful *manga* retelling of the acclaimed THE SANDMAN: SEASON OF MISTS and part original story of the party from Hell.

DEATH: THE HIGH COST OF LIVING
Neil Gaiman/Chris Bachalo/ Mark Buckingham
One day every century, Death assumes mortal form to learn more about the lives she must take.

DEATH: THE TIME OF YOUR LIFE
Neil Gaiman/Chris Bachalo/ Mark Buckingham/Mark Pennington
A young lesbian mother strikes a deal with Death for the life of her son in a story about fame, relationships, and rock and roll.

THE EXTERMINATORS
Simon Oliver/Tony Moore/ Chris Samnee/Mike Hawthorne/ Darick Robertson
An ex-con begins a job as an exterminator, but soon finds himself on the front line of the battle between human and insect.
Vol 1: BUG BROTHERS
Vol 2: INSURGENCY
Vol 3: LIES OF OUR FATHERS
Vol 4: CROSSFIRE AND COLLATERAL

FABLES
Bill Willingham/Lan Medina/ Mark Buckingham/Steve Leialoha
The immortal characters of popular fairy tales have been driven from their homelands, and now live hidden among us, trying to cope with life in 21st-century Manhattan.
Vol 1: LEGENDS IN EXILE
Vol 2: ANIMAL FARM
Vol 3: STORYBOOK LOVE
Vol 4: MARCH OF THE WOODEN SOLDIERS
Vol 5: THE MEAN SEASONS
Vol 6: HOMELANDS
Vol 7: ARABIAN NIGHTS (AND DAYS)
Vol 8: WOLVES
Vol 9: SONS OF EMPIRE
Vol 10: THE GOOD PRINCE

HELLBLAZER
Jamie Delano/Garth Ennis/Warren Ellis/ Brian Azzarello/Steve Dillon/ Marcelo Frusin/various
Where horror, dark magic, and bad luck meet, John Constantine is never far away.
ORIGINAL SINS
DANGEROUS HABITS
FEAR AND LOATHING
TAINTED LOVE
DAMNATION'S FLAME
RAKE AT THE GATES OF HELL
SON OF MAN
HAUNTED
SETTING SUN
HARD TIME
GOOD INTENTIONS
FREEZES OVER
HIGHWATER

JACK OF FABLES
Bill Willingham/Matthew Sturges/ Mark Buckingham/Steve Leialoha
The irrepressible would-be hero is exiled from Fabletown, journeying across America in search of wine, women and song... and cash.
Vol 1: THE (NEARLY) GREAT ESCAPE
Vol 2: JACK OF HEARTS
Vol 3: THE BAD PRINCE

LUCIFER
Mike Carey/Peter Gross/ Scott Hampton/Chris Weston/ Dean Ormston/various
Walking out of Hell (and out of the pages of THE SANDMAN), an ambitious Lucifer Morningstar creates a new cosmos modelled after his own image.
Vol 1: DEVIL IN THE GATEWAY
Vol 2: CHILDREN AND MONSTERS
Vol 3: A DALLIANCE WITH THE DAMNED
Vol 4: THE DIVINE COMEDY
Vol 5: INFERNO
Vol 6: MANSIONS OF THE SILENCE
Vol 7: EXODUS
Vol 8: THE WOLF BENEATH THE TREE
Vol 9: CRUX
Vol 10: MORNINGSTAR
Vol 11: EVENSONG

PREACHER
Garth Ennis/Steve Dillon/various
A modern American epic of life, death, God, love, and redemption — filled with sex, booze, and blood.
Vol 1: GONE TO TEXAS
Vol 2: UNTIL THE END OF THE WORLD
Vol 3: PROUD AMERICANS
Vol 4: ANCIENT HISTORY
Vol 5: DIXIE FRIED
Vol 6: WAR IN THE SUN
Vol 7: SALVATION
Vol 8: ALL HELL'S A-COMING
Vol 9: ALAMO

THE SANDMAN
Neil Gaiman/various
One of the most acclaimed and celebrated comics titles ever published.
Vol 1: PRELUDES & NOCTURNES
Vol 2: THE DOLL'S HOUSE
Vol 3: DREAM COUNTRY
Vol 4: SEASON OF MISTS
Vol 5: A GAME OF YOU
Vol 6: FABLES & REFLECTIONS
Vol 7: BRIEF LIVES
Vol 8: WORLDS' END
Vol 9: THE KINDLY ONES
Vol 10: THE WAKE
Vol 11: ENDLESS NIGHTS

SCALPED
Jason Aaron/R. M. Guéra
An angry ex-soldier goes undercover for the FBI, posing as a cop on the reservation where he grew up.
Vol 1: INDIAN COUNTRY
Vol 2: CASINO BOOGIE
Vol 3: DEAD MOTHERS

SWAMP THING: DARK GENESIS
Len Wein/Berni Wrightson
A gothic nightmare is brought to life with this horrifying yet poignant story of a man transformed into a monster.

SWAMP THING
Alan Moore/Stephen Bissette/ John Totleben/Rick Veitch/various
The writer and the series that revolutionized comics — a masterpiece of lyrical fantasy.
Vol 1: SAGA OF THE SWAMP THING
Vol 2: LOVE & DEATH
Vol 3: THE CURSE
Vol 4: A MURDER OF CROWS
Vol 5: EARTH TO EARTH
Vol 6: REUNION
Vol 7: REGENESIS

TRANSMETROPOLITAN
Warren Ellis/Darick Robertson/various
An exuberant trip into a frenetic future, where outlaw journalist Spider Jerusalem battles hypocrisy, corruption, and sobriety.
Vol 1: BACK ON THE STREET
Vol 2: LUST FOR LIFE
Vol 3: YEAR OF THE BASTARD
Vol 4: THE NEW SCUM
Vol 5: LONELY CITY
Vol 6: GOUGE AWAY
Vol 7: SPIDER'S THRASH
Vol 8: DIRGE
Vol 9: THE CURE
Vol 10: ONE MORE TIME

Y: THE LAST MAN
Brian K. Vaughan/Pia Guerra/ José Marzán, Jr.
An unexplained plague kills every male mammal on Earth — all except Yorick Brown and his pet monkey. Will he survive this new, emasculated world to discover what killed his fellow men?
Vol 1: UNMANNED
Vol 2: CYCLES
Vol 3: ONE SMALL STEP
Vol 4: SAFEWORD
Vol 5: RING OF TRUTH
Vol 6: GIRL ON GIRL
Vol 7: PAPER DOLLS
Vol 8: KIMONO DRAGONS
Vol 9: MOTHERLAND
Vol 10: WHYS AND WHEREFORES

ARMY@LOVE: THE HOT ZONE CLUB
Rick Veitch/Gary Erskine

ARMY@LOVE: GENERATION PWNED
Rick Veitch/Gary Erskine

CROSSING MIDNIGHT: A MAP OF MIDNIGHT
Mike Carey/Jim Fern/Mark Pennington

FAKER
Mike Carey/Jock

HEAVY LIQUID
Paul Pope

A HISTORY OF VIOLENCE
John Wagner/Vince Locke

JONNY DOUBLE
Brian Azzarello/Eduardo Risso

KID ETERNITY
Grant Morrison/Duncan Fegredo

MR. PUNCH
Neil Gaiman/Dave McKean

STARDUST
Neil Gaiman/Charles Vess

NEIL GAIMAN'S MIDNIGHT DAYS
Neil Gaiman/Matt Wagner/various

ORBITER
Warren Ellis/Colleen Doran

THE ORIGINALS
Dave Gibbons

THE OTHER SIDE
Jason Aaron/Cameron Stewart

THE QUITTER
Harvey Pekar/Dean Haspiel

THE SANDMAN: THE DREAM HUNTERS
Neil Gaiman/Yoshitaka Amano

THE SANDMAN PRESENTS: THE FURIES
Mike Carey/John Bolton

THE SANDMAN PRESENTS: TALLER TALES
Bill Willingham/various

SKREEMER
Peter Milligan/Brett Ewins

SLOTH
Gilbert Hernandez

V FOR VENDETTA
Alan Moore/David Lloyd

Visit us at www.titanbooks.com for more information on these and many other titles.